W9-BWB-152

A Quick Guide to Key Topics by Paragraph Number

The
Gregg
Reference
Manual

The Gregg Reference Manual

Seventh Edition

William A. Sabin

GLENCOE

Macmillan/McGraw-Hill

New York, New York
Columbus, Ohio
Mission Hills, California
Peoria, Illinois

Library of Congress Cataloging-in-Publication Data

Sabin, William A.
    The Gregg reference manual/William A. Sabin—7th ed.
        p.   cm.
    Includes index.
    ISBN 0-02-819920-0 (hardcover text ed.)—ISBN
0-02-819921-9 (softcover text ed.)—ISBN 0-02-819922-7
(spiral bound text ed.)
        1. English language—Business English—Handbooks, manuals, etc.,
    2. English language—Grammar—1950—Handbooks, manuals, etc.
    3. English language—Transcription—Handbooks, manuals, etc.
    4. Business writing—Handbooks, manuals, etc.   I. Title.
    PE1479.B87S23   1992
    808'.042—dc20   92-2544
                                                                                                CIP

The Gregg Reference Manual, Seventh Edition

Imprint 1994
Copyright © 1992 by the Glencoe Division of Macmillan/McGraw-Hill School Publishing
Company. All rights reserved. Previously copyright © 1985, 1977, 1970, 1961, 1956 by
McGraw-Hill, Inc. Copyright 1951 by McGraw-Hill, Inc. Except as permitted under the
United States Copyright Act, no part of this publication may be reproduced or distributed
in any form or by any means, or stored in a database or retrieval system, without prior
written permission of the publisher.

Send all inquiries to:
GLENCOE DIVISION
Macmillan/McGraw-Hill
936 Eastwind Drive
Westerville, OH 43081

ISBN 0-02-819920-0 (hardcover text edition)

Printed in the United States of America.

        6 7 8 9 0   ACH/LH   99 98 97 96 95 94

Contents

Preface

The Gregg Reference Manual is intended for anyone who writes, edits, or prepares final copy for distribution or publication. It presents the basic rules that apply in virtually every piece of writing, as well as the fine points that occur infrequently but cause trouble when they do. It offers an abundance of examples and illustrations so that you can quickly find a model on which to pattern a solution to a specific problem. It also provides the rationale underlying specific rules so that you can manipulate the principles of style with intelligence and taste.

Features of the New Edition. The seventh edition of *The Gregg Reference Manual* has been considerably expanded and completely updated. The objective of this expansion has been to ensure that users will find definitive answers to all the problems they are likely to encounter in written communications. In deciding what kinds of additional coverage to provide, I was guided by the following considerations:

1. Today's users typically inhabit two worlds—the business world and the academic—either as full-time students who are working to cover their expenses or as full-time workers who are going to school to upgrade their skills or train for a new career or enrich their personal lives. Therefore, in whatever written work they do, they are bound to encounter different requirements, different formats, different styles. The seventh edition of *The Gregg Reference Manual* acknowledges this situation by providing guidelines for academic reports, notes, and bibliographies wherever they tend to differ from what is done in business writing. (See, for example, ¶¶1413–1414, 1508b, 1534c.)
2. Computers, word processors, and other types of electronic equipment have been integrated into today's offices and schools, supplying users with a new set of capabilities that create, in turn, both opportunities and problems. This new edition provides guidance on how to edit and proofread at the computer (see ¶1204). Moreover, it shows how the new electronic capabilities can affect the formatting of letters, memos, reports, tables, and a wide variety of other business documents. For example:
   - In Section 13 (dealing with letters), ¶1305b reflects the new emphasis on setting margins on the basis of *margin width* rather than line length, and it sanctions the standard use of 1-inch side margins and a 6½-inch line in light of the pervasive influence of software programs with 1-inch default margins.
   - In Section 14 (dealing with reports), the illustrations on pages 372–373 show how boldface type can be used in place of underscoring in the treatment of headings, and ¶1407 indicates how the traditional complexities in determining good page breaks can be avoided on a computer.
   - In Section 16 (dealing with tables), ¶1633d provides special guidance on inserting horizontal and vertical rules by means of a computer, and the section indicates throughout how a computer can greatly simplify the customary difficulties in centering a table both horizontally and vertically on a page.
   - In Section 17 (dealing with agendas, minutes, résumés, and other business documents), ¶1703 shows alternative ways a computer can be used to treat displayed elements.

But computers and other forms of electronic equipment have also introduced some problems. For example:

- How should you cope with standard spacing guidelines if your equipment has difficulty in switching from double to triple spacing? (See ¶¶1385a, 1406, 1425g, and 1604c.)
- How should you indicate that a particular letter is simply a confirmation of a faxed document rather than an entirely new communication? (See ¶1375b.)
- If the equipment you are using cannot produce superior figures easily, how do you handle footnote or endnote references in the text? (See ¶¶1502h, 1523b.)
- How should you handle an attention line in conjunction with an inside address if you plan to use the inside address to generate the envelope address? (See ¶¶1344–1345.)

Computers have brought with them a strange and continually evolving vocabulary. To deal with this phenomenon, the new edition:

- Provides a glossary of computer terms (see the updated Section 20).
- Interprets many of the common abbreviations and acronyms used in referring to computers (see the expanded ¶544).
- Describes the patterns and variations in capitalizing these terms (see the new ¶365).

3. With the passage of time, some things need to be updated. For example:

- The treatment of alphabetic filing rules in Section 12 has been completely recast in the form of 14 rules that are consistent with ARMA's latest standards. Special guidance has been provided on how to decide which name to use for filing purposes when you have more than one form to work with. (See ¶¶1208, 1212c, 1214e, 1215a, and 1216a.)
- The language itself is continually being enriched with new words and expressions. Throughout the new edition, examples have been refreshed to reflect this new language, and various lists of words and abbreviations have been expanded accordingly. For example, *workers' compensation insurance* in place of *workmen's compensation insurance* (¶809a), getting oneself "booted up" in the morning (¶235), *camcorder* and *Rollerblades* (¶356), *the rubber-chicken circuit* (¶814), *a go/no-go decision* (¶831d), *Tex-Mex cooking* (¶309b), and some wonderful new acronyms such as *NIMBY* (¶546), *WYSIWYG* (¶544), and *MEGO* (¶522a).

4. Questions and suggestions from users of the previous edition have had a major impact on what has been added to the new edition.* For example:

- An all-new 26-page section (17) has been created to show how to format a variety of executive, financial, and job-seeking documents. The coverage in this section includes annotated models for three types of *agendas* (one in informal memo style, one in formal style, and one representing a formal program of events), *minutes* (both formal and informal), an *itinerary*, and a *fax cover sheet*. It also provides formats for a *balance sheet*, two types of *income statements*, a *statement of cash flows*, and an *operational analysis*. Finally, it shows a *résumé* formatted in three different ways and provides guidelines on what to put in, what to leave out, and which format may be best for your purposes.

---

*Because of the immense value that readers' comments have in ensuring that each new edition is truly responsive to readers' needs, I invite you to submit your questions and suggestions to me through the publisher's office in Westerville, Ohio. Please see the copyright page for the full address.

· Specific queries from readers led to new coverage on whether to hyphenate terms like *African American* (¶348), *turnkey computer system* (¶830), and *small business owner* (¶818c); how to spell words like *Sunbelt* and *Rust Belt* when they occur in the same context (¶333a); how to form the plurals of compound foreign nouns like *chaise longue* (¶614); how to treat area codes in telephone numbers (¶454); how to handle expressions like *"must" reading* (¶237a); the circumstances under which you can "feel badly" (page 256); how to deal with nicknames inserted in a person's full name (¶311g); how to address correspondence to a young girl or boy (¶1322d–e); and how to avoid misplaced modifiers (¶1086), misdirected passives (¶1037c), and confusing possessives like *the owner of the horse's wife* (¶648).

Available for use with *The Gregg Reference Manual* is a set of worksheets designed to build three critical skills. First, the *Worksheets for the Gregg Reference Manual* will familiarize you with the wide range of potential problems you are likely to encounter in any material that you write, transcribe, or type. Second, these worksheets will direct you to the key rules in each section of *The Gregg Reference Manual* so that later on, when you encounter similar problems in your own work, you will know where to look. Third, they will sharpen your ability to apply the rules correctly under many different circumstances. As in the previous edition, this set of worksheets begins with a 4-page survey of your editing skills at the outset and then, after you have completed a series of twenty-seven 2-page worksheets, you will encounter a parallel 4-page "final" survey so that you can see how much your skills have increased. Moreover, four 2-page surveys have been interspersed at appropriate points within the sequence of worksheets to help you integrate the things you have been learning and to let you measure your progress.

An Overview of the Organization and the Coverage. This edition of *The Gregg Reference Manual* consists of 20 sections, organized as follows:

Part One (Sections 1–11) deals with grammar, usage, and the chief aspects of style—punctuation, capitalization, numbers, abbreviations, plurals and possessives, spelling, compound words, and word division.

Part Two (Sections 12–17) deals with techniques and procedures for producing all kinds of written communications—letters, memos, reports, manuscripts, tables, agendas, minutes, itineraries, fax cover sheets, balance sheets, income statements, statements of cash flows, operational analyses, and résumés.

Part Three (Sections 18–20) provides three appendixes for fast reference: a listing of model forms of address, a glossary of grammatical terms, and a glossary of computer terms.

As you make your own survey of the text, you will want to single out the key rules that deserve further study; these are the rules that deal with everyday situations, the rules you need to have at your command. You will also want to develop a passing acquaintance with the fine points of style. It is sufficient simply to know that such rules exist; then, when you need them, you will know where to find them. Finally, you will want to take note of special word lists, sentence patterns, and illustrations that could be useful to you later on. If you find out now what aids the manual provides, you will know what kind of help you can count on in the future. And what is more important, you will be able to find what you are looking for faster.

A Final Note. A book of this type cannot be put together without the help and support of many people. To my colleagues in McGraw-Hill and Macmillan/ McGraw-Hill, to my many good friends in business and office education, and to the countless teachers, students, and professionals who all helped me—by their questions and suggestions—to see what was missing and how things could be made better, I want to express a deep feeling of gratitude.

And to my family—to my mother, who gave me my first sense of what language could accomplish (and a good deal more); to Margaret, John, Kate, Chris, and Jim, to whom much has been entrusted and from whom I have gained much in return; and ultimately to my wife Marie, who has made the journey worth the struggle—my thanks and my love.

William A. Sabin

How to Look Things Up

Suppose you were writing to someone in another department:

> I understand you are doing a confidential study of the Bronson matter. May I please get an advance copy of your report [At this point you hesitate. Should this sentence end with a period or a question mark?]

This is the kind of problem that continually comes up in any type of written communication. How do you find a fast answer to such questions? In this manual there are several ways to proceed.

Using the Index. The surest approach, perhaps, is to check the detailed index at the back of the manual (12 pages, with over 1700 entries). For example, any of the following entries will lead you to the right punctuation for the problem sentence above:

> Periods, **101–109** Question marks, **110–118** Request, punctuation
>   . . . . . . of, **103**
> at end of requests, **103** at end of requests, **103, 113**

In each entry the **boldface number** refers to the proper rule, **¶103.** (If you look up ¶103, you will find that a question mark is the right punctuation for the sentence in question.)

In almost all of the index entries, references are made to specific rule numbers so that you can find what you are looking for fast. In a few cases, where a page reference will provide a more precise location (for example, when a rule runs on for several pages), a page number is given in lightface type. Suppose you were confronted with this problem:

> If you compare the performance records of Catano, Harris, and Williams, you won't find much difference (*between/among*) them.

The index will show the following entries:

> *among–between*, 257 **or** *between–among*, 257

The rule on page 257 indicates that *between* is correct in this situation.

Using a Fast-Skim Approach. Many users of reference manuals have little patience with detailed indexes. They would rather open the book and skim through the pages until they find what they are looking for. If you are the kind of person who prefers this approach, you will find several features of this manual especially helpful:

· The brief topical index on the inside front cover indicates the key paragraphs for each major topic.
· At the start of each section except the glossaries, you will find a detailed list of all the topics covered in that section. This list will help you quickly focus on the rule or rules that pertain to your problem. Suppose the following problem came up:

> The only point still at issue is whether or not new *Federal* [or is it *federal*?] legislation is required.

The index on the inside front cover indicates that ¶¶301–365 deal with the topic of capitalization. A fast skim of the outline preceding ¶301 will turn up the entry *Names of Government Bodies* (¶¶*325–330*). If you turn to that set of rules, you will find in ¶328 that *federal* is the proper form.

Extensive cross-references have also been provided throughout the manual so that you can quickly locate related rules that could prove helpful. Some cross-references take this form: *See* ¶*324;* others may read *See also* ¶*324.* The form *See* ¶*324* indicates that ¶324 contains significant information that adds to or qualifies the rule you are currently reading; the word *See* suggests that you really ought to pursue the cross-reference before making a decision. The form *See also* ¶*324* carries a good deal less urgency. It indicates that you will find some additional examples in ¶324 and perhaps a restatement of the rule you are currently reading but nothing altogether new. In effect, *See also* suggests that you don't have to pursue the cross-reference if you don't want to—but it couldn't hurt.

Playing the Numbers. There is still a third way to find the answer to a specific problem—and this is an approach that will grow in appeal as you become familiar with the organization and the content of the manual. From a fast inspection of the rule numbers, you will observe that they all carry a section number as a prefix. Thus Section 3 (on capitalization) has a "300" series of rules—from 301 to 365; Section 4 (on number style) has a "400" series—from 401 to 470; and so on. Once you become familiar with the section numbers and the section titles, you can find your way around fairly quickly, without reference to either index, by using the section number tabs. For example, you are about to write the following sentence:

> *43* percent of the questionnaires have now been returned. [Or should it be *"Forty-three* percent of the questionnaires . . ."?]

If you know that matters of number style are treated in Section 4, you can quickly turn to the pages tabbed "4," where a fast skim of the outline of topics at the start of the section will lead you to the answer in ¶421. (*Forty-three percent* is the right answer in this instance.)

A familiarity with the section numbers and section titles can also save you time when you are using the index. If your index entry lists several different paragraph numbers, you can often anticipate what the paragraphs will deal with. For example, if you want to know whether to write *5 lb* or *5 lbs* on a purchase order, you might encounter the following entry in the index:

> Weights, **429–430, 535–538, 621**

If you know that Section 6 deals with plurals, you will try ¶621 first.

Looking Up Specific Words. Many of the problems that arise deal with specific words. For this reason the index provides as many entries for such words as space will permit. For example, in the following sentence, should *therefore* be set off by commas or not?

> It is(,) *therefore*(,) essential that operations be curtailed.

A check of the index will show the following entry:

> *therefore,* **122, 138–142**

A reading of the rules in ¶141 will indicate that no commas should be used in this sentence. If you ask the same question about another specific word and do not find it listed as a separate entry in the index, your best approach will be to check the index under "Comma" and investigate the most promising references or make a direct scan of the comma rules in Section 1 until you find the answer you are looking for.

If you are having difficulty with words that look alike and sound alike—*gibe* and *jibe* or *affect* and *effect*—turn directly to ¶719. For other troublesome words and phrases, consult Section 11.

The six brief essays that follow deal with a number of points of style that cause great difficulty for those who work with words. Out of this consideration of specific problems, these essays attempt to draw broader conclusions about the nature of style and the art of tailoring one's use of language to fit the needs of each situation.

Mastering Number Style: One (or 1?) Approach

A number of years ago, while making a presentation on the subject of style, I asked the audience to select the preferable form in each of the following pairs of examples:

$87,525	OR	eighty-seven thousand five hundred and twenty-five dollars
$3.8 trillion	OR	$3,800,000,000,000
4:30 p.m., January 19	OR	half after four o'clock, on the nineteenth of January

No one could see any use for the forms in the second column. Those in the first column were far easier to read and simpler to write and were clearly to be preferred in business writing. However, after some discussion, we tended to agree that Tiffany's had had the right idea in a recent ad, where beneath a picture of an elegant diamond necklace was the legend "Eighty-seven thousand five hundred and twenty-five dollars." Somehow, we felt, if they were going to charge that elegant a price, the least they could do was spell it out. Moreover, we tended to agree that a liberal in fiscal matters might readily dismiss the federal debt as "only $3.8 trillion," whereas a fiscal conservative who wanted to emphasize the enormity of the amount might well have written "The federal debt now stands at $3,800,000,000,000" and thereby have forced upon us a sense of the magnitude of the amount by making us calculate it for ourselves. Finally, we agreed that we would much rather be married at "half after four o'clock, on the nineteenth of January" than at "4:30 p.m., January 19."*

---

*One dissenter indicated that she simply wanted to get married and didn't much care how the invitations read.

These, admittedly, are extreme examples of occasions on which an unusual number style could be justified, but they tend to throw light on the more customary style for expressing numbers and on the notion of style in general. At the very least, these examples suggest that style should not be thought of as a rigid set of rules but rather as a set of principles for adjusting one's means of expression to fit a particular set of circumstances. We express our style in clothes through a varied wardrobe that suits the needs not only of everyday situations but of formal and informal occasions as well. It is the impoverished person who meets every situation with the same set of clothes. By the same token, it is an impoverished writer who meets all situations with a rigid set of rules. The writer of the Tiffany ad, who chose words instead of figures to express an amount of money, in this instance had some true sense of how to vary style for best effect.

Manipulating principles of style for specific effect ought not to be a random, hit-or-miss exercise but should proceed from some coherent notion about style itself. In the case of numbers, an intelligent control of number style proceeds from an awareness of the difference in effect that results from using figures or words to express numbers.

Figures are big (like capital letters); when used in a sentence, they stand out clearly from the surrounding tissue of words. As a result, they are easier to grasp on first reading, and they are easier to locate for subsequent reference. Thus whenever quick comprehension and fast reference are important (and this is true of most business writing), figures are to be preferred to words.

But the very characteristics of figures that make them preferable to words can be disadvantageous in certain circumstances. Figures stand out so sharply against a background of words that they achieve a special prominence and obtain a special emphasis. Not all numbers warrant that kind of emphasis, however, and in such cases words are preferable to figures. Keep in mind, too, that figures have the conciseness and the informality of an abbreviation. Thus the more formal the occasion, the more likely one is to spell numbers out (as in the wedding announcement cited on page xiii).

Given these basic differences between using figures and using words, it is quite clear why figures are preferred in ordinary business letters. These are typically straightforward communications that pass between business firms and their suppliers or their customers, containing frequent references to price quotations, quantities, shipping dates, credit terms, and the like. Frequently, these numbers represent data that has to be extracted from the letter and processed in some way: they may have to be checked against other numbers or included in some computation or simply transferred to another document. The advantage of figures to words in these ordinary cases is so clear that the point does not need to be argued.

But there is another kind of business writing in which the writer is not typically dealing with the workaday transactions of the business. It may be a special promotion campaign with an air of elegance and formality; it may be a carefully constructed letter with special stylistic objectives in mind; or it may be a special report which involves community relations and will have a wider distribution than the normal technical business report. This kind of writing tends to occur more often at the executive level, and it tends to occur in the more creative departments of a business (such as sales promotion, advertising, public relations, and customer relations). In this kind of writing, numbers don't occur very frequently; when they do, they are usually expressed in words.

As a response to the different needs posed by these two kinds of writing, there are two basic number styles in use today. Both use figures and words but in different proportions. The *figure style* uses figures for all numbers above 10, whether exact or approximate; the *word style* spells out all numbers up through 100 and all numbers above 100 that can be expressed in one or two words (such as *twenty-five hundred*).

As a practical matter, your immediate job may require you to use only the figure style. However, your next job may call for the use of the word style. And if you are working and going to school at the same time (as more and more people are these days), you will probably find yourself following one style for office work and another for your academic work. Under these circumstances, if you grasp the basic difference between using words and figures to express numbers, you will be better able to decide how to proceed in specific situations without having to consult a style manual each time. In any case, keep the following ideas in mind:

1. There are no absolute rights and wrongs in number style—only varying sets of stylistic conventions that people follow in one set of circumstances or another. There are, however, effective differences in using words or figures, and you should take these differences into account.
2. Before deciding on which number style to follow for a given piece of writing, first determine the basic objective of the material. If the material is intended to communicate information as simply and as briefly as possible, use the *figure style*. If the material is of a formal nature or aspires to a certain level of literary elegance, use the *word style*.
3. Having decided on a basic style, *be consistent in context.* When related numbers occur together in the same context and according to the rules some should go in figures and some should go in words, treat these related numbers all the same way.
4. Treat an approximate number exactly the same way you would treat an exact number. If you would write *50 orders,* then you should also write *about 50 orders.* (If the figure 50 looks too emphatic to you when used in an approximation, the chances are that you should be using the word style—and not just for approximate numbers but throughout.)
5. In areas where the style could go either way (for example, *the 4th of June* vs. *the fourth of June* or *9 o'clock* vs. *nine o'clock*), decide in accordance with your basic style. Thus if you are following the figure style, you will automatically choose *the 4th of June* and *9 o'clock*.
6. In expressions involving ages, periods of time, and measurements, use figures whenever these numbers have technical significance or serve as measurements or deserve special emphasis; otherwise, use words. (For example, *you receive these benefits at 65, the note will be due in 3 months, the parcel weighs over 2 pounds;* but *my father will be sixty-five next week, that happened three months ago, I hope to lose another two pounds this week.*)
7. Use figures in dates (*June 6*) and in expressions of money (*$6*), except for reasons of formality or special effect (as in the wedding announcement or the Tiffany ad). Also use figures in percentages, proportions, ratios, scores, and with abbreviations and symbols.

8. Use words for numbers at the beginning of a sentence, for most ordinals (*the third time, the twentieth anniversary*), and for fractions standing alone (*one-third of our sales*).

All manuals of style (including this one) include many more than eight rules. They give exceptions and fine points beyond those just summarized. Yet for all practical purposes these eight rules—and the philosophy that underlies them—will cover almost every common situation. Just remember that the conventions of number style were meant to be applied, not as an absolute set of dogmas, but as a flexible set of principles that help to fit the form to the occasion. When manipulated with intelligence and taste, these principles of style can enhance and support your broader purposes in writing.

A Fresh Look at Capitalization

The rules on capitalization give most people fits. First of all, there are a seemingly endless number of rules to master; second, the authorities themselves don't agree on the rules; and third, the actual practices of writers often don't agree with any of the contradictory recommendations of the authorities.

A frequent solution is to pretend that disagreements on capitalization style don't exist; instead, people are given one fixed set of rules to be applied under all circumstances. Yet all too many people never do remember the full complement of rules, and those they do remember they apply mechanically without comprehension. As a result, they never get to see that capitalization can be a powerful instrument of style if it is shrewdly and knowingly used.

To understand the basic function of capitalization, you should know that capitalization gives importance, emphasis, and distinction to everything it touches. That's why we capitalize the first word of every sentence—to signify emphatically that a new sentence has begun. That's why we capitalize proper nouns like *Marianne* and *California* and *April*—to indicate distinctively that these are the official names of particular people, places, or things. Moreover, when we take a word that normally occurs as a common noun and capitalize it, we are loading into that word the special significance that a proper noun possesses. The *fourth of July,* for example, is just another day in the year; when it signifies a national holiday, it becomes the *Fourth of July.* In exactly the same way, the *white house* that stands at 1600 Pennsylvania Avenue becomes the *White House* when we think of it, not as one of many white houses, but as the residence of the *President,* who is himself something special compared to the *president* of a business firm.

This process of giving special significance to a common noun and transforming it into a proper noun explains why we capitalize names coined from common nouns—for example, the *Windy City,* the *First Lady,* the *Sunflower State,* the *Stars and Stripes, Mother's Day,* and the *Industrial Revolution.* And it also explains why manufacturers who coin trade names try to register them whenever possible. As long as they can get legal protection for these names, they are entitled to capitalize them. The owners of such trade names as *Coke, Kleenex, Photostat, Dacron, Levi's,* and *Xerox* are likely to take legal action against anyone who uses such words generically. They are determined to protect their rights zealously because they don't want to lose the distinctive forcefulness that a capitalized noun possesses. In this respect they demonstrate an understanding of the function of capitalization that few of us can compete with.

Once it becomes clear that capitalization is a process of loading special significance into words, it's easier to understand why capitalization practices vary so widely. Individual writers will assign importance to words from their own vantage points. The closer they are to the term in question, the more inclined they will be to capitalize it. Thus it is quite possible that what is important to me (and therefore worthy of capitalization) may not be important to you and thus will not be capitalized.

One could cite any number of examples to prove the point. A retail merchant will take out full-page ads so that he can exclaim in print about his *Year-End*

Clearance Sale. The rest of us can respect his right to capitalize the phrase, but we are under no obligation to share his enthusiasm for what is, after all, just another *year-end clearance sale.* In legal agreements, as another example, it's customary to load such terms as *buyer* and *seller* with the significance of proper nouns and thus write, "The *Buyer* agrees to pay the *Seller*. . ."; in all other contexts, however, this kind of emphasis would not be warranted.

When it is understood that it is appropriate to capitalize a given term in some contexts but not necessarily in all contexts, a lot of the agony about capitalization disappears. Instead of trying to decide whether *Federal Government* or *federal government* is correct, you should recognize that both forms are valid and that depending on the context and the importance you want to attach to the term, one form will be more appropriate to your purpose than another. If you are a federal employee, you are very likely to write *Federal Government* under all circumstances, out of respect for the organization that employs you. If you are not a government employee, you are more likely to write *federal government* under ordinary circumstances. If, however, you are writing to someone connected with the federal government or you are writing a report or document in which the federal government is strongly personified, you will probably choose the capitalized form.

By the same token, you need not agonize over the proper way to treat terms like *advertising department, finance committee,* and *board of directors.* These are well-established generic terms as well as the official names of actual units within an organization. Thus you are likely to capitalize these terms if they refer to units within your own organization, because you would be expected to assign a good deal of importance to such things. But you wouldn't have to capitalize these terms when referring to someone else's organization unless for reasons of courtesy or flattery you wanted to indicate that you considered that organization important. (For example, "I would like to apply for a job as copywriter in your Advertising Department.") Moreover, when writing to outsiders, you should keep in mind whether or not they would assign the same importance you do to units within your organization. In an interoffice memo you would no doubt write, "David Walsh has been appointed to the Board of Directors"; in a news release intended for a general audience, you would more likely write, "David Walsh has been appointed to the board of directors of the Wilmington Corporation."

This switch in form from one context to another will appear surprising only to those who assume that one form is intrinsically right and the other intrinsically wrong. Actually, there are many more familiar instances of this kind of flexibility. We normally write the names of seasons in lowercase (for example, *spring*), but when the season is meant to be personified, we switch to uppercase (*Spring*). The words *earth, sun,* and *moon* are normally expressed in lowercase, but when these terms are used in the same context with proper names like *Mars* and *Venus,* they also become capitalized. Or we write that we are taking courses in *history* and *art,* but once these terms become part of the official names of courses, we write *History 101* and *Art 5C.*

O nce you come to view capitalization as a flexible instrument of style, you should be able to cope more easily with ambiguous or conflicting rules. For example, one of the most troublesome rules concerns whether or not to capitalize titles when they follow a person's name or are used in place of the name. According to many authorities, only the titles of "high-ranking" officials and dignitaries should be capitalized when they follow or replace a person's name. But how high is high? Where does one draw the line? You can easily become confused at this point because the authorities as well as individual writers have drawn the line at various places. So it helps to understand that the answer to how high is high will depend on where you stand in relation to the person named. At the international level, a lot of us would be willing to bestow initial caps on the *Queen of England,* the *Premier of France,* the *Pope,* the *Secretary General of the United Nations,* and people of similar eminence. At the national level in this country, many of us would agree on honoring with caps the *President,* the *Vice President,* Cabinet members (such as the *Attorney General* and the *Secretary of Defense*), the heads of federal agencies and bureaus (such as the *Director* or the *Commissioner*), but probably not lower-ranking officials in the national government. (However, if you worked in Washington and were closer to those lower-ranking people, you might very well draw the line so as to include at least some of them.) At the state level, we would probably all agree to honor the *Governor* and even the *Lieutenant Governor,* but most of us would probably refer to the *attorney general* of the state in lowercase (unless, of course, we worked for the state government or had dealings with the official in question, in which case we would write the *Attorney General*). Because most people who write style manuals are removed from the local levels of government, they rarely sanction the use of caps for the titles of local officials; but anyone who works for the local government or on the local newspaper or has direct dealings with these officials will assign to the titles of these officials a good deal more importance than the writers of style manuals typically do. Indeed, if I were writing to the mayor of my town or to someone in the mayor's office, I would refer to the *Mayor.* But if I discuss this official with you in writing, I would refer to the *mayor;* in this context it would be bestowing excessive importance on this person to capitalize the title.

What about titles of high-ranking officials in your own organization? They certainly are important to you, even if not to the outside world. Such titles are usually capped in formal minutes of a meeting or in formal documents (such as a company charter or a set of bylaws). In ordinary written communications, however, these titles are not—as a matter of taste—usually capitalized, for capitalization would confer an excessive importance on a person who is neither a public official nor a prominent dignitary. But those who insist on paying this gesture of respect and honor to their top executives have the right to do it if they want to. (And in some companies this gesture is demanded.)

In the final analysis, the important thing is for you to establish an appropriate capitalization style for a given context—and having established that style, to follow it consistently within that context, even though you might well adopt a different style in another context. Though others may disagree with your specific applications of the rules, no one can fault you if you have brought both sense and sensitivity to your use of capitalization.

The Comma Trauma

C onsider the poor comma, a plodding workhorse in the fields of prose—
exceedingly useful but like most workhorses overworked. Because it can
do so many things, a number of writers dispense the comma to cure their
ailing prose the way doctors dispense aspirin: according to this prescription, you
take two at frequent intervals and hope the problem will go away. Other writers,
having written, stand back to admire their handiwork as if it were a well-risen
cake—and for the final touch they sprinkle commas down upon it like so much
confectioner's sugar. And one writer I know, when pushed to desperation, will
type several rows of commas at the bottom of her letter and urge you to insert
them in the copy above wherever you think it appropriate.

It's too bad that commas induce a trauma in so many writers. Despite the
seemingly endless set of rules that describe their varied powers, commas have
only two basic functions: they either separate or set off. Separating requires only
one comma; setting off requires two.

The separating functions of the comma, for the most part, are easy to spot
and not hard to master. A separating comma is used:

1. To separate the two main clauses in a compound sentence when they are
   joined by *and, but, or,* or *nor.*
2. To separate three or more items in a series (*Tom, Dick, and Harry*)—unless all
   the items are joined by *and* or *or* (*Bob and Carol and Ted and Alice*).
3. To signify the omission of *and* between adjectives of equal rank (as in *a quiet,
   unassuming personality*).
4. To separate the digits of numbers into groups of thousands (*30,000*).

Writers get into trouble here mostly as a result of separating things that
should not be separated—for example, a subject and a verb (*Bob, Carol, Ted, and
Alice*⌇*decided to see a movie*) or an adjective and a noun (*a quiet, unassuming*⌇
personality). Yet this is not where the comma trauma begins to set in.

T he real crunch comes with the commas that set off. These are the commas that are intended to set off words, phrases, or clauses that (1) provide additional but nonessential information or (2) are out of their normal order in the sentence or (3) manage, in one way or another, to disrupt the
flow of the sentence from subject to verb to object or complement. What makes
it so difficult for people to use these commas correctly is that they have a hard
time analyzing the difference between an expression used as an essential element in one context and as a nonessential element in another.

Consider the following example. I would venture that most people have
been taught to punctuate the sentence exactly as it is given here:

It is, therefore, essential that we audit all accounts at once.

To be specific, they have probably been taught that *therefore* is always nonessential
when it occurs within a sentence and that it must therefore always be set off by
commas. What they probably have not been taught is that commas that set off
(unlike commas that separate) usually signal the way a sentence should sound
when spoken aloud. For example, if I were to read the foregoing sentence aloud

the way it has been punctuated, I would pause slightly at the sign of the first comma and then let my voice drop on the word *therefore:*

>   IT IS, therefore, ESSENTIAL . . .

Now if this is the reading that is desired, then the use of commas around *therefore* is quite correct. Yet I would venture that most people would read the sentence this way:

>   It is THEREFORE essential . . .

letting the voice rise on *therefore* to give it the special emphasis it demands. If this is the desired reading, then commas would be altogether wrong in this sentence, for they would induce a "nonessential" inflection in the voice where none is wanted.

If people have been mechanically inserting commas around *therefore* and similar words where commas do not belong, it is because they have not been encouraged to listen to the way the sentences are supposed to sound. Certainly once you become aware of the differences in inflection and phrasing that accompany essential and nonessential elements, it becomes a lot easier for you to distinguish between them and to insert or omit commas accordingly. Given this kind of approach, sentences like the following pair are simple to cope with.

>   Please let me know *if I have remembered everything correctly.*
>
>   He said he would meet us at three, *if I remember correctly.*

Although it would be possible, by means of a structural analysis, to establish why the first *if* clause is essential and why the second is not, you would do well to be guided by the inflection implied in each sentence. In the first instance, the voice arcs as it bridges the gap between *Please let me know* and *if I have remembered everything correctly.* In the second instance, the inflectional arc embraces only the first part of the sentence, *He said he would meet us at three;* then comes a slight pause followed by the *if* clause, which is uttered in a much lower register, almost as if it were an afterthought.

As you gain confidence in your ability to detect the inflectional patterns characteristic of essential and nonessential expressions, you should have no difficulty in picking your way through a variety of constructions like these:

>   I must report, *nevertheless,* that his work is unsatisfactory.
>
>   I must *nevertheless* report that his work is unsatisfactory.
>
>   The location, *I must admit,* is quite attractive.
>
>   The location is one *I must admit* I find attractive.
>
>   There are, *of course,* other possible answers to the problem.
>
>   It is *of course* your prerogative to change your mind.

This awareness of inflectional patterns is especially helpful when it comes to coping with appositives, a frustrating area in which the use or omission of commas often seems illogical. When the appositive expression is truly nonessential, as in:

>   Ed Brown, *the president of Apex,* would like to meet you.

the customary pause and the characteristic drop in voice are there. And when the appositive expression is essential, as in phrases like *the year 1996* and *the term "recommend,"* you can hear the single inflectional arc that embraces each group of words in one closely knit unit. You can also hear the same continuous arc in the phrase *my wife Marie.* By all that is logical, the name *Marie* should be set off by commas because it is not needed to establish which of my wives I'm speaking about; unlike an Arabian sheik, I have only one wife. Yet according to today's standards, *my wife Marie* is considered good form. Although not essential to the meaning, the name *Marie* is treated as if it were essential because of what style manuals call "a very close relationship with the preceding words." Although it is difficult, if not impossible, to state in concrete terms what constitutes "a very close relationship," you can tell by the sound when it exists. There is a subtle but very real difference in the phrases *my sister Florence* and *my sister, Florence Stern.* Once the second name is added, there tends to be a slight pause after *sister* and the voice tends to drop while uttering the full name. Yet it is not safe to conclude that adding the second name accounts for the difference in the inflection, for when one speaks of *the composer John Cage* or *the author John Fowles,* one hears the same inflectional pattern as in *my wife Marie* or *the year 1990.* So in the case of appositives, it is wise to be wary of simple generalizations and to listen attentively in each case to the way the expression ought to sound.

In stressing, as I have, the significance of inflection and phrasing as a guide to the use of commas, I do not mean to suggest that one can punctuate by sound alone and can safely ignore structure and meaning. What I am suggesting is that in a number of cases, such as those I have cited, an awareness of the sound of sentences can help you grasp relationships that might otherwise be obscure.

There are many other problems involving the comma that should be discussed here, but someone else (Ogden Nash, perhaps) will have to take over . . .

> And now if you'll excuse me comma
> I must lie down and have my trauma . . . ,

The Plight of the Compound Adjective—
Or, Where Have All the Hyphens Gone?

The hyphen, it grieves me to report, is in trouble. Indeed, unless concerted action is taken at once, the hyphen is likely to become as extinct as the apostrophe in *ladies aid*. The problem can be traced to two dangerous attitudes that are afoot these days. One is revolutionary in tone; its motto: "Compound adjectives, unite! You have nothing to lose but your hyphens." The other attitude reflects the view of the silent majority. These are the people who don't pretend to know how to cope with the "hyphen" mess; they just earnestly wish the whole problem would quickly disappear. It may now be too late to reverse the long-range trend. For the present, however, the hyphen exists—and anyone who expects to work with words at an acceptable level of proficiency needs to come to terms with the noble beast. Here, then, is a last-ditch effort to make sense out of an ever-changing and possibly fast-disappearing (but not-soon-to-be-forgotten) aspect of style.

As a general rule, the English language depends largely on word order to make the relationships between words clear. When word order alone is not sufficient to establish these relationships, we typically resort to punctuation. It is in this context that the hyphen has a service to offer. The function of the hyphen is to help the reader grasp clusters of words—or even parts of words—as a unit. When a word has to be divided at the end of a line, the hyphen signifies the connection between parts. Whenever two or more words function as a unit but cannot (for one reason or another) be written either as a solid word or as separate words, the hyphen clearly establishes the relationship between these words and prevents a lapse in comprehension.

If hyphens are typically required in compound adjectives, it is because there is something "abnormal" about the word order of such expressions. Other kinds of modifiers, by contrast, do not require hyphens. For example, if I write about "a *long, hard* winter," I am actually referring to a winter *that will be long and hard;* so I need a comma—not a hyphen—to establish the fact that *long* and *hard* modify *winter* independently. If I write about "a *long opening* paragraph," the word order makes it clear that *opening* modifies *paragraph* and that *long* modifies the two words together; so no punctuation is needed to establish the fact that I'm speaking about *"an opening paragraph that is long."*

However, if I write about "a *long-term* loan," an entirely different relationship is established between the elements in the modifier. I am not speaking of a *loan* that is *long* and *term,* nor am I referring to a *term loan* that is *long.* I am speaking about a loan "that is to run for a *long term* of years." The words *long-term* (unlike *long, hard* or *long opening*) have an internal relationship all their own; it is only as an integral unit that these two words can modify a noun. Thus a hyphen is inserted to establish this fact clearly.

For a better understanding of the internal relationship that exists between the elements in a compound adjective, one has to go back to its origins. A compound adjective is actually a compressed version of an adjective phrase or clause. For example, if I describe a product as carrying "a *money-back* guarantee," I am actually talking about "a guarantee *to give you your money back if you are not satisfied with the product.*" Or if I refer to "a *take-charge* kind of guy," I am really speaking of "the kind of guy *who always takes charge of any situation he finds himself in.*" One can easily see from these examples why compound adjectives are so popular, for these expressions are usually a good deal crisper and livelier than the phrases or clauses they represent. These examples give further evidence of why a hyphen is needed. In each case we have zeroed in on a couple of words, we have wrenched them out of context and out of their normal order in a descriptive phrase or clause, and we have inserted them before a noun as if they were an ordinary adjective—a role these two words were never originally designed to play. Deprived of all the other words that would clearly establish the relationship between them, these elements require a hyphen to hold them together.

The two factors of compression and dislocation are all the justification one needs to hyphenate a compound adjective. However, there are often additional clues to the need for a hyphen. In the process of becoming a compound adjective, the individual words frequently undergo a change in form: "a contract for *two years*" becomes "a *two-year* contract"; a blonde with *blue eyes*" becomes "a *blue-eyed* blonde." Sometimes the words are put in inverted order: "lands *owned* by the *government*" becomes "*government-owned* lands." Sometimes the elements undergo a change both in form *and* in word order: "an employee *who works hard*" becomes "a *hard-working* employee"; "bonds *exempt from taxation*" becomes "*tax-exempt* bonds." The change in form or the inversion in word order is an additional signal that you are in the presence of a compound adjective and ought to hyphenate it.

I f the compound adjective is so simple to understand in theory, why is it so difficult to handle in practice? A good deal of the problem can be traced to that neat but now-discredited rule, "Hyphenate compound adjectives when they precede the noun but not when they follow the noun." It was indeed a very neat rule but not a very precise one. Let's take it apart and see why.

It is quite true that compound adjectives should be hyphenated when they occur *before* a noun—for the most part. There's the catch—"for the most part." The exceptions seem to occur in such a random, hit-and-miss, now-and-then, flip-a-coin, make-it-up-as-you-go-along fashion that one begins to lose respect for the rule. Yet there is a very definite pattern to the exceptions. Keep in mind that the hyphen serves to hold a cluster of words together as a unit. If, through some other means, these words make themselves clearly recognizable as a unit, the hyphen is superfluous and can be omitted. There are at least three such situations where a hyphen is unnecessary: when the compound modifier is a proper name, when it is a well-recognized foreign expression, and when it is a well-established compound noun serving as a compound adjective. Let's look at some samples.

If I speak of "a *Madison Avenue* agency," the capital *M* and *A* virtually guarantee that the expression will be quickly grasped as a unit. And if I talk about "a *bona fide* contract," the reader will recognize this Latin expression as a unit without the help of a hyphen. By the same token, terms like *social security, life insurance,* and *high school* are so well established as compound nouns that when they are used as adjectives, we immediately grasp such expressions as a unit, without the support of any punctuation.

If no hyphen is needed in "*social security* benefits," one may well ask why a hyphen is required in "*short-term* benefits." After all, words like *short term* and *long range* are adjective-noun combinations that closely resemble *social security, life insurance,* and *high school.* Why hyphenate some and not others? The reason is this: Words like *short term, long range,* and *high level* don't have any standing as compound nouns in their own right; they do not represent a concept or an institution (as terms like *social security* and *life insurance* do). Therefore, these words require a hyphen to hold them together when they occur before a noun.

Once you grasp the difference between *social security* and *short-term* as compound adjectives, you can use these two expressions as touchstones in deciding how to handle other adjective-noun combinations. With a principle like this in hand, you don't have to engage in profound analysis to resolve the "hyphen problem." Consider a random list of examples such as these:

a *red letter* day	a *white collar* worker
a *civil service* test	a *real estate* agent
mass production techniques	*word processing* equipment
long distance calls	*high level* decisions

The expressions *civil service, mass production, real estate,* and *word processing* all resemble *social security,* since they stand for well-known concepts or institutions; therefore, as compound adjectives they can all be written without hyphens. However, *red-letter, long-distance, white-collar,* and *high-level* are much more like *short-term* and should have a hyphen.

S o much for compound adjectives before the noun. When they occur *after* the noun, according to the traditional rule, they should not be hyphenated. Yet this traditional formulation is somewhat misleading. If we aren't supposed to hyphenate a "compound adjective" when it follows a noun, it's for the simple reason that the words in question no longer function as a compound adjective—they are playing a normal role in a normal order. It's one thing to use hyphens in the expression "an *up-to-date* report," for a prepositional phrase doesn't normally belong before a noun. However, if I said "This report is *up to date,*" there would be no more justification for hyphenating here than there would be if I said "This report is *in good shape.*" Both expressions—*in good shape* and *up to date*— are prepositional phrases playing a normal role in the predicate.

However, if the expression still exhibits an abnormal form or inverted word order in the predicate, it is still a compound adjective—and it must still be hyphenated. For example, whether I speak of *"tax-exempt* items" or say "these items are *tax-exempt,*" the hyphen must be inserted because regardless of where it appears—*before* or *after* the noun—the expression is a compressed version of the phrase "exempt from taxation."

There are at least four kinds of compound adjectives that must always be hyphenated *after* as well as *before* the noun (because of inverted word order or change of form). These compound adjectives consist of the following patterns:

noun + adjective (*duty-free*)
noun + participle (*interest-bearing*)
adjective + participle (*soft-spoken*)
adjective + noun + *ed* (*old-fashioned*)

Once you learn to recognize these four patterns, you can safely assume that any compound adjective that fits one of these patterns must always be hyphenated, no matter where it falls in a sentence.*

It does no good to pretend that compound adjectives are an easy thing to master. They aren't. And for that very reason people who have to cope with these expressions need more guidance than they get from a simple "hyphenate before but not after" kind of rule. In the final analysis, what becomes of the hyphen over the long run is of little consequence. What does matter is that we express ourselves with precision, verve, and grace. If the hyphen can help us toward that end, why not make use of it?

---

*There is only one worm in this rosy apple: some of the words that fit these patterns are now acceptably spelled as one word.

The Semicolon; and Other Myths

I
n certain circles that I move in, the fastest way I know to start a quarrel is to attack the semicolon. If I knocked my friends' politics or sneered at their religious beliefs, they would simply smile. But attack their views on the semicolon and they reach for a bread knife. Why this particular mark of punctuation should excite such intense passion escapes me. The semicolon has always been a neurotic creature, continually undergoing an identity crisis. After all, it is half comma and half period, and from its name you would think it is half a colon. It is hardly any wonder, then, that a lot of people are half crazy trying to determine who the semicolon really is and what its mission in life is supposed to be.

In the course of this brief essay, I am going to explore three myths that have grown up over the years about the semicolon and about some other marks of punctuation.

Myth No. 1: If either clause in a compound sentence contains an internal comma, use a semicolon (not a comma) before the coordinating conjunction that connects the clauses. According to this line of reasoning, it is all right to use a comma in a compound sentence like this:

> The regional meeting in Salem has been canceled, but all other meetings will go on as scheduled.

However, if I use commas for a lesser purpose within either clause (for example, by inserting *Oregon* after *Salem* and setting it off with commas), then the comma before the conjunction must be upgraded to a semicolon.

> The regional meeting in Salem, Oregon, has been canceled; but all other meetings will go on as scheduled.

It is harsh, I concede, to dismiss this rule as a myth when it has been taught for years in various classes and various texts. But the unhappy fact is that outside those classes and those texts, almost no one punctuates that way anymore. The trouble with using a semicolon in such sentences is that it creates a break that is too strong for the occasion. It closes down the action of the sentence at a point where the writer would like it to keep on going. So contemporary writers see nothing wrong with using commas simultaneously to separate clauses and to perform lesser functions within the clauses—unless, of course, total confusion or misreading is likely to result. But in most cases it doesn't. In the following sentence, commas are used both *within* clauses and *between* clauses without any loss of clarity and also without any loss of verbal momentum.

> On March 16, 1993, I wrote to your credit manager, Mr. Lopez, but I have not yet heard from him.

This simultaneous use of commas within and between clauses may look offensive to anyone accustomed to the traditional rule. The fact remains that we have been using commas for both purposes in *complex* sentences all along, and it has never occasioned any comment.

> Although I wrote to your credit manager, Mr. Lopez, on March 16, 1993, I have not yet heard from him.

It should be clearly understood that the use of a semicolon before the conjunction in a compound sentence is not wrong. If you want a strong break at that point, the semicolon can and should be used. But you ought to know that the reason for using it is the special effect it creates—and not the presence of internal commas. For example:

> I have tried again and again to explain to George why the transaction had to be kept secret from him; but he won't believe me.

Myth No. 2: Always use a semicolon before an enumeration or an explanation introduced by *for example, namely,* or *that is.* In many cases this rule is quite true, but in other cases either a colon or a comma is better suited to the occasion. Let's look at some examples.

> There are several things you could do to save your business (?) namely, try to get a loan from the bank, find yourself a partner with good business judgment, or pray that your competitor goes out of business before you do.

If you put a semicolon before *namely,* you will close the action down just when the sentence is starting to get somewhere. Because the first part of the sentence creates an air of anticipation, because it implicitly promises to reveal several ways of saving the business, you need not a mark that closes the action down but one that supports the air of anticipation. Enter the colon.

The colon is one of the underrated stars in the firmament of punctuation. It would be more widely used, perhaps, if its sound effects were better understood. The colon is the mark of anticipation. It is a blare of trumpets before the grand entrance; it is the roll of drums before the dive off the 100-foot tower. It marks the end of the buildup and gets you ready for "the real thing." Thus:

> There are several things you can do to save your business: namely, try to get a loan . . .

Consider this example, however:

> Always express numbers in figures when they are accompanied by abbreviations; for example, *4 p.m., 8 ft.*

The first part of this sample sentence expresses a self-contained thought. If the sentence ended right there, the reader would not be left up in the air. The examples that follow are unexpected, unanticipated, added on almost as an afterthought. We're glad to have them, but they aren't anything we were counting on. The semicolon here is quite appropriate; it momentarily closes down the action of the sentence after the main point is expressed.

In other situations a comma may be the best mark to use before *namely, for example,* or *that is.* Consider this sentence as an example:

> Do not use quotation marks to enclose an *indirect quotation,* that is, a restatement of a person's exact words.

In this case, a semicolon would be inappropriate before *that is* because it would close off the action just as we were about to get a definition of a term within the main clause. Moreover, a colon would be inappropriate because it would imply that the sentence up to that point was a buildup for what follows—and that is not true in this case. Here all that is needed is a simple comma to preserve the close relationship between the term *indirect quotation* and the explanatory expression that follows it.

Myth No. 3: When a polite request is phrased as a question, end it with a period. This is another statement that does not, unfortunately, always hold true. In fact, once a period is used at the end of some requests, they no longer sound very polite. I once posted the following note in my home: "Will you please close the door." My children knew this was not really a polite request but a firm parental command. When they chose to ignore it, I amended the sign to read, "Will you please close the door!" (I was relying on the exclamation point to carry the full force of my exasperation.) That approach failed too, so I tried a new tack in diplomacy, amending the sign once again: "Will you please close the door?" My children now knew they had broken my spirit. They now sensed in the sign a pleading note, a petitioning tone, the begging of a favor. They also knew that now I was asking them a real yes-or-no question (or at least I was creating the illusion of asking). Then, in the paradoxical way that children have, once they knew they had the chance to say no, they began to answer my question with tacit affirmations, tugging the door after them on the way out or kicking it shut behind them on the way in.

My problems with my kids are, of course, my own, but learning how to express and punctuate polite requests tends to be a problem for all of us. Consider, for a moment, the wording of those three signs, alike in all respects except for the final mark of punctuation. The version that ends with a period is really a quiet but nonetheless firm demand. There is no element of a question in it at all. The voice rises in an arc and then flattens out at the end on a note of resolution. In the version that ends with an exclamation point, the voice rises in a higher arc and resounds with greater intensity and force of feeling, but it, too, comes down at the end—this time with something of a bang. In the final version, the one with the question mark, the voice starts on an upward curve and then trails off, still on an upward note. Three different readings of the same words, each with a different impact on the reader—all evoked by three different punctuation marks at the end.

Once you become sensitive to the effects produced by these marks of punctuation, handling polite requests becomes quite simple. All you have to do is say the sentence aloud and listen to the sound of your own voice. If you end the sentence with your voice on an upward note, you know that a question mark is the right punctuation to use. If your voice comes down at the end, you know that you need a period. (And if you really feel forceful about it, you probably want an exclamation point.)

If there is any potential danger in so simple a rule, it is this: we sometimes express our requests orally as flat assertions ("Will you please do this for me.") when, as a matter of good taste and good manners, we ought to be asking a question ("Will you please do this for me?").

Now it is true that in the normal course of events we all make demands on one another, and though we tack on a "Will you please" for the sake of politeness, these are still demands, not questions. As long as your reader is not likely to consider them presumptuous, it is appropriate to punctuate these demands with periods:

> Will you please sign both copies of the contract and return the original to me.
>
> May I suggest that you confirm the departure time for your flight before you leave for the airport.
>
> Will you please give my best regards to your family.

As opposed to these routine demands, there is the kind of polite request that asks the reader for a special favor. Here, if you really want to be polite, you will punctuate your request as a question so as to give your reader the chance to say no.

> May I please see you sometime next week?
>
> May I please get an advance copy of the confidential report you are doing?
>
> Will you please acknowledge all my correspondence for me while I'm away?

In these cases you are asking for things that the reader may be unable or unwilling to grant; therefore, you ought to pose these requests as questions. (If you try reading them as statements, you will observe how quickly they change into peremptory demands.) Suppose, however, that these requests were addressed to your subordinates. Under those conditions you would have the right to expect your reader to make the time to see you, to supply you with an advance copy of the confidential report, and to handle your mail for you; therefore, you would be justified in ending these sentences with periods. But even when you have this authority over your reader, you ought to consider the alternative of asking. The inspired public official who replaced the "Keep Off the Grass" signs with a simple "PLEASE?" understood people and how they like to be talked to. If a question mark will get faster results or establish a nicer tone, why not use it?

There are other myths that one could discuss, but these three are sufficient to permit me to make one central point. Mastery over the rules of punctuation depends to a considerable extent on cultivating a sensitivity to the way a sentence moves and the way it sounds.

Punctuating by ear has come to be frowned on—and with much justification—for it has come to mean punctuating solely by feeling, by instinct, by intuition, without much regard for (or knowledge of) the structure of the language and the function of punctuation. Yet the solution, it seems to me, is not to abandon the technique of punctuating by ear but to cultivate it, to develop in yourself a disciplined sense of the relationship between the sound and the structure and the mechanics of language. Many authorities on language, if pressed, have to concede that they often consider first whether a thing sounds right or looks right; only then do they utter a pronouncement as to why it is right. If they rely on their ears for this kind of assurance, then why don't you cultivate the same skill?

Re Abbrevs.

Sensitive environmentalists will tell you that emissions from smokestacks and automobile exhaust pipes are not the only forms of pollution that are potentially deadly to human beings. All about us are forces of depersonalization that continually menace the human touches that have previously graced our lives. Most of us have become reconciled to being numerical entities on computer printouts. We have adjusted—many of us—to the loss of those elegant telephone exchanges (*PLaza 9, ASpinwall 7*).

But new forms of pollutants continually appear on the atmospheric scene. We are beginning to choke—some of us—on the fog of initials and abbreviations and "memorable" acronyms that are intended to identify worthwhile examples of human endeavor. One gem is *HURRAH* (*H*elp *U*s *R*each & *R*ehabilitate *A*merica's *H*andicapped), an instance where a dignified cause is demeaned by a fatuous label, a hollow cheer, an irrelevant salute. Perhaps in self-defense I ought to found a group called *HELP* (*H*elp *E*liminate *L*inguistic *P*ollution).

To put matters in perspective, it may help to think of abbreviations as belonging to the same class of objects as instant coffee, powdered eggs, and TV dinners. They don't take up much space and they're great when you're in a hurry, but they never have the taste of the real thing. Abbreviations are always appropriate in highly expedient documents (such as invoices, pur-. chase orders, low-level interoffice memos, and routine correspondence), where the emphasis is on precise communication of data in the briefest possible space without concern for style or elegance of expression. But in other kinds of writing, where some attention is given to the *effect* to be made on the reader, a more formal style prevails—and under these circumstances only certain kinds of abbreviations are acceptable.

Some that are always acceptable, even in the most formal contexts, are those that precede or follow personal names (*Mr., Mrs., Jr., Sr., Ph.D., Esq.*), those that are part of an organization's legal name (*Inc., Ltd., Co.*), those used in expressions of time (*a.m., p.m., PST, EDT*), and a few miscellaneous expressions (such as *B.C.* and *A.D.*).

Those venerable Latin abbreviations *etc., i.e., e.g.,* and the like are usually acceptable, but in writing that aspires to a certain elegance or formality they ought to be replaced, not by the full Latin expressions, but rather by the English expressions *and so forth* (or *and the like*), *that is, for example,* or appropriate equivalents.

Organizations with long names are now commonly identified by their initials in all but the most formal writing—*IBM, AT&T, AFL-CIO, UNICEF, FBI, CBS.* Even the initials *U.S.* are now acceptable in all but the most formal writing when used in the names of federal agencies (such as the *U.S. Department of Labor*); however, using the initials by themselves (as in *throughout the U.S.*) is bad form.

Abbreviations of days of the week, of names of months, of geographic names, and of units of measure are appropriate only in business forms, in correspondence that is clearly expedient, and in tables where space is tight.

Although it may seem troublesome knowing *when* to abbreviate, it is often more troublesome knowing *how* to abbreviate. There are so many variations in style (involving the use of caps or small letters, the use or omission of periods, and the use or omission of internal space) that it is often difficult to find an authoritative source to follow. (*Webster's Ninth New Collegiate Dictionary*, for example, omits virtually all periods from its list of abbreviations, as if this were now the commonly accepted practice. Webster, of course, uses periods with many of the abbreviations that appear in the main text. See ¶503, note.)

Here are a few safe guidelines:

1. An all-capital abbreviation made up of the initials of several words is normally written without periods and without internal space (for example, *IBM, UAW, BPOE, SEC, IQ*). The only major exceptions are geographic names (such as *U.S.A.*), academic degrees (such as *B.A., M.D.*), and a few odd expressions (such as *A.D., B.C.,* and *P.O.*).
2. A small-letter abbreviation that consists of the initials of several words is normally written *with* a period after each initial but *without* space after internal periods (for example, *a.m., e.g.*).
3. When an abbreviation can be styled in all caps (*COD, FOB*) or in small letters (*c.o.d., f.o.b.*), reserve the use of all caps for business forms and similar documents where the blatant look of the capitals will not matter.
4. When an abbreviation stands for several words and consists of more than initials, insert a period and a space after each element in the abbreviation (for example, *Lt. Col., op. cit.*). Academic degrees, however, are an exception: write them *with* the periods but *without* internal space (for example, *Ph.D., Ed.D., LL.B.*).
5. A person's initials are now usually written without periods and space (as in *JFK*) unless they are part of the full name (as in *J. F. Kennedy*).

So much, in brief, for abbreviations. Useful devices on many occasions, but— except for an *R.S.V.P.* delicately scripted in the lower left corner of a formal invitation—not very elegant.

The
Gregg
Reference
Manual

PART 1

Grammar, Usage, and Style

SECTION

1

Punctuation: Major Marks

The Semicolon

The Colon

Punctuation marks are the mechanical means for making the meaning of a sentence easily understood. They indicate the proper relationships between words, phrases, and clauses when word order alone is not sufficient to make these relationships clear.

One important caution about punctuation. If you find it particularly hard to determine the appropriate punctuation for a sentence you have written, the chances are that the sentence is improperly constructed. To be on the safe side, recast your thought in a form you can handle with confidence. In any event, do not try to save a badly constructed sentence by means of punctuation.

Section 1 deals with the three marks of terminal punctuation (the period, the question mark, and the exclamation point) plus the three major marks of internal punctuation (the comma, the semicolon, and the colon). All other marks of punctuation are covered in Section 2.

The Period

At the End of a Statement or Command

101 Use a period to mark the end of a sentence that makes a statement or expresses a command. (Leave two spaces between the period and the start of the next sentence. For complete guidelines on spacing, see ¶299.)

> John W. Hirsch, president of Seglin Controls Inc., has announced the company's plan to acquire Parker Associates before the end of this year.
>
> I question the need to cut advertising and promotion expenses at this time.
>
> All monthly expense reports must be submitted no later than the 10th of the following month.
>
> Make sure that Kate gets to the airport by 10 a.m. (The period that marks the end of the abbreviation also serves to mark the end of the sentence.)

102 Use a period to mark the end of an *elliptical* (condensed) expression that represents a complete statement or command. Elliptical expressions often occur as answers to questions or as transitional phrases.

> Yes.   No.   Of course.   Indeed.   By all means.
>
> Enough on that subject.   Now, to proceed to your next point.

NOTE: Do not confuse elliptical expressions with sentence fragments. An elliptical expression represents a complete sentence. A sentence fragment is a word, phrase, or clause that is incorrectly treated as a separate sentence when in fact it ought to be incorporated with adjacent words to make up a complete sentence.

> Great news! The laser printer arrived yesterday. After we had waited for six weeks. (*Great news* is an elliptical expression; it represents a complete sentence, *I have great news. After we had waited for six weeks* is a sentence fragment, incorrectly treated as a sentence in its own right; this dependent clause should be linked with the main clause that precedes it.)
>
> REVISED: Great news! The laser printer arrived yesterday, after we had waited for six weeks.

¶103

1

At the End of a Polite Request or Command

103 a. Requests, suggestions, and commands are often phrased as questions out of politeness. Use a period to end this kind of sentence if you expect your reader to respond *by acting* rather than by giving you a yes-or-no answer.

Will you please call us at once if we can be of further help.

Would you please send all bills to my bank for payment while I'm out of the country.

May I suggest that you put your request in writing and send it to Mr. Herzog for his approval.

If you can't attend the meeting, could you please send someone else in your place.

NOTE: Use a period only when you are sure that your reader is not likely to consider your request presumptuous.

b. If you are asking a favor or making a request that your reader may be unable or unwilling to grant, use a question mark at the end of the sentence. The question mark offers your reader a chance to say no to your request and helps to preserve the politeness of the situation.

May I ask a favor of you? Could you spare fifteen minutes to tell my son about career opportunities in your company?

Will you be able to have someone in your department help me on the Woonsocket project?

Will you please handle the production reports for me while I'm away?

c. If you are not sure whether to use a question mark or a period, reword the sentence so that it is clearly a question or a statement; then punctuate accordingly. For example, the sentence directly above could be revised as follows:

Would you be willing to handle the production reports for me while I'm away?

I would appreciate your handling the production reports for me while I'm away.

d. When you are addressing a request to someone who reports to you, you expect that person to comply. Therefore, a period can properly be used to punctuate such requests. However, since most people prefer to be *asked* to do something rather than be *told* to do it, a question mark establishes a nicer tone and often gets better results. Consider using a question mark when your request to a subordinate involves something beyond the routine aspects of the job.

Will you please let me know what your vacation plans are for the month of August. (Routine request to a subordinate.)

May I ask that you avoid scheduling any vacation time during August this year? I will need your help in preparing next year's forecasts and budgets. (Special request to a subordinate. The question mark suggests that the writer is sensitive to the problems this request could cause.)

NOTE: If you are unwilling to give your subordinate the impression that your request allows for a yes-or-no answer, simply drop the attempt at politeness and issue a straightforward command.

I must ask that you not schedule any vacation time during August this year. I will need your help in preparing next year's forecasts and budgets.

At the End of an Indirect Question

104 Use a period to mark the end of an indirect question. (See also ¶¶115–116.)

> Frank Wilcox has asked whether an exception can be made to our leave-of-absence policy.
>
> The only question she asked was when the report had to be on your desk.
>
> Why Janet Murray left the company so quickly has never been explained.
>
> We know what needs to be done; the question is how to pay for it.

With Decimals

105 Use a period (without space before or after it) to separate a whole number from a decimal fraction; for example, *$5.50, 33.33 percent.*

In Outlines and Displayed Lists

106 Use periods after numbers or letters that enumerate items in an outline or a displayed list—unless the numbers or letters are enclosed in parentheses. (See ¶¶107, 199c, 223, 1357d, 1424f for illustrations.)

107 a. Use periods after independent clauses, dependent clauses, or long phrases that are displayed on separate lines in a list. Also use periods after short phrases that are essential to the grammatical completeness of the statement introducing the list. (In the following example the three listed items are all objects of the preposition *on* in the introductory statement.)

> Please get me year-end figures *on*:
>> a. Domestic sales revenues.
>> b. Total operating costs.
>> c. Net operating income.

b. No periods are needed after short phrases in a list if the introductory statement is grammatically complete (as in the first example below) or if the listed items are like those on an inventory sheet or a shopping list.

> This computer offers features that are typically found on much more expensive models:
>> 1. Built-in graphics capability
>> 2. A space-saving configuration
>> 3. An up-front power switch for easy access

> When you come to take the qualifying examination, please bring:
>> 2 No. 2 pencils
>> 1 ballpoint pen

With Headings

108 a. Use a period after a *run-in* heading (one that begins a paragraph and is immediately followed by text matter on the same line) unless some other mark of punctuation, such as a question mark, is required.

(Continued on page 8.)

Insuring Your Car. Automobile insurance is actually a package of six different types of coverage. . . .

How Much Will It Cost? How much automobile insurance will cost you depends on your driving record, your age, and how much shopping around you do. . . .

b. Omit the period if the heading is *freestanding* (displayed on a line by itself). However, retain a question mark or an exclamation point with a freestanding head if the wording requires it.

TAX-SAVING TECHNIQUES

Tax Elimination or Reduction

Nontaxable Income. Of the various types of nontaxable income, the most significant is the interest paid on municipal bonds. Investment in municipals has become one of the most popular ways to avoid . . .

Is It Legal? Investing your money so as to avoid taxes is perfectly legal. It is quite different from tax evasion, a deliberate attempt to . . .

NOTE: A period follows a run-in expression like *Table 6,* even though the heading as a whole is freestanding.

Table 6. Revised Salary Ranges   Figure 2-4. Departmental Staff Needs

For the treatment of headings in reports and manuscripts, see ¶1425; for the treatment of headings in tables, see ¶¶1612–1615.

A Few Don'ts

109 Don't use a period:

a. After letters used to designate persons or things (for example, *Manager A, Class B, Grade C, Brand X*). **EXCEPTION:** Use a period when the letter is the initial of a person's last name (for example, *Mr. A.* for *Mr. Adams*).

b. After contractions (for example, *cont'd;* see ¶505).

c. After ordinals expressed in figures (*1st, 2d, 3d, 4th*).

d. After roman numerals (for example, *Volume I, David Weild III*).

EXCEPTION: Periods follow roman numerals in an outline. (See ¶223.)

Periods with abbreviations: see ¶¶506–513.
Periods with brackets: see ¶¶296.
Periods with dashes: see ¶¶213, 214a, 215a.
Periods with parentheses: see ¶¶224c, 225a, 225c, 226c.
Periods with quotation marks: see ¶¶247, 252, 253, 257, 258, 259.
Three spaced periods (ellipsis marks): see ¶¶274–280, 291.
Spacing with periods: see ¶299.

The Question Mark

To Indicate Direct Questions

110 **a.** Use a question mark at the end of a direct question. (Leave two spaces between the question mark and the start of the next sentence. For complete guidelines on spacing, see ¶299.)

Will you be able to meet with us after 5 p.m.?

Either way, how can we lose?

NOTE: Be sure to place the question mark at the *end* of the question.

How do you account for this entry: "Paid to E. M. Johnson, $300"?

(**NOT:** How do you account for this entry? "Paid to E. M. Johnson, $300.")

For the punctuation of indirect questions, see ¶¶104, 115, 116.

   b. Use a question mark (or, for special emphasis, an exclamation point) after a *rhetorical question,* a question to which no reply is expected. (See also ¶119b.)

Why not come in and see for yourself?

Wouldn't you rather be stuck in the sands of Florida this winter than in the snowdrifts of New England?

Isn't it incredible that people could actually fall for a scheme like that?

OR: Isn't it incredible that people could actually fall for a scheme like that!

111 Use a question mark at the end of an *elliptical* (condensed) *question,* that is, a word or phrase that represents a complete question.

Marion tells me that you are coming to the Bay Area. When? (The complete question is, "When are you coming?")

NOTE: Punctuate complete and elliptical questions separately, according to your meaning.

When will the job be finished? In a week or two?
(**NOT:** When will the job be finished in a week or two?)

Where shall we meet? At the airport? (With this punctuation, the writer allows for the possibility of meeting elsewhere.)

Where shall we meet at the airport? (With this punctuation, the writer simply wants to pinpoint a more precise location within the airport.)

112 Use a question mark at the end of a sentence that is phrased like a statement but spoken with the rising intonation of a question.

You expect me to believe this story?

Now that he has all the facts, he still intends to proceed?

113 A request, suggestion, or command phrased as a question out of politeness may not require a question mark. (See ¶103.)

To Indicate Questions Within Sentences

114 When a short direct question falls *within a sentence,* set the question off with commas and put a question mark at the end of the sentence. However, when a short direct question falls *at the end of a sentence,* use a comma before it and a question mark after.

I can alter the terms of my will, *can't I,* whenever I wish?

We aren't obligated to attend the meeting, *are we?*

NOTE: Short questions falling within a sentence may also be set off with dashes or parentheses in place of commas. For examples, see ¶¶214b, 224d.

115 When a longer direct question comes *at the end of a sentence,* it starts with a capital letter and is preceded by a comma or a colon. The question mark that ends the question also serves to mark the end of the sentence.

(Continued on page 10.)

The key question is, Whom *shall we* nominate for next year's election?

This is the key question: Whom *shall we* nominate for next year's election? (Use a colon if the introductory matter is an independent clause.)

BUT: We now come to the key question of whom *we shall* nominate for next year's election. (An indirect question requires no special punctuation or capitalization. See ¶116, note.)

OR: We now come to the key question of whom to nominate for next year's election.

116 When a longer direct question comes *at the beginning of a sentence,* it should be followed by a question mark (for emphasis) or simply a comma.

How *can we* achieve these goals? is the next question. (Leave one space after a question mark within a sentence.)

OR: How *can we* achieve these goals, is the next question.

BUT: How *we can* achieve these goals is the next question. (Indirect question; no special punctuation is needed.)

NOTE: In the examples in ¶¶115–116 notice how a simple shift in word order converts a direct question to an indirect question. When the verb precedes the subject *(shall we, can we),* the question is direct. When the verb follows the subject *(we shall, we can),* the question is indirect.

117 a. A series of brief questions at the end of a sentence may be separated by commas or (for emphasis) by question marks. Do not capitalize the individual questions.

Who will be responsible for drafting the proposal, obtaining comments from all the interested parties, preparing the final version, and coordinating the distribution of copies?

OR: Who will be responsible for drafting the proposal? obtaining comments from all the interested parties? preparing the final version? coordinating the distribution of copies?

NOTE: Leave one space after a question mark within a sentence and two spaces after a question mark at the end of a sentence. For complete guidelines on spacing, see ¶299.

b. The brief questions in *a* above are all related to the same subject and predicate *(Who will be responsible for).* Do not confuse this type of sentence pattern with a series of independent questions. Each independent question must start with a capital and end with a question mark.

Before you accept the job offer, think about the following: Will this job give you experience relevant to your real career goal? Will it permit you to keep abreast of the latest technology? Will it pay what you need?

NOTE: Leave two spaces after a question mark that marks the end of an independent question. For complete guidelines on spacing, see ¶299.

c. Independent questions in a series are often elliptical (condensed) expressions. (See ¶111.)

Has Walter's loan been approved? *When? By whom? For what amount?* (In other words: *When* was the loan approved? *By whom* was the loan approved? *For what amount* was the loan approved?)

(**NOT:** Has Walter's loan been approved, when, by whom, and for what amount?)

To Express Doubt

118 A question mark enclosed in parentheses may be used to express doubt or uncertainty about a word or phrase within a sentence. Do not insert any space before the opening parenthesis; leave one space after the closing parenthesis unless another mark of punctuation is required at that point.

> He joined the firm after his graduation from Columbia Law School in 1988(?).

NOTE: When dates are already enclosed within parentheses, question marks may be inserted as necessary to indicate doubt.

> the explorer Verrazano (1485?–1528?)

Question marks with dashes: see ¶¶214b, 215a.
Question marks with parentheses: see ¶¶224d, 225a, 225d, 226c.
Question marks with quotation marks: see ¶¶249, 252, 254, 257, 258, 259.
Spacing with question marks: see ¶299.

The Exclamation Point

The exclamation point is an "emotional" mark of punctuation that is most often found in sales and advertising copy. Like the word *very*, it loses its force when overused, so avoid it wherever possible.

NOTE: If an exclamation point is not a standard character on your equipment, you can construct it with an apostrophe and a period.

To Express Strong Feeling

119 **a.** Use an exclamation point at the end of a sentence (or an elliptical expression that stands for a sentence) to indicate enthusiasm, surprise, disbelief, urgency, or strong feeling. (Leave two spaces between the exclamation point and the start of the next sentence. For complete guidelines on spacing, see ¶299.)

> Yes! We're selling our entire inventory below cost! Doors open at 9 a.m.!
>
> No! I don't believe it!   What a fantastic achievement!   Incredible!

b. An exclamation point may be used in place of a question mark to express strong feeling. (See also ¶110b.)

> How could you do it! What made you think I'd welcome a call at 2:30 a.m.!

c. The exclamation point may be enclosed in parentheses and placed directly after a word that the writer wants to emphasize. Do not insert any space before the opening parenthesis; leave one space after the closing parenthesis unless another mark of punctuation is required at that point.

> We won exclusive(!) distribution rights in the Western Hemisphere.

120 **a.** A single word may be followed by an exclamation point to express intense feeling. The sentence that follows it is punctuated as usual.

> Congratulations! Your summation at the trial was superb.

b. When such words are repeated for emphasis, an exclamation point follows each repetition.

> Going! Going! Our bargains are almost gone!

c. When exclamations are mild, a comma or a period is sufficient.

> Well, well, things could be worse.   No. I won't accept those conditions.

With *Oh* and *O*

121   The exclamation *oh* may be followed by either an exclamation point or a comma, depending on the emphasis desired. It is capitalized only when it starts a sentence. The capitalized *O,* the sign of direct address, is not usually followed by any punctuation.

     Oh! I didn't expect that!   O Lord, help me!

     Oh, what's the use?   O America, where are you headed?

Exclamation point with dashes: see ¶¶214b, 215a.
Exclamation point with parentheses: see ¶¶224d, 225a, 225d, 226c.
Exclamation point with quotation marks: see ¶¶249, 252, 254, 257, 258, 259, 261.
Spacing with exclamation points: see ¶299.

The Comma

The comma has two primary functions: it *sets off* nonessential expressions that interrupt the flow of thought from subject to verb to object or complement, and it *separates* elements within a sentence to clarify their relationship to one another. Two commas are typically needed to "set off," but only a single comma is needed to "separate."

The following rules (¶¶122–125) present an overview of the rules governing the use of the comma. For a more detailed treatment of the specific rules, see ¶¶126–175.

Basic Rules for Commas That Set Off

122   Use commas to set off *nonessential expressions*—words, phrases, and clauses that are not necessary for the meaning or the structural completeness of the sentence.

     IMPORTANT NOTE: In many sentences you can tell whether an expression is nonessential or essential by trying to omit the expression. If you can leave it out without affecting the meaning or the structural completeness of the sentence, the expression is nonessential and should be set off by commas.

     NONESSENTIAL: Let's get the advice of Harry Stern, *who has in-depth experience with all types of personal computers.*

     ESSENTIAL: Let's get the advice of someone *who has in-depth experience with all types of personal computers.* (Without the *who* clause, the meaning of the sentence would be incomplete.)

     NONESSENTIAL: There is, *no doubt,* a reasonable explanation for his behavior at the board meeting.

     ESSENTIAL: There is *no doubt* about her honesty. (Without *no doubt,* the structure of the sentence would be incomplete.)

However, in other sentences the only way you can tell whether an expression is nonessential or essential is by the way you would say it aloud. If your voice tends to *drop* as you utter the expression, it is nonessential; if your voice tends to *rise,* the expression is essential.

1

NONESSENTIAL: Finch and Helwig would prefer, *therefore,* to limit the term of the agreement to two years.

ESSENTIAL: Finch and Helwig would *therefore* prefer to limit the term of the agreement to two years.

For additional examples, see ¶141, note.

a. **Interrupting Elements.** Use commas to set off words, phrases, and clauses when they break the flow of a sentence from subject to verb to object or complement. (See also ¶¶144–147.)

We can deliver the car on the day of your husband's birthday or, *if you wish,* on the Saturday before then. (When this sentence is read aloud, notice how the voice drops on the nonessential expression *if you wish.*)

They have sufficient assets, *don't they,* to cover these losses?

Let's take advantage of the special price and order, *say,* 200 reams this quarter instead of our usual quantity of 75.

Mary Cabrera, *rather than George Spengler,* has been appointed head of the Phoenix office.

BUT: Mary Cabrera has been appointed head of the Phoenix office *rather than George Spengler.* (The phrase is not set off when it does not interrupt.)

b. **Afterthoughts.** Use commas to set off words, phrases, or clauses loosely added onto the end of a sentence. (See also ¶144.)

Send us your check as soon as you can, *please.*

Grant promised to share expenses with us, *if I remember correctly.*

It is not too late to place an order, *is it?*

c. **Transitional Expressions and Independent Comments.** Use commas to set off transitional expressions (like *however, therefore, on the other hand*) and independent comments (like *obviously, in my opinion, of course*) when they interrupt the flow of the sentence. Do not set these elements off, however, when they are used to emphasize the meaning; the voice goes up in such cases. In the examples that follow, consider how the voice drops when the expression is nonessential and how it rises when the expression is essential. (See also ¶¶138–143.)

NONESSENTIAL: We are determined, *nevertheless,* to finish on schedule.

ESSENTIAL: We are *nevertheless* determined to finish on schedule.

NONESSENTIAL: It is, *of course,* your prerogative to change your mind. (Here the voice rises on *is* and drops on *of course.*)

ESSENTIAL: It is *of course* your prerogative to change your mind. (Here the voice rises on *of course.*)

d. **Descriptive Expressions.** When descriptive expressions *follow* the words they refer to and provide additional but nonessential information, use commas to set them off. (See also ¶¶148–153.)

NONESSENTIAL: His most recent article, "How to Make a Profit With High-Tech Investments," appeared in the June 1 issue of *Forbes.* (*His most recent* indicates which article is meant; the title gives additional but nonessential information.)

ESSENTIAL: The article "How to Make a Profit With High-Tech Investments" appeared in the June 1 issue of *Forbes.* (Here the title is needed to indicate which article is meant.)

(Continued on page 14.)

NONESSENTIAL: Thank you for your letter of April 12, in which you questioned our discount terms. (The date indicates which letter; the *in which* clause gives additional information. See also ¶152.)

ESSENTIAL: Thank you for your letter in which you questioned our discount terms. (Here the *in which* clause is needed to indicate which letter is meant.)

    e. Dates. Use commas to set off the year in complete dates (for example, Sunday, May 1, *1994,* . . .). (See also ¶¶154–155.)

    f. Names. Use commas to set off abbreviations that follow a person's name (Julie Merkin, *Ph.D.*, announces the opening . . .) and to set off names of states or countries following city names (Rye, *New York,* will host . . .). In personal names and company names, the trend is not to set off elements like *Jr., Sr., III, Inc.,* or *Ltd.* (for example, *Guy Tracy Jr.* and *Redd Inc.*); however, individual preferences should be respected when known. (See also ¶¶156–161.)

Basic Rules for Commas That Separate

123   Use a single comma:

    a. To separate the two main clauses in a compound sentence when they are joined by *and, but, or,* or *nor.* (See also ¶¶126–129.)

        We can't accept the marketing restrictions you proposed, *but* we think there is some basis for a mutually acceptable understanding.

    b. To separate three or more items in a series—unless all the items are joined by *and* or *or.* (See also ¶¶162–167.)

        It takes time, effort, *and* a good deal of money.

        BUT: It takes time *and* effort *and* a good deal of money.

    c. To separate two or more adjectives that both modify the same noun. (See also ¶¶168–171.)

        We need to mount an *exciting, hard-hitting* ad campaign.

    d. To separate the digits of numbers into groups of thousands. (See ¶461.)

        Sales projections for the Southern Region next year range between $900,000 and $1,000,000.

    e. To indicate the omission of key words or to clarify meaning when the word order is unusual. (See also ¶¶172–175.)

        Half the purchase price is due on delivery of the goods; the balance, in three months. (The comma here signifies the omission of *is due.*)

        What will happen, we don't know. (The comma here helps the reader cope with the unusual word order; it separates the object, *What will happen,* from the subject, *we,* which follows.)

124   Use a single comma after *introductory elements*—items that begin a sentence and come before the subject and verb of the main clause.

        Yes, we can deliver your new printer by Wednesday. (Introductory word.)

        Taking all the arguments into consideration, we have decided to modernize these facilities rather than close them down. (Introductory participial phrase.)

        To determine the proper mix of ingredients for a particular situation, see the table on page 141. (Introductory infinitive phrase.)

        Before we can make a final decision, we will need to run another cost-profit analysis. (Introductory dependent clause.)

a. Use a comma after an *introductory request or command.*

Look, we've been through tougher situations before.

You see, the previous campaigns never did pan out.

Please remember, all expense reports must be on my desk by Friday.

BUT: *Please remember that* all . . . (With the addition of *that, please remember* becomes the main verb and is no longer an introductory element.)

b. Commas are not needed after *ordinary introductory adverbs* or *short introductory phrases* that answer such questions as:

WHEN: tomorrow, yesterday, recently, early next week, in the morning, soon, in five years, in 1994

HOW OFTEN: occasionally, often, frequently, once in a while

WHERE: here, in this case, at the meeting

WHY: for that reason, because of this situation

However, commas are used after introductory adverbs and phrases:

(1) When they function as *transitional expressions* (such as *well, therefore, however, for example, in the first place*), which provide a transition in meaning from the previous sentence.

(2) When they function as *independent comments* (such as *in my opinion, by all means, obviously, of course*), which express the writer's attitude toward the meaning of the sentence. (See also ¶¶138–143.)

In the morning things may look better. (Short prepositional phrase telling *when;* no comma needed.)

In the first place, they don't have sufficient capital. (Transitional expression; followed by comma.)

In my opinion, we ought to look for another candidate. (Independent comment; followed by comma.)

Recently we had a request for school enrollment trends. (Introductory adverb telling *when;* no comma needed.)

Consequently, we will have to cancel the agreement. (Transitional expression; followed by comma.)

Obviously, the request will have to be referred elsewhere. (Independent comment; followed by comma.)

NOTE: Many writers use commas after *all* introductory elements to avoid having to analyze each situation.

125 Separating commas are often improperly used in sentences. In the following examples the diagonal marks indicate points at which single commas *should not* be used.

a. Do not separate a subject and its verb.

The person she plans to hire for the job/ is Peter Crotty.

BUT: The person she plans to hire for the job, *I believe,* is Peter Crotty. (Use *two* commas to set off an interrupting expression.)

Whether profits can be improved this year/ depends on several key variables. (Noun clause as subject.)

BUT: *Anyone who contributes, contributes* to a most worthy cause. (In special cases like this, a comma may be required for clarity. See also ¶175b.)

(Continued on page 16.)

b. Do not separate a verb and its object or complement.

The test mailing *has not produced/ the results* we were hoping for. (Verb and object.)

Mrs. Paterra *will be/ the Hapworth Corporation's new director of marketing.* (Verb and complement.)

The equipment *is/ easy to operate, inexpensive to maintain, and built to give reliable service for many years.* (Verb and complement.)

Rebecca Hingham *said/ that the research data would be on your desk by Monday morning.* (Noun clause as object.)

BUT: Rebecca Hingham *said,* "The research data will be on your desk by Monday morning." (A comma ordinarily follows a verb when the object is a direct quotation. See also ¶256.)

OR: The question we really need to address *is, Do we have a better solution to propose?* (A comma also follows a verb when the object or complement is a direct question. See also ¶115.)

c. Do not separate an adjective and a noun.

The project requires a highly motivated, research-oriented, cost-conscious/ manager.

d. Do not separate a noun and a prepositional phrase that follows.

The board of directors/ of the Fastex Corporation will announce its decision this Friday.

BUT: The board of directors, *of necessity,* must turn down the merger at this time. (Use *two* commas to set off an interrupting expression.)

e. Do not separate a coordinating conjunction (*and, but, or,* or *nor*) and the following word.

You can read the draft of the division's medium-range plan now *or/ when* you get home tonight.

BUT: You can read the draft of the division's medium-range plan now or, *if you prefer,* when you get home tonight. (Use *two* commas to set off an interrupting expression.)

f. Do not separate *two* words or phrases that are joined by a coordinating conjunction.

The letters on the Gray case/ and those concerning Mr. Pendleton should be shown to Mrs. Almquist. (Two subjects.)

I *have read Ms. Berkowitz's capital spending proposal/ and find it well done.* (Two predicates. See also ¶127.)

We hope *that you will visit our store soon/ and that you will find the styles you like.* (Two objects of the verb *hope.*)

The CEO plans *to visit the Western Region/ and call personally on the large accounts that have stopped doing business with us.* (Two infinitive phrases serving as objects of the verb *plans.*)

He may go on to graduate school at *Stanford/ or Harvard.* (Two objects of the preposition *at.*)

BUT: *Frank Albano will handle the tickets,* and *Edna Hoehn will be responsible for publicity.* (A comma separates two independent clauses joined by a coordinating conjunction. See ¶126.)

The following rules (¶¶126–137) deal with the punctuation of clauses and phrases in sentences.

With Clauses in Compound Sentences

126 **a.** When a compound sentence consists of *two* independent clauses joined by a coordinating conjunction (*and, but, or,* or *nor*), place a separating comma before the conjunction. (See ¶129.)

> Mrs. Fenster noticed a small discrepancy in the figures, *and* on that basis she began to reanalyze the data.

> **BUT:** Mrs. Fenster noticed a small discrepancy in the figures *and* on that basis began to reanalyze the data. (See ¶127a–b.)

> Show this proposal to Mr. Florio, *and* ask him for his reaction. (See ¶127c.)

> Either we step up our promotion efforts, *or* we must be content with our existing share of the market.

> Not only were we the developers of this process, *but* we were the first to apply it to the field of pollution control.

b. For special effect, the comma before the coordinating conjunction can be replaced by a period, a question mark, or an exclamation point. The coordinating conjunction is then capitalized, and the second independent clause is treated as a separate sentence. However, this treatment, if overused, quickly loses its effectiveness.

> Is it self-confidence that makes you successful? Or is it success that makes you self-confident?

> I told Callahan that we would not reorder from his company unless he cut his prices by 20 percent. And he did.

> **NOTE:** Do not insert a comma directly after the coordinating conjunction unless a parenthetical element begins at that point.

> I told Callahan that we would not reorder from his company unless he cut his prices by 20 percent. And, to my total amazement, he did.

c. When a compound sentence consists of *three* or more independent clauses, punctuate this series like any other series. (See also ¶162.)

> Bob can deal with the caterer, Nora can handle publicity, and Bev and I can take care of the rest.

127 Do not confuse a *compound sentence* with a simple sentence containing a *compound predicate.*

a. A *compound sentence* contains at least two independent clauses, and each clause contains a subject and a predicate.

> *Barbara just got her master's in economics,* and *she is now looking for a job in corporate planning.*

b. A sentence may contain one subject with a *compound predicate,* that is, two predicates connected by a coordinating conjunction. In such sentences no comma separates the two predicates.

> Barbara *just got her master's in economics* and *is now looking for a job in corporate planning.* (When *she* is omitted from the example in *a* above, the sentence is no longer a compound sentence. It is now a simple sentence with a compound predicate.)

> Ogleby not only *wants a higher discount* but also *demands faster turnarounds on his orders.* (Compound predicate; no comma before *but.*)

> **BUT:** *Ogleby not only wants a higher discount,* but *he also demands faster turnarounds on his orders.* (Compound sentence; comma before *but.*)

(Continued on page 18.)

1

   c. When one or both verbs are in the imperative and the subject is not expressed, treat the sentence as a compound sentence and use a comma between the clauses.

Please look at the brochure I have enclosed, and then *get* back to me if you have additional questions.

You may not be able to get away right now, but *do plan* to stay with us whenever you find the time.

Call Ellen Chen sometime next week, and *ask* her whether she will speak at our conference next fall.

BUT: *Call* Ellen Chen and *ask* her whether she will speak at our conference next fall. (Omit the comma if the first clause is short. See ¶129.)

   d. When nonessential elements precede the second part of a *compound predicate,* they are treated as interrupting expressions and are set off by two commas. When these same expressions precede the second clause of a *compound sentence,* they are treated as introductory expressions and are followed by one comma.

We can bill you on our customary terms or, *if you prefer,* can offer you our new deferred payment plan. (Interrupting expression requires two commas.)

We can bill you on our customary terms, or *if you prefer,* we can offer you our new deferred payment plan. (Introductory expression requires one comma.)

Frank Bruchman went into the boardroom and, *without consulting his notes,* proceeded to give the directors precise details about our financial situation. (Interrupting expression.)

Frank Bruchman went into the boardroom, and *without consulting his notes,* he proceeded to give the directors precise details about our financial situation. (Introductory expression.)

See also ¶¶131c, 136a, 142.

128   Do not use a comma between two independent clauses that are not joined by a coordinating conjunction *(and, but, or,* or *nor).* This error of punctuation is known as a *comma splice* and produces a *run-on sentence.* Use a semicolon, a colon, or a dash (whichever is appropriate), or start a new sentence.

    WRONG: Please review these spreadsheets quickly, I need them back tomorrow.

    RIGHT: Please review these spreadsheets quickly; I need them back tomorrow.

    OR: Please review these spreadsheets quickly. I need them back tomorrow.

129   If the first clause of a compound sentence is short, the comma may be omitted before the conjunction.

Their prices are low and their service is efficient.

Please initial these forms and return them by Monday.

Consider leasing and see whether it costs less in the long run than buying.

With Clauses in Complex Sentences

A complex sentence contains one independent clause and one or more dependent clauses. *After, although, as, because, before, if, since, unless, when,* and *while* are among the words most frequently used to introduce dependent clauses. (See ¶132 for a longer list.)

130 Introductory Dependent Clauses

a. When a dependent clause *precedes* the independent clause, separate the clauses with a comma.

Before we can make a decision, we must have all the facts.

When you read the Weissberg study, look at Appendix 2 first.

If, however, they had watched their investments more closely, do you think they could have avoided bankruptcy?

After we have studied all aspects of the complaint, <u>we will make</u> a recommendation.

BUT: *Only after we have studied all aspects of the complaint* <u>will we make</u> a recommendation. (No comma follows the introductory clause when the word order in the main clause is abnormal. Compare the abnormal *will we make* here with the normal *we will make* in the preceding example.)

b. Be sure you can recognize an introductory dependent clause, even if some of the essential words are omitted from the clause. (Such constructions are known as *elliptical clauses.*)

Whenever possible, he leaves his office by six. (Whenever *it is* possible, . . .)

If so, I will call you tomorrow. (If *that is* so, . . .)

Should you be late, just call to let me know. (*If* you should be late, . . .)

c. Use a comma after an introductory clause when it serves as the *object* of a sentence (but not when it serves as the *subject*).

Whomever you nominate, I will support. (Introductory clause as object.)

Whomever you nominate will have my support. (Introductory clause as subject.)

That the department must be reorganized, I no longer question. (Introductory clause as object.)

That the department must be reorganized is no longer questioned. (Introductory clause as subject.)

d. Sentences like those illustrated in ¶130a–c are often introduced by an expression such as *he said that, she believes that,* or *they know that.* In such cases use the same punctuation as prescribed in *a–c.*

Liz believes that *before we can make a decision,* we must have all the facts. (A separating comma follows the dependent clause, just as if the sentence began with the word *Before.* No comma precedes the dependent clause because it is considered introductory, not interrupting.)

BUT: He said that, *as you may already know,* he was planning to take early retirement. (Two commas are needed to set off an interrupting dependent clause. See also ¶131c.)

Harry says that *whenever possible,* he leaves his office by six.

Everyone knows that *whomever you nominate* will have my support in the next election.

131 Dependent Clauses Elsewhere in the Sentence

When a dependent clause *follows* the main clause or *falls within* the main clause, commas are used or omitted depending on whether the dependent clause is essential (restrictive) or nonessential (nonrestrictive).

(Continued on page 20.)

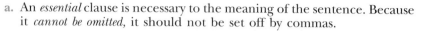

a. An *essential* clause is necessary to the meaning of the sentence. Because it *cannot be omitted*, it should not be set off by commas.

The person *who used to be Englund's operations manager* is now doing the same job for Jenniman Brothers. (Tells which person.)

The Pennington bid arrived *after we had made our decision.* (Tells when.)

Damato's suggestion *that we submit the issue to arbitration* may be the only sensible alternative. (Tells which of Damato's suggestions is meant.)

Mrs. Foy said *that she would send us an advance program.* (Tells what was said.)

b. A *nonessential* clause provides additional descriptive or explanatory detail. Because it *can be omitted* without changing the meaning of the sentence, it should be set off by commas.

George Pedersen, *who used to be Englund's operations manager,* is now doing the same job for Jenniman Brothers. (The name indicates which person; the *who* clause simply gives additional information.)

The Pennington bid arrived on Tuesday, *after we had made our decision.* (*Tuesday* tells when; the *after* clause simply adds information.)

Damato's latest suggestion, *that we submit the issue to arbitration,* may be the only sensible alternative. (*Latest* tells which suggestion is meant; the *that* clause is not essential.)

c. A dependent clause occurring within a sentence must always be set off by commas when it *interrupts* the flow of the sentence.

We can review the wording of the announcement over lunch or, *if your time is short,* over the phone.

Please tell us when you plan to be in town and, *if possible,* where you will be staying. (The complete dependent clause is *if it is possible.*)

Senator Hemphill, *when offered the chance to refute his opponent's charges,* said he would respond at a time of his own choosing.

Mrs. Kourakis is the type of person who, *when you need help badly,* will be the first to volunteer.

If, *when you have weighed the alternatives,* you choose one of the models that cost over $500, we can arrange special credit terms for you.

BUT: He said that *if we choose one of the models that cost over $500,* his firm can arrange special credit terms for us. (See ¶130d for dependent clauses following *he said that, she knows that,* and similar expressions.)

132 The following list presents the words and phrases most commonly used to introduce dependent clauses. For most of these expressions two sentences are given: one containing an essential clause and one a nonessential clause. In a few cases only one type of clause is possible. If you cannot decide whether a clause is essential or nonessential (and therefore whether commas are required or not), compare it with the related sentences that follow.

After. ESSENTIAL: His faxed response came *after you left last evening.* (Tells when.)

NONESSENTIAL: His faxed response came this morning, *after the decision had been made.* (The phrase *this morning* clearly tells when; the *after* clause provides additional but nonessential information.)

All of which. ALWAYS NONESSENTIAL: The rumors, *all of which were unfounded,* brought about his defeat in the last election.

Although, even though, and **though.** ALWAYS NONESSENTIAL: She has typed her letter of resignation, *although I do not believe she will submit it.*

As. ESSENTIAL: The results of the mailing are *as you predicted they would be.* NONESSENTIAL: The results of the mailing are disappointing, *as you predicted they would be.* (See page 255 for a usage note on *as.*)

As . . . as. ALWAYS ESSENTIAL: He talked *as* persuasively at the meeting *as* he did over the telephone. (See page 256 for a usage note on *as . . . as.*)

As if and **as though.** ESSENTIAL: She drove *as if* (or *as though*) *the road were a minefield.* (The *as if* clause tells how she drove.) NONESSENTIAL: She drove cautiously, *as if* (or *as though*) *the road were a minefield.* (The adverb *cautiously* tells how she drove; the *as if* clause provides additional but nonessential information.)

As soon as. ESSENTIAL: We will fill your order *as soon as we receive new stock.* NONESSENTIAL: We will fill your order next week, *as soon as we receive new stock.*

At, by, for, in, and **to which.** ESSENTIAL: I went to the floor *to which I had been directed.* NONESSENTIAL: I went to the tenth floor, *to which I had been directed.*

Because. *Essential* or *nonessential,* depending on closeness of relation. ESSENTIAL: She left *because she had another appointment.* (Here the reason expressed by the *because* clause is essential to complete the meaning.) NONESSENTIAL: I need to have two copies of the final report by 5:30 tomorrow, *because I am leaving for Chicago on a 7:30 flight.* (Here the meaning of the main clause is complete; the reason expressed in the *because* clause offers additional but nonessential information.)

Before. ESSENTIAL: The shipment was sent *before your letter was received.* NONESSENTIAL: The shipment was sent on Tuesday, *before your letter was received.* (*Tuesday* tells when the shipment was sent; the *before* clause provides additional but nonessential information.)

Even though. See *Although.*

For. ALWAYS NONESSENTIAL: He read the book, *for he was interested in psychology.* (A comma should always precede *for* as a conjunction to prevent misreading *for* as a preposition.)

If. ESSENTIAL: Let us hear from you *if you are interested.* NONESSENTIAL: She promised to write from Toronto, *if I remember correctly.* (Clause added loosely.)

In order that. *Essential* or *nonessential,* depending on closeness of relation. ESSENTIAL: Please notify your instructor promptly *in order that a makeup examination may be scheduled.* NONESSENTIAL: Please notify your instructor promptly if you will be unable to attend the examination on Friday, *in order that a makeup examination may be scheduled.*

No matter what (why, how, etc.**).** ALWAYS NONESSENTIAL: The order cannot be ready by Monday, *no matter what the store manager says.*

None of which. ALWAYS NONESSENTIAL: We received five boxes of samples, *none of which are in good condition.*

None of whom. ALWAYS NONESSENTIAL: We have interviewed ten applicants, *none of whom were satisfactory.*

Not so . . . as. ALWAYS ESSENTIAL: The second copy was *not so* clear *as* the first one. (See page 265 for a usage note on *not so . . . as.*)

Since. ESSENTIAL: We have taken no applications *since we received your memo.* NONESSENTIAL: We are taking no more applications, *since our lists are now closed.* (Clause of reason.)

(Continued on page 22.)

So that. *Essential* or *nonessential,* depending on closeness of relation.
ESSENTIAL: Examine all shipments *so that any damage may be detected promptly.*
NONESSENTIAL: Examine all shipments as soon as they arrive, *so that any damage may be detected promptly.*

So . . . that. ALWAYS ESSENTIAL: The costs ran *so* high *that we could not make a profit on the job.*

Some of whom. ALWAYS NONESSENTIAL: The agency has sent us five applicants, *some of whom seem promising.*

Than. ALWAYS ESSENTIAL: The employees seem to be more disturbed by the rumor *than they care to admit.*

That. When used as a relative pronoun, *that* refers to things; it also refers to persons when a class or type is meant. ALWAYS ESSENTIAL: Enclosed is a picture of the plane *that Lynn now owns.* She is the kind of candidate *that I prefer.* (See also ¶1062.)
When used as a subordinating conjunction, *that* links the dependent clause it introduces with the main clause. ALWAYS ESSENTIAL: We know *that we will have to make concessions in the upcoming talks.* (See page 270 for a usage note on *that.*)

Though. See *Although.*

Unless. ESSENTIAL: This product line will be discontinued *unless customers begin to show an interest in it.*
NONESSENTIAL: I plan to work on the Aspen proposal all through the weekend, *unless Cindy comes into town.* (Clause added loosely as an afterthought.)

Until. ALWAYS ESSENTIAL: I will continue to work *until my children are out of school.*

When. ESSENTIAL: The changeover will be made *when Mr. Ruiz returns from his vacation.*
NONESSENTIAL: The changeover will be made next Monday, *when Mr. Ruiz returns from his vacation.* (*Monday* tells when; the *when* clause provides additional but nonessential information.)

Where. ESSENTIAL: I plan to visit the town *where I used to live.*
NONESSENTIAL: I plan to stop off in Detroit, *where I used to live.*

Whereas. ALWAYS NONESSENTIAL: The figures for last year cover urban areas only, *whereas those for this year include rural areas as well.* (Clause of contrast.)

Which. Use *which* (rather than *who*) when referring to animals, things, and ideas. Always use *which* (instead of *that*) to introduce nonessential clauses: The revised report, *which was done by Mark,* is very impressive. *Which* may also be used to introduce essential clauses. (See ¶1062b, note.)

While. ESSENTIAL: The union has decided not to strike *while negotiations are still going on.* (Here *while* means ''during the time that.'')
NONESSENTIAL: The workers at the Apex Company have struck, *while those at the Powers Company are still at work.* (Here *while* means ''whereas.'')

Who. ESSENTIAL: All students *who are members of the Backpackers Club* will be leaving for Maine on Friday.
NONESSENTIAL: John Behnke, *who is a member of the Backpackers Club,* will be leading a group on a weekend trip to Maine.

Whom. ESSENTIAL: This package is for the friend *whom I am visiting.*
NONESSENTIAL: This package is for my cousin Amy, *whom I am visiting.*

Whose. ESSENTIAL: The prize was awarded to the employee *whose suggestion yielded the greatest cost savings.*
NONESSENTIAL: The prize was awarded to Joyce Bruno, *whose suggestion yielded the greatest cost savings.*

With Clauses in Compound-Complex Sentences

133 A compound-complex sentence typically consists of two independent clauses (joined by *and, but, or,* or *nor*) and one or more dependent clauses. To punctuate a sentence of this kind, first place a separating comma before the conjunction that joins the two main parts. Then consider each half of the sentence alone and provide additional punctuation as necessary.

> The computer terminals were not delivered until June 12, five weeks after the promised delivery date, and *when I wrote to complain to your sales manager,* it took another three weeks simply for him to acknowledge my letter. (No comma precedes *when* because the *when* clause is considered an introductory expression, not an interrupting expression. See also ¶127d.)

> Jeff Adler, the CEO of Marshfield & Duxbury, is eager to discuss a joint venture with my boss, *who is off on a six-week trip to the Far East,* but the earliest date I see open for such a meeting is Wednesday, October 20.

NOTE: If a misreading is likely or a stronger break is desired, use a semicolon rather than a comma to separate the two main clauses. (See ¶177.)

134 When a sentence starts with a dependent clause that applies to both independent clauses that follow, no comma separates the independent clauses. (A comma would make the introductory dependent clause seem to apply only to the first independent clause.)

> Before you start to look for venture capital, you need to prepare an analysis of the market *and* you must make a detailed set of financial projections. (The *before* clause applies equally to the two independent clauses that follow; hence no comma before *and.*)

> **BUT:** Before you start to look for venture capital, you need to prepare an analysis of the market, *but* don't think that's all there is to it. (The *before* clause applies only to the first independent clause; hence a comma is used before *but.*)

With Participial, Infinitive, and Prepositional Phrases

135 Introductory Phrases

a. Use a comma after an *introductory participial phrase.*

> *Seizing the opportunity,* I presented an overview of our medium-range plans.
> *Established in 1905,* our company takes great pride in its reputation for high-quality products and excellent service.
> *Having checked the statements myself,* I feel confident that they are accurate.

NOTE: Watch out for phrases that look like introductory participial phrases but actually represent the subject of the sentence or part of the predicate. Do not put a comma after these elements.

> *Looking for examples of good acknowledgment letters in our files* has taken me longer than I had hoped. (Gerund phrase as subject.)

> **BUT:** *Looking for examples of good acknowledgment letters in our files,* I found four that you can use. (Participial phrase used as an introductory element; the subject is *I.*)

(Continued on page 24.)

Following Mrs. Fahnstock's speech was a presentation by Ms. Paley. (With normal word order, the sentence would read, "A presentation by Ms. Paley was *following Mrs. Fahnstock's speech."* The introductory phrase is actually part of the predicate; the subject is *a presentation by Ms. Paley.*)

BUT: *Following Mrs. Fahnstock's speech,* Ms. Paley made her presentation. (Participial phrase used as an introductory element; the subject is *Ms. Paley.*)

b. Use a comma after an *introductory infinitive phrase* unless the phrase is the subject of the sentence. (Infinitive phrases are introduced by *to.*)

To get the best results from your dishwasher, follow the printed directions. (The subject *you* is understood.)

To have displayed the goods more effectively, he should have consulted a lighting specialist. (The subject is *he.*)

BUT: *To have displayed the goods more effectively* would have required a lighting specialist. (Infinitive phrase used as subject.)

c. As a general rule, use a comma after all *introductory prepositional phrases.* A comma may be omitted after a *short* prepositional phrase if (1) the phrase does not contain a verb form, (2) the phrase is not a transitional expression or an independent comment, or (3) there is no sacrifice in clarity or desired emphasis. (Many writers use a comma after all introductory prepositional phrases to avoid analyzing each situation.)

In response to the many requests of our customers, we are opening a branch in Kenmore Square. (Comma required after a long phrase.)

On Monday morning the first mail delivery is always late. (No comma required after a short phrase.)

In 1991 our entire inventory was destroyed by fire. (No comma required after a short phrase.)

BUT: *In 1991,* 384 cases of potential lung infections were reported. (Comma required to separate two numbers. See ¶456.)

At the time you called, I was tied up in a meeting. (Comma required after a short phrase containing a verb form.)

In preparing your report, be sure to include last year's figures. (Comma required after a short phrase containing a verb form.)

In addition, a 6 percent city sales tax must be imposed. (Comma required after a short phrase used as a transitional expression. See ¶¶138a, 139.)

In my opinion, your ads are misleading as they now appear. (Comma required after short phrase used as an independent comment. See ¶¶138b, 139.)

In legal documents, amounts of money are often expressed both in words and in figures. (Comma used to give desired emphasis to the introductory phrase.)

CONFUSING: After all you have gone through a great deal.

CLEAR: *After all,* you have gone through a great deal. (Comma required after a short phrase to prevent misreading.)

NOTE: Omit the comma after an introductory prepositional phrase if the word order in the rest of the sentence is inverted.

Out of an initial investment of $5000 came a stake that is currently worth over $2,500,000. (Normal word order: A stake that is currently worth over $2,500,000 came out of an initial investment of $5000.)

In an article I read in Time last week was an account of our company's decision to go public. (Omit the comma after the introductory phrase when the verb in the main clause immediately follows.)

BUT: *In an article I read in Time last week,* there was an account . . .

136 Phrases at the Beginning of a Clause

a. When a participial, infinitive, or prepositional phrase occurs *at the beginning of a clause within the sentence,* insert or omit the comma following, just as if the phrase were an introductory element at the beginning of the sentence. (See ¶135.)

I was invited to attend the monthly planning meeting last week, and *seizing the opportunity,* I presented an overview of our medium-range plans. (A separating comma follows the participial phrase just as if the sentence began with the word *Seizing.* No comma precedes the phrase because the phrase is considered introductory, not interrupting. See also ¶127d.)

The salesclerk explained that *to get the best results from your dishwasher,* you should follow the printed directions.

We would like to announce that *in response to the many requests of our customers,* we are opening a branch in Kenmore Square.

Last year we had a number of thefts, and *in 1991* our entire inventory was destroyed by fire. (No comma is needed after a short introductory prepositional phrase.)

b. If the phrase interrupts the flow of the sentence, set it off with two commas.

Pamela is the type of person who, *in the midst of disaster,* will always find something to laugh about.

If, *in the attempt to push matters to a resolution,* you offer that gang new terms, they will simply dig in their heels and refuse to bargain.

137 Phrases Elsewhere in the Sentence

When a participial, infinitive, or prepositional phrase occurs *at some point other than the beginning of a sentence* (see ¶135) *or the beginning of a clause* (see ¶136), commas are omitted or used depending on whether the phrase is essential or nonessential.

a. An *essential* participial, infinitive, or prepositional phrase is necessary to the meaning of the sentence and cannot be omitted. Therefore, do not use commas to set it off.

The catalog *scheduled for release in November* will have to be delayed until January. (Participial.)

The decision *to expand our export activities* has proved sound. (Infinitive.)

The search *for a new general manager* is still going on. (Prepositional.)

b. A *nonessential* participial, infinitive, or prepositional phrase provides additional information but is not needed to complete the meaning of the sentence. Set off such phrases with commas.

This new collection of essays, *written in the last two years before his death,* represents his most distinguished work. (Participial.)

I'd rather not attend her reception, *to be frank about it.* (Infinitive.)

Morale appears to be much better, *on the whole.* (Prepositional.)

c. A phrase occurring within a sentence must always be set off by commas when it *interrupts* the flow of the sentence.

The commission, *after hearing arguments on the proposed new tax rate structure,* will consider amendments to the tax law.

The company, *in its attempt to place more women in high-level management positions,* is undertaking a special recruitment program.

1

The following rules (¶¶138–161) deal with the various uses of commas to set off nonessential expressions. See also ¶¶201–202 and ¶¶218–219 for the use of dashes and parentheses to set off these expressions.

With Transitional Expressions and Independent Comments

138 **a.** Use commas to set off *transitional expressions.* These nonessential words and phrases are called *transitional* because they help the reader mentally relate the preceding thought to the idea now being introduced. They express such notions as:

ADDITION:	also, besides, furthermore, in addition, moreover, too (see ¶143), what is more
CONSEQUENCE:	accordingly, as a result, consequently, hence (see ¶139b), otherwise, so (see ¶179), then (see ¶139b), therefore, thus (see ¶139b)
SUMMARIZING:	after all, all in all, all things considered, briefly, by and large, in any case, in any event, in brief, in conclusion, in short, in summary, in the final analysis, in the long run, on balance, on the whole, to sum up
GENERALIZING:	as a rule, as usual, for the most part, generally, generally speaking, in general, ordinarily, usually
RESTATEMENT:	in essence, in other words, namely, that is, that is to say
CONTRAST AND COMPARISON:	by contrast, by the same token, conversely, instead, likewise, on one hand, on the contrary, on the other hand, rather, similarly, yet (see ¶179)
CONCESSION:	anyway, at any rate, be that as it may, even so, however, in any case (event), nevertheless, still, this fact notwithstanding
SEQUENCE:	afterward, at first, at the same time, finally, first, first of all, for now, for the time being, in conclusion, in the first place, in time, in turn, later on, meanwhile, next, second, then (see ¶139b), to begin with
DIVERSION:	by the by, by the way, incidentally
ILLUSTRATION:	for example, for instance, for one thing

See ¶¶139–142 for the punctuation of transitional expressions depending on where they occur in a sentence.

NOTE: The coordinating conjunctions *and, but, or,* or *nor* are sometimes used as transitional expressions at the beginning of a sentence. See ¶126b.

b. Use commas to set off *independent comments,* that is, nonessential words or phrases that express the writer's attitude toward the meaning of the sentence. By means of these independent comments, the writer indicates that what he is about to say carries his wholehearted endorsement *(indeed, by all means)* or deserves only his lukewarm support *(apparently, presumably)* or hardly requires saying *(as you already know, clearly, obviously)* or represents only his personal views *(in my opinion, personally)* or arouses some emotion in him *(unfortunately, happily)* or presents his honest position *(frankly, actually, to tell the truth).* Such terms modify the meaning of the sentence as a whole rather than a particular word within the sentence.

AFFIRMATION:	by all means, indeed, of course, yes
DENIAL:	no
REGRET:	alas, unfortunately
PLEASURE:	fortunately, happily
QUALIFICATION:	ideally, if necessary, if possible, literally, strictly speaking, theoretically
PERSONAL VIEWPOINT:	according to her, as I see it, in my opinion, personally
ASSERTION OF CANDOR:	actually, frankly, in reality, to be honest, to say the least, to tell the truth
ASSERTION OF FACT:	as a matter of fact, as it happens, as you know, believe it or not, certainly, clearly, doubtless, in fact, naturally, needless to say, obviously, without doubt
WEAK ASSERTION:	apparently, perhaps, presumably

See ¶¶139–142 for the punctuation of independent comments depending on where they occur in a sentence.

139 At the Beginning of a Sentence

a. When the words and phrases listed in ¶138a–b appear at the beginning of a sentence, they should be followed by a comma unless they are used as essential elements.

NONESSENTIAL: *After all*, you have done more for him than he had any right to expect.

ESSENTIAL: *After all* you have done for him, he has no right to expect more.

NONESSENTIAL: *However*, you look at the letter yourself to see whether you interpret it as I do.

ESSENTIAL: *However* you look at the letter, there is only one interpretation.

NONESSENTIAL: *Obviously*, the guest of honor was quite moved by the welcome she received.

ESSENTIAL: *Obviously* moved by the welcome she received, the guest of honor spoke with an emotion-choked voice. (Here *obviously* modifies *moved*. In the preceding sentence, *obviously* modifies the meaning of the sentence as a whole.)

b. When *hence, then,* or *thus* occurs at the beginning of a sentence, the comma following is omitted unless the connective requires special emphasis or a nonessential element occurs at that point.

Thus they thought it wise to get an outside consultant's opinion.

Then they decided to go back to their original plan.

BUT: *Then*, after they rejected the consultant's recommendation, they decided to go back to their original plan.

See also ¶142a, note.

c. When an introductory transitional expression or independent comment is incorporated into the flow of the sentence without any intervening pause, the comma may be omitted.

Of course I can handle it.   *Perhaps* she was joking.
No doubt he meant well.   *Indeed* she was not.

140   At the End of a Sentence

Use one comma to set off a transitional expression or an independent comment at the end of a sentence. However, be sure to distinguish between nonessential and essential elements.

NONESSENTIAL: Philip goes to every employee reception, *of course.*

ESSENTIAL: Philip goes to every employee reception as a matter *of course.*

NONESSENTIAL: The deal is going to fall through, *in my opinion.*

ESSENTIAL: She doesn't rank very high *in my opinion.*

141   Within the Sentence

Use two commas to set off a transitional expression or an independent comment when it occurs as a nonessential element *within the sentence.*

I, *too,* was not expecting a six-month convalescence.

The doctors tell me, *however,* that I will regain full use of my left leg.

If, however, the expression is used as an essential element, leave the commas out.

NONESSENTIAL: Let me say, *to begin with,* that I have always thought highly of him.

ESSENTIAL: If you want to improve your English, you ought *to begin with* a good review of grammar.

NOTE: In many sentences the only way you can tell whether an expression is nonessential or essential is by the way you say it. If your voice tends to *drop* as you utter the expression, it is nonessential and should be set off by commas.

We concluded, *nevertheless,* that their offer was not serious.

Millie understands, *certainly,* that the reassignment is only temporary.

It is critical, *therefore,* that we rework all these cost estimates.

If your voice tends to *rise* as you utter the expression, it is essential and should not be set off by commas.

We *nevertheless* concluded that their offer was not serious.

Millie *certainly* understands that the reassignment is only temporary.

It is *therefore* critical that we rework all these cost estimates.

If commas are inserted in the previous example, the entire reading of the sentence will be changed. The voice will rise on the word *is* and drop on *therefore.* (If this is the inflection intended, then commas around *therefore* are appropriate.)

It is, *therefore,* critical that we rework all these cost estimates.

142   At the Beginning of a Clause

a. When a transitional expression or independent comment occurs *at the beginning of the second independent clause* in a compound sentence and is *preceded by a semicolon,* use one comma following the expression.

I would love to work in a side trip to Vail; *however,* I don't think I can pull it off.

My boss just approved the purchase order; *therefore,* let's confirm a delivery date.

NOTE: When *hence, then,* or *thus* appears at the beginning of an independent clause, the comma following is omitted unless the connective requires special emphasis or a nonessential element occurs at that point. (See also ¶139b.)

Melt the butter over high heat; *then* add the egg.

BUT: Melt the butter over high heat; *then,* when the foam begins to subside, add the egg.

For the use of a semicolon before a transitional expression, see ¶¶178–180.

b. When the expression occurs *at the beginning of the second independent clause* in a compound sentence and is *preceded by a comma and a coordinating conjunction,* use one comma following the expression. (See also ¶127d.)

The location of the plant was not easy to reach, and *to be honest about it,* I wasn't very taken with the people who interviewed me.

The job seemed to have no future, and *to tell the truth,* the salary was pretty low.

In the first place, I think the budget for the project is unrealistic, and *in the second place,* the deadlines are almost impossible to meet.

NOTE: If the expression is a simple adverb like *therefore,* the comma following the expression is usually omitted. (See also ¶180.)

The matter must be resolved by Friday, and *therefore* our preliminary conference must be held no later than Thursday.

All the general managers have been summoned to a three-day meeting at the home office, and *consequently* I have had to reschedule all my meetings.

c. If the expression occurs *at the beginning of a dependent clause,* either treat the expression as nonessential (and set it off with two commas) or treat it as essential (and omit the commas).

If, *moreover,* they do not meet the deadline, we can cancel the contract.

If *indeed* they want to settle the dispute, why don't they agree to arbitration?

He is a man who, *in my opinion,* will make a fine marketing director.

She is a woman who *no doubt* knows how to run a department smoothly and effectively.

The situation is so serious that, *strictly speaking,* bankruptcy is the only solution.

The situation is so serious that *perhaps* bankruptcy may be the only solution.

143 With the Adverb *Too*

a. When the adverb *too* (in the sense of "also") occurs at the end of a clause or a sentence, the comma preceding is omitted.

If you feel that way *too,* why don't we just drop all further negotiation?

They are after a bigger share of the market *too.*

b. When *too* (in the sense of "also") occurs elsewhere in the sentence, particularly between subject and verb, set it off with two commas.

You, *too,* could be in the Caribbean right now.

Then, *too,* there are the additional taxes to be considered.

c. When *too* is used as an adverb meaning "excessively," it is never set off with commas.

The news is almost *too* good to be believed.

With Interruptions and Afterthoughts

144 Use commas to set off words, phrases, or clauses that interrupt the flow of a sentence or that are loosely added at the end as an afterthought.

Pam is being pursued, *so I've been told,* by three headhunters.

Bob spoke on state-of-the-art financial software, *if I remember correctly.*

Our order processing service, *you must admit,* leaves much to be desired.

His research work has been outstanding, *particularly in the field of ergonomics.*

This book is as well written as, *though less exciting than,* her other books.

This course of action is the wisest, *if not the most expedient,* one under the given circumstances.

See also ¶¶131c, 136b, 137c.

CAUTION: When enclosing an interrupting expression with two commas, be sure the commas are inserted accurately.

WRONG: That is the best, *though not the cheapest way,* to proceed.

RIGHT: That is the best, *though not the cheapest,* way to proceed.

WRONG: Glen has a deep interest in, *as well as a great fondness,* for jazz.

RIGHT: Glen has a deep interest in, *as well as a great fondness for,* jazz.

With Direct Address

145 Names and titles used in direct address must be set off by commas.

We agree, *Mrs. Connolly,* that your order was badly handled.

No, *sir,* that is privileged information.

I count on your support, *Bob.*

With Additional Considerations

146 **a.** When a phrase introduced by *as well as, in addition to, besides, along with, including, accompanied by, together with, plus,* or a similar expression falls between the subject and the verb, it is ordinarily set off by commas. Commas may be omitted, however, if the phrase fits smoothly into the flow of the sentence or is essential to the meaning.

Everyone, *including the top corporate managers,* will be required to attend the in-house seminars on the ethical dimensions of business.

The business plan *including strategies for the new market segments we hope to enter* is better than the other plans I have reviewed. (The *including* phrase is needed to distinguish this plan from the others; hence no commas.)

One *plus one* doesn't always equal two, as we have seen in the Parker-Jackel merger. (The *plus* phrase is essential to the meaning; hence no commas.)

Stephanie *as well as George* should be asked to attend the convention in Vancouver. (The *as well as* phrase flows smoothly in the sentence.)

For the effect these phrases have on the choice of a singular or a plural verb, see ¶¶1007; for a usage note on as well as, *see page 256.*

b. When the phrase occurs elsewhere in the sentence, commas may be omitted if the phrase is closely related to the preceding words.

The refinancing terms have been approved by the trustees *as well as the creditors.*

BUT: I attended the international monetary conference in Bermuda, *together with five associates from our Washington office.*

With Contrasting Expressions

147 Contrasting expressions should be set off by commas. (Such expressions often begin with *but, not,* or *rather than.*)

> The Sanchezes are willing to sell, *but only on their terms.*
>
> He had changed his methods, *not his objectives,* we noticed.
>
> Paula, *rather than Al,* has been chosen for the job.
>
> The CEO and not the president will make that decision. (See ¶1006b.)

NOTE: When such phrases fit smoothly into the flow of the sentence, no commas are required.

> It was a busy *but enjoyable* trip.   They have chosen Paula *rather than Al.*

For the punctuation of balancing expressions, see ¶172c.

The following rules (¶¶148–153) deal with descriptive expressions that immediately follow the words to which they refer. When nonessential, these expressions are set off by commas.

With Identifying, Appositive, or Explanatory Expressions

148 Use commas to set off expressions that provide additional but *nonessential* information about a noun or pronoun immediately preceding. Such expressions serve to further identify or explain the word they refer to.

> Harriet McManus, *an independent real estate broker for the past ten years,* will be joining our agency on Tuesday, *October 1.* (Phrases such as those following *Harriet McManus* and *Tuesday* are appositives.)
>
> Acrophobia, *that is, the fear of great heights,* can now be successfully treated. (See also ¶¶181–183 for other punctuation with *that is, namely,* and *for example.*)
>
> His first book, *written while he was still in graduate school,* launched a successful writing career.
>
> Our first thought, *to run to the nearest exit,* would have resulted in panic.
>
> Ms. Ballantine, *who has been a copywriter for six years,* will be our new copy chief.
>
> Everyone in our family likes outdoor sports, *such as tennis and swimming.* (See ¶149, note.)

NOTE: In some cases other punctuation may be preferable in place of commas.

> **CONFUSING:** Mr. Newcombe, *my boss,* and I will discuss this problem next week. (Does *my boss* refer to Mr. Newcombe, or are there three people involved?)
>
> **CLEAR:** Mr. Newcombe (my boss) and I will be discussing this problem next week. (Use parentheses or dashes instead of commas when an appositive expression could be misread as a separate item in a series.)
>
> There are two factors to be considered, *sales and collections.* (A colon or a dash could be used in place of the comma. See ¶¶189, 201.)
>
> **BUT:** There are three factors to be considered: sales, collections, and inventories. (When the explanatory expression consists of a series of *three* or more items and comes at the end of the sentence, use a colon or dash. See ¶¶189, 201.)
>
> **OR:** These three factors—sales, collections, and inventories—should be considered. (When the explanatory series comes within the sentence, set it off with dashes or parentheses. See ¶¶183, 202, 219.)

149 When the expression is *essential* to the completeness of the sentence, do not set it off. (In the following examples the expression is needed to identify which particular item is meant. If the expression were omitted, the sentence would be incomplete.)

The year *1994* marks the one hundredth anniversary of our company.

The word *liaison* is often misspelled.

The novelist *Anne Tyler* gave a reading last week from a work in progress.

The statement *"I don't remember"* was frequently heard in court yesterday.

The impulse *to get away from it all* is very common.

The notes *in green ink* were made by Mrs. Long.

The person *who takes over as general manager* will need everyone's support.

NOTE: Compare the following sets of examples:

Her article *"Color and Design"* was published in June. (The title is essential; it identifies *which* article.)

Her latest article, *"Color and Design,"* was published in June. (Nonessential; the word *latest* already indicates which article.)

Her latest article *on color and design* was published in June. (Without commas, this means she had earlier articles on the same subject.)

Her latest article, *on color and design,* was published in June. (With commas, this means her earlier articles were on other subjects.)

Everyone in our family likes such outdoor sports *as tennis and swimming.* (The phrase *as tennis and swimming* is essential; without it, the reader would not know which outdoor sports were meant.)

Everyone in our family likes outdoor sports, *such as tennis and swimming.* (The main clause, *Everyone in our family likes outdoor sports,* expresses a complete thought; the phrase *such as tennis and swimming* gives additional but nonessential information. Hence a comma is needed before *such as.*)

Words *such as peak, peek, and pique* can be readily confused. (The *such as* phrase indicates which words are meant.)

A number of Fortune 500 companies, *such as GE, TRW, and Du Pont,* have introduced new programs to motivate their middle managers. (The *such as* phrase provides additional but nonessential information.)

150 A number of expressions are treated as essential simply because of a very close relationship with the preceding words. (If read aloud, the combined phrase sounds like one unit, without any intervening pause.)

After a while Gladys *herself* became disenchanted with the Washington scene.

We *legislators* must provide funds for retraining displaced workers.

My wife Patricia has begun her own consulting business. (Strictly speaking, *Patricia* should be set off by commas, since the name is not needed to indicate *which* wife. However, commas are omitted in expressions like these because they are read as a unit.)

My brother Paul may join us as well.
BUT: My brother, *Paul Engstrom,* may join us.

The composer *Stephen Sondheim* has many Broadway hits to his credit.
BUT: My favorite composer, *Stephen Sondheim,* has many Broadway hits . . .

The Story of English by Robert McCrum, William Cran, and Robert MacNeil has been made into a highly praised television series. (Unless there is another book with the same title, the *by* phrase identifying the authors is not essential and should be set off by commas. However, since a book title and a *by* phrase are typically read as a unit, commas are usually omitted.)

151 When *or* introduces a word or a phrase that identifies or explains the preceding word, set off the explanatory expression with commas.

> Determine whether the clauses are coordinate, *or of equal rank*. (The nonessential *or* phrase may also be set off by parentheses.)

However, if *or* introduces an alternative thought, the expression is essential and should not be set off by commas.

> Determine whether the clauses are coordinate *or noncoordinate*.

152 When a business letter is referred to by date, any related phrases or clauses that follow are usually nonessential.

> Thank you for your letter of February 27, *in which you questioned the balance on your account*. (The date is sufficient to identify which letter is meant; the *in which* clause simply provides additional but nonessential information.)

However, no comma is needed after the date if the following phrase is short and closely related.

> Thank you for your letter of February 27 *about the balance on your account*.

With Residence and Business Connections

153 Use commas to set off a *long phrase* denoting a person's residence or business connections.

> Gary Kendall, *of the Van Houten Corporation in Provo, Utah,* will be visiting us next week.
>
> Gary Kendall *of Provo, Utah,* will be visiting us next week. (Omit the comma before *of* to avoid too many breaks in a short phrase. The state name must always be set off by commas when it follows a city name. See also ¶160.)
>
> Gary Kendall *of the Van Houten Corporation* will be visiting us next week. (Short phrase; no commas.)
>
> Gary Kendall *of Provo* will be visiting us next week. (Short phrase; no commas.)

The following rules (¶¶154–161) deal with the "nonessential" treatment of certain elements in dates, personal names, company names, and addresses. Because these elements cannot truly be called nonessential, the established tradition of setting them off with commas has in many cases begun to change.

In Dates

154 a. Use two commas to set off the year when it follows the month and day.

> On July 1, *1996,* I hope to retire from my present job and start on a second career.
>
> The January 28, *1991,* issue of *Business Week* correctly forecast that corporate mergers and acquisitions would face a "tough slog" in the 1990s.
>
> **NOTE:** Some writers omit the comma following the year.

b. When the month, day, and year are used as a nonessential expression, be sure to set the entire phrase off with commas.

> On Friday, *December 17, 1993,* the court declared a mistrial in the Jacobs trial and scheduled a new trial for February 2, 1994.
>
> Payment of estimated income taxes for the fourth quarter of 1994 will be due no later than Friday, *January 16, 1995*.

155 Omit the commas when only the month and year are given.

In *August 1991* Glen and I dissolved our partnership and went our independent ways.

Isn't it about time for *Consumer Reports* to update the evaluation of personal word processors that appeared in the *November 1991* issue?

For additional examples involving dates, see ¶410.

With *Jr., Sr.,* Etc.

156 Do not use commas to set off *Jr., Sr.,* or roman or arabic numerals following a person's name unless you know that the person in question prefers to do so.

Kelsey R. Patterson Jr.	Benjamin Hart 2d
Christopher M. Gorman Sr.	Anthony Jung III

John Bond Jr.'s resignation will be announced tomorrow.

NOTE: When a person prefers to use commas in his name, observe the following style:

Peter Passaro, Jr. (Use one comma when the name is displayed on a line by itself.)

Peter Passaro, Jr., director of . . . (Use two commas when other copy follows.)

Peter Passaro, Jr.'s promotion . . . (Drop the second comma when a possessive ending is attached.)

157 Abbreviations like *Esq.* and those that stand for academic degrees or religious orders are set off by two commas when they follow a person's name.

Address the letter to Helen E. Parsekian, *Esq.,* in New York.

Roger Farrier, *LL.D.,* will address the Elizabethan Club on Wednesday.

The Reverend James Hanley, *S.J.,* will serve as moderator of the panel.

158 When a personal name is given in inverted order, set off the inverted portion with commas.

McCaughan, James W., Jr.

With *Inc.* and *Ltd.*

159 Do not use commas to set off *Inc., Ltd.,* and similar expressions in a company name unless you know that a particular company prefers to do so. (See also ¶¶1328–1329.)

Time Inc.	Field Hats, Ltd.

Time *Inc.* has expanded its operations beyond magazine publishing.

Field Hats, *Ltd.,* should be notified about this mistake.

NOTE: When commas are to be used in a company name, follow this style:

McGraw-Hill, Inc. (Use one comma when the name is displayed on a line by itself.)

McGraw-Hill, Inc., announces the publication of . . . (Use two commas when other copy follows.)

McGraw-Hill, Inc.'s annual statement . . . (Drop the second comma after a possessive ending.)

For the use of commas with other parts of a company name, see ¶163.

In Geographic References and Addresses

160 Use two commas to set off the name of a state, country, or the equivalent when it directly follows the name of a city or a county.

> Four years ago I was transferred from Bartlesville, *Oklahoma,* to Kinshasa, *Zaire.*
>
> Could Pickaway County, Ohio, become a haven for retired and unemployed editors?
>
> Our Pierre, *South Dakota,* office is the one nearest to you.
>
> **OR:** Our Pierre (South Dakota) office is the one nearest to you. (Parentheses are clearer than commas when a city-state expression serves as an adjective.)
>
> Washington, *D.C.'s* transportation system has improved greatly since I was last there. (Omit the second comma after a possessive ending.)

161 When expressing complete addresses, follow this style:

> **IN SENTENCES:** During the month of August you can send material directly to me at 402 Woodbury Road, Pasadena, CA 91104, or you can ask my secretary to forward it. (Note that a comma follows the ZIP Code but does not precede it.)
>
> **IN DISPLAYED BLOCKS:** 402 Woodbury Road
> Pasadena, CA 91104

The following rules (¶¶162–175) deal with various uses of separating commas: to separate items in a series, to separate adjectives that precede a noun, and to clarify meaning in sentences with unusual word order or omitted words.

In a Series

162 When three or more items are listed in a series and the last item is preceded by *and, or,* or *nor,* place a comma before the conjunction as well as between the other items. (See also ¶126c.)

> Study the rules for the use of the comma, the semicolon, *and* the colon.
>
> The consensus is that your report is well written, that your facts are accurate, *and* that your conclusions are sound.
>
> The show will appeal equally to women and men, adults and children, *and* sophisticates and innocents. (See page 254 for a usage note on *and.*)

NOTE: If a nonessential element follows the conjunction *(and, or,* or *nor)* in a series, omit the comma before the conjunction to avoid excessive punctuation.

> We invited Ben's business associates, his friends and, of course, his parents.
>
> (**RATHER THAN:** . . . his friends, and, of course, his parents.)

163 For a series in a company name, always follow the style preferred by the particular firm.

> Merrill Lynch, Pierce, Fenner & Smith, Inc.   Legg Mason Wood Walker
>
> Smith Barney, Harris Upham & Co.   Rauscher Pierce Refnes, Inc.

If you do not have the company's letterhead or some other reliable resource at hand, follow the standard rule on commas in a series (see ¶162).

> Our primary supplier is *Ames, Koslow, Milke, and Company.*

NOTE: Do not use a comma before an ampersand (&) in a company name unless you know that a particular company prefers to do so.

> Aspinwall, Bromley, Carruthers & Dalgleish

164 When an expression such as *and so on* or *etc.* closes a series, use a comma before and after the expression (unless the expression falls at the end of a sentence).

> Our sale of suits, coats, hats, *and so on,* starts tomorrow.
>
> Tomorrow morning we will start our sale of suits, coats, hats, *etc.*

For a usage note on etc., see page 259.

165 Do not insert a comma after the last item in a series unless the sentence structure demands a comma at that point.

> May 8, June 11, and July 14 are the dates for the next three hearings.
>
> May 8, June 11, and July 14, 1995, are the dates for the next three hearings. (The comma following the year is one of the pair that sets off the year. See ¶154.)

166 When *and, or,* or *nor* is used to connect all the items in a series, do not separate the items by commas. (See also ¶123b.)

> Copies of our recently published company history are being distributed to employees *and* stockholders *and* major customers.

167 If a series consists of only two items, do not separate the items with a comma. (See also ¶125f.)

> We can send the samples to you *by regular mail* or *by one of the express services.*

NOTE: Use a comma, however, to separate two independent clauses joined by *and, but, or,* or *nor.* (See ¶126a.)

For the use of the semicolon in a series, see ¶¶184–185.

With Adjectives

168 When two consecutive adjectives modify the same noun, separate the adjectives with a comma.

> Most people think of her as a *generous, outgoing* person. (A person who is *generous and outgoing.*)

NOTE: Do *not* use a comma between the adjectives if they are connected by *and, or,* or *nor.*

> Most people think of her as a *generous* and *outgoing* person.

169 When two adjectives precede a noun, the first adjective may modify the combined idea of the second adjective plus the noun. In such cases do not separate the adjectives by a comma.

> The estate is surrounded by an *old stone* wall. (A *stone* wall that is *old.*)
>
> Ms. Klaussen is working on the *annual financial* statement. (A *financial* statement that is *annual.*)

TEST: To decide whether consecutive adjectives should be separated by a comma or not, try using them in a relative clause *after* the noun, with *and* inserted between them. If they read smoothly and sensibly in that position, they should be separated by a comma in their actual position.

> We need an *intelligent, enterprising* person for the job. (One can speak of "a person who is *intelligent* and *enterprising,*" so a comma is correct in the original wording.)
>
> Throw out your *old winter* coat. (One cannot speak of "a coat that is *old* and *winter,*" so no comma should be used in the actual sentence.)

170 When more than two adjectives precede a noun, insert a comma only between those adjectives where *and* could have been used.

> a relaxed, unruffled, confident manner (a relaxed *and* unruffled *and* confident manner)

> an experienced, efficient legal secretary (an experienced *and* efficient legal secretary)

> the established American political system (*and* cannot be inserted between these three adjectives)

171 Do not use a comma between the final adjective in a series and the following noun.

> I put in a long, hard, *demanding day* on Monday.

> (**NOT:** I put in a long, hard, *demanding, day* on Monday.)

To Indicate Omitted Words

172 a. **Omission of Repetitive Wording.** Use a comma to indicate the omission of repetitive wording in a compound sentence. (This use of the comma usually occurs when clauses are separated by semicolons.)

> Employees aged 55 and over are eligible for a complete physical examination every year; those between 50 and 54, every two years; and those under 50, every three years.

> **NOTE:** If the omitted words are clearly understood from the context, simpler punctuation may be used.

> Employees aged 55 and over are eligible for a complete physical examination every year, those between 50 and 54 every two years, and those under 50 every three years.

b. **Omission of *That*.** In some sentences the omission of the conjunction *that* creates a definite break in the flow of the sentence. In such cases insert a comma to mark the break.

> Remember, this offer is good only through May 31.

> The problem is, not all of these assumptions may be correct.

> The fact is, things are not working out as we had hoped.

> Chances are, the deal will never come off.

> **NOTE:** In sentences that are introduced by expressions such as *he said, she thinks, we feel,* or *they know,* the conjunction *that* is often omitted following the introductory expression. In such cases no comma is necessary because there is no break in the flow of the sentence.

> We know you can do it. She said she would handle everything.
> They think our price is too high. We believe we offer the best service.

c. **Balancing Expressions.** Use a comma to separate the two parts of a balancing expression from which many words have been omitted.

> First come, first served. The more we give, the more they take.
> First in, last out. GIGO: garbage in, garbage out.
> Here today, gone tomorrow. The less I see of him, the better I like it.

> **NOTE:** The phrase *The sooner the better* usually appears without a separating comma.

1

To Indicate Unusual Word Order

173   In some colloquial sentences, clauses or phrases occur out of normal order and connective words may be omitted. Use a comma to mark the resulting break in the flow of the sentence.

> You must not miss the play, it was that good.
>
> (NORMAL ORDER: The play was so good that you must not miss it.)
>
> Why he took the money, I'll never understand.
>
> That the shipment would be late, we were prepared to accept; that you would ship the wrong goods, we did not expect.

NOTE: In formal writing, these sentences should be recast in normal word order.

See also ¶135c, note.

For Special Emphasis

174   Individual words may be set off by commas for special emphasis.

> I have tried, *sincerely,* to understand your problems.
>
> They contend, *unrealistically,* that we can cut back on staff and still generate the same amount of output.

NOTE: The use of commas in the examples above forces the reader to dwell momentarily on the word that has been set off in each case. Without this treatment *sincerely* and *unrealistically* would not receive this emphasis.

For Clarity

175   a. Use a comma to prevent misreading.

> As you know, nothing came of the meeting.
> (NOT: As you know nothing came of the meeting.)
>
> To a liberal like Bill, Buckley seems hard to take.
>
> Soon after, the committee disbanded without accomplishing its goal.

b. Sometimes, for clarity, it is necessary to separate even a subject and a verb.

> All any insurance policy is, is a contract for services.

c. Use a comma to separate repeated words.

> It was a *long, long* time ago.
>
> That was a *very, very* old argument.
>
> *Well, well,* we'll find a way.
>
> *Now, now,* you don't expect me to believe that!

Commas with dashes: see ¶¶213, 215b.
Commas in numbers: see ¶¶461–463.
Commas with questions within sentences: see ¶¶114–117.
Commas with parentheses: see ¶224a.
Commas inside closing quotation marks: see ¶247.
Commas at the end of quotations: see ¶¶253–255.
Commas preceding quotations: see ¶256.
Commas with quotations within a sentence: see ¶¶259–261.
Commas to set off interruptions in quoted matter: see ¶¶262–263.
Spacing with commas: see ¶299.

The Semicolon

Between Independent Clauses—
And, But, Or, or *Nor* Omitted

176   a. When a coordinating conjunction *(and, but, or,* or *nor)* is omitted between two independent clauses, use a semicolon—not a comma—to separate the clauses. (See ¶187.)

Most of the stockholders favored the sale; the management and the employees did not.

(NOT: Most of the stockholders favored the sale, the management and the employees did not.)

Bob is going for his M.B.A.; Janet already has hers.

b. If the clauses are not closely related, treat them as separate sentences.

WEAK: Thank you for your letter of September 8; your question has already been passed on to the manager of mail-order sales, and you should be hearing from Mrs. Livonia within three days.

BETTER: Thank you for your letter of September 8. Your question has already been passed on to the manager of mail-order sales, and you should be hearing from Mrs. Livonia within three days.

c. The omission of *but* between two independent clauses requires, strictly speaking, the use of a semicolon between the two clauses. However, when the clauses are short, a comma is commonly used to preserve the flow of the sentence.

Not only was the food bad, the portions were minuscule.

Between Independent Clauses—
And, But, Or, or *Nor* Included

177   A comma is normally used to separate two independent clauses joined by a coordinating conjunction. However, under certain circumstances a semicolon is appropriate before the coordinating conjunction.

a. Use a semicolon in order to achieve a stronger break between clauses than a comma provides.

NORMAL BREAK: Many people are convinced that they could personally solve the problem if given the authority to do so, but no one will come forward with a clear-cut plan that we can evaluate in advance.

STRONG BREAK: Many people are convinced that they could personally solve the problem if given the authority to do so; but no one will come forward with a clear-cut plan that we can evaluate in advance.

b. Use a semicolon when one or both clauses have internal commas and a misreading might occur if a comma were also used to separate the clauses.

CONFUSING: I sent you an order for copier paper, computer paper, and No. 10 envelopes, and shipping tags, cardboard cartons, stapler wire, and binding tape were sent to me instead.

CLEAR: I sent you an order for copier paper, computer paper, and No. 10 envelopes; and shipping tags, cardboard cartons, stapler wire, and binding tape were sent to me instead.

(Continued on page 40.)

c. If no misreading is likely, a comma is sufficient to separate the clauses, even though commas are also used within the clauses.

> On June 8, 1993, I discussed this problem with your customer service manager, Betty Dugan, but your company has taken no further action.

> All in all, we're satisfied with the job Bergquist Associates did, and in view of the tight deadlines they had to meet, we're pleased that they came through as well as they did.

> *For additional examples, see ¶133.*

With Transitional Expressions

178 When independent clauses are linked by transitional expressions (see a partial list below), use a semicolon between the clauses. (If the second clause is long or requires special emphasis, treat it as a separate sentence.)

accordingly	however	so (see ¶179)
besides	moreover	that is (see ¶181)
consequently	namely (see ¶181)	then
for example (see ¶181)	nevertheless	therefore
furthermore	on the contrary	thus
hence	otherwise	yet (see ¶179)

> They have given us an oral okay to proceed; *however,* we're still waiting for written confirmation.

> Our costs have started to level off; our sales, *moreover,* have continued to grow.

> Let's give them another month; *then* we can pin them down on their progress.

NOTE: Use a comma after the transitional expression when it occurs at the start of the second clause. (See the first example above.) However, no comma is needed after *hence, then, thus, so,* and *yet* unless a pause is wanted at that point. (See the third example above.)

For the use of commas with transitional expressions, see ¶¶138–143.

179 An independent clause introduced by *so* (in the sense of "therefore") or *yet* may be preceded by a comma or a semicolon. Use a comma if the two clauses are closely related and there is a smooth flow from the first clause to the second. Use a semicolon if the clauses are long and complicated or if the transition between clauses calls for a long pause or a strong break.

> Sales have been good, *yet* profits are low.

> This report explains why production has slowed down; *yet* it does not indicate how to avoid future glitches.

> These sale-priced attaché cases are going fast, *so* don't delay if you want one.

> We have been getting an excessive number of complaints during the last few months about our service; *so* I would like each of you to review the operations in your department and indicate what corrective measures you think ought to be taken.

180 If both a coordinating conjunction and a transitional expression occur at the start of the second clause, use a comma before the conjunction.

> The site has a number of disadvantages, *and furthermore* the asking price is quite high. (See ¶142b and note.)

REMEMBER: A semicolon is needed to separate independent clauses, not so much because a transitional expression is present but because a coordinating conjunction is absent.

With *For Example, Namely, That Is,* Etc.

181 Before an Independent Clause

a. In general, when two independent clauses are linked by a transitional expression such as *for example (e.g.), namely,* or *that is (i.e.),* use a semicolon before the expression and a comma afterward.

> She is highly qualified for the job; *for example,* she has had ten years' experience as a research chemist. (The second independent clause may also be treated as a separate sentence.)

b. If the first clause serves to anticipate the second clause and the full emphasis is to fall on the second clause, use a colon before the transitional expression.

> Your proposal covers all but one point: *namely,* who is going to foot the bill?

c. For a stronger but less formal break between clauses, the semicolon or the colon may be replaced by a dash.

> Hampton says he will help—*that is,* he will help if you ask him to.

NOTE: Use the abbreviated forms *e.g.* and *i.e.* only in informal, technical, or "expedient" material. (See ¶502.)

182 At the End of a Sentence

When *for example, namely,* or *that is* introduces words, phrases, or a series of clauses *at the end of a sentence,* the punctuation preceding the expression may vary as follows:

a. If the first part of the sentence expresses the complete thought and the explanation seems to be added on as an afterthought, use a semicolon before the transitional expression.

> Always use figures with abbreviations; *for example,* 6 m, 9 sq in, 4 p.m. (Here the earlier part of the sentence carries the main thought; the examples are a welcome but nonessential addition.)

b. If the first part of the sentence suggests that an important explanation or illustration will follow, use a colon before the transitional expression to throw emphasis on what *follows.*

> My assistant has three important duties: *namely,* attending all meetings, writing the minutes, and sending out notices. (The word *three* anticipates the enumeration following *namely.* The colon suggests that what follows is the main thought of the sentence.)

> **NOTE:** Use a comma before the transitional expression to throw emphasis on what *precedes.*

> I checked these figures with three people, *namely, Alma, Andy, and Jim.* (This punctuation emphasizes *three people* rather than the specific names.)

c. If the expression introduces an appositive that explains a word or phrase immediately preceding, a comma should precede the transitional expression.

> Do not use quotation marks to enclose an indirect quotation, *that is, a restatement of a person's exact words.* (Here again, a comma is used because what precedes the transitional expression is more important than what follows.)

d. The semicolon, the colon, and the comma in the examples above may be replaced by a dash or by parentheses. The dash provides a stronger but less formal break; the parentheses serve to subordinate the explanatory element. (See also ¶¶201–205, 219.)

183 **Within a Sentence**

When *for example, namely,* or *that is* introduces words, phrases, or clauses *within a sentence,* treat the entire construction as nonessential and set it off with commas, dashes, or parentheses. Dashes will give emphasis to the interrupting construction; parentheses will make the construction appear less important than the rest of the words in the sentence.

> Many of the components, *for example, the motor,* are manufactured by outside suppliers.

> Many of the components—*for example, the motor*—are manufactured by outside suppliers.

> Many of the components *(for example, the motor)* are manufactured by outside suppliers.

NOTE: Commas can be used to set off the nonessential element so long as it contains no internal punctuation (other than the comma after the introductory expression). If the nonessential element is internally punctuated with several commas, set it off with either dashes or parentheses.

> Many of the components—*for example, the motor, the batteries, and the cooling unit*—are manufactured by . . . (Use dashes for emphasis.)

> **OR:** Many of the components *(for example, the motor, the batteries, and the cooling unit)* are manufactured by . . . (Use parentheses for subordination.)

In a Series

184 Use a semicolon to separate items in a series if any of the items already contain commas.

> The company will be represented on the Longwood Environmental Council next year by Martha Janowski, director of public affairs; Harris Mendel, vice president of manufacturing; and Daniel Santoya, director of environmental systems.

NOTE: As an alternative the title following each name may be enclosed in parentheses. In that case, commas can be used to separate the items in the series.

> The company will be represented on the Longwood Environmental Council next year by Martha Janowski (director of public affairs), Harris Mendel (vice president of manufacturing), and Daniel Santoya (director of environmental systems).

185 Avoid starting a sentence with a series punctuated with semicolons. Try to recast the sentence so that the series comes at the end.

> **AWKWARD:** New offices in Framingham, Massachusetts; Rochester, Minnesota; Metairie, Louisiana; and Bath, Maine, will be opened by the middle of next year.

> **IMPROVED:** By the middle of next year we will open new offices in Framingham, Massachusetts; Rochester, Minnesota; Metairie, Louisiana; and Bath, Maine.

With Dependent Clauses

186 Use semicolons to separate a series of parallel dependent clauses if they are long or contain internal commas. (However, a simple series of dependent clauses requires only commas, just like any other kind of series. For an illustration, see the second example in ¶162.)

They promised that they would review the existing specifications, costs, and sales estimates for the project; that they would analyze Merkle's alternative figures; and that they would prepare a comparison of the two proposals and submit their recommendations.

If you have tried special clearance sales but have not raised the necessary cash; if you have tried to borrow the money and have not been able to find a lender; if you have offered to sell part of the business but have not been able to find a partner, then it seems to me that your only course of action is to go out of business. (See ¶185.)

Semicolons with dashes: see ¶¶213, 215c.
Semicolons with parentheses: see ¶224a.
Semicolons with quotation marks: see ¶248.
Spacing with semicolons: see ¶299.

The Colon

Between Independent Clauses

187 a. Use a colon between two independent clauses when the second clause explains or illustrates the first clause and there is no coordinating conjunction or transitional expression linking the two clauses. (Leave two spaces after a colon. See also ¶299.)

I have a special fondness for the Maine coast: it reminds me of the many happy summers we spent there before our children went off to college.

I have two major hurdles to clear before I get my Ph.D.: pass the oral exam and write a dissertation.

NOTE: The second clause that explains or illustrates the first clause may itself consist of more than one independent clause.

It has been said that a successful project goes through three stages: it won't work, it costs too much, and I always knew it was a good idea.

b. Compare the use of the colon and the semicolon in the following sentences.

The job you have described sounds very attractive: the salary is good, and the opportunities for advancement seem excellent. (Use a colon when the second clause explains the first.)

The job you have described sounds very attractive; it is the kind of job I have been looking for. (Use a semicolon when the second clause does not explain the first clause.)

The job you have described sounds very attractive; for example, the salary is good, and the opportunities for advancement seem excellent. (Use a semicolon when a transitional expression links the clauses.)

c. If you aren't sure whether to use a semicolon or a colon between two independent clauses, you can always treat each clause as a separate sentence and use a period at the end of each.

The job you have described sounds very attractive. For example, the salary is good, and the opportunities for advancement seem excellent.

1

Before Lists and Enumerations

188 Place a colon before such expressions as *for example, namely,* and *that is* when they introduce words, phrases, or a series of clauses anticipated earlier in the sentence. (See ¶¶181–182.)

> The company provides a number of benefits not commonly offered in this area: for example, free dental insurance, low-cost term insurance, and personal financial counseling services.

189 When a clause contains an anticipatory expression (such as *the following, as follows, thus,* and *these*) and directs attention to a series of explanatory words, phrases, or clauses, use a colon between the clause and the series.

> *These* are some of the new features in this year's models: a fuel economy indicator, a new rear suspension, and a three-year limited warranty.

> *The following* staff members have been selected to attend the national sales conference in Honolulu:
>
> Frances Berkowitz
> Thomas Gomez
> Thomas Miscina

190 Use a colon even if the anticipatory expression is only implied and not stated.

> The house has attractive features: cross ventilation in every room, a two-story living room, and two terraces.

> Scientists have devised a most appropriate name for a physical property opposed to gravity: levity. (The colon may be used even when what follows is only a single word. See also ¶210.)

191 Do not use a colon in the following cases:

a. If the anticipatory expression occurs near the beginning of a long sentence.

> We have set *the following* restrictions on the return of merchandise, so please be aware of this new policy when dealing with customers. Goods cannot be returned after five days, and price tags must not be removed.
>
> **BUT:** We have set *the following* restrictions on the return of merchandise: goods cannot be returned . . .

b. If the sentence containing the anticipatory expression is followed by another sentence.

> Campers will find that *the following* small items will add much to their enjoyment. These articles may be purchased from a store near the camp.
>
> Flashlight   Hot-cold food bag
> Camera   Fishing gear

c. If an explanatory series follows an introductory clause that does not express a complete thought. (In such cases the introductory element often ends with a verb or a preposition.)

> **WRONG:** Some of the questions that this book answers are: How can you reduce your insurance expenses without sacrificing protection? How can you avoid being over- or underinsured? How can you file a claim correctly the first time around? (Here the introductory clause is incomplete. It has a subject, *Some,* and a verb, *are,* but it lacks a complement.)

> **RIGHT:** Some of the questions that this book answers are these: How can you . . . ? (Here the introductory clause is complete; hence a colon is acceptable.)

RIGHT: Here are some of the questions that this book answers: How can you . . . ? (Here again the introductory clause is complete; hence a colon is acceptable.)

WRONG: The panel consists of: Ms. Seidel, Mrs. Kitay, and Mr. Haddad.

RIGHT: The panel consists of Ms. Seidel, Mrs. Kitay, and Mr. Haddad.

RIGHT: The panel consists of the following people: Ms. Seidel, Mrs. Kitay, and Mr. Haddad.

WRONG: This set of china includes: 12 dinner plates, 12 salad plates, and 12 cups and saucers.

RIGHT: This set of china includes 12 dinner plates, 12 salad plates, and 12 cups and saucers.

RIGHT: This set of china includes the following items: 12 dinner plates, 12 salad plates, and 12 cups and saucers.

NOTE: A colon may be used after an incomplete introductory clause if the items in the series are listed on separate lines.

This set of china includes:	The panel consists of:
12 dinner plates	Ms. Seidel
12 salad plates	Mrs. Kitay
12 cups and saucers	Mr. Haddad

In Expressions of Time and Proportions

192 When hours and minutes are expressed in figures, separate them with a colon, as in the expression *8:25*. (No space precedes or follows this colon. See also ¶299.)

193 A colon is used to represent the word *to* in proportions, as in the ratio *2:1*. (No space precedes or follows this colon. See also ¶299.)

After Salutations

194 In business letters, use a colon after the salutation (see also ¶1346). In social-business letters, use a comma (see also ¶1395b).

In References to Books or Publications

195 a. Use a colon to separate the title and the subtitle of a book.

William Least Heat Moon, in *Blue Highways: A Journey Into America,* has provided an extraordinary portrait of a country and its people.

b. A colon may be used to separate volume number and page number in footnotes and similar references. (Leave no space before or after the colon. See also ¶299.)

8:763–766 (meaning *Volume 8, pages 763–766;* see also ¶1512, note)

NOTE: A reference to chapter and verse in the Bible is handled the same way:

Is. 55:10 (meaning *Chapter 55, verse 10* in the Book of Isaiah)

Capitalizing After a Colon

196 Do not capitalize after a colon if the material that follows cannot stand alone as a sentence.

(Continued on page 46.)

1

All cash advances must be countersigned by me, with one exception: when the amount is less than $50. (Dependent clause following a colon.)

Two courses are required: algebra and English. (Words following a colon.)

EXCEPTION: Capitalize the first word after the colon if it is a proper noun, a proper adjective, or the pronoun *I*.

Two courses are required: English and algebra.

197 Do not capitalize the first word of an independent clause after a colon if the clause explains, illustrates, or amplifies the thought expressed in the first part of the sentence. (See ¶196, exception.)

Essential and nonessential elements require altogether different punctuation: the latter should be set off by commas; the former should not.

198 Capitalize the first word of an independent clause after a colon if it requires special emphasis or is presented as a formal rule. (In such cases the independent clause expresses the main thought; the first part of the sentence usually functions only as an introduction.)

Let me say this: If the company is to recover from its present difficulties, we must immediately devise an entirely new marketing strategy.

Here is the key principle: Nonessential elements must be set off by commas; essential elements should not.

199 Also capitalize the first word after a colon under these circumstances:

When the material following the colon consists of two or more sentences.

There are several drawbacks to this proposal: First, it will tie up a good deal of capital for the next five years. Second, the likelihood of a significant return on the investment has not been shown.

b. When the material following the colon is a quoted sentence.

Frederick Fontina responded in this way: "We expect to win our case once all the facts are brought out in the trial." (See ¶256 for the use of a colon before a quoted sentence.)

c. When the material following the colon starts on a new line (for example, the body of a letter following the salutation or the individual items displayed on separate lines in a list).

Dear John:

I have read your latest draft, and I find it much improved. However, on page 4 I wish you would redo . . .

Capitalize the first word of:

a. Every sentence.
b. Direct quotations.
c. Salutations in letters.

d. When the material *preceding* the colon is a short introductory word such as *Note, Caution,* or *Wanted.*

Note: All expense reports must be submitted no later than Friday.

Remember: All equipment must be turned off before you leave.

Colons with dashes: see ¶¶213, 215c.
Colons with parentheses: see ¶224a.
Colons with quotation marks: see ¶¶248, 256.
Spacing with colons: see ¶299.

SECTION

2

Punctuation: Other Marks

The Dash

Although the dash has a few specific functions of its own, it most often serves in place of the comma, the semicolon, the colon, or parentheses. When used as an alternative to these other marks, it creates a much more emphatic separation of words within a sentence. Because of its versatility, some writers are tempted to use a dash to punctuate almost any break within a sentence. However, this indiscriminate use of dashes destroys the special forcefulness that a dash can convey. So please use the dash sparingly—and then only for deliberate effect.

In Place of Commas

201 Use dashes in place of commas to set off a nonessential element that requires special emphasis.

> At this year's annual banquet, the speakers—and the food—were superb.
>
> Of all the color samples you sent me, there was only one I liked—taupe.

202 If a nonessential element already contains internal commas, use dashes in place of commas to set the element off. (If dashes provide too emphatic a break, use parentheses instead. See ¶¶183, 219.)

> Our entire inventory of Oriental rugs—including a fine selection of Sarouks, Kashans, and Bokharas—will be offered for sale at a 40 percent discount.

203 To give special emphasis to the second independent clause in a compound sentence, use a dash rather than a comma before the coordinating conjunction.

> The information I sent you is true—and you know it!

In Place of a Semicolon

204 For a stronger but less formal break, use a dash in place of a semicolon between closely related independent clauses.

> I do the work—he gets the credit!
>
> The job needs to be done—moreover, it needs to be done well.
>
> Wilson is totally unqualified for a promotion—for example, he still does not grasp the basic principles of good management.

In Place of a Colon

205 For a stronger but less formal break, use a dash in place of a colon to introduce explanatory words, phrases, or clauses.

> I need only a few items for my meeting with Kaster—namely, a copy of his letter of May 18, a copy of the contract under dispute, and a bottle of aspirin.
>
> My arrangement with Gina is a simple one—she handles sales and promotion, and I take care of production.

In Place of Parentheses

206 Use dashes instead of parentheses when you want to give the nonessential element strong emphasis. (See ¶¶183, 219.)

> Call Mike Habib—he's with Jax Electronics—and get his opinion.

To Indicate an Abrupt Break or an Afterthought

207 Use a dash to show an abrupt break in thought or to separate an afterthought from the main part of a sentence. When a sentence breaks off after a dash, leave two spaces before the next sentence. (See ¶208.)

> I wish you would— Is there any point in telling you what I wish for you?
>
> We offer the best service in town—and the fastest!
>
> George Parrish's plane will be landing at O'Hare—or did he say Midway?

208 If a *question* or an *exclamation* breaks off abruptly before it has been completed, use a dash followed by a question mark or an exclamation point as appropriate and then two spaces. If the sentence is a *statement,* however, use a dash alone, followed by two spaces.

> Do you want to tell him or—? Suppose I wait to hear from you.
>
> If only— Yet there's no point in talking about what might have been.
> (NOT: If only—. Yet there's no point in talking about what might have been.)

For the use of ellipsis marks to indicate a break in thought, see ¶291b.

To Show Hesitation

209 Use a dash to indicate hesitation, faltering speech, or stammering.

> The work on the Patterson project was begun—oh, I should say—well, about May 1—certainly no later than May 15.

To Emphasize Single Words

210 Use dashes to set off single words that require special emphasis.

> Jogging—that's what he lives for.
>
> There is, of course, a secret ingredient in my pasta sauce—fennel.

With Repetitions and Restatements

211 Use dashes to set off and emphasize words that repeat or restate a previous thought.

> Next week—on Thursday at 10 a.m.—we will be making an important announcement at a press conference.
>
> Don't miss this opportunity—the opportunity of a lifetime!

Before Summarizing Words

212 Use a dash before such words as *these, they,* and *all* when these words stand as subjects summarizing a preceding list of details.

> Network television, magazines, and newspapers—*these* will be the big gainers in advertising revenues next year.
>
> India, Korea, and Australia—*all* are important new markets for us.
>
> BUT: India, Korea, and Australia are all important new markets for us. (No dash is used when the summarizing word is not the subject.)

Punctuation Preceding an Opening Dash

213 Do not precede an opening dash with a comma, a semicolon, a colon, or a period (except a period following an abbreviation).

> Quality circles boost productivity—and they pay off in higher profits too.
> (NOT: Quality circles boost productivity,—and they pay off in higher profits too.)
>
> The catalog proofs arrived before 11 a.m.—just as you promised.

Punctuation Preceding a Closing Dash

214 a. When a *statement* or a *command* is set off by dashes within a sentence, do not use a period before the closing dash (except a period following an abbreviation).

> Ernie Krauthoff—he used to have his own consulting firm—has gone back to his old job at Marker's.
>
> (NOT: Ernie Krauthoff—He used to have his own consulting firm.—has gone back to his old job at Marker's.)
>
> Your proposal was not delivered until 6:15 p.m.—more than two hours after the deadline.

b. When a *question* or an *exclamation* is set off by dashes within a sentence, use a question mark or an exclamation point before the closing dash.

The representative of the Hitchcock Company—do you know her?—has called again for an appointment.

The new sketches—I can't wait to show them to you!—should be ready by Monday.

NOTE: When a complete sentence is set off by dashes, do not capitalize the first word unless it is a proper noun, a proper adjective, the pronoun *I,* or the first word of a quoted sentence.

Punctuation Following a Closing Dash

215 When the sentence construction requires some mark of punctuation following a closing dash, either retain the dash or use the sentence punctuation—but do not use both marks together.

a. When a closing dash falls at the end of a sentence, it should be replaced by the punctuation needed to end the sentence—a period, a question mark, or an exclamation point. (See ¶208 for exceptions.)

Wheeler's Transport delivers the goods—on time!

(**NOT:** Wheeler's Transport delivers the goods—on time—!)

b. When a closing dash occurs at a point where the sentence requires a comma, retain the closing dash and omit the comma.

The situation has become critical—indeed dangerous—but no one seems to care. (Here the closing dash is retained, and the comma before the coordinating conjunction is omitted.)

If you feel you are qualified for the job—and you may very well be—you ought to take the employment test and go for an interview. (Here the closing dash is retained, and the comma that separates a dependent clause from an independent clause is omitted.)

Brophy said—and you can check with him yourself—"This office must be vacated by Friday." (Here the closing dash is retained, and the comma before the quotation is omitted.)

NOTE: Do not put a phrase in dashes if the closing dash occurs at a point where a comma is needed after an item in a series. Put the phrase in parentheses instead.

CONFUSING: I plan to ask Spalding, Crawford—Betty, not Harold—Higgins, and Martin to investigate why sales have fallen off so sharply.

CLEAR: I plan to ask Spalding, Crawford (Betty, not Harold), Higgins, and Martin to investigate why sales have fallen off so sharply.

c. If a closing dash occurs at a point where the sentence requires a semicolon, a colon, or a closing parenthesis, drop the closing dash and use the required sentence punctuation.

Please try to get your sales projections to us by Wednesday—certainly by Friday at the latest; otherwise, they will be of no use to us in planning next year's budget.

Here is what Marsha had to say—or at least the gist of it: look for new opportunities in niche marketing, and move quickly to capitalize on them.

You need a volunteer (for example, someone like Louis Morales—he's always cooperative) to play the part of the customer.

Constructing Dashes

216 The dash is constructed by striking the hyphen key *twice*, with no space before, between, or after the hyphens.

> Don't believe him--ever! **NOT:** Don't believe him -- ever!

> **BUT:** If I had only realized how the news would affect her--

(Two spaces follow a dash when a statement breaks off abruptly. See ¶208.)

NOTE: Do not use a single hyphen with space before and after it. (For an exception, see the writer's identification line in the simplified letter style, illustrated on page 305.)

217 Type a dash at the end of a line (rather than at the start of a new line).

> Next year our national sales conference is in Hawaii--
> on Maui, I believe.

> **NOT:** Next year our national sales conference is in Hawaii
> --on Maui, I believe.

Parentheses

Parentheses and dashes serve many of the same functions, but they differ in one significant respect: parentheses can set off only nonessential elements, whereas dashes can set off essential and nonessential elements.

REMEMBER: In setting off elements, dashes emphasize; parentheses de-emphasize.

With Explanatory Matter

218 Use parentheses to enclose explanatory material that is independent of the main thought of the sentence. The material within parentheses may be a single word, a phrase, or even an entire sentence.

> We called him Mr. B. for so long that when I ran into him last week, I couldn't remember his last name (Bertolucci). (A single word.)

> By Friday (and sooner if at all possible) I will have an answer for you. (A phrase.)

> Our competitors (we consistently underprice them) can't understand how we do it. (A sentence.)

NOTE: Be sure that the parentheses enclose only what is truly parenthetical and not words essential to the construction of the sentence.

> **WRONG:** I merely said I was averse (not violently opposed *to*) your suggestion.

> **RIGHT:** I merely said I was averse (not violently opposed) *to* your suggestion.

219 Use parentheses to set off a nonessential element when dashes would be too emphatic and commas would be inappropriate or might prove to be confusing.

a. Parentheses are clearer than commas when a city-state expression occurs as an adjective.

> Sales are down in our Middletown (Connecticut) office.

> **BETTER THAN:** Sales are down in our Middletown, Connecticut, office.

b. Parentheses are clearer than commas when the nonessential element already contains commas.

> In three of our factories (Gary, Detroit, and Milwaukee) output is up.

With References

220 Use parentheses to set off references and directions.

> When I last wrote to you (see my letter of July 8 attached), I enclosed photo-copies of checks that you had endorsed and deposited.

When a reference falls *at the end of a sentence,* it may be treated as part of the sentence or as a separate sentence.

> This point is discussed at greater length in Chapter 7 (see pages 90–101).
>
> **OR:** This point is discussed at greater length in Chapter 7. (See pages 90–101.)

See also the note following ¶225d.

With Dates

221 Use parentheses to enclose dates that accompany a person's name, a publication, or an event.

> He claims that he can trace his family back to Charlemagne (742–814).
>
> The "Sin On" Bible (1716) got its name from an extraordinary typographical error: instead of counseling readers to "sin no more," it urged them to "sin on more."

With Enumerated Items

222 **a. Within a Sentence.** Use parentheses to enclose numbers or letters that accompany enumerated items within a sentence.

> We need the following information to complete our record of Ms. Pavlick's experience: (1) the number of years she worked for your company, (2) a description of her duties, and (3) the number of promotions she received.
>
> **NOT:** . . . our record of Ms. Pavlick's experience: 1) the number of years she worked for your company, 2) a description of her duties, and 3) the number of promotions she received. (The only acceptable use of a single closing parenthesis is in an outline. See ¶223.)

> **NOTE:** Letters are used to enumerate items within a sentence when the sentence itself is part of a *numbered* sequence.

> 3. Please include these items on your expense report: (a) the cost of your hotel room; (b) the cost of meals, including tips; and (c) the amount spent on transportation.

b. In a Displayed List. If the enumerated items appear on separate lines, the letters or numbers are usually followed only by periods. (See ¶107.)

223 Subdivisions in outlines are often enclosed in parentheses. It is sometimes necessary to use a single closing parenthesis to provide another level of subdivision.

> **NOTE:** At every level of an outline there should be at least two items. If an item is labeled *A,* there must be at least one more item (labeled *B*) at the same level.

Parenthetical Items Within Sentences

224 If the item in parentheses falls *within a sentence:*

a. Make sure that any punctuation that comes after the item (such as a comma, a semicolon, a colon, or a dash) falls *outside* the closing parenthesis.

Unless I hear from you within five working days (by May 3), I will turn this matter over to my attorney.

I tried to reach you last Monday (I called just before noon); however, no one in your office knew where you were.

For Jane there is only one goal right now (and you know it): getting that M.B.A.

I saw your picture in a magazine last week (in *People,* I think)—and how I laughed when I saw who was standing next to you!

NOTE: Do not insert a comma, a semicolon, a colon, or a dash *before* an opening parenthesis.

b. Do not capitalize the first word of the item in parentheses, even if the item is a complete sentence. **EXCEPTIONS:** Proper nouns, proper adjectives, the pronoun *I,* and the first word of a quoted sentence. (See examples in *c* and *d.*)

c. Do not use a period before the closing parenthesis except with an abbreviation.

Plan to stay with us (we're only fifteen minutes from the airport) whenever you come to New Orleans.

NOT: Plan to stay with us (We're only fifteen minutes from the airport.) whenever you come to New Orleans.

Paul Melnick (Bascomb's new sales manager) wants to take you to lunch.

At last week's hearing (I had to leave at 4 p.m.), was the relocation proposal presented?

d. Do not use a question mark or an exclamation point before the closing parenthesis unless it applies solely to the parenthetical item *and* the sentence ends with a different mark of punctuation.

At the coming meeting (will you be able to make it on the 19th?), let's plan to discuss next year's budget. (Question mark used in parentheses because the sentence ends with a period.)

May I still get tickets to the show (and may I bring a friend), or is it too late? (Question mark omitted in parentheses because the sentence ends with a question mark.)

NOT: May I still get tickets to the show (and may I bring a friend?), or is it too late?

Parenthetical Items at the End of Sentences

225 If the item in parentheses is to be incorporated *at the end of a sentence:*

a. Place the punctuation needed to end the sentence *outside* the closing parenthesis.

Please return the payroll review sheets by Monday (October 8).

How can I reach Jan Weidner (she spoke at yesterday's seminar)?

What a prima donna I work with (you know the one I mean)!

b. Do not capitalize the first word of the item in parentheses, even if the item is a complete sentence. **EXCEPTIONS:** Proper nouns, proper adjectives, the pronoun *I,* and the first word of a quoted sentence. (See examples in *c* and *d.*)

c. Do not use a period before the closing parenthesis except with an abbreviation.

Our office is open late on Thursdays (until 9 p.m.).

Our office is open late on Thursdays (we're here until nine).

NOT: Our office is open late on Thursdays (We're here until nine.).

d. Do not use a question mark or an exclamation point before the closing parenthesis unless it applies solely to the parenthetical element *and* the sentence ends with a different mark of punctuation.

My new assistant is Bill Romero (didn't you meet him once before?).

Be sure to send the letter to Portland, Oregon (not Portland, Maine!).

Then he walked out and slammed the door (can you believe it?)!

Do you know Ellen Smyth (or is it Smythe)?

NOT: Do you know Ellen Smyth (or is it Smythe?)?

I'm through with the job (and I mean it)!

NOT: I'm through with the job (and I mean it!)!

NOTE: When a complete sentence occurs within parentheses at the end of another sentence, it may be incorporated into the sentence (as in the examples above) so long as it is fairly short and closely related. If the sentence in parentheses is long or requires special emphasis, it should be treated as a separate sentence (see ¶226).

Parenthetical Items as Separate Sentences

226 If the item in parentheses is to be treated as a *separate sentence:*

a. The preceding sentence should close with a punctuation mark of its own.

b. The item in parentheses should begin with a capital.

c. A period, a question mark, or an exclamation point (whichever is appropriate) should be placed *before* the closing parenthesis.

d. No other punctuation mark should follow the closing parenthesis, but leave two spaces before the start of the next sentence.

Then Steven Pelletier stood up and made a motion to replace the existing board of directors. (He does this at every stockholders' meeting.) However, this year . . .

I was most impressed with the speech given by Helena Verdi. (Didn't you used to work with her?) She knew her subject, and perhaps more important, she knew her audience.

Parentheses around question marks: see ¶118.
Parentheses around exclamation points: see ¶119c.
Parentheses around confirming figures: see ¶420.
Parentheses around area codes in telephone numbers: see ¶454.
Parenthetical elements within parenthetical elements: see ¶297.

Quotation Marks

Quotation marks have three main functions: to indicate the use of someone else's exact words (see ¶¶227–234), to set off words and phrases for special emphasis (see ¶¶235–241), and to display the titles of literary and artistic works (see ¶¶242–244).

2

For guidance on how to position punctuation marks in relation to the closing quotation mark—*inside* or *outside*—see ¶¶247–251.

For more specific guidance on when to use punctuation with quoted matter and which punctuation to use, refer to the following paragraphs:

Quotations standing alone: see ¶252.
Quotations at the beginning of a sentence: see ¶¶253–255.
Quotations at the end of a sentence: see ¶¶256–258.
Quotations within a sentence: see ¶¶259–261.
Quotations with interrupting expressions: see ¶¶262–263.
Quotations within quotations: see ¶¶245–246.
Long quotations: see ¶¶264–265.
Quoted letters: see ¶266.
Quoted poetry: see ¶¶267–268.
Quoted dialogues and conversations: see ¶¶269–270.

With Direct Quotations

227   Use quotation marks to enclose a *direct quotation,* that is, the exact words of a speaker or a writer.

> When the final gavel sounded, Ferguson merely said, "Let's get out of here before someone reconsiders the verdict."

> When I asked Diana whether she liked the new format of the magazine, all she said was "No." (See ¶¶233, 256a.)

> According to *New York* magazine, William Homisak has defined a vegetarian as "someone who gives peas a chance."

228   a. Do not use quotation marks for an *indirect quotation,* that is, a restatement or a rearrangement of a person's exact words. (An indirect quotation is often introduced by *that* or *whether* and usually differs from a direct quotation in person, verb tense, or word order.)

> DIRECT QUOTATION: Mrs. Knudsen asked her boss, "Am I still being considered for the transfer?"

> INDIRECT QUOTATION: Mrs. Knudsen asked her boss whether she was still being considered for the transfer.

> DIRECT QUOTATION: Her boss said, "You're still in the running, but don't expect a quick decision."

> INDIRECT QUOTATION: Her boss said that she was still in the running but should not expect a quick decision.

> NOTE: Sometimes *direct* quotations are introduced by *that*. See ¶¶256f and 272, note.

   b. In some cases a person's exact words may be treated as either a direct or an indirect quotation, depending on the kind of emphasis desired.

The chairman himself said, "The staff should be told at once that the reloca-tion rumors have no foundation." (The use of quotation marks emphasizes that these are the chairman's exact words.)

The chairman himself said the staff should be told at once that the relocation rumors have no foundation. (Without quotation marks, the emphasis falls on the message itself. The fact that the chairman used these exact words is not important.)

229 Do not use quotation marks to set off a *direct question* at the end of a sentence unless it is also a *direct quotation* of someone's exact words.

DIRECT QUESTION: The question is, Who will pay for the restoration of the land-mark?

DIRECT QUOTATION: Mrs. Burchall then asked, "Who will pay for the restoration of the landmark?"

DIRECT QUOTATION: Mrs. Burchall then replied, "The question is, Who will pay for the restoration of the landmark?" (See also ¶115.)

230 When only a word or phrase is quoted from another source, be sure to place the quotation marks only around the words extracted from the original source and not around any rearrangement of those words.

Tanya said she would need "more help" in order to finish your report by this Friday. (Tanya's exact words were, "How can he expect me to finish his report by this Friday without more help?")

NOTE: When a quoted word or phrase comes at the end of a sentence, the period goes *inside* the closing quotation mark.

Barbara described the plain white shift she wore to the masquerade party as a "Freudian slip." (See also ¶247a, particularly examples 2–4.)

231 Be particularly sure not to include such words as *a* and *the* at the begin-ning of the quotation or *etc.* at the end unless these words were actually part of the original material.

Ben thought you did a "super" job on the packaging design. (Ben's exact words were, "Tell Bonnie I thought the job she did on the packaging design was super.")

Explain the decision any way you want, but tell George I said, "I'm truly sorry about the way things turned out," etc., etc.

232 When quoting a series of words or phrases in the exact sequence in which they originally appeared, use quotation marks before and after the com-plete series. However, if the series of quoted words or phrases did not appear in this sequence in the original, use quotation marks around each word or phrase.

According to Selma, the latest issue of the magazine looked "fresh, crisp, and appealing." (Selma's actual words were, "I think the new issue looks especially fresh, crisp, and appealing.")

BUT: Selma thinks the magazine looks "fresh" and "crisp."
(NOT: Selma thinks the magazine looks "fresh and crisp.")

233 Do not quote the words *yes* and *no* unless you wish to emphasize that these were (or will be) the exact words spoken.

Please answer the question yes or no.

Don't say no until you have heard all the terms of the proposal.

Once the firm's board of directors says yes, we can draft the contract.

(Continued on page 58.)

When asked if he would accept a reassignment, Nick thought for a moment; then, without any trace of emotion, he said "Yes." (The quotation marks imply that Nick said precisely this much and no more. See ¶256a, note, for the use or omission of a comma after *he said*.)

NOTE: When quoting these words, capitalize them if they represent a complete sentence.

All she said was "No."

I would have to answer that question by saying "Yes and no."
BUT: That question requires something more than a yes-or-no answer.

234 Do not use quotation marks with well-known proverbs and sayings. They are not direct quotations.

Sidney really believes that an apple a day keeps the doctor away.

For Special Emphasis

235 When using technical terms, business jargon, or coined words not likely to be familiar to your reader, enclose them in quotation marks when they are first used.

Don't be alarmed if your editor tells you your book is "on the skids." It simply means that your books are now stacked on pallets (skids) and are ready for distribution.

It takes Joe a long time to get himself "booted up" in the morning. (The quoted phrase refers to the technique whereby a computer gets itself up and running.)

236 a. Words used humorously or ironically may be enclosed in quotation marks. However, unless you are convinced your reader will otherwise miss the humor or the irony, omit the quotation marks.

We were totally underwhelmed by his ideas on reorganizing the order processing procedures.

Nothing would please me more than looking at the slides of Mike's tour of Egypt. (One might reasonably conclude that the writer takes unalloyed pleasure at the prospect.)

BUT: "Nothing" would please me more than looking at the slides of Mike's tour of Egypt. (When *Nothing* is enclosed in quotation marks, the writer makes it clear that doing nothing would be preferable to looking at Mike's slides.)

b. A slang expression, the use of poor grammar, or a deliberate misspelling is enclosed in quotation marks to indicate that such usage is not part of the writer's normal way of speaking or writing.

Now that his kids have run off to Europe with the college tuition money, Bob has stopped boasting about his close-knit "nucular" family. (The writer is mimicking Bob's habitual mispronunciation of *nuclear*.)

As far as I'm concerned, Polly Harrington's version of what happened "ain't necessarily so."

c. Quotation marks are not needed for colloquial expressions.

She cares less about the salary than she does about the *perks*—you know, chauffeured limousine, stock options, and all the rest of it. (*Perks* is short for perquisites, meaning "special privileges.")

Pam is planning *to temp* until she's sure about staying in Los Angeles. (*To temp* means "to do temporary work.")

237 **a.** Use quotation marks to enclose words and phrases that have been made to play an abnormal role in a sentence—for example, verb phrases made to function as adjectives.

> We were all impressed by her "can do" attitude. (*Can do* is a verb phrase used here as an adjective modifying *attitude*.)
>
> OR: We were all impressed by her can-do attitude. (A hyphen may also be used to hold together a phrase used as an adjective before a noun. See ¶828.)
>
> BUT NOT: We were all impressed by her "can-do" attitude. (Do not use both quotation marks and a hyphen for the same purpose.)
>
> NOTE: When a verb like *must* or a preposition-adverb like *in* becomes established as a noun or an adjective (as indicated in the dictionary), use quotation marks only in those constructions where confusion could otherwise result.
>
> You have to read that book; it's a must.
>
> BUT: You have to get that book; it's "must" reading.
>
> Frank must have an in with their purchasing department.
>
> BUT: I guess she thinks it's still the "in" thing to do.

b. Do not use quotation marks to enclose phrases that are taken from other parts of speech and are now well established as nouns; for example, *haves and have-nots, pros and cons, ins and outs.* (See also ¶626.)

> My predecessor left me a helpful list of dos and don'ts.
>
> This document will explain all the whys and wherefores.
>
> Give me an agreement without a lot of ifs, ands, or buts. (See also ¶285.)

238 When a word or an expression is formally defined, the word to be defined is usually underscored (*italicized* in print) and the definition is usually quoted so that the two elements may be easily distinguished. (See ¶286.)

NOTE: Many types of electronic equipment now have the capability of printing italic type. If you have access to such equipment, use italics in place of underscoring.

239 A word referred to as a word may be enclosed in quotation marks but is now more commonly underscored or italicized. (See ¶285.)

240 **a.** Words and phrases introduced by such expressions as *marked, labeled, signed,* and *entitled* are enclosed in quotation marks.

> The carton was marked "Fragile."
>
> He received a message signed "A Friend."
>
> The article entitled "Write Your Senator" was in that issue.
>
> NOTE: Titles of complete published works following the expression *entitled* require underscoring or italics rather than quotation marks. (See ¶289 for titles to be underscored or italicized; ¶¶242–244 for titles to be quoted.)

b. Words and phrases introduced by *so-called* require neither quotation marks nor underscoring. The expression *so-called* is sufficient to give special emphasis to the term that follows.

> The so-called orientation session struck Paula and me as more of an exercise in outright brainwashing.

241 The translation of a foreign expression is enclosed in quotation marks; the foreign word itself is underscored or italicized. (See ¶287.)

With Titles of Literary and Artistic Works

242 Use quotation marks around the titles that represent only *part* of a complete published work—for example, the titles of chapters, lessons, topics, sections, and parts within a book; the titles of articles and feature columns in newspapers and magazines; and the titles of essays, short poems, lectures, sermons, and conference themes. (Underscore or italicize titles of *complete* published works. See ¶289.)

> The heart of her argument can be found in Chapter 3, "The Failure of Traditional Therapy." You'll especially want to read the section entitled "Does Father Know Best?"

> An exciting article—"Can Cancer Now Be Cured?"—appears in the magazine I'm enclosing. (See ¶¶260–261 for the use of commas, dashes, and parentheses with quoted titles.)

> The theme of next month's workshop is "Imperatives for the Nineties—From the Ragged Edge to the Cutting Edge."

> The title of my speech for next month's luncheon will be "Reforming Our Local Tax Policy."

> **BUT:** At next month's luncheon I will be talking about reforming our local tax policy. (Do not enclose the words with quotation marks when they describe the topic rather than signify the exact title.)

NOTE: The titles *Preface, Contents, Appendix,* and *Index* are not quoted, even though they represent parts within a book. They are often capitalized, however, for special emphasis.

> All the supporting data is given in the Appendix. (Often capitalized when referring to another section within the same work.)

> **BUT:** You'll find that the most interesting part of his book is contained in the appendix. (Capitalization is not required when reference is made to a section within another work.)

243 Use quotation marks around the titles of *complete but unpublished* works, such as manuscripts, dissertations, and reports.

> I would like to get a copy of Sandor's study, "Criteria for Evaluating Staff Efficiency."

> Thank you for giving us the chance to review "Working out of Your Home." I have given your manuscript to an editor with a good deal of personal experience in this field.

244 Use quotation marks around the titles of songs and other short musical compositions and around the titles of individual segments or programs that are part of a larger television or radio series. (Series titles are underscored or italicized.)

> Just once I would like to get through a company party without having to hear Reggie sing "Danny Boy."

> I understand that our company was briefly mentioned on the <u>Frontline</u> program entitled "Pentagon, Inc.," which was shown last Tuesday night.

Quotations Within Quotations

245 A quotation within another quotation is enclosed in single quotation marks. Use the apostrophe for a single quotation mark.

> Fowler then said, "We were all impressed by her 'can do' attitude."

246 If a quotation appears within the single-quoted matter, revert to double quotation marks for the inner portion.

> Mrs. DeVries then remarked, "I thought it a bit strange when Mr. Fowler said, 'Put these checks in an envelope marked "Personal Funds," and set them aside for me.' " (When single and double quotation marks occur together, do not insert any extra space between them in typewritten material.)

NOTE: For the positioning of punctuation in relation to a single quotation mark, see the following paragraphs:

For placement of periods and commas, see ¶247b.
For placement of semicolons and colons, see ¶248b.
For placement of question marks and exclamation points, see ¶249d.
For placement of dashes, see ¶250b.

The following rules (¶¶247–251) indicate how to position punctuation marks in relation to the closing quotation mark—inside *or* outside.

With Periods and Commas

247 **a.** Periods and commas always go *inside* the closing quotation mark. This is the preferred American style. (Some writers in the United States follow the British style: Place the period *outside* when it punctuates the whole sentence, *inside* when it punctuates only the quoted matter. Place the comma *outside,* since it always punctuates the sentence, not the quoted matter.)

> Before the conference began, Mr. Karras made a point of saying, "Let me do the talking."
>
> He wants to change "on or about May 1" to read "no later than May 1."
>
> The price tag on the leather sofa was clearly marked "Sold."
>
> Sign your name wherever you see an "X."
>
> "Let's go over the details again," she said.
>
> "The date stamp indicates that my copy arrived at 10:50 a.m.," he said.
>
> Their latest article, "Scanning the Future," will appear in next month's issue of *Inc.* magazine.
>
> "Witty," "clever," "amusing," and "hilarious" are only a few of the adjectives that are being applied to her new book.
>
> The package was labeled "Fragile," but that meant nothing to your delivery crew.

b. Periods and commas also go *inside* the single closing quotation mark.

> Mr. Poston said, "Please let me see all the orders marked 'Rush.'"
>
> "All he would say was 'I don't remember,'" answered the witness.

NOTE: Do not confuse a single quotation mark with an apostrophe used to show possession. When a sentence requires the use of a comma or a period at the same point as an apostrophe showing possession, the comma or period *follows* the apostrophe.

> I recently took over the management of the Murrays', the Boyarskys', and the Cabots' investment portfolios.

With Semicolons and Colons

248 **a.** Semicolons and colons always go *outside* the closing quotation mark.

> Last Tuesday you said, "I will mail a check today"; it has not yet arrived.

> When the announcement of the changeover was made, my reaction was "Why?"; John's only reaction was "When?"

> Please send me the following items from the file labeled "In Process": the latest draft of the Berryman agreement and FASB Statement 33.

> The memo I sent you yesterday said that the new workstations would cost "a nominal egg"; it should have said "an arm and a leg."

b. Semicolons and colons also go *outside* the single quotation mark.

> Alice Arroyo called in from her country place to say, "Please send me the following items from the file labeled 'In Process': the latest draft of the Berryman agreement and FASB Statement 33."

With Question Marks and Exclamation Points

249 **a.** A question mark or an exclamation point goes *inside* the closing quotation mark when it applies only to the quoted material.

> His first question was, "How long have you worked here?" (Quoted question at the end of a statement.)

> Garland still ends every sales meeting by shouting, "Go get 'em!" (Quoted exclamation at the end of a statement.)

b. A question mark or an exclamation point goes *outside* the closing quotation mark when it applies to the entire sentence.

> When will she say, for a change, "You did a nice job on that"? (Quoted statement at the end of a question.)

> Stop saying "Don't worry"! (Quoted statement at the end of an exclamation.)

c. If the quoted material and the entire sentence each require the same mark of punctuation, use only one mark—the one that comes first. (See also ¶¶257–258.)

> Have you seen the advertisement that starts, "Why pay more?" (Quoted question at the end of a question.)

> Let's not panic and yell "Fire!" (Quoted exclamation at the end of an exclamation.)

d. These same principles govern the placement of a question mark or an exclamation point in relation to a single quotation mark.

> What prompted her to say, "Be careful in handling documents marked 'Confidential'"? (Quoted phrase within a quoted statement within a question.)

> Dr. Marks asked, "Was the check marked 'Insufficient Funds'?" (Quoted phrase within a quoted question within a statement.)

> Miss Parsons then said, "How did you answer him when he asked you, 'How do you know?'" (Quoted question within a quoted question within a statement.)

With Dashes

250 **a.** A dash goes *inside* the closing quotation mark to indicate that the speaker's or writer's words have broken off abruptly.

> It was tragic to hear Tom say, "If he had only listened—"

b. A dash goes *outside* the closing quotation mark when the sentence breaks off abruptly *after* the quotation.

If I hear one more word about "boosting productivity"—

BUT: Mrs. Halliday said, "If I hear one more word from the general manager about 'boosting productivity'—"

c. A closing dash goes *outside* the closing quotation mark when the quotation itself is part of a nonessential element being set off by a pair of dashes.

Get the latest draft—it's the one with the notation "Let's go with this"—and take it to Gladys Pomeroy for her approval.

With Parentheses

251 **a.** The closing parenthesis goes *inside* the closing quotation mark when the parenthetical element is part of the quotation.

Fox agreed to settle his account "by Friday (July 28)" when he last wrote us.

b. The closing parenthesis goes *outside* the closing quotation mark when the quotation is part of the parenthetical element.

Joe Elliott (the one everyone calls "Harper's gofer") will probably get the job.

The following rules (¶¶252–270) indicate what punctuation to use with various kinds of quoted matter.

Punctuating Quotations That Stand Alone

252 When a quoted sentence stands alone, put the appropriate mark of terminal punctuation—a period, a question mark, or an exclamation point—*inside* the closing quotation mark.

"I think we should switch suppliers at once."

"Can you send us your comments within two weeks?"

"I won't accept that kind of response!"

Punctuating Quotations That Begin a Sentence

253 When a quoted *statement* occurs at the beginning of a sentence, omit the period before the closing quotation mark and use a comma instead.

"I think we should switch suppliers at once," he said.
(NOT: . . . at once.," he said.)

EXCEPTION: Retain the period if it accompanies an abbreviation.

"I'm still planning to go on for an LL.B.," she said.

254 When a quoted *question* or *exclamation* occurs at the beginning of a sentence, retain the question mark or the exclamation point before the closing quotation mark and do *not* insert a comma.

"Can you send us your comments within two weeks?" she asked.
(NOT: . . . within two weeks?," she asked.)

"I won't accept that kind of response!" I told him.
(NOT: . . . that kind of response!," I told him.)

255 When a quoted *word* or *phrase* occurs at the beginning of a sentence, no punctuation should accompany the closing quotation mark unless required by the overall construction of the sentence.

> "An utter bore" was the general reaction to yesterday's speaker.

> "Managing Your Portfolio," the second chapter in the Klingenstein book, sets forth some guidelines I have never seen anywhere else. (The comma that follows the chapter title is the first of a pair needed to set off a nonessential expression.)

Punctuating Quotations That End a Sentence

256 a. When a quoted *statement, question,* or *exclamation* comes at the end of a sentence and is introduced by an expression such as *he said* or *she said,* a comma usually precedes the opening quotation mark.

> Mr. Kelley said, "We'll close early on Friday."

> In her letter Diana said, "I plan to arrive on Thursday at 6 p.m."

NOTE: If the quotation is quite short or is woven into the flow of the sentence, omit the comma.

> All she said was "No." **OR:** All she said was, "No." (The comma creates a slight pause and throws greater emphasis on the quotation.)

> Why does he keep saying "It won't work"?

b. Use a colon in place of a comma if the introductory expression is an independent clause.

> Jerry would say only this: "I'll send you my new address once I'm settled."

> Here is the key statement in his letter: "If my loan is approved, the deal is on."

c. Use a colon in place of a comma if the quotation contains more than one sentence.

> Mr. Bowles then said: "If the legislation is passed by Congress, we have an excellent chance to compete effectively in international markets. However, if the legislation gets bottled up in committee, our competitive position will worsen."

d. Use a colon in place of a comma if the quotation is set off on separate lines as an extract. (See also ¶265.)

> Sheila's letter said in part:

>> I have always valued your assistance on our various projects. You have always acted as if you were actually part of our staff, with our best interests in mind . . .

e. Do not use either a comma or a colon before an indirect quotation.

> Sheila said that she had always valued Bob's assistance on various projects.

f. Do not use either a comma or a colon when a direct quotation is introduced by *that* or is otherwise woven into the flow of the sentence.

> In a previous letter to you, I noted that "you have always acted as if you were actually part of our staff, with our best interests in mind."

NOTE: The first word of the quotation is not capitalized in this case, even though it was capitalized in the original. Compare *you* here with *You* in the example in *d* above. (See ¶272 for the rule on capitalizing the first word of a quoted sentence.)

257 When a quoted *sentence* (a statement, a question, or an exclamation) falls at the end of a larger sentence, do not use double punctuation—that is, one mark to end the quotation and another to end the sentence. Choose the stronger mark. (**REMEMBER:** *A question mark is stronger than a period; an exclamation point is stronger than a period or a question mark.*) If the same mark of punctuation is required for both the quotation and the sentence as a whole, use the first mark that occurs—the one within quotation marks.

Quoted Sentences at the End of a Statement

Bob said, "I can't wait to get back to work." (**NOT** .".)
Mrs. Fahey asked, "How long have you been away?" (**NOT** ?".)
Mr. Auden shouted, "We can't operate a business this way!" (**NOT** !".)

Quoted Sentences at the End of a Question

Did you say, "I'll help out"? (**NOT** .".?)
Why did Mary ask, "Will Joe be there?" (**NOT** ?".?)
Who yelled "Watch out!" (**NOT**!".?)

Quoted Sentences at the End of an Exclamation

How could you forget to follow up when you were specifically told, "Give this order special attention"! (**NOT** .".!)
Stop saying "How should I know"! (**NOT** ?".!)
How I'd like to walk into his office and say, "I quit!" (**NOT** !".!)

NOTE: When a quoted sentence ends with an abbreviation, retain the abbreviation period, even though a question mark or an exclamation point follows as the terminal mark of punctuation.

The reporter asked, "When did you first hear about the board's decision to sell Modem Inc.?"
Didn't Larry tell Meg, "I'll help you with the tuition for your M.D."?

However, if a period is required as the terminal mark of punctuation, use only one period to mark the end of the abbreviation and the end of the sentence.

Gloria said, "You can call as early as 6:30 a.m." (**NOT** .".)

For placement of periods, see ¶247; for placement of question marks and exclamation points, see ¶249.

258 When a quoted *word* or *phrase* occurs at the end of a sentence, punctuate according to the appropriate pattern in the following examples. (**NOTE:** If the quoted word or phrase represents a complete sentence, follow the patterns shown in ¶257.)

Quoted Words and Phrases at the End of a Statement

He says he is willing to meet "at your convenience." (**NOT** ".)
I thought her letter said she would arrive "at 10 p.m." (**NOT** .".)
I've been meaning to read "Who Pays the Bill?" (**NOT** ?".)
Critics have praised his latest article, "Freedom Now!" (**NOT** !".)

(Continued on page 66.)

Quoted Words and Phrases at the End of a Question

> Why is he so concerned about my "convenience"?
>
> Didn't she clearly state she would arrive "at 10 p.m."?
>
> Have you had a chance to read "Who Pays the Bill?" (NOT ?"?)
>
> What did you think of the article "Freedom Now!"?

Quoted Words and Phrases at the End of an Exclamation

> He couldn't care less about my "convenience"!
>
> You're quite mistaken—she clearly said "at 10 a.m."!
>
> Don't waste your time reading "Who Pays the Bill?"!
>
> What a reaction he got with his article "Freedom Now!" (NOT !"!)

Punctuating Quotations Within a Sentence

259 Do not use a comma before or after a quotation when it is woven into the flow of the sentence.

> Don't say "I can't do it" without trying.
>
> No considerate person would say "Why should I care?" under such desperate circumstances.
>
> The audience shouted "Bravo!" and "Encore!" at the end of Emanuel Ax's recital last night.

NOTE: In such cases do not use a period at the end of a quoted statement, but retain the question mark or the exclamation point at the end of a quoted question or exclamation (as illustrated in the examples above).

260 Do not use commas to set off a quotation that occurs within a sentence as an *essential* expression. (See ¶149.)

> The luxurious practice of booking passage between England and India on the basis of "Port Outward, Starboard Homeward" (so as to get a cabin on the cooler side of the ship) is said to be the origin of the word *posh*.
>
> The chapter entitled "Locating Sources of Venture Capital" will give you specific leads you can pursue.

261 a. When a quotation occurs within a sentence as a *nonessential* expression, use a comma before the opening quotation mark and before the closing quotation mark.

> His parting words, "I hardly know how to thank you," were sufficient.
>
> The next chapter, "The Role of Government," further clarifies the answer.

b. If the *nonessential* quoted matter requires a question mark or an exclamation point before the closing quotation mark, use a pair of dashes or parentheses (rather than commas) to set off the quoted matter.

> Your last question—"How can we improve communications between departments?"—can best be answered by you.
>
> RATHER THAN: Your last question, "How can we improve communications between departments?," can best be answered by you.

NOTE: When some or all of the quoted items in a series end with a question mark or an exclamation point, display them in a list to avoid the awkwardness of inserting commas before the quotation marks.

Next month's issue will feature the following articles:

"Is the Age of the Mainframe Over?"

"Tax Law Changes—Again!"

"Whither Wall Street?"

RATHER THAN: Next month's issue will feature the following articles: "Is the Age of the Mainframe Over?," "Tax Law Changes—Again!," and "Whither Wall Street?"

c. If *essential* quoted matter ends with a question mark or an exclamation point and occurs within a sentence where a comma would ordinarily follow (for example, at the end of an introductory clause or phrase), omit the comma.

Although we were all asked last week to read an article entitled "Can U.S. Manufacturers Prosper in Today's World Markets?" the topic was totally ignored in this week's seminar.

RATHER THAN: . . . an article entitled "Can U.S. Manufacturers Prosper in Today's World Markets?," the topic was . . .

NOTE: If the omission of a comma at this point could lead to confusion, reword the sentence to avoid the problem.

We were all asked last week to read an article entitled "Can U.S. Manufacturers Prosper in Today's World Markets?" Yet the topic was . . .

OR: We were all asked last week to read an article entitled "Can U.S. Manufacturers Prosper in Today's World Markets?"; yet the topic was . . .

Punctuating Quoted Sentences With Interrupting Expressions

262 When a quoted sentence is *interrupted* by an expression such as *he asked* or *she said,* use a comma and a closing quotation mark before the interrupting expression and another comma after it. Then resume the quotation with an opening quotation mark. Put the first word in small letters unless it is a proper noun, a proper adjective, or the pronoun *I.*

"During the past month," the memo said in part, "we have received some welcome news from our overseas branches."

263 If the interrupting expression ends the sentence and the quotation continues in a new sentence, put a period after the interrupting expression and start the new sentence with an opening quotation mark and a capital letter.

"Perhaps we should decline the invitation," he said. "It would be better not to go than to arrive late."

Punctuating Long Quotations

264 If a quotation consists of more than one sentence without any interrupting elements, use quotation marks only at the beginning and at the end of the quotation. Do not put quotation marks around each sentence within the quotation.

Here is the full text of the release he gave to the media: "I have decided to withdraw from the upcoming election. I wish to thank my supporters for their enormous help. I am sorry to disappoint them."

2

265 A long quotation that will make four or more lines may be handled in one of the following ways:

a. The preferred style for displaying the quoted matter is to treat it as a single-spaced extract. Indent the extract five spaces from each side margin, and leave one blank line above and below the extract. Do not enclose the quoted matter in quotation marks; the indention replaces the quotation marks. (See page 304 for an illustration.)

NOTE: Ordinarily, start the quoted matter flush left on the shorter line length; however, if a paragraph indention was called for in the original, indent the first line five spaces. Indent the first line of any additional paragraphs five spaces also, but do not leave a blank line between indented paragraphs.

b. Use the same line length and spacing for the quoted matter as for other text material on the page.

(1) If the quoted matter consists of one paragraph only, place quotation marks at the beginning and end of the paragraph. Use the normal paragraph indention of five spaces.

(2) If the quoted matter consists of two or more paragraphs, place a quotation mark *at the start* of each paragraph but at the end of only one paragraph—the last one.

(3) Change double quotation marks within the quoted matter to single quotation marks, and vice versa. (See ¶¶245–246.)

"When you are writing a letter that grants a request, you can follow this pattern:

"First, express appreciation for the writer's interest in the company's product or service.

"Next, give the exact information requested and, if possible, additional information that may be of interest.

"Finally, express willingness to 'be of further help.' "

Quoting Letters

266 Letters and other business documents that are to be quoted word for word may be handled in one of the following ways:

a. Make a photocopy of the material. In this case no quotation marks are used.

b. If no photocopy equipment is available, put the material on a separate sheet of paper headed *COPY*. In this case no quotation marks are used.

c. The material, if short, may be treated like a long quotation (see ¶265). If you use a shorter line length, omit the quotation marks. If you use the same line length as you do for other material on the page, then place the opening quotation mark before the first word (in a letter, the date line); place the closing quotation mark after the last word (in a letter, the last word in the signature block).

Quoting Poetry

267 When quoting a complete poem (or an extended portion of one) in a letter or a report, type it line for line, single-spaced (except for stanza breaks). If the line length is shorter than that of the normal text above and below the poem, no quotation marks are needed; the poem will stand out sufficiently as an extract. If, however, quotation marks are needed to indicate the special nature of the material, place a quotation mark at the beginning of each stanza and at the end of only the last stanza. (See also ¶284b.)

268   A short extract from a poem is sometimes woven right into a sentence or a paragraph. In such cases use quotation marks at the beginning and end of the extract, and use a diagonal line (with one space before and after) to indicate where each line would break in the original arrangement of the poem.

> In a poem about the death of an American poet, Richard Wilbur refers scathingly to the more prominent notices given to a "cut-rate druggist, a lover of Giving, / A lender, and various brokers: gone from this rotten / Taxable world to a higher standard of living."

Quoting Dialogues and Conversations

269   When quoting dialogues and conversations, start the remarks of each speaker as a new paragraph, no matter how brief.

> "Waiter, what was in that glass?"
>
> "Arsenic, sir."
>
> "*Arsenic.* I asked you to bring me absinthe."
>
> "I thought you said arsenic. I beg your pardon, sir."
>
> "Do you realize what you've done, you clumsy fool? I'm dying."
>
> "I am extremely sorry, sir."
>
> "I DISTINCTLY SAID ABSINTHE."
>
> "I realize that I owe you an apology, sir. I am extremely sorry."
>
> —Myles na Gopaleen

270   In plays and court testimony, where the name of the speaker is indicated, quotation marks are not needed.

> CECILY: Uncle Jack is sending you to Australia.
>
> ALGER: Australia! I'd sooner die.
>
> CECILY: Well, he said at dinner on Wednesday night that you would have to choose between this world, the next world, and Australia.
>
> ALGER: Oh, well! The accounts I have received of Australia and the next world are not particularly encouraging. This world is good enough for me, cousin Cecily.
>
> —Oscar Wilde

The following rules (¶¶271–284) cover a number of stylistic matters, such as how to capitalize in quoted matter (¶¶272–273), how to handle omissions in quoted matter (¶¶274–280), and how to handle insertions in quoted matter (¶¶281–283).

Style in Quoted Matter

271   In copying quoted matter, follow the style of the extract exactly in punctuation, spelling, hyphenation, and number style. (See ¶282 for the use of [*sic*] to indicate errors in the original.)

Capitalization in Quoted Matter

272 Ordinarily, capitalize the first word of every complete sentence in quotation marks.

> I overheard Ellis mutter, "Only a fool would make such a claim."

> Here is the key sentence in her memo: "Despite the understaffing in the department, everyone is expected to meet the goals established for the coming year."

NOTE: If the quoted sentence is preceded by *that* or is otherwise incorporated into the flow of a larger sentence, do not capitalize the first word (unless it is a proper noun, a proper adjective, or the pronoun *I*).

> I overheard Ellis mutter that "only a fool would make such a claim."

> In essence, she says that "despite the understaffing in the department, everyone is expected to meet the goals established for the coming year."

273 When quoting a word or phrase, do not capitalize the first word unless it meets *one* of these conditions:

a. It is a proper noun, a proper adjective, or the pronoun *I*.

> No one is terribly impressed by his "Irish temper."

b. It was capitalized in its original use.

> I watched her scrawl "Approved" and sign her name at the bottom of the proposal.

c. The quoted word or phrase occurs at the beginning of a sentence.

> "Outrageous" was the publisher's reaction to Maxon's attempt to duck the questions of the reporters. (Even if the expression was not capitalized in the original material, it is capitalized here to mark the start of the sentence.)

d. It represents a complete sentence.

> The Crawleys said "Perhaps"; the Calnans said "No way."

> *See ¶¶277–278 on capitalizing the first word of a quoted sentence fragment.*

Omissions in Quoted Matter

274 If one or more words are omitted *within a quoted sentence,* use ellipsis marks (three spaced periods, with one space before and after each period) to indicate the omission.

> "During the past thirty-five years . . . we have been witnessing a change in buying habits, particularly with respect to food."

NOTE: Omit any marks of internal punctuation (a comma, a semicolon, a colon, or a dash) on either side of the ellipsis marks unless they are required for the sake of clarity.

> **ORIGINAL VERSION:** "The objectives of the proposed bill are admirable, I will cheerfully concede; the tactics being used to gain support for the bill are not."

> **CONDENSED VERSION:** "The objectives of the proposed bill are admirable . . .; the tactics being used to gain support for the bill are not." (The comma preceding the omitted phrase is not needed; however, the semicolon following the omitted phrase must be retained for clarity.)

275 If one or more words are omitted *at the end of a quoted sentence,* use three spaced periods followed by the necessary terminal punctuation for the sentence as a whole.

"Can anyone explain why . . . ?" (The original question read, "Can anyone explain why this was so?")

"During the past thirty-five years, starting in the late 1950s, we have been witnessing a change in buying habits . . . . Consumers have become more concerned with what's in the package rather than with the package itself." (The first three periods represent the omitted words "particularly with respect to food"; the fourth period marks the end of the sentence. Two spaces follow before the next sentence.)

NOTE: If the quotation is intended to trail off, use only three spaced periods at the end of the sentence. (See also ¶291b.)

His reaction was, "If I had only known . . ."

276   If one or more sentences are omitted *between other sentences* within a long quotation, use three spaced periods *after* the terminal punctuation of the preceding sentence.

"During the past thirty-five years, starting in the late 1950s, we have been witnessing a change in buying habits, particularly with respect to food. . . . How far this pattern of change will extend cannot be estimated."

NOTE: There is no space between *food* and the first period because that period marks the end of a sentence. The remaining three periods signify the omission of one or more complete sentences. Two spaces follow before the next sentence.

277   If only a fragment of a sentence is quoted within another sentence, it is not necessary to use ellipsis marks to signify the omission of words before or after the fragment.

According to Robertson's report, there has been "a change in buying habits" during the past thirty-five years.

Moreover, if the fragment as given can be read as a complete sentence, capitalize the first word in the quoted fragment, even though this word was not capitalized in the original. (Compare *We* in the following example with *we* in the example in ¶276.)

According to Robertson's report, "We have been witnessing a change in buying habits, particularly with respect to food."

278   If a displayed quotation starts in the middle of a sentence, use three spaced periods at the beginning of the quotation.

According to Robertson's report, there has been

. . . a change in buying habits, particularly with respect to food. . . . How far this pattern of change will extend cannot be estimated.

If the fragment, however, can be read as a complete sentence, capitalize the first word of the fragment and omit the ellipsis marks. (Compare *Starting* in the following example with *starting* in the example in ¶276.)

According to Robertson's report:

Starting in the late 1950s, we have been witnessing a change in buying habits, particularly with respect to food.

279   When a long quotation starts with a complete sentence and ends with a complete sentence, do not use three spaced periods at the beginning or the end of the quotation unless you need to emphasize that the quotation has been extracted from a larger body of material.

280   If one or more paragraphs are omitted within a long quotation, indicate the omission by adding three spaced periods *after* the terminal punctuation that concludes the preceding paragraph.

Insertions in Quoted Matter

281 For clarity, it is sometimes necessary to insert explanatory words or phrases within quoted matter. Enclose such insertions in brackets. (See also ¶¶296–298.)

> Miss Rawlings added, "At the time of the first lawsuit [1986], there was clear-cut evidence of an intent to defraud."

282 For special emphasis, you may wish to underscore words that were not so treated in the original. In such cases insert a phrase like *emphasis added* in brackets at the end of the quotation or immediately after the underscored words.

> In the course of testifying, she stated, "I never met Mr. Norman in my life, to the best of my recollection. [Emphasis added.]"

NOTE: Underscoring in typewritten material is the counterpart of *italic type* in printed material. Many types of electronic equipment now have the capability of printing italic type. If you have access to such equipment, use italics in place of underscoring.

283 When the original wording contains a misspelling, a grammatical error, or a confusing expression of thought, insert the term *sic* (meaning "so" or "this is the way it was") in brackets to indicate that the error existed in the original material.

> As he wrote in his letter, "I would sooner go to jail then [*sic*] have to pay your bill."

NOTE: The word *sic* is not underscored in typed material, but it is italicized in printed material and in versions produced on electronic equipment that provides italic type.

For simple interruptions such as he said *or* she said, *see* ¶¶262–263.

Aligning Quotation Marks

284 **a.** In a list, any opening quotation mark should align with the first letter of the other items.

> I urge you to read the following materials (which I am sending to you under separate cover):
>
> Federal Tax Policy by Joseph A. Pechman
>
> "Tax Policy and Capital Formation" by the Joint Committee on Taxation
>
> The Zero-Sum Society by Lester C. Thurow

b. In poems, the opening quotation mark at the beginning of each stanza should clear the left margin so that the first letter of each line will be in alignment. (See also ¶267.)

> "So here I am, in the middle way . . .
> Trying to learn to use words, and every attempt
> Is a wholly new start, and a different kind of failure
> Because one has only learnt to get the better of words
> For the thing one no longer has to say, or the way in which
> One is no longer disposed to say it. And so each venture
> Is a new beginning, a raid on the inarticulate
> With shabby equipment always deteriorating. . . ."
> —T. S. Eliot

The Underscore

IMPORTANT NOTE: Underscoring in typewritten material is the counterpart of *italic type* in printed material. Many types of electronic equipment now have the capability of printing italic type. If you have access to such equipment, use italics in place of underscoring.

For Special Emphasis

285 A word referred to as a word is usually underscored, but it may be enclosed in quotation marks instead. A word referred to as a word is often introduced by the expression *the term* or *the word*.

> The term green marketing refers to a company's attempt to persuade its customers that it has adjusted its products, packaging, and manufacturing processes to satisfy current environmental concerns.

> Did you know that ciao, the Italian word used as an expression of greeting or farewell, literally means "I am your slave"?

> If you used fewer compound sentences, you wouldn't have so many ands in your writing. (Only the root word is underscored, not the *s*.)

> **BUT:** She refused to sign the contract because she said it had too many ifs, ands, or buts. (No underscores are required for the phrase *ifs, ands, or buts* because the writer is not referring literally to these words as words. The phrase means "too many conditions and qualifications.")

NOTE: Letters referred to as letters are usually underscored if they are not capitalized.

dotting your i's	the three Rs
solving for x when y = 3	three Bs and one C
minding your p's and q's	**BUT:** to the nth degree

For the plurals of letters such as i's and Rs, see ¶¶623–624.

286 In a formal definition, the word to be defined is usually underscored and the definition quoted. In this way the two elements may be easily distinguished.

> The verb prevaricate (a polite way of saying "to lie") comes from the Latin word praevaricari, which means "to go zigzag, to walk crookedly."

NOTE: An informal definition does not require any special punctuation.

> A wainwright is a person who makes or repairs wagons.

> Thomas Hobson was an English stablekeeper who insisted that every customer take the horse nearest the door. Hence the term Hobson's choice means that you really have no choice at all. (Because the definition is informal, it does not have to be set off in quotation marks. However, *Hobson's choice* is underscored, as indicated in ¶285, because the words are referred to as words.)

287 Underscore foreign expressions that are not considered part of the English language. (Use quotation marks to set off translations of foreign expressions.)

> It's true, n'est-ce pas? (Meaning "isn't that so?")

NOTE: Once an expression of foreign origin has become established as part of the English language, underscoring is no longer necessary. (Most

2

dictionaries offer guidance on this point.) Here are some frequently used expressions that do not need underscoring or any other special display:

à la carte	de jure	magnum opus	quid pro quo
à la mode	double entendre	maven	raison d'être
a priori	en masse	modus operandi	rendezvous
ad hoc	en route	modus vivendi	repertoire
ad infinitum	esprit de corps	non sequitur	résumé
ad nauseam	et al.	ombudsman	savoir faire
alfresco	etc.	op. cit.	sic (see ¶282)
alma mater	ex officio	per annum	sine qua non
alter ego	fait accompli	per capita	sotto voce
bona fide	habeas corpus	per se	status quo
carte blanche	ibid. (see ¶1530)	prima facie	tête-à-tête
caveat emptor	in absentia	prix fixe	tour de force
chutzpah	in toto	pro forma	troika
cul-de-sac	joie de vivre	pro rata	vice versa
de facto	laissez-faire	pro tem	vis-à-vis

For the use of accents and other diacritical marks with foreign words, see ¶718.

288   The *individual* names of ships, trains, airplanes, and spacecraft may be underscored for special display or written simply with initial caps.

> The S.S. <u>Parlin</u> will sail on Thursday.   **OR:** The S.S. Parlin . . .

> **BUT:** I flew to Paris on a Concorde and came back on a DC-10. (No special display is needed for the names *Concorde* and *DC-10* because they identify classes of aircraft but are not the individual names of planes.)

With Titles of Literary and Artistic Works

289   Underscore titles of *complete* works that are published as separate items— for example, books, pamphlets, long poems, magazines, and newspapers. Also underscore titles of movies, plays, musicals, operas, television and radio series, long musical pieces, paintings, and works of sculpture.

> You will particularly enjoy (don't laugh!) a cookbook entitled <u>The Supper of the Lamb</u>.
> Our ads in <u>The Wall Street Journal</u> have produced excellent results.
> Next Friday we will go to hear <u>Der Rosenkavalier</u>, one of my favorite operas.
> The painting popularly referred to as <u>Whistler's Mother</u> is actually entitled <u>Arrangement in Gray and Black No. 1</u>.

NOTE: The titles of musical pieces that are identified by form (for example, symphony, concerto, sonata) or by key are neither underscored nor quoted. However, if a descriptive phrase accompanies this type of title, it is underscored if the work is long, quoted if the work is short.

> Beethoven's Sonata No. 18 in E Flat Minor, Op. 31, No. 3
> Tchaikovsky's Symphony No. 6 in B Flat Minor (the <u>Pathétique</u>)
> Chopin's Etude No. 12 (the "Revolutionary" Etude)

a. If you are using electronic equipment with the capability of printing italic type, use italics in place of underscoring.

> Our ads in *The Wall Street Journal* have produced excellent results.

b. Titles of complete works may be typed in all capitals as an alternative to underscoring.

> Every executive will find RIGHT ON TIME! a valuable guide.

NOTE: The use of all capitals is acceptable (1) in business correspondence where titles occur frequently (as in the correspondence of a publishing house) and (2) in advertising and sales promotion copy where the use of all capitals is intended to have an eye-catching effect. In other circumstances use underscoring.

c. In typewritten material that is *to be set in type,* titles of complete works must be underscored. The underscoring indicates to the printer that the title should be set in italics.

Every executive will find <u>Right on Time!</u> a valuable guide.

d. In titles of magazines, do not underscore or capitalize the word *magazine* unless it is part of the actual title.

<u>Time</u> magazine   **BUT:** <u>The New York Times Magazine</u>

e. In some cases the name of the publishing company is the same as the name of the publication. Underscore the name when it refers to *the publication* but not when it refers to *the company.*

I saw her column in <u>Business Week</u>.

BUT: I wrote to Business Week about a job.

Joe used to be <u>Fortune</u>'s management editor; now he works as a management consultant to half a dozen Fortune 500 companies.

f. Underscore a subtitle (but not an edition number) that accompanies the main title of a book.

If you're looking for a good overview of the subject, get hold of Kinnear and Taylor's <u>Marketing Research: An Applied Approach</u>, Fourth Edition.

For the use of quotation marks with titles of literary and artistic works, see ¶¶242–244; for the treatment of titles of sacred works, see ¶350.

Inserting Underscores

290   Underscore as a unit whatever should be grasped as a unit—individual words, titles, phrases, or even whole sentences.

a. When underscoring a unit consisting of two or more words, be sure to underscore the space between words.

I would not use the phrase <u>in a nutshell</u> in the sentence where you sum up your feelings about the place where you work.

BUT: Do you understand the meaning of terms like <u>ipso facto</u>, <u>sine qua non</u>, and <u>pro forma</u>? (Only the individual units are underscored in this case.)

b. Do not underscore a mark of *sentence punctuation* that comes directly after the underscored matter. (However, underscore all punctuation marks that are an integral part of the underscored matter.)

This week the Summertime Playhouse is presenting <u>Oklahoma!</u>, next week <u>Where's Charley?</u>, and the following week <u>My Fair Lady</u>.

c. Do not underscore a possessive or plural ending that is added on to an underscored word.

the <u>Times-Picayune</u>'s editorial   too many <u>and</u>s

d. When an underscored element has to be divided at the end of a line, underscore the dividing hyphen as well.

For a Wall Street exposé with ''the suspense of a first-rate thriller,'' read <u>Bar-barians at the Gate</u>.

Other Marks of Punctuation

The Apostrophe (')

The use of the apostrophe is covered in the following paragraphs:

As a single quotation mark, see ¶¶245–246, 247b.
To indicate the omission of figures in dates, see ¶412.
As a symbol for feet, see ¶¶432, 543.
To form contractions, see ¶505.
To form plurals of figures, letters, etc., see ¶¶623–626.
To form possessives, see ¶¶247b, 627–651.

Ellipsis Marks (. . .)

291   a. Ellipsis marks (three spaced periods, with one space before and after each period) are often used, especially in advertising, to display individual items or to connect a series of loosely related phrases.

Where can you match these services—
. . . Free ticket delivery
. . . Flight insurance
. . . On-time departures

The Inn at the End of the Road . . . where you may enjoy the epicure's choicest offerings . . . by reservation only . . . closed Tuesdays.

   b. Ellipsis marks are also used to indicate that a sentence trails off before the end. The three spaced periods create an effect of uncertainty or suggest an abrupt suspension of thought. (No terminal punctuation is used with ellipsis marks in this kind of construction.)

He could easily have saved the situation by . . .   But why talk about it?

For the use of ellipsis marks to indicate omissions in quoted matter, see ¶¶274–280.

The Asterisk (*)

292   The asterisk may be used to refer the reader to a footnote placed at the bottom of a page or a table. (See ¶¶1502f, 1636c.)

   a. When the asterisk and some other mark of punctuation occur together within a sentence, the asterisk *follows* the punctuation mark, with no intervening space. (See also ¶1502b.)

   b. In the footnote itself, leave no space after the asterisk.

293   Asterisks are used to replace words that are considered unprintable.

If the TV cameras had been present when Finney called Schultz a ***** (and about 50 other names as well), tonight's newscast would have contained the longest bleep in television history.

The Diagonal (/)

294   The diagonal occurs (without space before or after) in certain abbreviations and expressions of time.

B/L	bill of lading	w/	with
B/S	bill of sale	n/30	net amount due in 30 days
c/o	care of	/S/	signed (used before a copied signature)

The copy deadline for the fall '92/winter '93 catalog is April 15.

Please check the figures for fiscal year 1992/93.

I'm concerned about their P/E ratio. (Referring to the price-to-earnings ratio of a company's stock.)

295 **a.** The diagonal is used to express alternatives.

a go/no-go decision   an either/or proposition
input/output systems   meet on Monday and/or Tuesday
                              (see page 182)

b. The diagonal may be used to indicate that a person or thing has two functions.

the owner/manager   zoned for commercial/industrial activities
our secretary/treasurer   planning to hold a dinner/dance

NOTE: A hyphen is preferred in such expressions. (See ¶806.)

c. The diagonal is also used in writing fractions (for example, 4/5) and in some code and serial numbers (for example, 2S/394756).

For the use of the diagonal when quoting poetry, see ¶268.
For the use of the diagonal in telephone numbers, see ¶454.

Brackets ([ ])

296 A correction or an insertion in a quoted extract should be enclosed in brackets. (See also ¶¶281–283.)

His final request was this: "Please keep me appraised [*sic*] of any new developments." (See ¶283, note.)

The transcript of his testimony contains this incredible statement: "I did not approach Commissioner Zajac at any time [emphasis added] while my petition was being considered."

"If we all pull together, we can bring a new level of political leadership to this state. [Extended applause.] Please give me your support in this campaign." (Note the capitalization of *Extended* and the use of a period before the closing bracket when the bracketed element is treated as a separate sentence. See also ¶226.)

297 When a parenthetical element falls within another parenthetical element, enclose the smaller element in brackets and enclose the larger element in parentheses.

Scalzo said on television yesterday that prices would begin to fall sharply. (However, in an article published in the *Times* [May 12, 1995], he was quoted as saying that prices would remain at their current levels for the foreseeable future.)

298 If the equipment you are using does not provide brackets, either construct them (as shown in the illustration below) or leave a space at the point where each mark should appear and pen in the marks after you remove the paper from the machine.

"We returned to Salem /Massachusetts/ the following year."

NOTE: If the term to be enclosed in brackets has to be underscored, do the underscoring on the machine and insert the brackets by hand.

Halliburton's press release stated, "If it hadn't been for a certain newspaper [The Tribune], we never would have lost the election."

(**RATHER THAN:** /The Tribune/ **OR** /The Tribune/)

Spacing With
Punctuation Marks

299 Period

No space *before.*

Two spaces *after* the end of a sentence.

Two spaces *after* a period when it follows a number or letter that indicates an enumeration.

One space *after* an abbreviation within a sentence. (See also ¶511.)

No space *after* a decimal point.

No space *after* when another mark of punctuation follows the period (for example, a closing quotation mark; a closing parenthesis; a closing dash, comma, semicolon, or colon following an "abbreviation" period).

Question Mark or Exclamation Point

No space *before.*

Two spaces *after* the end of a sentence.

One space *after* a question mark within a sentence. (See ¶¶116–117.)

No space *after* when another mark of punctuation follows (for example, a closing quotation mark, closing parenthesis, or closing dash).

Comma

No space *before.*

One space *after* unless a closing quotation mark follows the comma.

No space *after* commas within a number.

Semicolon

No space *before;* one space *after.*

Colon

No space *before.*

Two spaces *after* within a sentence.

No space *before* or *after* in expressions of time *(8:20 p.m.)* or proportions *(2:1).*

Dash

No space *before, between,* or *after* two hyphens used to represent a dash.

Two spaces *after* a dash at the end of a statement that breaks off abruptly. (See ¶¶207–208.)

Hyphen

No space *before;* no space *after* except at the end of a line.

Opening Parenthesis or Bracket

One space *before* when parenthetic matter is within a sentence.

Two spaces *before* when parenthetic matter follows a sentence. In this case the parenthetic matter starts with a capital and closes with its own sentence punctuation. (See ¶¶226, 296.)

No space *after.*

Closing Parenthesis or Bracket

No space *before.*

One space *after* when parenthetic matter is within a sentence.

Two spaces *after* when parenthetic matter is itself a complete sentence and another sentence follows. (See ¶¶226, 296.)

No space *after* if another mark of punctuation immediately follows.

Opening Quotation Mark

Two spaces *before* when quoted matter starts a new sentence or follows a colon.

No space *before* when a dash or an opening parenthesis precedes.

One space *before* in all other cases.

No space *after.*

Closing Quotation Mark

No space *before.*

Two spaces *after* when quoted matter ends the sentence.

No space *after* when another mark of punctuation immediately follows (for example, a semicolon or colon).

One space *after* in all other cases.

Single Quotation Mark

No space between single and double quotation marks. (See ¶246.)

Apostrophe (')

No space *before,* either within a word or at the end of a word.

One space *after* only if it is at the end of a word within a sentence.

Ellipsis Marks (. . .)

One space *before* and *after* each of the three periods within a sentence. (See ¶¶274–275.)

No space *before* when an *opening* quotation mark precedes ellipsis marks.

No space *after* when a *closing* quotation mark follows ellipsis marks. (See last example in ¶275.)

Two spaces *after* ellipsis marks that follow a period, question mark, or exclamation point at the end of a sentence. (See example in ¶276.)

Asterisk (*)

No space *before* an asterisk following a word or punctuation mark within a sentence or at the end of a sentence.

Two spaces *after* an asterisk at the end of a sentence.

One space *after* an asterisk following a word or punctuation mark within a sentence.

No space *after* an asterisk in a footnote. (See ¶292.)

Diagonal (/)

No space *before* or *after* a diagonal line. (See ¶268 for an exception in poetry.)

SECTION

3

Capitalization

The function of capitalization is to give distinction, importance, and emphasis to words. Thus the first word of a sentence is capitalized to indicate distinctively and emphatically that a new sentence has begun. Moreover, proper nouns like *George, Chicago, Dun & Bradstreet, the Parthenon, January,* and *Friday* are capitalized to signify the special importance of these words as the official names of particular persons, places, and things. A number of words, however, may function either as proper nouns or as common nouns—for example, terms like *the board of directors* or *the company.* For words like these, capitalization practices vary widely, but the variation merely reflects the relative importance each writer assigns to the word in question.

Despite disagreements among authorities on specific rules, there is a growing consensus against overusing capitalization in business writing. When too many words stand out, none stand out. The current trend, then, is to use capitalization more sparingly—to give importance, distinction, or emphasis only when and where it is warranted.

The following rules of capitalization are written with ordinary situations in mind. If you work or study in a specialized field, you may find it necessary to follow a different style of capitalization.

Basic Rules

First Words

301 Capitalize the first word of:

a. Every sentence. (See ¶302 for exceptions.)

Medium-range plans must be submitted within two weeks.

Will you be able to pull everything together by then?

The deadline we have been given is absolutely impossible!

b. An expression used as a sentence. (See also ¶¶102, 111, 119–120.)

So much for that.   Really?   No!

Enough said.   How come?   Unbelievable!

c. A quoted sentence. (See also ¶¶272–273.)

Mrs. Eckstein herself said, "We surely have not heard the complete story."

d. An independent question within a sentence. (See also ¶¶115–117.)

The question is, Whose version of the argument shall we believe?

BUT: Have you approved the divisional sales forecasts? the expense projections? the requests for staff expansion? (See ¶117.)

e. Each item displayed in a list or an outline. (See also ¶¶107, 1357c, 1424e.)

Here is a powerful problem-solving tool that will help you:

• Become an effective leader.
• Improve your relations with subordinates, peers, and superiors.
• Cope with stressful situations on the job.

(Continued on page 82.)

f. Each line in a poem. (Always follow the style of the poem, however.)

> From wrong to wrong the exasperated spirit
> Proceeds, unless restored by that refining fire
> Where you must move in measure, like a dancer.
>
> —T. S. Eliot

g. The salutation and the complimentary closing of a letter. (See also ¶¶1348, 1359.)

Dear Mrs. Pancetta: *Sincerely* yours,

302 **a.** When a sentence is set off by *dashes* or *parentheses* within another sentence, do not capitalize the first word following the opening dash or parenthesis unless it is a proper noun, a proper adjective, the pronoun *I*, or the first word of a quoted sentence. (See ¶¶214, 224–225 for examples.)

b. Do not capitalize the first word of a sentence following a colon except under certain circumstances. (See ¶¶196–199.)

Proper Nouns

303 Capitalize every *proper noun,* that is, the official name of a particular person, place, or thing. Also capitalize the pronoun *I.*

William J. Clinton	Wednesday, February 8
Baton Rouge, Louisiana	the Great Depression
Xerox Corporation	the Civil Rights Act of 1964
the Red Cross	the Japanese
the Export-Import Bank	Jupiter and Uranus
Johns Hopkins University	French Literature 212
the World Trade Center	Scotch tape
the Statue of Liberty	*Gone With the Wind*
the Center for Science in the Public Interest	the Smithsonian Institution
	United Farm Workers of America
a Pulitzer Prize	the Commonwealth of Independent
Microsoft Word	States

NOTE: Prepositions (like *of, for,* and *in*) are not capitalized unless they have four or more letters (like *with* and *from*). (See also ¶¶360–361.) The articles *a* and *an* are not capitalized; the article *the* is capitalized only under special circumstances. (See ¶324.) Conjunctions (like *and* and *or*) are also not capitalized. However, follow the capitalization style used by the owner of the name; for example, *3-In-One oil, One-A-Day vitamins, dBase V,* the poet *e e cummings.*

304 Capitalize adjectives derived from proper nouns.

America (n.), American (adj.)	Machiavelli (n.), Machiavellian (adj.)
Norway (n.), Norwegian (adj.)	Hemingway (n.), Hemingwayesque (adj.)

EXCEPTIONS: Congress, congressional; the Senate, senatorial; the Constitution (U.S.), constitutional. (See also ¶306.)

305 Capitalize imaginative names and nicknames that designate particular persons, places, or things. (See ¶¶333–335 for imaginative place names; ¶344 for imaginative names of historical periods.)

the Founding Fathers	Bubba
the First Lady	Whoopi Goldberg
the White House	the Gray Panthers
the Oval Office	Big Mac
the Stars and Stripes	the Establishment
the Gopher State (Minnesota)	Down Under (Australia)
Mother Nature	a Green Beret
a Good Samaritan	the Little Dipper
Fannie Mae (from the initials *FNMA,*	the Top 40
referring to the Federal National	Bloody Mary
Mortgage Association)	the Third World

306 Some expressions that originally contained or consisted of proper nouns or adjectives are now considered common nouns and should not be capitalized. (See ¶309b.)

charley horse	napoleon	ampere	texas leaguer
plaster of paris	boycott	watt	arabic numbers
manila envelope	diesel	joule	roman numerals
bone china	macadam	kelvin	BUT: Roman laws

NOTE: Check an up-to-date dictionary to determine capitalization for words of this type.

Common Nouns

307 A *common noun* names a class of things (for example, *books*), or it may refer indefinitely to one or more things within that class (*a book, several books*). Nouns used in this way are considered general terms of classification and are often modified by indefinite words such as *a, any, every,* or *some*. Do not capitalize nouns used as general terms of classification.

a company	every board of directors
any corporation	some senators

308 A common noun may also be used to name a *particular* person, place, or thing. Nouns used in this way are often modified (a) by *the, this, these, that,* or *those* or (b) by possessive words such as *my, your, his, her, our,* or *their*. Do not capitalize a general term of classification, even though it refers to a particular person, place, or thing.

COMMON NOUN:	our doctor	the hotel	the river
PROPER NOUN:	Dr. Tsai	Hotel Algonquin	the Colorado River

309 **a.** Capitalize a common noun when it is part of a proper name but not when it is used alone in place of the full name. (For exceptions, see ¶310.)

Professor Perry	BUT: the professor
the Goodall Corporation	the corporation
the Easton Municipal Court	the court
Sunset Boulevard	the boulevard
the Clayton Antitrust Act	the act

NOTE: Also capitalize the plural form of a common noun in expressions such as *the Republican and the Democratic Parties, Main and Tenth Streets, the Missouri and Ohio Rivers,* and *the Atlantic and Pacific Oceans.*

(Continued on page 84.)

b. In a number of compound nouns, the first element is a proper noun or adjective and the second element is a common noun. In such cases capitalize only the first element, since the compound as a whole is a common noun.

Brownie points	a Ferris wheel	a Rhodes scholar	a Labrador retriever
a Dutch oven	Danish pastry	French doors	Tex-Mex cooking

NOTE: Check an up-to-date dictionary for words of this type. After extensive usage the proper noun or adjective may become a common noun and no longer require capitalization. (See ¶306.)

310 Some *short forms* (common-noun elements replacing the complete proper name) are capitalized when they are intended to carry the full significance of the complete proper name. It is in this area, however, that the danger of overcapitalizing most often occurs. Therefore, do not capitalize a short form unless it clearly warrants the importance, distinction, or emphasis that capitalization conveys. The following kinds of short forms are commonly capitalized:

PERSONAL TITLES: Capitalize titles replacing names of high-ranking national, state, and international officials (but not ordinarily local officials or company officers). (See ¶313.)

ORGANIZATIONAL NAMES: Do not capitalize short forms of company names except in formal or legal writing. (See ¶321.)

GOVERNMENTAL NAMES: Capitalize short forms of names of national and international bodies (but not ordinarily state or local bodies). (See ¶¶326–327, 334–335.)

PLACE NAMES: Capitalize only well-established short forms. (See ¶¶332, 335.)

NOTE: Do not use a short form to replace a full name unless the full name has been mentioned earlier or will be understood from the context.

Special Rules

Personal Names

311 a. Treat a person's name—in terms of capitalization, spelling, punctuation, and spacing—exactly as the person does.

Alice Mayer	Charles Burden Wilson
Alyce Meagher	L. Westcott Quinn
Steven J. Dougherty, Jr.	R. W. Ferrari
Stephen J. Dockerty Jr.	Peter B. J. Hallman

For the treatment of initials such as FDR, *see ¶516.*
For the use or omission of commas with terms such as Jr., *see ¶156.*

b. Respect individual preferences in the spelling of personal names.

Ann Marie, Anne Marie, Anna Marie, Annemarie, Annamarie, Anne-Marie, AnneMarie

Macmillan, MacMillan, Mac Millan, Macmillen, MacMillen, MacMillin, McMillan, Mc Millan, McMillen, McMillin, McMillon

c. In names containing the prefix *O'*, always capitalize the *O* and the letter following the apostrophe; for example, *O'Brian* or *O'Brien*.

d. Watch for differences in capitalization and spacing in names containing prefixes like *d', da, de, del, della, di, du, l', la, le, van,* and *von.*

D'Amelio, d'Amelio, Damelio   deLaCruz, DeLacruz, Dela Cruz, DelaCruz
LaCoste, Lacoste, La Coste   VanDeVelde, Van DeVelde, vandeVelde

e. When a surname with an uncapitalized prefix stands alone (that is, without a first name, a title, or initials preceding it), capitalize the prefix to prevent a misreading.

Anthony de Luca   Mr. de Luca   A. R. de Luca

BUT: I hear that *De Luca* is leaving the company.

f. When names that contain prefixes are to be typed in all-capital letters, follow these principles: If there is no space after the prefix, capitalize only the initial letter of the prefix. If space follows the prefix, capitalize the entire prefix.

Normal Form	**All-Capital Form**
MacDonald	MacDONALD
BUT: Mac Donald	MAC DONALD

g. When a nickname or a descriptive expression precedes or replaces a person's first name, simply capitalize it. However, if the nickname or descriptive expression falls between a person's first and last names, enclose it either in quotation marks or in parentheses.

Babe Ruth	**BUT:** George Herman "Babe" Ruth
	OR: George Herman (Babe) Ruth
Fats Waller	**BUT:** Thomas Wright "Fats" Waller
	OR: Thomas Wright (Fats) Waller
Tip O'Neill	**BUT:** Thomas Philip "Tip" O'Neill
	OR: Thomas Philip (Tip) O'Neill
Ol' Blue Eyes	**BUT:** Frank "Ol' Blue Eyes" Sinatra
	OR: Frank (Ol' Blue Eyes) Sinatra

For the plurals of personal names, see ¶¶615–616; for the possessives of personal names, see ¶¶630–633.

Titles With Personal Names

312   **a.** Capitalize all official titles of honor and respect when they *precede* personal names.

PERSONAL TITLES:
Mrs. Norma Washburn (see ¶517)   Miss Popkin
Ms. Terry Fiske   Mr. Benedict

EXECUTIVE TITLES:
President Julia McLeod   Vice President Saulnier

PROFESSIONAL TITLES:
Professor Henry Pelligrino   Dr. Khalil (see ¶517)

CIVIC TITLES:
Governor Samuel O. Bolling   Ambassador Staedler
Mayor-elect Louis K. Uhl (see ¶317)   ex-Senator Hausner (see ¶317)

MILITARY TITLES:
Colonel Perry L. Forrester   Commander Comerford

RELIGIOUS TITLES:
the Reverend William F. Dowd   Rabbi Gelfand

(Continued on page 86.)

b. Do not capitalize such titles when the personal name that follows is in apposition and is set off by commas.

Yesterday the *president*, Julia McLeod, revealed her plans to retire next June.

BUT: Yesterday *President* Julia McLeod revealed her plans to retire next June.

c. Do not capitalize occupational titles (such as *author, surgeon, publisher,* and *lawyer*) preceding a name.

The reviews of *drama critic* Simon Ritchey have a life-or-death effect on every play that opens in town.

NOT: The reviews of *Drama Critic* Simon Ritchey . . .

NOTE: Occupational titles can be distinguished from official titles in that only official titles can be used with a last name alone. Since one would not address a person as "Author Mailer" or "Publisher Johnson," these are not official titles and should not be capitalized.

313 a. In general, do not capitalize titles of honor and respect when they *follow* a personal name or are used *in place of* a personal name.

Julia McLeod, *president* of McLeod Inc., has revealed her plans to retire next June. During her sixteen years as *president,* the company grew . . .

However, exceptions are made for important officials and dignitaries, as indicated in the following paragraphs.

b. Retain the capitalization in the titles of high-ranking national, state, and international officials when they *follow* or *replace* a specific personal name. Below are examples of titles that remain capitalized.

NATIONAL OFFICIALS: the *President,* the *Vice President,* Cabinet members (such as the *Secretary of State* and the *Attorney General*), the heads of government agencies and bureaus (such as the *Director* or the *Commissioner*), the *Chief Justice,* the *Ambassador,* the *Senator,* the *Representative.*

STATE OFFICIALS: the *Governor,* the *Lieutenant Governor.* (**BUT:** the *attorney general,* the *senator.*)

FOREIGN DIGNITARIES: the *Queen of England,* the *King,* the *Prime Minister.*

INTERNATIONAL FIGURES: the *Pope,* the *Secretary General of the United Nations.*

NOTE: Some authorities now recommend that even these titles not be capitalized.

c. Titles of local governmental officials and those of lesser federal and state officials are not usually capitalized when they follow or replace a personal name. However, these titles are sometimes capitalized in writing intended for a limited readership (for example, in a local newspaper, in internal communications within an organization, or in correspondence coming from or directed to the official's office), where the person in question would be considered to have high rank by the intended reader.

The *Mayor* promised only last fall to hold the city sales tax at its present level. (Excerpt from an editorial in a local newspaper.)

BUT: Francis Fahey, *mayor* of Coventry, Rhode Island, appeared before a House committee today. The *mayor* spoke forcefully about the need to maintain federal aid to . . . (Excerpt from a national news service release.)

I would like to request an appointment with the *Attorney General.* (In a letter sent to the state attorney general's office.)

BUT: I have written for an appointment with the *attorney general* and expect to hear from his office soon.

d. Titles of *company officials* (for example, the *president,* the *general manager*) should not be capitalized when they follow or replace a personal name. Exceptions are made in formal minutes of meetings (see page 443) and in rules and bylaws.

The *president* will visit thirteen countries in a tour of company installations abroad. (Normal style.)

The *Secretary's* minutes were read and approved. (In formal minutes.)

NOTE: Some companies choose to capitalize these titles in all their communications because of the great respect the officials command within the company. However, this practice confers excessive importance on people who are neither public officials nor eminent dignitaries, and it should be avoided.

e. In general, do not capitalize job titles when they stand alone. However, in procedures manuals and in company memos and announcements, job titles are sometimes capitalized for special emphasis.

Marion Conroy has been promoted to the position of *senior accountant* (**OR** *Senior Accountant*).

f. Titles *following* a personal name or *standing alone* are sometimes capitalized in formal citations and acknowledgments.

314 Do not capitalize titles used as general terms of classification. (See ¶307.)

a United States senator	every king
a state governor	any ambassador

EXCEPTION: Because of the special regard for the office of the President of the United States, this title is capitalized even when used as a general term of classification (for example, a *President,* every *President*).

315 Capitalize any title (even if not of high rank) when it is used in *direct address* (that is, quoted or unquoted speech made directly to another person).

DIRECT ADDRESS: Please tell me, *Doctor,* what risks are involved in this treatment.

INDIRECT ADDRESS: I asked the *doctor* what risks were involved in this treatment.

NOTE: In direct address, do not capitalize a term like *madam, miss,* or *sir* if it stands alone without a proper name following.

Isn't it true, *sir,* that the defendant offered you money for trade secrets?

316 In the *inside address* of a letter, in the *writer's identification block,* and on an *envelope,* capitalize all titles whether they precede or follow the name. (See ¶¶1322–1325, 1362–1368, and the illustrations on page 337.)

317 Do not capitalize *former, late, ex-,* or *-elect* when used with titles. (See ¶363 for the style in headings.)

the late President Truman	ex-President Bush	Mayor-elect Bawley

Family Titles

318 Capitalize words such as *mother, father, aunt,* and *uncle* when they stand alone or are followed by a personal name.

Let me ask *Mother* and *Dad* if that date is open for them.

We'll be glad to put up *Aunt Peg* and *Uncle Fred* when they come to visit.

I hear that *Brother Bobby* has gone off the deep end again.

Do you think *Grandmother Harvey* will be pleased when she hears the news?

319   Do not capitalize family titles when they are preceded by possessives (such as *my, your, his, her, our,* and *their*) and simply describe a family relationship.

> Let me ask my *mother* and *dad* if that date is open for them.
>
> Do you think your *brother* Bobby would like to meet my *sister* Fern?

NOTE: If the words *uncle, aunt,* or *cousin* form a unit when used together with a first name, capitalize these titles, even when they are preceded by a possessive.

> Frank wants us to meet his *Uncle John.* (Here *Uncle John* is a unit.)
>
> **BUT:** Frank wants us to meet his *uncle,* John Cunningham. (Here *uncle* simply describes a family relationship.)
>
> I hope you can meet my *Cousin May.* (The writer thinks of her as *Cousin May.*)
>
> **BUT:** I hope you can meet my *cousin* May. (Here the writer thinks of her as *May;* the word *cousin* merely indicates relationship.)

Names of Organizations

320   a. Capitalize the names of companies, unions, associations, societies, independent committees and boards, schools, political parties, conventions, foundations, fraternities, sororities, clubs, and religious bodies.

BellSouth Corporation	the Hopewell Chamber of Commerce
the Transport Workers Union of America	the University of North Dakota
the American Society for Training and Development	the Democratic and Liberal Parties
	the Republican National Convention
the Committee for Economic Development	the Andrew W. Mellon Foundation
	the Overseas Press Club of America
the Financial Accounting Standards Board	Sigma Chi Fraternity
	St. Mark's United Methodist Church
	Parents Anonymous

NOTE: Try to follow the style established by the organization itself, as shown in the letterhead or some other written communication from the organization.

Disney World	Kmart Corporation	**BUT:** Toys "R" Us, Inc. (don't try
BUT: Disneyland	U-Haul International	to replicate the backward *R*)

b. Also capitalize imaginative names used to refer to specific organizations. (See also ¶333b.)

Big Blue (IBM)	the Big Board (the New York Stock Exchange)
Ma Bell (AT&T)	the Baby Bells (the U.S. regional phone companies)

For the treatment of articles (like the*), prepositions (like* of *or* for*), and conjunctions (like* and*), see* ¶*303, note. For the capitalization of abbreviations and acronyms used as organizational names, see* ¶¶*520, 522.*

321   When the common-noun element is used in place of the full name (for example, *the company* in place of *the Andersen Hardware Company*), do not capitalize the short form unless special emphasis or distinction is required (as in legal documents, minutes of meetings, bylaws, and other formal communications, where the short form is intended to invoke the full authority of the organization). In most cases, however, capitalization is unnecessary because the short form is used only as a general term of classification (see ¶¶307–308).

The *company* has always made a conscientious effort to involve itself in community affairs. However, our *company* policy specifically prohibits our underwriting any activity in support of a candidate for public office. (As used here, *company* is a term of general classification.)

BUT: On behalf of the *Company,* I am authorized to accept your bid. (Here the full authority of the company is implied; hence *Company* is spelled with a capital *C.*)

Mr. Weinstock has just returned from a visit to Haverford College. He reports that the *college* is planning a new fund-raising campaign to finance the construction of the new media center.

BUT: The *College* hopes to raise an additional $10,000,000 this year to finance the construction of the new media resource center. (Announcement in the alumni bulletin.)

NOTE: Do not capitalize the short form if it is modified by a word other than *the.* In constructions such as *our company, this company,* and *every company,* the noun is clearly a general term of classification. (See also ¶308.)

322 Common organizational terms such as *advertising department, manufacturing division, finance committee,* and *board of directors* are ordinarily capitalized when they are the actual names of units within the writer's own organization. These terms are not capitalized when they refer to some other organization unless the writer has reason to give these terms special importance or distinction.

The *Board of Directors* will meet next Thursday at 2:30. (From a company memo.)

BUT: Julia Perez, senior vice president of the Mulholland Bancorp, has been elected to the *board of directors* of the Kensington Trade Corporation. (From a news release intended for a general audience.)

The *Finance Committee* will meet all week to review next year's budget. (Style used by insiders.)

BUT: Gilligan says his company can give us no encouragement about the sponsorship of a new art center until its *finance committee* has reviewed our proposal. (Style normally used by outsiders.)

The *Advertising Department* will unveil the fall campaign this Friday. (Style used by insiders.)

BUT: The *advertising department* of Black & London will unveil its fall campaign this Friday. (Style used by outsiders.)

NOTE: Do not capitalize these organizational terms when they are modified by a word other than *the.* Constructions such as *this credit department, their credit department, every credit department, your credit department,* and *our credit department* are terms of general classification and should not be capitalized. (See also ¶321, note.)

Black & London always seems to have a great deal of turnover in *its advertising department.*

We don't have as much turnover in *our advertising department* as you may think. (Some insiders prefer to write "our Advertising Department" because of the special importance they attach to their own organizational structure.)

I would like to apply for the position of copywriter that is currently open in *your advertising department.* (Some outsiders might write "your Advertising Department" if they wanted to flatter the reader by giving special importance to the reader's organizational structure.)

323 Capitalize such nouns as *marketing, advertising,* or *promotion* when they are used alone to designate a department within an organization.

> Paul Havlicek in *Corporate Communications* is the person to talk with.
>
> I want to get a reaction from our people in *Marketing* first.
>
> **BUT:** I want to talk to our *marketing* people first. (Here *marketing* is simply a descriptive adjective.)

324 Capitalize the word *the* preceding the name of an organization only when it is part of the legal name of the organization.

> The Associated Press   The New York Times (see ¶289d)
> The Gap   The Wall Street Journal

     a. Even when part of the organizational name, *the* is often uncapitalized except in legal or formal contexts where it is important to give the full legal name.

     b. Do not capitalize *the* when the name is used as a modifier or is given in the form of an abbreviation.

> the Associated Press report   the AP   works for the Times

Names of Government Bodies

325 Capitalize the names of countries and international organizations as well as national, state, county, and city bodies and their subdivisions.

> the British Commonwealth   the Utah Bureau of Air Quality
> the Federal Republic of Germany   the Ohio Legislature
> the United Nations   the Court of Appeals of the State of
> the Bush Administration   Wisconsin (see ¶303, note)
> the Cabinet   the New York State Board of Education
> the Ninety-ninth Congress   the Coe County Shade Tree Commission
>   (see ¶363)   the Boston City Council
> the House of Representatives   the Small Business Development Agency

For city and state names, see ¶¶334–335.

326 Capitalize short forms of names of national and international bodies and their major divisions.

> the House (referring to the House of Representatives)
>
> the Department (referring to the Department of Justice, the State Department, the Department of the Treasury, etc.)
>
> the Bureau (referring to the Bureau of the Budget, the Federal Bureau of Investigation, the Bureau of the Census, etc.)
>
> the Court (referring to the United States Supreme Court, the International Court of Justice, etc.)
>
> the Fed (referring to the Federal Reserve Board)
>
> **BUT:** the feds (referring to federal regulators)

As a rule, do not capitalize short forms of names of state or local governmental groups except when special circumstances warrant emphasis or distinction. (See ¶327.)

327 Common terms such as *police department, board of education,* and *county court* need not be capitalized (even when referring to a specific body), since they are terms of general classification. However, such terms should be capitalized when the writer intends to refer to the organization in all of its official dignity.

The *Police Department* has announced the promotion of Robert Boyarsky to the rank of sergeant. (The short form is capitalized here because it is intended to have the full force of the complete name, the *Cranfield Police Department*.)

BUT: The Cranfield *police department* sponsors a youth athletic program that we could well copy. (No capitalization is used here because the writer is referring to the department in general terms and not by its official name.)

NOTE: Do not capitalize the short form if it is not actually derived from the complete name. For example, do not capitalize the short form *police department* if the full name is *Department of Public Safety*.

328   Capitalize *federal* only when it is part of the official name of a federal agency, a federal act, or some other proper noun.

the *Federal* Reserve Board   the *Federal* Insurance Contributions Act

BUT: . . . subject to *federal*, state, and local laws.

329   The terms *federal government* and *government* (referring specifically to the United States government) are now commonly written in small letters because they are considered terms of general classification. In government documents, however, and in other types of communications where these terms are intended to have the force of an official name, they are capitalized.

330   Capitalize the words *union* and *commonwealth* only when they refer to a specific government.

Wilkins has lectured on the topic in almost every state in the *Union*.

Names of Places

331   Capitalize the names of places, such as streets, buildings, parks, monuments, rivers, oceans, and mountains. Do not capitalize short forms used in place of the full name. (See ¶332 for a few exceptions.)

Montgomery Street	**BUT:** the street
Sears Tower	the tower
Stone Mountain Park	the park
Sacramento River	the river
Lake Pontchartrain	the lake
Colony Surf Hotel	the hotel
Rittenhouse Square	the square
Riverside Drive	the drive
Bighorn Mountain	the mountain
Shoshone Falls	the falls
the Washington Monument	the monument
Stapleton Airport	the airport
the Fogg Art Museum	the museum
Golden Gate Bridge	the bridge
Lincoln Park Zoo	the zoo
Nicollet Mall	the mall

For plural expressions like the Atlantic and Pacific Oceans, *see ¶309a, note. For the treatment of prepositions and conjunctions in proper names, see ¶303, note.*

332   A few short forms are capitalized because of clear association with one place.

the Coast (the West Coast)   the Hill (Capitol Hill)
the Continent (Europe)   the Street (Wall Street)
the Channel (English Channel)   the Village (Greenwich Village)

¶333

333 a. Capitalize imaginative names that designate specific places or areas.

the Bay Area (around San Francisco)
the Loop (in Chicago)
the Big Apple (New York)
the Big D (Dallas)
Back Bay (in Boston)
the Pacific Rim
the Right Bank (in Paris)
the Twin Cities (Minneapolis and St. Paul)
Tinseltown (Hollywood)
the Big Muddy (the Missouri River)
the Beehive State (Utah)
the French Quarter (in New Orleans)

NOTE: The terms *Sunbelt* and *Frostbelt* are now commonly spelled as one word; the terms *Farm Belt, Bible Belt,* and *Rust Belt* are still commonly spelled as two words. Within the same context treat these terms the same way—as two words; for example, *in the Farm Belt and the Frost Belt.*

b. Some place names are used imaginatively to refer to types of businesses or institutions.

Madison Avenue (the advertising industry)
Wall Street (the financial industry)
Foggy Bottom (the U.S. State Department)
Silicon Valley (the cluster of high-tech industries south of San Francisco)

334 Capitalize the word *city* only when it is part of the corporate name of the city or part of an imaginative name.

Kansas City
BUT: the city of San Francisco
the Windy City (Chicago)
the Eternal City (Rome)

335 Capitalize *state* only when it follows the name of a state or is part of an imaginative name.

New York *State* is also called the Empire *State.*

The *state* of Alaska is the largest in the Union.

Washington *State* entered the Union in 1889, the forty-second *state* to do so.

The *state* of Arizona is also known as the Grand Canyon *State.*

Next year we plan to return to the *States.* (Meaning the United States.)

NOTE: Do not capitalize *state* when used in place of the actual state name.

He is an employee of the *state.* (People working for the state government, however, might write *State.*)

336 Capitalize *the* only when it is a part of the official name of a place.

The Dalles
The Hague
BUT: the Bronx
the Netherlands

337 Capitalize the words *upper* and *lower* only when they are part of an actual place name or a well-established imaginative name.

Upper Montclair
Upper Peninsula
Upper West Side
Lower California
Lower East Side
Newton Lower Falls

Points of the Compass

338 a. Capitalize *north, south, east, west,* and derivative words when they designate definite regions or are an integral part of a proper name.

in the North
down South
out West
back East
the Far North
the Deep South
the Middle West
the Near East
the North Pole
the South Side
the West Coast
the Eastern Seaboard
OR: the East Coast

b. Do not capitalize these words when they merely indicate direction or general location.

Many factories have relocated from the *Northeast* to the *South.* (Region.)

BUT: They maintain a villa in the *south* of France. (General location.)

OR: Go *west* on Route 517 and then *south* on I-95. (Direction.)

John is coming back *East* after three years on the *West Coast.* (Region.)

BUT: The *west coast* of the United States borders on the Pacific. (Referring only to the shoreline, not the region.)

Most of our customers live on the *East Side.* (Definite locality.)
BUT: Most of our customers live on the *east side* of town. (General location.)

339 Capitalize such words as *Northerner, Southerner,* and *Midwesterner.*

340 Capitalize such words as *northern, southern, eastern,* and *western* when they refer to the people in a region or to their political, social, or cultural activities. Do not capitalize these words when they merely indicate general location or refer to the geography or climate of the region.

Eastern bankers	**BUT:** the eastern half of Pennsylvania
Southern hospitality	southern temperatures
Western civilization	westerly winds
the Northern vote	a northern winter

The *Northern* states did not vote as they were expected to. (Political activities.)
BUT: The drought is expected to continue in the *northern* states. (Climate.)

My sales territory takes in most of the *southeastern* states. (General location.)

NOTE: When terms like *western region* and *southern district* are used to name organizational units within a company, capitalize them.

The *Western Region* (referring to a part of the national sales staff) reports that sales are 12 percent over budget for the first six months this year.

341 When words like *northern, southern, eastern,* and *western* precede a place name, they are not ordinarily capitalized because they merely indicate general location within a region. However, when these words are actually part of the place name, they must be capitalized. (Check an atlas or the geographic listings in a dictionary when in doubt.)

Preceding a Place Name	**Part of a Place Name**
northern New Jersey	**BUT:** Northern Ireland
western Massachusetts	Western Australia

NOTE: Within certain regions it is not uncommon for many who live there to capitalize the adjective because of the special importance they attach to the regional designation. Thus people who live in southern California may prefer to write *Southern California.*

Days of the Week, Months, Holidays, Seasons, Events, Periods

342 Capitalize names of days, months, holidays, and religious days.

Tuesday	Mother's Day	Good Friday
February	Martin Luther King Day	All Saints' Day
New Year's Eve	Kamehameha Day	Rosh Hashanah
April Fools' Day	Oktoberfest	Yom Kippur
Veterans Day	Ramadan	Hanukkah

343 Do not capitalize the names of the seasons unless they are personified.

We hold our regional sales conferences during the *fall* and *winter,* but our national conference always takes place early in the *spring.*

We do not plan to announce our new line of software applications until our fall '93/winter '94 catalog.

> BUT: And this you can see is the bolt. The purpose of this
> Is to open the breech, as you see. We can slide it
> Rapidly backwards and forwards: we call this
> Easing the spring. And rapidly backwards and forwards
> The early bees are assaulting and fumbling the flowers:
> They call it easing the Spring.
>
> —Henry Reed

344 a. Capitalize the names of historical events and imaginative names given to historical periods.

the American Revolution	the Renaissance
World War II	the Counter-Reformation
the Holocaust	Prohibition
Fire Prevention Week	the Great Depression

b. References to cultural *ages* are usually capitalized. However, contemporary references are not usually capitalized unless they appear together with a capitalized reference.

the Bronze Age	BUT: the space age
the Dark Ages	the atomic age
the Middle Ages	the nuclear age

The course spans the development of civilization from the *Stone Age* to the *Space Age.*

c. References to cultural *eras* are usually capitalized, but references to cultural periods are usually not.

the Christian Era	BUT: the romantic period
the Victorian Era	the colonial period

345 Do not capitalize the names of decades and centuries.

during the fifties	in the twenty-first century
in the nineteen-eighties	during the nineteen hundreds

NOTE: Decades are capitalized, however, in special expressions.

the Gay Nineties	the Roaring Twenties

Acts, Laws, Bills, Treaties

346 a. Capitalize formal titles of acts, laws, bills, and treaties, but do not capitalize common-noun elements that stand alone in place of the full name.

the Airline Deregulation Act	the act
Public Law 480	the law
the Treaty of Versailles	the treaty
the First Amendment	the amendment
the Constitution of the United States	BUT: the Constitution (see ¶304)

b. Do not capitalize generic or informal references to existing or pending legislation except for proper nouns and adjectives.

environmental protection laws	the Brady gun control proposal

c. "Laws" that make humorous or satirical observations about human and organizational behavior are capitalized to suggest that they carry the same authority as an actual piece of legislation.

Parkinson's Law states that work expands to fill the time that has been allotted for its completion.

Murphy's Law holds that if something can go wrong, it will.

The *Peter Principle* maintains that people in an organization tend to be promoted until they reach their level of incompetence.

According to *Fudd's First Law of Opposition*, if you push something hard enough, it will fall over.

d. In the names of authentic scientific laws, capitalize only proper nouns and adjectives.

Gresham's law
Mendel's law

Newton's first law of motion
the first law of thermodynamics

Programs, Movements, Concepts

347 a. Do not capitalize the names of programs, movements, or concepts when used as general terms.

social security benefits
BUT: the Social Security Administration
medicare payments
BUT: the Medicare Act

the civil rights movement
BUT: the Civil Rights Act
glasnost and perestroika
existentialism and rationalism

b. Capitalize proper nouns and adjectives that are part of such terms.

the Socratic method
Keynesian economics

Newtonian physics
Marxist-Leninist theories

c. Capitalize imaginative names given to programs and movements.

the New Deal
the Great Society

the New Frontier
the War on Poverty

d. Capitalize terms like *democrat, socialist,* and *communist* when they signify formal membership in a political party but not when they merely signify belief in a certain philosophy.

a lifelong *Democrat* (refers to a person who consistently votes for candidates of the Democratic Party)

a lifelong *democrat* (refers to a person who believes in the principles of democracy)

independent voters
the right wing

leftists
fascist tendencies

Races, Peoples, Languages

348 Capitalize the names of races, peoples, tribes, and languages.

Caucasians   Americans   Native Americans   **BUT:** the blacks
the Chinese   Hispanics   Mandarin Chinese   the whites

NOTE: Do not hyphenate terms like *African Americans* or *French Canadians* when they are used as nouns, because the first word in each case modifies the second. However, hyphenate such terms when they are used as adjectives; for example, *African-American enterprises, French-Canadian voters.* Moreover, hyphenate such terms when the first element is a prefix; for example, *an Afro-American style, the Anglo-Saxons, the Indo-Chinese.*

Religious References

349 **a.** Capitalize all references to a supreme being.

God	the Supreme Being	Allah
the Lord	the Messiah	Yahweh
the Holy Spirit	the Almighty	Providence

NOTE: The word *God* is capitalized in such compound expressions as *God-fearing* and *Godspeed* but not in such terms as *godforsaken* and *god-awful*.

b. Capitalize personal pronouns referring to a supreme being when they stand alone, without an antecedent nearby.

Offer thanks unto *Him*.   BUT: Ask the Lord for *his* blessing.

NOTE: Some writers capitalize these personal pronouns under all circumstances.

c. Capitalize references to persons revered as holy.

the Prince of Peace	Buddha	John the Baptist
the Good Shepherd	the Prophet	Saint Peter (see ¶518e)
the Blessed Virgin	the Apostles	Luke the Evangelist

d. Capitalize the names of religions, their members, and their buildings.

Reform Judaism	Mormons	Saint Mark's Episcopal Church
Zen Buddhism	Methodists	Temple Beth Sholom

the Roman Catholic *Church* (meaning the institution as a whole)

BUT: the Roman Catholic *church* on Wyoming Avenue (referring to a specific building)

e. Capitalize references to religious events. (See also ¶342.)

the Creation	the Exodus	the Crucifixion
the Flood	the Second Coming	the Resurrection

f. In general, do not capitalize references to specific religious observances and services. However, if you are writing from the perspective of a particular religion, follow the capitalization style of that religion.

bar mitzvah	baptism	BUT: the Eucharist
seder	christening	the Mass

350 Capitalize (but do not quote, underscore, or italicize) references to works regarded as sacred.

the King James Bible	the Koran	the Ten Commandments
BUT: biblical sources	the Talmud	the Sermon on the Mount
the Revised Standard Version	the Torah	Psalms 23 and 24
the Old Testament	the Our Father	Kaddish
the Book of Genesis	the Lord's Prayer	Hail Mary
	Hebrews 13:8	the Apostles' Creed

Celestial Bodies

351 Capitalize the names of planets (*Jupiter, Mars*), stars (*Polaris, the North Star*), and constellations (*the Big Dipper, the Milky Way*). However, do not capitalize the words *sun, moon,* and *earth* unless they are used in connection with the capitalized names of other planets or stars.

With the weather we've been having, we haven't seen much of the *sun*.

We have gone to the ends of the *earth* to assemble this collection of jewelry.

Compare the orbits of *Mars, Venus,* and *Earth*.

Course Titles, Subjects, Academic Degrees

352 Capitalize the names of specific course titles. However, do not capitalize names of subjects or areas of study (except for any proper nouns or adjectives in such names).

> *American History 201* meets on Tuesdays and Thursdays. (Course title.)
>
> Harriet has decided to major in *American history.* (Area of study.)

353 Do not capitalize academic degrees used as general terms of classification. However, capitalize a degree used after a person's name.

a bachelor of arts degree	received his bachelor's
a master of science degree	working for a master's
a doctor of laws degree	will soon receive her doctorate

> **BUT:** Claire Hurwitz, Doctor of Philosophy

354 In references to academic years, do not capitalize the words *freshman, sophomore, junior,* and *senior.* In references to grade levels, capitalize the word *grade* when a number follows but not when a number precedes.

> All incoming *freshmen* must register by September 4.
>
> Harriet spent her *junior* year in Germany.
>
> Our oldest child is in *Grade 6;* our second child is in the *third grade.*

Commercial Products

355 Capitalize trademarks, brand names, proprietary names, names of commercial products, and market grades. The common noun following the name of a product should not ordinarily be capitalized; however, manufacturers and advertisers often capitalize such words in the names of their own products to give them special emphasis.

> Elmer's glue   **BUT:** Krazy Glue

NOTE: Be alert to the correct spelling of proper nouns.

> Macintosh computers   **BUT:** McIntosh apples

356 Capitalize all trademarks except those that have become clearly established as common nouns. To be safe, check an up-to-date dictionary or consult The United States Trademark Association (6 East 45 Street, New York, NY 10017).

Xerox, Photostat; **BUT:** photocopy, fax
LaserJet; **BUT:** laser printer
Telecopier, Teletype, TelePrompTer
  BUT: teleprinter, telex, teletext
Express Mail, Mailgram, Yellow Pages
  BUT: E-mail, voice mail, videotex
Scotch tape, Post-It notes, Magic
  Marker, Jiffy bag, White-Out
Acrilan, Dacron, Lycra, Orlon,
  Ultrasuede; **BUT:** nylon, spandex
Levi's, Windbreaker, Loafers,
  Top-Siders
Jeep, Dumpster, Hide-A-Bed,
  Quonset hut
Frisbee, Ping-Pong, Rollerblades
Monopoly, Scrabble, Trivial Pursuit
Dramamine, Aureomycin
  BUT: penicillin
Realtor; **BUT:** real estate agent

Teflon, Velcro, Ziploc, Baggies
Styrofoam, Lucite, Peg-Board
Fiberglas; **BUT:** fiberglass
Band-Aid, Ace bandage, Q-Tips,
  Vaseline, Kleenex
Tylenol, Novocain, Demerol,
  Valium; **BUT:** aspirin
diet Coke, diet Pepsi, Kool-Aid,
  7UP, Gatorade
Jell-O, Tabasco sauce, Popsicle,
  Turtles
Crock-Pot, Pyrex dish, Dixie cup,
  Formica
Frigidaire, Disposall, Jacuzzi,
  Laundromat
Kitty Litter, Seeing Eye dog
Day-Glo colors, Technicolor
Walkman stereo, Polaroid
  BUT: camcorder

Advertising Material

357 Words ordinarily written in small letters may be capitalized in advertising copy for special emphasis. (This style is inappropriate in all other kinds of written communication.)

> Save money now during our *Year-End Clearance Sale.*
>
> It's the event *Luxury Lovers* have been waiting for . . . from Whitehall's!

Legal Documents

358 In legal documents, many words that ordinarily would be written in small letters are written with initial capitals or all capitals—for example, references to parties, the name of the document, special provisions, and sometimes spelled-out amounts of money (see ¶420b).

> THIS AGREEMENT, made this 31st day of January 1995 . . .
>
> . . . hereinafter called the SELLER . . .
>
> WHEREAS the Seller has this day agreed . . .
>
> WITNESS the signatures . . .

Nouns With Numbers or Letters

359 Capitalize a noun followed by a number or a letter that indicates sequence. **EXCEPTIONS:** Do not capitalize the nouns *line, note, page, paragraph, size, step,* and *verse.*

Account 66160	Check 181	Invoice 270487	Platform 3
Act 1	Class 4	Item 9859D	Policy 394857
Appendix A	Column 1	Lesson 20	Room 501
Article 2	Diagram 4	line 4	Section 1
Book III	Exercise 8	Model B671-4	size 10
Building 4	Exhibit A	note 1	step 3
Bulletin T-119	Extension 2174	page 158	Table 7
Car 8171	Figure 9	paragraph 2a	Unit 2
Chapter V	Flight 626	Part Three	verse 3
Chart 3	Illustration 19	Plate XV	Volume II

> For a more detailed discussion of this argument, see *Chapters 5 and 6.*

NOTE: It is often unnecessary to use *No.* before the number. (See ¶455a.)

> Purchase Order 4713 (**RATHER THAN:** Purchase Order *No.* 4713)

Titles of Literary and Artistic Works; Headings

360 In titles of literary and artistic works and in displayed headings, capitalize all words with *four or more* letters. Also capitalize words with fewer than four letters except:

> **ARTICLES:** *the, a, an*
>
> **SHORT CONJUNCTIONS:** *and, as, but, if, or, nor*
>
> **SHORT PREPOSITIONS:** *at, by, for, in, of, off, on, out, to, up*
>
> *How to Succeed in Business Without Really Trying*
>
> "Redevelopment Proposal Is Not Expected to Be Approved"

NOTE: Be sure to capitalize short verb forms like *Is* and *Be.*

361 Even articles, short conjunctions, and short prepositions should be capitalized under the following circumstances:

a. Capitalize the first and last word of a title.

"*A* Home to Be Proud *Of* "

CAUTION: Do not capitalize *the* at the beginning of a title unless it is actually part of the title.

For further details check *the Encyclopaedia Britannica.*

This clipping is from *The New York Times.*

b. Capitalize the first word following a dash or colon in a title.

Abraham Lincoln—The Early Years

The Treaty of Versailles: A Reexamination

c. Capitalize short words like *in, out, off,* and *up* in titles when they serve as adverbs rather than as prepositions. (These words may occur as adverbs in verb phrases or in hyphenated compounds derived from verb phrases. See ¶¶803, 1070.)

"AT&T Chalks *Up* Record Earnings for the Year"

"LeClaire Is Runner-*Up* in Election" (see also ¶363)

BUT: "Sailing *up* the Mississippi"

The Spy Who Came In From the Cold

"Foxworth Is Considered a Shoo-*In* for Governor"

BUT: "Pollsters Project an Easy Win for Foxworth *in* Heavy Voter Turnout"

d. Capitalize short prepositions like *in* and *up* when used together with prepositions having four or more letters.

"Sailing *Up* and *Down* the Mississippi"

"Happenings *In* and *Around* Town"

"Mall Opening *On* or *About* May 1"

e. When a title or heading is displayed on more than one line, do not capitalize the first word of any turnover line unless it needs to be capitalized on the basis of the preceding guidelines.

Should You Invest for the Long Pull *or* Should You Trade Continually?	Millions *of* Dollars	Income *per* Capita

For the capitalization of Preface, Contents, Appendix, *and* Index, *see* ¶242, *note; for the use of all capitals with titles, see* ¶289a.

362 Do not capitalize a book title when it is incorporated into a sentence as a descriptive phrase.

In his book on *economics* Samuelson points out that . . .

BUT: In his book *Economics* Samuelson points out that . . .

Hyphenated Words

363 *Within a sentence,* capitalize only those elements of a hyphenated word that are proper nouns or proper adjectives. *At the beginning of a sentence,* capitalize the first element in the hyphenated word but not other elements unless they are proper nouns or adjectives. *In a heading or title,* capitalize all the elements except articles, short prepositions, and short conjunctions (see ¶360).

(Continued on page 100.)

Within Sentences	Beginning Sentences	In Headings
up-to-date	Up-to-date	Up-to-Date
Spanish-American	Spanish-American	Spanish-American
English-speaking	English-speaking	English-Speaking
mid-September	Mid-September	Mid-September
ex-President Reagan	Ex-President Reagan	Ex-President Reagan
Senator-elect Murray	Senator-elect Murray	Senator-Elect Murray
self-confidence	Self-confidence	Self-Confidence
de-emphasize	De-emphasize	De-Emphasize
follow-up	Follow-up	Follow-Up (see ¶361c)
Ninety-ninth Congress	Ninety-ninth Congress	Ninety-Ninth Congress
one-sixth	One-sixth	One-Sixth
post-World War II	Post-World War II	Post-World War II

Awards and Medals

364 Capitalize the names of awards and medals.

Pulitzer Prize winners	the Congressional Medal of Honor
the Nobel Prize	the Distinguished Service Medal
Oscars and Emmys	the Purple Heart

Computer Terminology

365 a. The names of many programming languages are written in all capitals. (See also ¶544.)

BASIC	FORTRAN	**BUT:** Pascal
COBOL	PROLOG	Ada

b. The names of many operating systems are also written in all capitals.

MS-DOS	UNIX	**BUT:** Macintosh
PC-DOS	OS/2	

c. The names of many software applications are compound nouns that are written solid but with a capital letter at the beginning of each element. (Follow the manufacturer's style in each case.)

WordPerfect	PageMaker	**BUT:** Microsoft Word
WordStar	MultiMate	dBASE V
DisplayWrite	DataEase	PC/FOCUS

Capitalization of questions within sentences: see ¶¶115, 117.
Capitalization after a colon: see ¶¶196–199.
Capitalization after an opening bracket: see ¶296.
Capitalization after an opening dash: see ¶214, note.
Capitalization after an opening parenthesis: see ¶¶224–226.
Capitalization after an opening quotation mark: see ¶¶272–273.
Capitalization of abbreviations: see ¶514.

Numbers

¶401

There is a significant difference between using figures and using words to express numbers. Figures are big (like capital letters) and compact and informal (like abbreviations); when used in a sentence, they stand out clearly from the surrounding words. By contrast, numbers expressed in words are unemphatic and formal; they do not stand out in a sentence. It is this functional difference between figures and words that underlies all aspects of number style.

Basic Rules

The rules for expressing numbers would be quite simple if writers would all agree to express numbers entirely in figures or entirely in words. But in actual practice the exclusive use of figures is considered appropriate only in tables and statistical matter, whereas the exclusive use of words to express numbers is found only in ultraformal documents (such as proclamations and social invitations). In writing that is neither ultraformal nor ultratechnical, most style manuals call for the use of both figures and words in varying proportions. Although authorities do not agree on details, there are two sets of basic rules in wide use: the *figure style* (which uses figures for most numbers above 10) and the *word style* (which uses figures for most numbers above 100). Unless you deal with a very limited type of business correspondence, you should be familiar with both styles and be prepared to use each appropriately as the situation demands.

Figure Style

The figure style is most commonly used in ordinary business correspondence (dealing with sales, production, finance, advertising, and other routine commercial matters). It is also used in journalistic and technical material and in academic work of a technical or statistical nature. In writing of this kind, most numbers represent significant quantities or measurements that should stand out for emphasis or quick comprehension.

401 Spell out numbers from 1 through 10; use figures for numbers above 10. This rule applies to both exact and approximate numbers.

> I would like *ten* copies of this article, but I need only *two* or *three* right away.
>
> At the convention we got over *75* requests for a copy of your report.
>
> We expect about *30* to *35* employees to sign up for the graphic arts course.
>
> The advertising is deliberately pitched at the *40-plus* age group.
>
> My letter in last Sunday's paper apparently provoked over *25* letters and some *60-odd* phone calls.
>
> One bookstore chain has already ordered *2500* copies. (See ¶461 on the omission of commas in four-digit figures.)
>
> The exhibition drew more than *12,000* people in the first month.
>
> We send out about 200,000 catalogs almost every month, but our year-end holiday catalog is mailed to over 1,000,000 households. (See ¶403b.)

> a. Use all figures—even for the numbers 1 through 10 (as in this sentence)—when they have technical significance or need to stand out for quick comprehension. This all-figure style is used in tables, in statistical matter, and in expressions of dates *(May 3)*, money *($6)*, clock time *(4 p.m.)*, proportions and ratios *(a 10-to-1 shot)*, scores *(3 to 1)*, and

percentages *(8 percent)*. This style is also used with abbreviations and symbols *(12 cm, 8°F)*, with numbers referred to as numbers *(think of a number from 1 to 10)*, with highway designations *(U.S. Route 1, I-80)*, and with technical or emphatic references to age *(a tristate clinical study of 5-year-olds)*, periods of time *(a 6-month loan)*, measurements *(parcels over 3 pounds)*, and page numbers *(page 1)*.

b. In isolated cases spell out a number above 10 in order to de-emphasize the number or make it seem indefinite.

Jonathan could give you *a thousand and one* reasons for his inability to find a job that's right for him.

I have *a hundred* things to do today. (In this context *100 things* would seem too precise, too exact.)

NOTE: Also use words for numbers at the beginning of a sentence, for most ordinals *(our twenty-fifth anniversary)*, for fractions *(one-third of our sales)*, and for nontechnical or nonemphatic references to age *(my son just turned twelve)*, periods of time *(twenty years ago)*, and measurements *(I need to lose another thirty pounds)*.

For rules on how to express numbers in figures, see ¶¶461–464.
For rules on how to express numbers in words, see ¶¶465–467.

402 Use the same style to express *related* numbers above and below 10. If any of the numbers are above 10, put them all in figures.

We used to have *two* dogs, *one* cat, and *one* rabbit.

BUT: We now have *5* dogs, *11* cats, and *1* rabbit. (The rabbit is male.)

Our *four* sons consumed a total of *18* hamburgers, *5* large bottles of diet Coke, *12* DoveBars, and about *2000* cookies—all at *one* sitting. (Figures are used for all the related items of food; the other numbers—*four* and *one*—are spelled out, since they are not related and are not over 10.)

NOTE: In the names of companies and products, follow the organization's style.

a 7-Eleven store   3-In-One oil   9-Lives cat food
a can of 7UP   3M office products   Lotus 1-2-3 software

403 For fast comprehension, numbers in the *millions* or higher may be expressed as follows:

21 million (in place of 21,000,000)
3 billion (in place of 3,000,000,000)
14½ million (in place of 14,500,000)
2.4 billion (in place of 2,400,000,000)

Bindel & Boggs is placing an order for *2.4 million* barrels of oil.
BUT: Bindel & Boggs is placing a *2.4-million-barrel* order. (See ¶817.)

a. This style may be used only when the amount consists of a whole number with nothing more than a simple fraction or decimal following. A number such as *4,832,067* must be written all in figures.

b. Treat related numbers alike.

Last year we sold *21,557,000* items; this year, nearly *23,000,000*.
(NOT: 21,557,000 . . . 23 million.)

For examples involving money, see ¶416.

Word Style

The word style of numbers is used in high-level executive correspondence (see ¶¶1394–1395) and in nontechnical material, where the writing is of a more formal or literary nature and the use of figures would give numbers an undesired emphasis and obtrusiveness. Here are the basic rules for the word style.

404 Spell out all numbers, whether exact or approximate, that can be expressed in one or two words. (A hyphenated compound number like *twenty-one* or *twenty-nine* counts as one word.) In effect, spell out all numbers from 1 through 100 and all round numbers above 100 that require no more than two words (such as *sixty-two thousand* or *forty-five million*).

> Mr. Ryan received *twenty-three* letters praising his talk last Wednesday at the Rotary Club.
>
> Last year more than *twelve million* people attended the art exhibition our company sponsored.
>
> Some *sixty-odd* people have called to volunteer their services.
>
> Over *two hundred* people attended the reception for Helen and Frank Russo.
>
> **BUT:** Over *250* people attended the reception. (Use figures when more than two words are required.)

NOTE: In writing of an ultraformal nature—proclamations, social invitations, and many legal documents—even a number that requires more than two words is spelled out. However, as a matter of practicality the word style ordinarily uses figures when more than two words are required.

For rules on how to express numbers in words, see ¶¶465–467.

405 Express related numbers the same way, even though some are above 100 and some below. If any are in figures, put all in figures.

> We sent out *three hundred* invitations and have already received over *one hundred* acceptances.
>
> **BUT:** We sent out *300* invitations and have already received *125* acceptances. (**NOT:** three hundred . . . 125.)

406 Numbers in the millions or higher *that require more than two words when spelled out* may be expressed as follows:

> 231 million (in place of 231,000,000)
> 9¾ billion (in place of 9,750,000,000)
> 671.4 million (in place of 671,400,000)

Even a two-word number such as *sixty-two million* should be expressed as *62 million* when it is related to a number such as *231 million* (which cannot be spelled in two words). Moreover, it should be expressed as *62,000,000* when it is related to a number such as *231,163,520.*

Special Rules

The preceding rules on figure style (¶¶401–403) and word style (¶¶404–406) are basic guidelines that govern in the absence of more specific principles. The following rules cover those situations that require special handling (for example, expressions of dates and money). In a number of cases where either figures or words are acceptable, your choice will depend on whether you are striving for emphasis or formality.

Dates

These rules apply to dates in sentences. See ¶1314 for date lines in business correspondence.

407 When the day *precedes* the month or *stands alone,* express it either in ordinal figures (*1st, 2d, 3d, 4th,* etc.) or in ordinal words (the *first,* the *twelfth,* the *twenty-eighth*).

> **FOR EMPHASIS:** This year's international sales conference runs from the *2d* of August through the *5th.*

> **FOR FORMALITY:** We leave for Europe on the *third* of June and don't return until the *twenty-fifth.*

408 When the day *follows* the month, use a cardinal figure (*1, 2, 3,* etc.) to express it.

> on March *6* (**NOT:** March *6th* **OR** March *sixth*)

409 a. Express complete dates in month-day-year sequence.

> March 6, 1995

> **NOTE:** In United States military correspondence and in letters from foreign countries, the complete date is expressed in day-month-year sequence.

> 6 March 1995

b. The form *3/6/95* (representing a *month*-day-year sequence) is acceptable on business forms and in informal letters and memos. Avoid this form, however, if there is any chance your reader could misinterpret it as a *day*-month-year sequence.

c. Avoid the following forms: *March 6th, 1995; Mar. 6, 1995; the 6th of March, 1995; the sixth of March, 1995.*

410 Note the use of commas and other punctuation with expressions of dates.

> On *August 13, 1992,* my husband and I received the bank loan that permitted us to start our own restaurant. (Two commas set off the year following the month and day.)

> We set a formal opening date of *November 15, 1992;* we actually opened on *March 18, 1993* (because of the flash fire that virtually destroyed the restaurant and forced us to start from scratch). (Note that the second comma is omitted after *1992* and *1993* because in each case some other punctuation mark—a semicolon or an opening parenthesis—is required at that point.)

> Sales for *February 1992* hit an all-time low. (Omit commas around the year when it follows the month alone.)

> **BUT:** Once we introduced our new product line in *September 1992,* it was clear that we were finally on the road to a strong recovery. (The comma following *1992* is needed to separate an introductory dependent clause from the rest of the sentence, not because of the date.)

> The *May 1992* issue of *The Atlantic* carries an excerpt from Brenda's forthcoming book. (No commas are used when the month-year expression serves as an adjective.)

> **BUT:** The *May 4, 1992,* issue of *Newsweek* broke the story. (Use two commas to set off the year when a complete date serves as an adjective. See ¶154.)

(Continued on page 106.)

In *1992* we opened six branch offices in the Southwest. (No comma follows the year in a short introductory phrase.)

On *February 28* the board will decide whether to sell off its holdings in Oregon real estate. (No comma follows the month and day in a short introductory phrase.)

BUT: On *February 28*, 27 managers from the Cincinnati plant will leave on a tour of Asian manufacturing facilities. (Insert a comma when another figure immediately follows. See ¶456.)

Yesterday, *April 3*, I spoke to a group of exporters in Los Angeles. Two days from now, *April 6*, I will speak to a similar group in San Francisco. Then on Wednesday, *April 11*, I will be speaking at an international trade fair in Honolulu. (Set off a month-day expression when it serves as an appositive. See ¶148.)

For the use or omission of a comma when a date is followed by a related phrase or clause, see ¶152.

411 In formal legal documents, formal invitations, and proclamations, spell out the day and the year. A number of styles may be used:

May twenty-first	nineteen hundred and ninety-three
the twenty-first of May	one thousand nine hundred and ninety-three
this twenty-first day of May	in the year of our Lord one thousand nine hundred and ninety-three

412 **a.** Class graduation years and well-known years in history may appear in abbreviated form.

the class of '96   the winter of '93

b. Years also appear in abbreviated form in certain business expressions. (See also ¶294.)

FY 1993/94 **OR** fiscal year 1993/94   the fall '93/'94 catalog

For the expression of centuries and decades, see ¶¶438–439; for dates in a sequence, see ¶¶458–460.

Money

413 **a.** Use figures to express exact or approximate amounts of money.

$7	about $1500	over $5,000,000 a year	a $50 bill
$13.50	nearly $50,000	a $5,000,000-a-year account	$350 worth

b. When amounts of money from different countries are referred to in the same context, the unit of currency in each case usually appears as an abbreviation or symbol (or both) directly preceding the numerical amount.

US$10,000	(refers to 10,000 U.S. dollars)
Can$10,000	(refers to 10,000 Canadian dollars)
Mex$10,000	(refers to 10,000 Mexican pesos)
DM10,000	(refers to 10,000 German deutsche marks)
£10,000	(refers to 10,000 British pounds)
¥10,000	(refers to 10,000 Japanese yen)

NOTE: If your equipment does not have the capability to print the symbols £ and ¥, you may be able to construct them as follows: To form the symbol for the British pound, type a capital *L* over a small *f*. To form the symbol for the Japanese yen, type a capital Y over an equal sign (=). The results will appear as follows:

£   ¥

c. An isolated, nonemphatic reference to money may be spelled out.

two hundred dollars	a half-dollar
nearly a thousand dollars	half a million dollars
a twenty-dollar bill	five thousand dollars' worth (note
a million-dollar beach house	the apostrophe with *dollars*)

414 Spell out indefinite amounts of money.

a few million dollars   many thousands of dollars

415 It is not necessary to add a decimal point or zeros to a *whole* dollar amount when it occurs in a sentence.

I am enclosing a check for *$125* as payment in full.

This model costs $12.50; that one costs *$10*.

In a column, however, if any amount contains cents, add a decimal point and two zeros to all *whole* dollar amounts to maintain a uniform appearance. (See also ¶1628.)

$150.50
25.00
8.05
$183.55

416 Money in round amounts of a million or more may be expressed partially in words. (The style given in the first column is preferred.)

$12 million	**OR**	12 million dollars		
$10½ million	**OR**	10½ million dollars		
$10.5 million	**OR**	10.5 million dollars		
$6¼ billion	**OR**	6¼ billion dollars	**OR**	$6250 million
$6.25 billion	**OR**	6.25 billion dollars	**OR**	6250 million dollars

a. This style may be used only when the amount consists of a whole number with nothing more than a simple fraction or decimal following. Write an amount like *$10,235,000* entirely in figures.

b. Express related amounts the same way.

from $500,000 to $1,000,000 (**NOT:** from $500,000 to $1 million)

c. Repeat the word *million* (*billion*, etc.) with each figure to avoid misunderstanding.

$5 million to $10 million (**NOT:** $5 to $10 million)

417 Fractional expressions of large amounts of money should be either completely spelled out or converted to an all-figure style.

one-quarter of a million dollars   **OR** $250,000
(**BUT NOT:** ¼ of a million dollars   **OR** $¼ million)

a half-billion dollars   **OR** $500,000,000
(**BUT NOT:** ½ billion dollars   **OR** $½ billion)

418 a. For amounts under a dollar, ordinarily use figures and the word *cents*.

I am sure that customers will not pay more than *50 cents* for this item.

This machine can be fixed with *80 cents'* worth of parts. (Note the apostrophe with *cents*.)

These *25-cent* tokens can be used at all tollbooths.

NOTE: An isolated, nonemphatic reference to cents may be spelled out.

I wouldn't give *two cents* for that car.

(Continued on page 108.)

b. Do not use the style *$.75* in sentences except when related amounts require a dollar sign.

It will cost you *$4.84* a copy to do the company manual: *$.86* for the paper, *$1.54* for the printing, and *$2.44* for the special binder.

c. The cent sign (*¢*) may be used in technical and statistical matter.

The price of lead, approximately *15.5¢* a pound in 1970, now runs around *37¢* a pound; zinc, averaging *15¢* a pound in 1970, now sells for *60¢* a pound.

419 When using the dollar sign or the cent sign with a price range or a series of amounts, use the sign with each amount.

$5,000 to $10,000 $10 million to $20 million
10¢ to 20¢   (**BUT NOT:** $10 to $20 million)

These three properties are valued at $832,900, $954,500, and $1,087,000, respectively.

If the term *dollars* or *cents* is to be spelled out, use it only with the final amount.

10 to 20 cents   10 million to 20 million dollars (see ¶416c)

420 In legal documents, amounts of money are often expressed first in words and then, within parentheses, in figures. (See also ¶¶465–467.)

One Hundred Dollars ($100)   **OR**   One Hundred (100) Dollars
(**BUT NOT:** One Hundred ($100) Dollars)

Three Thousand One Hundred and 50/100 Dollars ($3100.50)

a. When spelling out amounts of money, omit the *and* between hundreds and tens of dollars if *and* is used before the fraction representing cents.

Six Hundred Thirty-two and 75/100 Dollars
(**NOT:** Six Hundred *and* Thirty-two and 75/100 Dollars)

NOTE: In whole dollar amounts, the use of *and* between hundreds and tens of dollars is optional.

Six Hundred Thirty-two Dollars   **OR**   Six Hundred and Thirty-two Dollars

b. The capitalization of spelled-out amounts may vary. Sometimes the first letter of each main word is capitalized (as in the examples in ¶420a); sometimes only the first letter of the first word is capitalized (as on checks); sometimes the entire amount is given all in capitals.

The following rules (¶¶421–428) cover situations in which numbers are usually spelled out: at the beginning of sentences and in expressions using indefinite numbers, ordinal numbers, and fractions.

At the Beginning of a Sentence

421 Spell out a number that begins a sentence, as well as any related numbers.

Thirty-four former students of Dr. Helen VanVleck came from all parts of the country to honor their professor on the occasion of her retirement.

Eight hundred people have already signed the recall petition.

Forty to *fifty* percent of the people polled on different occasions expressed disapproval of the mayor's performance in office.

(**NOT:** *Forty* to *50* percent . . .)

422 If the number requires more than two words when spelled out or if figures are preferable for emphasis or quick reference, reword the sentence.

> The company sent out *298* copies of its consumer guidelines last month.
>
> (**NOT:** *Two hundred and ninety-eight* copies of its consumer guidelines were sent out by the company last month.)
>
> We had a good year in *1992*.
>
> (**NOT:** *Nineteen hundred ninety-two* [**OR** *1992*] was a good year for us.)
>
> Our mining operations in Nevada and Montana provide *60* to *70* percent of our revenues.
>
> (**NOT:** *Sixty* to *seventy* percent of our revenues come from our mining operations in Nevada and Montana.)

Indefinite Numbers and Amounts

423 Spell out indefinite numbers and amounts.

several hundred investors	hundreds of inquiries
a few thousand acres	thousands of readers
a multimillion-dollar sale	many millions of dollars
a man in his late forties	a roll of fifties and twenties

For approximate numbers, see ¶401 (figure style) and ¶404 (word style).

Ordinal Numbers

424 In general, spell out all ordinal numbers (*first, second, third,* etc.) that can be expressed in one or two words. (A hyphenated number like *twenty-first* counts as one word.)

in the twenty-first century	the firm's one hundredth anniversary
twentieth-century art (see ¶817)	(**BUT:** the firm's 125th anniversary)
on the forty-eighth floor	the Ninety-ninth Congress (in text)
on my fifty-fifth birthday	the Ninety-Ninth Congress (in head-
the Fourteenth Ward	ings and titles; see ¶363)
the two millionth visitor	the 104th Congress
to EPCOT	the Eighteenth Amendment

For the rule on how to express ordinal numbers in words, see ¶465; for the distinction between ordinals and fractions, see ¶427d.

425 Use figures for ordinals in certain expressions of dates (see ¶¶407–409), in numbered street names above 10 (see ¶1333b), and in situations call-ing for special emphasis.

In Advertising Copy

> Come to our *25th* Anniversary Sale! (Figures for emphasis.)
>
> Come to our *Twenty-fifth* Anniversary Sale! (Words for formality.)

In Ordinary Correspondence

> Watkins & Glenn is having a *twenty-fifth* anniversary sale.

NOTE: Ordinal figures are expressed as follows: *1st, 2d* or *2nd, 3d* or *3rd, 4th, 5th, 6th,* etc. Do not use an ''abbreviation'' period following an ordi-nal figure.

For the use of 2d in preference to 2nd, see ¶503.

426 Ordinals that follow a person's name may be expressed in arabic or roman numerals. As a rule, use arabic numerals unless you know that the person in question prefers roman numerals.

> James A. Wilson 3d **OR** James A. Wilson III
> C. Roy Post 4th C. Roy Post IV

For the use or omission of commas with numerals that follow a person's name, see ¶156.

Fractions

427 Fractions Standing Alone

a. Ordinarily, spell out a fraction that stands alone (that is, without a whole number preceding). Use figures, however, if the spelled-out form is long and awkward or if the fraction is used in a technical measurement or some type of computation.

> one-half the audience (see ¶427c)   three-fourths of the profits
>
> a two-thirds majority   nine-tenths of a mile away
>
> 3/4-yard lengths (**BETTER THAN:** three-quarter-yard lengths)
>
> 5/32 inch (**BETTER THAN:** five thirty-seconds of an inch)
>
> multiply by 2/5
>
> This recipe calls for only *a quarter pound* of butter.
>
> He came back *a half hour* later (**OR** *half an hour* later).

> **NOTE:** Hyphenate *half dozen* or *half a dozen* when this phrase is used as a compound modifier before a noun.

> I'll take *a half-dozen* eggs (**OR** *half-a-dozen* eggs).

> **BUT:** I'll take *a half dozen* (**OR** *half a dozen*).

b. When a fraction is spelled out, the numerator and the denominator should be connected by a hyphen unless either element already contains a hyphen.

> five-eighths   thirteen thirty-seconds
> thirteen-sixteenths   twenty-seven sixty-fourths

c. In constructions involving the balanced phrases *one half . . . the other half*, do not hyphenate *one half*.

> *One half* of the shipment was damaged beyond use; *the other half* was salvageable.

d. Distinguish between large spelled-out fractions (which are hyphenated) and large spelled-out ordinals (which are not).

> The difference is less than *one-hundredth* of 1 percent. (Hyphenated fraction meaning *1/100.*)

> **BUT:** This year the company will be celebrating the *one hundredth* anniversary of its founding. (Unhyphenated ordinal meaning *100th.*)

e. Fractions expressed in figures should not be followed by endings like *sts, ds, nds,* or *ths* or by an *of* phrase.

> 3/200 (**NOT:** 3/200ths)   9/64 inch (**NOT:** 9/64ths of an inch)

> If a sentence requires the use of an *of* phrase following the fraction, spell the fraction out.

> three-quarters of an hour (**NOT:** 3/4 of an hour)

428 Fractions in Mixed Numbers

a. A mixed number (a whole number plus a fraction) is written in figures except at the beginning of a sentence.

Retail sales are now *4½* times what they were in 1967.

Two and a quarter (**or** *Two and one-quarter*) inches of rain fell over the weekend. (Note the use of *and* between the whole number and the fraction.)

b. When constructing fractions that do not appear on the keyboard, use the diagonal (/). Separate a whole number from a fraction by means of a space (not with a hyphen).

I can remember when an *8 5/8* percent mortgage seemed high.

(**not:** . . . an 8-5/8 percent mortgage.)

c. In the same sentence, do not mix constructed fractions (7/8, 5/16) with those that appear on the keyboard (½, ¼).

The rate on prime commercial paper has dropped from *11 1/2* percent a year ago to *8 3/4* percent today.

(**not:** 11½ . . . 8 3/4.)

NOTE: To simplify typing, convert constructed fractions (and simpler ones used in the same context) to a decimal form whenever feasible.

The rate on prime commercial paper has dropped from *11.5* percent a year ago to *8.75* percent today.

The following rules (¶¶429–442) deal with measurements and with expressions of age and time (elements that often function as measurements). When these elements have technical or statistical significance, they are expressed in figures; otherwise, they are expressed in words.

Measurements

429 Most measurements have a technical significance and should be expressed in figures (even from 1 through 10) for emphasis or quick comprehension. However, spell out an isolated measurement that lacks technical significance.

A higher rate is charged on parcels over *2 pounds.*
but: I'm afraid I've gained another *two pounds* this week.

Add *1 quart* of sugar for each *4 quarts* of strawberries.
but: Last weekend we picked *four quarts* of strawberries from our own patch.

There is no charge for delivery within a *30-mile* radius of Chicago.
but: It's only a *thirty-mile* drive up to our summer place.

NOTE: Dimensions, sizes, and actual temperature readings are always expressed in figures.

I'm looking for a *4- by 6-foot* Oriental rug for my reception room. (See also ¶432.)

Please send me a half-dozen blue oxford shirts, size *17½/33.*

The thermometer now stands at *32,* a drop of five degrees in the past two hours.

but: The temperature has been in the low *thirties* (**or** *30s*) all week. (An indefinite reference to the temperature may be spelled out or expressed in figures.)

¶430

430 When a measurement consists of several elements, do not use commas to separate the elements. The measurement is considered a single unit.

> The package weighed *8 pounds 11 ounces.*
> The punch bowl holds *4 quarts 1 pint.*
> Hal is *6 feet 8 inches* tall in his stocking feet.

NOTE: If this type of measurement is used as a compound modifier before a noun, use hyphens to connect all the elements as a single unit. (See also ¶817.)

> a *6-foot-8-inch* man

431 The unit of measurement may be abbreviated (for example, *12 ft*) or expressed as a symbol (for example, *12'*) in technical material or in tables. If either an abbreviation or a symbol is used, the number must be expressed as a figure.

For the style of abbreviations for units of measure, see ¶¶535–538.
For the use of figures with abbreviations and symbols, see ¶453.

432 Dimensions may be expressed as follows:

GENERAL USAGE:	a room 15 by 30 feet	a 15- by 30-foot room
TECHNICAL USAGE:	a room 15 × 30 ft	a 15- × 30-ft room
	a room 15' × 30'	a 15' × 30' room
GENERAL USAGE:	a room 5 by 10 meters	a 5- by 10-meter room
TECHNICAL USAGE:	a room 5 × 10 m	a 5- × 10-m room
GENERAL USAGE:	15 feet 6 inches by 30 feet 9 inches	
TECHNICAL USAGE:	15 ft 6 in × 30 ft 9 in OR 15' 6" × 30' 9"	

Ages and Anniversaries

433 Express ages in figures (including 1 through 10) when they are used as significant statistics or as technical measurements.

> Ethel Kassarian, *38,* has been promoted to director of marketing services.
> The attached printout projects the amount of the monthly retirement benefit payable *at the age of 65.* (See the entry for *Age–aged–at the age of* on page 254.)
> A computer literacy program is being offered in the schools to all *8- and 9-year-olds.* (See ¶832.)
> This insurance policy is specially tailored for people in the *50-plus* age group.
> You cannot disregard the job application of a person *aged 58.* (NOT: age 58.)

NOTE: When age is expressed in years, months, and days, do not use commas to separate the elements; they make up a single unit.

> On January 1 she will be *19 years 4 months and 17 days old.* (The *and* linking months and days may be omitted.)

434 Spell out ages in nontechnical references and in formal writing.

> My son is *three years old*, and my daughter is *two.*
> Shirley is in her early *forties;* her husband is in his *mid-sixties.*
> Have you ever tried keeping a group of *five-year-olds* happy and under control at the same time?

435 Spell out ordinals in references to birthdays and anniversaries except where special emphasis or more than two words are required. (See also ¶¶424–425.)

on my thirtieth birthday   her forty-first class reunion
our twenty-fifth anniversary   the company's 135th anniversary

Periods of Time

436 Use figures (even from 1 through 10) to express periods of time when they are used as technical measurements or significant statistics (as in discounts, interest rates, and credit terms).

a 35-hour workweek   a 30-year mortgage   a note due in 6 months

437 Spell out nontechnical references to periods of time unless the number requires more than two words.

a twenty-minute wait   in twenty-four months   three hundred years ago
eight hours later   in the last thirty years   BUT: 350 years ago
twelve days from now   forty-odd years ago   two thousand years ago

438 Centuries may be expressed as follows:

the 1900s OR: the nineteen hundreds
the twenty-first century   twentieth-century literature

439 Decades may be expressed as follows:

the 1990s OR the nineteen-nineties OR the nineties OR the '90s

the mid-1960s OR the mid-sixties OR the mid-'60s

during the years 1985–1995 OR from 1985 to 1995 (see ¶459)

OR between 1985 and 1995

NOTE: Decades are not capitalized except in special expressions such as *the Gay Nineties, the Roaring Twenties.*

Clock Time

440 With *a.m., p.m., Noon,* and *Midnight*

  a. Always use figures with *a.m.* or *p.m.*

We take off at *8:45 a.m.*   The bus is due at *2 p.m.*

By *8 p.m.,* CST, the first election returns should be in.

OR: By *8 p.m.* (CST) the first election returns should be in.

  b. The abbreviations *a.m.* and *p.m.* should appear in small letters without internal space. (In printed matter they usually appear in small capitals: A.M., P.M.)

  c. For time "on the hour," zeros are not needed to denote minutes.

Our store is open from 9:30 a.m. to *6 p.m.* (NOT: 6:00 p.m.)
BUT: Our store is always open until 6:00. (See ¶442 for the use of zeros when *a.m.* or *p.m.* is omitted.)

We always close from *12 noon* to 1:30 p.m.

You can buy your tickets between *9* and *10 a.m.*

(Continued on page 114.)

In tables, however, when some entries are given in hours and minutes, add a colon and two zeros to exact hours to maintain a uniform appearance. (For more complex illustrations showing the alignment of clock times in columns, see ¶1626b.)

Arr.	Dep.
8:45	9:10
9:00	9:25
9:50	10:00

d. Do not use *a.m.* or *p.m.* unless figures are used.

this morning   tomorrow afternoon
(NOT: this a.m.)   (NOT: tomorrow p.m.)

e. Do not use *a.m.* or *p.m.* with *o'clock.*

6 o'clock OR 6 p.m.   ten o'clock OR 10 a.m.
(NOT: 6 p.m. o'clock)   (NOT: 10 a.m. o'clock)

NOTE: The expression *o'clock* is more formal than *a.m.* or *p.m.*

f. Do not use *a.m.* or *p.m.* with the expressions *in the morning, in the afternoon, in the evening,* and *at night.* The abbreviations themselves already convey one of these meanings.

at 9 p.m. OR at nine in the evening (NOT: at 9 p.m. in the evening)

g. Use a colon (without space before or after) to separate hours from minutes (as in *3:22*).

h. The times *noon* and *midnight* may be expressed in words alone. However, use the forms *12 noon* and *12 midnight* when these times are given with other times expressed in figures.

Dinner is served in the main dining room until *midnight.*

BUT: Dinner is served from *6 p.m.* until *12 midnight.*

441   With *O'Clock*

a. With *o'clock,* use figures for emphasis or words for formality.

3 o'clock (for emphasis)   three o'clock (for formality)

b. To express hours and minutes with *o'clock,* use this style:

half past four o'clock OR half after four o'clock
(BUT NOT: four-thirty o'clock)

c. Expressions of time containing *o'clock* may be reinforced by such phrases as *in the morning, in the afternoon,* and the like.

10 o'clock at night   seven o'clock in the morning

For quick comprehension, the forms *10 p.m.* and *7 a.m.* are preferable.

442   Without *a.m., p.m.,* or *O'Clock*

When expressing time without *a.m., p.m.,* or *o'clock,* either spell the time out or—for quick comprehension—convert the expression to an all-figure style.

arrive at eight OR arrive at 8:00 (NOT: at 8)
five after six OR 6:05
a quarter past ten OR 10:15
twenty of four OR 3:40
a quarter to five OR a quarter of five OR 4:45
half past nine OR nine-thirty OR 9:30
nine forty-two OR 9:42

NOTE: A hyphen is used between hours and minutes *(seven-thirty)* but not if the minutes must be hyphenated *(seven thirty-five).*

The following rules (¶¶443–455) deal with situations in which numbers are always expressed in figures.

Decimals

443   Always write decimals in figures. Never insert commas in the decimal part of a number.

> 665.3184368 (no comma in decimal part of the number)
> 58,919.23785 (comma used in whole part of the number)
>
> *For the metric style of writing decimals, see ¶461b.*

444   When a decimal stands alone (without a whole number preceding the decimal point), insert a zero before the decimal point. (Reason: The zero keeps the reader from overlooking the decimal point.)

> 0.55 inch   0.08 gram
> **EXCEPTIONS:** a Colt .45; a .36 caliber revolver

445   Ordinarily, drop the zero at the end of a decimal (for example, write *2.787* rather than *2.7870*). However, retain the zero (*a*) if you wish to emphasize that the decimal is an exact number or (*b*) if the decimal has been rounded off from a longer figure. In a column of figures add zeros to the end of a decimal in order to make the number as long as other numbers in the column. (For illustrations, see ¶¶1626, 1628, 1629, 1631.)

446   Do not begin a sentence with a decimal figure.

> The temperature at 8 a.m. was *63.7.*
>
> (**NOT:** *63.7* was the temperature at 8 a.m.)

Percentages

447   Express percentages in figures, and spell out the word *percent.* (See ¶¶421–422 for percentages at the beginning of a sentence.)

> Carpenter Industries has increased its prices by only *3 percent* this year.
>
> My client had been expecting at least a *25 percent* discount from you.
> (**NOT:** a 25-percent discount. See also ¶817.)
>
> Our terms are *2 percent* 10 days, net 30 days. (These credit terms may be abbreviated as *2/10, n/30* on invoices and other business forms.)

NOTE: The % symbol may be used in tables, on business forms, and in statistical or technical matter.

448   **a.** Fractional percentages *under 1 percent* may be expressed as follows:

> one half of 1 percent   **OR**   0.5 percent
>
> **NOTE:** The zero before the decimal point in *0.5 percent* prevents misreading the amount as *5 percent.*

b. Fractional percentages *over 1 percent* should be expressed in figures.

> 7½ percent   **OR**   7.5 percent   9¼ percent   **OR**   9.25 percent

449   In a range or series of percentages, the word *percent* follows the last figure only. If the symbol % is used (see ¶447, note), it must follow each figure.

> Price reductions range from *20 to 50 percent.* (**BUT:** from 20% to 50%.)
>
> We give discounts of *10, 20, and 30 percent.* (**BUT:** 10%, 20%, and 30%.)
>
> *For the use of % in a column of figures, see ¶1629; for the use of* percent *and* percentage, *see page 266.*

Ratios and Proportions

450   As a rule, write ratios and proportions in figures.

> a proportion of 5 to 1   **OR**   a 5-to-1 ratio   **OR**   a 5:1 ratio
> the odds are 100 to 1   **OR**   a 100-to-1 shot
> 7 parts benzene to 3 parts water

NOTE: A nontechnical reference to a ratio or a proportion may be spelled out.

> a *fifty-fifty* chance of success   **OR**   a *50-50* chance of success

Scores and Voting Results

451   Use figures (even for 1 through 10) to express scores and voting results.

> a score of 85 on the test   a vote of 17 to 6
> New York 8, Chicago 6   **BUT:** a 17-6 vote

Numbers Referred to as Numbers

452   Always use figures to express numbers referred to as numbers.

> pick a number from 1 to 10   divide by 16
> the number 7 is considered lucky   multiply by $7/8$

Figures With Abbreviations and Symbols

453   a. Always use figures with abbreviations and symbols.

> $50   10:15 a.m.   43%   2 in   **OR**   2″   FY1995 (see ¶1616c)
> 65¢   6 p.m.   No. 631   I-95   200 km (see ¶537)

  b. If a symbol is used in a range of numbers, it should be repeated with each number. A full word or an abbreviation used in place of the symbol is given only with the last number.

> 20°–30°C   **BUT:** 20 to 30 degrees Celsius (see ¶537, note)
> 5½″ × 8″   5½ by 8 inches   **OR**   5½ × 8 in
> 9′ × 12′   9 by 12 feet   **OR**   9 × 12 ft
> 30%–40%   30 to 40 percent
> 50¢–60¢   50 to 60 cents
> $70–$80   seventy to eighty dollars

NOTE: A symbol should be used with each number in a series.

> discounts of 5%, 10%, and 15%   **BUT:** discounts of 5, 10, and 15 percent

Telephone Numbers

454   a. Insert a hyphen after the first three digits of a telephone number; for example, *284–1789.*

  b. When the area code precedes a phone number, use a hyphen or a diagonal (with no space on either side) between the two elements, or enclose the area code in parentheses (followed by one space).

> 707-555-3998   **OR**   707/555-3998   **OR**   (707) 555-3998

NOTE: When the area code and the telephone number as a unit have to be enclosed in parentheses, use either a hyphen or a diagonal after the area code.

You can always reach me by phone (517-555-6939) between 8:30 and 11:30 a.m.

OR: . . . by phone (517/555-6939) between 8:30 and 11:30 a.m.

BUT NOT: . . . by phone ((517) 555-6939) between 8:30 and 11:30 a.m.

c. When an access code precedes the area code and the phone number, it is customary to use a hyphen to connect all the elements.

Please use our toll-free, 24-hour phone number: 1-800-555-6400.

NOTE: International phone numbers typically contain a series of special access codes. Hyphens are used to connect all the elements.

011-64-9-555-1523

└ international access code from the United States
  └ country access code
    └ city access code

d. When providing a telephone extension along with the main number, use the following form: *555-4890, Ext. 6041.* (In formal correspondence, spell out *Extension.*)

No. or # With Figures

455 If the term *number* precedes a figure, express it as an abbreviation (singular: *No.;* plural: *Nos.*). At the beginning of a sentence, however, spell out *Number* to prevent misreading.

Our check covers the following invoices: *Nos.* 8592, 8653, and 8654.

Number 82175 has been assigned to your new policy. (**NOT:** No. 82175 . . .)

a. If an identifying noun precedes the figure (such as *Invoice, Check, Room, Box,* or the like), the abbreviation *No.* is usually unnecessary.

Our check covers *Invoices* 8592, 8653, and 8654.

EXCEPTIONS: License No. HLM 744; Social Security No. 169-35-8142; Patent No. 953,461

b. The symbol # may be used on business forms (such as invoices) and in technical matter.

For the capitalization of nouns preceding figures, see ¶359.

The following rules (¶¶456–470) deal with two technical aspects of style: treating numbers that are adjacent or in a sequence and expressing numbers in figures, words, or roman numerals.

Adjacent Numbers

456 When two numbers come together in a sentence and both are in figures or both are in words, separate them with a comma.

In *1991, 78* percent of our field representatives exceeded their sales goal.

Although the meeting was scheduled for *two, ten* of the participants did not show up until two-thirty.

On page *192, 25* problems are provided for review purposes.

On Account *53512, $125.40* is the balance outstanding.

On May *8, 18* customers called to complain about the "incomprehensible" assembly instructions.

(Continued on page 118.)

NOTE: No comma is necessary when one number is in figures and the other is in words.

On May *9 seven* customers called to complain.

457 When two numbers come together and one is part of a compound modifier (see ¶817), express one of the numbers in figures and the other in words. As a rule, spell the first number unless the second number would make a significantly shorter word.

| two 8-room houses | **BUT:** 500 four-page leaflets |
| sixty $5 bills | 150 five-dollar bills |

Numbers in a Sequence

458 Use commas to separate numbers that do not represent a continuous sequence.

| on pages 18, 20, and 28 | the years 1988, 1990, and 1992 |

459 a. A hyphen in typewritten or computer-generated material (or an en dash in printed material) may be used in place of the word *to* to link two figures that represent a continuous sequence. (Do not leave any space before or after the hyphen.)

| on pages 18–28 | in Articles I–III |
| during the week of May 15–21 | during the years 1985–1995 |

b. Do not use the hyphen (or dash) if the sequence is introduced by the word *from* or *between*.

| from 1993 to 1996 | between 1991 and 1994 |
| (**NOT:** from 1993–1996) | (**NOT:** between 1991–1994) |

460 a. In a continuous sequence of figures connected by a hyphen or a dash, the second figure may be expressed in abbreviated form. This style is used for sequences of page numbers or years when they occur quite frequently. (In isolated cases, do not abbreviate.)

| 1980–95 (**OR** 1980–1995) | pages 110–12 (**OR** pages 110–112) |
| 1901–2 (**OR** 1901–1902) | pages 101–2 (**OR** pages 101–102) |

b. Do not abbreviate the second number when the first number ends in two zeros.

| 1900–1995 | pages 100–101 |

c. Do not abbreviate the second number when it starts with different digits.

| 1890–1902 | pages 998–1004 |

d. Do not abbreviate the second number when it is under 100.

| 46–48 A.D. (see page 253) | pages 46–48 |

Expressing Numbers in Figures

461 a. When numbers run to five or more figures, use commas to separate thousands, hundreds of thousands, millions, etc., in *whole* numbers. Do not use commas in the decimal part of a number.

| 12,375 | 147,300 | $11,275,478 | 4,300,000,000 | **BUT:** 70,650.37248 |

NOTE: The comma is now commonly omitted in four-digit numbers unless these numbers occur together with larger numbers that require commas.

3500   OR   3,500 $2000   OR $2,000

b. In metric quantities, use a space (not a comma) to separate digits into groups of three. Separate whole numbers and decimal fractions, counting from the decimal point.

12 945 181 (**RATHER THAN:** 12,945,181)   0.594 31 (**RATHER THAN:** 0.59431)

NOTE: When a four-digit number is used as a metric quantity, do not leave a space unless the number is used in a column that has larger numbers.

5181   OR   5 181   0.3725   OR   0.372 5

462   Do not use commas in year numbers, page numbers, house or building numbers, room numbers, ZIP Code numbers, telephone numbers, heat units, and decimal parts of numbers.

1986	8760 Sunset Drive	New York, New York 10021	1500°C
page 1246	Room 1804	602-555-2174 (see ¶454)	13,664.9999

463   Serial numbers (for example, invoice, style, model, or lot numbers) are usually written without commas. However, some serial numbers are written with hyphens, spaces, or other devices. In all cases follow the style of the source.

Invoice 38162   **BUT:** Social Security No. 152-22-8285
Model G-43348   License No. SO14 785 053
Lot 75/23512   Patent No. 222,341

For the capitalization of nouns before numbers, see ¶359.
For the use of No., see ¶455.

464   To form the plurals of figures, add *s*.

in the 1990s   temperatures in the 80s

Expressing Numbers in Words

465   When expressing numbers in words, hyphenate all compound numbers between *21* and *99* (or *21st* and *99th*), whether they stand alone or are part of a number over 100.

twenty-one   twenty-one hundred
twenty-first   twenty-one hundredth

seven hundred and twenty-five (*and* may be omitted)

five thousand seven hundred and twenty-five (no commas)

Do not hyphenate other words in a spelled-out number over 100.

one hundred   nineteen hundred
two thousand   three hundred thousand
four million   six hundred million
twenty-three billion   fifty-eight trillion

For the capitalization of hyphenated numbers, see ¶363.

466   When there are two ways to express a number in words, choose the simpler form. For example, use the form *fifteen hundred* rather than *one thousand five hundred*. (The longer form is rarely used except in formal expressions of dates. See ¶411 for examples.)

467 To form the plurals of spelled-out numbers, add *s* or *es*. (For numbers ending in *y*, change the *y* to *i* before *es*.)

| ones | twos | threes | sixes | twenty-fives |
| thirds | sixths | eighths | twenties | thirty-seconds |

For spelled-out dates, see ¶411; for spelled-out amounts of money, see ¶¶413c, 414, 417, 418, 420; for spelled-out fractions, see ¶¶427–428.

Expressing Numbers in Roman Numerals

468 Roman numerals are used chiefly for the important divisions of literary and legislative material, for main topics in outlines, in dates on public buildings, and in proper names.

Chapter VI	Books IV and V	Roy Ward II
Part IX	World Wars I and II	King Edward VII
Volume III	MCMXCIII (1993)	Pope John XXIII

NOTE: Pages in the front section of a book or a formal report (such as the preface and table of contents) are usually numbered in small roman numerals: *iii, iv, v,* etc. Other pages are numbered in arabic numerals: *1, 2, 3,* etc.

469 To form roman numerals, consult the following table.

1	I	19	XIX	300	CCC	1800	MDCCC
2	II	20	XX	400	CD	1900	MCM
3	III	21	XXI	500	D	2000	MM
4	IV	24	XXIV	600	DC	3000	MMM
5	V	25	XXV	700	DCC	4000	$\overline{\text{MV}}$
6	VI	29	XXIX	800	DCCC	5000	$\overline{\text{V}}$
7	VII	30	XXX	900	CM	6000	$\overline{\text{V}}$M
8	VIII	40	XL	1000	M	7000	$\overline{\text{V}}$MM
9	IX	50	L	1100	MC	8000	$\overline{\text{V}}$MMM
10	X	60	LX	1200	MCC	9000	$\overline{\text{M}}$X
11	XI	70	LXX	1300	MCCC	10,000	$\overline{\text{X}}$
12	XII	80	LXXX	1400	MCD	50,000	$\overline{\text{L}}$
13	XIII	90	XC	1500	MD	100,000	$\overline{\text{C}}$
14	XIV	100	C	1600	MDC	500,000	$\overline{\text{D}}$
15	XV	200	CC	1700	MDCC	1,000,000	$\overline{\text{M}}$

NOTE: A dash appearing over any roman numeral indicates that the original value of the numeral is to be multiplied by 1000.

Expressing Thousands and Millions in Abbreviated Form

470 In technical and informal contexts and in material where space is tight (for example, newspaper headlines and classified advertisements), numbers in the thousands or millions may be expressed as follows:

	Roman Style		Metric Style	
38,000	38M		38K	(short for *kilo*, a metric prefix signifying thousands)
3,500,000	3.5$\overline{\text{M}}$	(rarely used)	3.5M	(short for *mega*, a metric prefix signifying millions)

Division of larger numbers at the end of a line: see ¶915.
House, street, and ZIP Code numbers: see ¶¶1332–1333, 1339, 1341c.

SECTION 5

Abbreviations

Basic Rules

When to Use Abbreviations

501 An abbreviation is a shortened form of a word or phrase used primarily to save space. Abbreviations occur most frequently in technical writing, statistical matter, tables, and notes.

502 In business writing, abbreviations are appropriate in "expedient" documents (such as business forms, catalogs, and routine memos and letters between business offices), where the emphasis is on communicating data in the briefest form. In other kinds of writing, where a more formal style is appropriate, use abbreviations sparingly. When in doubt, spell it out.

a. Some abbreviations are always acceptable, even in the most formal contexts: those that precede or follow personal names (such as *Mr., Ms., Mrs., Jr., Sr., Esq., Ph.D., S.J.*); those that are part of an organization's legal name (such as *Co., Inc., Ltd.*); those used in expressions of time (such as *a.m., p.m., CST, EDT*); and a few miscellaneous expressions (such as *A.D.* and *B.C.*).

b. Organizations with long names are now commonly identified by their initials in all but the most formal writing (for example, *YMCA, NAACP, IBM, SEC*).

c. Days of the week, names of the months, geographic names, and units of measure should be abbreviated only on business forms, in "expedient" correspondence, and in tables, lists, and narrow columns of text (for example, in a newsletter or brochure) where space is tight.

d. When an abbreviation is only one or two keystrokes shorter than the full word (for example, *Pt.* for *Part*), do not bother to abbreviate except to achieve consistency in a context where similar terms are being abbreviated.

503 Consult a dictionary or an authoritative reference work for the acceptable forms of abbreviations. When a term may be abbreviated in several ways, choose the form that is shortest without sacrifice of clarity.

continued:	Use *cont.* rather than *contd.*
2 pounds:	Use *2 lb* rather than *2 lbs* (see ¶621).
Enclosures 2:	Use *Enc. 2* rather than *Encs. 2* or *Encl. 2.*
second, third:	Use *2d, 3d* rather than *2nd, 3rd* (see also ¶425, note).

NOTE: *Webster's Ninth New Collegiate Dictionary* (published by Merriam-Webster), the basic authority for all spelling in this manual, shows virtually every abbreviation without any periods, even though in actual practice many abbreviations are still written with periods.* Thus, for example, unless your Latin is very good, you may not realize that in the expression *et al.,* the word *et* is a full word (meaning "and") and requires no period, whereas *al.* is short for *alii* (meaning "others") and does require a period. Under these circumstances, for specific abbreviations not shown in this manual, you will need to consult another up-to-date dictionary.

---

*It is interesting to note that Merriam-Webster itself uses periods with certain abbreviations (for example, *masc., fem., neut., fr., prob., lit.,* and *ca.*) when they occur functionally within the main text of the dictionary, even though these same abbreviations are given *without* periods in the section on abbreviations at the back of the dictionary.

The forms shown here reflect the spellings found in Merriam-Webster, but the punctuation is based on observations of actual practice and is consistent with the style recommended by other authorities.

504 Be consistent within the same material: do not abbreviate a term in some sentences and spell it out in other sentences. Moreover, having selected one form of an abbreviation (say, *c.o.d.*), do not use a different style *(COD)* elsewhere in the same material.

NOTE: When using an abbreviation that may not be familiar to the reader, spell out the full term along with the abbreviation when it is first used.

> At the end of *fiscal year (FY)* 1991, we showed a profit of $1.2 million; at the end of FY1992, however, we showed a loss of $1.8 million.

505 a. Given a choice between an abbreviation and a contraction, choose the abbreviation. It not only looks better but is easier to read.

> cont. (**RATHER THAN:** cont'd) govt. (**RATHER THAN:** gov't)
> dept. (**RATHER THAN:** dep't) mfg. (**RATHER THAN:** m'f'g)

b. When a word or phrase is shortened by contraction, an apostrophe is inserted at the exact point where letters are omitted and no period follows the contraction except at the end of a sentence.

> let's doesn't
> ma'am o'clock
> rock 'n' roll sou'wester
> ne'er-do-well fo'c'sle

NOTE: Respect a company's preference when it uses a contraction in its corporate name or in the name of a product.

> Wash 'n Dri Chock Full o'Nuts
> Sweet 'n Low Land O Lakes
> Shake 'n Bake Ken-L Ration
> Light n' Lively La-Z-Boy

c. As a rule, contractions are used only in informal writing or in tabular matter where space is limited. However, contractions of verb phrases (such as *can't* for *cannot*) are commonly used in business letters where the writer is striving for an easy, colloquial tone. In formal writing, contractions are not used (except for *o'clock*, which is considered a more formal way to express time than *a.m.* or *p.m.*).

d. Be sure to distinguish certain contractions from possessive pronouns that sound the same but do not use an apostrophe.

> Ron has been pushing the Kirschner proposal for all *it's* worth. (In other words, for all *it is* worth.)

> Let's get an outside consultant to analyze the Kirschner proposal and assess *its* worth. (Here *its* is a possessive pronoun and should not be spelled with an apostrophe.)

See ¶1056e for further examples and a test on how to determine the correct form.

e. Note that certain contractions can have more than one meaning.

> What's her name? (What *is* her name?)
> What's he do for a living? (What *does* he do for a living?)
> What's been happening? (What *has* been happening?)
> When's the last time you saw her? (When *was* the last time you saw her?)
> Let's find out. (Let *us* find out.)

Punctuation and Spacing
With Abbreviations

506 The abbreviation of a single word requires a period at the end.

Mrs.	Jr.	Corp.	pp.	Wed.
misc.	Esq.	Inc.	Nos.	Oct.

NOTE: Units of measurement are now commonly written without periods. (See ¶¶535a, 538a.)

507 Almost all small-letter abbreviations made up of single initials require a period after each initial but no space after each internal period.

a.m.	i.e.	f.o.b.	**BUT:** rpm	mpg
p.m.	e.g.	e.o.m.	ips	mph

For the omission of periods with abbreviations of units of measure, see ¶535a. For the definition of business abbreviations like f.o.b. and e.o.m., see ¶541.

508 All-capital abbreviations made up of single initials normally require no periods and no internal space.

IBM	AMA	AICPA	IRS	TLC
MIT	UAW	NFL	UN	PSAT

EXCEPTIONS: Retain the periods in abbreviations of geographic names (such as *U.S.A.*), academic degrees (such as *B.A., M.S.*), and a few miscellaneous expressions (such as *A.D., B.C., P.O.,* and *V.P.*).

509 If an abbreviation stands for two or more words and consists of more than single initials, insert a period and a space after each element in the abbreviation.

N. Mex.	Lt. Col.	Rt. Rev.	loc. cit.	nol. pros.

EXCEPTIONS: Academic abbreviations, such as *Ph.D., Ed.D., LL.B.,* and *Litt.D.,* are written with periods but no spaces. Units of measurement such as *sq ft* and *cu cm* are written with spaces but no periods.

510 A number of shortened forms of words are not abbreviations and should not be followed by a period. (See also ¶524, note.)

ad	demo	limo	prep	specs
auto	exam	logo	promo	sync
caps	expo	math	rep	temp
comp	fax	memo	repro	trig
condo	hi-fi	perks	req	typo
co-op	info	phone	sci-fi	before the 2d
deli	lab	photo	stereo	after the 5th

A number of the sales *reps* have sent a *fax,* asking for some *info* on this year's incentive *comp* plans.

When you check the *repros* for *typos,* please watch out for the problems we had with *caps* in our last *promo* piece, and make sure our *logo* is not left off this time.

Also check everything against the original *specs,* and tell me what the total *prep* costs amount to.

511 *One space* should follow an abbreviation within a sentence unless another mark of punctuation follows immediately.

You ought to talk to your CPA about that problem.

Dr. Wilkins works in Washington, D.C., but his home is in Bethesda.

Please call tomorrow afternoon (before 5:30 p.m.).

When Jonas asked, "When do you expect to finish your Ph.D.?" Fred looked embarrassed. (See ¶261c regarding the omission of a comma after an introductory dependent clause.)

I'm waiting for some word on Harrison, Inc.'s stock repurchase plan. (See ¶¶638–639 for possessive forms of abbreviations.)

512 *Two spaces* should follow an abbreviation at the end of a sentence that makes a statement. If the abbreviation ends with a period, that period also serves to mark the end of the sentence. If the abbreviation ends without a period, insert one to mark the end of the sentence and then leave two spaces.

Helen has just returned from a trip to Washington, D.C.   Next year . . .

We're flying over on Air France and coming back on KLM.   If you . . .

513 *No space* should follow an abbreviation at the end of a question or an exclamation. The question mark or the exclamation point should come directly after the abbreviation.

Did you see Jack Hainey being interviewed last night on CBS?

Because of bad weather our flight didn't get in until 4 a.m.!

Capitalization

514 Most abbreviations use the same capitalization as the full words for which they stand.

| Mon. | Monday | a.m. | ante meridiem |
| Btu | British thermal unit | D.C. | District of Columbia |

EXCEPTIONS: CST   Central standard time   A.D.   anno Domini

For abbreviations with two forms (for example, COD or c.o.d.), see ¶542.

The following rules (¶¶515–549) offer guidance on how to treat specific types of abbreviations.

Special Rules

Personal Names and Initials

515 Use periods with abbreviations of first or middle names but not with nicknames.

Thos.	Jos.	Robt.	Benj.
Tom	Joe	Bob	Ben
Jas.	Wm.	Saml.	Edw.
Jim	Bill	Sam	Ed

NOTE: Do not abbreviate first and middle names unless (1) you are preparing a list or table where space is tight or (2) a person uses such abbreviations in his or her legal name. (See also ¶1321a, note.)

516 a. Each initial in a person's name should be followed by a period and one space.

John T. Noonan   Mr. L. Bradford Anders
J. T. Noonan & Co.   L. B. Anders Inc. (see also ¶159)

(Continued on page 126.)

NOTE: Respect the preference of the individual or of the company that uses a person's initials in its corporate name.

Harry S Truman   BFGoodrich
L.L. Bean, Inc.   JCPenney

b. When personal initials stand alone, type them preferably without periods or space. If periods are used, omit the internal space.

JTN   OR   J.T.N.

c. For names with prefixes, initials are formed as follows:

JDM (for John D. MacDonald)   FGO (for Frances G. O'Brien)

NOTE: If you know that an individual prefers some other form (for example, *FGO'B* rather than *FGO*), respect that preference.

d. Do not use a period when the initial is only a letter used in place of a real name. (See also ¶109a.)

I have selected three case studies involving a Ms. A, a Mr. B, and a Miss C. (Here the letters are used in place of real names, but they are not abbreviations of those names.)

BUT: Call Mrs. *G.* when you get a chance. (Here *G.* is an initial representing an actual name like *Galanos.*)

e. The abbreviation *NMI* is sometimes used on forms and applications to indicate that an individual has <u>no</u> <u>m</u>iddle <u>i</u>nitial.

Abbreviations With Personal Names

517   a. Always abbreviate the following titles when they are used with personal names:

SINGULAR: { Mrs. (for Mistress)   Ms.   Mr.   Dr.
            { Mme. (for Madame)

PLURAL: Mmes.   OR   Mesdames   Mses.   OR   Mss.   Messrs.   Drs.

Mr. and *Mrs.* Pollo both speak highly of *Dr.* Fry.

Ms. Harriet Porter will serve as a consultant to the Finance Committee.

NOTE: The abbreviation *Ms.* is used (1) when a woman has indicated that she prefers this title, (2) when a woman's marital status is unknown, or (3) when a woman's marital status is considered not relevant to the situation. Always respect the individual woman's preference. If her preference is unknown, use the title *Ms.* or omit the title altogether. (See also ¶¶618, 1322b, 1366a.)

For the proper use of the singular and plural forms of these titles, see ¶¶618–619; for the use of Dr. *with degrees, see ¶519c.*

b. The titles *Miss* and *Misses* are not abbreviations and should not be followed by periods.

c. In general, spell out all other titles used with personal names.

Vice President Howard Morse   Professor Harriman
Mayor Wilma Washington   Father Hennelly
Governor Warren R. Fishback   Dean Castaneda

d. Long military, religious, and honorable titles are spelled out in formal situations but may be abbreviated in informal situations as long as the surname is accompanied by a first name or initials.

Formal	**Informal**
Brigadier General Percy J. Cobb	Brig. Gen. P. J. Cobb
Lieutenant Governor Nancy Pulaski	Lt. Gov. Nancy Pulaski

(**BUT NOT:** Brig. Gen. Cobb, Lt. Gov. Pulaski)

NOTE: Do not abbreviate *Reverend* or *Honorable* when these words are preceded by *the*.

Formal	**Informal**
the Reverend William R. Bullock	Rev. W. R. Bullock
the Honorable Sarah T. McCormack	Hon. Sarah T. McCormack

For the treatment of titles in addresses, see ¶¶1322–1323; for the treatment of titles in salutations, see ¶¶1347–1350.

518   **a.** Always abbreviate *Jr.*, *Sr.*, and *Esq.* when these terms follow personal names.

b. The forms *Jr.* and *Sr.* should be used only with a full name or initials but not with a surname alone. A title like *Mr.* or *Dr.* may precede the name.

Mr. Henry J. Boardman *Jr.*

OR: Mr. H. J. Boardman *Jr.*

(**BUT NOT:** Mr. Boardman Jr.)

For the use or omission of commas with Jr. *and* Sr.*, see ¶156.*

c. The form *Esq.* should also be used only with a full name or initials, but no title should precede the name.

George W. LaBarr, *Esq.*

NOT: Mr. George W. LaBarr, Esq.

NOTE: In the United States the form *Esq.* is used primarily by lawyers. Although by derivation the title applies strictly to males, it is now common practice for women who are lawyers to use the title as a professional designation.

d. The terms *2d* or *II* and *3d* or *III* following personal names are not abbreviations and should not be used with periods.

e. When the word *Saint* is part of a person's name, follow that person's preference for abbreviating or spelling out the word.

Yves Saint-Laurent	Ruth St. Denis
Camille Saint-Saëns	St. John Perse

NOTE: When used with the name of a person revered as holy, the word *Saint* is usually spelled out, but it may be abbreviated in informal contexts and in lists and tables where space is tight.

Saint Martin	Saint Thérèse
Saint Francis	Saint Catherine

For the treatment of Saint *in place names, see ¶529b.*

Academic Degrees, Religious Orders, and Professional Designations

519 **a.** Abbreviations of academic degrees and religious orders require a period after each element in the abbreviation but no internal space.

B.S.	LL.B.	B.Ch.E.	M.D.	S.J.
M.B.A.	Litt.D.	B.Arch.	D.D.S.	O.S.B.
Ph.D.	Ed.D.	M.Div.	R.N.	S.N.D.

NOTE: The term *ABD* (without periods) is often used to identify a graduate student who has completed all the requirements for a doctorate except the dissertation. (The initials stand for *all but dissertation.*)

So far we have received résumés from two *Ph.D.s* and seven *ABDs*. (See ¶623 for guidelines on forming the plurals of these abbreviations.)

b. The term *M.B.A.* is now commonly written without periods when it is used to signify an executive with a certain type of training rather than the degree itself.

We have just hired two Stanford *MBAs* and one from Harvard.

BUT: After I get my *M.B.A.*, I plan to go on to law school.

c. When academic degrees follow a person's name, do not use such titles as *Dr., Mr., Ms., Miss,* or *Mrs.* before the name.

Dr. Helen Garcia   **OR**   Helen Garcia, M.D.

(**BUT NOT:** Dr. Helen Garcia, M.D.)

However, other titles may precede the name as long as they do not convey the same meaning as the degree that follows.

Professor Rex Ford, Ph.D.	the Reverend John Day, D.D.
President Jean Dill, L.H.D.	**OR:** the Reverend Dr. John Day
Dean May Ito, J.S.D.	(**BUT NOT:** the Reverend Dr. John Day, D.D.)

See also ¶¶1324c, 1324d, 1364a.

d. Academic degrees standing alone may be abbreviated except in very formal writing.

I am now completing my *Ph.D.* thesis.

She received her *M.A.* degree last year.
OR . . . her *master of arts* degree last year. (See also ¶353.)

e. Professional designations such as *CPA* (certified public accountant), *CPS* (certified professional secretary), *CFP* (certified financial planner), *CLU* (chartered life underwriter), and *FACS* (fellow of the American College of Surgeons) are commonly written *without* periods when they are used alone but *with* periods when they are used with academic degrees.

Anthony Filippo, CPA	**BUT:** Anthony Filippo, B.S., M.B.A., *C.P.A.*
Ruth L. Morris, CLU	Ruth L. Morris, B.A., *C.L.U.*

Names of Organizations

520 Names of well-known business organizations, labor unions, societies, associations (trade, professional, charitable, and fraternal), and government agencies are often abbreviated except in the most formal writing. When these abbreviations consist of all-capital initials, they are typed without periods or spaces.

AT&T	American Telephone & Telegraph Co.
AFL-CIO	American Federation of Labor and Congress of Industrial Organizations
ILGWU	International Ladies' Garment Workers' Union
ASCAP	American Society of Composers, Authors, and Publishers
NAACP	National Association for the Advancement of Colored People
NYSE	New York Stock Exchange
AMEX	American Stock Exchange (see ¶522b for *AmEx*)
NAM	National Association of Manufacturers
NIMH	National Institute of Mental Health
YMCA	Young Men's Christian Association
IOOF	Independent Order of Odd Fellows
IRS	Internal Revenue Service
SEC	Securities and Exchange Commission
SBA	Small Business Administration

521 The following terms are often abbreviated in the names of business organizations. However, follow the individual company's preference for abbreviating or spelling out.

Mfg.	Manufacturing	Co.	Company
Mfrs.	Manufacturers	Corp.	Corporation
Bro.	Brother	Inc.	Incorporated
Bros.	Brothers	Ltd.	Limited

Acronyms

522 a. An acronym—for example, *NOW*—is a shortened form derived from the initial letters of the words that make up the complete form. Thus *NOW* is derived from *National Organization for Women*. Like all-capital abbreviations such as *IBM* and *NAM*, acronyms are usually written in all capitals and without periods; however, unlike those abbreviations, which are pronounced letter by letter, acronyms are pronounced like words. Because they have been deliberately coined to replace the longer expressions they represent, acronyms are appropriate for use on all occasions.

CARE	Cooperative for American Relief to Everywhere
OPEC	Organization of Petroleum Exporting Countries
PERT	program evaluation and review technique
ZIP (Code)	Zone Improvement Plan
PIN	personal identification number
VISTA	Volunteers in Service to America
ACTION	American Council to Improve Our Neighborhoods
SADD	Students Against Drunk Driving
GAG	Graphic Artists Guild
NASDAQ	National Association of Security Dealers Automated Quotations
OSHA	Occupational Safety and Health Administration
ESOP	employee stock ownership plan
EPCOT	Experimental Prototype Community of Tomorrow
STEP	School to Employment Program
FONZ	Friends of the National Zoo
HOPE	Help Obese People Everywhere
MEGO	my eyes glaze over

NOTE: In a few cases acronyms derived from initial letters are written entirely in small letters without periods.

scuba	self-contained underwater breathing apparatus
laser	light amplification by stimulated emission of radiation

(Continued on page 130.)

b. Some coined names use more than the first letters of the words they represent. Such names are usually written with only the first letter capitalized.

Nabisco	National Biscuit Company
Delmarva	an East Coast peninsula made up of Delaware and parts of Maryland and Virginia
radar	radio detecting and ranging
sonar	sound navigation ranging
modem	modulator and demodulator
canola (oil)	Canada, oil low acid
op ed page	the page that is opposite the editorial page
BUT: AmEx	American Express
FedEx	Federal Express
INTELPOST	International Electronic Postal Service

c. In a few cases all-capital abbreviations such as *MC* (for *master of ceremonies*) or *DJ* (for *disc jockey*) may also be spelled out in an uncapitalized form (*emcee* and *deejay*). The spelled-out forms are preferable when such abbreviations are used as verbs.

Fran Zangwill *emceed* (RATHER THAN: MC'd) the fund-raiser kickoff dinner.

Who has been *okaying* (RATHER THAN: OK'ing) these bills? (See ¶548.)

Names of Broadcasting Stations and Systems

523 The names of radio and television broadcasting stations and the abbreviated names of broadcasting systems are written in capitals without periods and without spaces.

Portsmouth:	WRAP-AM	San Antonio:	KISS-FM
Houston:	KILT-FM	Pittsburgh:	WEEP-AM

According to *ABC* and *CBS* news reports, the earthquake registered 6.8 on the Richter scale.

Names of Government and International Agencies

524 The names of well-known government and international agencies are often abbreviated. They are written without periods or spaces.

FNMA	the Federal National Mortgage Association (often referred to as "Fannie Mae," the result of trying to sound out the initials *FNMA*)
HUD	the Department of Housing and Urban Development
GAO	the General Accounting Office
EEOC	the Equal Employment Opportunity Commission
SBA	the Small Business Administration
WHO	the World Health Organization

NOTE: Expressions such as *the Fed* (for the Federal Reserve Board) and *the Ex-Im Bank* (for the U.S. Export-Import Bank) involve shortened forms rather than true abbreviations and thus are written without periods.

525 The name *United States* is usually abbreviated when it is part of the name of a government agency. When used as an adjective, the name is often abbreviated, though not in formal usage. When used as a noun, the name is spelled out.

U.S. Employment Service	**OR**	USES
U.S. Department of Agriculture		USDA
U.S. Air Force		USAF
the United States government		the U.S. government
United States foreign policy		U.S. foreign policy

throughout the United States (**NOT:** throughout the U.S.)

Geographic Names

526 Do not abbreviate geographic names except in tables, business forms, and "expedient" correspondence (see ¶502). **EXCEPTION:** Because of its great length, the name *Union of Soviet Socialist Republics* is often replaced by the abbreviation *U.S.S.R.*

NOTE: In informal writing, the city of Washington may be referred to as *D.C.* and Los Angeles as *L.A.* In general, however, these city names should be spelled in full.

INFORMAL CONTEXT: Did you know that Liz has been transferred from the *D.C.* office to the branch in *L.A.?*

OTHER CONTEXTS: Did you know that Liz has been transferred from the *Washington, D.C.,* office to the branch in *Los Angeles?*

527 **a.** When abbreviating state names *in addresses,* use the two-letter abbreviations (without periods) shown in ¶1341 and on the inside back cover.

b. *In all situations other than addresses,* use the following abbreviations (with periods and spacing as shown).

Alabama	Ala.		Missouri	Mo.
Alaska	—		Montana	Mont.
Arizona	Ariz.		Nebraska	Nebr.
Arkansas	Ark.		Nevada	Nev.
California	Calif.		New Hampshire	N.H.
Canal Zone	C.Z.		New Jersey	N.J.
Colorado	Colo.		New Mexico	N. Mex.
Connecticut	Conn.		New York	N.Y.
Delaware	Del.		North Carolina	N.C.
District of Columbia	D.C.		North Dakota	N. Dak.
Florida	Fla.		Ohio	—
Georgia	Ga.		Oklahoma	Okla.
Guam	—		Oregon	Oreg.
Hawaii	—		Pennsylvania	Pa.
Idaho	—		Puerto Rico	P.R.
Illinois	Ill.		Rhode Island	R.I.
Indiana	Ind.		South Carolina	S.C.
Iowa	—		South Dakota	S. Dak.
Kansas	Kans.		Tennessee	Tenn.
Kentucky	Ky.		Texas	Tex.
Louisiana	La.		Utah	—
Maine	—		Vermont	Vt.
Maryland	Md.		Virgin Islands	V.I.
Massachusetts	Mass.		Virginia	Va.
Michigan	Mich.		Washington	Wash.
Minnesota	Minn.		West Virginia	W. Va.
Mississippi	Miss.		Wisconsin	Wis.
			Wyoming	Wyo.

NOTE: Alaska, Guam, Hawaii, Idaho, Iowa, Maine, Ohio, and Utah are not abbreviated.

528 **a.** Geographic abbreviations made up of single initials require a period after each initial but *no* space after each internal period.

U.K.   United Kingdom   N.A.   North America

NOTE: When a company uses a geographical abbreviation in its corporate name or in the name of a product, respect the company's style.

U.S.A.   BUT: *USA Today*   U.S.   BUT: U S WEST Communications

b. If the geographic abbreviation contains more than single initials, space once after each internal period.

N. Mex.   N. Dak.   W. Va.   W. Aust.

529 **a.** In place names, do not abbreviate *Fort, Mount, Point,* or *Port* except in tables and lists where space is tight.

Fort Wayne	Mount Pleasant	Point Pleasant	Port Arthur
Fort Myers	Mount Rainier	Point Pelee	Port Ludlow

b. In U.S. place names, abbreviate *Saint.* For other place names involving *Saint,* follow the style shown in an authoritative dictionary or atlas.

St. Louis, Missouri   St. Lawrence River
St. Petersburg, Florida   St. Charles Avenue

For the abbreviation or the spelling out of names of streets, cities, states, and countries, see also ¶¶1334–1337, 1340–1341, 1343.

Compass Points

530 **a.** Spell out compass points used as ordinary nouns and adjectives.

The company has large landholdings in the *Southwest.*

We purchased a lot at the *southwest* corner of Green and Union Streets.

For the capitalization of compass points, see ¶¶338–341.

b. Spell out compass points included in street names except in lists and tables where space is tight. (See also ¶1334.)

143 South Mountain Avenue   1232 East Franklin Street

531 **a.** Abbreviate compass points without periods when they are used *following* a street name to indicate the section of the city. (See also ¶1335.)

1330 South Bay Boulevard, SW

NOTE: In some communities the predominant style is to use periods in such abbreviations; for example, *S.W., N.E.* (See ¶1335.)

b. In technical material (especially pertaining to real estate and legal or nautical matters), abbreviate compass points without periods.

N   north   NE   northeast   NNE   north-northeast

Days and Months

532 Do not abbreviate names of days of the week and months of the year except in tables or lists where space is limited. In such cases the following abbreviations may be used:

Sun.	Thurs., Thu.	Jan.	May	Sept., Sep.
Mon.	Fri.	Feb.	June, Jun.	Oct.
Tues., Tue.	Sat.	Mar.	July, Jul.	Nov.
Wed.		Apr.	Aug.	Dec.

NOTE: When space is extremely tight, the following one- and two-letter abbreviations may be used.

| Su | M | Tu | W | Th | F | Sa | | Ja | Mr | My | Jl | S | N |
| F | Ap | Je | Au | O | D |

Time and Time Zones

533 Use the abbreviations *a.m.* and *p.m.* in expressions of time (see ¶440). Small letters are preferred for these abbreviations. For more formal expressions of time, use *o'clock* (see ¶441).

534 a. The standard time zones in the continental United States are abbreviated as follows:

EST (Eastern standard time) MST (Mountain standard time)
CST (Central standard time) PST (Pacific standard time)

See ¶440a for examples.

NOTE: When daylight saving time is in effect, use DST (daylight saving time) or one of the following forms:

EDT (Eastern daylight time) MDT (Mountain daylight time)
CDT (Central daylight time) PDT (Pacific daylight time)

b. Puerto Rico and the U.S. Virgin Islands are in the Atlantic standard time zone (AST). Hawaii is in the Hawaii-Aleutian time zone (abbreviated simply as HST with reference to Hawaii). Alaska falls in the Alaska time zone (which is commonly abbreviated as YST, referring to an earlier designation, the Yukon time zone). Within these areas only Alaska observes daylight saving time (YDT).

Customary Measurements

535 Abbreviate units of measure when they occur frequently, as in technical and scientific work, on invoices and other business forms, and in tables.

a. Units of measure are now commonly abbreviated without periods. The abbreviations are the same for the singular and the plural.

yd (yard, yards)   oz (ounce, ounces)   rpm (revolutions per minute)
ft (foot, feet)   gal (gallon, gallons) mpg (miles per gallon)
mi (mile, miles)   lb (pound, pounds)   mph (miles per hour)

NOTE: Even the abbreviation *in* (for inch or inches) may be written without a period so long as it is not likely to be confused with the preposition *in*.

8 in OR 8 in.   BUT: 8 sq in   8 ft 2 in

b. In a set of simple dimensions or a range of numbers, use an abbreviation only with the last number. Repeat a symbol with each number.

a room 10 × 15 ft   35° to 45°F
BUT: a room 10′ × 15′   OR: 35°–45°F

NOTE: In a set of complex dimensions, where more than one unit of measure is involved, repeat the abbreviations with each number.

a room 10 ft 6 in × 19 ft 10 in OR a room 10′ 6″ × 19′ 10″ (see ¶432)

536 In nontechnical writing, spell out units of measure.

a 20-gallon container   8½ by 11 inches
a 150-acre estate   an 8½- by 11-inch book (see ¶817)

Metric Measurements

The following rules of style are based on the *Metric Editorial Guide,* published by the American National Metric Council (Washington, D.C.). For a full listing of metric terms, consult a dictionary.

537 The most common metric measurements are derived from three basic units and several prefixes indicating multiples or fractions of a unit, as shown below. The abbreviations for these terms appear in parentheses in the first column below.

Basic Units

meter (m)	One meter is 10 percent longer than a yard (39.37 inches).
gram (g)	A thousand grams (a *kilogram*) is 10 percent heavier than 2 pounds (2.2 pounds).
liter (L)	A liter is about 5 percent bigger than a quart (1.057 quarts).

Prefixes Indicating Fractions

deci (d)	1/10	A *decimeter* (dm) equals 1/10 meter.
centi (c)	1/100	A *centigram* (cg) equals 1/100 gram.
milli (m)	1/1000	A *milliliter* (mL) equals 1/1000 liter.

Prefixes Indicating Multiples

deka (da)	10	A *dekameter* (dam) equals 10 meters (about 11 yards).
hecto (h)	100	A *hectogram* (hg) equals 100 grams (about 3½ ounces).
kilo (k)	1000	A *kilometer* (km) equals 1000 meters (about 5/8 mile).

NOTE: Temperatures are expressed in terms of the Celsius scale (abbreviated *C*).

Water freezes at 0°C (32°F) and boils at 100°C (212°F).

With a temperature of 37°C (98.6°F), you can't be very sick.

The temperature here on the island stays between 20° and 30°C (68° and 86°F).

For the use of spaces in figures expressing metric quantities, see ¶461b.

538 Metric units of measurement, like the customary units of measurement described in ¶535, are abbreviated in technical and scientific work, on business forms, and in tables. In nontechnical writing, metric units are ordinarily spelled out, but some expressions typically appear in abbreviated form (for example, *35-mm film*).

a. Abbreviations of metric units of measurement are written without periods except at the end of a sentence.

100-mm cigarettes (10 centimeters or about 4 inches)
a 30-cm width (about 12 inches or 1 foot)
an office 5 × 3 m (about 5.5 yards by 3.3 yards)
a 1000-km trip (620 miles)
weighs 100 kg (about 220 pounds)
50 to 75 kg (about 110 to 165 pounds)
feels like 10°C weather (50°F weather)

NOTE: In abbreviations of expressions like *kilometers per hour,* a diagonal is used to express *per.*

an 80 km/h speed limit (50 miles per hour)

b. Metric abbreviations are the same for the singular and the plural.

1 kg (1 kilogram)   5 kg (5 kilograms)

c. When expressing temperatures, leave no space between the number and the degree symbol or between the degree symbol and the abbreviation for Celsius.

14°C   (NOT: 14° C)

d. In printed material, metric measurements for area and volume are usually expressed with raised numbers.

m^2 square meter cm^3 cubic centimeter

If the equipment you are using makes it difficult or awkward to create raised numbers, use the following forms:

sq m   square meter   cu cm   cubic centimeter

NOTE: In material that uses raised numbers for footnote references, use the forms *sq m* and *cu cm* to avoid the possibility of confusion.

Chemical and Mathematical Expressions

539   Do not use a period after the symbols that represent chemical elements and formulas.

K (potassium)   NaCl (sodium chloride—table salt)

The chemical notations H_2O and CO_2 stand for "dihydrogen oxide" (namely, water) and "carbon dioxide." They do not refer, as one student observed, to hot water and cold water.

540   Do not use a period after such mathematical abbreviations as *log* (for *logarithm*) and *tan* (for *tangent*).

Business Expressions

541   A number of terms are commonly abbreviated on business forms, in tables, and in routine business correspondence. (See also ¶¶544–546.)

acct.	account	B/S OR	bill of sale
ack.	acknowledge	BS	
addl.	additional	B-school	graduate school of
agt.	agent		business
AI	artificial intelligence	bu	bushel(s)
a.k.a.	also known as	C	100; Celsius
amt.	amount		(temperature)
anon.	anonymous	CDC	community development
AP	accounts payable		corporation
approx.	approximately	CEO	chief executive officer
AR	accounts receivable	CFO	chief financial officer
ASAP	as soon as possible	cg	centigram(s)
Assn.	Association	chg.	charge
assoc.	associate(s)	c.i.f. OR	cost, insurance, and
asst.	assistant	CIF	freight (see ¶542)
att.	attachment	CIO	chief information officer
Attn.	Attention	cm	centimeter(s)
avg.	average	Co.	Company
bal.	balance	c/o	care of
bbl	barrel(s)	c.o.d. OR	cash (or collect) on
bl	bale(s)	COD	delivery (see ¶542)
B/L OR	bill of lading	COLA	cost-of-living adjustment
BL		cont.	continued
bldg.	building	COO	chief operating officer

(Continued on page 136.)

Corp.	Corporation	HQ	headquarters
CPA	certified public	hr	hour(s)
	accountant	in OR in.	inch(es)
	(see ¶519e)		(see ¶535a, note)
CPI	consumer price index	Inc.	Incorporated
cr.	credit	incl.	including, inclusive
ctn.	carton	ins.	insurance
cwt.	hundredweight	intl.	international
d.b.a. OR	doing business as	inv.	invoice
DBA	(see ¶542)	ips	inches per second
dept.	department	kg	kilogram(s)
dis.	discount	km	kilometer(s)
dist.	district	km/h	kilometers per hour
distr.	distributor, distribution,	L	liter(s) (see ¶537)
	distributed	l., ll.	line, lines
div.	division	lb	pound(s)
DJIA	Dow Jones industrial	LBO	leveraged buyout
	average	l.c.l. OR	less-than-carload lot
doz.	dozen	LCL	(see ¶542)
dr.	debit	LIFO	last in, first out
dstn.	destination	Ltd.	Limited
dtd.	dated	m	meter(s) (see ¶537)
ea.	each	M	1000
EEO	equal employment	M&A	mergers and acquisitions
	opportunity	max.	maximum
enc.	enclosed, enclosure	mdse.	merchandise
e.o.m. OR	end of month	mfg.	manufacturing
EOM	(see ¶542)	mfr.	manufacturer
Esq.	Esquire	mg	milligram(s)
ETA	estimated time of arrival	mgr.	manager
ETD	estimated time of	mgt. OR	management
	departure	mgmt.	
exec.	executive	min	minute(s)
F	Fahrenheit	min.	minimum
	(temperature)	misc.	miscellaneous
f.a.s. OR	free alongside ship	mL	milliliter(s)
FAS	(see ¶542)	mm	millimeter(s)
f.b.o. OR	for the benefit of	mo	month(s)
FBO	(see ¶542)	MO	mail order, money order
FIFO	first in, first out	mpg	miles per gallon
f.o.b. OR	free on board	mph	miles per hour
FOB	(see ¶542)	mtg.	mortgage
ft	foot, feet	n/30	net in 30 days
ft-tn	foot-ton(s)	NA	not applicable,
fwd.	forward		not available
FY	fiscal year (see ¶504)	NCR	no carbon required
FYI	for your information	n.d.	no date
g	gram(s) (see ¶537)	No., Nos.	number(s) (see ¶455)
GAAP	generally accepted	nt. wt.	net weight
	accounting	NV	no value
	principles	OAG	*Official Airline Guide*
gal	gallon(s)	opt.	optional
GM	general manager	OS	out of stock
gr.	gross	OTC	over the counter
gr. wt.	gross weight	oz	ounce(s)
hdlg.	handling	p., pp.	page, pages
HMO	health maintenance	P&H	postage and handling
	organization	P&L OR	profit and
HP OR hp	horsepower	P/L	loss (statement)

PC	personal computer, politically correct		ROE	return on equity
			ROI	return on investment
P.C.	professional corporation		rpm	revolutions per minute
pd.	paid		/S/	signed (before a copied signature)
P.E.	professional engineer			
PERT	program evaluation and review technique		S&H	shipping and handling
			SASE	self-addressed, stamped envelope
pkg.	package(s)			
PO	purchase order		sec	second(s)
P.O.	post office		sec.	secretary
p.o.e. OR POE	port of entry (see ¶542)		shtg.	shortage
			SO	shipping order
PP	parcel post		std.	standard
ppd.	postpaid, prepaid (postage paid in advance)		stge.	storage
			stmt.	statement
pr.	pair(s)		treas.	treasury, treasurer
PS, PS.	postscript		UPC	Universal Product Code
pt	pint(s)			
pt.	part, point(s), port		VAT	value-added tax
qr	quire(s)		V.P.	vice president
qt	quart(s)		vs.	versus (v. in legal citations)
qtr.	quarter(ly)			
qty.	quantity		w/	with
recd.	received		whsle.	wholesale
reg.	registered, regular		w/o	without, week of
ret.	retired		wt.	weight
rev.	revised		yd	yard(s)
rm	ream(s)		yr	year(s)
ROA	return on assets		YTD	year to date

542 A few common business abbreviations listed in ¶541 are frequently typed in small letters (with periods) when they occur within sentences but are typed in all-capital letters (without periods) when they appear on business forms.

c.i.f.	OR	CIF		f.o.b.	OR	FOB
c.o.d.	OR	COD		l.c.l.	OR	LCL
e.o.m.	OR	EOM		p.o.e.	OR	POE

Symbols

543 A number of symbols are commonly used on business forms, in tables and statistical matter, and in informal business communications.

@	at		#	number (before a figure)
&	and		#	pounds (after a figure)
%	percent		′	feet
$	dollar(s)		″	inches; ditto
¢	cent(s)		¶	paragraph
°	degree(s)		§	section
=	equals		×	by, multiplied by

a. Leave one space before and after the following symbols:

@	order 200 @ $49.95		=	if $a = 7$ and $b = 9$
&	Kaye & Elman Inc.		×	a room 12×18 ft

(Continued on page 138.)

(Continued on page 138.)

NOTE: As a rule, do not leave space before and after an ampersand (&) in all-capital abbreviations.

AT&T has always been heavily committed to a wide range of R&D [research and development] activities.

At the next shareholders' meeting we need to anticipate some tough queries during the Q&A [question and answer] session about our M&A [merger and acquisition] activities.

I have an uncontrollable passion for M&M's [candy].

BUT: These A & P stores do not give their customers S & H trading stamps. (Even these abbreviations should be closed up when they are used in the same context with other closed-up abbreviations or when you do not know a specific company's preference.)

b. Do not leave space between a figure and one of the following symbols:

%	a 65% sales increase	#	use 50# paper for the job
¢	about 30¢ a pound	'	a 9′ × 12′ Oriental carpet
°	reduce heat to 350°	″	an 8·½″ × 11″ sheet of paper

c. Do not leave any space after these symbols when they are followed by a figure:

$	in the $250–$500 range	¶¶	as explained in ¶¶1218–1220
#	reorder #4659 and #4691	§	will be covered in §14.26

Computer Abbreviations and Acronyms

544 The following list presents some of the abbreviations and acronyms commonly used in references to computers and office automation.

ADP	automatic data processing
ALGOL	algorithmic language
APL	a programming language
ASCII	American Standard Code for Information Interchange (pronounced *as-kee*)
BASIC	Beginner's All-Purpose Symbolic Instruction Code
BBS	bulletin board service
BIOS	basic input/output system
bit	binary digit
CAD	computer-aided design
CAI	computer-aided instruction
CAM	computer-aided manufacturing
CAR	computer-assisted retrieval
CD-ROM	compact disc–read-only memory
COBOL	common business-oriented language
CPU	central processing unit
CRT	cathode-ray tube
DBMS	database management system
DOS	disk operating system
DSS	decision support system
DTP	desktop publishing
EDP	electronic data processing
ET	electronic typewriter
FORTRAN	formula translation
GIGO	garbage in, garbage out
IC	integrated circuit
I/O	input/output
K	kilobyte
LAN	local area network
LQ	letter quality

MICR	magnetic ink character reader
MIS	management information system
OCR	optical character recognition **OR** reader
OS	operating system
PC	personal computer
PL/1	programming language/1
RAM	random-access memory
ROM	read-only memory
VAN	value-added network
VDT	video display terminal
VM	voice mail
WAN	wide area network
WORM	write once—read many times
WYSIWYG	what you see is what you get (pronounced *wissy-wig*)

For a glossary of computer terms, see Section 20.
For the capitalization of computer terms, see ¶365.

Foreign Expressions

545 Many foreign expressions contain or consist of short words, some of which are abbreviations and some of which are not. Use periods only with abbreviations.

ad hoc		(meaning "for a particular purpose")
ad val.		(*ad valorem*, meaning "according to the value")
c. **OR** ca.		(*circa*, meaning "approximately")
cf.		(*confer*, meaning "compare")
Cie.		(*Compagnie*, meaning "Company")
e.g.		(*exempli gratia*, meaning "for example")
et al.		(*et alii*, meaning "and other people")
etc.		(*et cetera*, meaning "and other things," "and so forth")
ibid.		(*ibidem*, meaning "in the same place")
idem		(meaning "the same")
i.e.		(*id est*, meaning "that is")
infra		(meaning "below")
inst.		(*instans*, meaning "the current month")
loc. cit.		(*loco citato*, meaning "in the place cited")
M.O.		(*modus operandi*, meaning "the way in which something is done")
N.B.		(*nota bene*, meaning "note well")
nol. pros.		(*nolle prosequi*, meaning "to be unwilling to prosecute")
non seq.		(*non sequitur*, meaning "it does not follow")
op. cit.		(*opere citato*, meaning "in the work cited")
p.a. **OR** PA		(*per annum*, meaning "for each year")
p.d. **OR** PD		(*per diem*, meaning "for each day")
pro tem.		(*pro tempore*, meaning "for the time being")
prox.		(*proximo*, meaning "in the next month")
Q.E.D.		(*quod erat demonstrandum*, meaning "which was to be demonstrated")
q.v.		(*quod vide*, meaning "which see")
re **OR** in re		(meaning "in the matter of," "concerning")
R.S.V.P. **OR** R.s.v.p.		(*Répondez s'il vous plaît*, meaning "please reply")
supra		(meaning "above")
ult.		(*ultimo*, meaning "in the last month")
viz.		(*videlicet*, meaning "namely")

Miscellaneous Expressions

546 The following list of expressions presents common abbreviations acceptable in general usage.

AIDS	acquired immune deficiency syndrome	supporting an AIDS research program
A-OK	very definitely OK	the morale of the sales rep is A-OK
A1	first-rate	his heart is now in A1 condition
ATM	automated teller machine	get $50 from the nearest ATM
AV	audiovisual	a list of AV materials
CAT	clear-air turbulence	a plane crash caused by CAT
CATV	community antenna television	an improvement in CATV programming
CB	citizens band	called in on her CB radio
CD	certificate of deposit,	investing in 8.5% CDs
	compact disc	the high quality of a CD recording
DAT	digital audio tape	the superior quality of DATs
ESP	extrasensory perception	their sales manager must have ESP
GNP	gross national product	the GNP for the fourth quarter
ID	identification data	show your user ID card
IOU	I owe you	holds my IOU for $500
IQ	intelligence quotient	take an IQ test
IRA	individual retirement account	make a tax-deductible deposit to your IRA
NIMBY	not in my backyard	a NIMBY protest against a homeless shelter
PA	public address	a problem with our PA system
PR	public relations	need to work on your PR campaign
R&D	research and development	need a bigger R&D budget
S&L	savings and loan association	more taxes for the S&L bailout
SOP	standard operating procedure	find out the SOP for submitting expense reports
SRO	standing room only	an SRO audience at our show
TLC	tender, loving care	give this customer some TLC
TV	television	watch for it on TV
UFO	unidentified flying object	took off like a UFO
VCR	videocassette recorder	play this tape on your VCR
VIP	very important person	treat these dealers like VIPs
WATS	Wide-Area Telecommunications Service	use our WATS line to place your order

547 Do not use periods with letters that are not abbreviations. (See also ¶109a.)

Brand X	T-bill	f-stop	J-bar lift	D-mark
X ray	T square	y-axis	U-turn	B picture

548 The abbreviation *OK* is written without periods. In sentences, the forms *okay, okayed,* and *okaying* look better than *OK, OK'd,* and *OK'ing,* but the latter forms may be used.

549 The dictionary recognizes *x* as a verb; however, *cross out, crossed out,* and *crossing out* look better than *x out, x-ed out,* and *x-ing out.*

Plurals of abbreviations: see ¶¶620–624.
Possessives of abbreviations: see ¶¶638–639.

SECTION

6

Plurals and Possessives

¶601

Forming Plurals

When you are uncertain about the plural form of a word, consult a dictionary. If no plural is shown, form the plural according to the rules in ¶¶601–605.

Basic Rule

601 Plurals are regularly formed by adding *s* to the singular form.

suburb	suburbs	quota	quotas
fabric	fabrics	idea	ideas
yield	yields	committee	committees
egg	eggs	lie	lies
length	lengths	league	leagues
check	checks	alibi	alibis
rhythm	rhythms	menu	menus
flight	flights	bayou	bayous

NOTE: A few words have the same form in the plural as in the singular. (See ¶¶603, 1013, 1016, 1017.)

Nouns Ending in *S, X, CH, SH,* or *Z*

602 When the singular form ends in *s, x, ch, sh,* or *z,* the plural is formed by adding *es* to the singular.

bias	biases	tax	taxes
summons	summonses	sketch	sketches
business	businesses	wish	wishes
process	processes	quartz	quartzes

603 Singular nouns ending in silent *s* do not change their forms in the plural. (However, the *s* ending is pronounced when the plural form is used.)

one corps	two corps	a rendezvous many rendezvous

Nouns Ending in *Y*

604 When a singular noun ends in *y* preceded by a *consonant,* the plural is formed by changing the *y* to *i* and adding *es* to the singular.

copy	copies	liability	liabilities
policy	policies	proxy	proxies

605 When a singular noun ends in *y* preceded by a *vowel,* the plural is formed by adding *s* to the singular.

delay	delays	guy	guys
attorney	attorneys	BUT: soliloquy	soliloquies
boy	boys	colloquy	colloquies

Nouns Ending in *O*

606 Singular nouns ending in *o* preceded by a *vowel* form their plurals by adding *s* to the singular.

stereo	stereos	shampoo	shampoos
ratio	ratios	boo	boos
portfolio	portfolios	tattoo	tattoos
scenario	scenarios	duo	duos

607 Singular nouns ending in *o* preceded by a *consonant* form their plurals in different ways.

a. Some nouns in this category simply add *s.*

ego	egos	memo	memos
photo	photos	placebo	placebos
auto	autos	two	twos
typo	typos	weirdo	weirdos
logo	logos	hairdo	hairdos

b. Some add *es.*

potato	potatoes	hero	heroes
tomato	tomatoes	embargo	embargoes
echo	echoes	fiasco	fiascoes

c. Some have two plural forms. (The preferred form is given first.)

cargo	cargoes, cargos	zero	zeros, zeroes
no	noes, nos	tuxedo	tuxedos, tuxedoes
motto	mottoes, mottos	innuendo	innuendos, innuendoes
proviso	provisos, provisoes	ghetto	ghettos, ghettoes

d. Singular musical terms ending in *o* form their plurals by simply adding *s.*

soprano	sopranos	piano	pianos
alto	altos	cello	cellos
basso	bassos	banjo	banjos

For foreign nouns ending in o, see ¶611.

Nouns Ending in *F, FE,* or *FF*

608 a. Most singular nouns that end in *f, fe,* or *ff* form their plurals by adding *s* to the singular form.

belief	beliefs	safe	safes
proof	proofs	tariff	tariffs

b. Some commonly used nouns in this category form their plurals by changing the *f* or *fe* to *ve* and adding *s.*

half	halves	self	selves
wife	wives	shelf	shelves
leaf	leaves	knife	knives
thief	thieves	life	lives

c. A few of these nouns have two plural forms. (The preferred form is given first.)

scarf	scarves, scarfs	dwarf	dwarfs, dwarves

Nouns With Irregular Plurals

609 The plurals of some nouns are formed by a change of letters within.

wom*a*n	wom*e*n	f*oo*t	f*ee*t
m*ou*se	m*i*ce	g*oo*se	g*ee*se

610 A few plurals end in *en* or *ren.*

ox	oxen	child	children
brother	brethren (*an alternative plural to* brothers)		

Compound Nouns

611   When a compound noun is a *solid* word, pluralize the final element in the compound as if it stood alone.

print*out*	print*outs*	birth*day*	birth*days*
flash*back*	flash*backs*	photo*copy*	photo*copies*
wine*glass*	wine*glasses*	grand*child*	grand*children*
hat*box*	hat*boxes*	foot*hold*	foot*holds*
eye*lash*	eye*lashes*	fore*foot*	fore*feet*
straw*berry*	straw*berries*	tooth*brush*	tooth*brushes*
book*shelf*	book*shelves*	mouse*trap*	mouse*traps*
stand*by*	stand*bys*	work*man*	work*men*
BUT: *passer*by	*passers*by	**BUT:** talisman	talisman*s*

612   **a.** The plurals of *hyphenated* or *spaced* compounds are formed by pluralizing the chief element of the compound.

father-in-law	*fathers*-in-law	*rule* of thumb	*rules* of thumb
senator-elect	*senators*-elect	*letter* of credit	*letters* of credit
looker-on	*lookers*-on	*leave* of absence	*leaves* of absence
runner-up	*runners*-up	*account* payable	*accounts* payable
grant-in-aid	*grants*-in-aid	*attorney* at law	*attorneys* at law
bill of lading	*bills* of lading	deputy *chief* of staff	deputy *chiefs* of staff
editor in chief	*editors* in chief	lieutenant *general*	lieutenant *generals*
BUT: time-*out*	time-*outs*	**BUT:** chaise *longue**	chaise *longues*

See ¶614 for the plurals of foreign compound words.

b. When a hyphenated compound does not contain a noun as one of its elements, simply pluralize the final element.

go-*between*	go-*betweens*	two-by-*four*	two-by-*fours*
get-*together*	get-*togethers*	shoo-*in*	shoo-*ins*
hang-*up*	hang-*ups*	has-*been*	has-*beens*
hand-me-*down*	hand-me-*downs*	have-*not*	have-*nots* (see ¶626a)
tie-*in*	tie-*ins*	know-it-*all*	know-it-*alls*
fade-*out*	fade-*outs*	so-and-*so*	so-and-*sos*
come-*on*	come-*ons*	do-it-*yourself*	do-it-*yourselfers*
show-*off*	show-*offs*	shoot-'em-*up*	shoot-'em-*ups*
run-*through*	run-*throughs*	no-see-*um*	no-see-*ums*

c. Some of these compounds have two recognized plural forms. (The first plural form shown below is preferred because it adds the plural sign to the chief element of the compound.)

court-martial	*courts*-martial, court-*martials*
notary public	*notaries* public, notary *publics*
attorney general	*attorneys* general, attorney *generals*

d. When the first element of a compound is a *possessive*, simply pluralize the final element.

collector's item	collector's items
traveler's check	traveler's checks
rabbit's foot	rabbit's feet
proofreaders' mark	proofreaders' marks
rogues' gallery	rogues' galleries
witches' brew	witches' brews
finder's fee	finder's fees
visitor's permit	visitor's permits

---

*Note that the correct spelling of this word is *longue* (not *lounge*).

NOTE: Do not convert a singular possessive form into a plural unless the context clearly requires it.

> The number of *driver's licenses* issued last year was 15 percent ahead of the number issued the year before.

> **BUT:** As a result of the highway checkpoints set up by the state police, over 200 *drivers' licenses* have been revoked in the past four weeks.

> *See also ¶651.*

613 The plurals of compounds ending in *ful* are formed by adding *s*.

armful   armfuls   handful   handfuls
cupful   cupfuls   teaspoonful teaspoonfuls

Compare the difference in meaning in these phrases:

> six *cupfuls* of sugar (a quantity of sugar that would fill one cup six times)

> six *cups full* of sugar (six separate cups, each filled with sugar)

Foreign Nouns

614 Many nouns of foreign origin retain their foreign plurals, others have been given English plurals, and still others have two plurals—an English and a foreign one. When two plural forms exist, one may be preferred to the other or there may be differences in meaning that govern the use of each. Consult your dictionary to be sure of the plural forms and the meanings attached to them.

For agreement of foreign-plural subjects with verbs, see ¶1018.

WORDS ENDING IN *US*

Singular	English Plural	Foreign Plural
alumnus		alumni
apparatus	apparatuses*	apparatus
cactus	cactuses	cacti*
census	censuses	
corpus		corpora
focus	focuses*	foci
genus		genera
nucleus	nucleuses	nuclei*
opus	opuses	opera*
prospectus	prospectuses	
radius	radiuses	radii*
status	statuses	
stimulus		stimuli
syllabus	syllabuses	syllabi*
terminus	terminuses	termini*

WORDS ENDING IN *A*

Singular	English Plural	Foreign Plural
agenda	agendas	
alumna		alumnae
antenna	antennas (of radios)	antennae (of insects)
formula	formulas*	formulae
minutia		minutiae
schema		schemata
stigma	stigmas	stigmata*
vertebra	vertebras	vertebrae*

*Preferred form.

(Continued on page 146.)

WORDS ENDING IN *UM*

Singular	English Plural	Foreign Plural
addendum		addenda
auditorium	auditoriums*	auditoria
bacterium		bacteria
colloquium	colloquiums*	colloquia
cranium	craniums*	crania
curriculum	curriculums*	curricula†
datum	datums	data* (see ¶1018)
erratum		errata
gymnasium	gymnasiums*	gymnasia
maximum	maximums*	maxima†
medium	mediums (spiritualists)	media (for advertising and communication)
memorandum	memorandums*	memoranda
millennium	millenniums*	millennia†
minimum	minimums*	minima†
momentum	momentums*	momenta†
optimum	optimums*	optima†
referendum	referendums*	referenda†
stadium	stadiums*	stadia†
stratum		strata
symposium	symposiums*	symposia†
ultimatum	ultimatums*	ultimata

WORDS ENDING IN *O*

Singular	English Plural	Foreign Plural
concerto	concertos	concerti*
graffito		graffiti
libretto	librettos*	libretti
paparazzo		paparazzi
tempo	tempos	tempi (in music)
virtuoso	virtuosos*	virtuosi

WORDS ENDING IN *ON*

Singular	English Plural	Foreign Plural
automaton	automatons*	automata
criterion	criterions	criteria*
phenomenon	phenomenons	phenomena*

WORDS ENDING IN *X*

Singular	English Plural	Foreign Plural
apex	apexes*	apices
appendix	appendixes*	appendices
codex		codices
crux	cruxes*	cruces
index	indexes (of books)	indices (math symbols)
larynx	larynxes	larynges*
matrix	matrixes	matrices*
vertex	vertexes	vertices*
vortex	vortexes	vortices*

*Preferred form.   †Merriam-Webster shows this form first.

WORDS ENDING IN *IS*

Singular	English Plural	Foreign Plural
analysis		analyses
axis		axes
basis		bases
crisis		crises
diagnosis		diagnoses
ellipsis		ellipses
emphasis		emphases
hypothesis		hypotheses
parenthesis		parentheses
synopsis		synopses
synthesis		syntheses
thesis		theses

WORDS ENDING IN *EAU*

Singular	English Plural	Foreign Plural
beau	beaus	beaux*
bureau	bureaus*	bureaux
plateau	plateaus*	plateaux
tableau	tableaus	tableaux*
trousseau	trousseaus	trousseaux*

NOTE: The *x* ending for these foreign plurals is pronounced like *z*.

COMPOUND WORDS

Singular	English Plural	Foreign Plural
chaise longue	chaise longues*	chaises longues
coup d'état		coups d'état
éminence grise		éminences grises
hors d'oeuvre	hors d'oeuvres*	hors d'oeuvre
idiot savant	idiot savants	idiots savants*
maître d'hôtel		maîtres d'hôtel
maître d'	maître d's	
nouveau riche		nouveaux riches
pas de deux		pas de deux

Proper Names

615 **a.** Most *surnames* are pluralized by the addition of *s*.

Mr. and Mrs. Brinton	the Brintons
Mr. and Mrs. Romano	the Romanos

b. When a surname ends in *s, x, ch, sh,* or *z*, add *es* to form the plural.

Mr. and Mrs. Banks	the Bankses
Mr. and Mrs. Van Ness	the Van Nesses
Mr. and Mrs. Maddox	the Maddoxes
Mr. and Mrs. March	the Marches
Mr. and Mrs. Welsh	the Welshes
Mr. and Mrs. Katz	the Katzes
Mr. and Mrs. Jones	the Joneses
Mr. and Mrs. James	the Jameses
Mr. and Mrs. Barnes	the Barneses

*Preferred form.

(Continued on page 148.)

NOTE: Omit the *es* ending if it makes the plural surname awkward to pronounce.

the Hodges (NOT: Hodgeses)   the Hastings (NOT: Hastingses)

c. Never change the original spelling of a surname when forming the plural. Simply add *s* or *es*, according to *a* and *b* on page 147.

Mr. and Mrs. McCarthy	the McCarthys (NOT: McCarthies)
Mr. and Mrs. Wolf	the Wolfs (NOT: Wolves)
Mr. and Mrs. Martino	the Martinos (NOT: Martinoes)
Mr. and Mrs. Goodman	the Goodmans (NOT: Goodmen)
Mr. and Mrs. Lightfoot	the Lightfoots (NOT: Lightfeet)
Mr. and Mrs. Fairchild	the Fairchilds (NOT: Fairchildren)

d. When a surname is followed by *Jr.*, *Sr.*, or a number like *2d* or *II*, the plural can be formed two ways:

ORDINARY USAGE: the Roy Van Allen *Jrs.*   the Ellsworth Hadley *3ds*
FORMAL USAGE: the Roy Van *Allens* Jr.   the Ellsworth *Hadleys* 3d

616   To form the plurals of *first names*, add *s* or *es* but do not change the original spellings.

Marie	Maries	Douglas	Douglases	Timothy	Timothys
Ralph	Ralphs	Dolores	Doloreses	Beatrix	Beatrixes
Waldo	Waldos	Gladys	Gladyses	Fritz	Fritzes

617   To form the plural of other proper names, add *s* or *es* but do not change the original spelling.

three Texans	two Christmases ago
the Norwegians	checked our Rolodexes
the Dakotas	bought six Macintoshes
Februarys	Marches (*es* after *ch* sound)
the two Kansas Citys (NOT: Cities)	Czechs (*s* after *k* sound)

EXCEPTIONS:

the Alleghenies (for Allegheny Mountains)
the Rockies (for Rocky Mountains)

Personal Titles

618   The plural of *Mr.* is *Messrs.*; the plural of *Ms.* is *Mses.* or *Mss.*; the plural of *Mrs.* or *Mme.* is *Mmes.* (for *Mesdames*); the plural of *Miss* is *Misses* (no period follows). However, the use of plural titles normally occurs only in formal situations. In ordinary usage, simply retain the singular form and repeat it with each name.

Formal Usage	Ordinary Usage
Messrs. Rae and Tate	Mr. Rae and Mr. Tate
Mmes. (OR Mesdames) Byrd and Clyde	Mrs. Byrd and Mrs. Clyde
Misses Russo and Dupree	Miss Russo and Miss Dupree
Mses. (OR Mss.) Lai and Cohen	Ms. Lai and Ms. Cohen

619   When personal titles apply to two or more people with the same surname, the plural may be formed in two ways: (a) pluralize only the title (formal usage); (b) pluralize only the surname (ordinary usage).

Formal Usage	Ordinary Usage
the Messrs. Steele	the Mr. Steeles
the Mmes. (OR Mesdames) Bergeret	the Mrs. Bergerets
the Misses Conroy	the Miss Conroys
the Mses. (OR Mss.) Purdy	the Ms. Purdys

Abbreviations, Letters, Numbers, and Words

620 Form the plurals of most abbreviations by adding *s* to the singular.

bldg.	bldgs.	No.	Nos.
vol.	vols.	Dr.	Drs.
par.	pars.	Bro.	Bros.

621 **a.** The abbreviations of many customary units of weight and measure, however, are the same in both the singular and plural.

oz (ounce **OR** ounces) ft (foot **OR** feet)
deg (degree **OR** degrees) in (inch **OR** inches)
bbl (barrel **OR** barrels) mi (mile **OR** miles)

NOTE: For a number of these abbreviations, two plural forms have been widely used: for example, *lb* or *lbs* (meaning "pounds"), *yd* or *yds* (meaning "yards"), *qt* or *qts* (meaning "quarts"). However, the trend is toward using *lb, yd,* and *qt* to signify the plural.

b. The abbreviations of metric units of weight and measure are the same in both the singular and plural. (See also ¶¶537–538.)

km (kilometer **OR** kilometers) cg (centigram **OR** centigrams)
mL (milliliter **OR** milliliters) dam (dekameter **OR** dekameters)

For the omission of periods with abbreviations of measurements, see ¶¶535a, 538a.

622 The plurals of a few single-letter abbreviations (such as *p.* for *page* and *f.* for *the following page*) consist of the same letter doubled.

p. 64 (page 64)
pp. 64–72 (pages 64 through 72)
pp. 291 f. (page 291 and the following page)
pp. 291 ff. (page 291 and the following pages)
l. 23 (line 23)
ll. 23–24 (lines 23 through 24)
n. 3 (note 3)
nn. 3–4 (notes 3 and 4)

623 Capital letters and abbreviations ending with capital letters are pluralized by adding *s* alone.

three Rs	CEOs	V.P.s
four Cs	IQs	M.D.s
five VIPs	PTAs	LL.B.s
six CPUs	YWCAs	Ph.D.s

NOTE: Some authorities still sanction the use of an apostrophe before the *s* (for example, *four C's, PTA's*). However, the apostrophe is functionally unnecessary except where confusion might otherwise result.

three A's too many I's two U's on his report card

624 For the sake of clarity, uncapitalized letters and uncapitalized abbreviations are pluralized by adding an apostrophe plus *s*.

dotting the *i*'s *p*'s and *q*'s four c.o.d.'s wearing pj's

NOTE: When initials are spelled out in letters, the plurals are formed normally.

emcees deejays okays Jaycees

625　Numbers expressed in figures are pluralized by the addition of *s* alone. (See, however, ¶623, note.)

in the 1990s	Catch-22s
sort the W-2s	temperature in the 20s

Numbers expressed in words are pluralized by the addition of *s* or *es*.

ones　　twos　　threes　　sixes　　twenties　　twenty-fives

626　**a.** When words taken from other parts of speech are used as nouns, they are usually pluralized by the addition of *s* or *es*.

ifs, ands, or buts	pros and cons
dos and don'ts	whys and wherefores
yeses and noes	yeas and nays
the haves and the have-nots	the ins and outs
this year's hopefuls	ups and downs

b. If the pluralized form is unfamiliar or is likely to be misread, use an apostrophe plus *s* to form the plural.

which's and that's　　　　or's and nor's

c. If the singular form already contains an apostrophe, simply add *s* to form the plural.

ain'ts　　mustn'ts　　　don'ts　　ma'ams

For the use of underscoring or italics with words referred to as words, see ¶¶285, 290c.

Forming Possessives

Possession Versus Description

627　A noun ending in the sound of *s* is usually in the possessive form if it is followed immediately by another noun. (An apostrophe alone or an apostrophe plus *s* is the sign of the possessive. See ¶¶630–640.)

the *company's* profits (meaning the profits *of the company*)

Hodgkins' product line (meaning the product line *of the Hodgkins Company*)

Faulkner's novels (meaning the novels *written by Faulkner*)

McTavish's property (meaning the property *belonging to McTavish*)

the *patient's* medicine (meaning the medicine *intended for the patient*)

a two *weeks'* vacation (meaning a vacation *for* or *lasting two weeks*)

BUT: a *two-week* vacation (see ¶817a, note)

NOTE: To be sure that the possessive form should be used, try substituting an *of* phrase or making a similar substitution as in the examples above. If the substitution works, the possessive form is correct.

628　Do not mistake a descriptive form ending in *s* for a possessive form.

sales effort (*sales* describes the kind of effort)

savings account (*savings* describes the kind of account)

news release (*news* describes the type of press release)

earnings record (*earnings* describes the type of record)

NOTE: Some cases can be difficult to distinguish. Is it *the girls basketball team* or *the girls' basketball team*? Try substituting an irregular plural like *women.* You wouldn't say *the women basketball team;* you would say *the wom-en's basketball team.* By analogy, *the girls' basketball team* is correct.

For descriptive and possessive forms in organizational names, see ¶640.

629   In a number of cases only a slight difference in wording distinguishes a descriptive phrase from a possessive phrase.

Descriptive	Possessive
a six-month leave of absence	a six months' leave of absence
the California climate	California's climate
the Burgess account	Burgess's account
the Crosby children	the Crosbys' children
	OR: Mr. and Mrs. Crosby's children

Singular Nouns

630   To form the possessive of a singular noun *not* ending in an *s* sound, add an apostrophe plus *s* to the noun.

my lawyer's advice	Illinois's highways
Gloria's career	Arkansas's mountains
Mr. and Mrs. Goodwin's party	Des Moines's mayor
Maine's coastline	the corps's leadership

631   To form the possessive of a singular noun that ends in an *s* sound, be guided by the way you pronounce the word.

a. If a new syllable is formed in the pronunciation of the possessive, add an apostrophe plus *s.*

your boss's approval	Mr. and Mrs. Morris's plane tickets
the witness's reply	Miss Knox's decision
Congress's intention	Ms. Lopez's application
my coach's training regimen	Mr. Marsh's office
Paris's boulevards	Dallas's business district
St. Louis's airport	Phoenix's suburbs

b. If the addition of an extra syllable would make a word ending in an *s* hard to pronounce, add the apostrophe only.

Mrs. Phillips' request	Jesus' parables
Mr. Hastings' proposal	Moses' flight from Egypt
the Burroughs' condominium	New Orleans' restaurants
Los Angeles' freeways	for goodness' sake (see ¶646)

NOTE: Individual differences in pronunciation will affect the way some of these possessives are written. For example, if you pronounce the possessive form of *Perkins* as two syllables, you will write *Mr. Perkins' kindness;* if you pronounce the possessive of *Perkins* as three syllables, you will write *Mr. Perkins's kindness.* The important thing is to listen to your own pronunciation. When you hear yourself pronounce the possessive of *boss* as two syllables *(boss's)* and the possessive of *witness* as three *(witness's),* you will not be tempted to write *your boss' approval* or *the witness' reply.* Naturally, tradition should take precedence over your ear. For example, the U.S. ambassador to Great Britain is appointed to the *Court of St. James's* (not to the less awkward-sounding *Court of St. James').*

c. When forming the possessive of any noun ending in *s* (for example, *Mr. Hodges),* always place the apostrophe at the end of the original word, never within it.

Mr. Hodges' message (**NOT:** Mr. Hodge's message)

Plural Nouns

632 **a.** For a *regular* plural noun (one that ends in *s* or *es*), add only an apostrophe to form the plural possessive. (See ¶¶639–640 for the use of the apostrophe in organizational names.)

investors' objectives   attorneys' fees
the witnesses' contradictions   the agencies' conflicting rules
the United States' policy   the Gaineses' legal residence

b. Since the singular and plural possessives for the same word usually sound exactly alike, pay particularly close attention to the meaning in order to determine whether the noun in question is singular or plural.

An *investor's* objectives should largely define investment strategy.
BUT: *Investors'* objectives are often not clearly defined.

We will need a ride to Mr. and Mrs. *Gaines's* party.
BUT: We will need a ride to the *Gaineses'* party.

I especially want to hear the last witness's testimony.
BUT: I especially want to hear the last two witnesses' testimony.

NOTE: In some cases only a dictionary can help you determine whether the possessive form should be singular or plural. For example, a plural possessive is used in *Legionnaires' disease,* but a singular possessive is used in *Hodgkin's disease* since the discoverer's name was Dr. Hodgkin (and not, as you might have expected, the more common name Hodgkins). Unlike the term *deacon's bench* (which uses a singular possessive), the term *Parsons table* involves no possessive form at all.

633 For an *irregular* plural noun (one that does not end in *s*), add an apostrophe plus *s* to form the plural possessive.

women's blouses   men's shirts
children's toys   **BUT:** menswear (originally, men's wear)

IMPORTANT NOTE: To avoid mistakes in forming the possessive of plural nouns, form the plural first; then apply the rule in ¶632 or ¶633, whichever fits.

Singular	Plural	Plural Possessive
boy	boys (regular)	boys'
boss	bosses (regular)	bosses'
hero	heroes (regular)	heroes'
Mr. and Mrs. Fox	the Foxes (regular)	the Foxes'
child	children (irregular)	children's
alumnus	alumni (irregular)	alumni's
mother-in-law	mothers-in-law (irregular)	mothers-in-law's

Compound Nouns

634 To form the *singular* possessive of a compound noun (whether solid, spaced, or hyphenated), add an apostrophe plus *s* to the last element of the compound.

my son-in-law's job prospects   my stockbroker's advice
the secretary-treasurer's report   the notary public's seal
the owner-manager's policies   an eyewitness's account
a do-it-your-selfer's obsession   the attorney general's decision

635 To form the *plural* possessive of a compound noun, first form the plural.

a. If the plural form ends in *s*, add only an apostrophe.

Singular	Plural	Plural Possessive
stockholder	stockholders	stockholders'
vice president	vice presidents	vice presidents'
clerk-typist	clerk-typists	clerk-typists'
salesclerk	salesclerks	salesclerks'

b. If the plural form does not end in *s*, add an apostrophe plus *s*.

Singular	Plural	Plural Possessive
editor in chief	editors in chief	editors in chief's
brother-in-law	brothers-in-law	brothers-in-law's

NOTE: To avoid the awkwardness of a plural possessive such as *editors in chief's* or *brothers-in-law's*, rephrase the sentence.

AWKWARD: We may have to invite my three *sisters-in-law's* parents too.
BETTER: We may have to invite the parents of my three *sisters-in-law* too.

AWKWARD: Mr. Ahmed's statement agrees with both *attorneys general's* views.
BETTER: Mr. Ahmed's statement agrees with the views of both *attorneys general.*

Pronouns

636 The possessive forms of *personal pronouns* and of the relative pronoun *who* do not require the apostrophe. These pronouns have their own possessive forms.

I: my, mine	she: her, hers	they: their, theirs
you: your, yours	it: its	who: whose
he: his	we: our, ours	

My copy of the letter arrived last week, so she should have received *hers* by now. (**NOT:** her's.)

Each unit comes carefully packed in *its* own carton. (**NOT:** it's.)

The two products look so much alike that it's (it is) hard to tell *ours* from *theirs.* (**NOT:** our's from their's.)

CAUTION: Do not confuse personal possessive pronouns with similarly spelled contractions. (See ¶1056e for examples.)

637 Some *indefinite pronouns* have regular possessive forms.

one's choice	the other's claim	anybody's guess
anyone else's job	the others' claim	no one's responsibility
one another's time	each other's claim	someone's chance

For those indefinite pronouns that do not have possessive forms, use an *of* phrase.

Although the children in this group seem very much alike, the needs *of each* are different. (**NOT:** each's needs.)

Abbreviations

638 To form the singular possessive of an abbreviation, add an apostrophe plus *s*. To form the plural possessive, add an *s* plus an apostrophe to the singular form. (See also ¶639.)

Singular	Plural
Mr. C.'s opinion	the M.D.s' diagnoses
the FCC's ruling	the Ph.D.s' theses
the CPA's audit	the CPAs' meeting

Personal and Organizational Names; Titles

639 To form the possessive of a personal or organizational name that ends with an abbreviation, a number, or a prepositional phrase, add an apostrophe plus *s* at the end of the complete name.

the Winger Co.'s new plant
the Knights of Columbus's drive
United Bank of Arizona's loan rates

McGraw-Hill, Inc.'s dividends
David Weild II's retirement
Walter Frick Jr.'s campaign

NOTE: If *no* extra *s* sound is created when you pronounce the possessive form, add only an apostrophe.

the Gerald Curry Jrs.' yacht

For the treatment of possessive forms when terms like Jr. *and* Inc. *are set off by commas, see* ¶¶*156 and 159.*

640 Many organizational names and titles contain words that could be construed as either possessive or descriptive terms.

a. As a rule, use an apostrophe if the term is a singular possessive noun or an irregular plural noun.

McCall's	*Harper's Bazaar*	*Women's Wear Daily*	Children's Hospital
McDonald's	Levi's jeans	Macy's	Reese's Pieces

b. Do not use an apostrophe if the term is a regular plural.

American Bankers Association
Government Employees Insurance Company
U.S. Department of Veterans Affairs

Chemical Workers Union
Investors Trust Company
Underwriters Laboratories Inc.

c. In all cases follow the organization's preference when known.

Investor's Management Services, Inc.
International Ladies' Garment Workers' Union
Boys' Clubs of America
Diners Club membership
Lands' End clothing

Ladies' Home Journal
Reader's Digest
Barron's
Mrs. Paul's frozen foods
Mrs. Fields cookies

d. When adding the sign of the possessive to a phrase that must be underscored (or italicized), do not underscore (or italicize) the possessive ending. (See also ¶290c.)

Gone With the Wind's main characters   The Wind in the Willows' author

Nouns in Apposition

641 Sometimes a noun that ordinarily would be in the possessive is followed by an *appositive,* a closely linked explanatory word or phrase. In such cases add the sign of the possessive to the appositive.

Rockport, *Massachusetts'* attraction for artists goes back many decades. (Note that the comma that normally follows an appositive is omitted after a possessive ending.)

You will faint when you see Paul *the plumber's* bill. (If the noun and the appositive are closely linked as a unit, even the first comma is omitted. See also ¶150.)

NOTE: To avoid an awkward construction, use an *of* phrase instead.

You will need to get the signature *of Mr. Bartel,* the executor.
(**BETTER THAN:** You will need to get Mr. Bartel, *the executor's* signature.)

6

Separate and Joint Possession

642 To indicate separate possession:

    a. Add the sign of the possessive to the name of each individual.

       the buyer's and the seller's signatures
       the Joneses' and the Browns' houses

       NOTE: The repetition of *the* with each name emphasizes that ownership is separate.

    b. If one or both of the individuals' names are replaced by a possessive pronoun, watch out for awkwardness and reword if necessary.

       AWKWARD: my and the seller's signatures
       BETTER: the seller's and my signatures
       OR: the seller's signature and mine
       AWKWARD: their and our houses
       BETTER: their house and ours

643 To indicate joint (or common) ownership:

    a. Add the sign of the possessive to the *final* name alone.

       the Barneses and the Terrys' property line

       NOTE: In organizational names, follow the company's preference.

       Ben & Jerry's ice cream   Kroch's & Brentano's bookstores

    b. If one of the owners is identified by a pronoun, make each name and pronoun possessive.

       Karen's and my ski lodge   **BUT:** Karen and Brian's ski lodge

Possessives Standing Alone

644 Sometimes the noun that the possessive modifies is not expressed but merely understood.

       Ask for it at your *grocer's* [store].

       Wear your oldest shirt and *Levi's* [jeans]. (The trademark *Levi's* is a singular possessive form.)

       We have been invited to dinner at the *Furnesses'* [house].

       BUT: We always enjoy an evening with the *Furnesses.* (The people themselves are referred to; hence no possessive.)

    NOTE: The possessive form must be used in the following construction in order to keep the comparison parallel.

       This year's product line is pulling better than *last year's* [product line].

       NOT: This year's product line is pulling better than *last year.* (Incorrectly compares *product line* with *last year.*)

Inanimate Possessives

645 As a rule, nouns referring to inanimate things should not be in the possessive. Use an *of* phrase instead.

       the bottom of the barrel (**NOT:** the barrel's bottom)
       the wording of the agreement (**NOT:** the agreement's wording)
       the lower level of the terminal (**NOT:** the terminal's lower level)

646 In many common expressions that refer to time and measurements, how-ever, and in phrases implying personification, the possessive form has come to be accepted usage. (See also ¶817a.)

one day's notice	a dollar's worth	a stone's throw
a nine days' wonder	several dollars' worth	for heaven's sake
an hour's work	two cents' worth	for conscience' sake
two years' progress	at arm's length	(see ¶631b)
the company's assets	New Year's resolutions	the earth's atmosphere
the sun's rays	this morning's news	the next world's fair

NOTE: Be sure to distinguish possessive expressions like those above from similar wording where no possessive relation is involved.

two weeks' salary   BUT: two weeks ago, two weeks later, two weeks overdue

I bought *five dollars' worth* of chocolate truffles.

BUT: I found *five dollars lying* on the sidewalk.

Possessives Preceding Verbal Nouns

647 **a.** When a noun or a pronoun modifies a *gerund* (the *ing* form of a verb used as a noun), the noun or pronoun should be in the possessive.

What was the point of *our* asking any further questions? (NOT: of us asking.)

NOTE: The use of a possessive form before a gerund can produce a sentence that is grammatically correct but awkward nonetheless. In such cases do not hesitate to reword the sentence.

AWKWARD: He wanted to be reassured about his *children's* being given a ride home.

BETTER: He wanted to be reassured that his children would be given a ride home.

b. Not every noun or pronoun preceding the *ing* form of a verb should be in the possessive form. Compare the following pairs of examples:

I heard *you* singing at the party. (Here the emphasis is on *you*, the object of *heard; singing* is a participle that modifies *you*.)

I liked *your* singing at the party. (Here the emphasis is on *singing*, a gerund that is the object of *liked;* the pronoun *your* is in the possessive form because it modifies *singing*.)

Our success in this venture depends on *Allen* acting as the coordinator. (This suggests that the success depends on Allen himself rather than on the role he is playing. Even if Allen's role should change, success seems likely as long as he is associated with the project in some way.)

Our success in this venture depends on *Allen's* acting as the coordinator. (This puts the emphasis squarely on Allen's acting in a certain role. If he ceases to function as the coordinator, the venture may not succeed.)

Possessives in *Of* Phrases

648 **a.** The object of the preposition *of* should not ordinarily be in the posses-sive form, since the *of* phrase as a whole expresses possession. How-ever, possessives are used in a few idiomatic expressions.

Tony and Fiona are good friends of *ours* as well as our *children's*.

Did you know that Polly and Fred are neighbors of the *Joneses'*?

Bobby Busoni is a business associate of *Gordon's*.

b. Avoid adding the sign of the possessive to an *of* phrase.

AWKWARD: A *friend of mine's house* burned down last night.

BETTER: The *house of a friend of mine* burned down last night.

AWKWARD: *One of my friends' son* has been named a Rhodes scholar. (NOT: One of my friend's son.)

BETTER: The *son of one of my friends* has been named a Rhodes scholar.

NOTE: Attaching the sign of the possessive to an *of* phrase can sometimes create humorous confusion in addition to awkwardness.

CONFUSING: You must negotiate the purchase price with the owner of the horse's wife.

CLEAR: You must negotiate the purchase price of the horse with the owner's wife.

Possessives Modifying Possessives

649   Avoid attaching a possessive form to another possessive. Change the wording if possible.

AWKWARD: I have not yet seen the *utility company's lawyer's* petition.

BETTER: I have not yet seen the petition of the *utility company's lawyer.*

Possessives in Holidays

650   Possessives in names of holidays are usually singular.

New Year's Eve	Valentine's Day	BUT: Presidents' Day
Lincoln's Birthday	Saint Patrick's Day	April Fools' Day
Mother's Day	Saint Agnes' Eve	All Saints' Day

NOTE: Some holiday names contain a plural form rather than a plural possessive; for example: *Armed Forces Day, Veterans Day, United Nations Day.*

Miscellaneous Expressions

651   A number of common expressions contain possessive forms. Most of these involve singular possessives.

driver's license	proofreaders' mark
traveler's check	lovers' lane
collector's item	workers' compensation (see ¶809a, note)
visitor's permit	witches' brew
seller's market	women's room
finder's fee	BUT: woman's rights
dog's life	states' rights
cat's-paw	BUT: state's evidence
mare's nest	citizen's arrest
rabbit's foot	BUT: citizens band
bull's-eye	teacher's pet
monkey's uncle	BUT: teachers college

For the plural forms of expressions like these, see ¶612c.

6

Spelling

Spelling Guides

Words That Sound or Look Alike (¶719)

Troublesome Words (¶720)

In matters of spelling, the most important rule is this: *When in doubt, consult the dictionary.* The next most important rule: *Try to master the principles of spelling so as to avoid frequent trips to the dictionary.*

Section 7 offers three kinds of assistance: ¶¶701–718 present the basic guidelines for correct spelling; ¶719 provides a 12-page list of look-alike and sound-alike words for review and fast reference; ¶720 presents a list of troublesome words—those that are frequently misspelled or that frequently send writers to their dictionaries.

NOTE: The authority for spelling in this manual is the 1990 printing of *Webster's Ninth New Collegiate Dictionary* and *Webster's Third New International Dictionary* (both published by Merriam-Webster, Springfield, Massachusetts). Whenever two spellings are allowable, only the first form is usually given here.

Spelling Guides

When a Final Consonant Is Doubled

701 When a word of one syllable ends in a single consonant (ba*g*) preceded by a single vowel (b*a*g), double the final consonant before a suffix beginning with a vowel (bagg*age*) or before the suffix *y* (bagg*y*). (See ¶703.)

rub	rub*b*ed	swim	swim*m*er	slip	slip*p*age
glad	glad*d*en	skin	skin*n*y	star	star*r*ing
beg	beg*g*ar	clan	clan*n*ish	bet	bet*t*or

EXCEPTIONS:

yes	yeses	dew	dewy	fix	fixed
bus	buses	bow	bowed	box	boxy

NOTE: When a one-syllable word ends in *y* preceded by a single vowel, do not double the *y* before a suffix beginning with a vowel. (See ¶711.)

pay	payee	joy	joyous	toy	toying
key	keyed	boy	boyish	buy	buyer

702 When a word of more than one syllable ends in a single consonant (refe*r*) preceded by a single vowel (ref*e*r) and the accent falls on the last syllable of the root word (re*fer*), double the final consonant before a suffix beginning with a vowel (referr*ed*). (See ¶704.)

forbid	forbid*d*en	begin	begin*n*ing	infer	infer*r*ed
unclog	unclog*g*ed	unzip	unzip*p*ed	occur	occur*r*ing
control	control*l*er	concur	concur*r*ent	regret	regret*t*able

EXCEPTIONS (SEE ¶711):

display	displaying	obey	obeyed	enjoy	enjoyable

NOTE: When a suffix beginning with a vowel is added, do not double the final consonant if the accent *shifts* from the second syllable.

refer	referred	prefer	preferred	transfer transferred
BUT: reference		**BUT:** preferable		**BUT:** transferee

When a Final Consonant Is Not Doubled

703 When a word of one syllable ends in a single consonant (ba*d*) preceded by a single vowel (b*a*d), *do not* double the final consonant before a suffix beginning with a *consonant* (bad*ly*).

glad	glad*ness*	star	star*dom*	play	play*ful*
ten	ten*fold*	wit	wit*less*	joy	joy*fully*
ship	ship*ment*	flag	flag*ship*	boy	boy*hood*

704 When a word of more than one syllable ends in a single consonant (bene-fi*t*) preceded by a single vowel (benef*i*t) and the accent *does not* fall on the last syllable of the root word (*ben*efit), *do not* double the final consonant before a suffix beginning with a vowel (benefit*ed*).

catalog	cataloged, cataloging	differ	differed, different
total	totaled, totaling	credit	credited, creditor
cancel	canceled, canceling	profit	profited, profiting
	(**BUT:** cancellation)	benefit	benefited, benefiting
diagram	diagramed, diagraming	borrow	borrowed, borrowing
worship	worshiped, worshiper	index	indexed, indexing

(Continued on page 160.)

EXCEPTIONS:

program	programmed, programming	kidnap	kidnapped,
format	formatted, formatting		kidnapping
overstep	overstepped, overstepping	handicap	handicapped,
outfit	outfitted, outfitting		handicapping

705 When a word of one or more syllables ends in a single consonant (clou*d*, repea*t*) preceded by more than one vowel (cl*ou*d, rep*ea*t), *do not* double the final consonant before any suffix, whether it begins with a consonant (cloud*less*) or a vowel (repeat*ing*).

gain	gain*ful*	bias	bias*ed*	wool	wool*en*
haul	haul*ing*	chief	chief*ly*		(**BUT:** wool*ly*)
dream	dream*y*	riot	riot*ous*	loud	loud*ness*
cheer	cheer*y*	broad	broad*ly*	equal	equal*ed*
deceit	deceit*ful*	poet	poet*ic*	duel	duel*ing*
feud	feud*al*	toil	toil*some*	buoy	buoy*ant*

EXCEPTIONS:

equip	equipped, equipping (**BUT:** equipment)	quit	quitting
quiz	quizzed, quizzing, quizzical	squat	squatter

706 When a word of one or more syllables ends with more than one consonant (wor*k*, deta*ch*), *do not* double the final consonant before any suffix (work*day*, detach*ed*).

comb	comb*ing*	back	back*ward*	shirr	shirr*ing*
hand	hand*y*	curl	curl*y*	mass	mass*ive*
self	self*ish*	warm	warm*ly*	slant	slant*wise*
swing	swing*ing*	return	return*ed*	jinx	jinx*ed*
wish	wish*ful*	harp	harp*ing*	blitz	blitz*ing*

NOTE: Words ending in *ll* usually retain both consonants before a suffix. However, when adding the suffix *ly*, drop one *l* from the root word. When adding the suffix *less* or *like*, insert a hyphen between the root and the suffix to avoid three *l*'s in a row.

skill	skillful	full	fully	hull	hull-less
install	installment	dull	dully	shell	shell-like

Final Silent *E*

707 **a.** Words ending in silent *e* usually *drop* the *e* before a suffix beginning with a vowel.

sale	sal*able*	sense	sens*ible*	propose	propos*ition*
move	mov*able*	argue	argu*ing*	execute	execut*ive*
store	stor*age*	issue	issu*ing*	sincere	sincer*ity*
arrive	arriv*al*	blue	blu*ish*	desire	desir*ous*
accuse	accus*ation*	true	tru*ism*	use	us*ual*

EXCEPTIONS:

agree	agreeing	mile	mileage	dye	dyeing
see	seeing	acre	acreage	hoe	hoeing

b. Words ending in silent *e* usually *drop* the *e* before the suffix *y*.

ease	easy	ice	icy	edge	edgy
chance	chancy	bounce	bouncy	range	rangy

EXCEPTIONS:

cage	cagey	dice	dicey	price	pricey

c. Words ending in *ce* or *ge* usually *retain* the *e* before a suffix beginning with *a* or *o*.

enforce	enforce*able*	courage	courag*eous*
notice	notic*eable*	outrage	outrag*eous*
peace	peac*eable*	change	chang*eable*
replace	replac*eable*	knowledge	knowledg*eable*
service	servic*eable*	manage	manag*eable*
advantage	advantag*eous*	marriage	marriag*eable*

EXCEPTIONS:

pledge	pledgor	mortgage	mortgagor

NOTE: Before suffixes beginning with *i*, the *e* is usually dropped.

force	forc*ible*	college	colleg*ial*	age	ag*ing*
reduce	reduc*ible*	finance	financ*ial*	enforce	enforc*ing*

EXCEPTIONS:

singe	singeing	tinge	tingeing	age	ageism

708 Words ending in silent *e* usually *retain* the *e* before a suffix beginning with a consonant.

hope	hope*ful*	flame	flame*proof*
care	care*less*	trouble	trouble*some*
sincere	sincere*ly*	nine	nine*ty*
manage	manage*ment*	subtle	subtle*ty*
like	like*ness*	edge	edge*wise*

EXCEPTIONS:

wise	wisdom	judge	judgment
awe	awful	acknowledge	acknowledgment
true	truly	subtle	subtly
due	duly	nine	ninth
gentle	gently	whole	wholly

709 Words ending in *ie* change the *ie* to *y* before adding *ing*.

die	dying	tie	tying	lie	lying

When Final *Y* Is Changed to *I*

710 Words ending in *y* preceded by a consonant change the *y* to *i* before any suffix except one beginning with *i*.

vary	vari*able*	accompany	accompani*ment*
custody	custod*ial*	happy	happi*ness*
Italy	Itali*an*	fallacy	fallaci*ous*
defy	defi*ant*	try	try*ing*
carry	carri*ed*	thirty	thirty*ish*
fly	fli*er*	lobby	lobby*ist*
easy	easi*er*	Kennedy	Kennedy*ite*
heavy	heavi*est* **BUT:**	dry	dry*ly*
fifty	fifti*eth*	shy	shy*ly*
fancy	fanci*ful*	country	country*wide*
likely	likeli*hood*	academy	academ*ic*
ordinary	ordinari*ly*	economy	econom*ist*

711 Words ending in *y* preceded by a vowel usually retain the *y* before any suffix.

okay	okay*ed*	convey	convey*ance*	employ	employ*able*
clay	clay*ey*	obey	obey*ing*	joy	joy*ful*
display	display*ing*	survey	survey*or*	buy	buy*er*

EXCEPTIONS:

pay	paid	day	daily	gay	gaily
lay	laid	say	said	slay	slain

EI and IE Words

712 According to the old rhyme:
Put *i* before *e*
Except after *c*
Or when sounded like *a*
As in *neighbor* and *weigh.*

I Before E

believe	brief	field	niece	**BUT:** either	height
relieve	chief	wield	piece	neither	leisure
belief	thief	yield	anxiety	seize	foreign
relief	friend	view	variety	weird	forfeit

After C

deceive	receive	conceive	perceive	**BUT:** ancient	species
deceit	receipt	conceit	ceiling	science	financier

Sounded Like A

freight	their	eight	vein
weight	heir	sleigh	skein

Words Ending in ABLE and IBLE

713 **a.** The ending *able* is more commonly used.

admirable	dependable	likable	probable	salable
advisable	doable	movable	reasonable	transferable
changeable	knowledgeable	payable	receivable	valuable

See ¶707 on dropping or retaining silent e *before the ending.*

b. However, a number of frequently used words end in *ible*.

compatible	eligible	irrepressible	possible	susceptible
convertible	feasible	irresistible	responsible	terrible
credible	flexible	legible	sensible	visible

Words Ending in ANT, ANCE, ENT, and ENCE

714 Words ending in *ant, ance, ent,* and *ence* follow no clear-cut pattern. Therefore, consult a dictionary when in doubt.

exist*ent*	persist*ent*	defend*ant*	descend*ant*	occur*rence*
insist*ent*	resist*ant*	depend*ent*	transcend*ent*	recur*rence*
assist*ance*	mainten*ance*	relev*ance*	surveill*ance*	intellig*ence*

Words Ending in IZE, ISE, and YZE

715 **a.** Most words end in *ize*.

apologize	criticize	minimize	realize	summarize
authorize	economize	organize	recognize	vandalize
characterize	emphasize	prize	specialize	visualize

b. A number of common words end in *ise*.

advertise	compromise	enterprise	improvise	supervise
advise	devise	exercise	merchandise	surprise
arise	disguise	franchise	revise	televise

c. Only a few words end with *yze*.

analyze	paralyze	catalyze

Words Ending in *CEDE*, *CEED*, and *SEDE*

716 **a.** Only *one* word ends in *sede: supersede.*

b. Only *three* words end in *ceed: exceed, proceed, succeed.* (Note, however, that derivatives of these three words are spelled with only one *e: excess, procedure, success.*)

c. All other words ending with the sound of "seed" are spelled *cede: precede, secede, recede, concede, accede, intercede.*

Words Ending in C

717 Words ending in *c* usually take the letter *k* before a suffix so as to preserve the hard sound of the *c*.

mimic	mimicked, mimicking (BUT: mimicry)
panic	panicked, panicking, panicky
picnic	picnicked, picnicking, picnicker
shellac	shellacked, shellacking
traffic	trafficked, trafficking

BUT: arc   arced, arcing

Words With Diacritical Marks

718 Many French words are now considered part of the English language and therefore do not require underscoring or italicizing (see ¶287). Nevertheless, some of these words retain diacritical marks from their original French form.

a. **Acute Accent.** An acute accent (´) over the letter *e* (*é*) signifies that the letter is to be pronounced "ay" (as in *may*). Moreover, it signifies that at the end of a word the letter *é* is to be pronounced as a separate syllable.

attaché	crudités	fiancé (m.)	risqué
blasé	détente	fiancée (f.)	sauté
café	éclair	habitué	soufflé
canapé	éclat	macramé	touché
cliché	élan	née	BUT: matinee
communiqué	entrée	outré	melee
consommé	exposé	passé	puree

A few words call for two acute accents:

résumé	protégé	décolleté	déclassé

NOTE: The word *forte* (meaning "one's strong point") does not have an acute accent over the *e*. It should be pronounced as if it were spelled *fort* (not *fortay*).

b. **Grave Accent.** A few expressions taken from the French retain a grave accent (`).

à la carte	vis-à-vis	déjà vu	pièce de résistance
à la mode	pied-à-terre	voilà	cause célèbre

c. **The Circumflex.** A few phrases derived from the French still retain a circumflex (ˆ).

maître d'hôtel	raison d'être	pâté	papier-mâché
table d'hôte	tête-à-tête	bête noire	BUT: fete

Words That Sound Alike or Look Alike

719   The following list contains two types of words: (a) words that are pro-nounced *exactly alike* though spelled differently; and (b) words that look and sound *somewhat alike*.

accede to comply with; to give consent
exceed to surpass

accent stress in speech or writing
ascent act of rising
assent consent

accept to take; to receive
except (v.) to exclude; (prep.) excluding (see page 260)

access admittance
excess surplus

ad short for *advertisement*
add to join

adapt to adjust
adept proficient
adopt to choose

addenda (see *agenda*)

addition something added
edition one version of a printed work

adherence attachment
adherents followers

adverse hostile; unfavorable
averse disinclined

advice (n.) information; recommendation
advise (v.) to recommend; to give counsel

affect to influence; to change; to assume (see page 253)
effect (n.) result; impression; (v.) to bring about

agenda list of things to be done
addenda additional items

aid (n.) a form of help; (v.) to help
aide an assistant

ail to be in ill health
ale a drink much like beer

air atmosphere
heir one who inherits

aisle (see *isle*)

allot to assign or distribute a share of something (see page 253)
a lot a great deal; NOT: alot

allowed permitted
aloud audibly

allusion an indirect reference
illusion an unreal vision; misapprehension
delusion a false belief
elusion adroit escape

almost nearly (see page 254)
all most all very much

already previously (see page 254)
all ready all prepared

altar part of a church
alter to change

alternate (n.) substitute; (v.) to take turns
alternative (n.) one of several things from which to choose

altogether entirely (see page 254)
all together everyone in a group

always at all times (see page 254)
all ways all means or methods

annual yearly
annul to cancel

ante- a prefix meaning "before"
anti- a prefix meaning "against"

antecedence priority
antecedents preceding things; ancestors

anyone anybody (see ¶1010)
any one any one person in a group

anyway in any case (see page 255)
any way any method

apportion (see *portion*)

appraise to set a value on (see page 255)
apprise to inform

arc something arched or curved
ark a ship; a place of protection and safety

are (see *hour*)

area surface; extent
aria a melody
arrears that which is due but unpaid

arrange to put in order
arraign to call into court

ascent (see *accent*)

assay to test, as an ore or a chemical
essay (n.) a treatise; (v.) to attempt

assent (see *accent*)

assistance help
assistants those who help

assure (see *ensure*)

ate past tense of *eat*
eight a number

attain to gain; to achieve
attend to be present at

attendance presence
attendants escorts; followers; companions; associates

aught (see *ought*)

averse (see *adverse*)

awhile (adv.) for a short time (see page 256)
a while (phrase) a short period of time

bail (n.) security; the handle of a pail; (v.) to dip water
bale a bundle

bare (adj.) naked; empty; (v.) to expose
bear (n.) an animal; (v.) to carry; to endure; to produce

base (n.) foundation; (adj.) mean
bass a fish (pronounced *mass*); lower notes in music (pronounced *base*)

bases plural of *base* and of *basis*
basis foundation

bazaar (see *bizarre*)

beat (n.) throb; tempo; (v.) to strike
beet a vegetable

berry a fruit
bury to submerge; to cover over

berth a bed
birth being born

beside by the side of; separate from (see page 256)
besides in addition to; also

biannual occurring twice a year (see page 257)
biennial occurring once in two years

bibliography list of writings pertaining to a given subject or author
biography written history of a person's life

billed charged
build to construct

birth (see *berth*)

bizarre fantastic; extravagantly odd
bazaar a place for selling goods

blew past tense of *blow*
blue a color

block (n.) a solid piece of material; (v.) to obstruct
bloc an interest group pursuing certain political or economic goals

board a piece of wood; an organized group; meals
bored penetrated; wearied

boarder one who pays for meals and often for lodging as well
border edge

bolder more daring
boulder a large rock

born brought into life
borne carried; endured

boy a male child
buoy a float

brake (n.) a retarding device; (v.) to retard
break (n.) an opening; a fracture; (v.) to shatter; to divide

bread food
bred brought up

breath respiration
breathe (v.) to inhale and exhale
breadth width

bridal concerning the bride or the wedding
bridle (n.) means of controlling a horse; (v.) to take offense

broach to open; to introduce
brooch ornamental clasp

build (see *billed*)

bullion uncoined gold or silver
bouillon broth

buoy (see *boy*)

bury (see *berry*)

cache (see *cash*)

calendar a record of time
calender a machine used in finishing paper and cloth
colander a strainer

callous (adj.) hardened
callus (n.) a hardened surface

7

cannot usual form (meaning "to be unable")
can not two words in the phrase *can not only* (where *can* means "to be able")

canvas (n.) a coarse cloth
canvass (v.) to solicit

capital (n.) city serving as the seat of government; a principal sum of money; a large-sized letter; (adj.) chief; foremost; punishable by death
capitol the building in which a state legislative body meets
Capitol the building in which the U.S. Congress meets

carton a pasteboard box
cartoon a caricature

cash ready money
cache a hiding place

casual incidental
causal causing

cease to stop
seize to grasp

cede to grant; to give up
seed that from which anything is grown

ceiling top of a room; any overhanging area
sealing closing

cell (see *sell*)

cellar (see *seller*)

census statistics of population
senses mental faculties

cent (see *scent*)

cereal any grain food
serial arranged in a series

cession a yielding up
session the sitting of a court or other body

choose to select
chose did choose (past tense of *choose*)
chews masticates

chord combination of musical tones
cord string or rope

chute (see *shoot*)

cite (v.) to quote; to summon
sight a view; vision
site a place

click a slight, sharp noise
clique an exclusive group
cliché a trite phrase

climatic referring to climate
climactic referring to a climax

clothes garments
cloths fabrics
close (n.) the end; (v.) to shut

coarse rough; common
course direction; action; a way; part of a meal

colander (see *calendar*)

collision a clashing
collusion a scheme to defraud

coma an unconscious state
comma a mark of punctuation

command (n.) an order; (v.) to order
commend to praise; to entrust

commence (v.) to begin
comments (n.) remarks

complement something that completes
compliment (n.) a flattering remark; (v.) to praise

comprehensible understandable
comprehensive extensive

confidant a friend; an adviser (feminine form: *confidante*)
confident sure; positive

confidently certainly; positively
confidentially privately

conscience (n.) the sense of right and wrong
conscious (adj.) cognizant; sensible; aware

conservation preservation
conversation a talk

consul (see *council*)

consular (see *councillor*)

continual occurring steadily but with occasional breaks
continuous uninterrupted; unbroken

cooperation working together
corporation a form of business organization

cord (see *chord*)

core the central part; the heart
corps a group of persons with a common activity

correspondence letters
correspondents those who write letters; journalists
corespondents certain parties in divorce suits

costume dress
custom habit

7

council an assembly
counsel (n.) an attorney; advice; (v.) to give advice
consul a foreign representative

councillor a member of a council
counselor one who advises
consular (adj.) of a consul

course (see *coarse*)

courtesy a favor; politeness
curtesy a husband's life interest in the lands of his deceased wife
curtsy a gesture of respect

credible believable
creditable meritorious; deserving of praise
credulous ready to believe

critic one who makes judgments
critique (n.) a critical assessment; (v.) to judge; to criticize

cue a hint
queue a line of people

currant a berry
current (adj.) belonging to the present; (n.) a flow of water or electricity

curser one who curses
cursor a symbol used as a pointer on a computer screen

custom (see *costume*)

dairy source of milk products
diary daily record

deceased dead
diseased sick

decent proper; right
descent going down
dissent disagreement

decree a law
degree a grade; a step

deduce to infer
deduct to subtract

defer to put off
differ to disagree

deference respect; regard for another's wishes
difference dissimilarity; controversy

delusion (see *allusion*)

deposition a formal written statement
disposition temper; disposal

depraved morally debased
deprived taken away from

deprecate to disapprove
depreciate to lessen in estimated value

desert (n.) barren land; (plural) a deserved reward; (v.) to abandon
dessert the last course of a meal

desolate lonely; sad
dissolute loose in morals

detract to take away from
distract to divert the attention of

device (n.) a contrivance
devise (v.) to plan; to convey real estate by will

dew (see *do*)

diary (see *dairy*)

die (n.) mold; (v.) to cease living
dye (n.) that which changes the color of; (v.) to change the color of

differ (see *defer*)

difference (see *deference*)

disapprove to withhold approval
disprove to prove the falsity of

disassemble to take apart
dissemble to disguise; to feign

disburse to pay out
disperse to scatter

discreet prudent
discrete distinct; separate

diseased (see *deceased*)

disinterested unbiased; impartial
uninterested bored; unconcerned

disposition (see *deposition*)

disprove (see *disapprove*)

dissemble (see *disassemble*)

dissent (see *decent*)

dissolute (see *desolate*)

distract (see *detract*)

divers (adj.) various or sundry; (n.) plural of *diver*
diverse different

do to perform
due owing
dew moisture

done finished
dun to demand payment

dose a measured quantity
doze to sleep lightly

dual double
duel a combat

due (see *do*)

dye (see *die*)

7

dying near death
dyeing changing the color of

edition (see *addition*)

effect (see *affect*)

eight (see *ate*)

elapse (see *lapse*)

elicit to draw forth
illicit unlawful

eligible qualified
illegible unreadable

elusion (see *allusion*)

elusive baffling; hard to catch
illusive misleading; unreal

emerge to rise out of
immerge to plunge into

emigrate to go away from a country
immigrate to come into a country

eminent well-known; prominent
imminent threatening; impending
emanate to originate from; to come out of

en route (see *root*)

ensure to make certain (see page 259)
insure to protect against loss
assure to give confidence to someone

envelop (v.) to cover; to wrap
envelope (n.) a wrapper for a letter

equable even; tranquil
equitable just; right

erasable capable of being erased
irascible quick-tempered

especially to an exceptional degree
specially particularly, as opposed to generally

essay (see *assay*)

everyday daily (see page 260)
every day each day

everyone each one (see ¶1010)
every one each one in a group

ewe (see *you*)

exalt to glorify
exult to be joyful

exceed (see *accede*)

except (see *accept*)

excess (see *access*)

expand to increase in size
expend to spend

expansive capable of being extended
expensive costly

expatiate to enlarge on
expiate to atone for

explicit easily understood
implicit unquestioning

extant still existing
extent measure

exult (see *exalt*)

facet aspect
faucet a tap

facetious witty
factitious artificial
fictitious imaginary

facilitate to make easy
felicitate to congratulate

facility ease
felicity joy

faint (adj.) dim; weak; (v.) to pass out
feint a trick; a deceptive move

fair (adj.) favorable; just; (n.) an exhibit
fare (n.) cost of travel; food; (v.) to go forth

farther at a greater distance, referring to *actual* distance (see page 260)
further to a greater extent or degree, referring to *figurative* distance; moreover; in addition

faucet (see *facet*)

faze to disturb
phase a stage in development

feet plural of *foot*
feat an act of skill or strength

fictitious (see *facetious*)

finale the end
finally at the end
finely in a fine manner

fineness delicacy
finesse tact

fir a tree
fur skin of an animal

fiscal (see *physical*)

flair aptitude
flare a light; a signal

flaunt to display showily
flout to treat with contempt

flew did fly
flue a chimney
flu short for *influenza*

flounder to move clumsily
founder to collapse; to sink; one who establishes something

7

flour ground meal
flower blossom

for a preposition
fore first; preceding; the front
four numeral

forbear to bear with
forebear an ancestor

forgo to relinquish; to let pass
forego to go before

formally in a formal manner
formerly before

fort a fortified place
forte (n.) area where one excels; (adv.) loud (musical direction)

forth away; forward
fourth next after third

forward ahead
foreword preface

foul unfavorable; unclean
fowl a bird

founder (see *flounder*)

four (see *for*)

fur (see *fir*)

further (see *farther*)

genius talent
genus a classification in botany or zoology

gibe (n.) a sarcastic remark; (v.) to scoff at
jibe to agree

grate (n.) a frame of bars (as in a fireplace); (v.) to scrape; to irritate
great large; magnificent

guessed past tense of *guess*
guest visitor

hail (n.) a shower of icy pellets; (v.) to call out to
hale (adj.) healthy; (v.) to compel to go

hall a corridor
haul to drag

heal to cure
heel part of a foot or a shoe

healthful promoting health (e.g., a *healthful* food)
healthy being in good health (e.g., a *healthy* person)

hear to perceive by ear
here in this place

heard past tense of *hear*
herd a group of animals

heir (see *air*)

higher at a greater height
hire to employ; to use someone's services

holy sacred
holey full of holes
wholly entirely
holly a tree

hour sixty minutes
our belonging to us
are a form of *to be* (as in *we are, you are, they are*)

human pertaining to humanity
humane kindly

hypercritical overcritical
hypocritical pretending virtue

ideal a standard of perfection
idle unoccupied; without worth
idol object of worship
idyll a description of rural life

illegible (see *eligible*)

illicit (see *elicit*)

illusion (see *allusion*)

illusive (see *elusive*)

imitate to resemble; to mimic
intimate (adj.) innermost; familiar; (v.) to hint; to make known

immerge (see *emerge*)

immigrate (see *emigrate*)

imminent (see *eminent*)

implicit (see *explicit*)

imply to suggest (see page 262)
infer to deduce; to guess; to conclude

inane senseless
insane of unsound mind

incidence range of occurrence
incidents occurrences; happenings

incinerate to burn
insinuate to imply

incite (v.) to arouse
insight (n.) understanding

indict to charge with a crime
indite to compose; to write

indifferent without interest (see page 262)
in different in other

indigenous native
indigent needy
indignant angry

indirect not direct (see page 262)
in direct *in* (preposition) + *direct* (adjective)

7

infer (see *imply*)

ingenious clever
ingenuous naive

insane (see *inane*)

insight (see *incite*)

insinuate (see *incinerate*)

insoluble incapable of being dissolved
insolvable not explainable
insolvent unable to pay debts

instants short periods of time
instance an example

insure (see *ensure*)

intelligent possessed of understanding
intelligible understandable

intense acute; strong
intents aims

interstate between states
intrastate within one state
intestate dying without a will

intimate (see *imitate*)

into, in to (see page 262)

irascible (see *erasable*)

isle island
aisle passage between rows

its possessive form of *it*
it's contraction of *it is* or *it has* (see ¶1056e)

jibe (see *gibe*)

key a means of gaining entrance or understanding
quay a wharf (also pronounced *key*)

knew understood
new fresh; novel

know to understand
no not any

lapse to become void
elapse to pass
relapse to slip back into a former condition

last final (see page 263)
latest most recent

later more recent; after a time
latter second in a series of two (see page 263)

lath a strip of wood
lathe a wood-turning machine

lay to place (see page 263)
lie (n.) a falsehood; (v.) to recline; to tell an untruth
lye a strong alkaline solution

lead (n.) heavy metal (pronounced like *led*); (v.) to guide (pronounced *leed*)
led guided (past tense of *to lead*)

lean (adj.) thin; (v.) to incline
lien a legal claim

leased rented
least smallest

legislator a lawmaker
legislature a body of lawmakers

lend to allow the use of temporarily
loan (n.) something lent; (v.) to lend
lone solitary

lessee a tenant
lesser of smaller size
lessor one who gives a lease

lessen (v.) to make smaller
lesson (n.) an exercise assigned for study

levee embankment of a river
levy (v.) to raise a collection of money; (n.) the amount that is thus collected

liable responsible
libel defamatory statement

lie (see *lay*)

lien (see *lean*)

lightening making lighter
lightning accompaniment of thunder
lighting illumination

loan, lone (see *lend*)

loath (adj.) reluctant
loathe (v.) to detest

local (adj.) pertaining to a particular place
locale (n.) a particular place

loose (adj.) not bound; (v.) to release
lose (v.) to suffer the loss of; to part with unintentionally
loss something lost

lye (see *lay*)

made constructed
maid a servant

magnificent having splendor
munificent unusually generous

mail correspondence
male masculine

main (adj.) chief; (n.) a conduit
mane long hair on the neck of certain animals

manner a way of acting (as in "to the manner born")
manor an estate

marital pertaining to marriage
martial military
marshal (n.) an official; (v.) to arrange

maybe perhaps (see page 265)
may be a verb consisting of two words

mean (adj.) unpleasant; (n.) the midpoint; (v.) to intend
mien appearance

meat flesh of animals
meet (v.) to join; (adj.) proper
mete to measure

medal a badge of honor
meddle to interfere
metal a mineral
mettle courage; spirit

mien (see *mean*)

miner a worker in a mine
minor (adj.) lesser, as in size, extent, or importance; (n.) a person who is under legal age

mist haze
missed failed to do

mite a tiny particle
might (n.) force; (v.) past tense of *may*

mood disposition
mode fashion; method

moral virtuous
morale spirit

morality virtue
mortality death rate

morning before noon
mourning grief

munificent (see *magnificent*)

naught (see *ought*)

new (see *knew*)

no (see *know*)

nobody no one (see page 265)
no body no group

none not one (see ¶1013)
no one nobody (see ¶1010)

oculist an ophthalmologist or an optometrist
ophthalmologist a doctor who treats eyes
optician one who makes or sells eyeglasses
optometrist one who measures vision

official authorized
officious overbold in offering services

one a single thing
won did win

ordinance a local law
ordnance arms; munitions

ought should
aught anything; all
naught nothing; zero

our (see *hour*)

overdo to do too much
overdue past due

packed crowded
pact an agreement

pail a bucket
pale (adj.) light-colored; (n.) an enclosure

pain suffering
pane window glass

pair two of a kind
pare to peel
pear a fruit

parameter a quantity with an assigned value; a constant
perimeter the outer boundary

partition division
petition prayer; a formal written request

partly in part
partially to some degree

past (n.) time gone by; (adj., adv., or prep.) gone by
passed moved along; transferred (past tense of *pass*)

patience composure; endurance
patients sick persons

peace calmness
piece a portion

peak the top
peek to look slyly at
pique (n.) resentment; (v.) to offend; to arouse
piqué cotton fabric

peal to ring out
peel (n.) the rind; (v.) to strip off

pear (see *pair*)

pedal (adj.) pertaining to the foot; (n.) a treadle
peddle to hawk; to sell

peek (see *peak*)

peer (n.) one of equal rank or age; (v.) to look steadily
pier a wharf

perfect without fault
prefect an official

perimeter (see *parameter*)

perpetrate to be guilty of
perpetuate to make perpetual

perquisite privilege
prerequisite a preliminary requirement

7

persecute to oppress
prosecute to sue

personal private
personnel the staff

perspective a view in correct proportion
prospective anticipated

peruse to read
pursue to chase

petition (see *partition*)

phase (see *faze*)

physic a medicine
physique bodily structure
psychic (adj.) pertaining
to the mind or spirit;
(n.) a medium

physical relating to the
body
fiscal pertaining to
finance
psychical mental

piece (see *peace*)

pier (see *peer*)

pique, piqué (see *peak*)

plain (adj.) undecorated;
(n.) prairie land
plane (n.) a level surface,
an airplane; (v.) to
make level

plaintiff party in a lawsuit
plaintive mournful

pleas plural of *plea*
please to be agreeable

pole a long, slender piece
of wood or metal
poll (n.) the casting of
votes by a body of
persons; (v.) to regis-
ter the votes of

poor (adj.) inadequate;
(n.) the needy
pore to study; to gaze in-
tently
pour to flow

populace the common
people; the masses
populous thickly settled

portend (see *pretend*)

portion a part
proportion a ratio of parts
apportion to allot

practicable workable; feasible
practical useful

pray to beseech
prey a captured victim

precede to go before
proceed to advance

precedence priority
precedents established
rules

prefect (see *perfect*)

preposition a part of
speech
proposition an offer

prerequisite (see *perquisite*)

prescribe to designate
proscribe to outlaw

presence bearing; being
present
presents gifts

presentiment a foreboding
presentment a proposal

pretend to make believe
portend to foreshadow

principal (adj.) chief;
leading; (n.) a capital
sum of money that
draws interest; chief
official of a school
principle a general truth;
a rule

proceed (see *precede*)

profit gain
prophet one who forecasts

prophecy a prediction
prophesy to foretell

propose to suggest
purpose intention

proposition (see *preposition*)

proscribe (see *prescribe*)

prosecute (see *persecute*)

prospective (see *perspective*)

psychic (see *physic*)

purpose (see *propose*)

pursue (see *peruse*)

quay (see *key*)

queue (see *cue*)

quiet calm; not noisy
quite entirely; wholly
quit to stop

rain falling water
rein part of a bridle; a
curb
reign (n.) the term of a
ruler's power; (v.) to
rule

raise to lift something
(see page 267)
raze to destroy
rays beams

rap to knock
wrap (n.) a garment;
(v.) to enclose

read to perform the act of
reading
reed a plant; a musical
instrument
red a color

real actual
reel (n.) a spool; a dance;
(v.) to whirl

reality actuality
realty real estate

7

receipt an acknowledgment of a thing
received
recipe a formula for mix-
ing ingredients

recent (adj.) relating to a
time not long past
resent (v.) to feel hurt by

reference that which refers to something
reverence profound
respect

reign, rein (see *rain*)

relapse (see *lapse*)

residence a house
residents persons who
reside in a place

respectably in a manner
worthy of respect
respectfully in a courte-
ous manner
respectively in the order
indicated

right (adj.) correct; (n.) a
privilege
rite a ceremony
wright a worker; a maker
(used as a combining
form, as in *playwright*)
write to inscribe

role a part in a play
roll (n.) a list; a type of
bread; (v.) to revolve

root (n.) underground
part of a plant; (v.) to
implant firmly
route (n.) an established
course of travel;
(v.) to send by a cer-
tain route
en route on or along the
way
rout (n.) confused flight;
(v.) to defeat

rote repetition
wrote did write

sail (n.) part of a ship's
rigging; (v.) to travel
by water
sale the act of selling

scene a setting; an exhibition of strong feeling
seen past participle of *to
see*

scent odor
sent did send
cent penny
sense meaning

sealing (see *ceiling*)

seam a line of junction
seem to appear

seed (see *cede*)

seize (see *cease*)

sell to transfer for a price
cell a small compartment

seller one who sells
cellar an underground
room

sense, sent (see *scent*)

senses (see *census*)

serge a kind of cloth
surge (n.) a billow; (v.) to
rise suddenly

serial (see *cereal*)

serve to help (see
page 268)
service to keep in good
repair

session (see *cession*)

sew (see *so*)

shear to cut; to trim
sheer transparent; unqual-
ified, utter

shoot to fire
chute a slide

shown displayed; revealed;
past participle of *show*
shone gave off light; did
shine

sight, site (see *cite*)

simple plain; uncompli-
cated
simplistic oversimplified;
falsely simple

sleight dexterity, as in
"sleight of hand"
slight (adj.) slender;
scanty; (v.) to make
light of

so therefore
sew to stitch
sow to scatter seed

soar (see *sore*)

soared did fly
sword weapon

sole one and only
soul the immortal spirit

soluble having the ability
to dissolve in a liquid
solvable capable of being
solved or explained

some a part of
sum a total

someone somebody (see
¶1010)
some one some person in
a group

sometime at some unspecified time (see
page 270)
some time a period of
time
sometimes now and then

son male child
sun the earth's source of
light and heat

sore painful
soar to fly

soul (see *sole*)

sow (see *so*)

spacious having ample room
specious outwardly correct but inwardly false

specially (see *especially*)

staid grave; sedate
stayed past tense and past participle of *to stay*

stair a step
stare to look at

stake (n.) a pointed stick; the prize in a contest; (v.) to wager
steak a slice of meat or fish

stationary fixed
stationery writing materials

statue a carved or molded figure
stature height
statute a law

steal to take unlawfully
steel a form of iron

straight not crooked; directly
strait a water passageway; (plural) a distressing situation

suit (n.) a legal action; clothing; (v.) to please
suite a group of things forming a unit
sweet having an agreeable taste; pleasing

sum (see *some*)

sun (see *son*)

superintendence management
superintendents supervisors

surge (see *serge*)

sweet (see *suit*)

sword (see *soared*)

tack (n.) direction; (v.) to change direction (see page 270)
tact considerate way of behaving so as to avoid offending others

tail the end
tale a story

tare allowance for weight
tear (n.) a rent or rip (pronounced like *tare*); a secretion from the eye (pronounced like *tier*); (v.) to rip
tier a row or layer

taught did teach
taut tight; tense

team a group
teem to abound

tenant one who rents property
tenet a principle

than conjunction of comparison (see page 270)
then (adv.) at that time

their belonging to them (see ¶1056e)
there in that place
they're contraction of *they are*

theirs possessive form of *they*, used without a following noun (see ¶1056e)
there's contraction of *there is* or *there has*

therefor for that thing
therefore consequently

throes a painful struggle
throws hurls; flings

through by means of; from beginning to end; because of
threw did throw
thorough carried through to completion

tier (see *tare*)

to (prep.) toward
too (adv.) more than enough; also
two one plus one

tortuous winding; twisty; devious
torturous cruelly painful

track a trail
tract a treatise; a piece of land

trial examination; an experiment; hardship
trail a path

undo to open; to render ineffective
undue improper; excessive

uninterested (see *disinterested*)

urban pertaining to the city
urbane polished; suave

vain proud; conceited; futile
vane a weathercock
vein a blood vessel; a bed of mineral materials

vale a valley
veil a concealing cover or cloth

vendee purchaser
vendor seller

veracious truthful
voracious greedy

veracity truthfulness
voracity ravenousness; greediness

7

vice wickedness; a prefix used with nouns to designate titles of office (see ¶808b)
vise a clamp

waist part of the body
waste (n.) needless destruction; useless consumption; (v.) to expend uselessly

wait to stay
weight heaviness

waive (v.) to give up
wave (n.) a billow; a gesture; (v.) to swing back and forth

waiver the giving up of a claim
waver to hesitate

want (n.) a need; (v.) to lack; to desire
wont a custom (pronounced like *want*)
won't contraction of *will not*

ware goods
wear to have on
were form of *to be*
where at the place in which

wave (see *waive*)

way direction; distance; manner
weigh to find the weight of

weak not strong
week period of seven days

weather (n.) state of the atmosphere; (v.) to come through safely
whether if (see page 272)

weight (see *wait*)

whoever anyone who
who ever *two words* (see page 272)

wholly (see *holy*)

whose possessive of *who*
who's contraction of *who is* (see ¶1063)

won (see *one*)

wont, won't (see *want*)

wood lumber
would an auxiliary verb form (as in *they would like some*)

wrap (see *rap*)

wright, write (see *right*)

wrote (see *rote*)

yoke a crosspiece that holds two things together; an oppressive constraint
yolk the yellow part of an egg

you second-person pronoun
yew an evergreen tree or bush
ewe a female sheep

your belonging to *you* (see ¶1056e)
you're contraction of *you are*

Troublesome Words

720   The following list presents a selection of words that business writers often misspell or stop and puzzle over. In some cases the difficulty results from the inability to apply an established rule; for such words, references to the rules are given. In many other instances, however, errors result from the peculiar spelling of the words themselves; in such cases the only remedy is to master the correct spelling of such words on an individual basis.

NOTE: For troublesome words that sound alike or look alike, see ¶719. For troublesome compound words, see Section 8.

abscess
absence
accessory
accidentally (see page 255)
accommodate
accompanying
achievement
acknowledgment (see ¶708)
acquaintance
acquiesce

acquire
acquisition
across
adjacent
advantageous (see ¶707)
aegis
affidavit
aggressive
aging (see ¶707)
aisle

Albuquerque
algorithm
alignment
all right (see page 254)
alleged
already (see page 254)
amateur
amortize (see ¶715)
analogous
analysis

analyze (see ¶715)
anomalous
answer
antecedent
appall
apparatus
architect
argument (see ¶708)
assistance (see ¶714)
asthma
attendance
attorney
autumn
auxiliary
bachelor
bankruptcy
bargain
basically
believe (see ¶712)
beneficiary
benefited (see ¶704)
benign
Berkeley (California)
biased (see ¶705)
biscuit
bizarre
boundary
breakfast
brochure
buoyant
bureau
business
busy
calendar
caliber
calorie
campaign
canceled (see ¶704)
cancellation (see ¶704)
candor
Caribbean
carriage
catalog
category
ceiling
cemetery
census
chaise longue (see ¶612a)
changeable (see ¶707)
chronological
Cincinnati
circuit
coincidence
collateral
colonel
colossal
column
comparison
concede (see ¶716)
conceive

condemn
Connecticut
connoisseur
conscience
conscientious
conscious
consensus
corduroy
correspondent
courtesy
debt
debtor
deductible
de-emphasize
defendant (see ¶714)
defense
deficit
definite
dependent (see ¶714)
Des Moines
descendant (see ¶714)
describe
desperately
detrimental
develop
dictionary
dilemma
disappear
disappoint
disastrous
dissatisfied
dissimilar
doctrinaire
dossier
double
ecstasy
eighth
cither
eliminate
embarrass
emphasize
empty
entrepreneur
enumerate
environment
erroneous
escrow
exaggerate
exceed (see ¶716)
excellent
exercise
exhaustible
exhibition
exhilarate
exonerate
exorbitant
extension
extraordinary
eyeing
facsimile

familiar
fantasy
fascinating
fatigue
February
fiery
financier
fluorescent
forbade
foreign (see ¶712)
foresee
forfeit
forty
fourteen
fourth
freight
fulfill
gauge
glamorous
glamour
goodwill
government
grammar
grateful
gray
grievous
gruesome (see ¶708)
guarantee
guardian
handkerchief
harass
height (see ¶712)
hemorrhage
heterogeneous
hindrance
hors d'oeuvre
hygiene
hypocrisy
impasse
inasmuch as
incidentally
indict
indispensable
innocuous
innuendo
inoculate
interim
intern
irrelevant (see ¶714)
itinerary
jeopardy
judgment (see ¶708)
khaki
labeled (see ¶704)
laboratory
league
ledger
leisure
liable
liaison

7

library
license
lien
lieutenant
lightning
liquefy
literature
maintenance
maneuver
marriage
marshaled
martyr
medieval
mediocre
memento
mileage (see ¶707)
milieu
millennium
millionaire
miniature
minuscule
miscellaneous
mischievous
misspell
mnemonic
mortgage
motor
necessary
negotiate
neighbor
neither (see ¶712)
nickel
niece (see ¶712)
ninety
ninth
noticeable (see ¶707)
nuclear
obsolescent
offense
omelet
omission
ophthalmology
pamphlet
panicky (see ¶717)
paradigm
parallel
parliament
pastime
patience
permissible (see ¶713)
perseverance
persistent
persuade
phase
phenomenal
Philippines
phony
physician
picnicking (see ¶717)
Pittsburgh

plagiarism
plausible (see ¶713)
practically
practice
prairie
preceding (see ¶716)
preferable (see ¶702)
prerogative
presumptuous
pretense
privilege
procedure (see ¶716)
proceed (see ¶716)
programmed (see ¶704)
prohibition
pronunciation
protégé
psalm
pseudonym
psychiatric
psychological
publicly
pursue
quantity
questionnaire
queue
rarefy
receipt
receive (see ¶712)
recommend
reconnaisance
recruit
reinforce
relevant (see ¶714)
renaissance
rendezvous
renowned
rescind
resistance (see ¶714)
restaurant
résumé (see ¶718)
rhapsody
rhetorical
rhyme
rhythm
rhythmic
sacrilegious
salable (see ¶707)
San Francisco
sandwich
satellite
schedule
scissors
secretary
seize (see ¶712)
separate
sergeant
siege (see ¶712)
sieve
similar

simultaneous
sincerely (see ¶708)
skeptic
skillful
souvenir
specimen
sponsor
stratagem
strength
subpoena
subtlety
subtly
succeed
summary
superintendent
supersede (see ¶716)
surgeon
surprise
surreptitious
surveillance (see ¶714)
synagogue
tariff
taxiing
technique
temperament
temperature
tempt
theater
their (see ¶712)
theory
thoroughly
threshold
through
totaled (see ¶704)
tragedy
traveler (see ¶704)
Tuesday
unctuous
unique
unmanageable (see ¶707)
unwieldy (see ¶712)
usage (see ¶707)
vaccinate
vacillate
vacuum
vegetable
victim
vinyl
volume
warrant
Wednesday
weird (see ¶712)
whether
whiskey
wholly
wield (see ¶712)
withhold
woeful
woolly (see ¶705)
yield (see ¶712)

7

SECTION 8

Compound Words

Some compound words are written as solid words, some are written as separate words, and some are hyphenated. As in other areas of style, authorities do not agree on the rules. Moreover, style is continually changing: many words that used to be hyphenated are now written solid or as separate words. The only complete guide is an up-to-date dictionary. However, a careful reading of the following rules will save you many a trip to the dictionary.

NOTE: The spellings in this section agree with those in the 1990 printing of *Webster's Ninth New Collegiate Dictionary* and *Webster's Third New International Dictionary* (published by Merriam-Webster, Springfield, Massachusetts) unless otherwise indicated.

Compound Nouns

801   Compound nouns follow no regular pattern. Some are written solid, some are spaced, and some are hyphenated.

airfreight	air bag	air-conditioning
checklist	check mark	check-in
closeout	close shave	close-up
crossroad	cross section	cross-reference
daytime	day care	day-tripper
doubleheader	double take	double-dipper
eyewitness	eye shadow	eye-opener
freeway	free lance	free-fall
goodwill	good sense	good-bye
halftime	half hour	half-truth
jobholder	job action	job-hopper
lifeline	life span	life-style
lightweight	light bulb	light-year
moneylender	money market	money-maker
placeholder	place mat	place-name
pocketbook	pocket money	pocket-handkerchief
showdown	show biz	show-off
sickroom	sick pay	sick-out
timetable	time deposit	time-saver
trademark	trade name	trade-off
bondholder	bond paper	
bookstore	book review	
cashbook	cash flow	
handbook	hand truck	
homeowner	home port	
masterpiece	master plan	
paperwork	paper clip	
payroll	pay dirt	
salespeople	sales tax	
schoolteacher	school board	
standby	stand-in	
workstation	work load	
bylaw	by-product	
voiceprint	voice-over	
wageworker	wage earner	

NOTE: To be sure of the spelling of a compound noun, check a dictionary. If the noun is not listed, treat the components as separate words. For the spelling of compounds in company names, check letterheads for possible variations. (Compare, for example, *United Airlines* with *Delta Air Lines*.)

8

802 Some solid and hyphenated compound nouns closely resemble verb phrases. Be sure, however, to treat the elements in a verb phrase as separate words.

Nouns	Verb Phrases
a *breakdown* in communications	when communications *break down*
a thorough *follow-up* of the report	to *follow up* on your recommendation
operate a *drive-in*	*drive in* to your dealer's
a high school *dropout*	don't *drop out* of high school
at the time of *takeoff*	planes cannot *take off* or land
when they give us a *go-ahead*	we can *go ahead* with the plan
come to a *standstill*	we can't *stand still*
let's have a *run-through*	let's *run through* the plan
plan a *get-together*	plan to *get together*
they have the *know-how*	they *know how* to handle it
expect a *turnaround* in sales	once our sales *turn around*
we have to make a *getaway*	we have to *get away*
to attempt a *takeover* of their firm	to attempt to *take over* their firm
I was a *standby* on Flight 968A	we can't *stand by* and do nothing
Paul's speech was merely a *put-on*	your requisition was *put on* hold
devise an alternative plan as a *fallback*	we can always *fall back* on Plan B if we have to
serve as a *go-between* in the labor dispute	this note should *go between* the two tables on page 5

803 a. *Up* **Words.** Compound nouns ending in *up* are either solid or hyphenated. For example:

backup	linkup	call-up	mock-up
blowup	makeup	catch-up	runner-up
breakup	markup	close-up	send-up
brushup	pasteup	cover-up	shake-up
buildup	pileup	flare-up	sign-up
checkup	roundup	follow-up	start-up
cleanup	setup	foul-up	tie-up
getup	slipup	hang-up	toss-up
holdup	smashup	jam-up	touch-up
letup	warmup*	lead-up	wrap-up
lineup	windup	mix-up	write-up

b. *Down* **Words.** Most compound nouns ending in *down* are solid. For example:

breakdown	lowdown	shakedown	**BUT:** dressing-down
closedown	markdown	showdown	put-down
comedown	meltdown	shutdown	sit-down
countdown	phasedown	slowdown	step-down
crackdown	rubdown	sundown	wind-down
letdown	rundown	turndown	write-down

c. *In* **Words.** Compound nouns ending in *in* are typically hyphenated. For example:

break-in	fill-in	shut-in	trade-in
buy-in	lead-in	sit-in	turn-in
cave-in	listener-in	stand-in	walk-in
check-in	run-in	teach-in	weigh-in
drive-in	shoo-in	tie-in	write-in

---

*Merriam-Webster shows this as a hyphenated word, but it frequently appears as a solid word in business.

d. Out Words. Compound nouns ending in *out* are typically solid. For example:

bailout	handout	rollout	**BUT:**	cop-out
blackout	hangout	sellout		diner-out
blowout	hideout	shakeout		fade-out
breakout	holdout	shutout		falling-out
burnout	knockout	standout		lights-out
buyout	layout	strikeout		shoot-out
checkout	lookout	tryout		sick-out
closeout	payout	turnout		time-out
cutout	phaseout	walkout		
dropout	printout	washout		
fallout	readout	workout		

e. On Words. Compound nouns ending in *on* are typically hyphenated. For example:

add-on	follow-on	lookers-on		slip-on
carryings-on	goings-on	put-on		turn-on
come-on	hangers-on	run-on	**BUT:**	carryon

f. Off Words. Compound nouns ending in *off* are either solid or hyphenated. For example:

checkoff	liftoff	brush-off	send-off
cutoff	payoff	drop-off	show-off
falloff	runoff	goof-off	sign-off
kickoff	shutoff	play-off	spin-off
knockoff	standoff	rake-off	tip-off
layoff	takeoff	rip-off	trade-off
leadoff	turnoff	sell-off	write-off

g. Over Words. Compound nouns ending in *over* are typically solid. For example:

carryover	layover	slipover		turnover
changeover	leftover	spillover		walkover
crossover	pushover	stopover	**BUT:**	going-over
hangover	rollover	strikeover		once-over
holdover	runover	takeover		voice-over

h. Back Words. Compound nouns ending in *back* are typically solid. For example:

buyback	drawback	payback	setback
callback	fallback	playback	snapback
carryback	feedback	pullback	throwback
comeback	kickback	rollback	tieback

i. Away Words. These compounds are typically solid. For example:

breakaway	hideaway	runaway	straightaway
getaway	layaway	stowaway	throwaway

j. Compounds Ending in *About, Around,* and *By*. These compounds are typically solid. For example:

knockabout	runabout	runaround	passersby
layabout	turnabout	turnaround	standbys

k. Compounds Ending in *Between, Through,* and *Together*. These compounds are typically hyphenated. For example:

go-between	follow-through	walk-through	**BUT:** breakthrough
in-between	run-through	get-together	

8

804   **a.** Hyphenate a compound noun that lacks a noun as one of its elements.

the also-rans	know-it-alls	a set-to
a cure-all	hand-me-downs	a lean-to
a go-getter	the well-to-do	a talking-to
a has-been	a shoot-'em-up	give-and-take
the have-nots	do-it-yourselfers	a five-and-ten
the higher-ups	a good-for-nothing	half-and-half
know-how	a ne'er-do-well	on the up-and-up
a look-alike	a merry-go-round	show-and-tell
make-believe	a free-for-all	a sing-along
say-so	the be-all and end-all	the old so-and-so
two-by-fours	hide-and-seek	**BUT:** ups and downs
the old one-two	no get-up-and-go	wear and tear
a nine-to-fiver	a sing-along	wannabes

b. Words coined from repeated syllables or rhyming syllables are typically hyphenated. Other coined words may be hyphenated or solid.

boo-boo	culture-vulture	one-upmanship
goody-goody	hurly-burly	stick-to-itiveness
no-no	nitty-gritty	comeuppance
yo-yo	walkie-talkie	whodunit
hanky-panky	**BUT:** wingding	twofers
hocus-pocus	mumbo jumbo	a gofer

c. Many compound nouns that end with a prepositional phrase are hyphenated.

ambassador-at-large	stick-in-the-mud	**BUT:** bill of lading
attorney-at-law	man-about-town	editor in chief
brother-in-law	right-of-way	line of credit
grants-in-aid	stay-at-home	power of attorney
jack-of-all-trades	stock-in-trade	rule of thumb
Johnny-on-the-spot	theater-in-the-round	standard of living

805   Treat a compound noun like *problem solving* as two words unless your dictionary specifically shows it as solid or hyphenated. (Most words of this pattern are not shown in a dictionary. However, the solid and hyphenated examples below have been taken from the 1990 printing of *Webster's Ninth New Collegiate Dictionary,* published by Merriam-Webster.)

data processing	brainstorming	belt-tightening
decision making	housewarming	consciousness-raising
plea bargaining	lawmaking	house-sitting
problem solving	letterspacing	name-dropping
profit sharing	lipreading	sight-seeing
skill building	logrolling	soul-searching
space heating	safekeeping	speed-reading
skin diving	trailblazing	whistle-blowing
(**BUT:** skydiving)	troubleshooting	witch-hunting

For words like air conditioning, *which are derived from hyphenated infinitives like* air-condition, *see ¶812.*

806   Hyphenate two nouns when they signify that one person or one thing has two functions. (See also ¶295b.)

actor-director	dinner-dance	secretary-treasurer
clerk-typist	owner-manager	wheeler-dealer

807   Compound nouns that have a single letter as their first element are either hyphenated or written as two words.

A-frame	f-stop	I beam	T square	X ray
B-school	G suit	J-bar lift	U-turn	x axis
D-mark	H-bomb	T-shirt	V neck	y coordinate

NOTE: The term *X ray* (which is two words when used as a noun) is hyphenated when used as a verb or an adjective. (See also ¶815a.)

808 Do not hyphenate civil, military, and naval titles of two or more words.

Chief of Police Potenza Attorney General Leibowitz
General Manager Werner Rear Admiral Byrd

a. Hyphenate compound titles containing *ex* and *elect*.

ex-President Reagan Vice President-elect Jordan

NOTE: Also use a hyphen when *ex* is attached to a noun (for example, *ex-wife, ex-convict*), but omit the hyphen in Latin phrases (for example, *ex officio, ex cathedra*).

For the capitalization of titles with ex *and* elect, *see ¶¶317 and 363; for the correct usage of* ex, *see the entry for* Ex—former *on page 260.*

b. The hyphen is still customary in *vice-chancellor* and *vice-consul,* but it is gone from *vice president* and *vice admiral.*

Vice-Chancellor Safran Vice President Quayle Vice Admiral Bissell

809 Compound nouns containing *man* or *men* as an element have traditionally been used generically to refer to males and females alike.

not for the average *layman* the history of *mankind*
of concern to all *businessmen* reduce the number of *man-hours*
write your *congressman* a new source of *manpower*

a. The *generic* use of such terms is offensive to many people, who feel that the masculine bias of these terms makes them unsuitable for reference to women as well as men. Therefore, avoid using such terms whenever possible. The following list suggests appropriate alternatives.

In Place of the Generic Term	Use
layman	layperson
businessmen	business owners, business executives, business managers, business people
congressmen	members of Congress, representatives
mankind	people, humanity, the human race, human beings
man-hours	worker-hours
manpower	work force, human resources, staff
salesmen	salespeople, sales representatives, salespersons, salesclerks, sales staff, sales force
foremen	supervisors
policemen	police officers
mailmen	mail carriers
workmen	workers

NOTE: The traditional term *workmen's compensation insurance* (or *workmen's comp*) is now commonly referred to as *workers' compensation insurance* (or *workers' comp*).

See ¶840 for alternatives to words ending with feminine suffixes.

(Continued on page 184.)

b. Whenever possible, replace a word like *salesmanship* with an alternative expression (for example, *selling skills*). However, words such as *craftsmanship, workmanship, sportsmanship, grantsmanship, brinkmanship,* and *one-upmanship* are still widely used because of the difficulty in devising alternative expressions.

c. When naming a job or role, avoid the use of compound terms ending in *man* or *woman* unless the term refers to a specific person whose gender is known.

There are ten candidates seeking election to the City *Council.* (NOT: . . . seeking election as city *councilmen.*)

BUT: *Councilwoman* Walters and *Councilman* Holtz will study the proposal.

Write to your *representative in Congress.* (NOT: Write to your *congressman.*)

BUT: I was very much impressed by *Congresswoman* Schroeder of Colorado.

Who will be appointed as *head* of the committee? OR Who will be appointed to *chair* the committee? (NOT: . . . appointed *chairman* of the committee?)

BUT: Robert Haas has been appointed *chairman* of the committee.

NOTE: Words like *chairperson* and *spokesperson* have been coined as a means of avoiding the generic use of masculine compound nouns. Personal taste or institutional policy will dictate whether to use these terms or not.

810 Terms like *doctor, lawyer,* and *nurse* are generic—that is, they apply equally to women and men. Therefore, do not use compound nouns like *woman lawyer* and *male nurse* unless there is a legitimate reason for making a distinction according to gender.

Next Wednesday there will be a seminar on the special problems facing *women lawyers* in the courtroom.

Capitalization of hyphenated compound nouns: see ¶363.
Plurals of compound nouns: see ¶¶611–613.
Possessives of compound nouns: see ¶¶634–635.

Compound Verbs

811 a. Compound verbs are usually hyphenated or solid.

to air-condition	to fine-tune	to backstop	to mastermind
to baby-sit	to off-load	to bulldoze	to moonlight
to bird-dog	to pinch-hit	to buttonhole	to pinpoint
to blue-pencil	to rubber-stamp	to downgrade	to proofread
to color-code	to second-guess	to download	to sandbag
to custom-tailor	to shrink-wrap	to downsize	to shortchange
to deep-six	to soft-pedal	to ghostwrite	to sidetrack
to double-space	to spot-check	to hamstring	to troubleshoot
to dry-clean	to test-drive	to handpick	to waterproof
to field-test	to window-shop	to highlight	to whitewash

NOTE: If you try to check the spelling of a compound verb in a dictionary and do not find the verb listed, hyphenate the components.

b. Do not hyphenate verb phrases combinations such as *make up, slow down, tie in.* (See ¶802 for examples.)

812 **a.** If the infinitive form of a compound verb contains a hyphen, retain the hyphen in the other forms of the verb. (See ¶812b for one type of exception.)

Would you like to *air-condition* your entire house?
The theater was not *air-conditioned.*
We need an *air-conditioning* expert to advise us.

You need to *double-space* all these reports.
Please *double-space* this letter.
This material should not be *double-spaced.*
BUT: Leave a *double space* between paragraphs. (No hyphen in *double space* as a compound noun.)

b. The gerund derived from a hyphenated compound verb requires no hyphen unless it is followed by an object.

Dry cleaning is the best way to treat this garment.
BUT: *Dry-cleaning* this *sweater* will not remove the spot.

Air conditioning is no longer as expensive as it used to be.
BUT: In *air-conditioning* an *office,* you must take more than space into account.

Spot checking is all we have time for.
BUT: In *spot-checking* the *data,* I found some disturbing errors.

Compound Adjectives

No aspect of style causes greater difficulty than compound adjectives. When a compound adjective is shown hyphenated in the dictionary, you can assume only that the expression is hyphenated when it occurs directly *before* a noun. When the same combination of words falls elsewhere in the sentence, the use or omission of hyphens depends on how the words are used.

For the basic rules, see ¶¶813–815. For detailed comments, see the following paragraphs:

Adjective + noun (as in short-term *note): see ¶816.*
Compound with number or letter (as in 40-hour *week): see ¶817.*
Compound noun (as in high school *graduate): see ¶818.*
Proper name (as in Madison Avenue *agencies): see ¶819.*
Noun + adjective (as in tax-free *imports): see ¶820.*
Noun + participle (as in time-consuming *details): see ¶821.*
Adjective + participle (as in nice-looking *layout): see ¶822.*
Adjective + noun + ed (as in quick-witted *assistant): see ¶823.*
Adverb + participle (as in privately owned *stock): see ¶824a.*
Adverb + participle (as in well-known *facts): see ¶824b.*
Adverb + adjective (as in very exciting *test results): see ¶825.*
Participle + adverb (as in warmed-over *ideas): see ¶826.*
Adjective + adjective (as in black leather *notebook): see ¶827.*
Verb + verb (as in stop-and-go *traffic): see ¶828.*
Verb + adverb (as in a read-only *memory): see ¶829.*
Verb + noun (as in take-home *pay): see ¶830.*
Phrasal compound (as in up-to-date *accounts): see ¶831.*

NOTE: If you try to check the spelling of a compound adjective in a dictionary and do not find it listed, match up the components with one of the patterns shown above and follow the standard style for that pattern.

Basic Rules

813   A compound adjective consists of two or more words that function as a unit and express a single thought. These one-thought modifiers are derived from (and take the place of) adjective phrases and clauses. In the following examples the left column shows the original phrase or clause; the right column shows the compound adjective.

Adjective Phrase or Clause	Compound Adjective
terminals *installed at the point of sale*	*point-of-sale* terminals
a career *moving along a fast track*	a *fast-track* career
imports *that are free of duty*	*duty-free* imports
a woman *who speaks quietly*	a *quiet-spoken* woman
an actor *who is well known*	a *well-known* actor
a conference *held at a high level*	a *high-level* conference
a building *ten stories high*	a *ten-story* building
a report *that is up to date*	an *up-to-date* report
an article *that is as long as a book*	a *book-length* article
an environment *where people work under high pressure*	a *high-pressure* environment

NOTE: In the process of becoming compound adjectives, the adjective phrases and clauses are usually reduced to a few essential words. In addition, these words frequently undergo a change in form (for example, *ten stories high* becomes *ten-story*); sometimes they are put in inverted order (for example, *free of duty* becomes *duty-free*); sometimes they are simply extracted from the phrase or clause without any change in form (for example, *well-known, high-level*).

814   Hyphenate the elements of a compound adjective that occurs *before* a noun. (**REASON:** The words that make up the compound adjective are not in their normal order or a normal form and require hyphens to hold them together.)

> *high-tech* equipment (equipment *that reflects a high level of technology*)
> a *worst-case* scenario (a scenario *based on the worst case that could occur*)
> an *old-fashioned* dress (a dress *of an old fashion*)
> a *$20,000-a-year* salary (a salary *of $20,000 a year*)
> *long-range* plans (plans *projected over a long range of time*)
> *machine-readable* copy (copy *readable by a machine*)
> an *eye-catching* display (a display *that catches the eye*)
> a *high-ranking* official (an official *who ranks high in the organization*)
> *same-day* service (service *completed the same day you bring the item in*)
> a *black-tie* affair (an affair *at which men must wear formal clothes with a black tie*)
> the *rubber-chicken* circuit (a circuit *or series of banquets at which speeches are given and rubbery chicken or some equally bad food is served*)
> *revolving-door* management (a management *with such rapid turnover that managers seem to be arriving and departing through a continuously revolving door*)
> *bottom-line* results (the results *shown on the bottom line of a financial statement*)

EXCEPTIONS: A number of compounds like *real estate* and *high school* do not need hyphens when used as adjectives before a noun. (See ¶818.)

815 **a.** When these expressions occur *elsewhere in the sentence,* drop the hyphen if the individual words occur in a normal order and in a normal form. (In such cases the expression no longer functions as a compound adjective.)

Before the Noun	Elsewhere in Sentence
an *X-ray* treatment	This condition can be treated by *X ray.* (Object of preposition.)
an *up-to-date* report	Please bring the report *up to date.* (Prepositional phrase.)
a *follow-up* letter	Let's *follow up* at once with a letter. (Verb + adverb.)
a *high-level* decision	The decision must be made at a *high level.* (Object of preposition.)
a *never-to-be-forgotten* book	Your latest book is *never to be forgotten.* (Adverb + infinitive phrase.)
an *off-the-record* comment	The next comment is *off the record.* (Prepositional phrase.)
a *no-nonsense* attitude	Marion will tolerate *no nonsense* from you. (Object of verb.)
a *low-key* sales approach	Christopher pitches his sales approach in a *low key.* (Object of preposition.)
a *cause-and-effect* relationship	Is there a relationship of *cause and effect* in this case? (Object of preposition.)
a *four-color* cover	Is this cover printed in *four colors?* (Object of preposition.)

b. When these expressions occur elsewhere in the sentence *but are in an inverted word order or an altered form,* retain the hyphen.

Before the Noun	Elsewhere in Sentence
a *tax-exempt* purchase	The purchase was *tax-exempt.* BUT: The purchase was *exempt from taxes.*
government-owned lands	These lands are *government-owned.* BUT: These lands are *owned by the government.*
a *friendly-looking* salesclerk	That salesclerk is *friendly-looking.* BUT: That salesclerk *looks friendly.*
high-priced goods	These goods are *high-priced.* BUT: These goods carry a *high price.*

NOTE: The following kinds of compound adjectives almost always need to be hyphenated:

Noun + adjective (for example, tax-exempt*): see ¶820.*
Noun + participle (for example, government-owned*): see ¶821.*
Adjective + participle (for example, friendly-looking*): see ¶822.*
Adjective + noun + ed (for example, high-priced*): see ¶823.*

Adjective + Noun (see also ¶¶817–819)

816 **a.** Hyphenate an adjective and a noun when these elements serve as a compound modifier *before* a noun. Do not hyphenate these elements when they play a normal role *elsewhere in the sentence* (for example, as the object of a preposition or of a verb). However, if the expression continues to function as a compound adjective, retain the hyphen.

(Continued on page 188.)

Before the Noun	Elsewhere in Sentence
high-speed printers	These printers run at *high speed*. (Object of preposition.)
random-access memory	This computer permits *random access* to the stored data. (Object of verb.)
red-carpet treatment	They plan to roll out the *red carpet*. (Object of infinitive.)
a *closed-door* discussion	The discussion was held behind *closed doors*. (Object of preposition.)
an *all-day* seminar	The seminar will last *all day*. (Normal adverbial phrase.)
a *long-term* investment in bonds	This investment in bonds runs for a *long term*. (Object of preposition.)
	BUT: This investment in bonds is *long-term*. (Compound adjective.)
a *part-time* job	This job is *part-time*. (Compound adjective.)
	I work *part-time*. (Compound adverb.)
	I travel *part of the time*. (Normal adverbial phrase.)

NOTE: Combinations involving comparative or superlative adjectives plus nouns follow the same pattern.

Before the Noun	Elsewhere in Sentence
a *larger-size* shirt	He wears a *larger size*. (Object of verb.)
the *finest-quality* goods	These goods are of the *finest quality*. (Object of preposition.)

b. A few compound adjectives in this category are now written solid—for example, *a commonsense solution, a freshwater pond, a surefire success.*

Compound With Number or Letter

817 **a.** When a number and a noun form a one-thought modifier *before* a noun (as in *six-story building*), make the noun singular and hyphenate the expression. When the expression has a normal form and a normal function *elsewhere in the sentence,* do not hyphenate it.

Before the Noun	Elsewhere in Sentence
a *one-way* street	a street that runs only *one way*
a *first-person* account	a story written in the *first person*
a *first-rate* job	a job that deserves the *first* (or highest) *rating*
	BUT: a job that is *first-rate*
a *two-piece* suit	a suit consisting of *two pieces*
a *three-ring* circus	a circus with *three rings*
a *four-color* illustration	an illustration printed in *four colors*
a *5-liter* container	a container that holds *5 liters*
an *8-foot* ceiling	a ceiling *8 feet* above the floor
a *20-year* mortgage	a mortgage running for *20 years*
twentieth-century art	art of the *twentieth century*
a *50-cent* fee	a fee of *50 cents*
an *$85-a-month* charge	a charge of *$85 a month*
a *100-meter* sprint	a sprint of *100 meters*
an *8½- by 11-inch* book (see ¶832)	a book *8½ by 11 inches*
a *55-mile-an-hour* speed limit	a speed limit of *55 miles an hour*

Before the Noun	Elsewhere in Sentence
a *2-million-ton* shipment	a shipment of *2 million tons*
a *10-inch-thick* panel	a panel *10 inches thick*
a *7-foot-2-inch* basketball player	a basketball player *7 feet 2 inches* tall (see ¶430)
24-hour-a-day service	service *24 hours a day*
300-dpi graphics	graphics composed of *300 dpi* (dots per inch)

EXCEPTIONS: a *15 percent* decline, a *$4 million* profit, a *twofold* increase (**BUT:** a *12-fold* increase), a *secondhand* car (**BUT:** a *second-degree* burn)

For the hyphenation of fractional expressions serving as compound adjectives (like half-dozen *or* 1/4-inch), *see* ¶427a.

NOTE: A hyphenated compound adjective and an unhyphenated possessive expression often provide *alternative* ways of expressing the same thought. Do not use both styles together.

a *one-year* extension	a *two-week* vacation
OR: a *one year's* extension	**OR:** a *two weeks'* vacation
(**BUT NOT:** a one-year's extension)	(**BUT NOT:** a two-weeks' vacation)

b. Hyphenate compound adjectives involving a number and *odd* or *plus*.

The embezzlement occurred some *twenty-odd* years ago.

I now give my age simply as *forty-plus*.

c. Compound adjectives involving two numbers (as in ratios and scores) are expressed as follows:

a *50-50* (**OR** *fifty-fifty*) chance	a *1000-to-1* possibility
20/20 (**OR** *twenty-twenty*) vision	a *3-to-1* ratio **OR** a *3:1* ratio
an *18-7* victory over the Giants	**BUT:** a ratio of *3 to 1*

See also ¶450–451.

d. Other compound expressions involving a number or letter are expressed as follows:

our *number-one** (**OR** *No. 1*) priority	*Class A* materials
BUT: our goal is to be *number one*	a grade of *A plus* (**OR** *A+*)
in *A1* condition	**BUT:** does *A-plus* (**OR** *A+*) work
BUT: *A.1.* steak sauce	a passing mark of *D minus* (**OR** *D−*)
Title IX provisions	**BUT:** a *D-minus* (**OR** *D−*) student

Compound Noun

818 a. A number of adjective-noun combinations (such as *real estate* or *social security*) and noun-noun combinations (such as *life insurance* or *money market*) are actually well-established compound nouns serving as adjectives. Unlike *short-term, low-risk,* and the examples in ¶816, these expressions refer to well-known concepts or institutions. Because they are easily grasped as a unit, they *do not* require a hyphen.

accounts payable records	*life insurance* policy	*public relations* adviser
branch office reports	*mass production* techniques	*real estate* agent
high school diploma	*money market* funds	*social security* tax
income tax return	*nuclear energy* plant	*word processing* center

EXCEPTION: a *mail-order* business

---

*Merriam-Webster does not hyphenate *number-one* before a noun.

(Continued on page 190.)

NOTE: When dictionaries and style manuals do not provide guidance on a specific adjective-noun combination, consider whether the expression is more like a well-known compound such as *social security* or whether it is more like *short-term*. Then space the combination or hyphenate it accordingly.

b. When a noun-noun combination involves two words of relatively equal rank, hyphenate the combination.

the *price-earnings* ratio   the *space-time* continuum   an *air-sea* search
cost-benefit analyses   *labor-management* relations   a *sand-gravel* mixture

c. As a general rule, when a compound noun is used as a compound adjective, the decision to hyphenate or not will depend on how familiar you think your reader is with the term in question. Thus a term like *small business owner* would not be hyphenated if you feel your reader is familiar with the concept of *small business*. However, if your reader could misinterpret *small business owner* as a reference to the size of the person rather than to the size of the business, write *small-business owner*.

d. A compound noun like *African American* is hyphenated when used as an adjective. (See ¶348, note.)

Proper Name

819 a. Do not hyphenate the elements in a proper name used as an adjective.

a *Supreme Court* decision   a *Rodeo Drive* location
a *Saks Fifth Avenue* store   *Mickey Mouse* procedures

b. When two or more distinct proper names are combined to form a one-thought modifier, use a hyphen to connect the elements.

a *German-American* restaurant   the cuisine is *German-American*

the *New York-Chicago-Los Angeles* flight (no hyphens within *New York* and *Los Angeles*)

BUT: the flight to *New York, Chicago, and Los Angeles*

NOTE: If one of the elements already contains a hyphen, use a dash in printed material (two hyphens in typed material) to connect the two proper names.

the *Winston-Salem--Atlanta* bus trip   the Scranton--Wilkes-Barre area

Noun + Adjective

820 a. When a compound adjective consists of a noun plus an adjective, hyphenate this combination whether it appears before or after the noun. (See ¶815b.)

accident-prone	color-blind	paper-thin	tone-deaf
age-old	cost-effective	pitch-dark	top-heavy
bone-dry	ice-cold	scot-free	trigger-happy
brain-dead	knee-deep	sky-high	user-friendly
capital-intensive	letter-perfect	street-smart	water-repellent
class-conscious	machine-readable	tax-exempt	year-round

Your suggestion is ingenious but not *cost-effective*.

You are trying to solve an *age-old* problem.

She wants everything to be *letter-perfect*.

We import these *water-repellent* fabrics *duty-free.*

I want a computer that is *IBM PC/AT-compatible.*

BUT: I want a computer that is compatible with an IBM PC/AT.

NOTE: Retain the hyphen in a noun + adjective combination when the expression functions as an adverb rather than as an adjective.

ADJECTIVE: Please call me on my *toll-free* number.
ADVERB: You can always call me *toll-free.*

ADJECTIVE: The information is encoded on *paper-thin* wafers.
ADVERB: The wafers have to be sliced *paper-thin.*

b. A few words in this category are now written solid. For example:

-wide:	worldwide, nationwide, countrywide, statewide, countywide, citywide, communitywide, industrywide, companywide, storewide
-proof:	waterproof, fireproof, shatterproof, weatherproof, shockproof, burglarproof, childproof
-worthy:	airworthy, seaworthy, praiseworthy, newsworthy, trustworthy, creditworthy, blameworthy
-sick:	homesick, airsick, carsick, heartsick
-long:	daylong, nightlong, yearlong, lifelong, agelong

Noun + Participle

821 **a.** When a compound adjective consists of a noun plus a participle, hyphenate this combination whether it appears before or after the noun. (See ¶815b.)

awe-inspiring	face-saving	law-abiding	panic-stricken
bell-shaped	habit-forming	market-tested	smoke-filled
computer-aided	hair-raising	mind-boggling	tailor-made
custom-tailored	interest-bearing	money-making	tax-sheltered
eye-catching	jet-propelled	nerve-racking	zero-based

Computer-aided design (CAD) was one of the technological breakthroughs of the 1980s.

The layout of the catalog cover is *eye-catching.*

Buying *custom-tailored* suits can easily become *habit-forming.*

b. When an open compound noun is combined with a participle to form a one-thought modifier, insert a hyphen only before the participle.

U.S. government-owned lands a *Pulitzer Prize-winning* play
a *Labor Department-sponsored* conference *health care-related* expenditures
a *Dayton, Ohio-based* consortium *solar energy-oriented* research
a *Frank Lloyd Wright-designed* building *property tax-based* revenues

c. A few words in this category are now written solid. For example:

hand-:	handmade, handpicked, handwoven, handwritten
heart-:	heartbreaking, heartbroken, heartfelt, heartrending, heartwarming
home-:	homebound, homegrown, homemade, homespun
time-:	timesaving, timeserving, timeworn
	BUT: time-consuming, time-honored, time-sharing, time-tested
pain-:	painkilling, painstaking

Adjective + Participle (see also ¶824b)

822 **a.** When a compound adjective consists of an adjective plus a participle, hyphenate this combination whether it appears before or after the noun. (See ¶815b.)

clean-cut	high-ranking	rough-hewn
friendly-looking (see ¶824a)	long-standing	smooth-talking
half-baked	odd-sounding	soft-spoken
hard-hitting	ready-made	sweet-smelling

EXCEPTIONS: easygoing, halfhearted

I'm *half-tempted* to apply for the Singapore opening myself.

He is a *smooth-talking* operator who never delivers what he promises.

Betty was anything but *soft-spoken* in arguing against the new procedures.

b. Retain the hyphen even when a comparative or superlative adjective is combined with a participle—for example, *nicer-looking, best-looking, oddest-sounding, better-tasting.*

As the *highest-ranking* official present, Mrs. Egan took charge of the meeting.

This year's brochure is *better-looking* than last year's.

Why can't we attract *better-qualified* people to our company?

Adjective + Noun + *ED*

823 **a.** When a compound adjective consists of an adjective plus a noun plus *ed,* hyphenate this combination whether it appears before or after the noun. (See ¶815b.)

broad-minded	empty-handed	open-ended
empty-headed	light-fingered	closed-captioned
quick-witted	two-fisted	low-pitched
hot-tempered	loose-jointed	high-priced
good-humored	double-breasted	middle-aged
high-spirited	long-winded	old-fashioned
fair-haired	good-hearted	short-lived (pronounced "līvd")
dog-eared	wasp-waisted	pint-sized (see ¶823d)
two-faced	deep-seated	fast-paced
clear-eyed	swivel-hipped	broad-based
hard-nosed	clean-limbed	coarse-grained
tight-mouthed	weak-kneed	double-edged
thin-lipped	long-legged	single-spaced (see ¶812)
sharp-tongued	flat-footed	deep-rooted
gap-toothed	hot-blooded	high-powered
red-cheeked	thin-skinned	one-sided
round-shouldered	full-bodied	BUT: lopsided

Our success was *short-lived:* the business folded after six months. (*Short-lived* is derived from the phrase *of short life.* For that reason the *i* in *lived* is pronounced like the long *i* in *life,* not like the short *i* in *given.*)

These symptoms commonly occur in *middle-aged* executives.

I'm too *old-fashioned* to be that *broad-minded.*

b. Retain the hyphen in comparative or superlative forms—for example, *smaller-sized, highest-priced, best-natured.*

Our *higher-priced* articles sold well this year.
These goods are *higher-priced* than the samples you showed me.

Fred is the *longest-winded* speaker I ever heard.
Fred's speech was the *longest-winded* I ever heard.

c. Some words in this category are now written solid. For example:

-headed: bareheaded, bullheaded, chowderheaded, clearheaded, fatheaded, hardheaded, hotheaded, levelheaded, muddleheaded, pigheaded, redheaded, softheaded, thickheaded, woodenheaded, wrongheaded
BUT: bald-headed, empty-headed, light-headed

-hearted: bighearted, brokenhearted, coldhearted, halfhearted, heavyhearted, lighthearted, openhearted, softhearted, stouthearted, tenderhearted, warmhearted, wholehearted
BUT: good-hearted, hard-hearted, single-hearted

-mouthed: closemouthed, openmouthed, widemouthed, bigmouthed, loudmouthed
BUT: tight-mouthed

-fisted: hardfisted, tightfisted, closefisted
BUT: two-fisted

-sighted: nearsighted, shortsighted, farsighted
BUT: clear-sighted, sharp-sighted

-brained: birdbrained, featherbrained, lamebrained, scatterbrained

-minded: feebleminded
BUT: broad-minded, civic-minded, high-minded, like-minded, low-minded, open-minded, serious-minded, single-minded, small-minded, strong-minded

d. Compound adjectives such as *pint-sized, pocket-sized, life-sized, full-sized, giant-sized, king-sized, queen-sized,* and *twin-sized* may also be written without the final *d.*

Adverb + Participle (see also ¶825)

824 **a.** Do not hyphenate an adverb-participle combination if the adverb ends in *ly.*

a *poorly constructed* house   a *wholly owned* corporation
a *highly valued* employee   a *newly formed* division
a *clearly defined* set of terms   an *extremely tiring* trip

NOTE: Hyphenate adjectives ending in *ly* when they are used with participles. (See ¶822.)

a *friendly-sounding* voice   a *motherly-looking* woman

To distinguish between adjectives and adverbs ending in ly, *see ¶1069.*

b. Other adverb-participle compounds are hyphenated *before* the noun. When these same combinations occur in the predicate, drop the hyphen if the participle is part of the verb.

Before the Noun	Elsewhere in Sentence
a *well-known* consultant	This consultant *is* well *known.*
much-needed reforms	These reforms *were* much *needed.*
the *above-mentioned* facts	These facts *were mentioned* above.
the *ever-changing* tides	The tides *are* ever *changing.*
a *long-remembered* tribute	Today's tribute *will be* long *remembered.*
a *soon-forgotten* achievement	Her achievement *was* soon *forgotten.*

(Continued on page 194.)

However, if the participle does not become part of the verb and continues to function with the adverb as a one-thought modifier in the predicate, retain the hyphen.

Before the Noun	Elsewhere in Sentence
a *well-behaved* child	The child is *well-behaved*.
a *clear-cut* position	Their position was *clear-cut*.
a *well-intentioned* proposal	The proposal was *well-intentioned*.

NOTE: You couldn't say, ''The child is behaved'' or ''Their position was cut'' or ''The proposal was intentioned.'' Since the participle is not part of the verb, it must be treated as part of a compound adjective. Compare the use of *fast-moving* in the following examples.

Before the Noun	Elsewhere in Sentence
a *fast-moving* narrative	The narrative is *fast-moving*.
	BUT: The narrative *is* fast *moving* toward a climax.

c. Hyphenated adverb-participle combinations like those in *b* retain the hyphen even when the adverb is in the comparative or superlative.

a *better-known* brand	the *hardest-working* secretary
the *best-behaved* child	a *faster-moving* stock clerk

d. A few words in this category are now written solid. For example:

-going: ongoing, outgoing, thoroughgoing

far-: farfetched, farsighted   BUT: far-flung, far-reaching

free-: freehanded, freehearted, freestanding, freethinking, freewheeling
BUT: free-floating, free-spoken, free-swinging

wide-: widespread   BUT: wide-eyed, wide-ranging, wide-spreading

Adverb + Adjective

825   **a.** A number of adverb-adjective combinations closely resemble the adverb-participle combinations described in ¶824. However, since an adverb normally modifies an adjective, do not use a hyphen to connect these words.

a *not too interesting* report	a *very moving* experience
a *rather irritating* delay	a *quite trying* day

NOTE: In these examples you can omit the adverb and speak of an *interesting* report, an *irritating* delay, a *moving* experience, and a *trying* day; hence no hyphen is needed. However, in the first set of examples at the top of this page, you cannot speak of a *behaved* child, a *cut* position, or an *intentioned* proposal; for that reason, the adverb preceding *behaved, cut,* and *intentioned* must be linked by a hyphen.

b. Do not hyphenate comparative and superlative forms where the adverbs *more, most, less,* and *least* are combined with an adjective.

a *more determined* person	a *less complicated* transaction
the *most exciting* event	the *least interesting* lecture

Participle + Adverb

826   Hyphenate a participle-adverb combination *before* the noun but not when it occurs elsewhere in the sentence.

Before the Noun	Elsewhere in Sentence
filled-in forms	These forms should be *filled in.*
worn-out equipment	The equipment was *worn out.*
a *tuned-up* engine	The engine has been *tuned up.*
a *scaled-down* proposal	The proposal must be *scaled down.*
baked-on enamel	This enamel has been *baked on.*
a *cooling-off* period	Don't negotiate without *cooling off* first.
unheard-of bargains	These bargains were *unheard of.*
an *agreed-upon* date	We *agreed upon* a date.
warmed-over ideas	He gave us stale ideas that were *warmed over* for the occasion.

See also the examples in ¶831.

Adjective + Adjective

827　**a.** Do not hyphenate independent adjectives preceding a noun.

a *long* and *tiring* trip (*long* and *tiring* each modify *trip*)

a *warm, enthusiastic* reception (*warm* and *enthusiastic* each modify *reception;* a comma marks the omission of *and*)

a *distinguished public* orator (*public* modifies *orator; distinguished* modifies *public orator*)

For the use of commas with adjectives, see ¶¶168–171.

b. In a few special cases two adjectives joined by *and* are hyphenated because they function as one-thought modifiers. These, however, are rare exceptions to the rule stated in *a.*

a *cut-and-dried* presentation	an *out-and-out* lie
a *hard-and-fast* rule	an *up-and-coming* lawyer
a *high-and-mighty* attitude	a *rough-and-tumble* environment
a *tried-and-true* method	a *spick-and-span* kitchen
an *open-and-shut* case	a *sweet-and-sour* sauce

Henry views the matter in *black-and-white* terms. (A one-thought modifier.)

BUT: Sue wore a *black and white* dress to the Mallory party. (Two independent adjectives.)

c. Hyphenate two adjectives that express the dual nature of the thing that they refer to. (See also ¶¶295b, 806.)

a *true-false* test　　　　　　a *compound-complex* sentence

BUT: a *bittersweet* ending

d. Hyphenate repeated or rhyming words used before a noun.

a *go-go* attitude	an *artsy-craftsy* boutique
a *rah-rah* spirit	a *fancy-schmancy* wedding
never-never land	a *rinky-dink* setup
a *teeny-weeny* salary increase	a *ticky-tacky* operation

e. Hyphenate expressions such as *blue-black, green-gray, snow-white,* and *red-hot* before and after a noun. However, do not hyphenate expressions such as *bluish green, dark gray,* or *bright red* (where the first word clearly modifies the second).

Sales have been *red-hot* this quarter.　　Her dress was *bluish green.*

Verb + Verb

828 a. Hyphenate a compound adjective consisting of two verbs (sometimes joined by *and* or *or*) when the adjective appears *before* the noun.

a *hit-or-miss* marketing strategy   graded on a *pass-fail* basis
a *make-or-break* financial decision   a *can-do* spirit
stop-and-go production lines   a *do-or-die* commitment
a *hunt-and-peck* attack on the keyboard   a *live-and-let-live* philosophy

b. Do not hyphenate these elements when they play a normal function *elsewhere in the sentence*. However, retain the hyphen if these expressions continue to function as a compound adjective.

They're never sure whether they'll *hit or miss* their marketing targets.

BUT: Their marketing strategy can best be described as *hit-or-miss*.

Verb + Adverb

829 a. Hyphenate a compound adjective consisting of a verb plus an adverb when the adjective appears *before* the noun.

our *break-even* point   a *drop-dead* party dress
a *read-only* memory   a *come-hither* look
the *trickle-down* theory of financing   a *zip-out* lining
a *get-well* card   a *tow-away* zone
a *live-in* housekeeper   *run-on* sentences
a *walk-in* closet   *carry-on* luggage

b. Do not hyphenate these elements when they play a normal function *elsewhere in the sentence*.

At what point will we *break even*?   Does this lining *zip out*?

Verb + Noun

830 a. Hyphenate a compound adjective consisting of a verb plus a noun (or pronoun) when the adjective appears *before* the noun.

take-home pay   a *show-me* kind of attitude
a *take-charge* kind of person   **BUT:** a *turnkey* computer system
a *thank-you* note   a *lackluster* approach

b. Do not hyphenate these elements when they play a normal function *elsewhere in the sentence*.

In terms of salary it's not so much what you gross as it is what you *take home*.
Betsy is inclined to *take charge* of any situation in which she finds herself.

Phrasal Compound

831 a. Hyphenate phrases used as compound adjectives *before* a noun. Do not hyphenate such phrases when they occur normally elsewhere in the sentence.

Before the Noun	Elsewhere in Sentence
up-to-date expense figures	The expense figures are *up to date*.
down-to-earth projections	These projections appear to be *down to earth*.
on-the-job training	I got my training *on the job*.
off-the-shelf software	You can buy that software *off the shelf*.

Before the Noun	Elsewhere in Sentence
an *in-depth* analysis	Carpentier has analyzed the subject *in depth*.
an *out-of-the-way* location	Why would they locate a shopping mall so far *out of the way?*
over-the-counter stocks	These stocks are sold only *over the counter*.
under-the-table payments	Don't promise to make any payments *under the table*.
an *above-average* rating	Our unit's performance was rated *above average*.
below-the-line charges	These charges will show up *below the line*.
a *middle-of-the-road* position	His political position never strays far from the *middle of the road*.
before-tax earnings	What were our earnings *before taxes?*
after-dinner speeches	Speeches *after dinner* ought to be prohibited by law.
around-the-clock service	We provide telephone order service *around the clock*.
across-the-board cuts	The CEO is demanding budget cuts *across the board*.
a *between-the-lines* reading	When you read *between the lines,* Jan's memo takes on a completely different interpretation.
behind-the-scenes contract negotiations	Contract negotiations are still going on *behind the scenes*.
a *state of the art* installation	This installation reflects the current *state of the art*.
a *spur-of-the-moment* decision	Barra's decision to resign was made on the *spur of the moment*.
a *change-of-address* form	Please show your *change of address*.
a *matter-of-fact* approach	Jan accepted the situation as a *matter of fact*.
a *dog-in-the-manger* attitude	Joe's attitude reminds me of the fable about the *dog in the manger*.
straight-from-the-shoulder talk	I gave it to him *straight from the shoulder*.
made-to-order wall units	These wall units were *made to order*.
a *pay-as-you-go* tax plan	The new tax plan requires you to *pay as you go*.
a *would-be* expert	Roy hoped he *would be* accepted as an expert.
coast-to-coast flights	I fly *coast to coast* about three times a month.
bumper-to-bumper traffic	The traffic stood *bumper to bumper*.
door-to-door selling	He goes from *door to door* selling housewares.
a *case-by-case* analysis	We must resolve these problems *case by case*.
a *by-invitation-only* seminar	Attendance at the seminar is *by invitation only*.
an *eight-year-old* boy	That boy is only *eight years old*.
a *$150,000-a-year* fee	Our legal fees run about *$150,000 a year*.
a *well-thought-of* designer	Our former designer was *well thought of*.
a *well-thought-out* plan	The plan was *well thought out*.
a *much-talked-about* party	Your party was *much talked about*.

BUT: in the *not too distant* future (see ¶825a)

(Continued on page 198.)

SECTION 8 □ COMPOUND WORDS   197

b. When two nouns joined by *and* are used as a compound adjective before a noun, hyphenate the phrase.

a *cock-and-bull* story	a *trial-and-error* approach
a *dog-and-pony** show	a *mom-and-pop* operation
a *chicken-and-egg* situation	a *carrot-and-stick* proposal
a *life-and-death* matter	a *meat-and-potatoes* kind of guy
a *cat-and-mouse* relationship	a *cause-and-effect* hypothesis

c. As a rule, do not hyphenate foreign phrases used as adjectives before a noun. (See also ¶287.)

an *ad hoc* committee	an *ex officio* member
an *à la carte* menu	a *pro rata* assessment
a *bona fide* transaction	a *per diem* fee

EXCEPTIONS: an *ad-lib* speech, a *laissez-faire* economic policy

d. When a compound modifier consists of two or more hyphenated phrases, separate the phrases with a comma.

a *penny-wise, pound-foolish* approach to handling money
a *knock-down, drag-out** fight over ownership of the company
the *first-in, first-out** method of accounting
a *first-come, first-served* policy of seating
a *chin-up, back-straight, stomach-in* posture
an *on-again, off-again* wedding

BUT: a *go/no-go** decision (see also ¶295a)

Suspending Hyphen

832 **a.** When a series of hyphenated adjectives has a common basic element and this element is shown only with the last term, insert a "suspending" hyphen after each of the incomplete adjectives to indicate a relationship with the last term.

long- and short-term securities	*8½- by 11-inch* paper
private- and public-sector partnerships	*10- and 20-year* bonds
single-, double-, or triple-spaced copy	a *three- or four-color* cover

b. Use one space after each suspending hyphen unless a comma is required at that point.

a *six- to eight-week* delay	*3-, 5-, and 8-gallon* buckets
a *10- to 12-hour* trip	*6-, 12-, and 24-month* CDs

c. When two or more solid compound adjectives with a common element are used together (for example, *lightweight* and *heavyweight*) and the common element is shown only with the last term, use a suspending hyphen with the incomplete forms to indicate a relationship with the common element.

This product is available in *light-* and *heavyweight* versions.
Please provide *day-* and *nighttime* phone numbers.

NOTE: Repeat the common element with each word if the use of the suspending hyphen looks odd or is likely to confuse your reader.

See ¶833d–e for the use of a suspending hyphen with prefixes or suffixes.

*Merriam-Webster treats this word differently.

Prefixes and Suffixes

833 **a.** In general, do not use a hyphen to set off a prefix at the beginning of a word or a suffix at the end of a word. (See ¶808a for two exceptions: *ex-* and *-elect.*)

*after*taste	*mini*bike	change*able*
*ambi*dextrous	*mis*spell	patron*age*
*ante*date	*mono*syllable	free*dom*
*anti*trust (see ¶834)	*multi*purpose	six*fold*
*audio*visual	*non*essential	meaning*ful*
*bi*weekly	*off*beat	cable*gram*
*by*line (**BUT:** by-product)	*out*run	photo*graph*
*circum*locution	*over*confident	convert*ible*
*co*author (see ¶835)	*para*medical	misspell*ing*
*counter*balance	*poly*syllabic	fifty*ish*
*de*centralize (see ¶835)	*post*test	thank*less*
*extra*legal	*pre*requisite (see ¶835)	book*let*
*fore*front	*pro*active	child*like*
*hyper*sensitive	*pseudo*scientific	induce*ment*
*hypo*critical	*re*organize (see ¶837)	upper*most*
*il*legal	*retro*active	happi*ness*
*im*material	*semi*annual (see ¶834)	computer*nik*
*in*defensible	*sub*division	fire*proof*
*infra*structure	*super*natural	censor*ship*
*inter*office	*supra*natural	hand*some*
*intra*mural (see ¶834)	*trans*continental	home*stead*
*intro*version	*ultra*conservative (see ¶834)	back*ward*
*macro*economics	*un*accustomed	nation*wide* (see ¶820b)
*micro*processor	*under*current	edge*wise*
*mid*stream	*up*shot	trust*worthy*

NOTE: Although a hyphen is not usually used to set off the prefix *mid-*, a hyphen normally follows *mid* in expressions of time (as in *mid-sixties*). (See ¶¶434, 439.) Also, in the addition of the suffix *less* or *like*, if three *l*'s occur in succession, a hyphen should be used; for example, *shell-less*, *bell-like*. (See ¶706, note.)

b. Whenever necessary, use a hyphen to prevent one word from being mistaken for another. (See ¶837.)

lock the *coop*	*multiply* by 12	a *unionized* factory
buy a *co-op*	a *multi-ply* fabric	an *un-ionized* substance

c. As a rule, when adding a prefix to a hyphenated or spaced compound word, use a hyphen after the prefix.

pre-high school texts	*non*-interest-bearing notes
post-bread-winning years	*non*-computer-literate adults
ex-attorney general	*non*-civil service position

EXCEPTIONS: coeditor in chief, unair-conditioned, unself-conscious

d. When two or more prefixes have a common element and this element is shown only with the final prefix, insert a "suspending" hyphen after each of the unattached prefixes to indicate a relationship with the common element.

pre- and *post*natal care	*maxi-*, *midi-*, and *mini*skirts
macro- and *micro*economics	*inter-* and *intra*office networks
pro- and *anti*union forces	*over-* and *under*qualified job applicants

(Continued on page 200.)

e. When two or more suffixes have a common element, it is possible to leave one of the suffixes unattached and insert a "suspending" hyphen to indicate the relationship with the common element. However, to avoid confusion or awkwardness, it is usually better to repeat the common element with each suffix.

AWKWARD: I thought Nancy's reaction was more *thoughtless* than *-ful.*
BETTER: I thought Nancy's reaction was more *thoughtless* than *thoughtful.*

AWKWARD: I would characterize his behavior as *childlike* rather than *-ish.*
BETTER: I would characterize his behavior as *childlike* rather than *childish.*

834 When the prefix ends with *a* or *i* and the base word begins with the same letter, use a hyphen after the prefix to prevent misreading.

ultra-active	anti-intellectual	semi-independent
intra-abdominal	anti-inflationary	semi-indirect

835 When the prefix ends with *e* or *o* and the base word begins with the same letter, the hyphen is almost always omitted.

coordinate	reeducate	preeminent	de-emphasize
cooperate	reelect	preemployment	de-escalate
BUT: co-op	reemphasize	preempt	
co-opt	reemploy	preexisting	
co-owner	reenforce	**BUT:** pre-engineered	

NOTE: In a few cases a hyphen follows *co,* even though the base word begins with a letter other than *o.*

co-anchor	**BUT:** coauthor	coeditor	copromoter
co-edition	cocaptain	cofounder	copublisher
co-occurrence	cochair	coholder	cosigner
co-officiate	cocontributor	copartner	cosponsor
co-organize	codefendant	copilot	costar
	codeveloper	coproducer	coworker

836 Use a hyphen after *self* when it serves as a prefix.

self-addressed	self-evident	self-important	self-study
self-confidence	self-fulfilling	self-paced	self-supporting
self-destruct	self-help	self-serving	self-worth

Omit the hyphen when *self* serves as the base word and is followed by a suffix.

selfdom	selfhood	selfness
selfish	selfless	selfsame

837 As a rule, the prefix *re* (meaning "again") should not be followed by a hyphen. A few words require the hyphen so that they can be distinguished from other words with the same spelling but a different meaning.

to *re-collect* the slips	to *recollect* the mistake
to *re-cover* a chair	to *recover* from an illness
to *re-form* the class	to *reform* a sinner
to *re-lease* the apartment	to *release* the hostage
she *re-marked* the ticket	as he *remarked* to me
to *re-press* the jacket	to *repress* one's emotions
to *re-sort* the cards	to *resort* to violence
to *re-sign* the contracts	to *resign* the position
to *re-treat* the cloth	to *retreat* to safer ground
a *re-creation* of the original sketches	a *recreation* program for employees

8

838 When a prefix is added to a word that begins with a capital, use a hyphen after the prefix.

anti-American   mid-January   pre-Revolutionary War days
non-Asiatic   trans-Canadian   post-World War II period

BUT: transatlantic, transpacific, the Midwest

839 Always hyphenate family terms involving the prefix *great* or the suffix *in-law,* but treat terms involving *step* and *grand* solid.

my great-grandfather   my grandmother   your brother-in-law
their great-aunt   his grandchild   my stepdaughter

840 Avoid feminine suffixes like *ess, ette,* and *trix.*

She has an established reputation as an *author* and a *poet.* (**NOT:** *authoress* and *poetess.*)

If you have any questions, ask your *flight attendant.* (**NOT:** *steward* or *stewardess.*)

NOTE: A few terms with feminine suffixes are still widely used; for example, *hostess, heroine,* and *fiancée.*

841 Use a hyphen after *quasi* when an adjective follows.

quasi-judicial   quasi-public
quasi-legislative   **BUT:** quasi corporation

Sometimes One Word, Sometimes Two Words

842 A number of common words may be written either as one solid word or as two separate words, depending on the meaning. See individual entries listed alphabetically in ¶1101 (unless otherwise indicated) for the following words:

Almost–all most
Already–all ready
Altogether–all together
Always–all ways
Anyone–any one (see ¶1010, note)
Anytime–any time
Anyway–any way
Awhile–a while
Everyday–every day
Everyone–every one (see ¶1010, note)
Indifferent–in different
Indirect–in direct

Into–in to (see *In*)
Maybe–may be
Nobody–no body
None–no one (see ¶1013)
Onto–on to (see *On*)
Someday–some day
Someone–some one (see ¶1010, note)
Sometime–sometimes–some time
Upon–up on (see *On*)
Whoever–who ever

Hyphens in spelled-out numbers: see ¶¶427, 465.
Hyphens in spelled-out dates: see ¶411.
Hyphens in spelled-out amounts of money: see ¶420.
Hyphens in spelled-out fractions: see ¶427.
Hyphens in numbers representing a continuous sequence: see ¶¶459–460.

Basic Rules (¶¶901–906)
Preferred Practices (¶¶907–918)
Breaks Within Word Groups (¶¶919–920)
Guides to Correct Syllabication (¶¶921–922)

Whenever possible, avoid dividing a word at the end of a line. Word divisions are unattractive, and they may slow down or even confuse the reader. When word division is unavoidable, try to divide at the point that is least likely to disrupt the reader's grasp of the word.

The rules that follow are intended for those who use a typewriter or a computer. (Typesetters may take greater liberties.) The rules fall into two categories: (1) those that must never be violated (see ¶¶901–906) and (2) those that should be followed whenever space permits a choice (see ¶¶907–920).

NOTE: The authority for the word divisions shown in this manual is the 1990 printing of *Webster's Ninth New Collegiate Dictionary,* published by Merriam-Webster, Springfield, Massachusetts.

Basic Rules

901 Divide words only between syllables. Whenever you are unsure of the syllabication of a word, consult a dictionary. (See also ¶¶921–922 for some guides to correct syllabication.)

NOTE: Some syllable breaks shown in the dictionary are not acceptable in typed or keyboarded material as points of word division. See ¶¶903–904.

902 Do not divide one-syllable words. Even when *ed* is added to some words, they still remain one-syllable words and cannot be divided.

stressed	through	spring	hour
planned	thoughts	straight	rhythm

903 Do not set off a one-letter syllable at the beginning or the end of a word.

amaze (**NOT:** a- maze)	media (**NOT:** medi- a)
ideal (**NOT:** i- deal)	lucky (**NOT:** luck- y)

NOTE: So as to discourage word division at the beginning or end of a word, some dictionaries no longer mark one-letter syllables at these points.

904   Do not divide a word unless you can leave a syllable of at least three characters (the last of which is the hyphen) on the upper line and you can carry a syllable of at least three characters (the last may be a punctuation mark) to the next line.

ad- mit	*de-* ter	*un-* der	*in-* ert
do- *ing*	re- *new*	set- *up,*	happi- *ly.*

NOTE: Whenever possible, avoid dividing any word with fewer than six letters.

905   Do not divide abbreviations.

ACTION	UNICEF	AMVETS	NASDAQ
irreg.	approx.	assoc.	introd.

NOTE: An abbreviation like *AFL-CIO* may be divided after the hyphen.

906   Do not divide contractions.

haven't	shouldn't	mustn't	o'clock

Preferred Practices

While it is acceptable to divide a word at any syllable break shown in the dictionary, it is often better to divide at some points than at others in order to obtain a more intelligible grouping of syllables. The following rules indicate preferred practices whenever you have sufficient space left in the line to permit a choice.

907   Divide a solid compound word between the elements of the compound.

eye- witness	time- saving	photo- copy	socio- economic

908   Divide a hyphenated compound word at the point of the hyphen.

self- confidence	father- in-law	cross- reference	senator- elect

909   Divide a word *after* a prefix (rather than within the prefix).

Preferred		Acceptable	
.... intro-		.... in-	
duce .... inter-		troduce .... in-	
national ... super-		ternational ... su-	
sonic .... circum-		personic .... cir-	
stances ..... ambi-		cumstances ... am-	
dextrous		bidextrous	

However, avoid divisions like the following, which can easily confuse a reader.

Confusing		Better	
.... inter-		.... in-	
rogate .... super-		terrogate .... su-	
lative ...... circum-		perlative ..... cir-	
ference ... ambi-		cumference ... am-	
tious ...... hyper-		bitious .... hy-	
bole .... extra-		perbole ...... ex-	
neous ..... coin-		traneous ..... co-	
cide		incide	

910 Divide a word *before* a suffix (rather than within the suffix).

> appli- cable (RATHER THAN: applica- ble)
>
> comprehen- sible (RATHER THAN: comprehensi- ble)

911 When a word has both a prefix and a suffix, choose the division point that groups the syllables more intelligibly.

> replace- ment (RATHER THAN: re- placement)

The same principle applies when a word contains a suffix added on to a suffix. Choose the division point that produces the better grouping.

> helpless- ness (RATHER THAN: help- lessness)

912 Whenever you have a choice, divide after a prefix or before a suffix (rather than within the root word).

> over- active (RATHER THAN: overac- tive)
>
> success- ful (RATHER THAN: suc- cessful)

NOTE: Avoid divisions that could confuse a reader.

> re- address (RATHER THAN: read- dress)
> re- allocate (RATHER THAN: real- locate)
> re- apportion (RATHER THAN: reap- portion)
> re- arrange (RATHER THAN: rear- range)
> re- invest (RATHER THAN: rein- vest)
> co- insure (RATHER THAN: coin- sure)
> co- operate (RATHER THAN: coop- erate)

913 When a one-letter syllable occurs within the root of a word, divide *after* it (rather than before it).

> impera- tive   pene- trate   simi- lar   congratu- late
> nega- tive   reme- dies   apolo- gize   salu- tary

914 When two separately sounded vowels come together in a word, divide between them.

ultra- ambitious	courte- ous	patri- otic	co- opting
ultra- exclusive	re- union	anti- union	situ- ated
recre- ation	medi- ation	pro- active	influ- ential
pre- eminent	experi- ence	po- etic	ingenu- ity
spontane- ity	anti- intellectual	auto- immune	continu- ous

NOTE: Do not divide between two vowels when they are used together to represent one sound.

main- tained	trea- surer	en- croaching	ac- quaint
extraor- dinary	es- teemed	amoe- ba	guess- ing
laugh- ter	per- ceive	ap- point	acquit- tal
pa- tience	sur- geon	ty- coon	mis- quoted
por- tion	neu- tral	pro- nounce	

915 When necessary, an extremely long number can be divided after a comma; for example, *24,358,- 692,000.* Try to leave at least four digits on the line above and at least six digits on the line below, but always divide after a comma.

916 Try not to end more than two consecutive lines in hyphens.

917 Try not to divide at the end of the first line or at the end of the last full line in a paragraph.

918 Do not divide the last word on a page.

Breaks Within Word Groups

919 Try to keep together certain kinds of word groups that need to be read together—for example, page and number, month and day, month and year, title and surname, surname and abbreviation (or number), number and abbreviation, or number and unit of measure.

page 203	September 1994	Paula Schein, J.D.	10:30 a.m.
April 29	Mrs. Connolly	Adam Hagerty Jr.	465 miles

920 When necessary, longer word groups may be broken as follows:

a. *Dates* may be broken between the day and year.

.... November 14, 1994 ....   NOT: .... November 14, 1994 ....

b. *Street addresses* may be broken between the name of the street and *Street, Avenue,* or the like. If the street name consists of two or more words, the break may come between words in the street name.

.... 1024 Westervelt Boulevard ....   NOT: .... 1024 Westervelt Boulevard ....

.... 617 North Fullerton Street ....   NOT: .... 617 North Fullerton Street ....

c. *Names of places* may be broken between the city and the state or between the state and the ZIP Code. If the city or state name consists of two or more words, the break may come between these words.

.... Portland, Oregon 97229, ...,,,   OR: .... Portland, Oregon 97229, ...

. ... Grand Rapids, MI 49505, ...   OR: .... Grand Forks, North Dakota, ...

d. *Names of persons* may be broken between the given name (including middle initial if given) and surname.

.... Mildred R. Palumbo ....   NOT: .... Mildred R. Palumbo ....

NOTE: If it is absolutely necessary, a person's name may be divided. Follow the same principles given for dividing ordinary words.

Samuel- son	Cala- brese	Spil- lane (see ¶922c)
Lind- quist	Eisen- hower	BUT: Spell- man (see ¶922a)

e. *Names preceded by long titles* may be broken between the title and the name (preferably) or between words in the title.

.... Assistant Commissioner Roy N. Frawley...........................   OR: .... Assistant Commissioner Roy N. Frawley...

f. *A numbered or lettered enumeration* may be broken before (but not directly after) any number or letter.

.... these points: (1) All cards should ....   NOT: .... these points: (1) All cards should ....

g. *A sentence with a dash in it* may be broken after the dash.

.... Early next year— say, in March—let's ....   NOT: .... Early next year —say, in March—let's ....

h. *A sentence with ellipsis marks in it* may be broken after the ellipsis marks.

Tennis . . . health spa . . . golf . . . and more . . . make this a world-class resort.   NOT: Tennis . . . health spa . . . golf . . . and more . . . make this a world-class resort.

9

Guides to Correct Syllabication

921   Syllabication is generally based on pronunciation rather than on roots and derivations. Careful pronunciation will often aid you in determining the correct syllabication of a word.

knowl- edge (NOT: know- ledge)   prod- uct (NOT: pro- duct)
chil- dren (NOT: child- ren)   ser- vice (NOT: serv- ice)

Note how syllabication changes as pronunciation changes.

Verbs	Nouns
pre- sent (to make a gift)	pres- ent (a gift)
re- cord (to make an official copy)	rec- ord (an official copy)
pro- ject (to throw forward)	proj- ect (an undertaking)

922   The following paragraphs offer some guides to syllabication. You are not obliged to divide a word at the points named, but you can safely do so without checking a dictionary.

a. If a word ends in double consonants *before* a suffix is added, you can safely divide *after* the double consonants (so long as the suffix creates an extra syllable).

sell- ers   bless- ing   staff- ing   buzz- ers

BUT: filled, distressed

b. If a final consonant of the base word is doubled *because* a suffix is added, you can safely divide *between* the double consonants (so long as the suffix creates an extra syllable).

ship- ping   omit- ted   begin- ner   refer- ral

BUT: shipped, referred

c. When double consonants appear elsewhere *within* the base word (but not as the final consonants), you can safely divide between them.

bub- bling   dif- fer   recom- mend   cur- rent
suc- cess   strug- gle   con- nect   neces- sary
mid- dle   mil- lion   sup- pose   bet- ter

Subjects and Verbs

Verbs

Subjects and Verbs

Basic Rule of Agreement

1001 a. A verb must agree with its subject in number and person.

> *I am* eager to get back to work. (First person singular subject *I* with first person singular verb *am.*)

> *It seems* odd that *Farmer hasn't followed up* on our last conversation. (Third person singular subjects *it* and *Farmer* with third person singular verbs *seems* and *hasn't followed up.*)

He is coming to stay with us for a week. (Third person singular subject *he* with third person singular verb *is coming*.)

She does intend to call you this week. (Third person singular subject *she* with third person singular verb *does intend*.)

We were delighted to read about your promotion. (First person plural subject *we* with first person plural verb *were*.)

They are convinced that the *Parkinsons are* worth millions. (Third person plural subjects *they* and *Parkinsons* with third person plural verbs *are convinced* and *are*.)

Your *order* for six laptop computers *was shipped* last Friday. (Third person singular subject *order* with third person singular verb *was shipped*.)

Our *efforts* to save the business *have been* unsuccessful. (Third person plural subject *efforts* with third person plural verb *have been*.)

NOTE: A plural verb is always required after *you*, even when *you* is singular, referring to only one person.

You alone *have understood* the full dimensions of the problem. (Second person singular subject *you* with second person plural verb *have understood*.)

You both *have been* a great help to us. (Second person plural subject *you* with second person plural verb *have been*.)

You do enjoy your work, *don't you?*

b. Although *s* or *es* added to a *noun* indicates the plural form, *s* or *es* added to a verb indicates the third person singular. (See ¶1035.)

Singular	**Plural**
The price *seems* reasonable.	The prices *seem* reasonable
The tax *applies* to everyone.	The taxes *apply* to everyone.

Subjects Joined by *And*

1002 a. If the subject consists of two or more words that are connected by *and* or by *both . . . and,* the subject is plural and requires a plural verb.

Ms. Rizzo and *Mr. Bruce have received* promotions.

Both the *collection* and the *delivery* of mail *are* to be curtailed as of July 1. (The repetition of *the* with the second subject emphasizes that two different items are meant.)

The *general managers* and the *controllers are attending* a three-day meeting in Chicago this week.

The *director of marketing* and the *product managers are reviewing* the advertising budgets for next year.

The *sales projections* and the *cost estimate do not have* to be revised.

b. Use a singular verb when two or more subjects connected by *and* refer to the same person or thing. (See also ¶1028a, fourth example.)

Our *secretary and treasurer is* Frances Eisenberg. (One person.)

Corned beef and cabbage was his favorite dish. (One dish.)

Wear and tear has to be expected when you're in the rental business. (One type of damage.)

c. Use a singular verb when two or more subjects connected by *and* are preceded by *each, every, many a,* or *many an.* (See also ¶1009b.)

Every computer, printer, and fax machine *is marked* for reduction.

Many a woman and man *has responded* to our plea for contributions.

10

¶1003

Subjects Joined by *Or* or Similar Connectives

1003 If the subject consists of two or more *singular* words that are connected by *or, either . . . or, neither . . . nor,* or *not only . . . but also,* the subject is singular and requires a singular verb.

> Either *July* or *August is* a good time for the sales conference.
>
> Neither the *Credit Department* nor the *Accounting Department has* the file.
>
> Not only a cost-profit *analysis* but also a marketing *plan needs* to be developed.

1004 If the subject consists of two or more *plural* words that are connected by *or, either . . . or, neither . . . nor,* or *not only . . . but also,* the subject is plural and requires a plural verb.

> Neither the regional *managers* nor the *salesclerks have* the data you want.
>
> Not only the *dealers* but also the *retailers are* unhappy about our new pricing policy.

1005 If the subject is made up of both singular and plural words connected by *or, either . . . or, neither . . . nor,* or *not only . . . but also,* the verb agrees with the nearer part of the subject. Since sentences with singular and plural subjects usually sound better with plural verbs, try to locate the plural subject closer to the verb whenever this can be done without sacrificing the emphasis desired.

> Either *Miss Hertig* or her *assistants have* copies of the new catalog. (The verb *have* agrees with the nearer subject, *assistants.*)
>
> Neither the *buyers* nor the *sales manager is* in favor of the system. (The verb *is* agrees with the nearer subject, *sales manager.*)
>
> **BETTER:** Neither the *sales manager* nor the *buyers are* in favor of the system. (The sentence reads better with the plural verb *are.* The subjects *sales manager* and *buyers* have been rearranged without changing the emphasis.)
>
> Not only the *teachers* but also the *superintendent is* in favor of the plan. (The verb *is* agrees with the nearer subject, *superintendent.* With the use of *not only . . . but also,* the emphasis falls on the subject following *but also.*)
>
> Not only the *superintendent* but also the *teachers are* in favor of the plan. (When the sentence is rearranged, the nearer subject, *teachers,* requires the plural verb *are.* However, the emphasis has now changed.)
>
> Not only my *colleagues* but *I am* in favor of the plan. (The first person verb *am* agrees with the nearer subject, *I.* Rearranging this sentence will change the emphasis.)

NOTE: When the subjects reflect different grammatical persons (first, second, or third), the verb should agree in person as well as number with the nearer subject. If the resulting construction seems awkward, reword as necessary.

> **ACCEPTABLE:** Neither you nor *I am* in a position to pay Ben's legal fees.
>
> **BETTER:** Neither *one* of us *is* in a position to pay Ben's legal fees. (See ¶1009a.)
>
> **ACCEPTABLE:** Neither you nor *she has* the time to take on the Fuller case.
>
> **ACCEPTABLE:** Neither she nor *you have* the time to take on the Fuller case.
>
> **BETTER:** *She* and *you are* each too busy to take on the Fuller case. (See ¶1009c.)

For neither . . . nor *constructions following* there is, there are, there were, *or* there was, *see the last four examples in ¶1028a; for examples of subject-verb-pronoun agreement in these constructions, see ¶1049c.*

Intervening Phrases and Clauses

1006 a. When establishing agreement between subject and verb, disregard intervening phrases and clauses.

The *purchase order* for new diskettes *has not been found*. (Disregard *for new diskettes. Purchase order* is the subject and takes the singular verb *has not been found*.)

The *prices* shown in our catalog *do not include* sales tax.

Only *one* of the items that I ordered *has been delivered*. (See also ¶1008.)

Her *experience* with banks and brokerage houses *gives* her excellent qualifications for the position.

Several *phases* of our order processing system *are* out of sync.

A key *factor*, the company's assets, *is not being given* sufficient weight in the analysis. (The subject *factor*, not the intervening appositive, determines that the verb should be singular in this case.)

BUT: The company's *assets*, a key factor, *are not being given* sufficient weight in the analysis.

NOTE: When certain indefinite pronouns (*all, none, any, some, more, most*) and certain fractional expressions (for example, *one-half of, a part of, a percentage of*) are used as subjects, you may have to look at an intervening phrase or clause to determine whether the verb should be singular or plural. See ¶¶1013, 1025 for examples.

b. When a sentence has both a positive and a negative subject, make the verb agree with the positive subject. Set off the negative subject with commas unless it is preceded by *and* or *but*.

Profit and not sales *is* the thing to keep your eye on. (The verb *is* agrees with the positive subject *profit*.)

The *design* of the container, not the contents, *determines* what the consumer's initial reaction to the product will be.

The *members* of the Executive Committee and not the president *wield* the real power in the corporation.

It is not the president but the *members* of the Executive Committee who *wield* the real power in the corporation. (In the main clause the verb *is* agrees with the subject *it;* the verb *wield* in the *who* clause is plural to agree with the antecedent of *who,* the positive subject *members.* See ¶1062c.)

BUT: It is the *president* and not the members of the Executive Committee who *wields* the real power in the corporation. (In this sentence the positive subject is *president,* a singular noun; therefore, the verb *wields* in the *who* clause must also be singular.)

1007 The number of the verb is not affected by the insertion between subject and verb of phrases beginning with such expressions as:

along with	as well as	plus	except
together with	in addition to	besides	rather than
and not (see ¶1006b)	accompanied by	including	not even

If the subject is singular, use a singular verb; if the subject is plural, use a plural verb.

Mrs. Swenson, together with her husband and daughter, *is going* to Arizona.

This *study,* along with many earlier reports, *shows* that the disease can be arrested if detected in time.

(Continued on page 212.)

No one, not even the executive vice presidents, *knows* whether the CEO plans to resign. (See ¶1010.)

The *director* of finance, not the divisional controllers, *is authorized* to approve unbudgeted expenditures over $5000. (See ¶1006b.)

NOTE: When the construction of a sentence like those above requires a singular verb but a plural verb would sound more natural, reword the sentence to create a plural subject.

CORRECT: The national sales *report*, along with the regional breakdowns you specifically requested plus the individual performance printouts, *was sent* to you last week.

BETTER: The national sales *report*, the regional *breakdowns* you specifically requested, and the individual performance *printouts were sent* to you last week. (The three subjects joined by *and—report, breakdowns,* and *printouts—*call for a plural verb.)

One of . . .

1008 a. Use a singular verb after a phrase beginning with *one of* or *one of the;* the singular verb agrees with the subject *one.* (Disregard any plural that follows *of* or *of the.*)

One of my backup disks *has been lost.*

One of the reasons for so many absences *is* poor motivation.

One of us *has* to take over the responsibility for in-service training.

One of you *is* to be nominated for the office.

One of the interviewers *is going* to call you early next week.

b. The phrases *one of those who* and *one of the things that* are followed by plural verbs because the verbs refer to *those* or *things* (rather than to *one*).

She is one of *those* who *favor* increasing the staff. (In other words, of *those* who *favor* increasing the staff, she is one. *Favor* is plural to agree with *those.*)

He is one of our *employees* who *are* never late. (Of our *employees* who *are* never late, he is one.)

I ordered one of the new *copiers* that *were advertised* in Monday's paper. (Of the new *copiers* that *were advertised* in Monday's paper, I ordered one.)

You are one of *those* rare individuals who *are* always honest with *themselves.* (Of those rare *individuals* who *are* always honest with *themselves,* you are one.)

EXCEPTION: When the words *the only* precede such phrases, the meaning is singular and a singular verb is required. Note that both words, *the* and *only,* are required to produce a singular meaning.

John is *the only one* of the staff members who *is going* to be transferred. (Of the staff members, John is *the only one* who *is going* to be transferred. Here the singular verb *is* is required to agree with *one.*)

BUT: John is only one of the *staff members* who *are going* to be transferred. (Of the *staff members* who *are going* to be transferred, John is only one.)

Indefinite Pronouns Always Singular

1009 a. The words *each, every, either, neither, one, another,* and *much* are always singular. When they are used as subjects or as adjectives modifying subjects, a singular verb is required.

Each has a clear-cut set of responsibilities.

Each employee is responsible for maintaining an orderly workstation.

One shipment *has* already gone out; *another is* to leave the warehouse tomorrow morning.

Neither one of the applicants *is* eligible.
OR: *Neither applicant is* eligible.

Much remains to be done on the Belgravia project.
OR: *Much work remains* to be done on the Belgravia project.

For the use of either . . . or *and* neither . . . nor, *see ¶¶1003–1005.*

b. When *each, every, many a,* or *many an* precedes two or more subjects joined by *and,* the verb should be singular.

Every customer and supplier *has been notified.*

See ¶1002c for other examples.

c. When *each* follows a plural subject, keep the verb plural. In that position, *each* has no effect on the number of the verb. To test the correctness of such sentences, mentally omit *each.*

The *members* each *feel* their responsibility.

They each *have* high expectations.

Twelve each of these items *are required.*

1010 The following compound pronouns are always singular and require a singular verb:

anybody	everybody	somebody	nobody
anything	everything	something	nothing
anyone	everyone	someone	no one
OR any one	OR every one	OR some one	

Everyone is required to register in order to vote.

Something tells me I'm wrong.

NOTE: Spell *anyone, everyone,* and *someone* as two words when these pronouns are followed by an *of* phrase or are used to mean ''one of a number of things.''

Every one of us (each person in the group) *likes* to be appreciated.

BUT: *Everyone* (everybody) *likes* to be appreciated.

1011 Use a singular verb when two compound pronouns joined by *and* are used as subjects.

Anyone and *everyone is entitled* to a fair hearing.

Nobody and *nothing is going* to stop me.

Indefinite Pronouns Always Plural

1012 The words *both, few, many, others,* and *several* are always plural. When they are used as subjects or as adjectives modifying subjects, a plural verb is required.

Several members *were invited;* the *others were overlooked.*

Both books *are* out of print.

Many were asked, but *few were* able to answer.

¶1013

Indefinite Pronouns Singular or Plural

1013 a. *All, none, any, some, more,* and *most* may be singular or plural, depending on the noun that they refer to. (The noun often occurs in an *of* phrase that follows immediately.)

All the manuscript *has been finished.*
All the reports *have been handed* in.

Some was acceptable. (Meaning some of the manuscript.)
Some were acceptable. (Meaning some of the reports.)

Is there *any* (money) left?
Are there *any* (bills) to be paid?

Do any of you *know* John Ferguson well? (*Any* is plural because it refers to the plural *you;* hence the plural verb *do know.*)
Does any one of you *know* John Ferguson well? (*Any* is singular because it refers to the singular *one;* hence the singular verb *does know.*)

More than one customer *has complained* about that item. (*More* refers to the singular noun *customer;* hence the singular verb *has complained.*)
More than five customers *have complained* . . . (*More* refers to the plural noun *customers;* hence the plural verb *have complained.*)

Most of the stock *has been sold.*
More of these computer stands *are* due.

Some of the software *seems* too high-priced.
Some of the videotapes *seem* too high-priced.

b. In formal usage, *none* is still considered a singular pronoun. In general usage, however, *none* is considered singular or plural, depending on the number of the noun to which it refers. *No one* or *not one* is often used in place of *none* to stress the singular idea.

None of the merchandise *was stolen.*
None of the packages *were* properly *wrapped.*
None were injured. (Meaning none of the passengers.)
Not one of the associates *has* a good word to say about the managing partner.

NOTE: The relative pronouns *who, which,* and *that* (like the indefinite pronouns discussed in *a* above) may be singular or plural, depending on the noun they refer to. (See ¶1062c.)

Nouns Ending in *S*

1014 Some nouns appear to be plural but are actually singular. When used as subjects, these nouns require singular verbs.

news *(no plural)*	measles *(no plural)*
lens *(plural:* lenses)	summons *(plural:* summonses)

The *news* from overseas *is* very discouraging.

The *lens has* to be reground.

1015 A number of nouns are always considered plural, even though they each refer to a single thing. As subjects, they require plural verbs.

assets	dues	grounds	proceeds	savings
belongings	earnings	odds	quarters	thanks
credentials	goods	premises	riches	winnings

The *premises are* now available for inspection.

My *earnings* this year *are* not what I had counted on.

NOTE: The following nouns are considered plural unless preceded by the term *a pair of.*

glasses	scissors	pliers	pants	trousers

The *scissors need* sharpening. (BUT: A *pair* of scissors *has been taken.*)

1016 A few nouns (not all of which end in *s*) have the same form in the plural as in the singular. When used as subjects, these nouns take singular or plural verbs according to the meaning.

series	means	chassis	headquarters	deer
species	gross	corps	sheep	moose

The *series* of concerts planned for the spring *looks* very exciting. (One series.)
Three *series* of tickets *are going* to be issued. (Three series.)

One *means* of breaking the impasse *is* to offer more money.
Other *means* of solving the problem *have* not *come* to mind.

Headquarters is not pleased with the performance of the Northeastern Region. (Referring to top management or central authority.)
The Pesco Corporation *headquarters are located* at the intersection of Routes 80 and 287. (Referring to the offices of top management.)

Nouns Ending in *ICS*

1017 Many nouns ending in *ics* (such as *economics, ethics, politics,* and *statistics*) take singular or plural verbs, depending on how they are used. When they refer to a body of knowledge or a course of study, they are *singular.* When they refer to qualities or activities, they are *plural.*

Economics (a course of study) *is* a prerequisite for advanced business courses.
The *economics* (the economic aspects) of his plan *are* not very sound.

Statistics is the one course I needed my wife's help in.
The *statistics indicate* that the market for this product line is shrinking at a rapid rate.

Nouns With Foreign Plurals

1018 Watch for nouns with foreign-plural endings (see ¶614). Such plural nouns, when used as subjects, require plural verbs.

No *criteria have been established.*
BUT: No *criterion has been established.*

Parentheses are required around such references.
BUT: The closing *parenthesis was omitted.*

The *media* through which we reach our clients *are* quality magazines and radio broadcasts.
BUT: The *medium* we find most effective *is* television.

NOTE: The noun *data,* which is plural in form, is commonly followed by a plural verb in technical and scientific usage. In general usage, *data* in the sense of "information" is followed by a singular verb; in the sense of "distinct bits of information," it is followed by a plural verb. Compare these examples:

The *data* obtained after two months of experimentation *is* now *being analyzed.* (Here *data* means "information.")

BUT: The *data* assembled by six researchers *are* now *being compared.* (Here *data* refers to several distinct bits of information.)

¶1019

Collective Nouns

1019 The following rules govern the form of verb to be used when the subject is a collective noun. (A *collective noun* is a word that is singular in form but represents a group of persons, animals, or things; for example, *army, audience, board, cabinet, class, committee, company, corporation, council, department, faculty, firm, group, jury, majority, minority, public, school, society*.)

a. If the group is thought of as acting as a unit, use the singular form of the verb.

The *Board of Directors meets* Friday.

The *firm is* one of the oldest in the field.

The *committee has agreed* to submit *its* report on Monday. (The pronoun *its* is also singular to agree with *committee*.)

b. If the members of the group are thought of as acting separately, the verb should be plural.

The *committee are* not in agreement on the action *they* should take. (The verb *are* and the pronoun *they* are plural to agree with the plural *committee*.)

NOTE: The use of a collective noun with a plural verb often produces an awkward sentence. Whenever possible, recast the sentence by inserting a phrase like *the members of* before the collective noun.

The *members of* the committee *are* not in agreement . . .

c. In a number of constructions, the choice of a singular or plural verb often depends on whether you wish to emphasize the group as a unit or as a collection of individuals. However, once the choice has been made, treat the collective noun consistently within the same context. If the resulting sentence sounds awkward, recast it as necessary.

I hope your *family is* well. (Emphasizes the family as a whole.)
OR: I hope your *family are* all well. (Emphasizes the individuals in the family.)
SMOOTHER: I hope all the *members of* your family *are* well.
OR: I hope *everyone* in your family *is* well.

The *couple was married* (**OR** *were married*) last Saturday.
OR: *Bob and Pauline were married* last Saturday.

The *couple have moved* into *their* new house. (More idiomatic than: "The *couple has moved* into *its* new house.")
OR: The *Goodwins have moved* into *their* new house.

NOTE: The expression *a couple of* is usually plural in meaning.

A *couple* of customers *have* already *reported* the error in our ad.
A *couple* of orders *have been shipped* to the wrong address.
BUT: A *couple* of days *is* all I need to complete the report. (When the phrase refers to a period of time, an amount of money, or a quantity that represents a total amount, treat the phrase as singular. See also ¶1024.)

Organizational Names

1020 Organizational names may be treated as either singular or plural. Ordinarily, treat the name as singular unless you wish to emphasize the individuals who make up the organization; in that case, use the plural. Once a choice has been made, use the singular or plural form consistently within the same context.

Brooks & Rice *has lost its* lease. *It is* now *looking* for a new location.

OR: Brooks & Rice *have lost their* lease. *They are* now *looking* for . . .

(**BUT NOT:** Brooks & Rice *has lost its* lease. *They are* now *looking* for . . .)

NOTE: If the organization is referred to as *they* or *who,* use a plural verb with the company name. If the organization is referred to as *it* or *which,* use a singular verb.

Geographic Names

1021 Geographic names that are plural in form are treated as *singular* if they refer to only one thing.

The *Netherlands is* the first stop on my itinerary.

The *Virgin Islands consists* of three large islands (St. John, St. Croix, and St. Thomas) and about 50 smaller islands.

The *United States has undertaken* a new foreign aid program.

BUT: These *United States are bound* together by a common heritage of political and religious liberty.

Titles of Publications

1022 The title of a book or magazine is considered singular, even though it is plural in form.

Physicians & Computers is one magazine you should consider if you want to market your software to doctors

Consumer Reports is publishing an update on automobile insurance costs.

Changing Times is offering new subscribers a special rate for a limited period of time.

The Number; A Number

1023 The expression *the number* has a singular meaning and requires a singular verb; *a number* has a plural meaning and requires a plural verb.

The number of branch offices we have in the Southeast *has increased* in each of the last five years.

A number of our branch offices *are* now *located* in suburban malls rather than in the central business district.

Expressions of Time, Money, and Quantity

1024 When subjects expressing periods of time, amounts of money, or quantities represent *a total amount,* use singular verbs. When these subjects represent *a number of individual units,* use plural verbs.

Three months is too long a time to wait.
BUT: *Three months have passed* since our last exchange of letters.

That *$10,000 was* an inheritance from my uncle.
BUT: *Thousands* of dollars *have* already *been spent* on the project.

Ten acres is considered a small piece of property in this area.
BUT: *Ten acres were plowed* last spring.

A psychotic is convinced that *2 and 2 equals* 5, whereas a neurotic recognizes that *2 plus 2 is* 4 but can't stand it.

Fractional Expressions

1025 When the subject is an expression such as *one-half of, two-thirds of, a part of, a majority of, a percentage of, a portion of,* or *the rest of:*

a. Use a *singular verb* if a *singular noun* follows *of* or is implied.

Three-fourths of the *mailing list has been checked.*

Part of our Norfolk *operation is being closed down.*

A *majority* of *2000 signifies* a landslide in this town. (The noun *2000* is considered singular because it is a total amount. See ¶1024.)

A large *percentage has* to be retyped. (Referring to a manuscript.)

b. Use a *plural verb* when a *plural noun* follows *of* or is implied.

Two-thirds of our *customers live* in the suburbs.

Part of the *walls are* to be papered.

A *majority* of our *employees have contributed* to the United Way fund drive.

A large *percentage work* part-time. (Referring to the students at a college.)

NOTE: In the following example, the word *half* is a condensed version of *one-half of.*

Over *half* the *staff have signed up* for the additional benefits. (A collective noun such as *staff*, though singular in form, takes a plural verb when it is plural in meaning. See ¶1019b.)

Phrases and Clauses as Subjects

1026 When a phrase or clause serves as the subject, the verb should be singular.

Analyzing financial reports takes all my time these days.

Whether the decision was right or not is no longer important.

That they will accept the offer is far from certain.

Whomever you support is likely to be elected.

Whatever sales brochure they mail me goes directly into the circular file.

EXCEPTION: Clauses beginning with *what* may be singular or plural according to the meaning.

What we need *is* a new *statement* of policy. (The *what* clause refers to *statement;* hence the verb is singular.)

What we need *are* some *guidelines* on personal time off. (Here the *what* clause refers to *guidelines;* hence the verb is plural.)

Subjects in Inverted Sentences

1027 In sentences in which the verb precedes the subject, make sure that the subject and verb agree.

On the results of this survey *depend* the *extent* and the *type* of campaign we shall wage.

Attached are two *copies* of the January mailing piece.

What *were* your *reasons* for resigning?

What *is* the *likelihood* of our persuading you to stay?

Where *are* the *reviews* of the Kelly book?
NOT: Where *is* (**OR** Where's) the *reviews* of the Kelly book?

What *is* missing from the report *is* the *rationale* for the decision.

What *appear* to be problems *are* often *opportunities.*

1028 a. In a sentence beginning with *there is, there are, here is, here are,* or similar constructions, the real subject follows the verb. Use *is* when the real subject is singular, *are* when it is plural.

There *is* a vast *difference* between the two plans.
There *are* a great many *angles* to this problem.

Here *are* a *catalog* and an *order blank.* (See ¶¶1002a, 1028b.)
Here *is* an old *friend* and former *partner* of mine. (The subject, *friend and partner,* is singular because only one person is referred to. See ¶1002b.)

There *is* *many an investor* who regrets not having bought our stock when it was only $5 a share. (See ¶1002c.)

There *is* a *branch office* or an *agency* representing us in every major city in the country. (See ¶1003.)

There *is* not only a 5 percent *state tax* but also a 2.5 percent *city tax.* (See ¶1003.)

There *is* the *cost* of your own time in addition to the substantial outlay for materials that must be figured in. (See ¶1007.)

There's (There *is*) *more* than one *way* to solve the problem. (See ¶1013a.)
There're (There *are*) *more* than five *candidates* running for mayor. (See ¶1056e.)
(**NOT:** There's more than five candidates running for mayor.)

There *are a number* of problems to be resolved. (See also ¶1023.)
Here *is the number* of orders received since Monday.

Here *is ten dollars* as a contribution. (See also ¶1024.)
Here *are ten* silver *dollars* for your collection.

There *is* neither a *hospital* nor a *clinic* on the island. (See ¶1003 for two singular subjects joined by *neither . . . nor.*)

There *are* neither *motel rooms* nor *condominiums* available for rent this late in the season. (See ¶1004 for two plural subjects joined by *neither . . . nor.*)

There *were* neither *tennis courts* nor a *swimming pool* in the hotel where we finally found a room. (*Were* agrees with the nearer subject, *tennis courts.* See also ¶1005 for singular and plural subjects joined by *neither . . . nor.*)

There *was* neither central *air conditioning* nor *fans* for any of the rooms in the hotel. (*Was* agrees with the nearer subject, *air conditioning.* See also ¶1005.)

b. When the subject consists of a series of singular nouns—or a series of nouns, the first of which is singular—*there is* or *here is* usually sounds more idiomatic (despite the fact that the subject is plural) than *there are* or *here are.* If you do not feel comfortable with this idiomatic construction, change the wording as necessary.

In the higher-priced model there *is* automatic number *alignment,* automatic right-margin *justification,* and proportional *spacing.* (In this construction, *there is* is understood to be repeated before the second and third subjects.)

OR: In the higher-priced model there *are* the following *features:* automatic number alignment, automatic right-margin justification, and proportional spacing. (In this version *are* agrees with the plural subject *features;* the three subjects in the sentence above are now simply appositives modifying *features.*)

Within a mile of the airport there *is* a full-service *hotel* and three *motels.*

OR: Within a mile of the airport there *is* a full-service hotel *plus* (**OR** *in addition to* **OR** *as well as*) three motels. (By changing the connective from *and* to *plus* or a similar connective, you are left with a singular subject, *hotel,* that calls for the singular verb *is.*)

OR: Within a mile of the airport there *are* three *motels* and a full-service *hotel.* (When the first subject in the series is plural, the verb *are* not only is grammatically correct but also sounds natural.)

Subjects and Predicate Complements

1029 Sentences containing a linking verb (such as *become* or some form of *to be*) sometimes have a plural subject and a singular complement or a singular subject and a plural complement. In such cases make sure that the verb agrees with the *subject* (and not with the complement).

> *Bicycles are* the only product we make.
>
> The key *issue is* higher wages.
>
> *One* of the things we have to keep track of *is* entertainment expenses. (Use *is* to agree with *one,* the subject.)
>
> *It is* they who are at fault. (Use *is* to agree with *it,* the subject.)

NOTE: Do not confuse the last two examples with the *inverted* sentences shown in ¶1028. In a sentence beginning with *here is* or *there is,* the subject *follows* the linking verb. In a sentence beginning with *it is* or *one . . . is,* the subject *precedes* the linking verb.

Verbs

This section deals with the correct use of verb tenses and other verb forms. For the rules on agreement of verbs with subjects, see ¶¶1001–1029.

Principal Parts

1030 The principal parts of a verb are the four simple forms upon which all tenses and other modifications of the verb are based.

a. For most verbs, the past and the past participle are formed simply by adding *d* or *ed* to the present form; the present participle is formed by adding *ing* to the present.

Present	Past	Past Participle	Present Participle	
taxi	taxied	taxied	taxiing	
drop	dropped	dropped	dropping	(see ¶701)
occur	occurred	occurred	occurring	(see ¶702)
offer	offered	offered	offering	(see ¶704)
need	needed	needed	needing	(see ¶705)
fill	filled	filled	filling	(see ¶706)
warm	warmed	warmed	warming	(see ¶706)
argue	argued	argued	arguing	(see ¶707)
hope	hoped	hoped	hoping	(see ¶708)
die	died	died	dying	(see ¶709)
try	tried	tried	trying	(see ¶710)
obey	obeyed	obeyed	obeying	(see ¶711)

b. Many frequently used verbs, however, have principal parts that are irregularly formed.

Present	Past	Past Participle	Present Participle	
choose	chose	chosen	choosing	
do	did	done	doing	
forget	forgot	forgotten	forgetting	
		OR forgot		
see	saw	seen	seeing	
write	wrote	written	writing	
lay	laid	laid	laying	(see page 263)
lie	lay	lain	lying	(see page 263)

10

NOTE: Dictionaries typically show the principal parts for all *irregular* verbs. If you are in doubt about any form, consult your dictionary. If the principal parts are not shown, the verb is regular (see ¶1030a).

c. The past participle and the present participle, if used as a part of a verb phrase, must *always* be used with one or more auxiliary verbs. The most common auxiliary verbs are:

is	was	can	do	has	have	might	shall	will
are	were	could	did	had	may	must	should	would

Verb Tenses

1031 The first principal part of the verb (the *present tense*) is used:

a. To express *present time*.

We *fill* all orders promptly.

She *does* what is expected of her.

b. To make a statement that is *true at all times*.

There *is* an exception to every rule (including this one).

c. With *shall* or *will* to express *future time*.

We *will order* (OR *shall order*) new stock next week. (For the use of the auxiliary verbs *shall* and *will* in the future tense, see page 268.)

For the third person singular form of the present tense, see ¶1035.

1032 The second principal part of the verb (the *past tense*) is used to express *past time*. (No auxiliary verb is used with this form.)

We *filled* the order yesterday.

She *did* what was expected of her.

NOTE: Do not use a past participle form to express the past tense.

He *drank* his coffee. (NOT: He *drunk* his coffee.)

I *saw* it. (NOT: I *seen* it.)

They *began* it together. (NOT: They *begun* it together.)

He was the one who *did* it. (NOT: He was the one who *done* it.)

I can't believe this sweater *shrank*. (NOT: . . . this sweater *shrunk*.)

1033 The third principal part of the verb (the *past participle*) is used:

a. To form the *present perfect tense*. This tense indicates action that was started in the past and has recently been completed or is continuing up to the present time. It consists of the verb *have* or *has* plus the past participle.

We *have filled* the orders. (NOT: We *have filled* the orders yesterday.)

She *has done* what was expected of her.

The consumer movement *has become* an articulate force in today's business world.

b. To form the *past perfect tense*. This tense indicates action that was completed *before another past action*. It consists of the verb *had* plus the past participle.

We *had filled* the orders before we saw your letter.

She *had finished* the job before we arrived.

(Continued on page 222.)

c. To form the *future perfect tense*. This tense indicates action that will be completed *before a certain time in the future*. It consists of the verb *shall have* or *will have* plus the past participle.

We *will have filled* the orders by that time. (See page 268 for the use of *shall* and *will*.)

She *will have finished* the job by next Friday.

NOTE: Be careful not to use a past tense form (the second principal part) in place of a past participle.

I have *broken* the racket. (**NOT:** I have *broke* the racket.)

The dress has *shrunk*. (**NOT:** The dress has *shrank*.)

Prices have *risen* again. (**NOT:** Prices have *rose* again.)

He has *worn* his shoes out. (**NOT:** He has *wore* his shoes out.)

1034 The fourth principal part of the verb (the *present participle*) is used:

a. To form the *present progressive tense*. This tense indicates action still in progress. It consists of the verb *am, is,* or *are* plus the present participle.

We *are filling* all orders as fast as we can.

She *is doing* all that can be expected of her.

b. To form the *past progressive tense*. This tense indicates action in progress sometime in the past. It consists of the verb *was* or *were* plus the present participle.

We *were waiting* for new stock at the time your order came in.

She *was doing* a good job when I last checked her work.

c. To form the *future progressive tense*. This tense indicates action that will be in progress in the future. It consists of the verb *shall be* or *will be* plus the present participle.

We *will be working* overtime for the next two weeks. (See page 268 for the use of *shall* and *will*.)

They *will be receiving* additional stock throughout the next two weeks.

d. To form the *present perfect progressive*, the *past perfect progressive*, and the *future perfect progressive tenses*. These tenses convey the same meaning as the simple perfect tenses (see ¶1033) except that the progressive element adds the sense of continuous action. These tenses consist of the verbs *has been, have been, had been, shall have been,* and *will have been* plus the present participle. Compare the following examples with those in ¶1033.

We *have been filling* these orders with Model 212A instead of 212. (Present perfect progressive.)

We *had been filling* these orders with Model 212A until we saw your directive. (Past perfect progressive.)

By next Friday we *will have been working* overtime for two straight weeks. (Future perfect progressive.)

1035 The first principal part of the verb undergoes a change in form to express the third person singular in the present tense.

a. Most verbs simply add *s* in the third person singular.

he feels	**BUT:** I feel, you feel, we feel, they feel
she thinks	I think, you think, we think, they think
it looks	I look, you look, we look, they look

b. Verbs ending in *s, x, z, sh, ch,* or *o* add *es.*

he misses	he wishes
she fixes	she watches
it buzzes	it goes

c. Verbs ending in a vowel plus *y* add *s;* those ending in a consonant plus *y* change *y* to *i* and add *es.*

say: he says	employ: she employs	try: it tries
convey: she conveys	buy: he buys	apply: she applies

d. Verbs ending in *i* simply add *s.*

taxi: he taxis	ski: she skis

e. The verb *to be* is irregular since *be,* the first principal part, is not used in the present tense.

I am	we are
you are	you are
he, she, it is	they are

f. A few verbs remain unchanged in the third person singular.

he may	she can	it will
he might	she could	it would

See the entry for Don't *on page 259.*

Passive Forms

1036 The passive forms of a verb consist of some part of the auxiliary verb *to be* plus the past participle of the main verb.

it is intended (present passive of *intend*)
we were expected (past passive of *expect*)
they will be audited (future passive of *audit*)
she has been notified (present perfect passive of *notify*)
you had been told (past perfect passive of *tell*)
he will have been given (future perfect passive of *give*)

1037 A *passive* verb directs the action toward the subject. An *active* verb directs the action toward an object.

ACTIVE: Melanie (*subject*) will lead (*verb*) the discussion (*object*).

PASSIVE: The discussion (*subject*) will be led (*verb*) by Melanie.

For additional examples, see the entry for Voice *in the Glossary of Grammatical Terms, page 479.*

a. The passive form of a verb is appropriate (1) when you want to emphasize the *receiver* of the action (by making it the subject) or (2) when the *doer* of the action is not important or is deliberately not mentioned.

I was seriously injured as a result of your negligence. (Emphasizes *I,* the receiver of the action. **RATHER THAN:** Your negligence seriously injured me.)

This proposal is based on a careful analysis of all available research studies. (Emphasizes the basis for the proposal; the person who drafted the proposal is not important.)

Unfortunately, the decision was made without consulting any of the board members. (Emphasizes how the decision was made and deliberately omits the name of the person responsible.)

(Continued on page 224.)

b. In all other cases use active verb forms to achieve a simpler and more vigorous style. Except in those circumstances cited in ¶1038a, passive verb forms typically produce awkward or stilted sentences.

WEAK PASSIVES: It *has been decided* by the Human Resources Committee that full pay *should be given* to you for the period of your hospitalization.

STRONG ACTIVES: The Human Resources Committee *has decided* that you *should receive* full pay for the period of your hospitalization.

c. Watch out for passive constructions that unintentionally point to the wrong *doer* of the action.

CONFUSING: Two computer terminals were reported stolen over the weekend by the head of corporate security.

CLEAR: The head of corporate security reported that two computer terminals were stolen over the weekend.

CONFUSING: One of our second-shift workers was found injured by a Good Samaritan outside the parking lot entrance last night.

CLEAR: Last night one of our second-shift workers was injured outside the parking lot entrance and was found there by a Good Samaritan.

Verbs Following Clauses of Necessity, Demand, Etc.

1038 Sentences that express *necessity, demand, strong request, urging,* or *resolution* in the main clause require a *subjunctive* verb in the dependent clause that follows.

a. If the verb in the dependent clause requires the use of the verb *to be,* use the form *be* with all three persons (not *am, is,* or *are*).

NECESSITY: It is necessary (OR important OR essential) that these questions *be answered* at once. (NOT: are answered.)

DEMAND: I insist that I *be allowed* to present a minority report at the next board meeting. (NOT: am allowed.)

REQUEST: They have asked that you *be notified* at once if matters do not proceed according to plan. (NOT: are notified.)

URGING: We urged (OR suggested) that he *be given* a second chance to prove himself in the job. (NOT: is given.)

RESOLUTION: The committee has resolved (OR decided OR ruled) that the decision *be deferred* until the next meeting. (NOT: is deferred.)

b. If the verb in the dependent clause is a verb other than *be,* use the ordinary *present tense* form for all three persons. However, do not add *s* (or otherwise change the form) for the third person singular.

NECESSITY: It is essential that he *arrive* on time. (NOT: arrives.)

DEMAND: They insist that he *do* the work over. (NOT: does.)

REQUEST: They have asked that she *remain* on the committee until the end of the year. (NOT: remains.)

URGING: I suggested that she *type* the material triple-spaced to allow room for some very heavy editing. (NOT: types.)

RESOLUTION: They have resolved that Fred *represent* them. (NOT: represents.)

See the entry for Mood, subjunctive *in the Glossary of Grammatical Terms, page 474.*

Verbs Following *Wish* Clauses

1039 Sentences that start with *I wish, she wishes,* and so on, require a subjunctive verb in the dependent clause that follows.

a. To express *present* time in the dependent clause, put the verb in the *past tense.*

I wish I *knew* how to proceed.

I wish I *could attend.*

NOTE: If the verb is *to be,* use *were* for all three persons.

I wish I *were going* to the reception. (**NOT:** was going.)

I wish he *were going* with me.

b. To express *past* time in the dependent clause, put the verb in the *past perfect tense.*

I wish that she *had invited* me.

I wish that I *had been* there.

I wish that I *could have attended.*

c. To express *future* time in the dependent clause, use the auxiliary verb *would* instead of *will.*

I wish he *would arrive* on time.

I wish she *would make* more of an effort.

Verbs in *If* Clauses

1040 When an *if* clause states a condition that is *highly improbable, doubtful,* or *contrary to fact,* the verb in the *if* clause requires special treatment, like that described in ¶1039: *to express present time, use the past tense; to express past time, use the past perfect tense.* (In the following examples note the relationship of tenses between the dependent clause and the main clause.)

If I *knew* the answer (but I don't), I *would* not *ask* you.

If I *had known* the answer (but I didn't), I *would* not *have asked* you.

If I *were* you (but I am not), I *would take* the job.

If I *had been* in your shoes (but I wasn't), I *would have taken* the job.

If he *were invited* (but he isn't), he *would be* glad to go.

If he *had been invited* (but he wasn't), he *would have been* glad to go.

NOTE: Do not use *would have* for *had* in an *if* clause. See page 272 for a usage note on *would have.*

1041 When an *if* clause states a condition that is *possible* or *likely,* the verb in the *if* clause requires no special treatment. *To express present time, use the present tense; to express past time, use the past tense.* Compare the following pairs of examples. Those labeled "Probable" reflect the verb forms described here in ¶1041. Those labeled "Improbable" reflect the verb forms described in ¶1040.

PROBABLE: If I *leave* this job (and I may do so), I *will take* a full-time teaching position.

IMPROBABLE: If I *left* this job (but I probably won't), I *would take* a full-time teaching position.

(Continued on page 226.)

10

PROBABLE: If I *go* to San Francisco (and I may), I *will want* you to go with me.

IMPROBABLE: If I *were going* to San Francisco (but I probably won't), I *would want* you to go with me.

PROBABLE: If she *was* in the office yesterday (and she may have been), I *did* not *see* her.

IMPROBABLE: If she *had been* in the office yesterday (but she wasn't), I *would have seen* her.

Verbs in *As If* or *As Though* Clauses

1042 When an *as if* or *as though* clause expresses a condition *contrary to fact*, the verb in the clause requires special treatment, like that described in ¶1040.

She acts as if she *were* the only person who mattered. (But she isn't.)

He talks as if he *knew* the facts of the situation. (But he doesn't.)

You act as if you *hadn't* a care in the world. (But you have.)

1043 *As if* or *as though* clauses are now often used to express a condition that is *highly probable*. In such cases do not give the verb special treatment. *Use the present tense to express present time, the future tense to express future time, and the past tense to express past time.*

It looks as if it *will* rain. (**OR:** It looks as if it *is going* to rain.)

She acted as if she *planned* to look for another job.

Infinitives

1044 An infinitive is the form of the verb preceded by *to* (for example, *to write, to do, to be*). When two or more infinitives are used in a parallel construction, the word *to* may be omitted after the first infinitive unless special emphasis is desired.

Ask Ruth Gonzales *to sign* both copies of the contract, *return* the original to us, and *keep* the other copy for her own files. (*Return* and *keep* are infinitives without *to.*)

I would like you *to explain* the job to Harry, *to give* him help if he needs it, and *to see* that the job is done properly. (For emphasis, *to* is used with all three infinitives—*explain, give,* and *see.*)

NOTE: The word *to* is usually dropped when the infinitive follows such verbs as *see, hear, feel, let, help,* and *need.*

Will you please help me *prepare* the report? (**RATHER THAN:** help me *to prepare* the report?)

You need not *return* the clipping. (**OR:** You do not need *to return* the clipping.)

1045 Infinitives have two main tense forms: the present infinitive and the perfect infinitive.

a. The perfect infinitive is used to express action that has been completed before the time of the main verb.

I *am sorry to have caused* you so much trouble last week. (The act of causing trouble was completed before the act of expressing regret; therefore, the perfect infinitive is used.)

b. The present infinitive is used in all other cases.

I planned *to leave* early. (**NOT:** *to have left.* The act of leaving could not have been completed before the act of planning; therefore, the present infinitive is used.)

1046 *Splitting an infinitive* (that is, inserting an adverb between *to* and the verb) should be avoided because (a) it typically produces an awkward construction and (b) the adverb usually functions more effectively in another location.

WEAK: It was impossible to *even* see a foot ahead.

BETTER: It was impossible to see *even* a foot ahead.

WEAK: He always tries to *carefully* do the work.

BETTER: He always tries to do the work *carefully*.

However, split the infinitive when alternative locations of the adverb produce an awkward or weakly constructed sentence.

a. Before splitting an infinitive, first try to place the adverb *after the object* of the infinitive. In many instances the adverb functions most effectively in that location.

You ought *to review* these plans *thoroughly*.
(BETTER THAN: You ought to thoroughly review these plans.)

I need *to make* the decision *quickly*.
(BETTER THAN: I need to quickly make the decision.)

b. If step *a* does not produce an effective sentence, try to locate the adverb directly *before* or directly *after* the infinitive. In some cases the adverb functions effectively in this position; in other cases the resulting sentence is awkward.

CONFUSING: I want you *to supervise* the work that is to be done *personally*. (When the object of the infinitive is long or involved, it is difficult to place the adverb after the object without creating confusion. Here *personally* seems to modify *to be done* when in fact it should modify *to supervise*.)

AWKWARD: I want you to supervise *personally* the work that is to be done.

GOOD: I want you *personally* to supervise the work that is to be done.

c. If steps *a* and *b* fail to produce an effective sentence, try splitting the infinitive. If a good sentence results, keep it; if not, try rewording the sentence.

CONFUSING: I want you *to consider* Jenkins' proposal to handle all our deliveries *carefully*. (When *carefully* is located after the complete object, it no longer clearly refers to *to consider*.)

AWKWARD: I want you *carefully* to consider Jenkins' proposal to handle all our deliveries.

AWKWARD: I want you to consider *carefully* Jenkins' proposal to handle all our deliveries.

GOOD: I want you to *carefully* consider Jenkins' proposal . . .

d. When an infinitive consists of *to be* plus a past or present participle of another verb, inserting an adverb before the participle is not considered splitting an infinitive. Nevertheless, in many such sentences it may be possible to locate the adverb to better advantage elsewhere in the sentence.

These plans need to be *thoroughly* reviewed.

Claude appears to be *continually* turning up with last-minute objections to any decision I make.

(Continued on page 228.)

10

NOTE: By the same token, it is perfectly acceptable to position an adverb between a helping verb and a past or present participle. It is even acceptable to position an adverb *within* the elements of a helping verb.

This new technology has *already* been *effectively* applied in many industries.
I hear that Martha has been *seriously* considering early retirement.

For dangling infinitive phrases, see also ¶1082b.

Sequence of Tenses

1047 When the verb in the main clause is in the past tense, the verb in a subordinate *that* clause should also express past time. Compare the tenses in the following pairs of examples:

She *says* (present) that she *is* now *working* (present) for CBS.
She *said* (past) that she *was* now *working* (past) for CBS.

He *says* (present) that he *has seen* (present perfect) your résumé.
He *said* (past) that he *had seen* (past perfect) your résumé.

I *think* (present) that he *will see* (future) you tomorrow.
I *thought* (past) that he *would see* (past form of *will see*) you tomorrow.

EXCEPTION: The verb in the subordinate clause should remain in the present tense if it expresses a general truth.

Our legal adviser *pointed out* (past) that all persons under 18 *are* (present) legally considered minors. (General truth.)

Omitting Parts of Verbs

1048 When compound verbs in the same sentence share a common element, that element does not need to be repeated.

We *have* received your letter and forwarded it to our St. Louis office. (The auxiliary verb *have* is shared by the two main verbs, *received* and *forwarded.*)

We can and will *achieve* these goals. (The main verb *achieve* is shared by the two auxiliary verbs, *can* and *will.*)

However, do not omit any element when different parts of the main verb are required.

WRONG: I never have and I never will forget what you have done for me.
RIGHT: I never have *forgotten* and I never will *forget* . . .

WRONG: We have and still are asking for an accounting of the assets.
RIGHT: We have *asked* and still are *asking* for . . .

Troublesome Verbs

See individual entries listed alphabetically in Section 11 for the following verbs:

Affect–effect	Enthused over	Raise–rise
Appraise–apprise	Graduated–was graduated	Serve–service
Appreciate	Help	Set–sit
Bring–take	Imply–infer	Shall–will
Come–go	Lay–lie	Should–would
Come and	Learn–teach	Supposed to
Comprise–Compose	Leave–let	Try and
Done	May–can (might–could)	Used to
Don't	Maybe–may be	Would have
Ensure–insure–assure	Of–have	

10

Pronouns
Agreement With Antecedents: Basic Rules

1049 **a.** A pronoun must agree with its *antecedent* (the word for which the pronoun stands) in number, gender, and person.

I must stand by *my* client, just as *you* must stand by *yours.*

Frank said that *he* could do the job alone.

Alice wants to know whether *her* proposal has been approved.

The *company* has not decided whether to change *its* policy on vacations. (See ¶¶1019–1020.)

We plan to explain *our* shift in corporate strategy at the next shareholders' meeting.

The company's *auditors* will issue *their* report tomorrow.

The *Vanderveers* are giving a party at *their* house.

The *grand jury* has completed *its* investigation. (See ¶1019 for collective nouns.)

Why not have *each witness* write *his* or *her* version of the accident? (See ¶1053 for indefinite pronouns as antecedents.)

It is *I* who *am* at fault. (*Who* agrees in person and number with the antecedent *I;* the verb *am* also agrees with *I.*)

It is *she* who *is* willing to compromise.

It is *we,* the individual taxpayers, who *have* to make up for the loss of commercial ratables.

It is *they* who *are* behind schedule.

It is *you* who *are* to blame. (*Who* refers to *you;* hence the verb *are* is plural to agree with *you.* See also ¶1001a, note.)

BUT: You are the *person* who *is* to blame. (Here *who* refers to *person;* hence the verb *is* is singular to agree with *person.*)

b. Use a plural pronoun when the antecedent consists of two nouns joined by *and.*

Harry and *I* think *we* can handle the assignment.

Can *Mary* and *you* give us *your* decision by Monday?

Sonia and *Dave* say *they* will attend.

The *Montaignes* and the *Reillys* have sent *their* regrets.

c. Use a singular pronoun when the antecedent consists of two *singular* nouns joined by *or* or *nor.* Use a plural pronoun when the antecedent consists of two *plural* nouns joined by *or* or *nor.* (See also ¶¶1003–1005.)

Either *Will* or *Ed* will have to give up *his* office. (**NOT:** their.)

Neither *Joan* nor *Helen* wants to do *her* share. (**NOT:** their.)

Either the *Kopecks* or the *Henleys* will bring *their* videocassette recorder.

NOTE: When *or* or *nor* joins a singular noun and a plural noun, a pronoun that refers to this construction should agree in number with the nearer noun. However, a strict application of this rule can lead to problems in sentence structure and meaning. Therefore, always try to make this kind of construction plural by locating the plural subject nearer the verb.

(Continued on page 230.)

10

Neither Mr. Wing nor his *employees have* reached *their* goal. (The plural pronoun *their* is used to agree with the nearer noun, *employees;* the verb *have* is also in the plural.)

NOT: Neither the employees nor *Mr. Wing has* reached *his* goal. (The sentence follows the rule—*his* agrees with *Mr. Wing,* the nearer noun, and the verb *has* is singular; however, the meaning of the sentence has been distorted.)

d. Make sure that the pronouns you use refer to the antecedents you intend. To avoid confusion, you may have to reword a particular sentence.

CONFUSING: Unrealistic deadlines, excessive pressures, and unsafe working conditions can be very damaging to your employees. You must do everything you can to eliminate them. (The employees or the destructive conditions?)

CLEAR: Unrealistic deadlines, excessive pressures, and unsafe working conditions can be very damaging to your employees. You must do everything you can to eliminate these destructive conditions.

Agreement With Common-Gender Antecedents

1050 Nouns that apply both to males and females have a *common* gender.

parent	doctor	boss	writer
child	lawyer	supervisor	speaker
customer	professor	employee	listener
manager	instructor	student	consultant

When a singular noun of common gender serves as a *definite* antecedent (one that names a specific person whose gender is known), use the pronoun *he* or *she* as appropriate.

My *boss* (previously identified as Robert Hecht) prefers to open *his* own mail.

Ask your *doctor* (known to be a woman) to sign *her* name on the attached forms.

1051 When a singular noun of common gender serves as an *indefinite* antecedent *(a doctor, any doctor, every doctor)* or as a *generic* antecedent *(the doctor,* meaning "doctors in general"), the traditional practice has been to use *he* as a generic pronoun applying equally to males and females.

The *writer* should include a table of contents with *his* manuscript.

When an indefinite or generic antecedent names an occupation or a role in which women predominate (for example, *the teacher, the secretary, the nurse*), the traditional practice has been to use *she* as a generic pronoun.

A *secretary* needs to organize *her* work and set priorities each day.

1052 The traditional use of *he* and *she* as generic pronouns (described in ¶1051 above) is offensive to many people, who feel that the masculine bias in the word *he* makes it unsuitable as a pronoun that applies equally to women and men. Moreover, they feel that the generic use of *she* serves to reinforce stereotyped notions about women's occupations or roles. The ideal solution would be a new generic pronoun without masculine or feminine connotations. However, until such a pronoun has been devised and accepted into common usage, here are a number of alternatives to the generic use of *he* or *she.*

a. Use *he or she, his or her,* or *him or her.* (This solution works well in isolated cases but can be clumsy if repeated frequently in the same context.)

An *instructor* should offer *his or her* students challenging projects.

(**RATHER THAN:** An instructor should offer *his* students . . .)

b. Change the wording from singular to plural.

Parents of teenage children often *wonder* where *they* went wrong.

(**RATHER THAN:** The *parent* of a teenage child often *wonders* where *he or she* went wrong.)

c. Reword to avoid the generic pronoun.

When a customer calls, be sure to ask for a phone number.

(**RATHER THAN:** When a customer calls, ask *him or her* to leave *his or her* phone number.)

A secretary tries to anticipate the needs of the boss.

(**RATHER THAN:** A secretary tries to anticipate the needs of *his or her* boss.)

d. If the application of these various alternatives produces wordiness or an unacceptable shift in meaning or emphasis, then as a last resort use the generic *he* or the generic *she* as described in ¶1051. However, try to avoid doing so whenever possible.

Agreement With Indefinite-Pronoun Antecedents

1053 a. Use a singular pronoun when the antecedent is a singular indefinite pronoun. The following indefinite pronouns are always singular:

anyone	everyone	someone	no one
anybody	everybody	somebody	nobody
anything	everything	something	nothing
each	every	either	one
each one	many a	neither	another

Every company has *its* own vacation policy. (**NOT:** their.)

Neither one of the campaigns did as well as *it* was supposed to. (**NOT:** they were.)

NOTE: These singular indefinite pronouns often call for the generic use of *he* or *she* (see ¶¶1051–1052). In the following sentences alternative wording is shown to suggest how the generic *he* or *she* can be avoided. The last sentence presents a situation for which no reasonable alternative exists.

Everyone should submit *his* expense report by Friday.

BETTER: All staff *members* should submit *their* expense reports by Friday.

OR: *Everyone* should submit *his or her* expense report by Friday.

If *anyone* should ask for me, tell *him* that I won't return until Monday.

BETTER: If anyone should ask for me, say that I won't return . . .

While the conference is in session, does *every secretary* know how *she* is to handle *her boss's* problem calls?

BETTER: . . . do *all the secretaries* know how *they* are to handle *their bosses'* problem calls?

Nobody could have helped *himself* in a situation like that.

For agreement of these indefinite pronouns with verbs, see ¶¶1009–1011; for possessive forms of these pronouns, see ¶637.

(Continued on page 232.)

10

b. Use a plural pronoun when the antecedent is a plural indefinite pronoun. The following indefinite pronouns are always plural:

many   few   several   others   both

Many customers prefer to help *themselves; others* usually like to have a salesperson wait on *them.*

A *few* of the secretaries have not yet taken *their* vacations.

Several sales representatives in the Southern Region made *their* annual goals in nine months.

Both managers have said that *they* want to be considered for Mr. Hall's job when he retires next year.

For agreement of these indefinite pronouns with verbs, see ¶1012.

c. The following indefinite pronouns may be singular or plural, depending on the noun they refer to.

all   none   any   some   more   most

When these words are used as antecedents, determine whether they are singular or plural. Then make the pronouns that refer to them agree in number.

Some employees have not yet had *their* annual physical checkup. (*Some* refers to *employees* and is plural; *some* is the antecedent of *their*.)

Some of the manuscript has been typed, but *it* has not been proofread. (*Some* refers to *manuscript* and is singular; *some* is the antecedent of *it* in the second clause.)

For agreement of these indefinite pronouns with verbs, see ¶1013.

d. Since indefinite pronouns express the third person, pronouns referring to these antecedents should also be in the third person *(he, she, it, they).*

If *anyone* wants a vacation pay advance, *he* or *she* should apply for it in writing.

(**NOT:** If *anyone* wants a vacation pay advance, *you* should apply for it . . .)

If the indefinite pronoun is modified so that it strongly expresses the first or second person, the personal pronoun must also agree in number. Compare the following examples:

Most parents want *their* children to go to college. (Third person.)
Most of *us* want *our* children to go to college. (First person.)

A *few* have missed *their* deadlines. (Third person.)
A *few* of *you* have missed *your* deadlines. (Second person.)

Each employee knows how much *he* or *she* ought to contribute to the United Way fund drive. (Third person.)
BUT: *Each* of us knows how much *he* or *she* ought to contribute to the United Way fund drive. (Third person. In this sentence, *of us* does not shift the meaning to the first person; the emphasis is on what the individual contributes, not on what *we* contribute.)

IMPORTANT NOTE: Pronouns take different forms, not only to indicate a difference in person *(I, you, he)*, number *(he, they)*, and gender *(he, she)* but also to indicate a difference in case *(nominative, possessive, objective)*. Although a pronoun must agree with its antecedent in person, number, and gender, it does *not* necessarily agree with its antecedent in case. The case of a pronoun depends on its own relation to the other words in the sentence. The rules in ¶¶1054–1064 indicate how to choose the right case for pronouns.

Personal Pronouns

1054 Nominative Forms of Personal Pronouns

Use *I, we, you, he, she, it, they:*

a. When the pronoun is the subject of a verb.

I wrote to Eileen McIntyre, but *she* hasn't answered.

Debbie and *I* can handle the job ourselves.
(NOT: Debbie and me OR: me and Debbie.)

Either *he* or *I* can work late tonight. (NOT: him or me.)

NOTE: In sentences like the last two above, try each subject alone with the verb. You would not say "Me can handle the job" or "Him can work late tonight." Therefore, *I* and *he* must be used.

b. When the pronoun appears in the predicate after some form of the verb *to be (am, is, are, was, were)* or after a verb phrase containing some form of *to be* (see the list below). Pronouns that follow these verb forms should be in the nominative.

shall (OR will) be
should (OR would) be
shall (OR will) have been
should (OR would) have been
can (OR could) be
could have been

have (OR has) been
had been
may (OR might) be
may (OR might) have been
must (OR ought to) be
must have (OR ought to have) been

It could have been *they.*

It is *I.*

Was it *he* or *she* who phoned?

This is *she.*

NOTE: A sentence like *It could have been they,* while grammatically correct, would sound better if reworded in idiomatic English: *They could have been the ones.* Moreover, a sentence like *It's me* is acceptable in colloquial speech but not in writing. When you hear a telephone caller ask for you by name, do not respond by saying *This is him* or *This is her.* If you wish to respond correctly (and somewhat pompously), say *This is he* or *This is she.* If you wish to respond correctly (and sound more natural), say *This is . . .* and then give your name.

For special rules governing pronouns with the infinitive to be, *see ¶1064.*

1055 Objective Forms of Personal Pronouns

Use *me, us, you, him, her, it, them:*

a. When the pronoun is the direct or indirect object of a verb.

Larry gave Maris and *us* tickets for the opening.

They invited my husband and *me* for the weekend.

NOTE: When *my husband and* is mentally omitted, the objective form *me* is clearly the correct pronoun ("They invited *me* for the weekend").

b. When the pronoun is the object of a preposition.

This is for *you* and *her.*

No one knows except *you* and *me.* (NOT: except you and I.)

Between *you* and *me,* that decision is unfair. (NOT: between you and I.)

EXCEPTION: He is a friend of *mine (yours, his, hers, ours, theirs).* (See ¶648.)

(Continued on page 234.)

10

   c. When the pronoun is the subject or object of an infinitive. (See ¶1064.)

     The department head asked *him* to resign. (*Him* is the subject of *to resign*.)

     Did you ask Janet to call *me*? (*Me* is the object of *to call*.)

1056 Possessive Forms of Personal Pronouns

   a. Most personal pronouns have two possessive forms:

my	your	his	her	its	our	their
mine	yours	....	hers	...	ours	theirs

   b. Use *my, your, his, her, its, our,* or *their* when the possessive pronoun immediately precedes the noun it modifies.

     That is *my* book.   It was *their* choice.   George is *her* neighbor.

   c. Use *mine, yours, his, hers, its, ours,* or *theirs* when the possessive pronoun stands apart from the noun it refers to.

     That book is *mine*.   The choice was *theirs*.   George is a neighbor of *hers*.

     NOTE: Do not insert an apostrophe before the final *s* in possessive pronouns.

   d. A pronoun that modifies a *gerund* (a verbal noun ending in *ing*) should be in the possessive. (See ¶647.)

     I appreciated *your shipping* the order so promptly.
     (**NOT:** I appreciated *you shipping* the order so promptly.)

     I was not happy about *his telling* the press why he had resigned.
     (**NOT:** I was not happy about *him telling* the press why he had resigned.)

   e. Do not confuse certain possessive pronouns with contractions and other phrases that sound like the possessive pronouns.

its (possessive)	it's (it is **OR** it has)
their (possessive)	they're (they are) **OR** there're (there are)
theirs (possessive)	there's (there is **OR** there has)
your (possessive)	you're (you are)

     As a test for the correct form, try to substitute *it is* (or *it has, they are, there are, there is, there has,* or *you are,* whichever is appropriate). If the substitution does not make sense, use the corresponding possessive form.

     The firm must protect *its* assets. ("Protect it is assets" makes no sense.)
     BUT: *It's* time to take stock of our achievements.

     How would you go about estimating *its* worth?
     BUT: How much would you say *it's* worth?

     Their investing in high-tech stocks was a shrewd idea.
     BUT: *They're* investing in high-tech stocks.

     Their complaints have proved to be unfounded.
     BUT: *There are* complaints that have proved to be unfounded.

     Theirs no longer works; that's why they borrow ours.
     BUT: *There's* no use expecting him to change.

     Your thinking is sound, but we lack the funds to underwrite your proposal.
     BUT: *You're* thinking of applying for a transfer, I understand.

     For other possessive pronouns, see also ¶¶636–637.

1057 When a pronoun follows *than* or *as* in a comparison, you can determine the correct form of the pronoun by mentally supplying any missing words.

> She writes better than *I*. (Than *I do*.)
>
> I like you better than *him*. (Than *I like him*.)
>
> Joe is not as talented as *she*. (As talented as *she is*.)

1058 When a pronoun is used to identify a noun or another pronoun, it is either nominative or objective, depending on how the antecedent is used.

> The committee has asked *us*, Ruth and *me*, to present the report. (Since *us* is objective, the identifying pronoun *me* is also objective.)
>
> The explanation was for the *newcomers*, Marie and *me*. (Was for *me*.)
>
> The exceptions were the *newcomers*, Marie and *I*. (Exception was *I*.)
>
> Let's *you* and *me* schedule a brown-bag lunch. (*Let's* is a contraction for *let us*. Since *us* is the objective form, the pronouns *you* and *me* are also objective.)

NOTE: In sentences like the following, mentally omit the noun *(employees)* to determine the correct form.

> The company wants *us* employees to work on Saturdays. (The company wants *us* to work on Saturdays.)
>
> *We* employees need to confer. (*We* need to confer.)

1059 Some writers consistently use *we* instead of *I* to avoid a seeming overemphasis on themselves. However, it is preferable to use *we* only when you are speaking on behalf of an organization you represent and to use *I* when speaking for yourself alone.

> *We* shall prepare the necessary forms as soon as you send *us* a signed release. (This writer is speaking on behalf of the firm.)
>
> It is *my* opinion that this patient may be discharged at once. (This writer is speaking only for himself. Under these circumstances it would sound pompous to say, "It is *our* opinion.")

Compound Personal Pronouns

1060 The *self-* or *selves*-ending pronouns *(myself, yourself, himself, herself, itself, ourselves, yourselves, themselves)* should be used:

a. To direct the action expressed by the verb back to the subject.

> *She* found *herself* the only one in favor of the move.
>
> *We* have satisfied *ourselves* as to the wisdom of the action.
>
> We think that *they* have insured *themselves* against a possible loss.

b. To emphasize a noun or pronoun already expressed.

> The *trainees themselves* arranged the program.
>
> *I myself* am bewildered.
>
> *I* will write her *myself*.

NOTE: Do not use a compound personal pronoun unless the noun or pronoun to which it refers is expressed in the same sentence.

> The tickets are for the Wrights and *me*. (**NOT:** myself.)
>
> Henry and *I* can handle all the mail. (**NOT:** Henry and myself.)

10

¶1061

Interrogative and Relative Pronouns

1061 *Who* and *Whom; Whoever* and *Whomever*

a. These pronouns are both *interrogative* pronouns (used in asking questions) and *relative* pronouns (used to refer to a noun in the main clause).

Who is going? (Interrogative.)

Mr. Sears is the one *who* is going. (Relative, referring to *one*.)

To *whom* shall I deliver the message? (Interrogative.)

Ms. DeAngelis, *whom* I have never met, is in charge of the program. (Relative, referring to *Ms. DeAngelis*.)

b. These pronouns may be either singular or plural in meaning.

Who is talking? (Singular.)   *Whom* do you prefer for this job? (Singular.)

Who are going? (Plural.)   *Whom* do you prefer for these jobs? (Plural.)

c. *Who* (or *whoever*) is the nominative form. Use *who* whenever *he, she, they, I,* or *we* could be substituted in the *who* clause. (If in doubt, mentally rearrange the clause as is done in parentheses after each of the following examples.)

Who is arranging the teleconference? (*She* is arranging the teleconference.)

Who booked our sales conference in a honeymooners' hideaway? (*He* booked the sales conference.)

Who shall we say referred us? (We shall say *he* referred us.)

Who did they say was chosen? (They did say *she* was chosen.)

Who could it have been? (It could have been *he*.)

The matter of *who* should pay was not decided. (*He* should pay.)

Everybody wants to know *who* you think should be appointed. (You think *she* should be appointed.)

Whoever wins the primary will win the election. (*She* wins the primary.)

We will select *whoever* meets our minimum qualifications. (*He* meets our minimum qualifications.)

I will speak to *whoever* answers the phone. (*He* answers the phone.)

Please write at once to *whoever* you think can supply the information desired. (You think *she* can supply the information desired.)

Gloria is the one *who* can best do the job. (*She* can best do the job.)

James is the one *who* we expect will win. (We expect *he* will win.)

Please vote for the member *who* you believe has done the most for the firm. (You believe *he* has done the most for the firm.)

We have referred your claim to our attorney, *who* we are sure will reply soon. (We are sure *she* will reply soon.)

We have sent this order blank to all *who* we have reason to believe are interested in our book. (We have reason to believe *they* are interested in our book.)

d. *Whom* (or *whomever*) is the objective form. Use *whom* whenever *him, her, them, me,* or *us* could be substituted as the object of the verb or as the object of a preposition in the *whom* clause.

Whom did you see today? (You did see *her* today.)

To *whom* were you talking? (You were talking to *him*.)

10

Whom were you talking about? (You were talking about *him*.)

Whom did you say you wanted to see? (You did say you wanted to see *her*.)

It depends on *whom* they mean. (They mean *him*.)

The question of *whom* we should charge is at issue. (We should charge *her*.)

Whomever you designate will get the promotion. (You designate *him*.)

I will hire *whomever* I can find. (I can find *her*.)

I will speak to *whomever* you suggest. (You suggest *her*.)

I will give the job to *whomever* you think you can safely recommend. (You think you can safely recommend *him*.)

BUT: I will give the job to *whoever* you think can be safely recommended. (You think *he* can be safely recommended.)

I need a cashier *whom* I can trust. (I can trust *her*.)

The man to *whom* I was referring is Ed Meissen. (I was referring to *him*.)

The person *whom* I was thinking of doesn't have all those qualifications. (I was thinking of *her*.)

The person *whom* we invited to address the committee cannot attend. (We invited *him* to address the committee.)

Jo Fry is the nominee *whom* they plan to support. (They plan to support *her*.)

Steve Koval is the person *whom* we all thought the committee would nominate. (We all thought the committee would nominate *him*.)

Elaine Gerrity, *whom* I considered to be their most promising representative, resigned. (I considered *her* to be their most promising representative.)

1062 *Who, Which,* and *That*

a. *Who* and *that* are used when referring to persons. Select *who* when the individual person or the individuality of a group is meant and *that* when a class, species, or type is meant.

She is the only one of my managers *who* can speak Japanese fluently.

He is the kind of student *that* should take advanced math.

b. *Which* and *that* are used when referring to places, objects, and animals. *Which* is always used to introduce nonessential clauses, and *that* is ordinarily used to introduce essential clauses.

Laura's report on employee benefits, *which* I sent you last week, should be of some help. (*Which* introduces a nonessential clause.)

The report *that* I sent you last week should be of some help. (*That* introduces an essential clause.)

NOTE: Many writers now use either *which* or *that* to introduce an essential clause. Indeed, *which* is to be preferred to *that* (1) when there are two or more parallel essential clauses in the same sentence, (2) when *that* has already been used in the sentence, or (3) when the essential clause is introduced by an expression such as *this . . . which, that . . . which, these . . . which,* or *those . . . which.*

Vivian is taking courses *which* will earn her a higher salary rating in her current job and *which* will qualify her for a number of higher-level jobs.

That is a movie *which* you must not miss.

We need to reinforce *those* ideas *which* were presented in earlier chapters.

(Continued on page 238.)

c. The verb in a relative clause introduced by *who, which,* or *that* should agree in number with the subject of the relative clause. In many cases the subject is clearly expressed.

The laser printer that *you have ordered* will be delivered in two weeks. (The subject of the relative clause is *you,* which requires a plural verb, *have ordered.*)

However, when the relative pronoun *who, which,* or *that* is itself the subject of the relative clause, the verb in the relative clause must agree with the antecedent of the relative pronoun.

The laser *printer* that *was ordered* on May 4 will be delivered in two weeks. (The relative pronoun *that* is the subject of the relative clause and refers to a singular antecedent, *printer.* Therefore, the verb in the relative clause—*was ordered*—must be singular.)

BUT: The laser *printers* that *were ordered* . . .

Sometimes it is difficult to determine the antecedent of the relative pronoun. In such cases mentally rearrange the wording, as is done in the following example.

Hyphenate the *elements* of a *compound adjective* that occur?/occurs? before a noun. (To determine whether the antecedent of *that* is the plural term *elements* or the singular term *compound adjective,* recast the sentence: "When a *compound adjective occurs* before a noun, hyphenate the elements." This makes it clear that in the original sentence *compound adjective* is the antecedent of *that;* thus the verb in the relative clause must be singular: *occurs.*)

Hyphenate the elements of a *compound adjective* that *occurs* before a noun.

d. *Which, that,* and *who* may be used to refer to organizations. When you are referring to the organization as a single entity (in other words, as *it*), then use *which* or *that* as indicated in ¶1062b above. However, when you are thinking of the organization in terms of the individuals who make up the organization (in other words, when you think of the organization as *they*), you may use *who* or *that* as indicated in ¶1062a. (See also ¶1020.)

Although you are free to choose your own doctor, medical care is also available through an HMO (a health maintenance organization) with *which* the company has a special contract. (Since the HMO is referred to as a single entity, use *with which,* not *with whom.*)

Whenever we run short of computer supplies, the Brown & Weiner Company is the one *that* gives us the best service and the best prices.

We really like doing business with the people at the Brown & Weiner Company. They are a customer-oriented group *who* give us the best service and the best prices. (*That* may also be used in this sentence in place of *who.*)

1063 *Whose* and *Who's*

Do not confuse *whose* (the possessive form of *who*) with *who's* (a contraction meaning "who is" or "who has").

Whose house is it? (It is *his.*)

Who's the owner of that house? (*She* is.)

Who's had the most experience in that position? (*She* has had the most experience in that position.)

Who's the most experienced person in that position? (*She* is the most experienced person in that position.)

Whose experience is best suited to that position? (*Her* experience is.)

Pronouns With *To Be*

1064 a. If a pronoun is the subject of *to be,* use the *objective* form.

I want *her* to be successful.   I expected *them* to be late.

Whom do you consider to be the more expert driver? (You do consider *whom* to be the more expert driver?)

b. If *to be* has a subject and is followed by a pronoun, put that pronoun in the *objective* case.

They mistook the *visitors* to be *us.* (*Visitors,* the subject of *to be,* is in the objective; therefore, the predicate pronoun following *to be* is objective, *us.*)

They took *her* to be *me.*

Whom did you take *him* to be? (You did take *him* to be *whom?*)

c. If *to be* has *no* subject and is followed by a pronoun, put that pronoun in the *nominative* case.

The *caller* was thought to be *I.* (*I* agrees with the subject of the sentence, *caller.*)

The *Macauleys* were thought to be *we.*

Who was *he* thought to be? (*He* was thought to be *who?*)

NOTE: The examples above are all grammatically correct, but they also sound quite awkward. Whenever possible, use more idiomatic wording. For example, the three sentences above could be recast as follows:

They thought I was the one who called.

The Macauleys were mistaken for us.

What did they think his name was?

Troublesome Pronouns

See the paragraphs indicated for each of the following pronouns. Entries listed in Section 11 are in alphabetic order.

All of (see ¶1101)	Each other–one another (see ¶1101)	Someone–some one (see ¶1010, note)
Anyone–any one (see ¶1010, note)	Everyone–every one (see ¶1010, note)	That–which–who (see ¶1062)
Between you and me (see ¶1055b)	Most (see ¶1101)	These sort–these kind (see ¶1101)
Both–each (see ¶1101)	Nobody–no body (see ¶1101)	Who–whom (see ¶1061)
Both alike (see ¶1101)	None–no one (see ¶1013)	Whoever–who ever (see ¶1061)

Adjectives and Adverbs

For definitions of the terms *adjective* and *adverb,* see the appropriate entries in the Glossary of Grammatical Terms (page 470.)

1065 Only an adverb can modify an adjective.

Packard's will give you a *really* good buy on handheld calculators.

(**NOT:** Packard's will give you a *real* good buy on handheld calculators.)

1066 When a word in the predicate refers to the *action of the verb,* use an *adverb* (not an adjective).

> We guarantee *to ship* the portfolios *promptly.*
>
> They *were injured badly* in the accident.

TEST: If *in a . . . manner* can be substituted for the *ly*-ending word, choose the adverb.

> *Read* the directions *carefully* (in a careful manner).

1067 When a word in the predicate describes the *subject* of the sentence, use an *adjective* (not an adverb). Verbs of the *senses (feel, look, sound, taste, smell)* and *linking* verbs (the various forms of *be, seem, appear, become*) are followed in most cases by adjectives. A few other verbs (such as *grow, prove, get, keep, remain,* and *turn*) are sometimes followed by adjectives.

> I feel *bad* (**NOT** badly).   He has grown *tall.*
>
> She looked *happy.*   The work proved *hard.*
>
> Your voice sounded *strong.*   I got *lucky.*
>
> He seemed (**OR** appeared) *shy.*   Let's all keep (**OR** remain) *calm.*
>
> They became *famous.*   The weather has turned *cold.*

TEST: If *is, are, was, were,* or some other form of *be* can be substituted for the verb, choose the adjective.

> He *looks happy.*   He *is happy.*

NOTE: In the following group of examples, verbs of the senses and linking verbs are used as verbs of action (¶1066). Since the modifier refers to the action of the verb (and does not describe the subject), the modifier must be an adverb.

> She *looked suspiciously* at the visitor in the reception room.
>
> He *felt carefully* along the ledge for the key.
>
> Our market share *has grown quickly.*
>
> He *appeared quietly* in the doorway.

1068 Several of the most frequently used adverbs have two forms.

close, closely	fair, fairly	loud, loudly	short, shortly
deep, deeply	hard, hardly	quick, quickly	slow, slowly
direct, directly	late, lately	right, rightly	wide, widely

a. In a number of cases the two forms have different meanings.

> Ship the goods *direct.* (Meaning "straight," "without detour.")
> They were *directly* responsible. (Meaning "without any intervention.")

> They arrived *late.*   The truck stopped *short.*
> I haven't seen her *lately.*   You will hear from us *shortly.*

> You've been working too *hard.*   Turn *right* at the first traffic light.
> I could *hardly* hear him.   I don't *rightly* remember.

b. In some cases the choice is largely a matter of idiom. Some verbs take the *ly* form; others take the short form.

dig deep	go slow	open wide	come close	play fair
wound deeply	proceed slowly	travel widely	watch closely	treat fairly

c. In still other cases the choice is simply one of formality. The *ly* forms are more formal.

> sell cheap **OR** sell cheaply   talk loud **OR** talk loudly

1069 a. Although the *ly* ending usually signifies an adverb, a few adjectives also end in *ly*—for example, *costly, orderly, timely, motherly, fatherly, friendly, neighborly, worldly, earthly, lively, lovely, lonely.*

> Let's look for a less *costly* solution.
>
> Her offer to help you was intended as a *friendly* gesture.

b. A few common *ly*-ending words are used both as adjectives and adverbs—for example, *early, only, daily, weekly, monthly, yearly.*

> I always try to leave for work at an *early* hour. (Adjective.)
>
> The surge in sales began *early* last month. (Adverb.)

1070 Words such as *up, in, out, on,* and *off*—commonly recognized as prepositions—also function as adverbs, especially in verb phrases where these words are needed to complete the meaning of the verb. (See also ¶802.)

	Used as Adverbs	**Used as Prepositions**
up:	to look *up* the definition	to jog *up* the hill
in:	to trade *in* your old car	to see *in* the dark
out:	to phase *out* operations	to look *out* the window
on:	to put *on* a performance	to act *on* the stage
off:	to write *off* our losses	to drive *off* the road

NOTE: When used in headings and titles as *adverbs,* these short words are capitalized; when used as *prepositions,* they are not. (See ¶361c–d.)

1071 Problems of Comparison

a. Form the comparative degree of *one-syllable* adjectives and adverbs by adding *er* to the positive form. Form the superlative degree by adding *est.* (See ¶1071e for a few exceptions.)

> thin: thinner, thinnest   soon: sooner, soonest

b. Form the comparative degree of *two-syllable* adjectives and adverbs either by adding *er* to the positive form or by inserting either *more* or *less* before the positive form. Form the superlative degree by adding *est* in some cases or by inserting *most* or *least* before the positive form.

> happy: happier, more (**OR** less) happy
> likely: likeliest, most (**OR** least) likely
> often: oftener, more (**OR** less) often
> highly: highest, most (**OR** least) highly

NOTE: If the positive form ends in a consonant plus *y* (for example, *happy, likely*), change the *y* to *i* before adding *er* or *est.* Some *ly*-ending words drop the *ly* in the comparative and superlative (for example, *highly, higher, highest; deeply, deeper, deepest*). (See also ¶710.)

c. Form the comparative degree of adjectives and adverbs containing *three or more syllables* by inserting *more* or *less* before the positive form. Form the superlative degree by inserting *most* or *least* before the positive form.

> competent: more competent   adventurous: less adventurous
> acceptable: most acceptable   carefully: least carefully

d. Avoid double comparisons.

> cheaper (**NOT:** more cheaper)   unkindest (**NOT:** most unkindest)

(Continued on page 242.)

10

e. A few adjectives and adverbs have irregular comparisons. For example:

Positive	Comparative	Superlative
good or well (see page 261)	better	best
bad or ill	worse	worst
far	farther, further (see ¶719)	farthest, furthest
late	later, latter (see ¶719)	latest, last
little	littler, less, lesser	littlest, least
many, much	more	most

f. Some adjectives and adverbs—for example, *square, round, unique, completely, universally, correct, perfect, always, never, dead*—do not logically permit comparison. A square cannot be any *squarer;* a circle cannot be the *roundest of all circles.* Nevertheless, a number of these words may be modified by *more, less, nearly, hardly, virtually,* and similar adverbs to suggest something less than absolute perfection in each case.

Next year we hope to do a *more complete* study.

He is looking for a *more universally* acceptable solution.

Handicraft of this caliber is *virtually unique* these days.

We *almost never* increase our prices more than once a year.

g. When referring to *two* persons, places, or things, use the comparative form; when referring to *more than two,* use the superlative form.

That is the *finer* piece of linen. (Only two pieces are involved; hence the comparative.)

This is the *finest* piece of linen I could find. (Many pieces are involved; hence the superlative.)

Of the two positions open, you have chosen the *more* promising.
Of the three positions open, you have chosen the *most* promising.

That is the *more* efficient of the two methods.
This is the *most* efficient method that could be devised.

I like Evelyn's plan *better* than Joe's or Betty's. (Although three things are involved in this comparison, they are being compared two at a time; hence the comparative.)

h. When comparing a person or a thing *within* the group to which it belongs, use the superlative. When comparing a person or a thing with individual members of the group, use the comparative and the words *other* or *else.*

Susan is the *most* conscientious employee on the staff.

Susan is *more* conscientious than any *other* employee on the staff. (Without the word *other,* the sentence would imply that Susan is not on the staff.)

Los Angeles is the *largest* city in California.

Los Angeles is *larger* than any *other* city in California. (Without *other,* the sentence would imply that Los Angeles is not in California.)

Bert's proposal was the *best* of all that were presented to the committee.

Bert's proposal was *better* than anyone *else's.* (NOT: anyone's.)

i. Be sure to compare like things. (See also ¶644, note.)

This year's output is lower than last year's. (In other words, "This year's *output* is lower than last year's *output.*")
NOT: This year's output is lower than last year. (Incorrectly compares *this year's output* with *last year.*)

1072 The adverbs *only, nearly, almost, ever, scarcely, merely, too,* and *also* should be placed as close as possible to the word modified—usually directly before it. Putting the adverb in the wrong position may change the entire meaning of the sentence.

> Our list of depositors numbers *almost* 50,000. (**NOT:** almost numbers.)
>
> *Only* the Board of Directors can nominate the three new officers. (Cannot be nominated by anyone else.)
>
> The Board of Directors can *only* nominate the three officers. (They cannot elect.)
>
> The Board of Directors can nominate *only* the three officers. (They cannot nominate anyone else.)
>
> *Only* Robert liked her. (No one else liked her.)
>
> Robert *only* liked her. (Robert did not love her.)
>
> Robert liked *only* her. (Robert liked no one else.)

1073 Do not use an adverb to express a meaning already contained in the verb.

assemble (**NOT:** assemble together)	finish (**NOT:** finish up or off)
begin (**NOT:** first begin)	follow (**NOT:** follow after)
cancel (**NOT:** cancel out)	refer (**NOT:** refer back)
continue (**NOT:** continue on)	repeat (**NOT:** repeat again)
convert (**NOT:** convert over)	return (**NOT:** return back)
cooperate (**NOT:** cooperate together)	revert (**NOT:** revert back)

Troublesome Adjectives and Adverbs

For the following adjectives and adverbs, see individual entries listed alphabetically in ¶1101.

A–an	Ex–former	More important–
Accidentally	Farther–further	more importantly
All right	Fewer–less	Only
Almost–all most	First–firstly, etc.	Real–really
Already–all ready	Flammable–inflammable	Said
Altogether–all	Former–first	Same
together	Good–well	Scarcely
Always–all ways	Hardly	Someday–some day
Anxious–eager	Healthy–healthful	Sometime–
Anytime–any time	Hopefully	sometimes–some time
Anyway–any way	Incidentally	Sure–surely
Awhile–a while	Indifferent–in different	This here
Bad–badly	Indirect–in direct	Unique
Different–differently	Last–latest	Up
Equally as good	Latter–last	Very
Everyday–every day	Maybe–may be	Wise

Negatives

1074 To express a negative idea in a simple sentence, use only one negative expression in the sentence. (A *double negative*—two negative expressions in the same sentence—gives a *positive* meaning.)

> We can sit by and do *nothing.*
>
> We can*not* sit by and do *nothing.* (The *not* and *nothing* create a double negative; the sentence now has a positive meaning: "We ought to do something.")

(Continued on page 244.)

10

Jim is *un*aware of the facts. (Here the negative element is the prefix *un*.)

Jim is *not un*aware of the facts. (With the double negative, the sentence means "Jim *is* aware of the facts.")

NOTE: A double negative is not wrong in itself. As the examples above indicate, a double negative may offer a more effective way of expressing a *positive thought* than a straightforward positive construction would. However, a double negative *is* wrong if the sentence is intended to have a negative meaning. Remember, two negatives make a positive.

1075 A negative expression gives a negative meaning to the *clause* in which it appears. In a simple sentence, where there is only one clause, the negative expression affects the entire sentence (see ¶1074). In a sentence where there are two or more clauses, a negative expression affects only the clause in which it appears. Therefore, each clause may safely contain one negative expression. A double negative results when there are two negative expressions within the *same* clause.

If Mr. Bogosian can*not* lower his price, there is *no* point in continuing the negotiations. (The *if* clause contains the negative *not;* the main clause contains the negative *no*. Each clause has its own negative meaning.)

I have *not* met Halliday, and I have *no* desire to meet him.

OR: I have *not* met Halliday, *nor* do I have *any* desire to meet him. (When the negative conjunction *nor* replaces *and,* the adjective *no* changes to *any* so as to avoid a double negative in the second clause.)

We have *never* permitted, *nor* will we permit, any lowering of our standards. (Here the second clause interrupts the first clause. If written out in full, the sentence would read, "We have *never* permitted any lowering of our standards, *nor* will we permit any lowering of our standards.")

NOTE: A second negative expression may be used in a clause to repeat or intensify the first negative expression. This construction is not a double negative.

No, I did *not* make that statement.

He would *never, never* do a thing like that.

1076 To preserve the *negative* meaning of a clause, follow these basic principles:

a. If the clause has a *negative verb* (a verb modified by *not* or *never*), do not use an additional negative expression, such as *nor, neither . . . nor, no, none, no one,* or *nothing*. Instead, use the corresponding positive expression, such as *or, either . . . or, any, anyone,* or *anything.*

I have *not* invited *anyone*. (**WRONG:** I have *not* invited *no one*.)

She does *not* want *any*. (**WRONG:** She does *not* want *none*.)

Mary did *not* have *anything* to do. (**WRONG:** Mary did *not* have *nothing* to do.)

I can*not* find *either* the letter *or* the envelope. (**WRONG:** I can*not* find *neither* the letter *nor* the envelope.)

He did *not* say whether he would mail the money to us *or* whether he would bring it himself. (**WRONG:** He did *not* say whether he would mail the money to us *nor* whether he would bring it himself.)

b. If a clause contains any one of the following expressions—*no, no one, none, nothing,* or *neither . . . nor* (this counts as one expression)—make sure that the verb and all other words are *positive*.

I see *nothing* wrong with *either* proposal. (**NOT:** neither proposal.)

Neither Martha Gutowski *nor* Yvonne Christopher *can* handle the meeting for me next Thursday. (**NOT:** cannot.)

c. The word *nor* may be used alone as a conjunction (see the third and fourth examples in ¶1075) or together with *neither*. Do not use *nor* in the same clause with any other negative; use *or* instead.

There are *neither* diskettes *nor* data cartridges in the stockroom.
BUT: There are *no* diskettes *or* data cartridges in the stockroom.
(**NOT:** There are *no* diskettes *nor* data cartridges.)

There are *no* clear-cut rights *or* wrongs in the situation.
(**NOT:** There are *no* clear-cut rights *nor* wrongs in the situation.)

Francine has *not* called *or* written us for some time.
(**NOT:** Francine has *not* called *nor* written us for some time.)

Never try to argue *or* debate with Larry.
(**NOT:** *Never* try to argue *nor* debate with Larry.)

For Hardly, Only, *and* Scarcely, *which have a negative meaning, see the appropriate entries in Section 11.*

Prepositions

Words Requiring Certain Prepositions

1077 Usage requires that certain words be followed by certain prepositions. Some of the most frequently used combinations are given in the following list.

account for something or someone: I find it hard to *account for* his behavior.

account to someone: You will have to *account to* Anne Cuneo for the loss of the key.

agree on or **upon** (reach an understanding): We cannot *agree on* the price.

agree to (accept another person's plan): Will you *agree to* their terms?

agree with (concur with a person or an idea): I *agree with* your objectives.

angry at or **about** something: He was *angry about* the total disorder of the office.

angry with someone: You have every right to be *angry with* me.

apply for a position: You ought to *apply for* Harry's job, now that he has left.

apply to someone or something: You must *apply* yourself *to* the job in order to master it. I am thinking of *applying to* the Field Engineering Company.

argue about something: We *argued about* the terms of the contract.

argue with a person: It doesn't pay to *argue with* Bremer.

compare to (assert a likeness): She *compared* my writing *to* E. B. White's. (She said I wrote like E. B. White.)

compare with (analyze for similarities and differences): When she *compared* my writing *with* E. B. White's, she said that I had a similar kind of humor but that my sentences lacked the clean and easy flow of White's material.

conform to (preferred to *with*): These blueprints do not *conform to* the original plans.

consists in (exists in): Happiness largely *consists in* wanting what you have, not having what you want.

consists of (is made up of): Their new formula for a wage settlement *consists of* the same old terms expressed in different language.

convenient for (suitable): What time will be most *convenient for* you?

convenient to (near at hand): Our plant is *convenient to* all transportation facilities in the area.

(Continued on page 246.)

10

correspond to (agree with): The shipment does not *correspond to* the sample.

correspond with (exchange letters with): It may be better to see him in person than to *correspond with* him.

differ about (something): We *differed about* means but not about objectives.

differ from (something else): This job *differs* very little *from* the one that I used to have.

differ with (someone): I *differ with* you over the consequences of our plan.

different from: This product is *different from* the one I normally use.

different than: I view the matter in a *different* way *than* you do. (Although *from* is normally preferred, *than* is acceptable in order to avoid sentences like "I view the matter in a different way from the way in which you do.")

identical with (not *to*): This $180 suit is *identical with* one advertised for $235 at other stores.

independent of (not *from*): He wants to be *independent of* his family's money.

interested in: We are *interested in* discussing the matter further with you at the conference in July.

retroactive to (not *from*): This salary adjustment is *retroactive to* May 1.

speak to (tell something to): You must *speak to* them about their absences.

speak with (discuss with): It was good to *speak with* you yesterday.

Superfluous Prepositions

1078 Omit prepositions that add nothing to the meaning—as in the following examples. (See also page 254 for a usage note on *all of.*)

Where is she [at]?

Where did that paper go [to]?

The new applicant seems to be [of] about sixteen years of age.

She could not help [from] laughing.

His office is opposite [to] hers.

Your chair is too near [to] your terminal.

Why don't we meet at about one o'clock? (Omit either *at* or *about.*)

The carton apparently fell off [of] the truck.

The strike is now over [with].

Necessary Prepositions

1079 Conversely, do not omit essential prepositions.

I need to buy a couple *of* books.
(**NOT:** I need to buy a couple books.)

Of what use is this gadget?
(**NOT:** What use is this gadget?)

We don't stock that type *of* filter.
(**NOT:** We don't stock that type filter.)

You seem to have a great interest *in*, as well as a deep respect *for*, fine antiques.
(**NOT:** You seem to have a great interest, as well as a deep respect *for*, fine antiques.)

She frequently appears in movies, *in* plays, and on television.
(**NOT:** She frequently appears in movies, plays, and on television.)

NOTE: The preposition *of* is understood in expressions such as *what color cloth* and *what size shoes.*

Prepositions at the End of Sentences

1080 Whether or not a sentence should end with a preposition depends on the emphasis and effect desired.

> **INFORMAL:** I wish I knew which magazine her article appeared *in.*
>
> **FORMAL:** I wish I knew *in which* magazine her article appeared.
>
> **STILTED:** It is difficult to know *about* what you are thinking.
>
> **NATURAL:** It is difficult to know what you are thinking *about.*

Short questions frequently end with prepositions.

> How many can I count *on?*
> What is this made *of?*
> Where did he come *from?*
> He has nothing to worry *about.*
>
> What is this good *for?*
> We need tools to work *with.*
> That's something we must look *into.*
> There's a new computer I want to look *at.*

Troublesome Prepositions

For the following prepositions, see individual entries listed alphabetically in Section 11.

At about	From–off	Off
Beside–besides	In–into–in to	On–onto–on to
Between–among	In regards to	On–upon–up on
Due to–because of–	Indifferent–in different	Opposite
on account of	Indirect–in direct	Per–a
Except	Like–as, as if	Toward–towards
	Of–have	

For the treatment of words that can function as both prepositions and adverbs, see ¶¶802, 1070. For the capitalization of such words, see ¶361c–d.

Sentence Structure

Parallel Structure

1081 Express parallel ideas in parallel form.

> **a.** Adjectives should be paralleled by adjectives, nouns by nouns, infinitives by infinitives, subordinate clauses by subordinate clauses, and so on.
>
> **WRONG:** Your new sales training program was *stimulating* and a *challenge.* (Adjective and noun.)
>
> **RIGHT:** Your new sales training program was *stimulating* and *challenging.* (Two adjectives.)
>
> **WRONG:** The sales representatives have already started *using the new techniques* and *to produce higher sales.* (Participial phrase and infinitive phrase.)
>
> **RIGHT:** The sales representatives have already started *using the new techniques* and *producing higher sales.* (Two participial phrases.)
>
> **RIGHT:** The sales representatives have already started *to use the new techniques* and *produce higher sales.* (Two infinitive phrases.)
>
> **WRONG:** This desk copier is *easy* to operate, *efficient,* and *it is relatively inexpensive.* (Two adjectives and a clause.)
>
> **RIGHT:** This desk copier is *easy* to operate, *efficient,* and relatively *inexpensive.* (Three adjectives.)

(Continued on page 248.)

10

NOTE: Parallelism is especially important in displayed enumerations.

POOR: This article will discuss:

1. How to deal with corporate politics.
2. Coping with stressful situations.
3. What the role of the manager should be in the community.

BETTER: This article will discuss:

1. *Ways* to deal with corporate politics.
2. *Techniques* of coping with stressful situations.
3. The *role* of the manager in the community.

OR: This article will tell managers how to:

1. *Deal* with corporate politics.
2. *Cope* with stressful situations.
3. *Function* in the community.

b. Correlative conjunctions (*both . . . and, either . . . or, neither . . . nor, not only . . . but also, whether . . . or,* etc.) should be followed by elements in parallel form.

WRONG: Kevin is not only gifted as a painter but also as a sculptor.

RIGHT: Kevin is gifted not only *as a painter* but also *as a sculptor.*

WRONG: We are flying both to Chicago and San Francisco.

RIGHT: We are flying to both *Chicago* and *San Francisco.*

RIGHT: We are flying both *to Chicago* and *to San Francisco.*

WRONG: He would neither apologize nor would he promise to reform.

RIGHT: He would neither *apologize* nor *promise to reform.*

RIGHT: He would not apologize, nor would he promise to reform.

Dangling Constructions

1082 When a sentence begins with a participial phrase, an infinitive phrase, a gerund phrase, or an elliptical clause (one in which essential words are missing), make sure that the phrase or clause logically agrees with the subject of the sentence; otherwise, the construction will "dangle." To correct a dangling construction, make the subject of the sentence the doer of the action expressed by the opening phrase or clause. If that is not feasible, use an entirely different construction.

a. **Participial Phrases**

WRONG: Stashed away in the attic for the past hundred years, the owner of the painting has decided to auction it off. (Who was stashed in the attic: the owner of the painting?)

RIGHT: The owner of the painting that has been stashed away in the attic for the past hundred years has decided to auction it off.

WRONG: Having studied your cost estimates, a few *questions* occur to me about your original assumptions. (As worded, this version implies that the *questions* have studied the cost estimates.)

RIGHT: Having studied your cost estimates, I would like to ask you a few questions about your original assumptions. (In the correct version, the person who studied the cost estimates is now the subject of the sentence and is the one asking the questions.)

WRONG: Putting the matter of costs aside, the *matter* of production delays remains to be discussed.

RIGHT: Putting the matter of costs aside, *we* must still discuss the matter of production delays.

NOTE: A few words ending in *ing* (such as *concerning, considering, pending,* and *regarding*) have now become established as prepositions. Therefore, when they introduce phrases at the start of a sentence, it is not essential that they refer to the subject of the sentence.

Considering how long the lawsuit has dragged on, it might have been wiser not to sue.

b. Infinitive Phrases

WRONG: To appreciate the full significance of Fox's latest letter, all the previous correspondence should be read.

RIGHT: To appreciate the full significance of Fox's latest letter, you should read all the previous correspondence.

WRONG: To obtain this free booklet, the enclosed coupon should be mailed at once.

RIGHT: To obtain this free booklet, mail the enclosed coupon at once.

c. Prepositional-Gerund Phrases

WRONG: By installing a computerized temperature control system, a substantial saving in fuel costs was achieved.

RIGHT: By installing a computerized temperature control system, we achieved a substantial saving in fuel costs.

WRONG: In analyzing these specifications, several errors have been found.

RIGHT: In analyzing these specifications, I have found several errors.

d. Elliptical Clauses

WRONG: If ordered before May 1, a 5 percent discount will be allowed on these goods.

RIGHT: If ordered before May 1, these goods . . .

WRONG: When four years old, my family moved to Omaha.

RIGHT: When I was four years old, my family moved to Omaha.

e. Absolute Phrases

Absolute phrases (typically involving passive participles) are not considered to "dangle," even though they come at the beginning of a sentence and do not refer to the subject. Such constructions, though grammatically correct, are usually awkward and should be avoided.

WEAK: The speeches having been concluded, we proceeded to take a vote.

BETTER: After the speeches were concluded, we proceeded to take a vote.

1083 When verbal phrases and elliptical clauses fall elsewhere in the sentence, look out for illogical or confusing relationships. Adjust the wording as necessary.

WRONG: I saw two truck drivers get into a fistfight while jogging down the street.

RIGHT: While jogging down the street, I saw two truck drivers get into a fistfight.

1084 A prepositional phrase will dangle at the beginning of a sentence if it leads the reader to expect a certain word as the subject and then another word is used instead.

> **WRONG:** As head of the program committee, we think you should make immediate arrangements for another speaker. (The head of the committee is *you,* not *we.*)

> **RIGHT:** We think that as head of the program committee you should make immediate arrangements for another speaker.

> **WRONG:** As a young boy, the woman I was destined to marry did not appeal to me in any way. (That woman never was a ''young boy.'')

> **RIGHT:** When I was a young boy, the woman I was destined to marry did not appeal to me in any way.

1085 A verbal phrase will dangle at the end of a sentence if it refers to the meaning of the main clause as a whole rather than to the doer of the action.

> **WRONG:** Our sales have been steadily declining for the past six months, thus creating a sharp drop in profits. (As worded, the sentence makes it appear that *our sales,* by themselves, have created the drop in profits. Actually, it is *the fact* that our sales have been declining which has created the drop in profits.)

> **RIGHT:** The steady decline in our sales for the past six months has created a sharp drop in profits.

> **RIGHT:** Our sales have been steadily declining for the past six months. As a result, we have experienced a sharp drop in profits.

Misplaced Modifiers

1086 Watch out for misplaced modifiers (either words or phrases) that provide the basis for unintended (and sometimes humorous) interpretations.

> **WRONG:** I suspect that my assistant accidentally dropped the report I had been drafting in the wastebasket. (What an uncomfortable location in which to draft a report!)

> **RIGHT:** The report I had been drafting has disappeared. I suspect that my assistant accidentally dropped it in the wastebasket.

> **WRONG:** Here are some helpful suggestions for protecting your valuables from our hotel security staff. (Can no one be trusted?)

> **RIGHT:** Here are some helpful suggestions from our hotel security staff for protecting your valuables.

> **WRONG:** One of our assistant vice presidents has been referred to a personal finance counselor with serious credit problems. (Would you consult such a counselor?)

> **RIGHT:** One of our assistant vice presidents has serious credit problems and has been referred to a personal finance counselor.

SECTION 11

Usage

Former—First
From—Off
Good—Well
Graduated—Was Graduated
Hardly
Healthy—Healthful
Help
Hopefully
If—Whether
Imply—Infer
In—Into—In to
In Regards to
Incidentally
Indifferent—In Different
Indirect—In Direct
Individual—Party—Person—People
Irregardless
Is Where—Is When
Its—It's
Kind
Kind of—Sort of
Kind of a
Last—Latest
Latter—Last
Lay—Lie
Learn—Teach
Leave—Let
Like—As, As if
Literally
May—Can (Might—Could)
Maybe—May Be
Media
More Important—More Importantly
Most
Nobody—No Body
None—No One
Of—Have
Off
On—Onto—On to
On—Upon—Up on
Only

Opposite
Per—A
Percent—Percentage
Plus
Raise—Rise
Real—Really
Reason Is Because
Retroactive to
Said
Same
Scarcely
Serve—Service
Set—Sit
Shall—Will
Should—Would
So—So That
Someday—Some Day
Someone—Some One
Sometime—Sometimes—Some Time
Supposed to
Sure—Surely
Sure and
Tack—Tact
Than—Then
That
That—Which—Who
These Sort—These Kind
This Here
Toward—Towards
Try and
Unique
Up
Used to
Very
Ways
Where—That
Who—Which—That
Who—Whom
Whoever—Who Ever
Wise
Would Have

1101 The following entries will help you avoid a number of common mistakes in usage.

A–an. In choosing *a* or *an*, consider the sound (not the spelling) of the following word. Use the article *a* before all *consonant* sounds, including sounded *h*, long *u*, and *o* with the sound of *w* (as in *one*).

a day	a home	a unit	a youthful spirit	a one-week delay
a week	a house	a union	a euphoric feeling	a 60-day note
a year	a hotel	a uniform	a European trip	a CPA

Use *an* before all *vowel* sounds except long *u* and before words beginning with silent *h*.

an asset	an AT&T product
an essay	an EPA ruling
an input	an f.o.b. order
an outcome	an HMO physician
an upsurge	an IRS audit
an eyesore	an L.A.-based firm
an heir	an M.B.A. degree
an hour	an NBC news report
an honor	an OPEC price cut
an 8-hour day	an ROI objective
an 80-year-old man	an SRO performance
an 11 a.m. meeting	an X-ray reading

NOTE: In speech, both *a historic occasion* and *an historic occasion* are correct, depending on whether the *h* is sounded or left silent. In writing, *a historic occasion* is the form more commonly used.

A lot–alot–allot. The phrase *a lot* (meaning "to a considerable quantity or extent") always consists of two words. Do not spell this phrase as one word (*alot*).

Thanks *a lot* (**NOT** *alot*) for all your help on this year's budget.

Do not confuse this phrase with the verb *allot* (meaning "to distribute or assign a share of something").

You will have to *allot* a portion of next year's budget to cover unforeseen expenses, even though you are not likely to have *a lot* of money left over after you cover your basic operations.

A–of. Do not use *a* in place of *of*.

What sort *of* turnout did you have at your seminar?
(**NOT:** What sort *a* turnout did you have at your seminar?)

The weather has been kind *of* cool for this time of year.
(**NOT:** The weather has been *kinda* cool for this time of year.)

See Kind of–sort of *and* Kind of a.

A–per. See *Per–a.*

Accidentally. Note that this word ends in *ally*. (The form *accidently* is incorrect.)

A.D.–B.C. *A.D.* (abbreviation of *anno Domini,* Latin for "in the year of our Lord") and *B.C.* ("before Christ") are written in all capitals, with a period following each letter. Do not use a comma to separate *B.C.* or *A.D.* from the year.

150 B.C.   465 A.D. (ordinary usage)   **OR**   A.D. 465 (formal usage)

NOTE: In typeset material, these abbreviations are typically done in *small caps* (capital letters with the same height as a small *a* or *e*). Thus the phrase 150 B.C. would appear in print as 150 B.C.

Affect–effect. *Affect* is normally used as a verb meaning "to influence, change, assume." *Effect* can be either a verb meaning "to bring about" or a noun meaning "result, impression."

The court's decision in this case will not *affect* (change) the established legal precedent.

She *affects* (assumes) an unsophisticated manner.

(Continued on page 254.)

It is essential that we *effect* (bring about) an immediate improvement in sales.

It will be months before we can assess the full *effect* (result) of the new law.

NOTE: In psychology, *affect* is used as a noun meaning "feeling, emotion," and the related adjective *affective* means "emotional." Because of the limited context in which these terms are likely to be used with these meanings, it should be easy to distinguish them from *effect* as a noun and the related adjective *effective*.

We need to analyze the *effects* (results) of this new marketing strategy.
We need to analyze the *affects* (emotions) produced by this conflict.

Which technique is *effective* (capable of producing the desired results)?
Let's deal with the *affective* (emotional) factors first.

Age–aged–at the age of

I interviewed a man *aged 52* for the job. (**NOT:** a man age 52.)

I don't plan to retire *at the age of 65*. (**NOT:** *at age 65*.)

NOTE: Elliptical references to age—for example, *at age 65*—should not be used except in technical writing such as human resources manuals.

See the chart on page 6-4 for the schedule of retirement benefits for employees who retire *at age 65*.

All of. *Of* is not necessary after *all* unless the following word is a pronoun.

All the staff members belong to the softball team.
(**ALSO:** All of the staff members belong to the softball team.)

All of us belong to the softball team.

All right. Like *all wrong*, the expression *all right* should be spelled as two words. (While some dictionaries list *alright* without comment, this spelling is not generally accepted as correct.)

Almost–all most. See also *Most*.

The plane was *almost* (nearly) three hours late.

We are *all most* pleased (all very much pleased) with the new schedule.

Already–all ready

The order had *already* (previously) been shipped.

The order is *all ready* (all prepared) to be shipped.

Altogether–all together

He is *altogether* (entirely) too lazy to be a success.

The papers are *all together* (all in a group) in the binder I sent you.

Always–all ways

She has *always* (at all times) done good work.

We have tried in *all ways* (by all methods) to keep our employees satisfied.

Among–between. See *Between–among*.

Amount–number. Use *amount* for things in bulk, as in "a large amount of lumber." Use *number* for individual items, as in "a large number of inquiries."

And. Retain *and* before the last item in a series, even though that last item consists of two words joined by *and*.

We need to increase our expense budgets for advertising, staff training, *and* research and development.

(**NOT:** We need to increase our expense budgets for advertising, staff training, research and development.)

Beginning a sentence with *and* or some other coordinating conjunction (*but, or,* or *nor*) can be an effective means—*if not overused*—of giving special attention to the thought that follows the conjunction. No comma should follow the conjunction at the start of a new sentence unless a parenthetical element occurs at that point.

> Last Friday George promised to have the market analysis on my desk this Monday. *And* then he took off on a two-week vacation.

> Tell him to return to the office at once. *Or* else.

> **BUT:** George just called from Lake Tahoe to say that the report was in Word Processing for some last-minute changes and would be on my desk by 11 a.m. *And,* to my delight, it was!

NOTE: Each of the sentences above illustrates how this device can be effectively used. However, these sentences also illustrate, when taken as a whole, how quickly the overuse of this device dissipates its effectiveness.

And etc. Never use *and* before *etc.* (See *Etc.*)

And/or. Try to avoid this legalistic term in ordinary writing.

Anxious–eager. Both *anxious* and *eager* mean "desirous," but *anxious* also implies fear or concern.

> I'm *anxious* to hear whether we won the bid or not.

> I'm *eager* (**NOT** anxious) to hear about your new house.

Anyone–any one. See ¶1010, note.

Anytime–any time

> Come see us *anytime* you are in town. (One word meaning "whenever.")

> Did you have dealings with Crosby at *any time* in the past? (Two words after a preposition such as *at.*)

Anyway–any way

> *Anyway* (in any case), we can't spare him now.

> If we can help in *any way* (by any method), please phone.

Appraise–apprise

> We would like to *appraise* (set a value on) Mrs. Ellsworth's estate.

> I will *apprise* (inform) you of any new developments.

Appreciate. When used with the meaning "to be thankful for," the verb *appreciate* requires an object.

> **NOT:** We would appreciate if you could give us your decision by May 1.

> **BUT:** We would appreciate *it* if you could give us your decision by May 1. (Pronoun as object.)

> **OR:** We would appreciate *your* (**NOT** you) *giving us your decision by May 1.* (Noun clause as object. See ¶647b on the use of *your* before *giving.*)

> I will appreciate *whatever you can do for us.* (Relative clause as object.)

> We will always appreciate the *help* you gave us. (Noun as object.)

As. Do not use for *that* or *whether.*

> I do not know *whether* (**NOT** as) I can go.

Use *because, since,* or *for* rather than *as* in clauses of reason.

> I cannot attend the meeting in Omaha, *because* (**NOT** as) I will be out on the West Coast that day.

As–as if. See *Like–as, as if.*

As . . . as – not so . . . as. The term *as . . . as* is now commonly used in both positive and negative comparisons. Some writers, however, prefer to use *not so . . . as* for negative comparisons.

> Bob is every bit *as* bright *as* his older sister. (Positive comparison.)

> It is *not as* important *as* you think. **OR:** . . . *not so* important *as* you think. (Negative comparison.)

As well as. When using *as well as,* be on guard against the possibility of misleading your reader.

> **CONFUSING:** Ms. Paglia plans to meet with Mr. Pierce and Mrs. Hamer as well as Ms. Fieno. (Is Ms. Paglia planning to meet with three people, or are Ms. Paglia and Ms. Fieno both planning to meet with two people?)

> **CLEAR:** Ms. Paglia plans to meet *with* Mr. Pierce and Mrs. Hamer as well as *with* Ms. Fieno. (Repeating the preposition *with* makes it clear that Ms. Paglia will meet with three people.)

> **CLEAR:** Ms. Paglia *as well as Ms. Fieno* plans to meet with Mr. Pierce and Mrs. Hamer. (Rearranging the word order makes it clear that both Ms. Paglia and Ms. Fieno will meet with two people. Note that an *as well as* phrase following the subject, *Ms. Paglia,* does not affect the number of the verb. See ¶1007.)

Assure. See *Ensure – insure – assure.*

At about. Use either *at* or *about,* but not both words together. For example, "Plan to arrive *at* ten" **OR** "Plan to arrive *about* ten." (**BUT NOT:** Plan to arrive *at about* ten.)

Awhile – a while. One word as an adverb; two words as a noun.

> You may have to wait *awhile.* (Adverb.)

> You may have to wait for *a while.* (Noun; object of the preposition *for.*)

> I ran into him *a while* back.

Bad – badly. Use the adjective *bad* (not the adverb *badly*) after the verb *feel* or *look.* (See ¶1067.)

> I feel *bad* (**NOT** badly) about the mistake. **BUT:** He was hurt *badly.*

NOTE: The only way you can "feel badly" is to have your fingertips removed first.

Balance. Do not use *balance* to mean "rest" or "remainder" except in a financial or accounting sense.

> I plan to use the *rest* of my vacation time next February.

> (**NOT:** I plan to use the *balance* of my vacation time next February.)

> **BUT:** The *balance* of the loan falls due at the end of this quarter.

B.C. – A.D. See *A.D. – B.C.*

Because. See *Reason is because.*

Because of. See *Due to – because of – on account of.*

Being that. Do not use for *since* or *because.*

> *Because* I arrived late, I could not get a seat.

> (**NOT:** *Being that* I arrived late, I could not get a seat.)

Beside – besides

> I sat *beside* (next to) Mr. Parrish's father at the meeting.

> *Besides* (in addition), we need your support of the measure.

Between–among. Ordinarily, use *between* when referring to *two* persons or things and *among* when referring to *more than* two persons or things.

> The territory is divided evenly *between* the two sales representatives.
>
> The profits are to be evenly divided *among* the three partners.

Use *between* with more than two persons or things when they are being considered in pairs as well as in a group.

> There are distinct differences *between* New York, Chicago, and Dallas.
>
> In packing china, be sure to place paper *between* the plates.
>
> The memo says something different when you read *between* the lines.

Between you and me (not *I*). See ¶1055b.

Biannual–biennial–semiannual. *Biannual* and *semiannual* both mean "occurring twice a year." *Biennial* means "occurring every two years." Because of the possible confusion between *biannual* and *biennial*, use *semiannual* when you want to describe something that occurs twice a year.

> PREFERRED: our *semiannual* sales conference
>
> CLEARER THAN: our *biannual* sales conference

If you think that your reader could misconstrue *biennial*, avoid the term and use *every two years* instead.

> Within our global organization each national company holds its own sales conferences on a *semiannual* basis; an international sales conference is scheduled on a *biennial* basis.
>
> OR: . . . is scheduled *every two years.*

Both–each. *Both* means "the two considered together." *Each* refers to the individual members of a group considered separately.

> *Both* designs are acceptable.
> The designs are *each* acceptable.
>
> *Each* sister complained about the other.
> (NOT: *Both* sisters complained about the other.)

Both alike–equal–together. *Both* is unnecessary when used with *alike, equal,* or *together.*

> These ink-jet printers are *alike.* (NOT: both alike.)
>
> These tape systems are *equal* in cost. (NOT: both equal.)
>
> We will travel *together* to the Far East. (NOT: both travel together.)

Bring–take. *Bring* indicates motion toward the speaker. *Take* indicates motion away from the speaker.

> Please *bring* the research data with you when you next come to the office.
>
> Please *take* the enclosed letter to Farley when you go to see him.
>
> You may *take* my copy with you if you will *bring* it back by Friday.
>
> *See note under* Come–go.

But . . . however. Use one or the other.

> We had hoped to see the show, *but* we couldn't get tickets.
>
> OR: We had hoped to see the show; *however,* we couldn't get tickets.
>
> (BUT NOT: . . . *but* we couldn't get tickets, *however.*)

But what. Use *that.*

> I do not doubt *that* (NOT but what) he will be elected.

Can–could. See *May–can (might–could).*

Cannot help but. This expression is a confusion of two others, namely, *can but* and *cannot help.*

> I *can but* try. (**BETTER:** I *can only* try.)
>
> I *cannot help* feeling sorry for her. (**NOT:** cannot help but feel.)

Class. See *Kind.*

Come–go. The choice between verbs depends on the location of the speaker. *Come* indicates motion *toward; go,* motion *away from.* (See also *Bring–take.*)

> When Bellotti *comes* back, I will *go* to the airport to meet him.
>
> *A secretary speaking over the phone to an outsider:* Will it be convenient for you to *come* to our office tomorrow?

NOTE: When discussing your travel plans with a person at your destination, adopt that person's point of view and use *come.*

> *An outsider speaking over the phone to a secretary:* Will it be convenient for me to *come* to your office tomorrow?
>
> *Midwesterner to Californian:* I am *coming* to California during the week of the 11th. I will *bring* the plans with me if they are ready.

However, if you are discussing your travel plans with someone who is *not* at your destination, observe the regular distinction between *come* and *go.*

> *An outsider speaking to an outsider:* I hope it will be convenient for me to *go* to their office tomorrow.
>
> *Midwesterner to Midwesterner:* I am *going* to California during the week of the 11th. I will *take* the plans with me if they are ready.

Come and. In formal writing, use *come to* instead of the colloquial *come and.*

> Come *to* see me. (**NOT:** Come *and* see me.)

Comprise–compose. *Comprise* means "to include, contain, consist of"; *compose* means "to make up." The parts *compose* (make up) the whole; the whole *comprises* (includes) the parts; the whole *is composed of* (**NOT** is comprised of) the parts.

> The parent corporation *comprises* (consists of) three major divisions.
>
> Three major divisions *compose* (make up) the parent corporation.
>
> The parent corporation *is composed of* (is made up of) three major divisions.

Data. See ¶1018, note.

Different–differently. When the meaning is "in a different manner," use the adverb *differently.*

> I wish we had done it *differently.*
>
> It came out *differently* than we expected. (See ¶1077.)

After linking verbs and verbs of the senses, the adjective *different* is correct. (See ¶1067.)

> That music sounds completely *different.*
>
> He seems (appears) *different* since his promotion.
>
> Don't believe anything *different.* (Meaning "anything that is different.")

Different from–different than. See ¶1077.

Done. Do not say "I *done* it." Say "I *did* it." (See also ¶1032, note.)

Don't (do not). Do not use *don't* with *he, she,* or *it;* use *doesn't.*

He *doesn't* talk easily.

She *doesn't* need any help.

It *doesn't* seem right to penalize them.

BUT: I *don't* think so.

They *don't* want any help.

We *don't* understand.

Doubt that–doubt whether. Use *doubt that* in negative statements and in questions. Use *doubt whether* in all other cases. (See also *If–whether.*)

We do not *doubt that* she is capable. (Negative statement.)

Does anyone *doubt that* the check was mailed? (Question.)

I *doubt whether* I can go.

Due to–because of–on account of. *Due to* introduces an adjective phrase and should modify nouns. It is normally used only after some form of the verb *to be* (*is, are, was, were,* etc.)

Her success is *due to* talent and hard work. (*Due to* modifies *success.*)

Because of and *on account of* introduce adverbial phrases and should modify verbs.

He resigned *because of* ill health. (*Because of* modifies *resigned.*)

(NOT: He resigned *due to* ill health.)

Each–both. See *Both–each.*

Each other–one another. Use *each other* to refer to two persons or things; *one another* for more than two.

The two partners had great respect for *each other's* abilities.

The four winners congratulated *one another.*

Eager–anxious. See *Anxious–eager.*

Effect–affect. See *Affect–effect.*

Ensure–insure–assure. *Ensure* means "to make certain." *Insure* means "to protect against loss." *Assure* means "to give someone confidence"; the object of this verb should always refer to a person.

I want to *ensure* (make certain) that nothing can go wrong tomorrow.

I want to *assure* you (give you confidence) that nothing will go wrong.

I want to *insure* this necklace (protect it against loss) for $5000.

Enthused over. Use *was* or *were enthusiastic about* instead.

The sales staff *was enthusiastic about* (NOT enthused over) next year's styles.

Equal. See *Both alike–equal–together.*

Equally as good. Use either *equally good* or *just as good.*

This model is newer, but that one is *equally good.* (NOT: equally as good.)

Those are *just as good* as these. (NOT: equally as good.)

Etc. This abbreviation of *et cetera* means "and other things." Therefore, do not use *and* before it. A comma both precedes and follows *etc.* (see ¶164). In formal writing, avoid the use of *etc.;* use a phrase such as *and the like* or *and so on* instead.

NOTE: Do not use *etc.* or an equivalent expression at the end of a series introduced by *such as.* The term *such as* implies that only a few selected examples will be given; therefore, it is unnecessary to add *etc.* or *and so on,* which suggests that further examples could be given.

> As part of its employee educational program, the company offers courses in report writing, business correspondence, grammar and style, *and so on.*
>
> OR: . . . the company offers courses *such as* report writing, business correspondence, and grammar and style.
>
> (BUT NOT: . . . the company offers courses *such as* report writing, business correspondence, grammar and style, *and so on.*)
>
> *For the use or omission of a comma before* such as, *see ¶¶148–149.*

Everyday–every day

> You'll soon master the *everyday* (ordinary or daily) routine of the job.
>
> He has called *every day* (each day) this week.

Everyone–every one. See ¶1010, note.

Ex–former. Use *ex-* with a title to designate the person who *immediately* preceded the current titleholder in that position; use *former* with a title to designate an earlier titleholder.

> Charles Feldman is the *ex-president* of the Harrisburg Chamber of Commerce. (Held office immediately before the current president.)
>
> BUT: . . . is a *former* president of the Harrisburg Chamber of Commerce. (Held office sometime before the current president and that person's immediate predecessor.)

Except. When *except* is a preposition, be sure to use the objective form of a pronoun that follows. (See also ¶1055b.)

> Everyone has been transferred *except* Jean and *me.* (NOT: except Jean and I.)

Farther–further. *Farther* refers to actual distance; *further* refers to figurative distance and means "to a greater degree" or "to a greater extent."

> The drive from the airport was *farther* (in actual distance) than we expected.
>
> Let's plan to discuss the proposal *further* (to a greater extent).

Fewer–less. *Fewer* refers to number and is used with *plural* nouns. *Less* refers to degree or amount and is used with *singular* nouns.

> *Fewer* accidents (a smaller number) were reported than was expected.
>
> *Less* effort (a smaller degree) was put forth by the organizers, and thus *fewer* people (a smaller number) attended.

The expression *less than* (rather than *fewer than*) precedes plural nouns referring to periods of time, amounts of money, and quantities.

> less than ten years ago   FORMAL: fewer than 60 people
> less than $1 million   COLLOQUIAL: less than 60 people

The expression *or less* (rather than *or fewer*) is used after a reference to a number of items.

> in words of 100 or less   in groups of six people or less

First–firstly, etc. In enumerations, use the forms *first, second, third* (NOT firstly, secondly, thirdly).

Flammable–inflammable. Both terms mean "easily ignitable, highly combustible." However, since some readers may misinterpret *inflammable* to mean "*non*flammable," *flammable* is the clearer form.

Former–ex. See *Ex–former.*

Former–first. *Former* refers to the first of two persons or things. When more than two are mentioned, use *first.* (See also *Latter–last.*)

> This item is available in wool and in Dacron, but I prefer the *former.*
>
> This item is available in wool, in Dacron, and in Orlon, but I prefer the *first.*

From–off. Use *from* (**NOT** off) with persons.

> I got the answer I needed *from* Margaret. (**NOT:** off Margaret.)

Go–come. See *Come–go.*

Good–well. *Good* is an adjective. *Well* is typically used as an adverb, but it may be used as an adjective to refer to the state of someone's health.

> Marie got *good* grades in school. (Adjective.)
>
> I will do the job as *well* as I can. (Adverb.)
>
> He admits he does not feel *well* today. (Adjective.)
>
> The security guards look *good* in their new uniforms. (Adjective.)

NOTE: *To feel well* means "to be in good health." *To feel good* means "to be in good spirits."

Graduated–was graduated. Both forms are acceptable. However, use *from* after either expression.

> My daughter *graduated from* MIT last year.
>
> (**NOT:** My daughter *graduated* MIT last year.)

Hardly. *Hardly* is negative in meaning. To preserve the negative meaning, do not use another negative with it.

> You *could hardly* (**NOT** couldn't hardly) expect him to agree.

Have–of. See *Of–have.*

Healthy–healthful. People are *healthy;* a climate or food is *healthful.*

> You ought to move to a more *healthful* (**NOT** healthier) climate.

Help. Do not use *from* after the verb *help.* For example, "I couldn't *help* (**NOT** help from) telling her she was wrong."

Hopefully. Although the subject of much controversy, the use of *hopefully* at the beginning of a sentence is no different from the use of *obviously, certainly, fortunately, actually, apparently,* and similar words functioning as "independent comments" (see ¶138b). These adverbs express the writer's attitude toward what he is about to say; as such they modify the meaning of the sentence as a whole rather than a particular word.

> *Hopefully,* the worst is over and we will soon see a strong upturn in sales and profits.

However. See *But . . . however.*

If–whether. *If* is often used colloquially for *whether* in such sentences as "He doesn't know *whether* he will be able to leave tomorrow." In written material, use *whether,* particularly in such expressions as *see whether, learn whether, know whether,* and *doubt whether.* Also use *whether* when the expression *or not* follows or is implied.

> Find out *whether* (**NOT** if) this format is acceptable *or not.*

Imply–infer. *Imply* means "to suggest"; you imply something by *your own* words or actions.

> Verna *implied* (suggested) that we would not be invited.

Infer means "to assume, to deduce, to arrive at a conclusion"; you infer something from *another person's* words or actions.

> I *inferred* (assumed) from Verna's remarks that we would not be invited.

In–into–in to

> The correspondence is *in* the file. (*In* implies position within.)

> He walked *into* the outer office. (*Into* implies entry or change of form.)

> All sales reports are to be sent *in to* the sales manager. (*In* is an adverb in the verb phrase *are to be sent in; to* is a simple preposition.)

> Mr. Boehme came *in to* see me. (*In* is part of the verb phrase *came in; to* is part of the infinitive *to see*.)

In regards to. Substitute *in regard to, with regard to, regarding,* or *as regards*.

Incidentally. Note that this word ends in *ally*. Never spell it *incidently*.

Indifferent–in different

> She was *indifferent* (not caring one way or the other) to the offer.

> He liked our idea, but he wanted it expressed *in different* (in other) words.

Indirect–in direct

> *Indirect* (not direct) lighting will enhance the appearance of this room.

> This order is *in direct* (the preposition *in* plus the adjective *direct*) conflict with the policy of this company.

Individual–party–person–people. Use *individual* to refer to someone whom you wish to distinguish from a larger group of people.

> We wish to honor those *individuals* who had the courage to speak out at a time when popular opinion was defending the status quo.

Use *party* only to refer to someone involved in a legal proceeding.

> All the *parties* to the original agreement must sign the attached amendment.

Use *person* to refer to a human being in all other contexts.

> Please tell me the name of the *person* in charge of your credit department.

If reference is made to more than one person, the term *people* usually sounds more natural than the plural form *persons*. In any event, always use *people* when referring to a large group.

> If you like, I can send you a list of all the *people* in our corporation who will be attending this year's national convention.

Infer. See *Imply*.

Inflammable–flammable. See *Flammable–inflammable*.

Insure. See *Ensure–insure–assure*.

Irregardless. Use *regardless*.

Is where–is when. Do not use these phrases to introduce definitions.

> A dilemma is a situation in which you have to choose between equally unsatisfactory alternatives.

> (NOT: A dilemma *is where* you have to choose between equally unsatisfactory alternatives.)

However, these phrases may be correctly used in other situations.

The Ritz-Carlton *is where* the dinner-dance will be held this year.

Two o'clock *is when* the meeting is scheduled to begin.

Its–it's. See ¶1056e.

Kind. *Kind* is singular; therefore, write *this kind, that kind, these kinds, those kinds* (**BUT NOT** *these kind, those kind*). The same distinctions hold for *class, type,* and *sort.*

Kind of–sort of. These phrases are sometimes followed by an adjective (for example, *kind of sorry, sort of baffled*). Use this kind of expression only in informal writing. In more formal situations, use *rather* or *somewhat* (*rather sorry, somewhat baffled*).

I was *somewhat* (**NOT** kind of, sort of) surprised.

She seemed *rather* (**NOT** kind of, sort of) tired.

NOTE: When *kind of* or *sort of* is followed by a noun, the expression is appropriate in all kinds of situations.

What *sort of business* is Vern Forbes in?

See A–of *and* Kind of a.

Kind of a. The *a* is unnecessary. For example, "That *kind of* (**NOT** kind of a) material is very expensive."

Last–latest. *Last* means "after all others"; *latest,* "most recent."

Mr. Lin's *last* act before leaving was to recommend Ms. Roth's promotion.

Attached is the *latest* report we have received from the Southern Region.

Latter–last. *Latter* refers to the second of two persons or things mentioned. When more than two are mentioned, use *last.* (See also *Former–first.*)

July and August are good vacation months, but the *latter* is more popular.

June, July, and August are good vacation months, but the *last* is the most popular.

Lay–lie. *Lay* (principal parts: *lay, laid, laid, laying*) means "to put" or "to place." This verb requires an object to complete its meaning.

Please *lay* the *boxes* on the pallets with extreme care.

I *laid* the *message* right on your desk.

I *had laid* two other *notes* there yesterday.

He *is* always *laying* the *blame* on his assistants. (Putting the blame.)

The dress *was laid* in the box. (A passive construction implying that someone *laid* the dress in the box.)

Lie (principal parts: *lie, lay, lain, lying*) means "to recline, rest, or stay" or "to take a position of rest." It refers to a person or thing as either assuming or being in a reclining position. This verb cannot take an object.

Now he *lies* in bed most of the day.

The mountains *lay* before us as we proceeded west.

This letter *has lain* unanswered for two weeks.

Today's mail *is lying* on the receptionist's desk.

TEST: In deciding whether to use *lie* or *lay* in a sentence, substitute the word *place, placed,* or *placing* (as appropriate) for the word in question. If the substitute fits, the corresponding form of *lay* is correct. If it doesn't, use the appropriate form of *lie*.

I will *(lie* or *lay?)* down now. (You could not say, "I will *place* down now." Therefore, write "I will *lie* down now.")

I *(laid* or *lay?)* the pad on his desk. ("I *placed* the pad on his desk" works. Therefore, write "I *laid* the pad.")

I *(laid* or *lay?)* awake many nights. ("I *placed* awake" doesn't work. Write "I *lay* awake.")

These files have *(laid* or *lain?)* untouched for some time. ("These files have *placed* untouched" doesn't work. Write "These files have *lain* untouched.")

He has been *(laying* or *lying?)* down on the job. ("He has been *placing* down on the job" doesn't work. Write "He has been *lying* down.")

NOTE: When the verb *lie* means "to tell a falsehood," it has regularly formed principal parts *(lie, lied, lied, lying)* and is seldom confused with the verbs just described.

Learn–teach. *Learn* (principal parts: *learn, learned, learned, learning*) means "to acquire knowledge." *Teach* (principal parts: *teach, taught, taught, teaching*) means "to impart knowledge to others."

I *learned* from a master teacher.	A first-rate instructor *taught* me how.
(**NOT:** I *was learned* by a master teacher.)	I was *taught* by a first-rate instructor.

Leave–let. *Leave* (principal parts: *leave, left, left, leaving*) means "to move away, abandon, or depart." *Let* (principal parts: *let, let, let, letting*) means "to permit or allow." **TEST:** In deciding whether to use *let* or *leave*, try substituting the appropriate form of *permit*. If *permit* fits, use *let;* if not, use *leave*.

I now *leave* you to your own devices. (Abandon you.)

Mr. Morales *left* on the morning train. (Departed.)

Let me see the last page. (Permit me to see.)

Leave me alone. **OR:** *Let* me alone. (Either is acceptable.)

Less–fewer. See *Fewer–less.*

Lie. See *Lay.*

Like–as, as if. *Like* is correctly used as a preposition. Although *like* is also widely used as a conjunction in colloquial speech, use *as, as if,* or a similar expression in written material.

We need to hire another person *like* you.
Kate, *like* her predecessor, will have to cope with the problem.
As (**NOT** Like) I told you earlier, we will not reorder for six months.
It looks *like* snow.
It looks *as if* (**NOT** like) it will snow.
Mary looks *like* her mother.
Mary looks *as* (**NOT** like) her mother did at the same age.
BETTER: Mary looks the way her mother did at the same age.

Literally. This adverb means "actually, truly." Do not use it in the sense of "almost" to modify a reference to an exaggerated or unreal situation.

NOT: When Jensen got the bill for all the "minor changes" made at the last minute, he *literally* hit the ceiling. (Omit the word *literally* unless Jensen actually exploded out of his chair and hit the ceiling headfirst.)

May–can (might–could). *May* and *might* imply permission or possibility; *can* and *could,* ability or power.

> You *may* send them a dozen cans of paint on trial. (Permission.)
>
> The report *may* be true. (Possibility.)
>
> *Can* he present a workable plan? (Has he the ability?)
>
> Miss Kovacs said I *might* (permission) have the time off if I *could* (had the ability to) finish my work in time.
>
> Please call me if you think I *can* be of any help. (Emphasizes the ability to help.)
>
> Please call me if you think I *may* be of any help. (Emphasizes the possibility of helping.)

Maybe–may be. *Maybe* is an adverb; *may be* is a verb.

> If we don't receive a letter from them today, *maybe* (an adverb meaning ''perhaps'') we should call.
>
> Mr. Boston *may be* (a verb) out of town next week.

Media. *Media,* referring to various channels of communication and advertising, is a plural noun. *Medium* is the singular. (See ¶1018.)

More important–more importantly. *More important* is often used as a short form for ''what is more important,'' especially at the beginning of a sentence. *More importantly* means ''in a more important manner.''

> *More important,* we need to establish a line of credit very quickly. (What is more important.)
>
> The incident was treated *more importantly* than it deserved. (In a more important manner.)

Most. Do not use for *almost.*

> *Almost all* the money is gone.
>
> OR: *Most* of the money is gone.
>
> BUT NOT: *Most all* of the money is gone.

Nobody–no body

> There was *nobody* (no person) at the information desk when I arrived.
>
> *No body* (no group) of employees is more cooperative than yours.

NOTE: Spell *no body* as two words when it is followed by *of.* (See also ¶1010.)

None–no one. See ¶1013.

Not so . . . as. See *As . . . as–not so . . . as.*

Number. See *Amount–number.*

Of–a. See *A–of.*

Of–have. Do not use *of* instead of *have* in verb forms. The correct forms are *could have, would have, should have, might have, may have, must have, ought to have,* and so forth.

> What *could have* happened? (NOT: What could *of* happened?)

Off. Do not use *off of* or *off from* in place of *off.* (See also ¶1078.)

> The papers fell *off* the desk. (NOT: off of the desk.)

Off–from. See *From–off.*

On–onto–on to

It's dangerous to drive *on* the highway shoulder. (*On* implies position or movement over.)

He lost control of the car and drove *onto* the sidewalk. (*Onto* implies movement toward and then over.)

Let's go *on to* the next problem. (*On* is an adverb in the verb phrase *go on*; *to* is a preposition.)

She then went *on to* tell about her experiences in Asia. (*On* is part of the verb phrase *went on*; *to* is part of the infinitive *to tell*.)

On–upon–up on

His statements were based *on* (**or** *upon*) experimental data. (*On* and *upon* are interchangeable.)

Please follow *up on* the Updegraff case. (*Up* is part of the verb phrase *follow up*; *on* is a preposition.)

On account of. See *Due to–because of–on account of*.

One another–each other. See *Each other–one another*.

Only. The adverb *only* is negative in meaning. Therefore, do not use another negative with it unless you want a positive meaning. (See ¶1072 for the placement of *only* in a sentence.)

I use this letterhead *only* for foreign correspondence. (I do not use this letterhead for anything else.)

BUT: I do not use this letterhead *only* for foreign correspondence. (I use it for a number of other things as well.)

Opposite. When used as a noun, *opposite* is followed by *of*.

Her opinion is the *opposite of* mine.

In other uses, *opposite* is followed by *to* or *from* or by no preposition at all.

Her opinion is *opposite to* (**or** *from*) mine.

She lives *opposite* the school.

Party. See *Individual–party–person–people*.

Per–a. *Per*, a Latin word, is often used to mean "by the," as in *28 miles per gallon (mpg)* or *55 miles per hour (mph)*. Whenever possible, substitute *a* or *an*; for example, *at the rate of $8 an hour, 75 cents a liter*. *Per* must be retained, of course, in Latin phrases—for example, *per diem* (by the day) or *per capita* (for each person; literally, by the head).

NOTE: Do not use *per* in the sense of "according to" or "in accordance with."

We are sending you samples *as you requested*. (**NOT:** per your request.)

Percent–percentage. In ordinary usage, *percent* should always be accompanied by a number; for example, *20 percent, 0.5 percent, 150 percent*. Similarly, in a table a column of figures representing percentages may be headed *Percent of Total* or something comparable. Otherwise, use the term *percentage*.

A large *percentage* of the calls we got yesterday came from customers who misread our ad. (**NOT:** A large *percent* of the calls . . .)

What *percentage* of our subscribers are in the 30–49 age group? (See ¶1025.)

NOTE: In the percentage formula used in mathematics (base × rate = amount), the rate is called a *percent* and the amount is called a *percentage*. Thus you might be asked to calculate the *percentage* if a sales tax of 6 percent (the rate) was applied to a purchase of $50 (the base). By the same token, you might be asked to calculate the *percent* (the rate) if you knew that a tax of $5 (the amount, or percentage) had been paid on an order of $200. Outside of this special context, *percent* and *percentage* should be used as noted at the start of this entry on page 266.

Person–people. See *Individual–party–person–people.*

Plus. This word can be correctly used as a noun, an adjective, or a preposition. However, do not use it as a conjunction (with the sense of "and").

> Your presence at the hearing was a real *plus* for our cause. (*Plus* used correctly as a noun.)

> The decision to offer a 10 percent discount on all orders received by June 1 was a *plus* factor in the campaign. (*Plus* used correctly as an adjective.)

> Your willingness to innovate *plus* your patient perspective on profits has permitted this company to grow at an astonishing rate. (*Plus* used correctly as a preposition. Note that a *plus* phrase following the subject of a sentence does not affect the number of the verb. See ¶1007.)

> **BUT NOT:** You have always been willing to innovate, *plus* you have been patient about the profits to be derived from the innovations. (Do not use *plus* as a conjunction; use *and* instead.)

Raise–rise. *Raise* (principal parts: *raise, raised, raised, raising*) means "to cause to lift" or "to lift something." This verb requires an object to complete its meaning.

> Mr. Pinelli *raises* a good *question.*

> Most growers *have raised* the *price* of coffee.

> We *are raising money* for the United Fund.

> Our rent *has been raised.* (A passive construction implying that someone *has raised* the rent.)

Rise (principal parts: *rise, rose, risen, rising*) means "to ascend," "to move upward by itself," or "to get up." This verb cannot be used with an object.

> We will have to *rise* to the demands of the occasion.

> The sun *rose* at 6:25 this morning.

> The river *has risen* to flood level.

> The temperature *has been rising* all day.

TEST: Remember, you cannot "rise" anything.

Real–really. *Real* is an adjective; *really,* an adverb. Do not use *real* to modify another adjective; use *very* or *really.*

> One taste will tell you these cookies were made with *real* butter. (Adjective.)

> We were *really* expecting a lower price from you this year. (Adverb.)

> **BUT:** It was *very* nice (**NOT:** real nice) to see you and your family again.

Reason is because. Substitute *reason is that.* For example, "The *reason* for such low sales *is that* (**NOT** because) prices are too high."

Retroactive to (**NOT** from)

> These improvements in benefits under the company dental plan will be *retroactive to* July 1. (See also ¶1077.)

Said. The use of *said* in a phrase like "the *said* document" is appropriate only in legal writing. In normal usage write "the document referred to above." (In many cases the document being referred to will be clear to the reader without the additional explanation.)

Same. Do not use *same* to refer to a previously mentioned thing.

> We are now processing your order and will have *it* ready for you Monday. (**NOT:** We are now processing your order and will have *same* ready . . .)

Scarcely. The adverb *scarcely* is negative in meaning. To preserve the negative meaning, do not use another negative with it. (See ¶1072 for the placement of *scarcely*.)

> I *scarcely* recognized (**NOT** didn't scarcely recognize) you.

Semiannual. See *Biannual–biennial–semiannual.*

Serve–service. Things can be *serviced*, but people are *served*.

> We take great pride in the way we *serve* (**NOT** service) our clients.
>
> For a small additional charge we will *service* the equipment for a full year.

Set–sit. *Set* (principal parts: *set, set, set, setting*) means "to place something somewhere." In this sense, *set* requires an object to complete its meaning. **REMEMBER:** You cannot "sit" anything.

> It's important to *set* down your *recollections* while they are still fresh.
>
> I must have dropped my wallet when I *set* my *suitcase* down.
>
> I *have set* my *alarm* for six in the morning.
>
> The crew *was setting* the *stage* for the evening performance.
>
> The date *was set* some time ago. (A passive construction implying that someone *set* the date.)

NOTE: *Set* has a few other meanings in which the verb does *not* require an object, but these meanings are seldom confused with *sit.*

> They *set* out on the trip in high spirits.
>
> The sun *set* at 5:34 p.m. Wednesday.
>
> Allow a full hour for the mixture to *set.*

Sit (principal parts: *sit, sat, sat, sitting*) means "to be in a position of rest" or "to be seated." This verb cannot be used with an object.

> So here we *sit,* waiting for a decision from top management.
>
> I *sat* next to Ebbetsen at the board meeting.
>
> They *had sat* on the plane a full hour before the flight was canceled.
>
> They *will be sitting* in the orchestra.

Shall–will. The auxiliary verb *shall* has largely given way to the verb *will* in all but the most formal writing and speech. The following rules reflect both ordinary and formal usage:

a. To express simple future time:

>   (1) In *ordinary* circumstances use *will* with all three persons.
>
>> *I* (**OR** *we*) *will* be glad to help you plan the program.
>>
>> *You will* want to study these recommendations before the meeting.
>>
>> *He* (**OR** *she, it, they*) *will* arrive tomorrow morning.
>
>   (2) In *formal* circumstances use *shall* with the first person (*I, we*) and *will* with the second and third persons (*you, he, she, it, they*).

I (**OR** *we*) *shall* be glad to answer all inquiries promptly.

You will meet the McGinnesses at the reception this evening.

They (**OR** *he, she*) *will* not find the trip too tiring.

b. To indicate *determination, promise, desire, choice,* or *threat:*

(1) In *ordinary* circumstances use *will* with all three persons.

(2) In *formal* circumstances use *will* for the first person (*I, we*) and *shall* for the second and third persons (*you, he, she, it, they*).

In spite of the risk, *I will* go where I please. (Determination.)

They shall not interfere with my department. (Determination.)

I will send my check by the end of the week. (Promise.)

We will report you to the authorities if this is true. (Threat.)

You shall regret your answer. (Threat.)

He shall study, or *he shall* leave college. (Threat.)

c. To indicate *willingness* (to be willing, to be agreeable to) in both *ordinary* and *formal* circumstances, use *will* with all persons.

Yes, I *will* meet you at six o'clock.

Should–would. *Should* and *would* follow the same rules as *shall* and *will* (see preceding entry) in expressions of future time, determination, and willingness. The distinctions concerning ordinary and formal usage also apply here.

ORDINARY: I *would* like to hear from you.

FORMAL: I *should* like to hear from you.

ORDINARY: We *would* be glad to see her.

FORMAL: We *should* be glad to see her.

ORDINARY: I *would* be pleased to serve on that committee.

FORMAL: I *should* be pleased to serve on that committee.

a. Always use *should* in all persons to indicate ''ought to.''

I *should* study tonight.

You *should* report his dishonesty to the manager.

He *should* pay his debts.

b. Always use *would* in all persons to indicate customary action.

Every day I *would* swim half a mile.

They *would* only say, ''No comment.''

She *would* practice day after day.

c. Use *should* in all three persons to express a condition in an *if* clause.

If I *should* win the prize, I will share it with you.

If you *should* miss the train, please call me collect.

d. Use *would* in all three persons to express willingness in an *if* clause.

If he *would* apply himself, he could win top honors easily.

If you *would* delay your decision, I could offer you more attractive terms.

So–so that. *So* as a conjunction means ''therefore''; *so that* means ''in order that.''

The work is now finished, *so* you can all go home. (See also ¶179.)

Please finish what you are doing *so that* we can all go home.

Someday–some day

Please set up a meeting with Al and Jerry *someday* (on an unspecified day) next week.

BUT: Please set up a meeting with Al and Jerry *for some day* next week. (Two words when used as the object of a preposition such as *for*.)

Someone–some one. See ¶1010, note.

Sometime–sometimes–some time

The order will be shipped *sometime* (at some unspecified time) next week. *Sometimes* (now and then) reports are misleading.

It took me *some time* (a period of time) to complete the job.

I saw him *some time* ago (a long time ago).

NOTE: Spell *some time* as two words when the term follows a preposition.

We will be happy to reconsider your proposal *at some time* in the future.

I've been thinking about retiring *for some time*.

Sort. See *Kind*.

Sort of–kind of. See *Kind of–sort of*.

Such as . . . etc. See *Etc*.

Supposed to. Be sure to spell *supposed* with a *d*.

Under the circumstances what was I *supposed to* think? (**NOT:** suppose to.)

Sure–surely. *Sure* is an adjective, *surely* an adverb.

I am *sure* that I did not make that mistake. (Adjective.)
You can *surely* count on our help. (Adverb.)

Do not use *sure* as an adverb; use *surely* or *very*.

I was *very* glad to be of help. (**NOT:** sure glad.)

Sure and. In formal writing use *sure to* in place of the colloquial *sure and*.

Be *sure to* give my best regards to the Meltzers.

(**NOT:** Be *sure and* give my best regards to the Meltzers.)

Tack–tact. Use *tack* (not *tact*) in the expression *to take a different tack* (meaning "to move in a different direction"). *Tact* means "a considerate way of behaving so as to avoid offending others."

We may have to take a different *tack* in our negotiations with Firebridge.

Please use a great deal of *tact* when you reply to Korbman's letter.

Take–bring. See *Bring–take*.

Teach–learn. See *Learn–teach*.

Than–then. *Than* is a conjunction introducing a subordinate clause of comparison. *Then* is an adverb meaning "at that time" or "next."

The compulsory retirement age is higher now *than* it was *then*.

They *then* asserted that they could handle the account better *than* we. (See ¶1057 for the case of pronouns following *than*.)

NOTE: Remember that *then* (like *when*) refers to time.

That. As a subordinating conjunction, *that* links the dependent clause it introduces with the main clause. *That* is often omitted (but understood).

We realize *that* our bargaining position is not a strong one.

OR: We realize our bargaining position is not a strong one.

However, under certain circumstances *that* should not be omitted:

a. When the word or phrase following *that* could be misread as the object of the verb in the main clause.

NOT: I heard your speech next Wednesday had to be rescheduled.

BUT: I heard *that* your speech next Wednesday had to be rescheduled.

b. When *that* introduces two or more parallel clauses.

NOT: Hilary said she had narrowed the applicants for the job down to three people and *that* she would announce her choice by this Friday.

BUT: Hilary said *that* she had narrowed the applicants for the job down to three people and *that* she would announce her choice by this Friday.

c. When an introductory or interrupting element comes between *that* and the subject of the dependent clause.

NOT: I think whenever possible, you should consult everyone involved before making your decision.

BUT: I think *that* whenever possible, you should consult everyone involved before making your decision. (See ¶130d.)

NOTE: If you are in doubt, do not omit *that*.

That–where. See *Where–that*.

That–which–who. See ¶1062.

These sort–these kind. Incorrect; the correct forms are *this* sort, *this* kind, these *sorts*, these *kinds*. (See also *Kind*.)

This here. Do not use for *this;* for example, ''*this* (**NOT** this here) word processor.''

Together. See *Both alike–equal–together*.

Toward–towards. *Toward* is more common, but both forms are correct.

Try and. In written material use *try to* rather than the colloquial *try and*. For example, ''Please *try to* be here on time.'' (**NOT:** try and be here.)

Type. See *Kind*.

Unique. Do not use *unique* in the sense of ''unusual.'' A unique thing is one of a kind. (See ¶1071f.)

Up. Many verbs (for example, *end, rest, lift, connect, join, hurry, settle, burn, drink, eat*) contain the idea of ''up''; therefore, the adverb *up* is unnecessary. In the following sentences, *up* should be omitted.

You need to rest (up) for a bit. Save $50 if you join (up) now.
Let's divide (up) the work load. I will call him (up) tomorrow.

Upon–up on. See *On–upon–up on*.

Used to. Be sure to spell *used* with a *d*.

We *used* to use Forsgate as our main supplier. (**NOT:** We *use* to use . . .)

Very. This adverb can be used to modify an adjective, another adverb, a present participle, or a ''descriptive'' past participle.

(Continued on page 272.)

We are *very happy* with the outcome. (Modifying an adjective.)

This finish dries *very quickly*. (Modifying an adverb.)

It was a *very disappointing* showing. (Modifying a present participle.)

I was *very pleased* with the pictures. (Modifying a descriptive past participle.)

When the past participle expresses action rather than description, insert an adverb like *much* after *very*.

They are *very much opposed* to your plan. (*Opposed* is part of the complete verb *are opposed* and expresses action rather than description.)

(**NOT:** They are *very opposed* to your plan.)

Ways. Do not use for *way* in referring to distance. For example, "I live a short *way* (**NOT** ways) from here."

Well–good. See *Good–well.*

Where–that. Do not use *where* in place of *that.*

I saw in yesterday's paper *that* Schuster's had changed its mind about closing its midtown store.

(**NOT:** I saw in yesterday's paper *where* Schuster's had changed its mind about closing its midtown store.)

Whether–if. See *If–whether.*

Who–which–that. See ¶1062.

Who–whom. See ¶1061.

Whoever–who ever

Whoever (anyone who) made such a statement should be fired.

Who ever made such a statement? (*Ever* is an adverb.)

Will–shall. See *Shall–will.*

Wise. Avoid the temptation to coin new words by attaching the suffix *wise* to various nouns. (Stylewise, it's considered bad form.)

NOT: *Costwise,* we're already 20 percent over budget.

BUT: We're already 20 percent over budget on costs.

NOT: *Sizewise,* what comes after extra large? Gross? (Even when used in a conscious attempt at humor, the approach leaves much to be desired. Once again, avoid the temptation.)

Would–should. See *Should–would.*

Would have. Note that the second word in this verb phrase is *have.* (The spelling *would of* is wrong.)

I myself *would have* (**NOT** would of) taken a different tack.

In a clause beginning with *if,* do not use *would have* in place of *had.*

If you *had* come early, you could have talked with Dr. Fernandez yourself.

NOT: If you would have come early, you could have talked with Dr. Fernandez yourself.

PART

2

Techniques and Formats

Editing and Proofreading

1201 The Editing and Proofreading Process

a. *Proofreading* is the process by which you confirm that the copy you are looking at faithfully reproduces the original material in the intended form. If the copy deviates in any way from the original, you have to mark it for correction. Once the corrections are made, you have to read the copy again to ensure that everything is now as it should be.

NOTE: Ordinarily, one person can handle the task of comparing the copy against the original and noting any necessary corrections. However, if the material is complex or involves many statistics or formulas, it is wise for two people to share the proofreading function—one (known as the *copyholder*) to read the original material aloud and also indicate the intended punctuation, capitalization, and paragraphing, as well as other significant details of style and format, while the other person (the *proofreader*) examines the copy closely to ensure that everything appears as it ought to.

b. *Editing* is the process by which you examine material on its own terms (either in its original form or at a later stage). You question the material on the grounds of accuracy, clarity, coherence, consistency, and effectiveness. When you encounter problems, you resolve the ones you are equipped (and authorized) to handle, and you refer the other problems to the author of the original material.

c. If you were to encounter a set of figures as a proofreader, your responsibility—strictly speaking—would be only to ensure that the figures on the copy agreed with the corresponding figures in the original. However, as an editor, you might well question whether the figures in the original were correct as given or even the best figures that might be supplied. By the same token, if you were to examine running text as a proofreader, your responsibility would be only to confirm that the copy agreed with the original in wording and in stylistic intent. However, as an editor, you might question—and change—the wording, the format, and the style in the interests of accuracy, clarity, coherence, consistency, and effectiveness.

d. Many people often function simultaneously as editors and proofreaders without realizing that they are operating at two different levels—one essentially *mechanical* (checking for similarities and differences) and the other essentially *analytical* and *judgmental* (looking for problems and solving them). Ideally, editing should be done on the original material so that all problems of substance, grammar, style, and format are resolved before a copy is executed in "final form." However, it would be a mistake to read the final copy merely as a mechanical proofreader, assuming that the original is perfect and that you need only to look for places where the copy deviates from the original. On the chance that problems may have gone undetected in the earlier editing, you need to read the final copy in that challenging, questioning way that distinguishes editing from simple proofreading. You may be able to edit and proofread at the same time, or you may need to make several readings, focusing each time on different things. The following paragraphs will suggest the kinds of things you should be looking for when you edit and proofread.

1202 What to Look for When Proofreading

When *proofreading* a document, be especially watchful for the following types of mistakes:

a. Repeated words (or parts of words), especially at the end of one line and the beginning of the next.

What are the chances of your your coming to see us some-time this summer?	I have been awaiting some indi-indication of a willingness to compromise.
I can help you in the event in the event you have more work than you can handle.	We are looking forward to the to the reception you are plan-ning for the Lockwoods.

b. Substitutions and omissions, especially those that change the meaning.

Original Material	**Erroneous Copy**
The courts have clearly ruled that this kind of transaction is now legal.	The courts have clearly ruled that this kind of transaction is not legal.
In my opinion, there is no reason to suspect Fred.	In my opinion, there is reason to suspect Fred.
I hereby agree to pay you $87.50 in full settlement of your claim.	I hereby agree to pay you $8750 in full settlement of your claim.
Tom has probably reached the acme of his career.	Tom has probably reached the acne of his career.
When provoked, Gail has been known to turn violent.	When provoked, Gail has been known to turn violet.
We want our managers to live in the communities where our plants are located.	We want our managers to lie in the communities where our plants are located.
He is quite proud of his flat stomach.	He is quite proud of his fat stomach.
I'll gladly give you the job if you'll do it in a week and if you'll reduce your price by $200.	I'll gladly give you the job if you'll reduce your price by $200.

c. Errors in copying key data.

	Original Material	**Erroneous Copy**
NAMES:	Katharine Ann Jorgensen	Katherine Anne Jorgenson
TITLES:	Ms. Margaret A. Kelly	Mrs. Margaret A. Kelly
ADDRESSES:	1640 Vauxhall Road Union, NJ 07083	140 Vauxhall Road Union, NH 07803
DATES:	October 13, 1993	October 31, 1994
PHONE NOS.:	419-555-1551	418-555-1515
AMOUNTS OF MONEY:	$83,454,000,000	$38,454,000
DECIMALS:	sales fell 5.2 percent	sales fell 52 percent

CLOCK TIME: arrive at 4:15 p.m.	arrive at 4:51 p.m.
PERIODS OF TIME: boil for 2 minutes	boil for 20 minutes

d. Transpositions in letters, numbers, and words as well as other typographical errors (such as strikeovers, floating capitals, and faint or broken letters).

Original Material	**Erroneous Copy**
I'll buy two boats this May.	I'll buy tow boats this May.
a process of trial and error	a process of trail and error
Let's form a committee to review our pricing policy.	Let's from a committee to biew our pricing policy.
We'll need 82 binders for the seminar beginning July 12.	We'll need 28 binders for the seminar beginning July 21.
How can we thank you all for your thoughtfulness?	How can we thank you for all your thoughtfulness?

e. Errors in spacing and inconsistencies in format (for example, indenting some paragraphs but not others, leaving too little or too much space between words or after punctuation, improperly aligning or centering lines).

Original Material	**Erroneous Copy**
Dear Mrs. Neilson:	Dear Mrs. Neilson:
Thank you for your letter of April 24. Let me try to answer each of the questions you raised.	Thankyou for your letter of April 24. Let me try to answer each of the questions you raised.
First, we do not sell the components separately; they only come packaged as a set.	First,we do not sell the components separately; they only come pack aged as a set.

NOTE: As a final step in proofreading, check the appearance of the document. Have the corrections been neatly made and properly aligned? Are there any smudges or marks that need to be cleaned up? Does each page as a whole look attractive? Apply standards that are appropriate for the occasion. Documents prepared for higher management and for clients or customers of your organization should meet the highest standards of appearance. On the other hand, manuscripts, drafts, and even rush memos to coworkers can be sent forward with minor corrections neatly inserted by hand. Naturally, if you have access to some type of electronic equipment, you should be able to input the corrections and quickly obtain a clean (and correct) page. (See ¶1204.)

1203 What to Look for When Editing

When *editing* a document—either in its original form or in its final form—consider the material in light of the following factors.

For an explanation of the proofreaders' *marks used to indicate the necessary corrections in the following examples, see ¶1205.*

(Continued on page 278.)

12

a. Check for errors in *spelling* (see Section 7). Give special attention to compound words (see Section 8) and those with plural and possessive endings (see Section 6). Keep an up-to-date dictionary or a wordbook like *20,000+ Words* at hand.

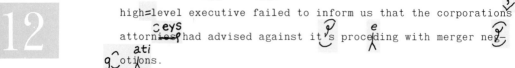

We had a similar break down in communications last May when a high=level executive failed to inform us that the corporations attornies had advised against it's proceeding with merger neg- otions.

NOTE: When the material is in its final form, also confirm the correctness of all word divisions. (See Section 9.)

b. Make sure that every necessary mark of *punctuation* is correctly inserted. (See Sections 1 and 2.)

How do you account for the fact that whenever we are about to launch a new product the company cuts our marketing dollars?

c. Inspect the material for possible errors in *capitalization, number,* and *abbreviation style.* (See Sections 3, 4, and 5.)

Please be sure to attend the Managers' meeting scheduled for june 4th at three p. m. There will be 5 or 6 announcements of special interest.

d. Correct any errors in *grammar* and *usage.* (See Sections 10 and 11.)

Everyone of the sales representatives have made less calls in the past six months then they did in the previous six-month period.

e. Be on the lookout for *inconsistencies* in the document. Resolve any problems that you can, and refer the rest to the person who wrote the original material.

When I met with you, Harry Mills, and Paula Fierro on May 8, we agreed that . . . Ed: Wasn't Paula at the 5/8 meeting?

I think that as a next move you ought to fill Paula Fierro in on what happened at our May 8 meeting and get her thoughts about how we ought to proceed.

NOTE: Be especially alert to wording that conveys a meaning you did not intend.

BAD: We take pride in offering excellent food and service every day except Sunday. (Does this mean that on Sundays the food and service are perfectly dreadful?)

BETTER: We take pride in offering excellent food and service. We are open every day except Sunday.

BAD: To enjoy our specially priced pretheater menu, you must be seated by 6 p.m. Remember, the early bird gets the worm. (Does the menu offer anything more appetizing?)

BETTER: To enjoy our specially priced pretheater menu, you must be seated by 6 p.m. Please try to come earlier if you can.

f. Look for problems in *organization* and *writing style*. The material could be entirely correct in terms of grammar, style, and usage and still contain clumsy sentences, a weak organization, and a tone that is not appropriate for the occasion.

g. Look at the document as a whole, and consider whether it is likely to accomplish its *objective*. If the document is intended to persuade readers to accept a recommendation that they currently tend to oppose, has the writer anticipated their objections and dealt with them? Or has the writer ignored the existence of such objections and thereby created the need for a follow-up document—or, worse, made it likely that the readers' negative leanings will harden into a flat rejection of the writer's recommendations?

NOTE: If you are editing material you yourself have written, consider all the points noted in ¶1203a–g. However, if you are editing material written by someone else, the extent of your editing will depend on your experience and your relationship with the writer. If you are on your first job and working for a literate boss, determine whether your boss has any special preferences with regard to matters of style. (What may look like an error to you could be an acceptable practice that you are not familiar with.) On the other hand, a boss who does not pretend to grasp the technical points of style will no doubt welcome your editing for such things as spelling, punctuation, capitalization, grammar, usage, and inconsistencies (see ¶1203a–e). How much your boss—or anyone else for that matter—will appreciate your comments about the organization, writing style, and effectiveness of the material (see ¶1203f–g) will depend not only on your relationship with the writer but also on the tact with which you make your comments. Do not assume that because you have a close relationship with the writer, you can speak bluntly. Indeed, the closer the relationship, the more tact you may need to exercise.

1204 Editing and Proofreading at the Computer

The computer provides some wonderful enhancements to the editing process. You can insert new copy, kill old copy, rearrange copy as many times as you like, and then print out a clean version without any evidence of all the foregoing changes. Yet in the process of all this electronic "cutting and pasting," you may have failed to remove every bit of the old version you rejected; you may have changed the subject of a sentence from singular to plural without realizing the effect this change would have on the verb; you may even have inserted new copy in the wrong place and thus unintentionally produced pure gibberish. It is imperative, therefore, that copy that has been rewritten and edited on a computer be carefully proofread. Yet it is harder to catch errors when proofing copy on a terminal screen than it is when reading hard copy. Moreover, if you try to proofread copy on the screen for any length of time, you are more likely to develop a bad case of eyestrain than you are to catch all the mistakes. To maximize the benefits from a computer and minimize the drawbacks, follow these guidelines.

(Continued on page 280.)

12

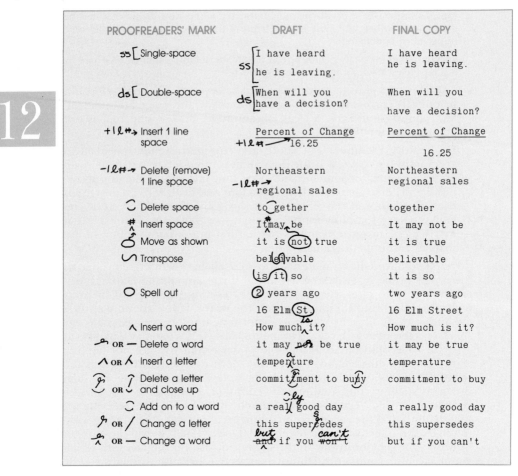

PROOFREADERS' MARK	DRAFT	FINAL COPY
ss[Single-space	I have heard he is leaving.	I have heard he is leaving.
ds[Double-space	When will you have a decision?	When will you have a decision?
+1 l #→ Insert 1 line space	Percent of Change 16.25	Percent of Change 16.25
−1 l #→ Delete (remove) 1 line space	Northeastern regional sales	Northeastern regional sales
⌣ Delete space	to gether	together
# Insert space	It may be	It may not be
⌒ Move as shown	it is (not) true	it is true
∽ Transpose	believable is it so	believable it is so
◯ Spell out	2 years ago 16 Elm St	two years ago 16 Elm Street
∧ Insert a word	How much it?	How much is it?
✎ OR — Delete a word	it may not be true	it may be true
∧ OR ⋏ Insert a letter	temperture	temperature
✎ OR ⌣ Delete a letter and close up	committment to buyy	commitment to buy
⌒ Add on to a word	a real good day	a really good day
✎ OR / Change a letter	this superfedes	this supersedes
✎ OR — Change a word	and if you won't	but if you can't

a. If you are inputting material from hard copy, first edit it carefully for all the factors noted in ¶1203. If the copy was written by someone else, then before you input it, get the writer's help in resolving any questions about content and style that you do not feel equipped (or authorized) to resolve yourself. By carefully editing this material prior to keying it in, you greatly reduce the likelihood of undetected errors in the final document.

b. If you are transcribing from recorded input, the first version you output may have to be considered a draft that must be shown to the dictator for alteration or approval.

c. By the same token, if you receive input in the form of a disk or via a modem, you may have to give the person who originated the document a chance to review and alter the document before you undertake the final editing and proofreading.

d. Before you print out the material you have input, check the spelling against your electronic dictionary (if your software program has this feature) and make the necessary corrections. Also scan the material on the screen for any obvious mistakes (such as those noted in ¶¶1202 and 1203), and make the necessary changes. However, do not assume that no further editing or proofreading will be required. (See ¶1201d.)

PROOFREADERS' MARK	DRAFT	FINAL COPY
.... Stet (don't delete)	I was ~~very~~ glad	I was very glad
/ Lowercase a letter (make it a small letter)	Federal Government	federal government
≡ Capitalize	Janet L. greyston	Janet L. Greyston
V Raise above the line	in her new book	in her new book*
∧ Drop below the line	H2SO4	H_2SO_4
⊙ Insert a period	Mr Henry Grenada	Mr. Henry Grenada
⌄ Insert a comma	a large old house	a large, old house
⌄ Insert an apostrophe	my childrens car	my children's car
⌄⌄ Insert quotation marks	he wants a loan	he wants a "loan"
= Insert a hyphen	a first rate job	a first-rate job
	ask the coowner	ask the co-owner
OR 1/M Insert a dash or change a hyphen to a dash	Success at last! Here it is cash!	Success—at last! Here it is—cash!
___ Insert underscore	an issue of _Time_	an issue of _Time_
Delete underscore	a very long day	a very long day
( ) Insert parentheses	left today(May 3)	left today (May 3)
¶ Start a new paragraph	¶ If that is so	If that is so
Indent 2 spaces	Net investment in tangible assets	Net investment in tangible assets
Move to the right	$38,367,000	$38,367,000
Move to the left	Anyone can win!	Anyone can win!
= Align horizontally	TO Bob Muller	TO: Bob Muller
‖ Align vertically	Jon Peters Ellen March	Jon Peters Ellen March

NOTE: If you have transcribed from recorded dictation, you will have no original copy to proofread against. Moreover, in the act of transcribing, it is easy to misinterpret and mispunctuate words and phrases or to omit them altogether. Therefore, while you should try to identify and correct as many errors on the screen as you can, you need to recognize that the editing you have done at this stage is not likely to be sufficient.

e. After you print out the material, examine it carefully for all types of errors as well as possible instances of inconsistency and incoherence. Make the necessary corrections, and then review the new material—first on the screen and then again on the final printout—to make sure that the corrections have been properly executed in the proper location. Also make sure that no new errors have been inadvertently introduced.

1205 Proofreaders' Marks

Whether you are editing or proofreading, use the proofreaders' marks shown on page 280 and above to indicate the corrections that need to be made. Minor variations in the way these marks are formed are unimportant as long as the marks clearly indicate what corrections have to be made.

Rules for Alphabetic Filing

There are three types of alphabetic filing: (1) letter by letter (in which spaces between words are disregarded); (2) word by word; and (3) unit by unit (in which every word, abbreviation, and initial is considered a separate unit). The Association of Records Managers and Administrators (ARMA) recommends the use of the unit-by-unit method.

The basic principles of the unit-by-unit method (see ¶¶1206–1208) and the more specific rules that follow (see ¶¶1209–1222) are consistent with ARMA standards.* There are, however, many acceptable alternative rules and variations that are currently in use. The important thing to remember is that the goal of any set of filing standards and rules is to establish a consistent method of sorting and storing materials so that you and others you work with can retrieve these materials quickly and easily. Therefore, it makes sense to modify or change the following rules as necessary to accommodate the specific needs of your office or organization. Make sure, however, that everyone with access to your files knows what the modifications are so that a consistent set of standards can be maintained.

Basic Principles
1206 Alphabetizing Unit by Unit

a. Alphabetize names by comparing the first units letter by letter.

Name	Unit 1	Unit 2	Unit 3
Alphanumerics	ALPHANUMERICS		
Butterfield	BUTTERFIELD		
Eagleton	EAGLETON		
Eaton	EATON		
Eberhardt	EBERHARDT		
Eberhart	EBERHART		
ERGOnomics	ERGONOMICS		
Office Space Designers	OFFICE	SPACE	DESIGNERS
Offices Incorporated	OFFICES	INCORPORATED	
Official Stationers	OFFICIAL	STATIONERS	
OFFshore Vacations	OFFSHORE	VACATIONS	

NOTE: For purposes of alphabetizing, it makes no difference whether a letter is capitalized or not. Therefore, all filing units are shown in capitals so that the letters can all be considered without regard to size.

b. Consider second units only when the first units are identical.

Name	Unit 1	Unit 2
Foley Enterprises	FOLEY	ENTERPRISES
Foley Industries	FOLEY	INDUSTRIES

*Alphabetic Filing Rules, Association of Records Managers and Administrators, Inc., Prairie Village, Kans., 1986.

c. Consider additional units only when the first two units are identical.

Name	Unit 1	Unit 2	Unit 3	Unit 4
Fox Hill Company	FOX	HILL	COMPANY	
Fox Hill Farm	FOX	HILL	FARM	
Fox Hill Farm Supplies	FOX	HILL	FARM	SUPPLIES

NOTE: If two names are identical, they may be distinguished on the basis of geographical location. (See ¶1219.)

1207 Nothing Comes Before Something

a. A single letter comes before a name that begins with the same letter.

Name	Unit 1
O	O
Oasis	OASIS
Oberon	OBERON

b. A name consisting of one word comes before a name that consists of the same word plus one or more other words.

Name	Unit 1	Unit 2	Unit 3
Operations	OPERATIONS		
Operations Management Consultants	OPERATIONS	MANAGEMENT	CONSULTANTS
Operations Technologies	OPERATIONS	TECHNOLOGIES	

c. A name consisting of two or more words comes before a name that consists of the same two or more words plus another word, and so on.

Name	Unit 1	Unit 2	Unit 3	Unit 4
Oak Creek	OAK	CREEK		
Oak Creek Home Furnishings	OAK	CREEK	HOME	FURNISHINGS
Oak Creek Homes	OAK	CREEK	HOMES	

1208 Deciding Which Name to Use

ARMA advocates filing "under the most commonly used name or title." This helpful principle provides the basis for choosing which name you should use for a person or an organization when alternatives exist. For example, given the alternatives of the *American Telephone & Telegraph Co.* and the abbreviation *AT&T*, most people would choose the abbreviated form, but people in law offices might well prefer the full formal name. The practical solution here is to select the form most likely to be used and then provide cross-references for the alternatives. In that way anyone who is searching for material under an alternative name will be referred to the primary name being used for filing purposes.

The discussion that follows indicates specific instances in which this principle can be applied. (See ¶¶1212c, 1214e, 1215a, note, and 1216a, note.)

Personal Names

1209 Rule 1: Names of Persons

a. Treat each part of the name of a person as a separate unit, and consider the units in this order: last name, first name or initial, and any subsequent names or initials. Ignore any punctuation following or within an abbreviation.

Name	Unit 1	Unit 2	Unit 3	Unit 4
Jacobs	JACOBS			
L. Jacobs	JACOBS	L		
L. Mitchell Jacobs	JACOBS	L	MITCHELL	
Stephen Jacobson	JACOBSON	STEPHEN		
Stephen Brent Jacobson	JACOBSON	STEPHEN	BRENT	
Steven O'K Jacobson	JACOBSON	STEVEN	OK	
B. Jacoby	JACOBY	B		
B. T. Jacoby	JACOBY	B	T	
Bruce Jacoby	JACOBY	BRUCE		
C. Bruce Hay Jacoby	JACOBY	C	BRUCE	HAY

b. When you are dealing with a foreign personal name and cannot distinguish the last name from the first name, consider each part of the name in the order in which it is written. Naturally, whenever you can make the distinction, consider the last name first.

Name	Unit 1	Unit 2	Unit 3
Kwong Kow Ng	KWONG	KOW	NG
Ng Kwong Cheung	NG	KWONG	CHEUNG
Philip K. Ng	NG	PHILIP	K

c. In a name like *María López y Quintana*, the last name consists of three separate words. For purposes of alphabetizing, treat these separate words as a single unit (for example, *LOPEZYQUINTANA*).

For the treatment of hyphenated personal names, see ¶1211.

1210 Rule 2: Personal Names With Prefixes

a. Consider a prefix (such as O' in O'Keefe) as part of the name, not as a separate unit. Ignore variations in spacing, punctuation, and capitalization in names that contain prefixes (for example, *d', D', Da, de, De, Del, De la, Des, Di, Du, El, Fitz, L', La, Las, Le, Les, Lo, Los, M', Mac, Mc, Saint, San, Santa, Santo, St., Ste., Ten, Ter, Van, Van de, Van der, Von,* and *Von Der*).

Name	Unit 1	Unit 2	Unit 3
A. Serafino Delacruz	DELACRUZ	A	SERAFINO
Anna C. deLaCruz	DELACRUZ	ANNA	C
Michael B DeLacruz	DELACRUZ	MICHAEL	B
Victor P. De La Cruz	DELACRUZ	VICTOR	P
LaVerne F. Delano	DELANO	LAVERNE	F
Angela G. D'Elia	DELIA	ANGELA	G
Pierre Des Trempes	DESTREMPES	PIERRE	
Brian K. De Voto	DEVOTO	BRIAN	K

b. Consider the prefixes *M'*, *Mac*, and *Mc* exactly as they are spelled, but ignore the apostrophe in *M'*.

Name	Unit 1	Unit 2	Unit 3
Marilyn R. Mack	MACK	MARILYN	R
Irene J. MacKay	MACKAY	IRENE	J
Roy F. Mackay	MACKAY	ROY	F
Walter G. Mac Kay	MACKAY	WALTER	G
F. Timothy Madison	MADISON	F	TIMOTHY
Agnes U. M'Cauley	MCAULEY	AGNES	U
Patrick J. McKay	MCKAY	PATRICK	J
Andrew W. O'Hare	OHARE	ANDREW	W

c. Treat the prefixes *Saint, San, Santa, Santo, St.,* and *Ste.* exactly as they are spelled.

Name	Unit 1	Unit 2	Unit 3
George V. Sahady	SAHADY	GEORGE	V
Kyle N. Saint Clair	SAINTCLAIR	KYLE	N
Jeffrey T. Sakowitz	SAKOWITZ	JEFFREY	T
Annette San Marco	SANMARCO	ANNETTE	
Felix Santacroce	SANTACROCE	FELIX	
Peter St. Clair	STCLAIR	PETER	
O. M. Ste. Marie	STEMAIRE	O	M

1211 Rule 3: Hyphenated Personal Names

Consider the hyphenated elements of a name as a single unit. Ignore the hyphen.

Name	Unit 1	Unit 2	Unit 3
S. T. Laverty-Powell	LAVERTYPOWELL	S	T
Victor Puentes-Ruiz	PUENTESRUIZ	VICTOR	
Jean V. Vigneau	VIGNEAU	JEAN	V
Jean-Marie Vigneau	VIGNEAU	JEANMARIE	
Jean-Pierre Vigneau	VIGNEAU	JEANPIERRE	

1212 Rule 4: Abbreviated Personal Names, Nicknames, and Pseudonyms

a. Treat an abbreviated part of a name (such as *Wm.* for *William*) or a nickname (such as *Al* or *Kate*) as written if that is how the person is known.

Name	Unit 1	Unit 2	Unit 3
Chas. E. Kassily	KASSILY	CHAS	E
Bubbles Leaden	LEADEN	BUBBLES	
Peggy Sue Marker	MARKER	PEGGY	SUE
B. J. Purcell	PURCELL	B	J

b. If a person is known by a nickname alone (without a surname) or by a pseudonym, consider each word in the nickname or pseudonym as a separate unit. If the name begins with *The,* treat *The* as the last unit.

Name	Unit 1	Unit 2	Unit 3
Big Al	BIG	AL	
The Fat Lady	FAT	LADY	THE
Handy Joe Bob	HANDY	JOE	BOB
Harry the Horse	HARRY	THE	HORSE
Mad Man Marko	MAD	MAN	MARKO
Madonna	MADONNA		
Mr. Bill (see ¶1213b)	MR	BILL	

c. When you have to decide whether to file material under a person's formal name or under a nickname, pseudonym, or some abbreviated form, choose the form that best reflects how you and others you work with are most likely to look the person up. You should also enter the person's alternative names in the appropriate alphabetic sequence and make cross-references to the primary name you have selected. (See also ¶1208.)

1213 Rule 5: Personal Names With Titles and Suffixes

a. A title (such as *Dr., Major, Mayor, Miss, Mr., Mrs.,* or *Ms.*) may be used as the *last* filing unit in order to distinguish two or more names that are otherwise identical. Treat any abbreviated titles as written.

Name	Unit 1	Unit 2	Unit 3	Unit 4
Dr. Leslie G. Mabry	MABRY	LESLIE	G	DR
Miss Leslie G. Mabry	MABRY	LESLIE	G	MISS
Mr. Leslie G. Mabry	MABRY	LESLIE	G	MR
Mrs. Leslie G. Mabry	MABRY	LESLIE	G	MRS
Ms. Leslie G. Mabry	MABRY	LESLIE	G	MS
Major Felix Novotny	NOVOTNY	FELIX	MAJOR	
Mayor Felix Novotny	NOVOTNY	FELIX	MAYOR	

b. When a title is used with only one part of a person's name, treat it as the *first* unit. (See ¶1208.)

Name	Unit 1	Unit 2
Dr. Ruth	DR	RUTH
Grandma Moses	GRANDMA	MOSES
King Hussein	KING	HUSSEIN
Miss Manners	MISS	MANNERS
Mother Teresa	MOTHER	TERESA
Prince Andrew	PRINCE	ANDREW
Saint Elizabeth	SAINT*	ELIZABETH

*Note that *Saint* as a title is considered a separate unit, whereas *Saint* as a prefix in a personal name is considered only part of a unit. (See ¶1210c for examples of *Saint* as a prefix.)

c. Ordinarily, a married woman's name should be alphabetized on the basis of her own first name. However, consider the title *Mrs.* (as abbreviated) if a woman uses her husband's name and you do not know her first name.

Name	Unit 1	Unit 2	Unit 3	Unit 4
Mrs. June Y. Nearing	NEARING	JUNE	Y	
Mr. Peter J. Nearing	NEARING	PETER	J	
Mr. Harry L. Norton	NORTON	HARRY	L	MR
Mrs. Harry L. Norton (*whose own first name is unknown*)	NORTON	HARRY	L	MRS

d. Consider a seniority term (such as *Jr., Sr., 2d, 3d, II,* or *III*), a professional or academic degree (such as *CPA, M.D.,* or *Ph.D.*), or any other designation following a person's name in order to distinguish names that are otherwise identical. Numeric designations precede alphabetic designations. Moreover, arabic numerals precede roman numerals, and each set of numbers is sequenced in numeric order. When dealing with ordinal numbers such as *3d* or *4th*, ignore the endings.

Name	Unit 1	Unit 2	Unit 3	Unit 4
James R. Foster 2d	FOSTER	JAMES	R	2
James R. Foster 3d	FOSTER	JAMES	R	3
James R. Foster III	FOSTER	JAMES	R	III
James R. Foster IV	FOSTER	JAMES	R	IV
James R. Foster Jr.	FOSTER	JAMES	R	JR
James R. Foster, M.B.A.	FOSTER	JAMES	R	MBA
James R. Foster, M.D.	FOSTER	JAMES	R	MD
James R. Foster, Mr.	FOSTER	JAMES	R	MR
James R. Foster, Ph.D.	FOSTER	JAMES	R	PHD
James R. Foster, S.J.	FOSTER	JAMES	R	SJ
James R. Foster, Sr.	FOSTER	JAMES	R	SR

Organizational Names

1214 Rule 6: Names of Organizations

a. Treat each word in the name of an organization as a separate unit, and consider the units in the same order as they are written on the company letterhead or some other authoritative document.

Name	Unit 1	Unit 2	Unit 3	Unit 4
American Data Control	AMERICAN	DATA	CONTROL	
American Data Processing Corporation	AMERICAN	DATA	PROCESSING	CORPORATION
Computer Enterprises	COMPUTER	ENTERPRISES		
Computer Systems Unlimited	COMPUTER	SYSTEMS	UNLIMITED	
I Deal Card Shops	I	DEAL	CARD	SHOPS
Ideal Printers	IDEAL	PRINTERS		

b. When alphabetizing, ignore all punctuation—for example, periods, commas, hyphens, apostrophes, and diagonals. When two or more words are joined by a hyphen or a diagonal, treat the phrase as a single unit.

Name	Unit 1	Unit 2	Unit 3
Baskins and Fry	BASKINS	AND	FRY
Baskins' Artworks	BASKINS	ARTWORKS	
Baskin's Basket Shop	BASKINS	BASKET	SHOP
Baskin-Shaw Films	BASKINSHAW	FILMS	
Baskin/Shaw Foods	BASKINSHAW	FOODS	
Curtis Imports	CURTIS	IMPORTS	
Curtis's China Gallery	CURTISS	CHINA	GALLERY
Curtiss Couriers	CURTISS	COURIERS	
Curtis's Marina	CURTISS	MARINA	
Oleander's Displays!	OLEANDERS	DISPLAYS	
O'Leary's Camera Shop	OLEARYS	CAMERA	SHOP
What's New?	WHATS	NEW	

c. Treat prepositions (such as *of* and *in*), conjunctions (such as *and* and *or*), and articles (*the, a,* and *an*) as separate units. When *the, a,* or *an* is the first word in a name, treat it as the last unit.

Name	Unit 1	Unit 2	Unit 3	Unit 4
In-Plant Catering	INPLANT	CATERING		
Over the Rainbow Gifts	OVER	THE	RAINBOW	GIFTS
The Pen and Pencil	PEN	AND	PENCIL	THE
Photos in a Flash	PHOTOS	IN	A	FLASH
A Touch of Glass	TOUCH	OF	GLASS	A

d. When a compound expression is written as one word or hyphenated, treat it as a single unit. If the compound expression is written with spaces, treat each element as a separate unit.

Name	Unit 1	Unit 2	Unit 3
Aero Space Systems	AERO	SPACE	SYSTEMS
Aerospace Research	AEROSPACE	RESEARCH	
Aero-Space Unlimited	AEROSPACE	UNLIMITED	
Foy Brothers Associates	FOY	BROTHERS	ASSOCIATES
Foy North-South Properties	FOY	NORTHSOUTH	PROPERTIES
Foy-Brothers Financial Planners	FOYBROTHERS	FINANCIAL	PLANNERS
Pay Fone Systems	PAY	FONE	SYSTEMS
Paychex Incorporated	PAYCHEX	INCORPORATED	
Pay-O-Matic Company	PAYOMATIC	COMPANY	
South East Condos	SOUTH	EAST	CONDOS
Southeast Chemicals	SOUTHEAST	CHEMICALS	
South-East Medical Labs	SOUTHEAST	MEDICAL	LABS
Southeastern Medical Supplies	SOUTHEASTERN	MEDICAL	SUPPLIES

e. Although the words in an organizational name should normally be considered in the same order in which they are written, there are occasions when it makes good sense to allow exceptions to this rule. (See also ¶1208.) Suppose the name in question is *Hotel Plaza*. Strictly speaking, *Hotel* should be the first unit. However, if you and others are more likely to look for stored material in the P section of the files, choose *Plaza* as the first unit and *Hotel* as the second. On the other hand, suppose the name in question is *Motel 6*. Most people would look for material in the M section. Thus it would be best to treat this name exactly as written.

The formal name of a South Bend academic institution is the *University of Notre Dame*. Yet most people would not look for the name in the U section (as the formal rule suggests) but would turn instead to the Ns. However, for the *University of the South*, most people would turn to the U section rather than the S section.

One important caution: When introducing exceptions to the basic rule for organizational names, be sure that these exceptions are supported by cross-references for the sake of those who may search the files for an alternative name.

1215 Rule 7: Personal Names Within Organizational Names

a. When an organizational name includes a person's name, consider the parts of the personal name in the order in which they are written. Ignore any punctuation.

(Continued on page 290.)

12

Name	Unit 1	Unit 2	Unit 3	Unit 4
Frank Balcom Construction Company	FRANK	BALCOM	CONSTRUCTION	COMPANY
Frank Balcom, Jr., Paving	FRANK	BALCOM	JR	PAVING
M. Clausen Optical Supplies	M	CLAUSEN	OPTICAL	SUPPLIES
M. G. Clausen Autos	M	G	CLAUSEN	AUTOS
Mark Clausen Interiors	MARK	CLAUSEN	INTERIORS	
Mark G. Clausen Homes	MARK	G	CLAUSEN	HOMES

NOTE: A more traditional rule that is still widely followed requires that a person's name within an organizational name be considered in the same way as if the person's name stood alone—namely, last name first. (See ¶1209.) Regardless of which approach you are following, there are specific situations in which it would be wise to make exceptions, depending on the way you (and others with access to your files) are likely to look the name up.

For example, even if you follow the ARMA standard for personal names in organizational names (first name first), you might want to make an exception for the *John F. Kennedy Presidential Library,* since most people would look for the file under the Ks rather than the Js. Similarly, the file for the *Bernard J. Baruch College* might be more easily found if sequenced according to the surname, *Baruch,* rather than the first name, *Bernard.*

On the other hand, those who follow the last-name-first approach might be wiser to locate the *Sarah Lawrence College* file in the S section rather than the L, to file materials on the *John Hancock Mutual Life Insurance Company* in the J section rather than the H, to store the *Fred Astaire Dance Studios* file under F rather than A, and to put the *Mary Kay Cosmetics* file under M rather than K.

The key here is to consider the way in which the name is most likely to be looked up and then provide cross-references between the alternative form and the primary name that has been selected. (See also ¶1208.)

b. If a prefix is used in a personal name that is part of an organizational name, do not treat the prefix as a separate unit. (See ¶1210.)

Name	Unit 1	Unit 2	Unit 3	Unit 4
A. de La Cruz Securities Company	A	DELACRUZ	SECURITIES	COMPANY
A. D'Elia Boat Sales	A	DELIA	BOAT	SALES
Peter Saint Clair Boatels	PETER	SAINTCLAIR	BOATELS	
Peter St. Clair Insurance Agency	PETER	STCLAIR	INSURANCE	AGENCY
R. San Marco Environmental Controls	R	SANMARCO	ENVIRONMENTAL	CONTROLS

c. If a hyphenated personal name is part of an organizational name, treat the hyphenated elements as a single unit. (See ¶1211.)

Name	Unit 1	Unit 2	Unit 3	Unit 4
Mary Tom Packaging Consultants	MARY	TOM	PACKAGING	CONSULTANTS
Mary Tom-Katz Production Company	MARY	TOMKATZ	PRODUCTION	COMPANY

d. Consider a title in an organization's name as a separate unit in the order in which it occurs. Treat abbreviated titles as they are written and ignore punctuation.

Name	Unit 1	Unit 2	Unit 3	Unit 4
Capt. Jack Seafood	CAPT	JACK	SEAFOOD	
Captain Ahab Tours	CAPTAIN	AHAB	TOURS	
Dr. Popper Vision Services	DR	POPPER	VISION	SERVICES
Ma Blake Food Shops	MA	BLAKE	FOOD	SHOPS
Miss Celeste Sportswear	MISS	CELESTE	SPORTSWEAR	
Mother Goose Nurseries	MOTHER	GOOSE	NURSERIES	
Mr. George Limousine Service	MR	GEORGE	LIMOUSINE	SERVICE
Mrs. Ellis Bakeries	MRS	ELLIS	BAKERIES	
Princess Diana Gowns	PRINCESS	DIANA	GOWNS	
Saint Margaret Thrift Shop	SAINT*	MARGARET	THRIFT	SHOP

*When Saint is used as a title rather than as a prefix in a personal name, it is considered a separate unit. (See ¶1213b.)

1216 Rule 8: Abbreviations, Acronyms, Symbols, and Letters in Organizational Names

a. Treat an abbreviation as a single unit. Consider it exactly as it is written, and ignore any punctuation.

Name	Unit 1	Unit 2	Unit 3	Unit 4
AFL-CIO	AFLCIO			
IBM	IBM			
NAACP	NAACP			
Smyly Grain Corp.	SMYLY	GRAIN	CORP	
Smyly Industries Inc.	SMYLY	INDUSTRIES	INC	
Smyth Data Systems Co.	SMYTH	DATA	SYSTEMS	CO
Smyth Datafax Ltd.	SMYTH	DATAFAX	LTD	
U. S. Data Sources	U	S	DATA	SOURCES
U S Datalink	U	S	DATALINK	
U. S. Grant Foundation	U	S	GRANT	FOUNDATION
U.S. Data Files	US	DATA	FILES	
US Data Tracers	US	DATA	TRACERS	

NOTE: When organizations are better known by their abbreviated names (*AFL-CIO, IBM, NAACP*) or acronyms (*NOW, NYNEX, UNESCO*) than by their formal names, use these short forms for filing purposes and provide cross-references as necessary. (See also ¶¶520, 522.)

(Continued on page 292.)

b. Treat acronyms and the call letters of radio and TV stations as single units.

Name	Unit 1	Unit 2	Unit 3
NOW	NOW		
NYNEX	NYNEX		
UNESCO	UNESCO		
WBBM Radio Station	WBBM	RADIO	STATION

c. When the symbol & occurs in a name, consider it as if it were spelled out (that is, as *and*). If the symbol is freestanding (that is, with space on either side), treat it as a separate filing unit.

Name	Unit 1	Unit 2	Unit 3	Unit 4
A & L Fabrics	A	AND	L	FABRICS
A&B Publications	AANDB	PUBLICATIONS		
Allen & Korn	ALLEN	AND	KORN	
AT&T	ATANDT			

d. Treat single letters as separate units. If two or more letters in a sequence are written solid or are connected by a hyphen or a diagonal, treat the sequence as a single unit.

A & D Terminals	A	AND	D	TERMINALS
A D S Graphics	A	D	S	GRAPHICS
AAA	AAA			
A&D Printers Inc.	AANDD	PRINTERS	INC	
ADS Reports	ADS	REPORTS		
A/V Resources	AV	RESOURCES		
A-Z Rental Corp.	AZ	RENTAL	CORP	
Triple A Realty Trust	TRIPLE	A	REALTY	TRUST
W Z Leasing Co.	W	Z	LEASING	CO
W. Y. Yee (*person's name*)	YEE	W	Y	

1217 Rule 9: Geographic Names Within Organizational Names

a. Treat each part of a geographic name as a separate unit. However, treat hyphenated parts of a geographic name as a single unit.

Big Sur Tours	BIG	SUR	TOURS	
Lake of the Woods Camping Store*	LAKE	OF	THE	WOODS
New Jersey Shore Rentals	NEW	JERSEY	SHORE	RENTALS
Puerto Rico Sugar Traders	PUERTO	RICO	SUGAR	TRADERS
United States Telecom	UNITED	STATES	TELECOM	
West New York Bedding	WEST	NEW	YORK	BEDDING
Wilkes-Barre Mills	WILKESBARRE	MILLS		
Winston-Salem Movers	WINSTONSALEM	MOVERS		

*The words *Camping* and *Store* represent the fifth and sixth filing units in this name.

b. When a geographic name begins with a prefix followed by a space or hyphen, treat the prefix and the following word as a single unit. (See ¶1210a for a list of prefixes.)

Name	Unit 1	Unit 2	Unit 3
El Cajon Editorial Services	ELCAJON	EDITORIAL	SERVICES
La Crosse Graphics	LACROSSE	GRAPHICS	
Las Vegas Lenders	LASVEGAS	LENDERS	
Le Mans Auto Repairs	LEMANS	AUTO	REPAIRS
Los Angeles Film Distributors	LOSANGELES	FILM	DISTRIBUTORS
San Francisco Cable Systems	SANFRANCISCO	CABLE	SYSTEMS
Santa Fe Hotel Supplies	SANTAFE	HOTEL	SUPPLIES
Ste.-Julie Inn	STEJULIE	INN	
St. Louis Water Filters	STLOUIS	WATER	FILTERS

NOTE: A name like *De Kalb* or *Des Moines* is considered a single unit, whereas a name like *Fond du Lac* should be treated as three units (since the prefix *du* does not come at the beginning of the geographic name).

1218 Rule 10: Numbers in Organizational Names

a. Arabic numerals (*1, 3, 5*) and roman numerals (*IV, XIX*) are considered separate units. Treat ordinal numbers such as *1st, 3d,* and *5th* as if they were written *1, 3,* and *5.*

b. Units that contain arabic or roman numerals precede units expressed in words. Moreover, units with arabic numerals come ahead of units with roman numerals. Each sequence of numeric units—arabic or roman—is arranged in numeric order.

Name	Unit 1	Unit 2	Unit 3	Unit 4
21st Century Travel	21	CENTURY	TRAVEL	
210th St. Assn.	210	ST	ASSN	
1218 Corp.	1218	CORP		
III Brothers Outlets	III	BROTHERS	OUTLETS	
The VII Hills Lodge	VII	HILLS	LODGE	THE
AAA Leasing Company	AAA	LEASING	COMPANY	
ILGW Local 134	ILGW	LOCAL	134	
ILGW Local 145	ILGW	LOCAL	145	
Sixth Street Fashions	SIXTH	STREET	FASHIONS	
Third Avenue Elegance	THIRD	AVENUE	ELEGANCE	

c. Units containing numbers expressed in words are sequenced (along with other units containing words or letters) in alphabetic order.

d. When a number is written with a hyphen (*Seventy-Six*), ignore the hyphen and treat the number as a single unit (*SEVENTYSIX.*)

(Continued on page 294.)

Name	Unit 1	Unit 2	Unit 3	Unit 4
The Turtle Back Inn	TURTLE	BACK	INN	THE
Twelve Eighteen Realty Co.	TWELVE	EIGHTEEN	REALTY	CO
Twentieth Century Press	TWENTIETH	CENTURY	PRESS	
Twenty-Eight Benbow Street Studios	TWENTYEIGHT	BENBOW	STREET	STUDIOS
Twenty-Five Hundred Club	TWENTYFIVE	HUNDRED	CLUB	
The Warren 200 Colony	WARREN	200	COLONY	THE
The Warren House	WARREN	HOUSE	THE	
Warren Sixty-Fourth Street Salon	WARREN	SIXTYFOURTH	STREET	SALON

e. When a phrase consists of a number (in figures or words) linked by a hyphen or a diagonal to a letter or word (for example, *1-A, A-1, 1-Hour, 4/Way, One-Stop*), ignore the punctuation and treat the phrase as a single unit.

f. When the phrase consists of a figure linked to another figure by means of a hyphen or a diagonal (for example, *80-20* or *50/50*), consider only the number that precedes the punctuation.

g. When a phrase consists of a figure plus a letter or word (for example, *3M*) without any intervening space or punctuation, treat the phrase as a single unit.

Name	Unit 1	Unit 2	Unit 3	Unit 4
1-A Physical Trainers	1A	PHYSICAL	TRAINERS	
3 Pro Corp.	3	PRO	CORP	
3M	3M			
4X Investment Group	4X	INVESTMENT	GROUP	
5-10 Household Wares	5	HOUSEHOLD	WARES	
5 Star Video Arcade	5	STAR	VIDEO	ARCADE
5-Corners Pasta Dishes	5CORNERS	PASTA	DISHES	
7-Eleven Food Store	7ELEVEN	FOOD	STORE	
20/20 Eye Care	20	EYE	CARE	
The 30-45 Singles Club	30	SINGLES	CLUB	THE
A-1 Autos Inc.	A1	AUTOS	INC	
Adam's 10-Minute Pizza Service	ADAMS	10MINUTE	PIZZA	SERVICE
Adams' One-Hour Photos	ADAMS	ONEHOUR	PHOTOS	
Adam's One-Stop Shop	ADAMS	ONESTOP	SHOP	
The Fifty-Fifty Co-op	FIFTYFIFTY	COOP	THE	
The Tarragon Tree	TARRAGON	TREE	THE	
Three-Hour Cleaners	THREEHOUR	CLEANERS		

h. When a symbol appears with a number, treat the two elements as a single unit only if there is no space between the symbol and the number. Consider the symbol as if it were spelled out; for example, & (*and*), ¢ (*cent* or *cents*), $ (*dollar* or *dollars*), # (*number* or *pounds*), % (*percent*), and + (*plus*).

Name	Unit 1	Unit 2	Unit 3	Unit 4
The $50 Dress Shop	50DOLLAR*	DRESS	SHOP	THE
50% Off Clothing Outlet	50PERCENT	OFF	CLOTHING	OUTLET
The 50+ Retirement Community	50PLUS	RETIREMENT	COMMUNITY	THE
The #1 Pizza Parlor	NUMBER1	PIZZA	PARLOR	THE
The Original 5&10	ORIGINAL	5AND10	THE	
Plaza 5 & 10	PLAZA	5	AND	10

*When a $ sign precedes a number, consider the number and then the word DOLLAR (or DOLLARS) in that order.

1219 Rule 11: Alphabetizing by Addresses

When two organizational names are otherwise identical, alphabetize them according to address.

a. First alphabetize by city.

b. If the city names are the same, consider the state. (For example, *Charleston, South Carolina,* comes before *Charleston, West Virginia.*)

Name	Unit 1	Unit 2	Unit 3	Unit 4
McDonald's Durango, Colorado	MCDONALDS	DURANGO		
McDonald's Springfield, Missouri	MCDONALDS	SPRINGFIELD	MISSOURI	
McDonald's Springfield, South Dakota	MCDONALDS	SPRINGFIELD	SOUTH	DAKOTA

c. If both the city and the state are identical, alphabetize by street name.

d. If the street name is a number, treat it exactly as written. Numbered street names expressed *in figures* precede street names (numbered or otherwise) expressed *in words.* Numbered street names *in figures* are sequenced in numeric order. Numbered street names *in words* are sequenced (along with other street names in words) in alphabetic order.

Name	Unit 1	Unit 2	Unit 3	Unit 4
McDonald's 17th Street Tallahassee, Florida	MCDONALDS	TALLAHASSEE	17	STREET
McDonald's 41st Street Tallahassee, Florida	MCDONALDS	TALLAHASSEE	41	STREET
McDonald's Appleyard Drive Tallahassee, Florida	MCDONALDS	TALLAHASSEE	APPLEYARD	DRIVE
McDonald's Third Avenue Tallahassee, Florida	MCDONALDS	TALLAHASSEE	THIRD	AVENUE

e. If the street names are also the same, alphabetize by direction if it is part of the address (for example, *north, south, northeast, southwest*).

(Continued on page 296.)

12

Name	Unit 1	Unit 2	Unit 3	Unit 4	Unit 5
McDonald's N. 16th Street Tallahassee, Florida	MCDONALDS	TALLAHASSEE	N	16	STREET
McDonald's S. 16th Street Tallahassee, Florida	MCDONALDS	TALLAHASSEE	S	16	STREET
McDonald's Swan Avenue East Tallahassee, Florida	MCDONALDS	TALLAHASSEE	SWAN	AVENUE	EAST
McDonald's Swan Avenue West Tallahassee, Florida	MCDONALDS	TALLAHASSEE	SWAN	AVENUE	WEST

f. If all the foregoing units are identical, consider the house or building numbers and sequence them in numeric order.

McDonald's 23 Tier Street Tallahassee, Florida	MCDONALDS	TALLAHASSEE	TIER	STREET	23
McDonald's 870 Tier Street Tallahassee, Florida	MCDONALDS	TALLAHASSEE	TIER	STREET	870

Governmental Names

1220 Rule 12: Federal Government Names

a. For any organization that is part of the federal government, consider *United States Government* as the first three units.

b. If necessary, consider the name of the department, transposing *Department of* to the end. (For example, treat *Department of Labor* as three separate units: *LABOR DEPARTMENT OF.*)

c. Next consider the name of the office or bureau within the department. Transpose opening phrases such as *Office of* and *Bureau of* to the end. (For example, treat *Bureau of Labor Statistics* as four separate units: *LABOR STATISTICS BUREAU OF.*)

Name	Unit 4*	Unit 5	Unit 6	Unit 7
Office of Consumer Affairs	CONSUMER	AFFAIRS	OFFICE	OF
Federal Bureau of Investigation	FEDERAL	BUREAU	OF	INVESTIGATION
Food and Drug Administration	FOOD	AND	DRUG	ADMINISTRATION
General Accounting Office	GENERAL	ACCOUNTING	OFFICE	
National Labor Relations Board	NATIONAL	LABOR	RELATIONS	BOARD
National Park Service	NATIONAL	PARK	SERVICE	

*The first three units are *United States Government.*

1221 Rule 13: State and Local Government Names

a. For any organization (except an educational institution) that is part of a state, county, city, or town government, first consider the distinctive place name (for example, *Idaho* or *Sandpoint*).

b. Then consider the name of the department, bureau, or other subdivision, transposing elements (if necessary) as was done with federal departments and bureaus in ¶1220.

Name	Unit 1	Unit 2	Unit 3	Unit 4	Unit 5
Illinois State Board of Education	ILLINOIS	STATE	EDUCATION	BOARD	OF
Iowa Division of Labor	IOWA	LABOR	DIVISION	OF	
Water Commission, City of Yuma	YUMA	CITY	OF	WATER	COMMISSION
Registry of Deeds, Yuma County	YUMA	COUNTY	DEEDS	REGISTRY	OF

1222 Rule 14: Foreign Government Names

a. First consider the distinctive name of the country. (For example, select the distinctive name *Egypt* from the formal name *Arab Republic of Egypt*.)

b. Next, supply the appropriate term of classification—for example, *Republic, Commonwealth, Kingdom, State*.

c. Finally, consider the name of the department, bureau, or other subdivision.

Name	Unit 1	Unit 2
Commonwealth of Australia	AUSTRALIA	COMMONWEALTH
Republic of Austria	AUSTRIA	REPUBLIC
Kingdom of Belgium	BELGIUM	KINGDOM
State of Israel	ISRAEL	STATE

Letters and Memos

13

Section 13 provides format guidelines for letters and memos. These guidelines are not intended as inflexible rules; they can—and should—be modified to fit specific occasions as good sense and good taste require.

Parts of Letters

1301 A business letter has the following parts:

	Standard	Optional
Heading:	Letterhead or return address (¶¶1311–1313) Date line (¶1314)	Personal or confidential notation (¶1315) Reference notations (¶1316)
Opening:	Inside address (¶¶1317–1343) Salutation (¶¶1346–1351)	Attention line (¶¶1344–1345)
Body:	Message (¶¶1354–1357)	Subject line (¶¶1352–1353)
Closing:	Complimentary closing (¶¶1358–1360) Writer's identification (¶¶1362–1369) Reference initials (¶¶1370–1372)	Company signature (¶1361) Enclosure notation (¶¶1373–1374) Delivery notation (¶1375) Copy notation (¶¶1376–1380) Postscript (¶1381)

Each of these parts is illustrated in the model letters on pages 302–305.

1302 A business letter is usually arranged in one of the following styles:

a. **Modified-Block Style—Standard Format.** The date line, the complimentary closing, and the writer's identification all begin at center. All other lines begin at the left margin. This is the style most commonly used. (See page 302 for an illustration.)

b. **Modified-Block Style—With Indented Paragraphs.** This is exactly the same as the standard format described in ¶1302a except for one additional feature: the first line of each paragraph is indented 5 spaces. (See page 303 for an illustration.)

c. **Block Style.** All lines typically begin at the left margin. Nothing is indented except for displayed quotations, tables, and similar material. (See page 304 for an illustration.)

(Continued on page 300.)

d. **Simplified Style.** As in the block style, all lines begin at the left margin. However, the simplified style has these additional features: the salutation is replaced by an all-capital subject line, the complimentary closing is omitted, the writer's identification is typed in all-capital letters on one line, and open punctuation (see ¶1309b) is always used. (See page 305 for an illustration.)

Stationery Sizes

1303 The three sizes of stationery most commonly used are standard (8½″ × 11″), monarch (7¼″ × 10½″), and baronial (5½″ × 8½″).

Letter Placement

13

1304 Top Margin

a. **Printed Stationery.** Place the date (the first element to be typed) on the third line below the letterhead, or position it on line 13 (2 inches from the top of the page).

b. **Unprinted Stationery.** The top margin on the first page of a letter depends on whether you type a *letterhead* address for a standard business letter or a *return* address for a personal-business letter. (See ¶¶1312–1313 for positioning instructions.)

c. **Continuation Pages.** The top margin on each continuation page of a letter is 6 lines (1 inch). These pages are always typed on unprinted stationery (even if the first page is done on a printed letterhead). (See also ¶¶1382–1387.)

1305 Side Margins

a. The side margins will depend on what kind of stationery you are using and whether you are using 10-pitch or 12-pitch type.

NOTE: To identify *10-pitch* type (also called *pica* type) or *12-pitch* type (also called *elite* type), type a series of periods and compare them with the ones below.

10–PITCH TYPE . . . . 10 keystrokes to 1 inch

12–PITCH TYPE . . . . 12 keystrokes to 1 inch

b. Traditionally, business writers using standard (8½″ × 11″) stationery have set their margins for a 5- or 6-inch line. Now, however, there is widespread and ever-increasing use of computer software that calls for 1-inch side margins (and hence a 6½-inch line) in the absence of overriding instructions from the software user. For that reason the format guidelines given in Sections 13 to 17 sanction the use of 1-inch side margins for all material typed on 8½″ × 11″ stationery. However, a letter typed with wider side margins is more attractive and easier to read, so adjust your margin settings as you think appropriate.

If you are using a typewriter, the table on page 301 will give you the appropriate margin settings for different stationery and side margins.

If you are using a computer, you simply have to indicate what size stationery you are using. You do not have to specify side margins unless you want something wider than the standard 1-inch margins (also called the *default margins*) that have been preset in the software.

Standard Margin Settings With Stationery Starting at Zero

Stationery	Pitch/ Type Size	Equal Side Margins	Line Length	Margin Settings
Standard (8½″ × 11″)	10/Pica	1″	6½″	11–76
	12/Elite	1″	6½″	13–91
	10/Pica	1¼″	6″	13–73
	12/Elite	1¼″	6″	16–88
	10/Pica	1½″	5½″	16–71
	12/Elite	1½″	5½″	19–85
	10/Pica	1¾″	5″	18–68
	12/Elite	1¾″	5″	22–82
Monarch (7¼″ × 10½″)	10/Pica	1″	5¼″	11–63
	12/Elite	1″	5¼″	13–76
	10/Pica	1¼″	4¾″	13–60
	12/Elite	1¼″	4¾″	16–73
	10/Pica	1½″	4¼″	16–58
	12/Elite	1½″	4¼″	19–70
Baronial (5½″ × 8½″)	10/Pica	¾″	4″	8–48
	12/Elite	¾″	4″	10–58
	10/Pica	1″	3½″	11–46
	12/Elite	1″	3½″	13–55

13

1306 Bottom Margin

a. Leave a bottom margin of at least 6 lines (1 inch).

b. If the letter requires more than one page, the bottom margin on the first page can be increased up to 12 lines (2 inches).

For guidelines on carrying a letter over from one page to the next, see ¶¶1382–1387.

1307 Lengthening a Short Letter

To *spread* a short letter (under 75 words or about 8 lines of text) over one page, use any combination of the following techniques:

a. Lower the first line of typing by as many as 5 lines.

b. Allow up to 8 blank lines between the date and the inside address.

c. Use 1½ blank lines before and after the salutation, between the paragraphs, between the message and the complimentary closing, and between the complimentary closing and the company name.

d. Allow 4 to 6 blank lines for the signature.

e. Place the signer's name and title on separate lines.

f. Lower the reference initials 1 or 2 lines.

g. Increase the side margins from the standard 1 inch. (See the table above for alternative margin settings.)

h. Type the message double-spaced, and indent the first line of each paragraph.

Modified-Block Style—Standard Format

Heading

Opening

Body

Closing

Letterhead: The company's name and address, along with other information (such as a telephone number). (See ¶1311.)

Date Line: The date (month, day, and year) on which the letter is typed; starts at center on the third line below the letterhead or on line 13 (2 inches from the top of the page). (See ¶1314.)

Inside Address: The name and address of the person you are writing to. (See ¶¶1317–1343.)

Salutation: An opening greeting like *Dear Ms. Morales* (See ¶¶1346–1351.)

Message: The text of the letter; all paragraphs are typed single-spaced with no indentions; leave 1 blank line between paragraphs. (See ¶¶1354–1357.)

Complimentary Closing: A parting phrase like *Sincerely* or *Sincerely yours* starts at center. (See ¶¶1358–1360.)

Company Signature: An indication that the writer is acting on behalf of the company. (See ¶1361.)

Writer's Identification: The signer's name and title. (See ¶¶1362–1369.)

Reference Initials: The initials of the typist and sometimes those of the writer as well. (See ¶¶1370–1372.)

Enclosure Notation: A reminder that the letter is accompanied by an enclosure. (See ¶¶1373–1374.)

Delivery Notation: An indication that the letter has been sent a special way. (See ¶1375.)

Copy Notation: The names of those who will receive copies of this letter. (See ¶¶1376–1380.)

Compudata Systems Inc.

600 East Algonquin Road
Arlington Heights, Illinois 60005-4332
(312) 555-4605

→13

December 12, 19— →6

Ms. Susan N. Morales
2839 Clary Street
Fort Worth, Texas 76111-4326 →2

Dear Ms. Morales: →2

We were pleased to receive your letter of application
for a sales position with Compudata Systems. →2

At the moment we do not have an opening in the Fort
Worth area, but we do need a field representative
who is based in Lubbock and can cover the northwestern
part of the state. If you would like to be considered for this position, please fill in the enclosed
application and send it back to me. →2

As it happens, I will be attending a convention in Fort
Worth next month. I would be delighted to meet with
you while I'm in town and describe the job that is
available. If you have the qualifications we're looking for and you are interested in joining our staff,
we might be able to come to an agreement at that point. →2

When you return your completed application, please let
me know whether you would be free to meet at 4 p.m. on
Wednesday or Thursday of the first week of January. I
look forward to hearing from you. →2

Sincerely yours, →2

COMPUDATA SYSTEMS INC. →4

Kenneth R. Willmott

Kenneth R. Willmott
National Sales Manager →2

bjn
Enclosure
By Federal Express
cc: Miss A. Rossi

Modified-Block Style—With Indented Paragraphs

Heading

Opening

Body

Closing

```
                                        ¶3
                              1600 Fulton Road
                              Cleveland, Ohio 44113-3003
                              November 25, 19——    ↓2
                              In reply to:  Invoice 57389
                                                          ↓4

Byfield & Duff 268
Post Office Box 268
Freeport, Maine 04032-0268    ↓2
Attention:  Accounting Department    ↓2
                                     ↓2
Dear Byfield & Duff:    ↓2

    Over two months ago I ordered a pair of hiking
boots size 5.  You acknowledged my order, informed
me that you were temporarily out of stock, and told
me I could expect delivery within four weeks.    ↓2
    Today I received Invoice 57389, billing me for
two log carriers which I did not order and have not
received.  May I ask that you cancel this invoice.
If the log carriers arrive, I will refuse delivery
and ask to have them shipped back to you at once.
                                                   ↓2

                              Sincerely.    ↓4

                              (Mrs.) Doris T. Hagerty
                              Doris T. Hagerty    ↓2
                                                  ↓2
    PS:  I'm still eager to have those boots.  Can
you give me any word about them?
```

Return Address: The arrangement used in a personal-business letter, when an individual writes on blank stationery from home. (For an alternative placement of the return address and other details, see ¶1313.)

Reference Notation: A filing code used by the writer or the addressee. (See ¶1316.)

Attention Line: A means of directing the letter to a particular person or a specific department, even though the letter is addressed to an organization as a whole. (For an alternative placement of the attention line and other details, see ¶¶1344–1345.)

Paragraph Indentions: Customarily 5 spaces.

Postscript: A device for presenting a final idea or an afterthought. (See ¶1381.)

303

Block Style

Heading

Opening

Body

Closing

Confidential Notation: A note indicating that the letter should be read only by the person addressed. (See ¶1315.)

Foreign Address: The name of the country typed in all-capital letters on a line by itself. (See ¶1343.)

Subject Line: A means of stating what the letter is about. (See ¶¶1352–1353.)

Displayed Extract: Copy set off from the rest of the letter for emphasis; indented 5 spaces from the left and right margins. (See ¶1357a.)

SATELLITE TRADERS INC.
1500 Balboa Street
San Francisco, California 94118-3519
(415) 555-6000

April 24, 19—— ↓ 13
↓ 2

CONFIDENTIAL
↓ 4

Mr. Philip Wurlitzer Jr.
Executive Vice President
Satellite Traders Inc.
Apartado Aero 11255
Bogotá, D.E.
COLOMBIA
↓ 2

Dear Phil:
↓ 2

Subject: Your Request for Early Retirement ↓ 2

I presented your request to the board of directors
last Friday. They were entirely sympathetic to your
reasons for wanting to take early retirement, but
they expressed concern over the timing. Al Barnes,
in particular, raised the following points in a
memo he sent me today.
↓ 2

     Ask Phil to identify people in the Bogotá
     office he considers prospective candidates
     for his position. Please ask him to spell
     out their present qualifications and esti-
     mate the time it would take to groom any
     one of these people for his job. ↓ 2

If you and I can identify at least one qualified
candidate acceptable to Al and the other members
of the board, I know they will move quickly to
honor your request.
↓ 2

Sincerely, ↓ 4

Tom ↓ 2

Thomas P. Gagliardi
President
↓ 2

npl ↓ 2
c Mr. A. J. Barnes

Simplified Style

Heading

March 6, 19—

Opening

Mrs. Rita Selden
680 Forrest Road NE
Atlanta GA 30312

Body

THE SIMPLIFIED LETTER

You will be interested to know, Mrs. Selden, that a number of years ago the Administrative Management Society developed a new letter format called the simplified style. This is a sample.

1. It makes use of the block style as well as open punctuation.

2. It omits the salutation and the complimentary closing.

3. It makes use of a subject line, typed in all-capital letters and preceded and followed by two blank lines. The word Subject is omitted.

4. It identifies the signer by an all-capital line that is preceded by four blank lines and followed by one—if further notations are used.

5. It tries to achieve a brisk but friendly tone and uses the addressee's name at least in the first sentence.

Perhaps, Mrs. Selden, for the sake of efficiency, you ought to give this style a trial.

(Ms.) Helen F. Holub

HELEN F. HOLUB – DIRECTOR, SECRETARIAL TRAINING

jb

Closing

Subject Line: Replaces the salutation; typed in all-capital letters on the third line below inside address.

Complimentary Closing: Omitted.

Writer's Identification: Typed on one line in all-capital letters.

1308 Shortening a Long Letter

To *condense* a long letter (over 225 words or 23 lines of text), use any combination of the following techniques:

a. On a page of printed stationery, type the date on the third line below the printed letterhead. On a page of blank stationery that calls for a letterhead (see ¶1312), type the letterhead single-spaced (rather than double-spaced), starting on line 7. On a page of blank stationery that calls for a return address (see ¶1313), leave a top margin of only 6 blank lines (rather than the 12 blank lines noted in ¶1313a).

b. Reduce the space between the date and the inside address to 2 or 3 blank lines (instead of the customary 5).

c. Reduce the space for the signature from 3 blank lines to 2.

d. Put reference initials on the same line as the writer's identification.

e. On standard and monarch stationery, use 1-inch side margins; on baronial stationery, use 3/4-inch side margins. (For the appropriate margin settings, see the table on page 301.)

Punctuation Patterns

1309 The message in a business letter is always punctuated with normal punctuation (see Sections 1 and 2). The other parts may be punctuated according to one of the following patterns:

a. **Standard (Mixed) Pattern.** A colon is used after the salutation and a comma after the complimentary closing. (This is the style most commonly used.)

b. **Open Pattern.** No punctuation is used at the end of any line outside the body of the letter unless that line ends with an abbreviation.

c. **Close (Full) Pattern.** A colon is used after the salutation, and each line outside the body of the letter ends with a comma or a period. (This style is now rarely used.)

For an illustration of all three patterns, see page 308.

Spacing

1310 Ordinarily, type all letters single-spaced. (For the use of double spacing in very short letters, see ¶1307h.)

The following rules (¶¶1311–1316) deal with the *heading* of a letter. The heading must always include two elements: a letterhead or a return address (¶¶1311–1313) and a date line (¶1314). It may also include a personal or confidential notation (¶1315) and reference notations (¶1316). The model letters shown on pages 302–305 illustrate the position of these elements in the heading.

Letterhead or Return Address

1311 Using a Printed Letterhead

The first page of a standard business letter is customarily written on stationery with a *printed letterhead* containing at least these elements: company name, street address or post office box number, and city, state, and ZIP Code. Most printed letterheads also show area code and telephone number. Some also provide a special address for cable messages as well as special phone numbers for the transmission of information by means of facsimile (fax) or teletypewriter (telex) equipment.

For the use of the nine-digit ZIP Code, see ¶1339, note.

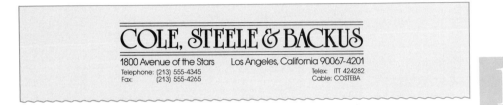

13

1312 Creating a Letterhead

If you are using plain paper and are writing a standard business letter on behalf of an organization, you can create a *typewritten letterhead* as shown below. Center the following information in four double-spaced lines, beginning on the seventh line from the top of the page: (1) the company name; (2) the street address or post office box number; (3) the city, state, and ZIP Code; (4) the telephone area code and number. (The date then follows on the third line below.)

```
                          ↓7
                  TURPIN AND KELLY INC.
                                      ↓2
                  250 Mulberry Street ↓2
            New York, New York 10012-4105 ↓2
                      212-555-3600 ↓3

                          September 28, 19---
```

NOTE: If you have access to electronic equipment and appropriate software, you can create your own professional-looking letterhead, using boldface type for special emphasis and incorporating a logo or some other image to enhance the look of your design.

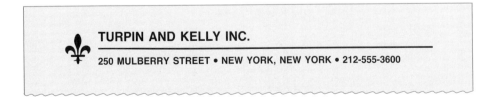

Standard Punctuation

May 3, 19—

Mr. Bernard Kraus Jr.
Purchasing Agent
The Bergen Press Inc.
313 North Street
San Jose, CA 95113

Dear Mr. Kraus:

Sincerely,
HUDSON COMPANY

Lee Brower

Lee Brower
Sales Manager

mr
Enclosure
cc: Ms. Loo

Open Punctuation

May 3, 19—

Mr. Bernard Kraus Jr.
Purchasing Agent
The Bergen Press Inc.
313 North Street
San Jose, CA 95113

Dear Mr. Kraus

Sincerely
HUDSON COMPANY

Lee Brower

Lee Brower
Sales Manager

mr
Enclosure
cc: Ms. Loo

Close Punctuation

May 3, 19—.

Mr. Bernard Kraus Jr.,
Purchasing Agent,
The Bergen Press Inc.,
313 North Street,
San Jose, CA 95113.

Dear Mr. Kraus:

Sincerely,
HUDSON COMPANY,

Lee Brower

Lee Brower,
Sales Manager.

mr.
Enclosure.
cc: Ms. Loo.

1313 Return Address

If you are using plain paper for a *personal-business letter* (one you write as an individual from your home), type a *return address*. There are three formats you can choose from.

a. Traditionally, the return address appears at the top of the page starting on line 13. The following information is provided on three or more single-spaced lines: (1) the street address; (2) the city, state, and ZIP Code; (3) the phone number (if you want the addressee to have it); and (4) the date (see ¶1314).

```
212 West 22d Street, Apt. 2B    OR    Apartment 2B
New York, NY 10011-2706               212 West 22d Street
212-555-9097                          New York, NY 10011-2706
January 24, 1994                      212-555-9097
                                      January 24, 1994
```

NOTE: For the *modified-block* letter style, start each line of the return address at the center of the page. (See page 303.) For the *block* and *simplified* styles, start each line at the left margin. (See pages 304–305.)

b. A style recently introduced locates the return address in the *closing* section of the letter, starting on the line directly below the writer's typed name.

```
Sincerely,
      ↓ 4


Josephine C. Carbonara
Apartment 2B
212 West 22d Street
New York, NY 10011-2706
212-555-9097
```

NOTE: Each line of the return address begins at the same point as the complimentary closing and the writer's typed name—at the center of the page for the *modified-block* style and at the left margin for the *block* and *simplified* styles.

c. If you are using electronic equipment with the appropriate software, you can create a personal letterhead.

Merle C. Forrest

SECOND WIND • BISCAY ROAD • DAMARISCOTTA, MAINE 04543 • 207-555-9097

Date Line

1314 a. The date line consists of the *name of the month* (written in full—never abbreviated or represented by figures), the *day* (written in figures and followed by a comma), and the *complete year*.

December 28, 1995 (NOT Dec. 28, 1995 OR December 28th, 1995)

NOTE: Do not use the style *12/28/95* or *'95* in the date line of a business letter.

(Continued on page 310.)

b. Some writers write the date line in this order: day, month, year. This is the style typically used in military correspondence and letters from abroad.

28 December 1995

c. When using letterhead stationery (printed or typewritten), position the date line on the third line below the letterhead or on line 13 (2 inches from the top of the page).

NOTE: For the *modified-block* letter style, you may position the date line as follows: (1) start it at the center of the page (preferred style); (2) position it so that it ends at the right margin; or (3) type it in some other position that is attractive in relation to the letterhead design (so long as it still stands out). For the *block* and the *simplified* styles, always start the date at the left margin.

d. When using a return address at the top of the letter, position the date as shown in ¶1313a. If the return address is placed at the bottom of the letter (as in ¶1313b), position the date on line 13 (2 inches from the top of the page).

See the illustrations on pages 302–305.

Personal or Confidential Notation

1315 If a letter is of a personal or confidential nature, provide the appropriate notation on the second line below the date, at the *left* margin. Type the notation in all-capital letters or in capital and small letters that are underscored. (See the illustration on page 304.)

PERSONAL OR Personal   CONFIDENTIAL OR Confidential

NOTE: If you are using electronic equipment, the notation may be done in boldface type without underscoring.

PERSONAL OR **Personal**   **CONFIDENTIAL** OR **Confidential**

Reference Notations

1316 a. Printed letterheads for large organizations sometimes contain a line in the upper right corner that reads *When replying, refer to:* or something similar. When using this kind of letterhead, type the appropriate reference number or filing code 2 spaces after the colon. Align the number or code at the bottom with the printed words.

NOTE: If the guide words *When replying, refer to:* are not printed on the stationery but are desired, type them on the second line below the date (or on the second line below any notation that follows the date). Start typing at the same point as the date.

When replying, refer to: ALG–341

b. When you are replying to a letter that contains a reference number or when you want to emphasize the fact that your letter concerns an insurance policy, an order, or a similar document, type a reference notation on the second line below the date (or on the second line below any notation that follows the date). Start typing at the same point as the date. (See the illustration on page 303.)

In reply to: G241 782 935   Refer to: Policy 234844

c. When there are two reference notations to be given, type your own reference notation first (as indicated in ¶1316a). Then type the addressee's reference notation on the second line below.

```
When replying, refer to:  F-17865
                                   ↓ 2
Your reference:  GAR-X-7
```

NOTE: Some writers prefer to give the addressee's reference notation in a subject line. (See ¶1353d.)

The following rules (¶¶1317–1351) deal with the opening of a letter. The opening typically includes two elements: the inside address (¶¶1317–1343) and the salutation (¶¶1346–1351). It may also include an attention line (¶¶1344–1345).

Inside Address

1317 Letters to an Individual

a. The inside address should include the following information: (1) the name of the person to whom you are writing; (2) the street address, the post office box number, or the rural route number; and (3) the city, state, and ZIP Code.

```
Dr. Margaret P. Vanden Heuvel      Mr. Albert W. Clemons Jr.
615 University Boulevard, NE        Meads Creek Road, R.R. 2
Albuquerque, NM 87106-4553         Painted Post, NY 14870
```

For the placement of the inside address, see ¶1319a; for the use of the nine-digit ZIP Code, see ¶1339, note.

b. If the person lives in an apartment building, give the apartment number after the street address or on the line above.

```
Miss Susan H. Ellington            Mrs. Lorraine Martineau
Apartment 10G                      6834 Creston Road, Apt. 4D
3864 South Kettering Boulevard     Edina, MN 55435
Dayton, Ohio 45439-2017
```

c. Sometimes the address for a person living in a small town consists only of (1) the name and (2) the city, state, and ZIP Code. In this case type the address on two lines. (Do not separate the city from the state to make three lines.)

```
Mrs. Marie S. Allen
Thompson, ND 58278-9998
```

1318 Letters to an Organization

a. The inside address should include the following information: (1) the name of the business or organization, (2) a street address or a post office box number, and (3) the city, state, and ZIP Code. Whenever possible, address the letter to a specific person in the organization and include that person's job title and department (if known). If you do not have the name of a specific person, use a title instead (for example, *Director of Marketing* or *Advertising Manager*).

```
Mr. Arthur L. Quintero             Director of Research
National Sales Manager             Stanton Chemical Company
Paragon Industries                 Post Office Box 21431
211 North Ervay Street             Chattanooga, TN 37421-0431
Dallas, Texas 75201
```

(Continued on page 312.)

b. When a room number or a suite number is included in the inside address, the following arrangements are acceptable:

```
Ms. Alice G. Alvarez            James W. Chiverton, M.D.
Woodruff Construction Company   Suite 1200
416 12th Street, Room 12        1111 West Mockingbird Lane
Columbus, Georgia 31901-2528    Dallas, Texas 75247

Mr. Raymond Kermian             Miss Pauline Leggett
Contemporary Tours Inc.         Steele & Leggett
Room 304, Tower Building        503 Hanna Building
2506 Willowbrook Parkway        1422 Euclid Avenue
Indianapolis, IN 46205          Cleveland, OH 44115-1901
```

13

1319 a. Whether a letter is going to an individual's home or to an organization, start the inside address on the *sixth* line below the date. If a notation falls between the date and the inside address (see ¶¶1315–1316), start the inside address on the *fourth* line below the notation.

See the illustrations on pages 302–305.

NOTE: In social-business correspondence (see ¶¶1394–1395), the inside address is typed at the bottom of the letter, aligned at the left margin and starting on the *sixth* line below the writer's signature or title (whichever comes last). In a purely personal letter, no inside address is given at all.

b. Single-space the inside address, and align each line at the left.

1320 a. If a letter is addressed to two or more people at different addresses, the individual address blocks may be typed one under the other (with 1 blank line between) or attractively positioned side by side. If the inside address blocks take up too much space at the opening of the letter, they may be typed at the end of the letter, starting on the second line below the final notation at the left or, if there are no notations, on the *sixth* line below the signature block.

b. If a letter is addressed to two or more people at the same address, list each name on a separate line. Do not show a position title for each person unless it is short and can go on the same line as the name. Moreover, omit the names of departments unless the persons are in the same department. In effect, type only those parts of the address that are common to the people named at the start. (On the respective envelopes for each individual, give the full address for that individual and omit all reference to others named in the inside address.)

```
Dr. Paul J. Rogers
Mr. James A. Dawes
Research Department
Sloan and Hewitt Advertising
700 North Harding Avenue
Chicago, Illinois 60624-1002
```

The following rules (¶¶1321–1343) provide additional details concerning the parts of inside addresses. See also the models in Section 18 for special forms of address used for individuals, couples, organizations, professional people, education officials, government officials, diplomats, military personnel, and religious dignitaries.

Name of Person and Title

1321 When writing the name of a person in an inside address or elsewhere in a letter, be sure to follow that person's preferences in the spelling, capitalization, punctuation, and spacing of the name. (See ¶311.)

    a. Do not abbreviate or use initials unless the person to whom you are writing prefers to use an abbreviation or initials. For example, do not write *Wm. B. Sachs* or *W. B. Sachs* if the person to whom you are writing used *William B. Sachs* in his correspondence.

    b. When writing to a married woman, follow her preference for first and last names if you know it. She may have decided not to adopt her husband's last name for business purposes (or for any purposes) and prefer to be addressed by her original name (for example, *Ms. Joan L. Conroy*). If you do know that she is using her husband's last name, continue to use her own first name and middle initial (for example, *Mrs. Joan L. Noonan*). The form that uses her husband's first name as well (for example, *Mrs. James W. Noonan*) is acceptable only for social purposes. It should never be used when addressing a business letter to a married woman, and it should not be used when a married woman becomes a widow unless she indicates that is her preference.

1322 In general, use a title before the name of a person in an inside address. (See ¶517 for appropriate abbreviations of such titles.)

    a. If the person has no special title (such as *Dr., Professor,* or *The Honorable*), use the courtesy title *Mr., Miss, Mrs.,* or *Ms.* (See also ¶1801.)

    b. In selecting *Miss, Mrs.,* or *Ms.,* always respect the individual woman's preference. If her preference is unknown, use the title *Ms.* or omit the courtesy title altogether. (See also ¶1801b–c.)

    NOTE: Follow the same practice in the salutation. (See ¶1349.)

    c. If you do not know whether the person addressed is a man or a woman, do not use any courtesy title. (See also ¶1801d.) Follow the same practice in the salutation. (See ¶1349.)

    NOTE: People who use initials in place of their first and middle names or who have ambiguous names (like *Marion, Leslie, Hilary,* and *Lee*) should always use a courtesy title when they sign their letters so that others may be spared the confusion over which title to use. (See also ¶¶1365–1366.)

    d. Address teenage girls as *Miss* or *Ms.,* and respect the individual's preference if you know it. For girls younger than 13, *Miss* or *Ms.* may be used or omitted.

    e. Address teenage boys as *Mr.* For boys younger than 13, omit the title. (*Master* is now rarely used except with the names of very young boys.)

1323 a. A letter to a husband and wife is customarily addressed in this form:

    Mr. and Mrs. Harold D. Bennisch (NOT: Mr. & Mrs.)

    b. If the husband has a special title such as *Dr.* or *Professor,* the couple is addressed as follows:

    Dr. and Mrs. Thomas P. Geiger

(Continued on page 314.)

13

c. If both husband and wife or the wife alone has a special title, list the names on separate lines.

Dean Walter O. Goetz   Dr. Eleanor V. Eberhardt-Ball
Professor Helen F. Goetz   Mr. Joseph L. Eberhardt-Ball

For other forms of address to use for couples in special circumstances, see ¶1802.

1324 a. When *Jr., Sr.,* or a roman numeral such as *III* is typed after a name, omit the comma before *Jr., Sr.,* or the roman numeral unless you know that the person being addressed prefers the use of a comma. (See also ¶156.)

b. Do not use a title before a name if the term *Esq.* follows the name. (See also ¶¶518c, 1804a.)

Rita A. Henry, Esq. (NOT: Ms. Rita A. Henry, Esq.)

NOTE: A comma separates the last name from the term *Esq.*

c. As a rule, do not use an academic degree with a person's name in an inside address. However, some doctors of medicine and divinity prefer the use of the degree after their names (rather than the title *Dr.* before). (See also ¶1804b.)

NOTE: If an academic degree follows the person's name, separate it from the last name with a comma. Also omit the titles *Dr., Miss, Mr., Mrs.,* and *Ms.* before the name. Another title (for example, *Professor, The Reverend, Captain, Dean*) may be used before the name as long as it does not convey the same meaning as the degree that follows. (See ¶519c.)

Reva C. Calhoun, M.D.   The Reverend Ernest G. Wyzanski, D.D.

d. Abbreviations of religious orders, such as *S.J.* and *S.N.D.,* are typed after names and preceded by a comma. An appropriate title should precede the name, even though the abbreviation follows the name; for example, *The Reverend John DeMaio, O.P.* (See also ¶1809.)

1325 a. A title of position, such as *Vice President* or *Sales Manager,* should be included in an inside address whenever possible. Ordinarily, place it on the line following the name; if the title requires a second line, indent the turnover 2 spaces. Capitalize the first letter of every word in the title except (1) prepositions under four letters (like *of* and *for*), (2) conjunctions under four letters (like *and*), and (3) the articles *the, a,* and *an* when they appear *within* the title.

```
Mrs. Martha Hansen            Mr. Ralph Nielsen
Executive Vice President      Vice President and   (NOT &)
                                General Manager

Mr. Harry F. Benjamin         Ms. Evangeline S. Palmer
Chairman of the Board         Director of In-Service Training
```

NOTE: In the last example above, *In* is capitalized because it is the first element in a compound adjective (rather than a pure preposition as in *Editor in Chief*). By the same token, in the title *Coordinator of On-the-Job Training, On* is capitalized as the first element in a compound adjective but *of* and *the* are not.

b. If the title is very short, it may be typed on the same line as the person's name or the person's department in order to balance the length of the lines in the address. However, do not type a title on the same line as the name of an organization. (See ¶1327.)

```
Mr. J. C. Lee, President          Mr. Armand F. Aristides
Merchants National Bank           Controller
                                  Dahl, Inc.


Mrs. Lucinda Hollingsworth  NOT:  Mr. Armand F. Aristides
Manager, Support Services         Controller, Dahl, Inc.
E. J. Haines & Company
```

In Care of . . .

1326 Sometimes a letter cannot be sent to the addressee's home or place of business; it must be directed instead to a third person who will see that the letter reaches the addressee. In such cases use an "in care of" notation as shown below.

```
Professor Eleanor Marschak    OR  Professor Eleanor Marschak
In care of Henry Wardwell, Esq.   c/o Henry Wardwell, Esq.
```

Name of Organization

1327 Type the organization's name on a line by itself. If the name of a division or a department is needed in the address, it should precede the name of the organization on a line by itself.

```
Ms. Laura J. Kidd
Assistant Vice President
Department of Corporate Planning
Holstein, Brooks & Co.
```

1328 When writing the name of an organization in an inside address, always follow the organization's style for spelling, punctuation, capitalization, spacing, and abbreviations. The letterhead on incoming correspondence is the best source for this information. Note the variations in style in these names.

Time Inc.	BankAmerica Corp.
Newsweek, Inc.	Rogers Cablesystems of America, Inc.
Prudential Securities	USLife Corp.
Incorporated	U S WEST Communications
Parker Pen Co.	Merrill Lynch, Pierce, Fenner & Smith Inc.
PepsiCo, Inc.	Janney Montgomery Scott Inc.
The Singer Company	MGM/UA Communications Co.
Engelhard Corp.	Ply*Gem Industries
Horizon Bancorp	Ex-Cell-O Corporation
Microsoft Corporation	La-Z-Boy Chair Co.
Frye & Smith Ltd.	Fisher - Price Toys
Fujitsu, Ltd.	The Robinson-Humphrey Company, Inc.
Canadian Pacific Limited	1 Potato 2 Inc.
INCO LTD	Toys "R" Us, Inc. (see ¶320a)

NOTE: If the name is long and requires more than one line, indent any turnover line 2 spaces. (See ¶1329e for examples.)

1329 If you do not have some way of determining the official form of a company name, follow these rules:

a. Spell out the word *and.* Do not use an ampersand (&).

Haber, Curtis, and Hall Inc.   Acme Lead and Tin Company

b. Write *Inc.* for *Incorporated* and *Ltd.* for *Limited.* Do not use a comma before the abbreviation.

c. As a rule, spell out *Company* or *Corporation;* if the name is extremely long, however, use the abbreviation *Co.* or *Corp.*

d. Do not use the word *the* at the beginning of a name unless you are sure it is part of the official name; for example, *The Wall Street Journal* (as illustrated in *e* below).

e. Capitalize the first letter of every word except (1) prepositions under four letters (like *of* and *for*), (2) conjunctions under four letters (like *and*), and (3) the articles *the, a,* and *an* when they appear *within* the organization's name.

```
Department of Health and          American Society for the
   Human Services                    Prevention of Cruelty
200 Independence Avenue, SW          to Animals
Washington, DC 20201-0001         441 East 92d Street
                                  New York, New York 10128
```

NOTE: In the following example note that the article *the* is capitalized because it comes at the start of the organization's official name. Note also that the name of the newspaper is not underscored because it refers to the organization rather than to the actual newspaper. (See also ¶289d.)

```
The Wall Street Journal
200 Liberty Street
New York, New York 10281-1099
```

For the use or omission of apostrophes in company names, see ¶640.

Building Name

1330 If the name of a building is included in the inside address, type it on a line by itself immediately above the street address. A room number or a suite number should accompany the building name.

```
Room 118, Acuff Building          858 Park Square Building
904 Bob Wallace Avenue, SW        31 St. James Avenue
Huntsville, AL 35801              Boston, MA 02116-4255
```

For additional examples, see ¶1318b.

Street Address

1331 Always type the street address on a line by itself, immediately preceding the city, state, and ZIP Code. (See ¶¶1317–1318 for examples.)

1332 Use figures for house and building numbers. Do not include the abbreviation *No.* or the symbol # before such numbers. **EXCEPTION:** For clarity, use the word *One* instead of the figure *1* in a house or building number; for example, *One Park Avenue.*

1333 Numbers used as street names are written as follows:

    a. Spell out the numbers 1 through 10; for example, *177 Second Avenue.*

    b. Use figures for numbers over 10; for example, *627 East 202d Street* or *144 65th Street.* (See also ¶425, note.)

1334 When a compass point (for example, *East, West, Southeast, Northwest*) appears *before* a street name, do not abbreviate it except in a very long street address when space is tight.

    330 West 42d Street   3210 Northwest Grand Avenue

1335 When a compass point appears *after* a street name, follow the local style that predominates. In the absence of a local style, follow these guidelines:

    a. Abbreviate compound directions (*NE, NW, SE, SW*) that represent a section of the city. Do not use a period with these abbreviations (see ¶531a). Insert a comma before them.

    817 Peachtree Street, NE   120 112th Street, NW

    b. Spell out *North, South, East,* and *West* following a street name, and omit the comma. (In such cases these compass points are typically an integral part of the street name rather than a designation of a section of the city.)

    10 Park Avenue South   2049 Century Park East

1336 Use the word *and,* not an ampersand (&), in a street address; for example, *Tenth and Market Streets.* However, avoid the use of such "intersection" addresses if a house or building number plus a single street name is available.

1337 Avoid abbreviating such words as *Street* and *Avenue* in inside addresses. (It may be necessary to abbreviate in envelope addresses. See ¶1390.)

For apartment and room numbers with street addresses, see ¶¶1317b, 1318b, 1330.

Box Number

1338 a. A post office box number may be used in place of the street address.

    Post Office Box 1518 **or** P.O. Box 1518 **or** Box 1518

    b. A station name, if needed, should follow the post office box number (and a comma) on the same line. If very long, the station name may go on the line below.

```
Box 76984, Sanford Station        P.O. Box 11215
Los Angeles, CA 90076-0984        Linda Vista Station
                                  San Diego, CA 92111
```

    c. Some companies show both a street address and a post office box number in their mailing address. Whatever information appears in the line immediately preceding the city, state, and ZIP Code determines where the mail will be delivered.

```
Henson Supply Corp.        The mail will be delivered to this address.
315 South Water Street
Post Office Box 181        Be sure that the ZIP Code refers in this case
Hartford, CT 06101-0181    to the post office in the line above (and not
                           to the street address).
```

(Continued on page 318.)

NOTE: When you are writing to a company that provides a street address and a post office box number in its mailing address, you are not obliged to use both forms either in the inside address or on the envelope. Simply choose the form you prefer and use it consistently in both places.

City, State, and ZIP Code

1339 The city, state, and ZIP Code must always be typed on one line, immediately following the street address. Type the name of the city (followed by a comma and 1 space), the state (followed by 1 space but no comma), and the ZIP Code.

> Denver, Colorado 80217 OR Denver, CO 80217-9999

NOTE: The U.S. Postal Service encourages the use of a nine-digit ZIP Code (consisting of the basic five digits followed immediately by a hyphen and another four digits). The use of the additional four digits is voluntary, but as an inducement the Postal Service offers discounts on postage fees. To qualify for a discount, mailers must submit a minimum of 500 *first-class* letters or postcards at one time; moreover, the envelope addresses must be readable by electronic (OCR) equipment (see ¶¶1389–1390) and satisfy a number of other criteria.

1340 When writing the name of a city in an inside address:

   a. Do not use an abbreviation (for example, *Chic.* for *Chicago* or *L.A.* for *Los Angeles*).

   b. Do not abbreviate the words *Fort, Mount, Point,* or *Port.* Write the name of the city in full; for example, *Fort Dodge, Mount Vernon, Point Pleasant, Port Huron.* (See also ¶529a.)

   c. Abbreviate the word *Saint* in the names of American cities; for example, *St. Louis, St. Paul, St. Petersburg.* (See also ¶529b.)

NOTE: It may be necessary, for reasons of space, to abbreviate city names in envelope addresses. (See ¶1390a.)

1341 **a.** In an address, spell out the name of the state or use a two-letter abbreviation of the state name (as shown at the top of page 319).

   NOTE: The two-letter abbreviations (for example, *AL* for *Alabama*) were created by the U.S. Postal Service and should be used only with ZIP Codes in addresses. The more traditional abbreviations of state names (for example, *Ala.* for *Alabama*) should be used in other situations where abbreviations are appropriate. (See ¶¶526–527 for a list of the traditional abbreviations.)

   b. When using two-letter state abbreviations, type them in capital letters, with no periods after or space between the letters.

   c. When giving an address in a sentence, insert a comma after the street address and after the city. Leave 1 space between the state and the ZIP Code. Insert a comma after the ZIP Code unless a stronger mark of punctuation is required at that point.

> My address next month will be 501 South 71st Court, Miami, Florida 33144-2728, but mail sent to my office will reach me just as easily.

Alabama	AL	Missouri	MO
Alaska	AK	Montana	MT
American Samoa	AS	Nebraska	NE
Arizona	AZ	Nevada	NV
Arkansas	AR	New Hampshire	NH
California	CA	New Jersey	NJ
Colorado	CO	New Mexico	NM
Connecticut	CT	New York	NY
Delaware	DE	North Carolina	NC
District		North Dakota	ND
of Columbia	DC	Northern Mariana	
Federated States		Islands	MP
of Micronesia	FM	Ohio	OH
Florida	FL	Oklahoma	OK
Georgia	GA	Oregon	OR
Guam	GU	Palau	PW
Hawaii	HI	Pennsylvania	PA
Idaho	ID	Puerto Rico	PR
Illinois	IL	Rhode Island	RI
Indiana	IN	South Carolina	SC
Iowa	IA	South Dakota	SD
Kansas	KS	Tennessee	TN
Kentucky	KY	Texas	TX
Louisiana	LA	Utah	UT
Maine	ME	Vermont	VT
Marshall Islands	MH	Virgin Islands	VI
Maryland	MD	Virginia	VA
Massachusetts	MA	Washington	WA
Michigan	MI	West Virginia	WV
Minnesota	MN	Wisconsin	WI
Mississippi	MS	Wyoming	WY

13

1342 Omit the name of the county or area (such as *Long Island*) in an address. However, the name of a community, subdivision, or real estate development may be included so long as it comes before the lines containing the mail delivery address.

```
Ms. Janet G. Arnold          NOT:  Ms. Janet G. Arnold
Muir Meadows                        1039 Erica Road
1039 Erica Road                     Muir Meadows
Mill Valley, CA 94941-3748          Mill Valley, CA 94941-3748
```

1343 In foreign addresses, type the name of the country on a separate line in all-capital letters. Do not abbreviate the name of the country.

```
Graf-Adolf Strasse 100        Rua Tabapua, 1105
Dusseldorf 4000               Caixa Postal 20689
GERMANY                       Itaim-Bibi, Sao Paulo, S.P.
                              BRAZIL


134 Piccadilly                21 St. Claire Avenue East
London W1V 9FJ                Toronto, Ontario M4T 1L9
ENGLAND                       CANADA
```

Attention Line

1344 a. When a letter is addressed directly to a company, an attention line may be used to route the letter to a particular person (by name or title) or to a particular department. For example:

```
Shelton & Warren Industries        Carrolton Labs
6710 Squibb Road                   1970 Briarwood Court
Mission, Kansas 66202-3223         Atlanta, GA 30329

Attention:  Mr. John Ellery        ATTENTION:  SALES MANAGER
```

NOTE: This form of address is intended to emphasize the fact that the letter deals with a business matter (rather than a personal matter) and may be handled by someone other than the person named in the attention line. However, it is simpler to type the name of the person or department above the company name and omit the attention line. When a letter without a personal or confidential notation is received by a company, it will be presumed to deal with company business and will be handled by others in the absence of the person named in the address. For this reason an attention line is not really needed.

b. If you use an attention line, type it on the second line below the inside address, starting at the left margin.

c. The attention line may be typed in capital and small letters or in all-capital letters.

d. Do not abbreviate the word *Attention.* Use a colon after *Attention.*

e. Do not underscore the attention line unless you feel that extra emphasis is warranted.

For the salutation to use with an attention line, see ¶1351.

1345 If you are using (a) window envelopes or (b) electronic equipment with the aim of generating the envelope address by repeating the inside address as typed, you should insert the attention line in the inside address—as the first line. (See also ¶¶1389m, 1390h.)

```
Attention:  Mr. John Ellery        Attention:  Sales Manager
Shelton & Warren Industries        Carrolton Labs
6710 Squibb Road                   1970 Briarwood Court
Mission, Kansas 66202-3223         Atlanta, GA 30329
```

NOTE: Once the attention line is placed on the first line of the address block, the argument for omitting the word *Attention* is further strengthened. (See the note in ¶1344 above.) Indeed, when the U.S. Postal Service (USPS) illustrates the use of an attention line, it typically omits the word *Attention* or the abbreviation *ATTN.* In fact, the USPS uses the term *attention line* to refer to *any* information—whether a person's name (*Ms. Hilary Edwards*), a person's title (*Marketing Director*), or a departmental name (*Research Department*)—that appears on the line above the organizational name (*The E. J. Monagle Publishing Company*). If you read somewhere that the USPS wants the first line of a business address to be an "attention line," do not conclude that it is pushing the use of the word *Attention.* The USPS simply wants to have personal or departmental names or titles come above the name of the organization.

Salutation

1346 Type the salutation, beginning at the left margin, on the second line below the attention line (if used) or on the second line below the inside address. Follow the salutation with a colon unless you are using open punctuation (see ¶1309) or you are typing a social-business letter (see ¶1395b). Omit the salutation if you are using the simplified style, and replace it with a subject line. (See ¶1352.)

1347 Abbreviate only the titles *Mr., Ms., Mrs., Messrs.,* and *Dr.* All other titles, such as *Professor* and *Father,* should be written out. (See Section 18 for titles used by officials, dignitaries, and military personnel.)

1348 Capitalize the first word as well as any nouns and titles in the salutation; for example, *Dear Sir, My dear Mrs. Brand.*

1349 A list of commonly used forms of salutation begins below and continues on the next page. (See also Section 18.)

To One Person (Name, Gender, and Courtesy Title Preference Known)

Dear Mr. Smith: Dear Ms. Simpson:
Dear Mrs. Gray: Dear Miss Wells:

To One Person (Name Known, Gender Unknown)

Dear Marion Parker: Dear R. V. Moore:

To One Person (Name Unknown, Gender Known)

Dear Madam: **OR** Madam: (more formal)
Dear Sir: **OR** Sir: (more formal)

To One Person (Name and Gender Unknown)

Dear Sir or Madam: **OR** Sir or Madam: (more formal)
OR Dear Madam or Sir: **OR** Madam or Sir: (more formal)

To Whom It May Concern: (see ¶1349c)

To One Woman (Courtesy Title Preference Unknown)

Dear Ms. Malloy: **OR** Dear Ruth Malloy: (see ¶1322b)

To Two or More Men

Dear Mr. Gelb and Mr. Harris: **OR** Gentlemen:
OR Dear Messrs. Gelb and Harris: (more formal)

To Two or More Women

Dear Mrs. Allen, Ms. Ott, and Miss Day:

Dear Mrs. Jordan and Mrs. Kent: (see ¶618)
OR Dear Mesdames Jordan and Kent: (more formal)

Dear Ms. Scott and Ms. Gomez: (see ¶618)
OR Dear Mses. (**OR** Mss.) Scott and Gomez: (more formal)

Dear Miss Winger and Miss Rossi: (see ¶618)
OR Dear Misses Winger and Rossi: (more formal)

(Continued on page 322.)

To a Woman and a Man

Dear Ms. Kent and Mr. Winston: Dear Mrs. Kay and Mr. Fox:
Dear Mr. Fong and Miss Landis: Dear Mr. and Mrs. Green:

To Several Persons

Dear Mr. Anderson, Mrs. Brodsky, Ms. Carmino,
Mr. Dellums, and Miss Eustace:

Dear Friends (Colleagues, Members, *or some other suitable collective term*):

To an Organization Composed Entirely of Men

Gentlemen:

To an Organization Composed Entirely of Women

Mesdames: OR   Ladies:

To an Organization Composed of Men and Women

See ¶1350.

a. Be sure that the spelling of the surname in the salutation matches the spelling in the inside address. If the person you are writing to has a hyphenated last name (for example, *Mrs. Hazel Merriman-Sparks*), the salutation should read *Dear Mrs. Merriman-Sparks.*

b. When writing to someone you know well, use a first name or nickname in place of the more formal salutations shown above. However, once you start using an informal salutation, be sure that anyone who prepares your letters for you maintains that form of address. Otherwise, a person who is used to getting *Dear Mike* letters from you may one day receive a *Dear Mr. Romano* letter and waste a good deal of time brooding over what could have caused the sudden chill in your relationship. (See also ¶1360d.)

c. When you are preparing a letter that may be sent or shown to a number of as yet undetermined recipients, it is permissible to use *To Whom It May Concern* as a salutation. However, when you are writing to one specific person whose name and gender you do not know, use *Dear Sir or Madam* or one of the other forms shown on the preceding page.

d. In extremely formal letters, *My dear* may be used in place of *Dear.*

1350   For an organization composed of both men and women, the salutation traditionally used was *Gentlemen.*

```
United Services Corporation
100 Kendall Parkway
Somerset, NJ 08873
```

```
Gentlemen:
```

However, this generic use of *Gentlemen* is now considered unsuitable for reference to a group that includes women as well as men. Here are some alternatives:

a. Use *Ladies and Gentlemen* or *Gentlemen and Ladies* in place of *Gentlemen* alone.

b. Address the letter, not to the organization as a whole, but to the head of the organization—by name and title if known, otherwise by title alone. Then the salutation would appear as shown in ¶1349.

```
Mr. James V. Quillan          President
President                     (OR Chief Executive Officer)
United Services Corporation   United Services Corporation
100 Kendall Parkway           100 Kendall Parkway
Somerset, NJ 08873            Somerset, NJ 08873

Dear Mr. Quillan:             Dear Sir or Madam:
```

c. Use the name of the organization in the salutation.

```
Dear United Services Corporation:
```

NOTE: This approach is acceptable in routine or informal letters but should not be used in formal communications.

See also ¶1803c.

d. Use the simplified letter style and omit the salutation.

1351 When an attention line is used (see ¶1344), the letter is considered to be addressed to the organization rather than to the person named in the attention line. Therefore, use one of the organizational salutations shown in ¶¶1349 and 1350. (Whenever possible, omit the attention line and address the letter directly to an individual in the organization—either by name or by title.)

The following rules (¶¶1352–1357) deal with the *body* of a letter. The body contains the text of the letter —in other words, the message (see ¶¶1354–1357). The body may also begin with a subject line (see ¶¶1352–1353), which briefly identifies the main idea in the message.

Subject Line

1352 In the *simplified letter style:*

a. A subject line is used in place of the salutation.

b. Start the subject line on the third line below the inside address. Begin at the left margin and type the subject line in all-capital letters.

c. Do not use a term like *Subject:* to introduce the subject line. (See the illustration on page 305.)

1353 In *other letter styles:*

a. The subject line (if used) appears between the salutation and the body of the letter, with 1 blank line above and below. (See the illustration on page 304.)

b. Ordinarily, the subject line starts at the left margin, but it may be centered for special emphasis. In a letter with indented paragraphs, the subject line may also be indented the same number of spaces.

c. Type the subject line either in capital and small letters or in all-capital letters. The subject line is customarily typed without underscoring, but for special emphasis the complete subject line may be underscored.

(Continued on page 324.)

The term *Subject:* or *In re:* or *Re:* usually precedes the actual subject but may be omitted.

```
Subject:  Introductory Offer to        SUBJECT:  MORAN LEASE
New Subscribers and Renewal Offer
to Present Subscribers                  In re:  Moran Lease
```

NOTE: If the subject line is long, type it in two or more single-spaced lines of roughly equal length.

d. When replying to a letter that carries a "refer to" notation, you may put the desired reference number or filing code in a subject line or below the date line. (See ¶1316.)

```
Refer to:  Policy 668485
```

13 Message

1354 Begin the text of the letter—the message—on the second line below the subject line, if used, or on the second line below the salutation.

1355 Use single spacing, and leave 1 blank line between paragraphs. (Very short letters may be double-spaced or lengthened by means of other techniques. See ¶1307.)

1356 a. Ordinarily, start each paragraph at the left margin. However, indent the first line of each paragraph 5 spaces if:

(1) You are using the modified-block style with indented paragraphs. (See the illustration on page 303.)

(2) You are typing the body of the letter double-spaced.

NOTE: Some writers indent more than 5 spaces for special effect.

b. If a letter takes two or more pages, do not divide a short paragraph (with only two or three lines) at the bottom of a page. Always leave at least two lines of the paragraph at the foot of one page and carry over at least two lines to the top of the next page. (See ¶¶1382–1387.)

NOTE: Some software programs have a feature that prevents the creation of *orphans* (printing the first line of a new paragraph as the last line on a page) and *widows* (printing the last line of a paragraph as the first line of a new page).

See the entries on orphan adjust *and* widow adjust *in Section 20.*

1357 a. **Quoted Material.** If a quotation will make four or more printed lines, type it as a single-spaced extract. Indent the extract 5 spaces from each side margin, and leave 1 blank line above and below the extract. (See page 304 for an illustration.) If the quoted matter represents the start of an indented paragraph in the original, indent the first word an additional 5 spaces.

For different ways of handling a long quotation, see ¶265.

b. **Tables.** When a table occurs in the text of a letter, center it between the left and right margins. Try to indent the table at least 5 spaces from each side margin. (If the table is very wide, reduce the normal 6 spaces between columns to as few as 2 spaces to prevent the table from extending beyond the width of the text.) Leave 1 to 3 blank lines above and below the table to set it off from the rest of the text. (See Section 16 for a full discussion on how to plan and execute tables.)

c. **Items in a List.** Type the list single-spaced with one blank line above and below the list as a whole. Either type the list on the full width of the letter (see the second illustration below), or indent the list 5 spaces from each side margin (see the first illustration below). If any item in the list requires more than one line, leave a blank line between all items in the list; moreover, align any turnovers with the first word in the line above.

```
When your analysis is ready to be distributed for the first
round of comments, I suggest you send it to the following
people inside the company:
                                2

     Angela Lawless, director of information systems
     Thomas Podgorski, manager of corporate planning
     Herschel Farmer, vice president of finance
                                            2
In addition, you may want to get reactions from two trust-
worthy consultants we have called on in the past:
                                                  2

     Dr. Harriet E. Fenster, professor of computer
     science at Michigan State University
                                          2

     Wilson G. Witherspoon, president of Witherspoon
     Associates in Princeton, New Jersey
                                         2
I can give you mailing addresses for these consultants if you
decide to get in touch with them.
```

d. **Enumerated Items in a List.** If the items each begin with a number or letter, insert a period after the number or letter and leave 2 spaces before starting the text that follows. Align the numbers or letters on the period. If an item requires more than one line, indent any turnover so that it aligns with the first word in the line above.

```
When I review the situation as you described it in your letter
of June 24, it seems to me that you have only two alternatives:
                                                                2
 1.  Agree to pay the additional amount that Henning now demands
     before he will start construction.
                                        2
 2.  Drop Henning and start the search all over again to find a
     firm qualified to handle a project of this size and this
     complexity.
                 2
As painful as it may be, you may find it easier to start looking
for a new contractor than to have to deal with new demands from
Henning once he is a quarter of the way through the job.
```

(Continued on page 326.)

NOTE: Ordinarily, an enumerated list may be typed to the full width of the letter or indented 5 spaces from each side margin. However, if the first line of each text paragraph is indented 5 spaces, then for better appearance indent the enumerated list as well.

Preferred Style	Avoid

```
 When I review the situation as        When I review the situation as
letter of June 24, it seems to me t   letter of June 24, it seems to me t

 1.  Agree to pay the additiona        1.  Agree to pay the additional amo
     demands before he will sta            before he will start constructi

 2.  Drop Henning and start the        2.  Drop Henning and start the sear
     find a firm qualified to h            firm qualified to handle a proj
     and this complexity.                  complexity.

 As painful as it may be, you m        As painful as it may be, you m
looking for a new contractor than t   looking for a new contractor than t
mands from Henning once he is a qua   mands from Henning once he is a qua
```

The following rules (¶¶1358–1381) deal with the *closing* of a letter. The closing typically includes a complimentary-closing phrase (¶¶1358–1360), the writer's name and title (¶¶1362–1369), and reference initials (¶¶1370–1372). It may also include a company signature line (¶1361), an enclosure notation (¶¶1373–1374), a delivery notation (¶1375), a copy notation (¶¶1376–1380), and a postscript (¶1381).

Complimentary Closing

1358 Type the complimentary closing on the second line below the last line of the body of the letter. Ordinarily, start the closing at center. In a block-style letter, start the closing at the left margin. In a simplified letter, omit the closing. (See the illustrations on pages 302–305.)

1359 Capitalize only the first word of a complimentary closing. Place a comma at the end of the line (except when open punctuation is used).

1360 a. The following complimentary closings are commonly used:

PERSONAL IN TONE:	Sincerely,	Sincerely yours,
	Cordially,	Cordially yours,
MORE FORMAL IN TONE:	Very truly yours,	Very cordially yours,
	Very sincerely yours,	Respectfully yours,

b. An informal closing phrase may be inserted in place of one of the more conventional closings shown above. If the wording is an adverbial phrase (one that tells *how* or *in what manner*—for example, *With all best wishes* or *With warmest regards*), follow the closing with a comma. If the wording is a complete sentence (for example, *See you in New Orleans*), follow the closing with a period. In each case the comma or the period may be replaced with stronger punctuation as appropriate—that is, a question mark, an exclamation point, or a dash.

c. If both a complimentary closing and an informal closing phrase are used, type the complimentary closing in its regular position, and (1) type the informal phrase at the end of the last paragraph or (2) treat it as the final paragraph with the appropriate terminal punctuation.

d. Once a pattern of personal or informal closings is begun, it should not be discontinued without good reason. Otherwise, if a later letter returns to a more formal closing, the person who receives the letter may wonder what has happened to the established relationship. (See also ¶1349b.)

Company Signature

1361 A company signature may be used to emphasize the fact that a letter represents the views of the company as a whole (and not merely the individual who has written it). If included, the company signature should be typed in all capitals on the second line below the complimentary closing. Begin the company signature at the same point as the complimentary closing. (See the illustration on page 302.)

```
Very truly yours, ↓2

HASKINS & COHEN INC.
```

Writer's Name and Title

1362 **a.** Ordinarily, type the writer's name on the fourth line below the company signature, if used, or on the fourth line below the complimentary closing. (See the illustrations on pages 302–305.)

NOTE: If the letter is running short, you can leave up to 6 blank lines for the signature. If the letter is running long, you can reduce the signature space to 2 blank lines. (See also ¶¶1307–1308.)

b. Start typing at the same point as the company signature or the complimentary closing.

NOTE: In the simplified letter style, type the writer's name and title on the *fifth* line below the body, in all-capital letters starting at the left margin. (See ¶1363.)

c. Although some writers prefer to give only their title and department name in the signature block, a typewritten signature should also be included so that the unsigned copies will clearly show who sent the letter. If the writer prefers to omit his or her name from the signature block, then it should be spelled out in the reference initials. (See ¶1370a, d.)

d. Top-level executives usually have special stationery with their name and title imprinted along with other elements of the letterhead. When using this type of stationery, supply a typewritten signature but omit the title.

1363 Arrange the writer's name, title, and department on two or more lines to achieve good visual balance. If a title takes more than one line, align all turnovers at the left.

```
Janice Mahoney, Manager          Ernest L. Welhoelter
Data Processing Division         Head, Sales Department

Charles Saunders                 Franklin Browning
Assistant Manager                Vice President and
Credit Department                General Manager
```

```
CHARLES SAUNDERS — ASSISTANT MANAGER, CREDIT DEPARTMENT
(simplified style)
```

For guidance on capitalizing in signature blocks, see ¶1325a.

1364 A person who has a special title should observe the following guidelines in the signature block.

    a. A person who wants to be addressed as *Dr.* should use an appropriate academic degree after his or her name (not *Dr.* before it).

Jane Bishop, M.D.
Charles Burgos, D.D.S.
Lee Toniolo, D.O.

Nancy Buckwalter, Ph.D.
Morris Finley, D.D.
Henry Krawitz, D.H.L.

    b. A person who wishes to be addressed by a title of academic or military rank *(Dean, Professor, Major)* should type this title *after* the name or on the next line, not before it.

Helene C. Powell
Dean of Students

Joseph F. Corey
Major, USAF

(**NOT:** Dean Helene C. Powell)   (**NOT:** Major Joseph F. Corey)

    c. When a title of address cannot be placed after a surname or cannot be inferred from the initials of an academic degree, then it may precede the name.

Rev. Joseph W. Dowd   Mother Ellen Marie O'Brien

1365 Ordinarily, a man should not include *Mr.* in his signature. However, if he has a name that could also be a woman's name *(Kay, Adrian, Beverly, Lynn)* or if he uses initials in place of a first and middle name *(J. G. Eberle)*, he should use *Mr.* in either his handwritten or his typewritten signature when writing to people who do not know him. If given in the handwritten signature, *Mr.* should be enclosed in parentheses. If given in the typewritten signature, *Mr.* should appear without parentheses.

Sincerely,   Sincerely,

(Mr.) Lynn Treadway   *Lynn Treadway*

Lynn Treadway   Mr. Lynn Treadway

1366 A woman should include a courtesy title *(Ms., Miss,* or *Mrs.)* in her signature unless she is called by a special title (see ¶1364). If she gives her name without any title at all, the reader of the letter is put in the awkward position of having to decide which title to use in a letter of reply.

NOTE: The courtesy title is enclosed in parentheses in the handwritten signature but not in the typewritten signature.

    a. A woman who does not want to indicate whether she is married or single should use *Ms.* in either her handwritten or her typewritten signature.

Sincerely yours,   Sincerely yours,

(Ms.) Constance G. Booth   *Constance G. Booth*

Constance G. Booth   Ms. Constance G. Booth

    b. A single woman who wants to indicate that she is a single woman should include *Miss* in her handwritten or her typewritten signature (but not both).

Cordially,

(Miss) Margaret L. Galloway

Margaret L. Galloway

Cordially,

Margaret L. Galloway

Miss Margaret L. Galloway

c. A married woman who retains her original name for career purposes or who does not change her surname at all may use either *Ms.* or *Miss,* as illustrated in ¶1366a–b.

d. A married woman or a widow who prefers to be addressed as *Mrs.* has many variations to choose from. The following examples show the possible styles for a woman whose maiden name was Nancy O. Ross and whose husband's name is (or was) John A. Wells.

Cordially yours,

(Mrs.) Nancy O. Wells

Nancy O. Wells

Cordially yours,

Nancy O. Wells

Mrs. Nancy O. Wells

Cordially yours,

(Mrs.) Nancy R. Wells

Nancy R. Wells

Cordially yours,

Nancy R. Wells

Mrs. Nancy R. Wells

Cordially yours,

(Mrs.) Nancy Ross Wells

Nancy Ross Wells

Cordially yours,

Nancy Ross Wells

Mrs. Nancy Ross Wells

Cordially yours,

(Mrs.) Nancy O. Ross-Wells

Nancy O. Ross-Wells

Cordially yours,

Nancy O. Ross-Wells

Mrs. Nancy O. Ross-Wells

NOTE: Giving the husband's full name in the typewritten signature (as in the example below) is a style often used for social purposes. It should not be used in business, and it should not be used when a married woman becomes a widow unless she indicates that that is her preference.

Cordially yours,

Nancy O. Wells

Mrs. John A. Wells

e. A divorced woman who has resumed her maiden name may use *Ms.* or *Miss* in any of the styles shown in ¶1366a–b. If she retains her ex-husband's surname, she may use *Ms.* or *Mrs.* in any of the styles shown in ¶1366a and d. (**EXCEPTION:** The style that uses the husband's full name in the typewritten signature is not appropriate for a divorcée.)

13

1367 A secretary who signs a letter at the boss's request customarily signs the boss's name and adds his or her initials. However, if the boss prefers, the secretary may sign the letter in his or her own name.

Sincerely yours,

Robert H. Benedict
DK

Robert H. Benedict
Production Manager

Sincerely yours,

Dorothy Kozinski

Ms. Dorothy Kozinski
Secretary to Mr. Benedict

1368 If the person who signs for another is not the secretary, either of the following forms may be used:

Sincerely yours,

(Miss) Alice R. Brentano

For Robert H. Benedict
Production Manager

Sincerely yours,

Robert H. Benedict
ARB

Robert H. Benedict
Production Manager

1369 When two people have to sign a letter, arrange the two signature blocks side by side or one beneath the other.

a. If they are placed side by side, start the first signature block at the left margin and the second block at center. If this arrangement is used, the complimentary closing should also begin at the left margin. (This arrangement is appropriate for all letter styles.)

b. If the signature blocks are positioned one beneath the other, start typing the second block on the fourth line below the end of the first block, aligned at the left. Ordinarily, begin typing at center; however, in a block-style or simplified letter, begin typing at the left margin.

Reference Initials

1370 a. Type the initials of the typist alone (or those of the writer and the typist) at the left margin, on the second line below the writer's name and title. If the writer's name is typed in the signature block, the writer's initials are unnecessary here. However, if the writer wants his or her initials used, they should precede the initials of the typist.

b. Type the initials either in capital letters or in small letters. When giving two sets of initials, type them both the same way for speed and simplicity. If you are using a typewriter, you can avoid shifting up or down by using a *colon* to separate two sets of all-capital initials and a *diagonal* to separate two sets of small-letter initials. If you are using electronic equipment, you can avoid shifting by putting both sets of initials in small letters and using a diagonal to separate them.

TYPIST ONLY: GDL   OR   gdl

WRITER AND TYPIST: DMD:MHS   OR   dmd/mhs

c. Include *Jr.* or *Sr.* with initials only if father and son work in the same office; for example, *EJM Jr:FWL.* (However, it would be simpler to omit the writer's initials and type the writer's full name in the signature block.)

For initials with names like McFarland *and* O'Leary, *see* ¶516c.

d. If the writer's name is not given in the signature block, type the writer's initials and surname before the initials of the typist; for example, *BSDixon/rp.*

NOTE: When the writer's name is given in the signature block, the simplest and most unobtrusive way to provide the necessary information is to give the typist's initials alone in small letters. (See the illustrations on pages 302, 304, and 305.)

1371 When the letter is written by someone other than the person who signs it, this fact may be indicated by showing the writer's and the typist's initials (not the signer's and the typist's).

```
                              Sincerely yours,  ↓4

                              Herbert Heymann

                              Herbert Heymann
                              President  ↓2
         pbr/jbp
```

13

1372 Do not include reference initials in a personal-business letter (see ¶1313 and the illustration on page 303) or a social-business letter (see ¶¶1394–1395 and the illustration on page 347).

Enclosure Notation

1373 **a.** If one or more items are to be included in the envelope with the letter, indicate that fact by typing the word *Enclosure* (or an appropriate alternative) at the left margin, on the line below the reference initials.

NOTE: Before sending the letter, make sure that the number of enclosures shown in the enclosure notation agrees with (1) the number cited in the body of the letter and (2) with the number of items actually enclosed.

b. The following styles are commonly used:

```
Enclosure              2 Enclosures          Enclosures:
Enc.                   2 Enc.                1.  Check for $500
1 Enc.                 Enclosures 2          2.  Invoice A37512
1 Enclosure            Enclosures (2)
Check enclosed         Enc. 2  (see ¶503)
```

c. Some writers use the term *Attachment* or *Att.*

1374 If material is to be sent separately instead of being enclosed with the letter, indicate this fact by typing *Separate cover* or *Under separate cover* on the line below the enclosure notation (if any) or on the line directly below the reference initials. The following styles may be used:

```
Separate cover 1       Under separate cover:
                       1.  Annual report
                       2.  Product catalog
                       3.  Price list
```

Delivery Notation

1375 a. If a letter is to be delivered in a special way (other than ordinary first-class mail), type an appropriate notation on the line below the enclosure notation (if used) or on the line below the reference initials. Among the notations that could be used are *By certified mail, By Express Mail, By fax, By Federal Express* (**OR** *FedEx*), *By messenger, By registered mail,* and *By special delivery.*

```
crj                     HWM:FH                   tpg/wwc
Enc. 2                  By Federal Express       Enclosures 4
By certified mail       cc Mr. Fry               By messenger
```

b. When a letter is first faxed to the addressee and then sent through the mail as a confirmation copy, it is helpful to provide a "confirmation" notation on the letter being mailed so that the addressee will realize at once that the document now in hand is not a new letter but simply a duplicate of the fax. Type the confirmation notation on the second line below the date line or on the second line below any notation that follows the date (see ¶¶1315–1316). Starting at the left margin, type *Confirmation of fax sent on* and then supply the date on which the fax was transmitted.

Copy Notation

1376 a. A copy notation lets the addressee know that one or more persons will also be sent a copy of the letter. The initals *cc* are still the most commonly used device for introducing this notation. Although the abbreviation originally stood for *carbon copies, cc* also means *copies* (in the same way that *pp.* means *pages* and *ll.* means *lines*). Some writers object to using *cc,* especially now that the widespread use of photocopying has made the use of carbons virtually obsolete when it comes to preparing duplicates of letters and memos. However, *cc* and its related form *bcc* (see ¶1378) continue to be widely used (regardless of how the copies are made), in much the same way that a *dial tone* continues to be heard on telephone instruments that use buttons rather than a rotary dial.

NOTE: Writers looking for an alternative to *cc* may use a single *c* or the phrase *Copies to:* (**OR** *Copy to:*).

b. Type *cc* or *c* at the left margin, on the line below the mailing notation, the enclosure notation, or the reference initials, whichever comes last. If several persons are to receive copies, list the names according to the rank of the persons or in alphabetic order.

```
AMH:HT          mfn                  lbw/ncy
Enclosure       Enc. 4               cc:  Contract File
Registered      c Mrs. A. C. Case         Houston Office
cc Ms. Hoey       Mr. R. G. Flynn         Sales Department
```

c. Type the initials *cc* or *c* with or without a colon following. When there are two or more names to be listed, type *cc* or *c* only with the first name. Align all the other names with the start of the first name.

```
cc:  Ms. Abernathy    OR    cc Ms. Abernathy
     Mrs. Bernardo            Mrs. Bernardo
     Mr. Cohen               Mr. Cohen
```

1377 When first names or initials are given along with last names, personal titles *(Mr., Miss, Mrs., and Ms.)* may be omitted except in formal letters. Moreover, do not use personal titles if nicknames are given with last names.

```
c:  James Diaz        cc:  J. Diaz       cc  Jim Diaz
    Kenneth Eustis         K. Eustis         Ken Eustis
    Margaret Falmouth      M. Falmouth       Peggy Falmouth
    Katherine Gabor        K. Gabor          Kay Gabor
```

1378 If the addressee is not intended to know that one or more persons are also being sent a copy of the letter, use a *blind copy notation*. First remove the original letter and any copies on which the *bcc* notation is not to appear. Then on each of the remaining copies, type a *bcc* notation in the upper left corner (starting at the left margin on the seventh line from the top). As an alternative, type the *bcc* notation on the second line below the last item in the letter (whether reference initials, an enclosure notation, a mailing notation, a *cc* notation, or a postscript). The file copy should show all the *bcc* notations, even though the individual copies do not.

NOTE: The form of a blind copy notation should follow the form of the copy notation. If you have used *cc* or *c,* then use *bcc* or *bc* accordingly. If you have used *Copies to:* for the copy notation, use *Blind copies to:* for a blind copy notation.

1379 When a letter carries both an enclosure notation and a copy notation, it is assumed that the enclosures accompany only the original letter. If a copy of the enclosures is also to accompany a copy of the letter, this fact may be indicated as follows:

```
cc:     Mr. D. R. Wellak  (received only the letter)
        Ms. N. A. Warren  (received only the letter)
cc/enc: Mr. J. Baldwin    (received the letter and the enclosures)
        Mrs. G. Conger    (received the letter and the enclosures)
```

1380 A copy is not usually signed unless the letter is addressed to several people and the copy is intended for one of the people named in the salutation. However, a check mark is usually made on each copy next to the name of the person or department for whom that copy is intended.

```
c:  Ms. A. M. Starr✓   c:  Ms. A. M. Starr✓   c:  Ms. A. M. Starr
    Mr. H. W. Fried         Mr. H. W. Fried✓        Mr. H. W. Fried
    Mrs. C. Quigley         Mrs. C. Quigley         Mrs. C. Quigley✓
```

NOTE: When an unsigned copy is likely to strike the recipient as cold and impersonal, it is appropriate for the writer to add a brief handwritten note at the bottom of the copy and sign or initial it.

Postscript

1381 **a.** A postscript can be effectively used to express an idea that has been deliberately withheld from the body of a letter; stating this idea at the very end gives it strong emphasis. A postscript may also be used to express an afterthought; however, if the afterthought contains something central to the meaning of the letter, the reader may conclude that the letter was badly organized.

(Continued on page 334.)

b. When a postscript is used:

(1) Start the postscript on the second line below the copy notation (or whatever was typed last). If the paragraphs are indented, indent the first line of the postscript (see page 303); otherwise, begin it at the left margin.

(2) Type *PS:* or *PS.* before the first word of the postscript, or omit the abbreviation altogether. (If *PS* is used, leave 2 spaces between the colon or period and the first word.)

(3) Use *PPS:* or *PPS.* (or no abbreviation at all) at the beginning of an additional postscript, and treat this postscript as a separate paragraph.

```
PS:  Instead of dashing for the airport as soon as the meeting
is over, why don't you have dinner and spend the night with us
and then go back on Saturday morning?

PPS: Better yet, why don't you bring Joyce with you and plan
to stay for the whole weekend?
```

Continuation Pages

1382 Use plain paper of the same quality as the letterhead (but never a letterhead) for all but the first page of a long letter.

1383 Use the same left and right margins that you used on the first page.

1384 On the seventh line from the top of the page, type a continuation-page heading consisting of the following: the name of the addressee, the page number, and the date. Either of the following styles is acceptable:

```
    ↓7
    Mrs. Laura R. Austin        2              September 30, 1993
                                                                 ↓3
    ↓7
OR  Mrs. Laura R. Austin
    Page 2
    September 30, 1993
```

1385 a. Leave 2 blank lines below the last line of the continuation-page heading and resume typing the letter. (If you are using the header feature of a software program, only 1 blank line will be left between the continuation-page heading and the text of the letter.)

b. Do not divide a short paragraph (one that contains only two or three lines) at the bottom of a page. For a paragraph of four or more lines, always leave at least two lines of the paragraph at the bottom of the previous page. Carry over at least two lines to the continuation page. (See also ¶1356b.)

c. Never use a continuation page just for the closing section of a business letter. (The complimentary closing should always be preceded by at least two lines of the message.)

1386 Try to leave a uniform margin of 6 to 12 lines at the foot of each page of a letter (except the last page, which may run short).

1387 Do not divide the last word on a page.

Addressing Envelopes

1388 The following table indicates which envelopes may be used, depending on the size of the stationery and the way in which the stationery is folded (see ¶1391).

Stationery	Fold	Envelope
Standard (8½″ × 11″)	In thirds	No. 10 (9½″ × 4⅛″)
	In half, then in thirds	No. 6¾ (6½″ × 3⅝″)
Monarch (7¼″ × 10½″)	In thirds	No. 7 (7½″ × 3⅞″)
Baronial (5½″ × 8½″)	In thirds	No. 6¾ (6½″ × 3⅝″)
	In half	No. 5⅜ (5¹⁵⁄₁₆″ × 4⅝″)

NOTE: If you are using stationery and envelopes other than those shown above, keep in mind the Postal Service's standards for envelope size and thickness in order to qualify for automated processing:

Minimum size: 3½″ × 5″   Minimum thickness: ⁷⁄₁₀₀₀″
Maximum size: 6⅛″ × 10½″   Maximum thickness: ³⁄₁₆″

1389 Typing an Address

When typing an address on an envelope:

a. Always use single spacing, and block each line at the left.

See the examples on page 337. For specific details on the handling of elements within the address block, see ¶¶1317–1343.

b. Capitalize the first letter of every word in an address except (1) prepositions under four letters (like *of* and *for*), (2) conjunctions under four letters (like *and*), and (3) the articles *the, a,* and *an* when they are used within a name or title. (Under certain circumstances even some of these short words are capitalized. See ¶¶1325a, 1329e.)

NOTE: The U.S. Postal Service has issued many brochures indicating that the use of all-capital letters "is preferred but not required" and that punctuation (such as periods with abbreviations and the comma between city and state) is not needed. Keep in mind that this style was devised primarily for the benefit of high-volume mailers, who must contend with space limitations for the address blocks they generate by computer or other automated equipment. (See ¶1390.) The traditional style (which uses capital and small letters plus punctuation as appropriate) is the style still universally seen on envelopes that are individually typed. Moreover, the Postal Service's OCRs (optical character readers) are programmed to read the traditional style of address as well as the all-cap style.

c. Type the city, state, and ZIP Code on the last line. If space limitations make it impossible for the ZIP Code to fit on the same line, the ZIP Code may be typed on the line directly below, blocked at the left.

d. Leave 1 space between the state name and the ZIP Code. (The U.S. Postal Service recommends either 1 or 2 spaces.)

e. The state name may be spelled out or given as a two-letter abbreviation. The OCRs can read both forms. (See ¶1341.)

(Continued on page 336.)

f. The next-to-last line in the address block should contain a street address or post office box number. (See ¶1338c.)

```
Elvera Agresta, M.D.              Mr. Christopher Schreiber
218 Oregon Pioneer's Building     Director of Manufacturing
320 Southwest Stark Street        Colby Electronics Inc.
Portland, Oregon 97204-2628       P.O. Box 6524
                                  Raleigh, NC 27628
```

g. When using a large envelope (No. 10), start the address on line 14 about 4 inches (40 spaces in 10-pitch or pica type, 48 spaces in 12-pitch or elite type) from the left edge. When using a small envelope (No. 7, 6¾, or 5⅜) or a postcard, start the address on line 13 about 2½ inches (25 spaces in 10-pitch or pica type, 30 spaces in 12-pitch or elite type) from the left edge.

NOTE: For OCR processing there should be a minimum margin of 1 inch at the left and right of the mailing address block. Therefore, decrease the left margins given above (4 inches for large envelopes, 2½ inches for small) if necessary to keep extremely wide address blocks from intruding into the 1-inch right margin.

h. When using a window envelope, position the address block on the material to be inserted so that there will be a minimum clearance of ⅛ inch (and preferably ¼ inch) between the edges of the window and all four sides of the address block, no matter how much the inserted material shifts around inside the envelope. (See also ¶1391d.)

i. To facilitate OCR processing under any circumstances, make sure that the mailing address starts no higher than 2¾ inches from the bottom edge, falls no lower than ⅝ inch from the bottom edge, and comes no closer to the left or the right edge than 1 inch. Do not allow any notations or graphics to fall alongside or below the area established for the mailing address. Moreover, make sure that the lines in the address block are parallel to the bottom edge of the envelope and that there is good contrast between the typed address and the color of the envelope. In addition, do not use a script or italic typeface, and avoid dot matrix print, especially if the dots that make up each character do not touch. The type should be clear and sharp, and adjacent characters should not touch or overlap.

j. When the envelope contains a printed return address for a company or an organization, type the name of the writer on the line above the return address. If all the lines in the printed return address are blocked at the left, align the writer's name at the left (as in the second illustration on page 337). However, if all the lines in the printed return address are centered on the longest line, center the writer's name accordingly.

NOTE: With some types of electronic equipment, it may not be feasible to insert the writer's name over the printed address. In such cases you may have to resort to using a typewriter, writing the name in by hand, or omitting the name altogether.

k. If a printed return address does not appear on the envelope, type a return address in the upper left corner, beginning on line 3 about a half inch in from the left edge. The return address should contain the

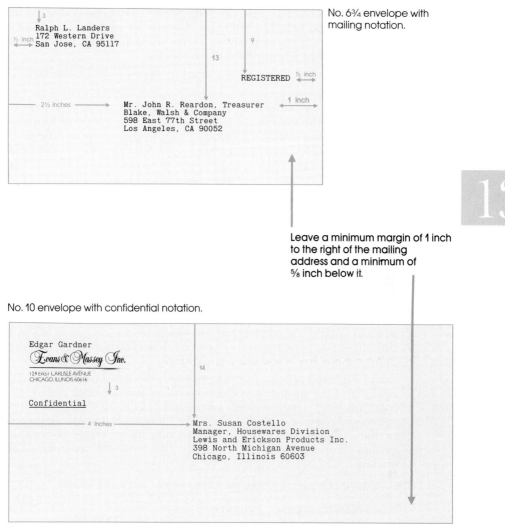

No. 6¾ envelope with mailing notation.

Ralph L. Landers
172 Western Drive
San Jose, CA 95117

REGISTERED

Mr. John R. Reardon, Treasurer
Blake, Walsh & Company
598 East 77th Street
Los Angeles, CA 90052

Leave a minimum margin of 1 inch to the right of the mailing address and a minimum of ⅝ inch below it.

No. 10 envelope with confidential notation.

Edgar Gardner
Evans & Massey Inc.
129 EAST CARLISLE AVENUE
CHICAGO, ILLINOIS 60616

Confidential

Mrs. Susan Costello
Manager, Housewares Division
Lewis and Erickson Products Inc.
398 North Michigan Avenue
Chicago, Illinois 60603

following information, arranged on separate lines: (1) the name of the writer; (2) the name of the company (if appropriate); (3) a street address or post office box number; and (4) the city, state, and ZIP Code. (See the first illustration above.)

1. A notation such as *Personal, Confidential, Please Forward,* or *Hold for Arrival* goes below the return address. It should begin on line 9 or on the third line below the return address, whichever is lower. Begin each main word with a capital letter, and use underscoring. The notation should align at the left with the return address.

NOTE: Do not allow any notations or graphics to fall alongside or below the area established for the mailing address (see ¶1389i). Copy placed in these locations will interfere with OCR processing.

(Continued on page 338.)

m. If an attention line was used within the letter itself, it should appear on the envelope as well. The attention line may be treated exactly like a personal or confidential notation, as described in ¶1389l, or it may be typed as the first line of the address block.

See ¶1344a, note, on avoiding the use of attention lines.

n. If a special mailing procedure is used, type the appropriate notation (such as *SPECIAL DELIVERY* or *REGISTERED*) in all-capital letters in the upper right corner of the envelope. Type the notation on line 9 or on the third line below the bottom edge of the stamp, whichever is lower. Position the notation so that it ends a half inch from the right margin.

See the illustration at the top of page 337.

o. Make sure that the spelling of the name and address on the envelope agrees with the spelling shown in the inside address (and with the spelling shown on your records or the incoming document).

For letters being sent to two or more people at the same address, see ¶1320b.

1390 Preparing an Address for Imprinting

When preparing an address that will be imprinted by means of electronic equipment:

a. Keep in mind the maximum number of strokes you can get in any one line (typically, 28 keystrokes). Therefore, if necessary to save space, use abbreviations freely and omit punctuation.

NOTE: To help keep the line length down, the U.S. Postal Service has provided three special sets of abbreviations: one for state names; another for long names of cities, towns, and places; a third for names of streets and roads and general terms like *University* or *Institute*. By means of these abbreviations (see the ZIP Code directory), it is possible to limit the last line of any domestic address to 28 keystrokes. For example:

```
Pass-a-Grill Beach, Florida 33741-9999    (38 keystrokes)

12345678901234567890123456789012345678

PAS-A-GRL BCH FL 33741-9999               (27 keystrokes)
```

Abbreviations such as those shown above serve to facilitate OCR processing, but they also serve to make the address incomprehensible to all except devoted students of USPS manuals. (See also ¶1389b, note, and ¶1390b, note.)

b. Type the lines in all-capital letters, single-spaced and blocked at the left.

```
MR HENRY T MACMILLAN JR
CAMPING ENTERPRISES INC
412 HIGH ST ROOM 980
WASHINGTON DC 20017
```

NOTE: If your organization maintains its mailing lists on tapes or disks and uses these to generate inside addresses in business letters (as well as address blocks on envelopes), the all-cap, no-punctuation style designed for the envelope will look inappropriate inside the letter. In such cases use the traditional style described in ¶1389. You will then have a format that looks attractive as an inside address and that is also OCR-readable when used on an envelope. This approach is quite acceptable to the U.S. Postal Service.

c. Type the city, state, and ZIP Code on the last line. If space limitations make it impossible for the ZIP Code to fit on the same line, the ZIP Code may be typed on the line directly below, blocked at the left.

d. Leave 1 space between the state name and the ZIP Code. (The U.S. Postal Service recommends either 1 or 2 spaces.)

e. The state name is customarily given as a two-letter abbreviation.

f. The next-to-last line in the address block should contain a street address or post office box number. (See ¶1338c.)

g. If a room number, a suite number, or an apartment number is part of the address, it should appear immediately after the street address on the same line. (See examples in ¶1390b and h.) When it is impossible to fit this information on the same line as the street address, it may go on the line above but never on the line below. (See examples in ¶¶1317b, 1318b.)

h. If an attention line is to be included in the address, it should appear on the line directly above the organizational name or (in the absence of an organizational name) on the line directly above the street address or post office box number. If a serial number of some kind (for example, an account number or a file reference number) is required, enter it as the first line of the address block.

```
H 048469 1078 AT5
ATTN MRS M R TURKEVICH
BROCK & WILSON CORP
79 WALL ST SUITE 1212
NEW YORK NY 10005-4101
```

i. To facilitate OCR processing, make sure that the mailing address starts no higher than 2¾ inches from the bottom edge, falls no lower than ⅝ inch from the bottom edge, and comes no closer to either the left or the right edge than 1 inch. Do not allow any notations or graphics to fall alongside or below the area established for the mailing address. Moreover, make sure that the lines in the address block are parallel to the bottom edge of the envelope and that there is good contrast between the typed address and the color of the envelope. In addition, do not use a script or italic typeface, and avoid dot matrix print, especially if the dots that make up each character do not touch. The type should be clear and sharp. Adjacent characters should not touch or overlap.

Folding and Inserting Letters

1391 The following paragraphs describe several methods for folding letters and inserting them into envelopes. See the table in ¶1388 to determine which method is appropriate for the stationery and envelope you are using.

(Continued on page 340.)

a. To fold a letter in thirds:

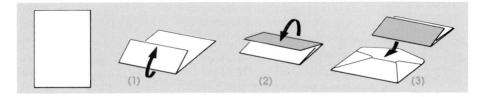

(1) Bring the bottom third of the letter up and make a crease.
(2) Fold the top of the letter down to within ⅜ inch of the crease you made in step 1. Then make the second crease.
(3) The creased edge made in step 2 goes into the envelope first.

NOTE: Use this method for 8½″ × 11″ stationery with a No. 10 envelope; 7¼″ × 10½″ stationery with a No. 7 envelope; 5½″ × 8½″ stationery with a No. 6¾ envelope. (See also ¶1388.)

b. To fold a letter in half and then in thirds:

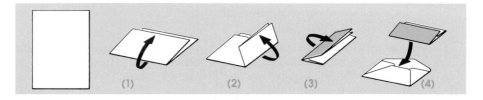

(1) Bring the bottom edge to within ⅜ inch of the top edge and make a crease.
(2) Fold from the right edge, making the fold a little less than one-third the width of the sheet before you crease it.
(3) Fold from the left edge, bringing it to within ⅜ inch of the crease you made in step 2 before you crease the sheet again.
(4) Insert the left creased edge into the envelope first. This will leave the crease you made in step 2 near the flap of the envelope.

NOTE: Use this method for 8½″ × 11″ stationery with a No. 6¾ envelope. (See also ¶1388.)

c. To fold a letter in half:

(1) Bring the bottom edge to within ⅜ inch of the top edge and make a crease.
(2) Insert the creased edge into the envelope first.

NOTE: Use this method for 5½″ × 8½″ stationery with a No. 5⅜ envelope. (See also ¶1388.)

d. To fold a letter for insertion into a window envelope:

(1) (2) (3)

13

(1) Bring the bottom third of the letter up and make a crease.

(2) Fold the top of the letter *back* to the crease you made in step 1. (The inside address should now be facing you.)

(3) Insert the letter with the inside address toward the *front* of the envelope. The inside address should now be fully readable through the window of the envelope. There should be at least ⅛ inch (and preferably ¼ inch) between all four sides of the address and the edges of the window, no matter how much the letter slides around in the envelope.

Memos

An interoffice memorandum is intended to expedite the exchange of written messages within an organization. For that reason many organizations provide printed forms that simplify and standardize the treatment of key information (such as the names of the writer and the addressee, the subject of the memo, and the date). Depending on the circumstances, a memo may be as terse as a telegram, as impersonal as a formal announcement, or as warm and casual as a personal note.

1392 When typing a memo on a *printed form:*

a. Set the left margin stop at a point 2 spaces after the longest guide word in the left half of the printed heading—for example, after *Subject* in the illustration on page 342.

NOTE: Some writers prefer to set the left margin stop at the point where the printed guide words begin. In this case it is necessary to set a tab stop 2 spaces after the longest guide word in the left half of the printed heading.

b. Set a tab stop 2 spaces after the longest guide word in the right half of the printed heading—for example, after *Floor and Ext.* (floor number and telephone extension) in the illustration on page 342.

c. Set the right margin stop so as to leave a right margin approximately equal to the left margin.

d. Insert the appropriate information after each printed guide word, using capital and small letters. The fill-ins should block at the left and align at the bottom with the printed guide words.

NOTE: If you are sending the memo to someone within your own department (or to someone elsewhere in the company with whom you have a close working relationship), you can omit the fill-ins after the guide words *Dept.* and *Floor and Ext.*

(Continued on page 342.)

13

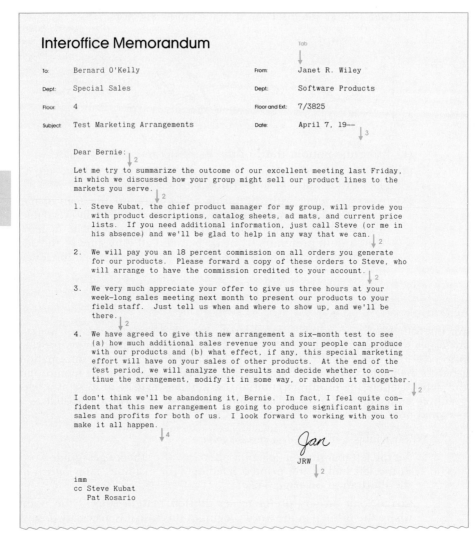

Interoffice Memorandum   Tab
↓

To: Bernard O'Kelly   From: Janet R. Wiley

Dept: Special Sales   Dept: Software Products

Floor: 4   Floor and Ext: 7/3825

Subject: Test Marketing Arrangements   Date: April 7, 19—
                                                                         ↓3

        Dear Bernie:
                    ↓2
        Let me try to summarize the outcome of our excellent meeting last Friday,
        in which we discussed how your group might sell our product lines to the
        markets you serve.
                          ↓2
        1. Steve Kubat, the chief product manager for my group, will provide you
            with product descriptions, catalog sheets, ad mats, and current price
            lists. If you need additional information, just call Steve (or me in
            his absence) and we'll be glad to help in any way that we can.
                                                                          ↓2
        2. We will pay you an 18 percent commission on all orders you generate
            for our products. Please forward a copy of these orders to Steve, who
            will arrange to have the commission credited to your account.
                                                                          ↓2
        3. We very much appreciate your offer to give us three hours at your
            week-long sales meeting next month to present our products to your
            field staff. Just tell us when and where to show up, and we'll be
            there.
                  ↓2
        4. We have agreed to give this new arrangement a six-month test to see
            (a) how much additional sales revenue you and your people can produce
            with our products and (b) what effect, if any, this special marketing
            effort will have on your sales of other products. At the end of the
            test period, we will analyze the results and decide whether to con-
            tinue the arrangement, modify it in some way, or abandon it altogether.
                                                                               ↓2
        I don't think we'll be abandoning it, Bernie. In fact, I feel quite con-
        fident that this new arrangement is going to produce significant gains in
        sales and profits for both of us. I look forward to working with you to
        make it all happen.
                           ↓4
                                                         Jan
                                                         JRW
                                                            ↓2
        imm
        cc Steve Kubat
           Pat Rosario

e. After the guide words *To* and *From,* the names of the addressee and the writer are usually given without personal titles *(Mr., Miss, Mrs., Ms.).* Indeed, when you are doing a memo to someone within your immediate unit, the use of initials or simply a first name may suffice. In short, the way you treat these names will depend on the relative formality or informality of the occasion.

f. If the memo is being sent to more than one person in another department, it may be possible to fit two or three names in the space following *To.*

To:	Hal Parker, Meryl Crawford, Mike Monagle	From:
Dept:	Profit Planning	**Dept:**

g. If fill-ins are omitted following such guide words as *Dept.* and *Floor* because the memo is going to two or more people in different departments and on different floors, you may list the names of the addressees vertically as long as you leave at least 1 blank line before the next fill-in.

```
To:       Louise Landes
          Fred Mendoza
Dept.:    Jim Norton
          Ruth O'Hare
Floor:.   Neil Sundstrom


Subject:  Revised Overhead Rates
```

h. If it is not possible to fit the names of the addressees in the heading of the memo, then after the guide word *To,* type *Distribution* or *See distribution below* or something similar (see the illustration on page 344). Then on the third line below the reference initials or the enclosure notation (whichever comes last), type <u>*Distribution*</u>. Use capital and small letters, followed by a colon, and underscore the word (but not the colon) for emphasis. Leave 1 blank line, and then list the names of the individuals who are to receive a copy of the memo. Arrange the names either by rank or in alphabetic order, and type them blocked at the left margin. (If space is tight, the names may be arranged in two or more columns.)

NOTE: For purposes of actual distribution, simply place a check mark next to one of the listed names to indicate who is to receive that particular copy.

i. If the fill-in after the guide word *Subject:* is long, type it in two or more single-spaced lines of roughly equal length. Align all turnover lines with the start of the first line of the fill-in. (For illustrations, see ¶1353c, page 359, and page 441.)

j. Begin typing the body of the memo on the third line below the last fill-in line in the heading.

NOTE: An interoffice memo ordinarily does not require a salutation, especially if the memo is an impersonal announcement being sent to a number of people or the staff at large (like the illustration on page 344). However, when a memo is directed to one person (like the illustration on page 342), many writers use a salutation—such as *Dear Andy:* or *Andy:* alone—to keep the memo from seeming cold or impersonal. (If a salutation is used, begin typing the body of the memo on the second line below.)

k. Use single spacing, and either block or indent the paragraphs. Leave 1 blank line between paragraphs.

l. Type the writer's name or initials on the second line below the last line of the message, beginning at the tab stop you set in accordance with ¶1392b.

NOTE: Although memos do not require a signature, many writers prefer to sign or initial their memos. In such cases type the writer's name or initials on the *fourth* line below the end of the message.

m. Type the reference initials (see ¶1370–1371) on the second line below the writer's name, initials, or title; block them at the left margin.

(Continued on page 344.)

13

Interoffice Memorandum   Tab ↓

To: Distribution   From: Stanley W. Venner

Dept: Dept: Accounting

Floor: Floor and Ext: 3 – x2291

Subject: Car Rentals   Date: May 10, 19— ↓3

We have just been informed that car rental rates will be increased by \$1 to \$2 a day, effective July 1. ↓2

This daily rate increase can be more than offset if you refill the gasoline tank before returning your rental car to the local agency. According to our latest information, the car rental companies are charging an average of 32 percent more per gallon than gas stations in the same area. Therefore, you can help us achieve substantial savings and keep expenses down by remembering to fill up the gas tank before turning your rental car in. ↓2

                                          SWV ↓2

jmb ↓3

Distribution: ↓2

G. Bonardi
D. Catlin
S. Folger
✓V. Jellinek
E. Kasendorf
P. Legrande
T. Pacheco
F. Sullivan
J. Trotter
W. Zysk

n. Type an enclosure notation, if needed, on the line below the reference initials, beginning at the left margin. (See ¶1373.)

o. Type a copy notation, if needed, on the line below the enclosure notation, if used, or on the line below the reference initials. (See the illustration at the top of page 342.) As an alternative, place the copy notation in the heading, 1 line below and aligned with the name of the person(s) to whom the memo is addressed. Use the same style for the copy notation as in a letter. (See ¶¶1376–1380.) If the addressee of the memo is not intended to know that a copy of the memo is being sent to one or more other persons, use a blind copy notation. (See ¶1378.)

p. If the memo is of a confidential nature, type the word *CONFIDENTIAL* in all-capital letters (and underscored for special emphasis), centered on the third line below the heading. Begin typing the body of the memo on the third line below the confidential notation.

↓3   ↓3

CONFIDENTIAL ↓3 OR C O N F I D E N T I A L ↓3

q. If the memo continues beyond the first page, type a continuation heading on a fresh sheet of paper. (Use the same style as shown in ¶1384 for a letter.) Then continue typing the message on the third line below the last line of the continuation-page heading. (See ¶1385 for additional details on continuing the message from one page to another.)

1393 When typing a memo on *plain paper* or *letterhead stationery:*

a. Set 1-inch side margins for a 6½-inch line. (See ¶1305b.)

b. *On plain paper,* ordinarily begin typing the heading of the memo on line 13 (2 inches from the top of the page). However, to fit more copy on the page (and avoid the need for a continuation page), you can reduce the top margin to 1 inch and begin typing on line 7. *On letterhead stationery,* begin typing on the third line below the letterhead.

c. The heading of the memo should include the following guide words—*MEMO TO, FROM, DATE, SUBJECT,* plus any others you wish to add. Start typing the guide words at the left margin, and use double spacing. Type the guide words in all-capital letters, and follow each with a colon.

d. Set a tab stop 10 spaces in from the left margin. In this way the entries following the guide words will all block at the left and will clear the longest guide words (*MEMO TO:* and *SUBJECT:*) by 2 spaces. (If you add longer guide words to the heading, you will have to adjust the tab setting as necessary.)

13

Tab 10

↓13

MEMO TO: Joanne Malik, Forrest Talbot, Lee Wriston ↓2

FROM: Sally Klein ↓2

DATE: February 9, 19— ↓2

SUBJECT: Convention Invitation ↓3

We have just been invited to make a one-hour presentation on catalog marketing at the annual convention of the International Marketing Institute. The convention will be held on November 12–15 at the Camelback Inn in Scottsdale, Arizona. I don't have all the details we need in order to start planning the presentation, but I would like you to block out these dates on your calendar now so as to avoid any schedule conflicts later on. ↓2

This invitation represents an excellent opportunity for us to show the profession some of the exciting things we have done in the past few years, and it could bring us a number of new clients next year. Let's give it our best shot. ↓2

As soon as I receive more information from the program coordinator, I'll set up a luncheon at which we can decide how best to proceed. ↓2

SK ↓2

jam

(Continued on page 346.)

e. Begin typing the rest of the memo on the third line below the final guide word, starting at the left margin.

f. Type the writer's name or initials on the second line below the last line of the message, beginning at center. (Some writers prefer to omit this element.)

For other guidelines to observe when typing the memo, see ¶1392d–q.

NOTE: There is no one correct format for memos typed on plain paper or letterhead. The format illustrated on page 345 has the advantage of being easy and quick to execute. Some writers prefer to use the two-column arrangement for guide words that is commonly found on printed memo forms (like the one illustrated on page 344); indeed, with a computer and the appropriate software, one can execute a heading design that looks professionally done. In any event, the memo format can and should be modified to fit the needs of your organization.

Social-Business Correspondence

1394 The term *social-business correspondence* applies to the following types of letters:

a. Executive correspondence addressed to high-level executives, officials, and dignitaries. Unlike ordinary business correspondence (which deals with sales, production, finance, advertising, and other routine commercial matters), these letters deal with such topics as corporate policy and issues of social responsibility, and they are written in a more formal style.

b. Letters expressing praise, concern, or condolence to someone within or outside the organization. The occasion that prompts the letter could be exceptional performance on the job or in the community, an employment anniversary, the death or serious illness of a family member, or an upcoming retirement. Such letters may be formal or informal, depending on the relationship between the writer and the person addressed.

c. Letters to business associates within or outside the company on purely social matters.

1395 Social-business correspondence differs from ordinary business correspondence in several ways:

a. The inside address is typed at the bottom of the letter, aligned at the left margin and starting on the sixth line below the writer's signature or title (whichever comes last).

b. The salutation is followed by a comma rather than a colon.

c. Reference initials and notations pertaining to enclosures, copies, and mailing are typically omitted. (It would make good sense, however, to put such notations on the file copy in case this information is needed later on.)

d. If the letter requires a *Personal* or *Confidential* notation, place the notation only on the envelope, not on the letter itself. (For the appropriate placement of the notation on an envelope, see ¶1389l and the second illustration on page 337.)

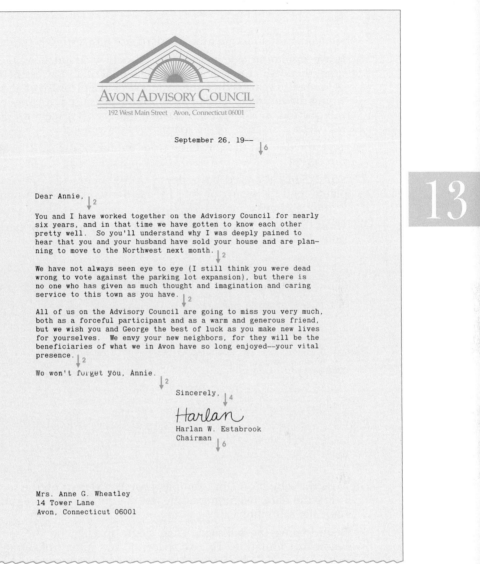

AVON ADVISORY COUNCIL
192 West Main Street | Avon, Connecticut 06001

September 26, 19--
↓6

Dear Annie,
↓2

You and I have worked together on the Advisory Council for nearly
six years, and in that time we have gotten to know each other
pretty well. So you'll understand why I was deeply pained to
hear that you and your husband have sold your house and are planning to move to the Northwest next month.
↓2

We have not always seen eye to eye (I still think you were dead
wrong to vote against the parking lot expansion), but there is
no one who has given as much thought and imagination and caring
service to this town as you have.
↓2

All of us on the Advisory Council are going to miss you very much,
both as a forceful participant and as a warm and generous friend,
but we wish you and George the best of luck as you make new lives
for yourselves. We envy your new neighbors, for they will be the
beneficiaries of what we in Avon have so long enjoyed--your vital
presence.
↓2

We won't forget you, Annie.
↓2

                        Sincerely,
                        ↓4

                        Harlan

                        Harlan W. Estabrook
                        Chairman
                        ↓6

Mrs. Anne G. Wheatley
14 Tower Lane
Avon, Connecticut 06001

e. Social-business correspondence also differs by being *more* formal or *less* formal than ordinary business correspondence. For example, correspondence to high-level officials and dignitaries is customarily more formal. In such cases use the word style for numbers (see ¶¶404–406) and one of the special salutations listed in Section 18. However, in letters to business associates who are also close friends, the salutation and the complimentary closing may be very informal, and the writer's typewritten signature and title—and even the inside address—may be omitted. Moreover, when such letters are purely personal in nature, the writer may use plain stationery and omit the return address.

Postcards

1396 When typing the message on a standard-size postcard (5½ by 3½ inches):

    a. Leave minimum side margins of ½ inch. If 10-pitch or pica type is used, the 5½-inch width will provide a total of 55 spaces; an allowance of ½ inch (5 spaces) on either side will yield a measure of 45 spaces for typing the message. If 12-point or elite type is used, the 5½-inch width will provide 66 *elite* spaces; a ½-inch margin (6 spaces) on either side will yield a measure of 54 spaces.

    b. Type the date on the third line from the top of the card, beginning at the center.

    NOTE: Since the card has a depth of 3½ inches (21 lines), you must plan to end the typing on line 18 in order to leave a bottom margin of ½ inch (3 lines).

    c. Omit the name and address of the person to whom the card is being sent.

    d. Type the salutation (for example, *Dear Mrs. Davis:*) on the second line below the date, beginning at the left margin. If space is tight, you can omit the salutation.

    e. Begin typing the message, using single spacing, on the second line below the salutation. To save space, do not indent paragraphs.

    f. Type the closing lines starting on the second line below the last line of the message; begin each line at the center. In order to leave a bottom margin of ½ inch, omit the following elements if necessary: the complimentary closing (for example, *Sincerely*), the handwritten signature, the writer's title, and reference initials.

1397 On the front side of the card, type a return address and the mailing address just as you would on a No. 6¾ envelope. (See ¶¶1389–1390 and the illustration at the top of page 337.)

SECTION 14

Reports and Manuscripts

Reports

14

Reports serve all kinds of purposes. Some simply communicate information—such as monthly sales figures or survey results—without any attempt to analyze or interpret the data. Others offer extensive analyses and make detailed recommendations for further action. As a result, reports come in all sizes and shapes. Some are done informally as memos or letters (depending on whether they are to be distributed inside or outside the organization). Some consist simply of fill-ins on preprinted forms. Many, however, are done in a more formal style. As you might expect, there is a wide variation to be found in what is considered acceptable—from one authority to another and from one organization to another. Regardless of which guidelines you follow, be prepared to modify them to fit a specific situation.

Choosing a Format

1401 If you are doing a report at the request of someone else, always try to get some guidelines from that person on such matters as format, length, amount of detail desired, and distribution. Check the files for copies of similar reports done in the past. If guidelines or models are not provided or if you are doing the report on your own initiative, consider the following factors in choosing a format.

a. *For whom are you writing the report?* (If intended for your boss or a colleague on staff, the report could be done simply as a memo. If intended for top management or the board of directors, the report will often require a more formal approach. By the same token, an academic term paper will require a simpler format than a thesis for an advanced degree.)

b. *What outcome do you hope to achieve?* (If you are merely providing information without attempting to win someone over to your point of view, the simplest and clearest presentation of the information will suffice. If you are trying to persuade the reader to adopt your viewpoint and accept your recommendations, you will probably need to make a detailed argument and devise a more complex structure for your report.)

c. *What is the existing mind-set of your reader?* (If you will have to argue long and hard to win your reader over, you may need to develop a number of chapters, grouped by part. If you need to demonstrate that your argument is supported by much detailed research, you may have to quote from published sources and provide an elaborate set of data in the form of tables and charts. If you know that your intended reader already supports your argument or simply wants your judgment on a certain matter, a shorter and simpler document will usually suffice.)

Parts of a Formal Report

1402 A *formal* report typically has three parts: front matter, body, and back matter. Each of these parts, in turn, typically contains some (if not all) of the following elements in the sequence indicated.

a. Front Matter

TITLE PAGE	*In a business report:* gives the full title, the subtitle (if any), the writer's name, title, and department, and the date of submission; may also indicate for whom the report was written. *In an academic report:* gives the name of the writer, the instructor, and the course, along with the date of submission. (See ¶1414.)
LETTER OR MEMO OF TRANSMITTAL	May be done as a letter (for distribution outside the company) or as a memo (for inside distribution); may be clipped to the front of the report (or to the binder in which the report is inserted); may be inserted in the report itself as the page preceding the title page. (See ¶1415.)
TABLE OF CONTENTS	A list of all chapters (by number and title), along with the opening page number of each chapter. If chapters are grouped by part, the titles of the parts also appear in the table of contents. Sometimes main headings within the chapters are also given under each chapter title. (See ¶1416.)
LISTS OF TABLES AND ILLUSTRATIONS	Separate lists of tables and illustrations are included if they are numerous and likely to be frequently referred to by the reader. (See ¶1417.)
FOREWORD	Written by someone other than the author of the report. May explain who commissioned the report, the reasons for doing so, and the qualifications of the writer to prepare the report. May also offer an evaluation of the report, and may ask those who receive copies of the report to give their assessment or take some other action after they have read the report. (See ¶1418.)
PREFACE	Written by the author of the report. Indicates for whom the report is written, the objectives and the scope of the report, and the methods used to assemble the material in the report (see ¶1418). Acknowledgments of help received on the report are usually included here (placed at the end), but if special emphasis is desired, the acknowledgments can be treated as a separate element of the front matter, immediately following the preface.
SUMMARY	A one-page document (two pages at most) designed to save the reader's time by presenting conclusions and recommendations right at the outset of the report. If a preface is not provided, the summary also includes some of the material that would have gone there. (See ¶1419.)

(Continued on page 352.)

¶1403

b. **Body**

INTRODUCTION   Sets forth (in greater detail than the preface) the objectives, the scope, and the methods, along with any other relevant background information. In a report with several chapters, this may precede the first chapter of the text or be labeled as Chapter 1. (See ¶1421.)

MAIN DISCUSSION   Sets forth all the pertinent data, evidence, analyses, and interpretations needed to fulfill the purpose of the report. May consist of one long chapter that opens with an introduction and closes with conclusions and recommendations. May consist of several chapters; these may be grouped into *parts,* with a part-title page inserted to introduce each sequence of chapters. May use different levels of headings throughout the text to indicate what the discussion covers and how it is organized. (See ¶¶1422–1426.)

CONCLUSIONS   Presents the key points and the recommendations that the writer hopes the reader will be persuaded to accept. In a report with several chapters, this material represents the final chapter or the final part.

c. **Back Matter**

APPENDIXES   A collection of tables, charts, or other data too specific to be included in the body of the report but provided here as supporting detail for the interested reader. (See ¶1428.)

ENDNOTES   A collection—all in one place at the end of the report—of what would otherwise appear as footnotes at the bottom of various pages in the report. A device that simplifies the preparation of the report. (See ¶¶1501–1502, 1504–1505.)

BIBLIOGRAPHY   A list of all sources (1) that were consulted in the preparation of the report and (2) from which material was derived or directly quoted. (See ¶¶1532–1536.)

GLOSSARY   A list of terms (with definitions) that may not be readily understood when encountered in the body of the report. (See ¶1430.)

Parts of an Informal Report

1403 a. An *informal* report has no front matter. The information that would go on a separate title page appears at the top of the first page and is immediately followed by the body of the report. (See ¶¶1411–1413 for format guidelines.)

b. An informal report typically contains no back matter except possibly a list of *endnotes* (in place of separate footnotes throughout the body of the report) and a *bibliography.*

Margins

1404 Side Margins

a. **Unbound Reports.** If a report is to remain unbound or will simply be stapled in the upper left corner, use a 6½-inch line with 1-inch side margins. Use the following margin settings when the left edge of your standard (8½" × 11") stationery is positioned at zero:

Type of Report	Pitch/ Type Size	Line Length (Spaces)	Margin Settings
Unbound	10/Pica	65	11–76
	12/Elite	78	13–91
Bound	10/Pica	60	16–76
	12/Elite	72	19–91

b. **Bound Reports.** Use a 6-inch line with a 1½-inch left margin and a 1-inch right margin. (The extra half inch at the left will provide space for the binding.) Use the margin settings shown above.

1405 Top and Bottom Margins of Opening Pages

The following guidelines apply to (1) the first page of each chapter, (2) the first page of each distinct element in the front matter and back matter, and (3) the first page of an informal report that consists of only one chapter (without any separate title page or other front matter).

a. On these opening pages, leave a top margin of 12 lines (2 inches) and a bottom margin of 6 lines (1 inch). Since a standard page is 66 lines deep, the area for typing falls between line 13 and line 60. (On the title page and on part-title pages, where the copy is centered as a whole on the page, leave a top and bottom margin of at least 6 lines.)

b. Ordinarily, nothing is typed in the space that represents the top margin. However, in informal academic reports, certain information is often typed in the upper right corner. (See ¶1413.)

c. On these opening pages, the first line of typing—typically a heading—starts on line 13. On a full page of copy, the last line of text typically falls on line 57 and the page number is centered on line 60. (See ¶¶1406c, 1408, and 1410a for exceptions to this standard.)

```
                        ↓13
line 13           CHAPTER 2.  ADMINISTRATIVE SERVICES
                                                     ↓3

        As part of a broad-based investigation into ways of increasing ↓2

productivity and improving operating efficiency, the managers of all
```

```
        will entail a substantial investment in state-of-the-art desktop
   ⌐ line 57
   └→ publishing equipment and will require hiring a number of trained
                                                              ↓3

line 60                        14
```

1406 Top and Bottom Margins of Other Pages

a. Leave 6 blank lines (1 inch) at both the top and the bottom of other pages in a report. (See ¶¶1408 and 1410b–c for exceptions to this standard.)

b. In the *body* and *back matter* of a report, type the page number on line 7 at the right margin (see ¶1426) and continue the text on line 10. (If you are using the header feature of a software program, only 1 blank line will be left beneath the page numbers.) The last line of copy on a full page of text should fall on line 60.

```
                                                          ↓7
line 7                                                   23
                                                           ↓3
line 10
 → Both sides are motivated to forge a new partnership.  Industry

   has seen its technological base erode in the face of foreign


        Meanwhile, the universities are caught in a financial
line 60
 → squeeze that is being intensified by dwindling enrollments
```

c. In the *front matter* of a report, the page number always goes at the foot of the page. Therefore, begin typing the text on line 7. On a full page of text, type the last line of text on line 57 and center the page number on line 60. (If you are using the footer feature of a software program, only 1 blank line will be left above the page number.)

```
line 7 Part Three will explore alternative recommendations for

   improving relations between factory personnel and first-line


        Part Six will analyze the pros and cons of constructing
line 57
 → all-new manufacturing facilities versus upgrading the existing
                                                           ↓3
line 60                         vii
```

1407 Handling Page Breaks on a Computer

If you are using electronic equipment with the appropriate features, you can avoid virtually every problem that could arise in connection with deciding where to end each page. (See ¶1408.) For example, if you make use of *automatic pagination,* the computer will end each page so as to maintain a minimum bottom margin of 1 inch. If you make use of such features as *orphan adjust* and *widow adjust,* the computer will ensure that at least two lines of a new paragraph appear at the bottom of the page and that at least two lines of that paragraph are carried over to the top of the next page. If you make use of a feature called *block protect*, the computer will ensure that a designated block of copy (such as a table or an enumerated list) will not be broken at the bottom of the page but will, if necessary, be carried over intact to the top of the next page.

For a formal definition of terms such as automatic pagination, block protect, orphan adjust, *and* widow adjust, *see Section 20.*

1408 Handling Page Breaks on a Typewriter

As indicated in ¶¶1405–1406, if you want to maintain a consistent bottom margin of 6 blank lines in a typed report, then strictly speaking, the last typing on a page should appear on line 60. In most cases this should be easy to achieve. However, in a few situations you may have to end the page one line long or several lines short.

a. On full pages of text where the page number must be typed at the bottom (see ¶¶1405 and 1406c), your goal is to type the last line of text on line 57 and the page number on line 60.

Standard Page-Ending Arrangement

However, if you are typing double-spaced text on even-numbered lines, it will be impossible for you to end the text on line 57. In such a case try to end the text on line 56 and keep the page number on line 60. In order to avoid a bad page break, you can end the text on line 58 and center the page number on line 61.

For examples of bad page breaks, see ¶1408c–h.

Preferable Variation   **Acceptable Variation**

(Continued on page 356.)

b. On full pages of text where the page number goes in the upper right corner on line 7, try to type the last line of text on line 60.

Standard Page-Ending Arrangement

line 54	xxxxxxxxxxxxxxxxxxxxxxxxxxxxxxx
line 56	xxxxxxxxxxxxxxx .
line 58	Xxxxxxxxxxxxxxxxxxxxxxxxxx
line 60	xxxxxxxxxxxxxxxxxxxxxxxxxxxxxxx

However, if you are typing double-spaced copy on odd-numbered lines, aim for line 59 but continue the text on line 61 if necessary to avoid a bad break.

Preferable Variation   **Acceptable Variation**

	Preferable Variation	Acceptable Variation
line 53	xxxxxxxxxxxxxxxxxxxxxxxxxxx	xxxxxxxxxxxxxxxxxxxxxxxxxx
line 55	xxxxxxxxxxxxxxx .	xxxxxxxxxxxxxxxxxxxxxxxxxx
line 57	Xxxxxxxxxxxxxxxxxxxxxx	xxxxxxxxxxxxxxxxxxxxx .
line 59	xxxxxxxxxxxxxxxxxxxxxxxxxxx	Xxxxxxxxxxxxxxxxxxxxxx
line 61		xxxxxxxxxxxxxxxxxxxxxxxxxx

c. In breaking a paragraph at the bottom of a page, always leave at least two lines at the bottom of the page and carry at least two lines to the top of the next. Three-line paragraphs pose a special problem: you must either fit all three lines at the bottom of one page or carry all three lines over to the top of the next page.

NOTE: Some software programs have a feature that prevents the creation of *orphans* and *widows*. An orphan is the *first* line of a new paragraph that appears as the last line on a page. A widow is the *last* line of a paragraph that appears as the first line on a page. (See the entries on *orphan adjust* and *widow adjust* in Section 20.)

d. Do not type a *centered heading* or a *side heading* near the bottom of a page unless you can fit at least the first two lines of copy after the heading. (For illustrations, see ¶1425d–f.)

NOTE: A *run-in heading* (in the first line of a paragraph) can fall near the bottom of a page if one additional line of the paragraph will also fit there. (For an illustration, see ¶1425f.)

For a discussion of centered, side, and run-in headings, see ¶1425c–g.

e. Do not divide a quoted extract (see ¶1424d) unless you can leave at least two lines at the bottom of one page and carry over at least two lines to the top of the next (as has been done in dividing this paragraph between the bottom of page 356 and the top of page 357.)

f. If a list of items (see ¶1424e) has to be broken at the bottom of a page, try to break *between* items (not within an item). Moreover, try to leave at least two items at the bottom of one page and carry over at least two items to the top of the next.

NOTE: If you need to break *within* an item, leave at least two lines at the bottom of one page and carry over at least two lines to the next.

g. If it is not possible to start typing a table at the desired point of reference and have it all fit on the same page, then insert a parenthetical note at the appropriate point in the text (referring the reader to the next page) and continue with the text to the bottom of the page. Then at the top of the next page, type the complete table, leave 1 to 3 blank lines, and resume typing the text. (See Section 16 for guidelines on the typing of tables.)

NOTE: If a table is so long that it will not fit on one page even when typed single-spaced, then look for a sensible division point in the body of the table and end the first page there. At the top of the next page, repeat the complete title of the table (with *Continued* or *Cont.* inserted in parentheses at the end) and also repeat any column heads before continuing with the rest of the table. If there is any possibility that a reader could mistake the first part of the divided table as the complete table, then type a continuation line (in parentheses or brackets) at the point where the table breaks off. (See ¶1638 for details.)

h. If a footnote cannot all fit on the page where the text reference occurs, continue it at the bottom of the following page. (See ¶1503f.)

1409 Controlling Bottom Margins

a. If you are using a computer, the automatic pagination feature will end each page so as to maintain a minimum bottom margin of 1 inch.

b. If you are using a typewriter, draw a pencil mark 6 lines above the point where the last line is to be typed. (Make the mark before inserting the paper into the machine; then erase it later on.)

1410 Shortening a Long Report

When the cost of reproducing and mailing a large number of copies of a long report becomes prohibitively expensive, consider the following devices for reducing the number of pages without having to cut the copy. (Note that these devices will also reduce the readability and the attractiveness of the report, so use them only in extreme circumstances.)

a. Reduce the standard 2-inch top margin for all "opening" pages to 1½ inches, and begin typing on line 10 (rather than line 13). (See ¶1405.)

b. Reduce the standard 1-inch top margin for all other pages to a half inch, and place the page number on line 4 (rather than line 7). Begin typing the text on line 7 (rather than line 10). (See ¶1406b.)

c. As an alternative to *b*, retain a top margin of 1 inch and reduce the bottom margin to a half inch. Start typing the text on line 7, and try to end the text on line 60. Place all the page numbers at the bottom of the page, centered on line 63. (See ¶1406c.)

(Continued on page 358.)

d. Type the report single-spaced, and leave 1 blank line between paragraphs.

e. If the report has only one level of heading, use run-in heads rather than side heads. (See ¶1425.)

f. Wherever the guidelines call for 2 blank lines between elements, use only 1 blank line. Wherever 1 blank line is called for, reduce it to half a line (if your equipment offers this option).

Informal Business Reports

These guidelines apply to business reports that consist of only one chapter and have no separate title page or other front matter.

1411 If the first page is typed on a *blank sheet of paper* (as in the illustration below):

a. Leave a top margin of 12 lines (2 inches).

b. On line 13 type the title of the report centered in all-capital letters. If a subtitle is used, type it centered in capital and small letters on the second line below the main title. (If the title or subtitle is long, break it into sensible phrases and arrange them on two or more single-spaced lines.)

NOTE: Use boldface for the title and the subtitle if the equipment you are using provides that option.

c. Type *By* and the writer's name centered in capital and small letters on the second line below the title or subtitle.

	↓ 13
line 13	CHANGES IN DISCOUNT POLICY ↓ 2
line 15	An Analysis of the Impact of Suggested Revisions
line 16	on Sales Revenues and Net Operating Income ↓ 2
line 18	By Catherine R. Hemphill ↓ 2
line 20	September 20, 19— ↓ 3

line 23 In a memo dated August 13, the Marketing Managers Committee asked

again that certain discounts in our pricing schedule be increased at

the beginning of next year in order to stimulate larger orders from

customers and to permit larger and more profitable production runs.

At the request of the Executive Committee, I have prepared the follow-

ing analysis, working on the basis of projections supplied by a number

---

line 59 If we were to increase our ⍵ discount from 33 1/3 percent to

┌line 61
└→ 40 percent, it is estimated that the immediate increase in sales

---

d. Type the date on which the report is to be submitted on the second line, centered, below the writer's name.

NOTE: Additional details that appear on a title page (such as the writer's title and affiliation or the name and affiliation of the person or group for whom the report has been prepared) are omitted when the title starts on the same page as the body. If these elements need to be provided, you will have to prepare a separate title page. (See ¶1414.)

e. On the third line below the date, start the body of the report. (See ¶¶1424–1426.)

NOTE: On the first page of an informal business report, there should be no page number. Therefore, the text can continue to line 60 (or line 61 to avoid a bad page break). However, count this page as page 1.

f. If the report requires more than one page, then on each continuation page leave 6 blank lines at the top, type the page number on line 7, and resume the text on line 10. (See ¶1406b.)

14

2 ↓7

↓3

are expected to produce sales increases of over 20 percent in the first

quarter of next year, 18 percent in the second quarter, 15 percent in

g. If the report requires one or more elements of back matter—for example, endnotes or a bibliography—follow the style established for a formal report. (See ¶¶1501–1502, 1504–1505, 1532–1536.)

1412 If the first page of a report is done in *memo form:*

a. Give the report title (and subtitle, if any) as the *subject* of the memo. Supply all the other elements called for in the heading of the memo in the usual way. (See ¶¶1392–1393.)

b. Then begin typing the body of the report on the third line below the last fill-in line in the heading. (See ¶¶1424–1426.)

Interoffice Memorandum

To: Executive Committee   From: Catherine R. Hemphill

Dept.:   Dept.: Profit Planning

Subject: Changes in Discount Policy—   Date: September 20, 19—
An Analysis of the Impact of
Suggested Revisions on Sales
Revenues and Net Operating
Income
↓3

In a memo dated August 13, the Marketing Managers Committee asked again that certain discounts in our pricing schedule be increased at the be-

(Continued on page 360.)

c. If the report requires more than one page, then type each continuation page on a blank sheet of paper. Beginning on line 7, use the same kind of continuation heading called for in any long memo (see also ¶1392q), and resume the text on the third line below the last line of the continuation heading. (If you are using the header feature of a software program, only 1 blank line will be left beneath the page number.)

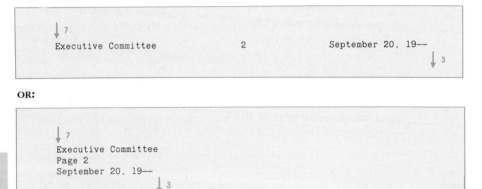

```
↓ 7
Executive Committee              2              September 20, 19--
                                                               ↓ 3
```

OR:

```
↓ 7
Executive Committee
Page 2
September 20, 19--
                ↓ 3
```

Informal Academic Reports

1413 An academic report that consists of only one chapter and has no separate title page or other front matter is typed exactly like an informal business report (see ¶¶1411–1412) except for the opening of the first page.

a. Type the following information in a block in the upper right corner of the first page: the writer's name on line 7, the instructor's name on line 8, the course title on line 9, and the date on line 10—all aligned at the left, with the longest line ending at the right margin.

b. Starting on line 13, type the title and subtitle (if any) just as in an informal business report. (See ¶1411b.)

c. Start typing the body of the report on the third line below the preceding copy (the title or subtitle).

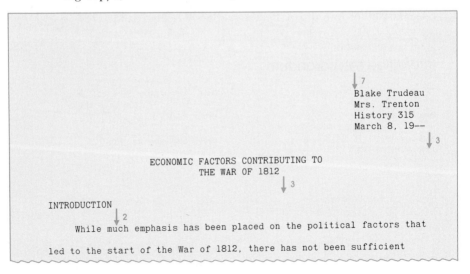

```
                                                         ↓ 7
                                                  Blake Trudeau
                                                  Mrs. Trenton
                                                  History 315
                                                  March 8, 19--
                                                               ↓ 3

          ECONOMIC FACTORS CONTRIBUTING TO
                THE WAR OF 1812
                            ↓ 3

INTRODUCTION
         ↓ 2
     While much emphasis has been placed on the political factors that

led to the start of the War of 1812, there has not been sufficient
```

The Front Matter of Formal Reports

The following guidelines deal with the preparation of a title page, a letter or memo of transmittal, a table of contents, a list of tables, a list of illustrations, a preface or foreword, and a summary. For a formal report, only a separate title page is essential; all the other elements are optional.

1414 Title Page

There is no one correct arrangement for the elements on a title page. Here are two acceptable formats.

a. Three-Block Arrangement. Group the material into three blocks of type, and leave equal space (at least 3 blank lines) above and below the middle block. Position the material as a whole so that it appears centered horizontally and vertically on the page. (See the illustrations below and at the top of page 362.)

Business Report

Academic Report

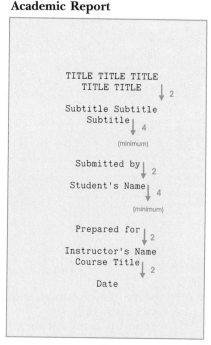

(Continued on page 362.)

```
ACQUISITION OF DESKTOP PUBLISHING EQUIPMENT
                                          ↓ 2
     A Comparative Cost-Benefit Analysis of
           Four Alternative Systems
                                    ↓ 4 (minimum)




              Submitted by
                           ↓ 2
            Ruth Mendelsohn
         Senior Systems Analyst
        Office Systems Department
                                 ↓ 4 (minimum)



              Prepared for
                           ↓ 2
          George F. Pendergast
             Vice President
        Corporate Administration
           and Communications
                             ↓ 2
           February 4, 19--
```

b. Two-Block Arrangement. Group the material into two blocks of type, and leave at least 5 blank lines between blocks. Position the material as a whole so that it appears centered horizontally and vertically on the page.

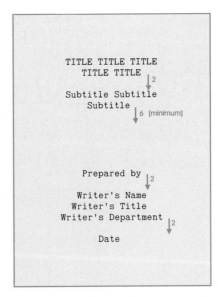

```
              TITLE TITLE TITLE
                TITLE TITLE
                          ↓ 2
           Subtitle Subtitle
               Subtitle
                       ↓ 6 (minimum)




              Prepared by
                         ↓ 2
             Writer's Name
             Writer's Title
          Writer's Department
                            ↓ 2
                 Date
```

NOTE: The two-block arrangement works well when the title page does not attempt to show the name of the person or group to whom the report is being submitted (as in the illustration above).

c. **Margins.** Regardless of which arrangement you use, leave a minimum margin of 6 lines (1 inch) at the top and bottom of the title page. Also leave minimum side margins equivalent to those used for the body of the report. (See ¶1404.)

d. **Title.** Type the title in all-capital letters, using boldface if you have that option. If the title is long, type it on two or more lines, single-spaced; try to break the title into meaningful phrases. (See the illustration at the top of page 362, which uses boldface for the title.)

e. **Subtitle.** Type the subtitle, if any, in capital and small letters, using boldface if you have that option. If the subtitle requires more than one line, type it single-spaced. Leave 1 blank line between the main title and the subtitle. (See the illustration at the top of page 362.)

f. **Writer's Identification.** Leave a minimum of 3 blank lines before typing the writer's identification block. The writer's name may be preceded by the word *By* on the same line or by a phrase such as *Prepared by* or *Submitted by* (or simply *By*) typed 2 lines above. If appropriate, the writer's name may be followed by a title on the next line and by an organizational affiliation on the following line.

14

```
    ↓ 4 (minimum)
    By Patricia C. Shea
  Manager, Accounts Payable
Financial Services Department
```

```
      ↓ 4 (minimum)
      Prepared by
                ↓ 2
      Floyd Welliman
      Acting Director
  Marketing Research Unit
```

g. **Reader's Identification.** It is customary (but not essential) to identify the individual or group for whom the report has been prepared. Leave a minimum of 3 blank lines before typing *Submitted to* or *Prepared for* or a similar phrase. Then on the second line below, type the name of the individual or the group. On succeeding lines, supply a title, an organizational affiliation, or both.

```
    ↓ 4 (minimum)
     Submitted to
              ↓ 2
   Robert G. Paterno
    General Manager
  Corporate Graphic Arts
```

```
    ↓ 4 (minimum)
     Prepared for
              ↓ 2
  The Finance Committee
   Davenport, Pierson,
     and Associates
```

NOTE: As an alternative, the reader's identification may be provided in the form of a subtitle.

```
AN ANALYSIS OF COMPUTERIZED GRAPHICS EQUIPMENT
                                          ↓ 2
       A Report to Robert G. Paterno
   General Manager, Corporate Graphic Arts
```

(Continued on page 364.)

¶1415

h. **Date.** Supply the date (month, day, and year) on which the report is being submitted. Type it on the second line below the reader's identification block (or, if none is given, on the second line below the writer's identification).

1415 Letter or Memo of Transmittal

a. A formal report is often accompanied by a letter or memo of transmittal. If the report is to be sent to people outside the company, use the letter format; if the report is to be sent only to people within the company, use a memo.

b. The message typically covers the following points: (1) a brief description of what is being transmitted; (2) a brief reference to the circumstances that prompted the report; (3) if necessary, a brief indication of why the report is being sent to the addressee; and (4) a statement about what action the addressee is expected to take. (See the illustration below.)

c. The letter or memo of transmittal is typically clipped to the front of the report. If the report is in a binder, the transmittal document may be clipped to the front of the binder or inserted in the binder preceding the title page.

ATLANTIC ENTERPRISES INCORPORATED
44 Exchange Street / Portland, Maine 04107 / 207-555-5166

February 5, 19—

Mr. Frank M. Eggleston
Back Meadow Road
Damariscotta, Maine 04543

Dear Frank:

I am enclosing a copy of a report entitled "Acquisition of Desktop Publishing Equipment," which I just completed for George Pendergast. Because of your expertise in this area, George has suggested that I send you the report with the hope that you might have time to read it and give us your comments and suggestions.

Because we need to make a decision by April 1 on what equipment to buy, it would help us greatly if we could hear from you by March 15. I know that given your busy schedule, you may not be able to get back to us in writing that quickly. If you would let George and me take you to lunch, we could talk about the report then and spare you the need to put your thoughts in writing.

I'll call you early next week so that we can decide what would be the best way to proceed.

Sincerely,

(Ms.) Ruth Mendelsohn

Ruth Mendelsohn
Senior Systems Analyst
Office Systems Department

ctl
Enclosure

1416 Table of Contents

a. On a fresh page type *CONTENTS* (or *TABLE OF CONTENTS*) in all-capital letters (using boldface if you have that option), and center the heading on line 13. On the third line below, begin typing the table double-spaced. Use the same side and bottom margins as for the text pages in the body of the report. (See ¶¶1404–1408.)

↓ 13

CONTENTS
↓ 3

b. In typing the body of the table of contents, list every separate element that *follows* the table of contents in sequence—whether in the front matter, the body of the report, or the back matter. In the illustration above, note the following aspects of the format:

(Continued on page 366.)

¶1417

(1) Individual entries pertaining to *chapters* begin with a chapter number (roman or arabic), followed by a period, 2 spaces, and then the chapter title typed in capital and small letters or in all-capital letters. Align the chapter numbers at the right, with the longest number positioned flush with the left margin. After each chapter title leave 1 space and type a solid row of leaders to guide the eye to the column of page numbers at the right. Leave 1 space between the final leader and the widest page number; all other page numbers should align at the right. (See the illustration below and on page 365.)

NOTE: If any chapter title should require more than one line, type the turnover line single-spaced and align it with the first letter of the chapter title in the line above.

(2) Individual entries pertaining to *front matter* and *back matter* begin at the left margin, with the title typed in capital and small letters or in all-capital letters, followed by a row of leaders and a page number (roman for front matter and arabic for back matter). Leave 2 blank lines *after* the front matter entries and 2 blank lines *before* the back matter entries.

(3) Individual entries pertaining to *part titles* are typed in all-capital letters and centered. The part numbers that precede the titles may be in arabic or roman numerals or (for formality) may be spelled out. Leave 2 blank lines before each part title and 1 blank line after. (See ¶1405b, note.)

c. The *main headings* within each chapter may be included in the table of contents. One acceptable arrangement is to indent each heading 2 spaces from the start of the chapter title and type it in capital and small letters. The list of headings for each chapter should be typed as a single-spaced block, with 1 blank line above and below it. Page numbers may be provided with the headings if desired.

1417 List of Tables or Illustrations

a. Start each list on a fresh page. Type the heading—*TABLES* (or *LIST OF TABLES*) or *ILLUSTRATIONS* (or *LIST OF ILLUSTRATIONS*)—in all-capital letters (using boldface if you have that option), and center the heading on line 13. (See the illustration on page 367.)

    b. On the third line below, begin typing the first entry in the list. Use the same format as for chapter titles in a table of contents. (See ¶1416.)

    NOTE: The tables or the illustrations may be numbered consecutively throughout the report or consecutively within each chapter. The latter technique (which is recommended whenever last-minute additions and deletions are likely) uses the chapter number as a prefix in the numbering scheme. (See the illustration below.)

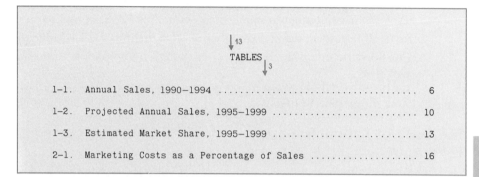

```
                              ↓13
                            TABLES
                                 ↓3

  1-1.   Annual Sales, 1990-1994 .....................................  6

  1-2.   Projected Annual Sales, 1995-1999 .........................  10

  1-3.   Estimated Market Share, 1995-1999 .........................  13

  2-1.   Marketing Costs as a Percentage of Sales ..................  16
```

1418 Preface or Foreword

    a. If a preface (written by the author) or a foreword (written by someone else) is to be provided, then on a fresh page type the appropriate title in all-capital letters (using boldface if you have that option), and center the heading on line 13. Note that the correct spelling is *FOREWORD* (NOT FORWARD).

    b. On the third line below, begin typing the actual text. Use the same side and bottom margins as for the text pages in the body of the report (see ¶¶1404–1408). Also follow the same guidelines for spacing, indentions, and headings as in the body of the report (see ¶¶1424–1425).

    c. The preface should cover the following points: (1) for whom the report is written, (2) what prompted the writing of the report, (3) what the report aims to accomplish, (4) what the report covers and what it does not try to deal with, (5) how the data and the conclusions were arrived at, and (6) acknowledgments of those individuals and organizations who helped the writer of the report.

    NOTE: The acknowledgments may be treated as a separate element in the front matter, following the foreword and the preface (in that sequence if both are given) and using the same format.

    d. The foreword typically deals with these topics: (1) who commissioned the report, (2) the reasons for doing so, (3) the writer's qualifications for undertaking the assignment, (4) an assessment of the job that the writer has done, and (5) a call for some follow-up action on the part of those who receive copies of the report.

1419 Summary

    a. If a summary (frequently called an *executive summary*) is to be provided, follow the format guidelines provided for a preface in ¶1418a–b above.

(Continued on page 368.)

b. Since this element is intended to be a time-saver, keep it short—ideally one page, at most two pages. The summary may be handled as a series of ordinary text paragraphs or as a series of numbered paragraphs typed with hanging indention (see ¶1424e–f).

1420 Numbering Front Matter Pages

a. On all pages of front matter except the title page, type a page number centered on line 60, the seventh line from the bottom of the page. Type the page number in small roman numerals (*ii, iii, iv,* and so on).

NOTE: If necessary, the page number may fall on line 61. (See ¶1408a.)

b. Consider the title page as *page i,* even though no number is typed on that page.

c. Leave 2 blank lines above the page number, more if the text above runs short. (See ¶1406c.)

The Body of Formal Reports

1421 Introduction

a. If the body of a report contains several chapters and begins with a formal introduction, treat the introduction either as Chapter 1 or as a distinct element preceding Chapter 1.

 (1) If you decide to treat it as Chapter 1, then consider *INTRODUC-TION* to be the title of this chapter and handle it as you would any other title on a chapter-opening page. (See ¶1423.)

 (2) If you decide to have the introduction precede Chapter 1, then on a fresh sheet type *INTRODUCTION* in all-capital letters (and bold-face if available), and center the heading on line 13. On the third line below, begin typing the actual text.

 (3) In either case treat the first page of the introduction as page 1 of the report. (See ¶1426.)

 For guidelines on margins, see ¶¶1404–1408; for guidelines on spacing, indentions, and headings, see ¶¶1424–1425.

b. If a report contains only one chapter and begins with an introductory section, treat the title *INTRODUCTION* as a first-level head (see ¶1425) and type it on the third line below the block of copy (title, etc.) at the top of the page. (See the illustration at the bottom of page 360.)

1422 Part-Title Pages

a. If the report contains several chapters organized in parts, insert a separate part-title page directly in front of the chapter that begins each part. (See the illustration at the top of page 369.)

NOTE: If the body of the report begins with a formal introduction (see ¶1421a), then the part-title page for Part 1 should *follow* the introduction. (REASON: The introduction embraces the whole work and not simply Part 1.)

b. Type the word *PART* and the part number on one line. Underneath type the part title on one or more lines as appropriate. Use all-capital letters (and boldface if available) for emphasis, and arrange the copy for maximum display effect. Center the copy as a whole horizontally and vertically.

PART 3

STRATEGIES FOR

REGAINING MARKET SHARE

1423 Chapter-Opening Pages

a. Leave 12 blank lines (2 inches) at the top of each chapter-opening page.

b. Type the chapter number and title in all-capital letters (and boldface if available), and center this element on line 13.

↓ 13
CHAPTER II. THE COMPUTER REVOLUTION
↓ 3

14

c. If the title is long, break it into sensible phrases and arrange them on two or more single-spaced lines. Put the chapter number on a line by itself, and leave 1 blank line before starting the chapter title.

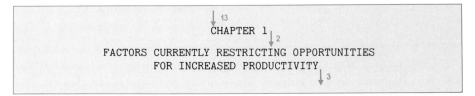

↓ 13
CHAPTER 1 ↓ 2

FACTORS CURRENTLY RESTRICTING OPPORTUNITIES
FOR INCREASED PRODUCTIVITY ↓ 3

d. Begin typing the first line of copy (whether text matter or a heading) on the third line below the title.

1424 Text Spacing and Indentions

a. **Running Text.** Ordinarily, double-space all text matter. However, use single spacing or 1½-line spacing in business reports when the costs of paper, reproduction, file space, and mailing are important considerations. (See ¶1410 for a number of ways to shorten a long report.)

For guidelines on dividing words and word groups at the ends of lines and between one page and the next, see ¶¶901–920; for guidelines on the use of footnotes, endnotes, or textnotes, see Section 15.

b. **Drafts.** Always double-space drafts that are to be submitted for editing or evaluation.

c. **Paragraphs.** Indent text paragraphs 5 spaces. Leave 1 blank line between paragraphs, whether the text is typed with single, double, or 1½-line spacing.

For guidelines on breaking short paragraphs at the bottom of a page, see ¶1408c.

(Continued on page 370.)

d. **Quoted Material.** If a quotation will make four or more lines, treat it as a single-spaced extract. Indent the extract 5 spaces from each side margin, and leave 1 blank line above and below the extract. If the quoted matter represents the start of a paragraph in the original, indent the first word an additional 5 spaces.

For an illustration, see page 304.

e. **Items in a List.** Type the list single-spaced with 1 blank line above and below the list as a whole. Either type the list on the full width of the text, or indent the list 5 spaces from each side margin. If any item in the list requires more than one line, leave a blank line after each item in the list. If an item requires more than one line, use hanging indention—that is, align any turnover with the first word in the line above.

NOTE: Sometimes a list of one-line items (with no turnovers) is typed double-spaced to enhance the readability.

For an example, see the illustration on page 441.

f. **Enumerated Items in a List.** If the items each begin with a number or letter, type a period after the number or letter and leave 2 spaces before typing the text that follows. Align the numbers or letters on the period. If an item requires more than one line, align any turnover with the first word in the line above.

NOTE: When the first line of each text paragraph is indented 5 spaces (as is typically done in reports), an enumerated list that falls within the text looks best when indented 5 spaces from each margin.

See ¶1357d, note, for a detailed explanation.

g. **Tables.** Tables may be typed with single, double, or 1½-line spacing. However, establish one style of spacing for all tables within a given report.

See Section 16 for a full discussion on how to plan and execute tables and for numerous illustrations.

1425 Text Headings

Headings (or heads) are the key technique for letting readers see at a glance the scope of the writer's discussion and the way in which it is organized. Therefore, make sure that the heads used throughout the report properly reflect the coverage and the structure of the material. It is also essential that the heads be typed in a way that clearly indicates different levels of importance or subordination.

Here are several techniques for achieving these objectives:

a. Try to limit yourself to three levels of text heads (not counting the chapter title). If you use more than three, it will be difficult for the reader to grasp the typographical distinction between one level and another.

NOTE: If you feel you need more than three levels, you may be trying to cram too much into one chapter. Consider a different organization of the material to solve this problem.

b. Before preparing the final version of the report, make an outline of the heading structure as it then stands and analyze it for:

(1) *Comprehensiveness.* When the heads are viewed as a whole, do they cover all aspects of the discussion, or are some topics not properly represented?

(2) *Balance.* Is one part of a chapter loaded with heads while a comparable part has only one or two?

(3) *Parallel structure.* Are the heads all worded in a similar way, or are some complete sentences and others simply phrases?

On the basis of this analysis, revise the heads as necessary.

c. Headings come in three styles:

(1) A *centered head* is one centered on a line by itself, with 2 blank lines above (see ¶1425g) and 1 blank line below. Type it in all-capital letters. If the head is too long to fit on one line, center the turnover on the following line. (See ¶1425f for illustrations.)

(2) A *side head* starts flush with the left margin, on a line by itself. Ordinarily, it should have 2 blank lines above (see ¶1425g) and

1 blank line below. (See the illustrations in ¶1425d.) However, if a side head comes directly below a centered head (without any intervening text), leave only 1 blank line above the side head. (See the second row of illustrations in ¶1425e.) A side head may be typed either in all-capital letters or in capital and small letters that are underscored. If the head is too long to fit on one line, type the turnover flush left on the following line.

(3) A *run-in head* (also called a *paragraph heading*) is one that begins a paragraph and is immediately followed by text matter on the same line. Like all new paragraphs, a paragraph that begins with a run-in head should be preceded by 1 blank line (whether the text is typed with single, double, or 1½-line spacing). A run-in head should begin 5 spaces in from the left margin. It should be typed in capital and small letters, underscored, and followed by a period (unless some other mark of punctuation, such as a question mark, is required). The text then begins 2 spaces after the mark of punctuation. (See the illustrations in ¶1425f.)

NOTE: Put all centered, side, and run-in headings in boldface if the equipment you are using offers that option. However, do not underscore side and run-in headings when they are done in boldface. (See the illustrations in the second column below and on page 373.)

For capitalization in headings, see ¶¶360–361, 363.

d. In a report that calls for only *one* level of heading, choose a side heading and type it in one of the styles shown below. (See ¶1425g.)

Typewriter Style   **Computer Style**

```
XXXXXXXXXXXXXXXXXXXXXXXXX          XXXXXXXXXXXXXXXXXXXXXXXXX
XXXXXXXXXXXXXXXXXXXXXXXXX          XXXXXXXXXXXXXXXXXXXXXXXXX
XXXXXXXXXXXX.  ↓3                  XXXXXXXXXXXX.  ↓3

SIDE HEAD ↓2                       SIDE HEAD ↓2

     Xxxxxxxxxxxxxxxxxxxx               Xxxxxxxxxxxxxxxxxxxx
XXXXXXXXXXXXXXXXXXXXXXXXX          XXXXXXXXXXXXXXXXXXXXXXXXX
XXXXXXXXXXXXXXXXXXXXXXXXX          XXXXXXXXXXXXXXXXXXXXXXXXX
```

```
XXXXXXXXXXXXXXXXXXXXXXXXX          XXXXXXXXXXXXXXXXXXXXXXXXX
XXXXXXXXXXXXXXXXXXXXXXXXX          XXXXXXXXXXXXXXXXXXXXXXXXX
XXXXXXXXXXXX.  ↓3                  XXXXXXXX.  ↓3

Side Head                         Side Head ↓2

     Xxxxxxxxxxxxxxxxxxxx               Xxxxxxxxxxxxxxxxxxxx
XXXXXXXXXXXXXXXXXXXXXXXXX          XXXXXXXXXXXXXXXXXXXXXXXXX
XXXXXXXXXXXXXXXXXXXXXXXXX          XXXXXXXXXXXXXXXXXXXXXXXXX
```

e. In a report that calls for *two* levels of headings, choose one of the styles shown below. (See ¶1425g.)

Typewriter Style   **Computer Style**

f. In a report with *three* levels of headings, choose one of the following styles. (See ¶1425g.)

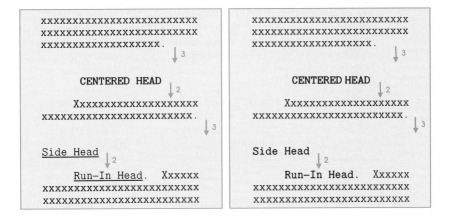

g. If the equipment you are using makes it difficult or awkward to leave 2 blank lines above centered heads and side heads, insert 3 blank lines above centered heads and 1 blank line above side heads.

1426 Numbering Text Pages

a. When the first page contains the title of the report and the body starts on the third line below, count this as page 1 but do not type the number on the page.

b. When the report begins with a formal title page and one or more additional pages of front matter, give these pages a separate numbering sequence, using small *roman* numerals. (See ¶1420.)

c. In a formal report, consider the first page *following* the front matter as page 1 in the *arabic* numbering sequence.

d. If part-title pages are included in the report (see ¶1422), consider them in the numbering sequence for the body of the report, but do not type a number on these pages. (Thus if the first page following the front matter is the part-title page for Part I, it will count as page 1 but no number will appear.)

e. On the first page of each new element in the body or back matter of the report (a title starts on line 13 of such pages), the page number should appear at the bottom of the page, as follows:

(1) Try to have the last line of the text fall on line 57 (the tenth line from the bottom of the page).

(2) Leave 2 blank lines (see ¶1406c), and then center the page number (without the word *Page*) on line 60 (the seventh line from the bottom).

For alternative ways to end a page, see ¶1408.

f. On all other pages in the body or back matter of the report, place the page number on the seventh line from the top, and have it end at the right margin. The word *Page* may precede the number. After typing the page number, begin the first line of text on the third line below. (See ¶1406b.)

g. In a long report with several chapters written by different authors under a tight deadline, it may be necessary to prepare the final version of the chapters out of order. In such cases, you may use a separate sequence of page numbers for each chapter, with the chapter number serving as a prefix. Thus, for example, the pages in Chapter 1 would be numbered 1-1, 1-2, 1-3, . . .; those in Chapter 2 would be numbered 2-1, 2-2, 2-3, . . .; and so on.

h. If you are using electronic equipment with the automatic page numbering feature, the appropriate page number will be properly positioned on each page in the correct sequence. If you later add or delete copy in a way that changes the overall length of the draft, the page numbering will be automatically adjusted in the next printout.

The Back Matter of Formal Reports

1427 Following the last page of the body of the report are those elements of back matter that may be needed: appendixes, endnotes, bibliography, and glossary. Begin each of these elements on a fresh page. Use the same margins as for other pages in the report (see ¶¶1404–1409), and treat the numbering of these pages as discussed in ¶1426e–g.

1428 Appendixes

a. If more than one appendix is to be included, number or letter each in sequence. (See the illustration of the table of contents on page 365 for an example.)

b. Type the word *APPENDIX* (plus a number or letter, if appropriate) and the appendix title in all-capital letters (and boldface if available), and center this element on line 13.

```
          ↓13

    APPENDIX A.   PROFILES OF MAJOR COMPETITORS ↓ 3
                                                  ↓
```

NOTE: If the title is long, type it in two or more centered lines, single-spaced. Leave 1 blank line before starting the appendix title.

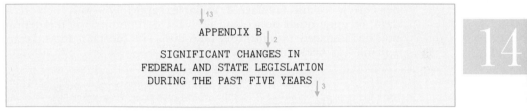

```
              ↓13

          APPENDIX B ↓ 2
                      ↓

     SIGNIFICANT CHANGES IN
   FEDERAL AND STATE LEGISLATION
   DURING THE PAST FIVE YEARS ↓ 3
                               ↓
```

c. Leave 2 blank lines before typing the body of the appendix. Since this material may be a table, a chart, a list, or straight text, choose the format that displays this copy to best effect.

1429 Endnotes and Bibliography

For detailed guidelines, see ¶¶1501–1502, 1504–1505, 1532–1536.

1430 Glossary

If this element is to be provided, then on a fresh sheet type *GLOSSARY* or some other heading in all-capital letters (and boldface if available), and center it on line 13. Leave 2 blank lines, and begin the text on line 16. There are a variety of ways to set up a glossary.

a. **Two Columns.** List the terms in alphabetic order in the left column and put the corresponding definitions in the right column. Begin the right column at least 2 spaces to the right of the longest term in the left column. Single-space each definition, and align turnover lines flush with the left margin of this column. Leave 1 blank line between entries.

```
Elliptical expression   A condensed expression from which key words
                        are omitted. ↓ 2
                                      ↓
Essential elements      Words, phrases, or clauses that are necessary
                        to the completeness of the structure or the
                        meaning of a sentence.
```

(Continued on page 376.)

b. Hanging Indention. Begin each term at the left margin, underscore it (or use boldface if available), and follow with a colon, a dash, or some other device and then the definition. Type the definition single-spaced, and indent turnover lines 5 spaces from the left margin so that the term in the first line will stand out. Leave 1 blank line between entries.

```
elliptical expression:  a condensed expression from which key words
     are omitted
                    ↓ 2
essential elements:  words, phrases, or clauses that are necessary
     to the completeness of the structure or the meaning of a
     sentence
```

c. Paragraph Style. Indent each term 5 spaces from the left margin, underscore it (or use boldface if available), and follow with a colon, a dash, or some other device and then the definition. Type the definition single-spaced, with turnover lines flush with the left margin. Leave 1 blank line between entries.

```
     Elliptical expression--a condensed expression from which key
words are omitted.
                    ↓ 2
     Essential elements--words, phrases, or clauses that are necessary
to the completeness of the structure or the meaning of a sentence.
```

NOTE: Regardless of the format selected, the terms may be typed with initial caps or all in small letters (except for proper nouns and adjectives). The definitions may also be styled either way; however, if they are written in sentence form, it is best to use initial caps for both the term and the definition. The use of periods at the end of definitions is optional unless, of course, the definitions are written as complete sentences. (See the illustration in ¶1430a for an example of the use of initial caps for both the term and the definition.)

Manuscripts

The preparation of manuscripts is subject to virtually the same considerations that apply to the preparation of reports (¶¶1401–1430). However, manuscripts differ from reports in one fundamental way: they are written with the idea of publication in mind—whether as a self-contained book, as an article in a magazine or some other printed periodical, or as an item to be included in a bulletin or newsletter prepared on a computer or a typewriter. As a result, manuscripts require some special considerations concerning format.

Preparing Manuscript for an Article

1431 If you have been invited to write an article for a specific publication, ask the editor for concrete guidelines on line length, spacing, paragraph indention, heading style, preferences in capitalization and punctuation, overall length of the article, and so on.

1432 If you are writing an article only with the hope that it may be accepted by a certain publication, you will enhance your chances of favorable consideration by imitating all aspects of the publication's format and style.

   a. In particular, try to type your manuscript on a line length that equals an average line of copy in the finished publication. A manuscript prepared in this way will make it easy for the editor to determine how much space your article will fill in the publication. To determine the appropriate line length, copy 10 to 20 lines—on a line-for-line basis—from a representative article. Observe at what point most lines end, and set your margins accordingly.

   b. Even if the publication puts two or more columns on a page, type only one column on a manuscript page. The wider margins will provide space for editing.

   c. Type your manuscript double-spaced to allow room for editing.

   d. Consistently type 25 lines of copy on a manuscript page (counting blank space above and below freestanding heads as lines of copy). In this way you and the editor can quickly calculate the total number of lines of copy.

   NOTE: Be sure to keep the overall length of your manuscript within the range of the materials typically used by the intended publication. There is little point in submitting a 2000-line manuscript to a publication that carries articles of no more than 500 lines.

   e. In trying to simulate the character count of a printed line on your computer or typewriter, you may have to adjust some of the normal standards for spacing and indentions. For example, leave only 1 space after periods, question marks, exclamation points, and colons (instead of the customary 2 spaces), and use only 2 or 3 spaces for paragraph indentions (instead of the usual 5 spaces).

Preparing Manuscript for a Book

If you are writing a book or assisting someone who is, consider the following guidelines.

1433 If your manuscript will consist essentially of straight text matter (with perhaps a few tables and illustrations), then in establishing a format for your manuscript, you can follow the standard guidelines for a formal report with respect to spacing, headings, page numbering, and other aspects involved in typing the front matter, the body, and the back matter. Use a 6-inch line, with a left margin of 1½ inches and a right margin of 1 inch. These margins (and the margin settings that go with them) are the same as those shown for a *bound* report in ¶1404b. A book manuscript, however, should not be bound. The 1½-inch left margin provides extra space for editing.

(Continued on page 378.)

NOTE: If the manuscript is done in 12-pitch (elite) type on a 6-inch line, with 26 lines on a page (starting the text on line 10 and ending the text on line 60), then as a rule of thumb, three manuscript pages will convert to two typeset pages in a standard 6- by 9-inch book.

1434 If you think your manuscript, when set in type, will require a special format—for example, a larger-than-usual page size to accommodate extremely wide tables or to permit notes and small illustrations to run alongside the text or to allow for a two-column arrangement of the printed text—then the easiest way to establish a format for your manuscript page is to select a published work that has the kind of format you have in mind. Then, on your computer or typewriter, copy a full page of representative printed text—on a line-for-line basis, if possible—to determine the manuscript equivalent of a printed page. (If a printed line is too long to fit on one manuscript line and still leave a margin of 1½ inches on the left side and 1 inch on the right side, choose some other typewritten format that you can readily execute.) The important thing is to determine how many pages of manuscript equal a page of printed text. Then, as you develop the manuscript, you can exercise some real control over the length of your material.

14

Precautions for All Manuscripts

1435 When sending material to a publisher, always retain a duplicate copy in case the material goes astray in the mail.

1436 Your unpublished manuscript is automatically protected by the copyright law as soon as it is written, without your putting a copyright notice on it or registering it with the U.S. Copyright Office. If you are concerned that someone may copy your material without giving you appropriate credit or compensation, you may place a copyright notice on the first page *(Copyright © [current year] by [your name])* to call attention to your ownership of the material. Since the copyright law protects only the written expression of your ideas and not the ideas themselves, you should obtain the help of a lawyer if you have an original publishing idea that you are afraid may be misappropriated.

Footnotes, Endnotes, and Textnotes

Functions of Notes

1501 a. In a report or manuscript, *notes* serve two functions: (1) they provide *comments* on the main text, conveying subordinate ideas that the writer feels might be distracting if incorporated within the main text; and (2) they serve as *source references*, identifying the origin of a statement quoted or cited in the text.

Comment

     1.   The actual date on which Governor Galloway made this statement is uncertain, but there is no doubt that the statement is his.

Source Reference

     2.   Sylvia Ann Hewlett, When the Bough Breaks: The Cost of Neglecting Our Children, Basic Books, New York, 1991, p. 297.

For a discussion of whether to type the note number on the line (as shown above) or raised slightly above the line, see ¶1523b.

b. When notes appear at the foot of a page, they are called *footnotes*. (See ¶1503.)

> an incredible range of bloopers to be found in classified ads. One
>
> anthology contains these gems: "Dog for sale: eats anything and is
>
> fond of children." "Illiterate? Write today for free help." "Auto
>
> Repair Service. . . . Try us once, you'll never go anywhere again."
>
> "Man, honest. Will take anything."[1]
>
> _____
>
>   1.   Richard Lederer, Anguished English, Wyrick, Charleston, S.C., 1987, p. 38.

c. When notes appear all together at the end of a complete report or manuscript (or sometimes at the end of each chapter), they are called *endnotes*. (See ¶¶1504–1505.)

> NOTES
>
>   1.   Richard Lederer, Anguished English, Wyrick, Charleston, S.C., 1987, p. 38.
>
>   2.   Ibid., pp. 39–40.

d. When source references appear parenthetically within the main text, they are called *textnotes*. (See ¶¶1506–1507.)

---

but the proper use of punctuation can sometimes have serious financial

consequences. Consider the following predicament.

    We came upon a writer at his work . . . . Quite casually he
    mentioned that he was getting fifty cents a word. A moment
    or two later his face became contorted with signs of an in-
    ternal distress. With his hand poised above the machine,
    he seemed to be fighting something out with himself. . . .
    "Listen," he said, grimly, "do you hyphenate 'willy-nilly'?"
    We nodded, and saw him wince as he inserted the little mark,
    at the cost of half a dollar. (E. B. White, "The Cost of
    Hyphens," Writings From The New Yorker: 1925–1976, Harper-
    Collins, New York, 1990, p. 17.)

---

e. Footnotes or endnotes are ordinarily keyed by number to a word, phrase, or sentence in the text. Textnotes (which appear parenthetically at the desired point of reference right in the text itself) do not have to be keyed this way.

f. Endnotes are growing in popularity because (1) they are easier to type and (2) they leave the text pages looking less cluttered and less complicated. They do present one drawback, however: the reader does not know in each instance whether the endnote will contain a comment of substance (which is typically worth reading) or simply a source reference (which is usually of interest only in special cases).

g. Textnotes are also growing in popularity for the same reasons: ease of execution and lack of clutter. While it is possible to provide in a textnote all the information that a source reference typically contains, writers more often use the textnote to provide an abbreviated reference in the text, with the understanding that the reader who wants complete information will be able to consult a bibliography at the back of the report or manuscript. (See ¶1507 for examples of these abbreviated references.)

h. If you have access to electronic equipment with the appropriate features, much of the difficulty associated with the typing of footnotes can be avoided. For example, a feature known as *automatic footnote tie-in* will automatically position a footnote on the same page where the related text reference occurs. If subsequent additions or deletions in the text cause the text reference to shift to another page, the related footnote will automatically shift as well. If the footnotes are numbered in sequence, then in the event that a footnote is subsequently inserted or deleted, all the footnotes (and their related text references) will be automatically renumbered from that point on. Some programs even offer a variety of common footnote formats so that the user can select the format best suited for the occasion.

i. To take advantage of the benefits and avoid the drawbacks of these three types of notes, some writers use a hybrid system: they treat *comments* as footnotes and *source references* as endnotes or textnotes. In this way comments of substance are conveniently at hand, whereas all or most of the information about sources is tucked out of sight but accessible when needed. (See ¶1502g.)

¶1502

Text References to Footnotes or Endnotes

1502 a. To indicate the presence of a comment or a source reference at the bottom of the page or in a special section at the end, insert a *superior* (raised) figure following the appropriate word, phrase, or sentence in the text. (See ¶1502b for examples.)

NOTE: To create a superior figure on a typewriter, turn the cylinder back slightly with one hand and type the figure with the other hand. If you are using electronic equipment with the appropriate features, you can execute superior figures without difficulty. However, if your equipment will not permit you to do so easily, consider an alternative to the use of superior figures, as indicated in ¶1502h.

b. Do not leave any space between the superior figure and the preceding word. If a punctuation mark follows the word, place the superior figure immediately after the punctuation mark. (EXCEPTION: The superior figure should precede, not follow, a dash.)

A research study published last month by a leading relocation consulting firm[2] provides the basis for the recommendations offered in Chapter 5.

The alternative approaches discussed in this report have been taken largely from an article entitled "Getting a Handle on Health Care Costs."[1]

c. While the superior figure should come as close as possible to the appropriate word or phrase, it is often better to place the superior figure at the end of the sentence (if this will cause no misunderstanding) so as to avoid distracting the reader in the midst of the sentence.

ACCEPTABLE: Her latest article, "Automating the Small Legal Office,"[1] was published about three months ago. I urge you to read it.

PREFERABLE: Her latest article, "Automating the Small Legal Office," was published about three months ago.[1] I urge you to read it.

NOTE: Leave 2 spaces after a superior figure that follows the punctuation at the end of a sentence.

d. When a paragraph calls for two or more footnotes or endnotes, try to combine all the necessary information within one note if this can be done without any risk of confusing the reader. This approach will reduce the sense of irritation that a large number of footnotes or endnotes tend to produce.

NOTE: When this approach is used, the superior figure is typically placed after the last word in the sentence or paragraph, depending on how the text references are dispersed.

AVOID: The following analysis draws heavily on recent studies undertaken by Andrew Bowen,[1] Frances Kaplan,[2] and Minetta Coleman.[3]

---

1.   Andrew Bowen, . . .

2.   Frances Kaplan, . . .

3.   Minetta Coleman, . . .

PREFERABLE: The following analysis draws heavily on recent studies undertaken by Andrew Bowen, Frances Kaplan, and Minetta Coleman.[1]

---

1.   Andrew Bowen, . . .; Frances Kaplan, . . .; and Minetta Coleman, ...

e. The numbering of footnotes or endnotes may (1) run consecutively throughout, (2) begin again with each new chapter, or (3) begin again with each new page.

NOTE: The third method should not be used for materials to be set in type unless the printed material will have the same pagination.

f. Footnotes are sometimes keyed by symbol rather than by number. This often occurs in tables with figures and in technical material with many formulas, where a raised figure—though intended to refer to a footnote or endnote—could be mistaken for part of the table text or the formula. When the use of symbols is appropriate, choose one of the following sequences: *, **, ***, etc. (these can be done on a typewriter or a computer); *, †, ‡, §, ¶ (these usually must be inserted by hand, but some electronic equipment can generate these symbols); or *a, b, c, d, e*, etc. (small letters—in italics if you have that option—may be used when there are more than five footnotes for a given table or page).

These tests confirmed that there was a reduction over time of the flexural strength of the marble unit from 1400 to 1200 lb/in^{2}.**

NOT: These tests confirmed that there was a reduction over time of the flexural strength of the marble unit from 1400 to 1200 lb/in^{2}.[2]

When the new process is designed, it is essential to maintain a pressure ratio of 1:8.**

NOT: When the new process is designed, it is essential to maintain a pressure ratio of 1:8.[2]

g. If you wish to treat *comments* as footnotes and *source references* as endnotes or textnotes (as suggested in ¶1501i), use *symbols* for the notes containing comments and use *figures* for the notes containing source references.

h. While the use of *superior* figures in the text is the style most commonly seen in business and academic reports, manuscripts, and published materials, some business writers are now using an "on-the-line" style for one of two reasons: (1) they dislike having to break their typing pace in order to adjust the cylinder each time they want to type a superior figure, or (2) they are using electronic equipment that cannot readily execute superior figures. If you wish to use this "on-the-line" style, follow these guidelines:

(1) Enclose the figure in brackets (if your equipment has bracket keys); otherwise, enclose it in parentheses.

(2) Try to position the figure so that it *follows* the end of a sentence or, better yet, the end of a paragraph. Leave 1 space before the opening bracket or parenthesis; leave 2 spaces after the closing bracket or parenthesis if a new sentence begins on the same line.

```
. . . is "the age of instability." [1]  He goes on . . .
```

(3) If the figure has to go *within* a sentence, leave 1 space before the opening bracket or parenthesis and 1 space after the closing bracket or parenthesis. Try to place the enclosed figure so that it is not next to any other mark of sentence punctuation; otherwise, a cluttered and possibly confusing situation could result. Do not use a figure enclosed in parentheses within a sentence where it could be mistaken for part of an enumeration.

Footnotes

1503 When notes are to be placed at the foot of a page:

a. Insert an underscore 2 inches long (20 strokes in 10-pitch or pica type, 24 strokes in 12-pitch or elite type) to separate footnote material from the main text above. Position the underscore 1 line below the last line of text, starting at the left margin. (Some software programs will automatically insert a horizontal rule before printing the first footnote.)

NOTE: If the text runs short on a page (say, the last page of a chapter), any footnotes related to that text must still be positioned at the *foot* of the page. In that case estimate the number of lines the footnote will occupy, and determine on which line the footnote material should begin in order to end at the foot of the page. Then insert the underscore on the second line above the line on which the footnote material should begin.

---

into the next century.[1] According to one authority:

Technology is helping distribute economic power throughout the American landscape. Major advances in telecommunications are creating a footloose economy that permits firms to locate where they want to be, not where the traditional centers of finance and commerce dictate they have to be.[2] ↓1

──────────────────────── ↓2

  1. For a detailed analysis of these technological developments, see Chapter 4, pp. 58–72.

  2. David A. Heenan, The New Corporate Frontier: The Big Move to Small Town, U.S.A., McGraw–Hill, New York, 1991, p. 9.

---

b. Start the first footnote on the second line below the underscore.

For guidelines on how to construct source reference footnotes, see ¶¶1508–1531.

c. Ordinarily, single-space each footnote, but in a manuscript to be set in type, use double spacing to allow room for editing. In either case leave 1 blank line between footnotes.

d. Indent the first line of each footnote 5 spaces. Type the footnote number on the line or as a superior figure (see ¶1523b). Start any additional lines within the same footnote at the left margin.

e. As a rule, allow three to four lines for each source reference footnote; this estimate allows for space above and below each footnote. Footnotes that contain comments may run longer. Remember that on pages with a page number in the upper right corner, the last line of copy (whether text or footnote) should fall on line 60 or (to avoid a bad page ending) on line 61; on pages where the page number falls at the bottom of the page, the last line of text or footnote should come no farther down than line 57 or (to avoid a bad break) line 58.

For additional details on ending pages, see ¶¶1406b and c, 1407, and 1408a and h.

f. Ideally, the *complete* footnote should appear on the same page as the superior figure or symbol that refers to it. Occasionally, however, a footnote may be so long that it will not all fit on the page, even if it begins immediately following the line of text in which the superior figure or symbol occurs. In such a case follow this procedure:

(1) Once you have completed the line of text in which the footnote reference occurs, type a 2-inch underscore on the following line (see ¶1503a).

(2) If the long footnote is the only footnote on the page, start it on the second line below the underscore (as directed in ¶1503b–e). If other footnotes come before this long one on the page, begin the long one on the second line below the preceding footnote.

(3) Type as much of the footnote on the page as possible. Try to end at a point that is obviously incomplete so that the reader will realize the footnote runs on to the next page. If that is not possible, you may need to insert a continuation line—for example, *Footnote continued on next page*—typed within parentheses or brackets and positioned at the right margin on the line directly below the last line of the footnote.

(4) At the top of the next page, resume typing the text (along with any needed text references to further footnotes), but plan to end the text at a point that leaves enough space to (a) finish the footnote carried over from the preceding page and (b) insert any new footnotes called for in the text above.

Starting a Long Footnote

```
a problem for businesswomen who continue to work after they marry.²  ↓₁
                              ↓₂
     1.  Letitia Baldrige, Letitia Baldrige's Complete Guide to the New
Manners for the '90s, Rawson, New York, 1990, p. 591. ↓₂

     2.  Judith Martin (in Miss Manners' Guide for the Turn-of-the-
Millenium, Simon & Schuster, 1990, pp. 57–58) offers this advice to the
"conservative" businesswoman who is wondering whether or not to adopt
her husband's surname for business purposes: "At work, she is known by
her original surname, or the one under which she happened to make her
professional reputation (which might be the name of a previous husband——
```

Continuing a Footnote on the Next Page

```
on which there still is a considerable difference of opinion.³  ↓₁
                              ↓₂
conservativeness does not guarantee prudence), and is addressed as 'Ms.'
This form meets Miss Manners' standard of old-fashioned propriety for
married, single, or divorced ladies." ↓₂

     3.  Baldrige, p. 593.
```

NOTE: If you expect to encounter a number of long notes that may not easily fit on the page where they are first referred to, you have an excellent reason for abandoning the footnote format and using endnotes instead.

For the treatment of footnotes that pertain to a table, see ¶¶1634–1636.

Textnotes

1506 In a report or manuscript with only a few source references and no bibliography at the end, the complete source data may be inserted within the text in the form of parenthetical textnotes.

```
                                                              2-5



If we decide to switch to a strategy of niche marketing, we have to re-

train our people.  Two experts on the subject have this to say:

          Don't expect your typical mass-market manager automati-
     cally to become a niche marketer.  Niche marketing, especi-
     ally if initiated under the big bang approach, may differ
     too much from management's past practices.
          With niche marketing you're focusing your energy on
     smaller target markets as opposed to larger, more visible
     segments.  That makes a lot of people nervous.  They think
     you're giving up a larger market.  They don't realize that
     the sum of the smaller markets might be bigger than the
     mass market.
          Any time you start talking niche marketing, some execu-
     tives will still insist on going after the entire market.
     (Robert E. Linneman and John L. Stanton, Jr., Making Niche
     Marketing Work, McGraw-Hill, New York, 1991, p. 183.)
```

For guidelines on how to construct these source reference textnotes, see ¶¶ 1508–1531.

NOTE: If some of the data called for in a source reference is already provided in the main text, there is no need to repeat it in the textnote.

```
                                                              2-5



If we decide to switch to a strategy of niche marketing, we have to re-

train our people.  Two experts on the subject, Robert E. Linneman and

John L. Stanton, Jr., have this to say:

          Don't expect your typical mass-market manager automati-
     cally to become a niche marketer.  Niche marketing, especi-
     ally if initiated under the big bang approach, may differ
     too much from management's past practices.
          With niche marketing you're focusing your energy on
     smaller target markets as opposed to larger, more visible
     segments.  That makes a lot of people nervous.  They think
     you're giving up a larger market.  They don't realize that
     the sum of the smaller markets might be bigger than the
     mass market.
          Any time you start talking niche marketing, some execu-
     tives will still insist on going after the entire market.
     (Making Niche Marketing Work, McGraw-Hill, New York, 1991,
     p. 183.)
```

1507 In a report or manuscript that contains a number of source references *and* a complete bibliography, textnotes may be used as follows:

a. At the appropriate point in the main text, supply the author's last name and the appropriate page number in parentheses. The reader who wants more complete information can consult the full entry in the bibliography.

According to an excellent book on time management (Bittel, p. 27), your ability to manage time depends in part on the way you experience the passage of time.

NOTE: Some authorities omit *p.* and *pp.* as well as the comma between the name and the page number; for example, (*Bittel 27*).

b. If the author's name already appears in the main text, give only the page number in parentheses.

Lester R. Bittel, in his excellent book Right on Time! (p. 27), says that . . .

c. If the bibliography lists more than one publication by the same author, then in the textnote use an abbreviated title or the year of publication to indicate which publication is being referred to.

According to an excellent book on time management (Bittel, Time, p. 27), . . .

OR: . . . an excellent book on time management (Bittel, 1991, p. 27), . . .

d. If the bibliography lists publications by two or more authors with the same surname, use each author's first name or initial along with the surname.

According to an excellent book on time management (L. Bittel, p. 27), . . .

e. If the entries in the bibliography are numbered in sequence (see ¶1535c), then the textnote can simply list the appropriate "entry number" along with the page reference. Underscore the entry number to distinguish it from the page number, especially if the abbreviation *p.* or *pp.* is omitted.

According to an excellent book on time management (18, p. 27), . . .

Constructing Source Reference Notes

The following guidelines for constructing source reference notes deal with the situations that most commonly occur—whether in the form of footnotes, endnotes, or the type of textnote discussed in ¶1506. There is no clear-cut agreement among authorities on how these notes should be constructed; rather, there are several schools of thought on the subject, and within each school there are variations between one reference manual and another.

Of all the well-established conventions and variations, the style best suited for business use—and the one presented here—is a style that employs the simplest punctuation and the most straightforward presentation of the necessary data without any sacrifice in clarity or completeness. However, certain professional organizations—for example, the American Psychological Association, the American Medical Association, and the American Chemical Society—have each established a distinctive style, the use of which sometimes shows up in other fields. Moreover, slightly different patterns are often used in academic materials, such as those featured in *The MLA [Modern Language Association] Style Manual*. If you are one of the many full-time business workers who are simultaneously taking one or more academic courses or one of the many full-time academic students who are concurrently holding down part- or full-time office jobs, you may need to familiarize yourself with more than one style. Note that along with the basic pattern for citing book titles (see ¶1508), you will find an "academic" variation that you may need to use from time to time. However, unless you are specifically directed to follow a particular style, the following "all-purpose" patterns—based on well-established conventions—should meet your needs in virtually every type of situation you encounter.

NOTE: For detailed information about specific elements within these patterns, see the following paragraphs:

Note number: see ¶1523.
Names of authors: see ¶1524.
Title of the work: see ¶1525.
Publisher's name: see ¶1526.

Place of publication: see ¶1527.
Date of publication: see ¶1528.
Page numbers: see ¶1529.
Subsequent references: see ¶¶1530–1531.

1508 Book Title: Basic Pattern

a. Business Style

1. Author, <u>book title</u>, publisher, place of publication, year of publication, page number [if reference is being made to a specific page].

1. Guy Kawasaki, <u>The Macintosh Way</u>, Scott, Foresman, Glenview, Ill., 1990, p. 56.

OR

1. Guy Kawasaki, *The Macintosh Way*, Scott, Foresman, Glenview, Ill., 1990, p. 56. (If you are using electronic equipment with the capability of generating italic type, then any element that is shown underscored in these patterns may be rendered in italics instead. See also ¶289.)

NOTE: If any of these elements have already been identified in the text (for example, the author's name and the book title), they need not be repeated in the note. Moreover, if reference is made to the book as a whole rather than to a particular page, omit the page number. In the following illustration, observe that the quoted material requires more than three lines. For that reason, it is indented 5 spaces from each side margin. (See ¶1424d.)

---

the right kind of people. According to Guy Kawasaki, in his provocative book <u>The Macintosh Way</u>:

Four kinds of people are required to understand people's needs and to develop great products. They are: Visionary, Architect, Producer, and Grunt. The Visionary anticipates the wants, needs, and dreams of the market. The Architect figures out how to build the product. The Producer keeps the team together and moving forward. The Grunt implements features. Sometimes all four people are combined in one--that's called genius.[1]

---

1. Scott; Foresman, Glenview, Ill., 1990, p. 56.

(Continued on page 390.)

b. Academic Style

    1. Author, <u>book title</u> (place of publication: publisher, year of publication), page number [if reference is being made to a specific page].

```
    1.  Guy Kawasaki, The Macintosh Way (Glenview, Ill.:
Scott, Foresman, 1990), p. 56. (In endnotes, the note number is typed
on the line; in academic-style footnotes, the note number is typically typed
above the line. See ¶1523b.)
```

NOTE: The key distinction between these two styles lies in a slightly different sequence of elements and a slightly different form of punctuation:

    BUSINESS STYLE: ... publisher, place of publication, year of publication ...

    ACADEMIC STYLE: ... (place of publication: publisher, year of publication) ...

The following patterns for books (in ¶¶1509–1516) show only the business style. However, you can readily convert them to the academic style by simply changing the treatment of these three elements.

For the academic style for entries in bibliographies, see ¶1534c.

1509 Book Title: With Edition Number

    1. Author, <u>book title</u>, edition number [if not the first edition], publisher, place, year, page number.

```
    1.  Andrew Tobias, Managing Your Money, 2d ed., Prentice-
Hall, Englewood Cliffs, N.J., 1991, p. 14.
```

NOTE: Use an edition number only when the book is not in the first edition. If included, the edition number follows the main title and any related elements, such as the subtitle or the volume number and title. (For an example, see ¶1511.) The following abbreviated forms are commonly used: *2d ed., 3d ed., 4th ed.,* and *rev. ed.* (for "revised edition").

1510 Book Title: With Subtitle

    1. Author, <u>book title: subtitle</u>, edition number [if not the first edition], publisher, place, year, page number.

```
    1.  Steven P. Schnaars, Marketing Strategy:  A Customer-
Driven Approach, Free Press, New York, 1991, p. 228.
```

```
    2.  Al Ries and Jack Trout, Positioning:  The Battle for
Your Mind, 1st ed. rev., McGraw-Hill, New York, 1986, p. 46.
```

NOTE: Do not give the subtitle of a book unless it is significant in identifying the book or in explaining its basic nature. If a subtitle is to be shown, separate it from the main title with a colon (unless the title page shows some other mark such as a dash). Type an underscore (without a break) from the start of the main title to the end of the subtitle. If you are using electronic equipment with the capability of generating italic type, the main title and the subtitle may be done in italics. Capitalize the first word of the subtitle, even if it is a short preposition like *for,* a short conjunction like *or,* or an article like *the* or *a.* (See ¶361.)

```
    3.  Roy Blount, Jr., One Fell Soup:  Or I'm Just a Bug on
the Windshield of Life, Little, Brown, Boston, 1983, p. 84.
```

1511 Book Title: With Volume Number and Volume Title

1. Author, <u>book title</u>, volume number, <u>volume title</u>, edition number [if not the first edition], publisher, place, year, page number.

1. E. Lipson, <u>The Economic History of England</u>, Vol. 1, <u>The Middle Ages</u>, 12th ed., Adam & Charles Black, London, 1959, pp. 511–594.

NOTE: As a rule, do not show the volume title in a note unless it is significant in identifying the book. When the volume title is included, both the volume number and the volume title follow the book title (and subtitle, if any) but precede the edition number. The volume number is usually preceded by the abbreviation *Vol.* or by the word *Book* or *Part* (depending on the actual designation). The volume number may be arabic or roman, depending on the style used in the actual book. Some writers prefer to use one style of volume number throughout the notes.

See also ¶1512.

1512 Book Title: With Volume Number Alone

1. Author, <u>book title</u>, edition number [if not the first edition], publisher, place, year, volume number, page number.

1. Robert E. Spiller et al. (eds.), <u>Literary History of the United States</u>, Macmillan, New York, 1948, Vol. II, pp. 639–651.

NOTE: When the volume number is shown without the volume title, it follows the date of publication. When the volume number and page number occur one after the other, they may be styled as follows:

Style for Roman Volume Number
Vol. III, p. 197   **OR**   III, 197

Style for Arabic Volume Number
Vol. 5, pp. 681–684   **OR**   5:681–684

1. Robert E. Spiller et al. (eds.), <u>Literary History of the United States</u>, Macmillan, New York, 1948, II, 639–651.

Do not use the forms with figures alone if there is a chance your reader will not understand them.

1513 Book Title: With Chapter Reference

1. Author, <u>book title</u>, publisher, place, year, chapter number, "chapter title" [if significant], page number.

1. Will Durant and Ariel Durant, <u>The Age of Napoleon</u>, Simon and Schuster, New York, 1975, Chap. XII, "Napoleon and the Arts," pp. 278–285.

NOTE: When a note refers primarily to the title of a book, a chapter number and a chapter title are not usually included. If considered significant, however, these details can be inserted just before the page numbers. The word *chapter* is usually abbreviated as *Chap.*, the chapter number is arabic or roman (depending on the original), and the chapter title is enclosed in quotation marks. Some writers prefer to use one style of chapter number throughout the notes.

1514 Selection From Collected Works of One Author

> 1. Author, "title of selection," book title, publisher, place, year, page number.

> 1. Sylvia Plath, "The Courage of Shutting Up," Winter Trees, Harper & Row, New York, 1972, pp. 8–9.

1515 Selection in Anthology

> 1. Author of selection, "title of selection," **in** editor of anthology **(ed.)**, book title, publisher, place, year, page number.

> 1. Robert M. Clark, "Water Supply," in Robert A. Corbitt (ed.), Standard Handbook of Environmental Engineering, McGraw–Hill, New York, 1990, p. 5–3.

> 2. James Thurber, "The Unicorn in the Garden," in Frank Muir (ed.), The Oxford Book of Humorous Prose, Oxford Univ. Press, 1990, p. 573.

> 3. Herbert Marks, "The Twelve Prophets," in Robert Alter and Frank Kermode (eds.), The Literary Guide to the Bible, Harvard Univ. Press, 1987, pp. 207–233.

> 4. Lindsy Van Gelder, "The Great Person–Hole Cover Debate: A Modest Proposal for Anyone Who Thinks the Word 'He' Is Just Plain Easier," in 75 Readings: An Anthology, 2d ed., McGraw–Hill, 1989, pp. 347–349.

1516 Article in Reference Work

> 1. Author [if known], "article title," name of reference work, edition number [if not the first edition], publisher [usually omitted], place [usually omitted], year, page number [may be omitted].

> 1. Grace M. Booth, "Distributed Systems (Computers)," McGraw–Hill Encyclopedia of Science and Technology, 7th ed., 1992.

> 2. "Information Theory," The New Encyclopedia Brittanica: Macropaedia, 15th ed., 1990.

> 3. "Ellison, Ralph," Encyclopedia of Southern Culture, Univ. of North Carolina Press, Chapel Hill, 1989.

> 4. "Foreign Visa Requirements," The New York Public Library Desk Reference, Webster's New World, New York, 1989, p. 471.

NOTE: It is not necessary to give the name of the publisher or the place of publication unless there is some possibility of confusion or the reference is not well known.

> 5. Webster's Ninth New Collegiate Dictionary, Merriam, Springfield, Mass., 1990, pp. 24–28.

> 6. Random House Webster's College Dictionary, 1991, pp. 1564–1565.

Moreover, if you are making reference to an article or an entry that appears in alphabetic order in the main portion of the work, even the page number may be omitted. If the reference work carries the name of an editor rather than an author, the editor's name is also usually omitted.

> 7. "Green Revolution," The Concise Columbia Encyclopedia, 2d ed., 1989.

1517 Article in Newspaper

> 1. Author [if known], "article title," name of newspaper, date, page number, column number.

> 1. Edith Herman, "Switching to Switched Data," Communications Week, July 8, 1991, p. 30, cols. 3–5.

> 2. Jonathan R. Laing, "Are the Glory Years Over?" Barron's, July 8, 1991, p. 22, col. 3.

See ¶1518, note.

NOTE: If a particular issue of a newspaper is published in several sections and the page numbering begins anew with each section, include the section letter or number before the page number.

> 3. Elizabeth M. Fowler, "Creating Jobs by Building Export Trade," The New York Times, July 2, 1991, Sec. D, p. 6, col. 2. (**OR:** . . . July 2, 1991, p. D6, col. 2.)

1518 Article in Magazine

> 1. Author [if known], "article title," name of magazine, date, page number.

> 1. "The Best (and Worst) Airlines," Consumer Reports, July 1991, pp. 462–469.

> 2. Patricia Sellers, "Winning Over the New Consumer," Fortune, July 29, 1991, p. 113.

> 3. Constance M. Green, "How to Turn Your Staff Into Star Performers," Black Enterprise, July 1991, p. 64.

NOTE: Omit the comma between the article title and the name of the periodical if the article title ends with a question mark or an exclamation point.

> 4. Alan Tonelson, "What Is the National Interest?" The Atlantic, July 1991, p. 35.

> 5. Susan Kerr, "Inventory Your LAN--Automatically!" Datamation, July 1, 1991, pp. 47–48.

See also the second example in ¶1517.

1519 Article in Professional Journal

> 1. Author, "article title," title of journal [frequently abbreviated], series number [if given], volume number, issue number [if given], date, page number.

> 1. Andrea Gabor, "Rochester Focuses: A Community's Core Competence," Harvard Business Review, Vol. 69, No. 4, July–August 1991, pp. 116–126.

OR:

> 1. Andrea Gabor, "Rochester Focuses: A Community's Core Competence," HBR, Vol. 69, No. 4, July–August 1991, pp. 116–126.

NOTE: Titles of journals are often abbreviated in notes whenever these abbreviations are likely to be familiar to the intended readership or are clearly identified in a bibliography at the end.

1520 Bulletin, Pamphlet, or Monograph

1. Author [if given], "article title" [if appropriate], <u>title of bulletin</u>, series title and series number [if appropriate], volume number and issue number [if appropriate], sponsoring organization, place [may be omitted], date, page number.

1. Carolena L. Lyons–Smith and Richard A. Hatch, "Selection of an Integrated Software Package for the Business Communication Course," <u>The Bulletin of the Association for Business Communication</u>, Vol. LIV, No. 2, June 1991, p. 32. (The name of the sponsoring organization has not been listed separately because it is incorporated in the title of the bulletin.)

2. "Appropriations Fiscal Year 1992," <u>ALA Washington Newsletter</u>," Vol. 43, No. 6, American Library Association, Washington, June 27, 1991, p. 1. (The name of the sponsoring organization can be omitted from this note if you are sure your reader will understand that *ALA* in the bulletin title refers to the American Library Association.)

NOTE: Because the pertinent data used to identify bulletins, pamphlets, and monographs may vary widely, adapt the pattern shown above as necessary to fit each particular situation.

1521 Unpublished Dissertation or Thesis

1. Author, "title of thesis," **doctoral dissertation OR master's thesis** [identifying phrase to be inserted], name of academic institution, place, date, page number.

1. David Harry Weaver, "An Experimental Study of the Relative Impact of Controllable Factors of Difficulty in Typewriting Practice Material," doctoral dissertation, Syracuse University, Syracuse, N.Y., 1966, p. 121.

1522 Quotation From a Secondary Source

1. Author, <u>book title</u>, publisher, place, date, page number, **quoted by** author, <u>book title</u>, publisher, place, date, page number.

1. Herbert Marcuse, <u>One Dimensional Man</u>, Beacon, Boston, 1964, p. 7, quoted by William J. McGill, <u>The Year of the Monkey: Revolt on Campus, 1968–69</u>, McGraw–Hill, New York, 1982, p. 49.

2. <u>Newsweek</u>, May 2, 1988, p. 51, cited by Seymour Chatman, "The Pajama Man: Idyll Without Words," in Christopher Ricks and Leonard Michaels (eds.), <u>The State of the Language</u>, Univ. of California Press, Berkeley, 1990.

NOTE: While it is always preferable to take the wording of a quotation from the original source, it is sometimes necessary to draw the wording from a secondary source. In such cases construct the note in two parts: in the first part, give as much information as possible about the *original* source (derived, of course, from the reference note in the secondary source); in the second part, give the necessary information about the *secondary* source (which is at hand). Bridge the two parts of the note with a phrase such as *quoted by* or *cited by*. The pattern shown above assumes that the quotation originally appeared in a book and that the secondary source for the quoted matter was also a book. Naturally, if the original source or the secondary source is a work other than a book, use the pattern appropriate for that work in place of the "book" pattern shown above.

Elements of Source Reference Notes

1523 Note Number

a. Make sure that the number at the start of a footnote or an endnote corresponds to the appropriate reference number in the text.

b. Indent the note number 5 spaces, and type it (1) on the line (like an ordinary number), followed by a period and 2 spaces, or (2) as a superior (raised) figure without any space following it. Although the second style has traditionally been the one more commonly used (and is still preferred in academic work), the on-the-line style is now increasingly seen in business material because it is easier to execute. Moreover, the on-the-line style is always used in endnotes. (See ¶1504.)

[1]Michael Lewis, Liar's Poker: Rising Through the Wreckage on Wall Street, Norton, New York, 1989, p. 134.

OR:

1. Michael Lewis, Liar's Poker: Rising Through the Wreckage on Wall Street, Norton, New York, 1989, p. 134.

See ¶1502e on numbering notes; ¶1502f–g on the use of symbols in place of figures.

1524 Names of Authors

a. Type an author's name (first name first) exactly as it appears on the title page of a book or in the heading of an article. (See ¶1508a, note.)

1. Arthur M Schlesinger, Jr., A Thousand Days, Houghton Mifflin, Boston, 1965, p. 31.

2. William Strunk Jr. and E. B. White, The Elements of Style, 3d ed., Macmillan, New York, 1979, pp. 32–33.

3. Clark Clifford with Richard Holbrooke, Counsel to the President, Random House, New York, 1991, p. 170.

4. John A. Byrne with a team of Business Week editors, Business Week's Guide to the Best Business Schools, 2d ed., McGraw–Hill, New York, 1991, p. 67.

b. When two authors have the same surname, show the surname with each author's listing.

5. John–Roger McWilliams and Peter McWilliams, Life 101: Everything We Wish We Had Learned About Life in School––But Didn't, Prelude Press, Los Angeles, 1990, p. 326.

c. When there are three or more authors, list only the first author's name followed by *et al.* (meaning "and others"). Do not underscore or italicize *et al.*

6. E. Raymond Corey et al., Going to Market: Distribution Systems for Industrial Products, Harvard Business School Press, Boston, 1989, p. 104.

NOTE: The names of all the authors may be given, but once this style is used in a source reference note, it should be used consistently.

7. E. Raymond Corey, Frank V. Cespedes, and V. Kasturi Rangan, Going to Market: Distribution Systems for Industrial Products, Harvard Business School Press, Boston, 1989, p. 104.

(Continued on page 396.)

d. When an organization (rather than an individual) is the author of the material, show the organization's name in the author's position.

8. Society for Creative Anachronism, <u>Giants in the Earth</u>, Bennett & Kitchel, East Lansing, Mich., 1991, p. 54.

However, if the organization is both the author and the publisher, show the organization's name only once—as the publisher.

9. <u>Patterson's American Education, 1991</u>, Educational Directories, Mount Prospect, Ill., 1990, Vol. LXXXVII.

10. "Combating Air Travel Fatigue," <u>The Book of Inside Information</u>, Boardroom Classics, New York, 1989, p. 370.

e. When a work such as an anthology carries an editor's name rather than an author's name, list the editor's name in the author's position, followed by the abbreviation *ed.* in parentheses. (If the names of two or more editors are listed, use the abbreviation *eds.* in parentheses.)

11. David Rosenberg (ed.), <u>Congregation: Contemporary Writers Read the Jewish Bible</u>, Harcourt, New York, 1987.

12. Christopher Ricks and Leonard Michaels (eds.), <u>The State of the Language</u>, Univ. of California Press, Berkeley, 1990.

NOTE: If a reference work (such as an encyclopedia, a dictionary, or a directory) carries the name of an editor rather than an author, the editor's name is usually omitted. (See ¶1516.)

13. <u>Dictionary of American Regional English</u>, Harvard Univ. Press, Cambridge, Mass., 1985, Vol I, p. xxxii.

RATHER THAN:

13. Frederic G. Cassidy (ed.), <u>Dictionary of American Regional English</u>, Harvard Univ. Press, Cambridge, Mass., 1985, Vol. I, p. xxxii.

f. If the author of a work is unknown, begin the note with the title of the work. Do not use *Anonymous* in place of the author's name.

1525 Title of the Work

a. In giving the title of the work, follow the title page of a book or the main heading of an article for wording, spelling, and punctuation. However, adjust the capitalization as necessary so that all titles cited in the notes conform to a standard style. For example, a book entitled *Assertiveness*, with a subtitle (*the right to be you*) shown entirely in small letters on the title page for graphic effect, would appear in a note as follows: Claire Walmsley, *Assertiveness: The Right to Be You.*

For the capitalization of titles, see ¶¶360–363.

b. If a title and a subtitle are shown on separate lines in the original work without any intervening punctuation, use a colon to separate them in the source reference note. (See ¶1510 for an example.)

c. In general, use underscoring or italics for titles of *complete* published works and quotation marks for titles that refer to *parts* of complete published works.

For the use of underscoring or italics with titles, see ¶¶289, 1508a; for the use of quotation marks with titles, see ¶¶242–243.

1526 Publisher's Name

a. List the publisher's name as it appears on the title page (for example, *Macmillan Publishing Co., Inc.*) or in a shortened form that is clearly recognizable *(Macmillan)*; use one form consistently throughout. If a division of the publishing company is also listed on the title page, it is not necessary to include this information in the footnote. Publishers, however, often do so in references to their own materials.

b. The following list of examples shows acceptable patterns for abbreviating publishers' names. If in doubt, do not abbreviate.

Full Name	Acceptable Short Form
Alfred A. Knopf	Knopf
John Wiley & Sons	Wiley
William Morrow and Company, Inc.	Morrow
Random House	——
The Brookings Institution	Brookings
Macmillan Publishing Co., Inc.	Macmillan
Houghton Mifflin Company	Houghton Mifflin
Addison-Wesley Publishing Co.	Addison-Wesley
HarperCollins Publisher	HarperCollins
McGraw-Hill, Inc.	McGraw-Hill
Simon & Schuster Inc.	Simon & Schuster
Little, Brown & Co.	Little, Brown
Farrar Straus Giroux	
Yale University Press	Yale Univ. Press
University of California Press	Univ. of California Press
Penguin Books	Penguin
BUT: Basic Books	——

NOTE: The patterns of abbreviation typically depend on how the publishers are referred to in speech. Since one never hears Random House referred to as *Random,* the name is not abbreviated. By the same token, one hears Little, Brown & Co. referred to as *Little, Brown,* never simply as *Little.* Penguin Books is typically referred to as *Penguin,* whereas Basic Books is never referred to as *Basic;* hence the difference in the treatment of these names.

c. Omit the publisher's name from references to magazines, newspapers, and journals. The publisher's name is also usually omitted from references to dictionaries and similar works unless confusion might result or the work is not well known. (For examples, see ¶1516.)

1527 Place of Publication

a. As a rule, list only the city of publication (for example, *New York, Boston, Washington, Toronto*). If the city may not be well known to your intended audience (for example, readers from abroad) or the city is likely to be confused with another city of the same name, add the state or the country (for example, *Cambridge, Mass.; Cambridge, England*). If the title page lists several cities in which the publisher has offices, use only the first city named.

b. Omit the place of publication from references to magazines, journals, and well-known reference works.

c. Incorporate the city name in the name of a newspaper that might otherwise be unrecognized. For example, *The Star-Ledger* (published in Newark, New Jersey) should be referred to in a note as *The Newark (N.J.) Star-Ledger.*

1528 Date of Publication

    a. For books, show the year of publication. (Use the most recent year shown in the copyright notice.)

    b. For monthly periodicals, show both the month and the year. (See ¶1518 for examples.)

    c. For weekly or daily periodicals, show the month, day, and year. (See ¶¶1517–1518 for examples.)

1529 Page Numbers

    a. Page references in notes occur in the following forms:

        p. 3   p. v
        pp. 3–4   pp. v–vi

        pp. 301 f. (meaning ''page 301 and the following page'')
        pp. 301 ff. (meaning ''page 301 and the following pages'')

    NOTE: Whenever possible, avoid using the indefinite abbreviations *f.* and *ff.*, and supply a specific range of page numbers instead.

    b. In a range of page numbers the second number is sometimes abbreviated; for example, *pp. 981–983* may be expressed as *pp. 981–83*. (See ¶460.)

    c. There is a trend toward dropping *p.* and *pp.* when there is no risk of mistaking the numbers for anything but page numbers.

Subsequent References

1530 a. When a note refers to a work that was fully identified in the note *immediately preceding*, it may be shortened by use of the abbreviation *ibid.* (meaning ''in the same place''). *Ibid.* replaces all those elements that would otherwise be carried over intact from the previous note. Do not underscore or italicize *ibid.*

        1.   William Safire, <u>Fumblerules</u>, Doubleday, New York, 1990, pp. 67–69.

        2.   Ibid., p. 73. (*Ibid.* represents all the elements in the previous note except the page number.)

        3.   Ibid. (Here *ibid.* represents everything in the preceding note, including the same page number.)

    b. If you plan to use *ibid.* in a *footnote,* make sure that the footnote ''immediately preceding'' is no more than a few pages back. Otherwise, the interested reader will be put to the irritating task of having to riffle back through the pages in order to find the ''immediately preceding'' footnote. To spare your reader this inconvenience, use the forms suggested in ¶1531.

    c. Do not use *ibid.* in a *textnote* unless the one ''immediately preceding'' is on the same page and easy to spot; otherwise, your reader will have to search through lines and lines of text to find it. To spare your reader, construct these ''subsequent reference'' textnotes along the same lines as ''first reference'' textnotes. (See ¶1507a–e.)

    NOTE: With *endnotes,* the use of *ibid.* will cause no inconvenience, since it refers to the note directly above.

1531 **a.** When a note refers to a work fully identified in an earlier note but *not the one immediately preceding*, it may be shortened as follows:

    1.   Author's surname, page number.

    8.   Safire, p. 78. (Referring to the work fully identified in an earlier note; see note 1 in ¶1530a.)

NOTE: When this short form is used for a subsequent reference, it is desirable to provide a complete bibliography as well, so that the interested reader can quickly find the complete reference in an alphabetic listing.

b. When previous reference has been made to different authors with the same surname, the use of a surname alone in a subsequent reference would be confusing. Therefore, the basic pattern in ¶1531a must be modified in the following way:

    1.   Author's initial(s) plus surname, page number.

OR: 2.   Author's full name, page number.

    1.   Denys Wilkinson, Man's Universe, Columbia Univ. Press, New York, 1991, p. 29.

    2.   Carroll W. Wilkinson, Women in Nontraditional Occupations, G. K. Hall, Boston, 1991, p. 46.

    3.   D. Wilkinson, pp. 35–36.

    4.   C. Wilkinson, p. 53.

c. If previous reference has been made to different works by the same author, any subsequent reference should contain the title of the specific work now being referred to. This title may be shortened to a key word or phrase; the word or phrase should be sufficiently clear, however, so that the full title can be readily identified in the bibliography or in an earlier note.

    1.   Author's surname, book title [shortened if feasible], page number.

    1.   Peter F. Drucker, Managing the Nonprofit Organization, HarperCollins, New York, 1990, p. 143.

    2.   Peter F. Drucker, Managing for Results, Harper & Row, New York, 1986, pp. 201–2.

    3.   Peter F. Drucker, Managing for the Future: The 1990s and Beyond, Dutton, New York, 1992, p. 89.

    4.   Drucker, Results, p. 144.

    5.   Drucker, Future, p. 93.

If referring to an article in a periodical, use the periodical title rather than the article title.

    2.   Author's surname, periodical title [shortened if feasible], page number.

    4.   Elaine Segal, "You Should Have Seen the Onethatgotaway," Smithsonian, July 1991, p. 138.

    5.   Tracy Kidder,...

    6.   Segal, Smithsonian, p. 140. (Referring to the work identified in note 4 above.)

(Continued on page 400.)

d. A more formal style in subsequent references uses the abbreviations *loc. cit.* ("in the place cited") and *op. cit.* ("in the work cited").

  1. Author's surname, **loc. cit.** (This pattern is used when reference is made to the *very same page* in the work previously identified.)

  2. Author's surname, **op. cit.,** page number. (This pattern is used when reference is made to a *different page* in the work previously identified.)

  1. Helen Kennerly, <u>Managing Anxiety</u>, Oxford Univ. Press, New York, 1990, p. 167.

  2. Larry Hirschhorn, <u>Managing in a Team Environment</u>, Addison–Wesley, Reading, Mass., 1991, p. 73.

  3. Kennerly, op. cit., p. 173. (Referring to a different page in <u>Managing Anxiety</u>.)

  4. Hirschhorn, loc. cit. (Referring to the same page in <u>Managing in a Team Environment</u>.)

  5. Ibid. (Referring to exactly the same page as shown in note 4. *Ibid.* may be used only to refer to the note immediately preceding. See ¶1530.)

NOTE: Do not underscore or italicize *loc. cit., op. cit.* or *ibid.*

Bibliographies

15

1532 A bibliography at the end of a report or a manuscript typically lists all the works *consulted* in the preparation of the material as well as all the works that were actually *cited* in the notes. The format of a bibliography is also used for any list of titles, such as a list of recommended readings or a list of new publications.

1533 a. On a new page put *BIBLIOGRAPHY* (or some other appropriate title) in all-capital letters (and boldface if available), and center the head on line 13. Leave 2 blank lines, and begin the first entry on line 16. (See the illustration on page 401.)

  b. Use the same margins as for other pages in the body of the report or manuscript (see ¶¶1404–1409), and treat the numbering of these pages as indicated in ¶1426e–f.

  c. Begin each entry at the left margin. Ordinarily, single-space the entries, but use double spacing if the material is to be set in type.

  d. Indent turnover lines 5 spaces so that the first word in each entry will stand out.

  e. Leave 1 blank line between entries (whether they are single- or double-spaced).

1534 a. List the entries alphabetically by author's last name.

  b. Entries lacking an author are alphabetized by title. Disregard the word *The* or *A* at the beginning of a title in determining alphabetic sequence. (For an example, see the next-to-last entry in the illustration on page 401. Note that this entry is alphabetized on the basis of *Guide,* following *Galbraith.*)

  c. There is no need to number the alphabetized entries in a bibliography unless you plan to use the style of textnotes described in ¶1507e. In that case begin each entry of the bibliography with a number typed at the left margin, followed by a period and 2 spaces. Then type the rest of the entry in the customary way, but indent any turnover so that it begins under the first word in the line above. (In the parenthetical textnotes, you can then make reference to different works by their bibliographic "entry number" instead of by author.)

9. Bamford, Janet, et al., <u>Complete Guide to Managing Your Money</u>, Consumers Union, Mount Vernon, N.Y., 1989.

10. Beard, Henry, <u>Latin for All Occasions</u>, Villard, New York, 1990.

NOTE: In a bibliography with numbered entries, align the numbers on the period. On a page where the numbers shift from single digits to double digits (as in the illustration above) or from double digits to triple digits, start the smaller numbers 1 space in from the left margin.

1535 When a bibliography contains more than one work by the same author, replace the author's name with a long dash (six hyphens) in all the entries after the first. List the works alphabetically by title. (For examples, see the fifth, sixth, and seventh entries in the illustration below. Note that these titles are alphabetized on the key words *Anatomy, Short,* and *Tenured.* The eighth entry involves a coauthor and therefore follows the works written by the first author alone.)

NOTE: As an alternative, multiple entries pertaining to the same author may be listed in chronological sequence according to the date of each publication.

15

↓ 43

BIBLIOGRAPHY ↓ 3

Bernheim, B. Douglas, and John B. Shoven (eds.), <u>National Saving and Economic Performance</u>, Univ. of Chicago Press, Chicago, 1991. ↓ 2

Biven, W. Carl, <u>Who Killed John Maynard Keynes?: Conflicts in the Evolution of Economic Policy</u>, Dow Jones–Irwin, Homewood, Ill., 1989.

Bruno, Michael, et al. (eds.), <u>Lessons of Economic Stabilization and Its Aftermath</u>, MIT Press, Cambridge, Mass., 1991.

Galbraith, James K., <u>Balancing Acts: Technology, Finance, and the American Future</u>, Basic Books, New York, 1990.

Galbraith, John Kenneth, <u>The Anatomy of Power</u>, Houghton Mifflin, Boston, 1983.

------, <u>A Short History of Financial Euphoria: Financial Genius Is Before the Fall</u>, Whittle, Knoxville, 1990.

------, <u>A Tenured Professor</u>, Houghton Mifflin, Boston, 1990.

------ and Paul W. McCracken, <u>Reaganomics: Meaning, Means, and Ends</u>, Free Press, New York, 1984.

<u>A Guide for Selecting Automated Risk Analysis Tools</u>, Gordon Press, New York, 1990

Harvard Business Review, <u>Strategic Management</u>, Wiley, New York, 1983.

1536 Entries in bibliographies contain the same elements and follow the same style as source reference notes except for two key differences.

a. Begin each entry with the name of the author listed in inverted order (last name first). When an entry includes two or more authors' names, invert only the first author's name. When an organization is listed as the author, do not invert the name.

> Andrews, Kenneth R. (ed.), <u>Ethics in Practice: Managing the Moral Corporation</u>, Harvard Business School Press, Boston, 1989.

> Burrough, Bryan, and John Helyar, <u>Barbarians at the Gates: The Rise and Fall of RJR Nabisco</u>, Harper & Row, New York, 1990.

> J. K. Lasser Tax Institute, <u>How to Run a Small Business</u>, 6th ed., McGraw-Hill, New York, 1989.

For additional examples, see the illustration on page 401.

b. Include page numbers in bibliographic entries only when the material being cited is part of a larger work. In such cases show the range of pages (for example, *pp. 215–232*) on which the material appears.

> Finegan, Jay, "The Smart T&E Expense Report," <u>Inc.</u>, July 1991, pp. 57–59.

c. In academic material, bibliographic entries typically follow a slightly different style. In the examples below, note that a period follows the three main parts of the entry (author's name, the title, and the publishing information). Also note that the parentheses that normally enclose the publishing information in an academic-style footnote or endnote (see ¶1508b) are omitted in the bibliographic entry.

> Andrews, Kenneth R. (ed.). <u>Ethics in Practice: Managing the Moral Corporation</u>. Boston: Harvard Business School Press, 1989.

> Finegan, Jay. "The Smart T&E Expense Report." <u>Inc.</u>, July 1991, pp. 57–59. (Note that the magazine title—in this case <u>Inc.</u>—is considered part of the publishing information. Thus a period follows the article title here to mark the end of the title information in the entry.)

SECTION 16

Tables

¶1601

You can fit a good deal of material into a compact space when you present it in the form of a table—with items arranged in *rows* (to be read horizontally) and in *columns* (to be read vertically). However, in designing a table, you should aim for more than compactness. Your reader should be able to locate specific information faster—and detect significant patterns or trends in the data more quickly—than if the same information were presented in the running text.

The following section presents guidelines on setting up and executing well-designed tables. Modify these guidelines as necessary in specific situations to achieve results that are easy to understand, attractive to look at, and as simple as possible to execute.

With the advent of the computer and a wide array of software packages, it is now possible to eliminate much (and in some cases all) of the tedious calculations entailed in planning the layout of multicolumn tables. There are software packages, for example, for financial spreadsheets and various types of statistical analyses that require you simply to input the variable data; the software will then perform all the necessary calculations and print the results out in a preset format (unless you have called for specific format modifications). Moreover, you can take advantage of the automatic centering capabilities in many programs to center copy within a table and then center the table as a whole, both horizontally and vertically, on a full sheet of paper.

The following guidelines assume that you may have to perform all the necessary operations by hand. However, if you are using a software program, be sure to exploit its timesaving features whenever you can.

Types of Tables

1601 a. **Table Text Only.** A table may simply consist of two columns of data with as few as two rows in each column.

```
                                                              4


        Our analysis of the latest reports indicates that sales are up by
    at least 10 percent in all regions:
                                          ↓ 2
                        Eastern Region            16.2%
                        North Central Region      11.0%
                        Southern Region           18.4%
                        Western Region            13.9%
                                                          ↓ 2
        The primary reason for this upsurge, according to the managers of
    these regions, is the rebuilding of inventories, which were allowed to
```

NOTE: When a single-spaced table is inserted in the midst of single-spaced running text, leave 1 blank line above and below the table (as shown above). If the table is typed with double or 1½-line spacing or if the table is inserted in the midst of running text typed with double or 1½-line spacing, leave 2 blank lines above and below. (See ¶1604c, note.)

b. Open (Unruled) Table. An open table may consist of nothing more than two columns of data, each labeled with a column head. The table is called *open* because no horizontal rules are used in the table design.

NOTE: When a table begins with unruled column heads, leave 2 blank lines above and below the table as a whole. (See also ¶1604c.)

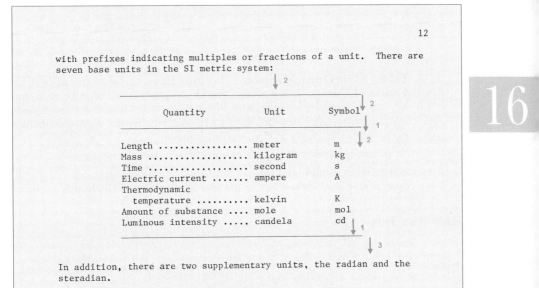

```
     When designing buildings for New England sites, keep in mind the

typical outdoor winter temperatures.  For example: ↓ 3


                                    Temp.
                                     (°F)
                      City                    ↓ 2
                  Boston, Mass.          0
                  Burlington, Vt.      -10
                  Concord, N.H.        -15
                  Hartford, Conn.        0
                  Portland, Maine       -5
                  Providence, R.I.       0  ↓ 3
```

c. Ruled Table. A ruled table is so called because it has three horizontal rules: one above the column heads, one below the column heads, and one below the last line of the table text.

```
                                                                    12

with prefixes indicating multiples or fractions of a unit.  There are
seven base units in the SI metric system:
                              ↓ 2

        ────────────────────────────────────────────
                                                      ↓ 2
            Quantity        Unit        Symbol▼
        ────────────────────────────────────────────
                                                     ↓ 1
        Length ................ meter        m        ↓ 2
        Mass .................. kilogram     kg
        Time .................. second       s
        Electric current ....... ampere      A
        Thermodynamic
            temperature ......... kelvin     K
        Amount of substance .... mole        mol
        Luminous intensity ..... candela     cd  ↓ 1
        ────────────────────────────────────────────
                                                      ↓ 3
In addition, there are two supplementary units, the radian and the
steradian.
```

NOTE: When a table begins with ruled column heads, leave 2 blank lines above and below the table as a whole. (See also ¶1604c.) Type the first underscore on the second line beneath the running text to create the appearance of 2 blank lines.

For the use of leaders between columns, see ¶1631d, note; for the use of rules within a table, see ¶1633.

(Continued on page 406.)

d. **Boxed Table.** This is a ruled table to which vertical rules have been added.

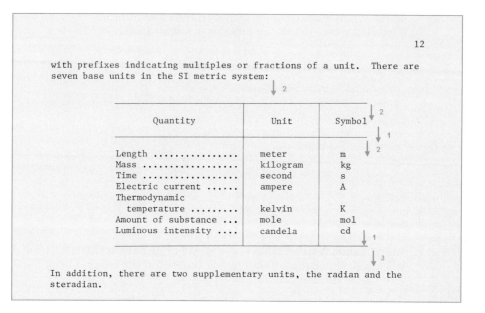

12

with prefixes indicating multiples or fractions of a unit. There are seven base units in the SI metric system:
↓ 2

Quantity	Unit	Symbol
Length	meter	m
Mass	kilogram	kg
Time	second	s
Electric current	ampere	A
Thermodynamic temperature	kelvin	K
Amount of substance ...	mole	mol
Luminous intensity	candela	cd

In addition, there are two supplementary units, the radian and the steradian.

For the use of leaders in a boxed table, see ¶1631e; for the use of rules within a table, see ¶1633.

e. **Tables With Other Elements.** The four types of tables identified in ¶1601a–d frequently carry additional elements, such as a table number, a table title, a subtitle, and notes. Moreover, *leaders* (rows of periods) may be used to lead the eye from items in the first column to corresponding items in the second column.

For the use of leaders between columns, see ¶1631d, note.

NOTE: When a table begins with a title or a table number, leave 3 blank lines above and below the table as a whole. (See ¶1604c–d.)

Table With Title

ESTIMATED NUMBER OF EMPLOYEES IN
MAJOR OCCUPATIONAL GROUPS IN 1990

Managerial and professional specialty ...	12,588,000
Technical, sales, and administrative support	9,472,000
Service occupations	4,229,000
Precision production, craft, and repair	10,109,000
Operators, fabricators, and laborers	10,758,000
Farming, forestry, and fishing	1,020,000

Table With Number, Title, and Subtitle

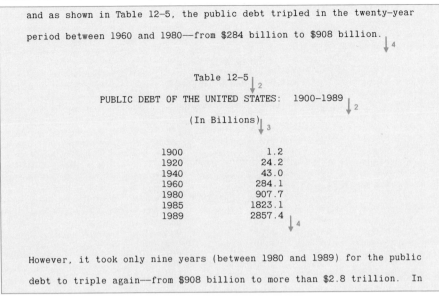

and as shown in Table 12-5, the public debt tripled in the twenty-year

period between 1960 and 1980—from $284 billion to $908 billion. ↓4

Table 12-5 ↓2

PUBLIC DEBT OF THE UNITED STATES: 1900-1989 ↓2

(In Billions) ↓3

1900	1.2
1920	24.2
1940	43.0
1960	284.1
1980	907.7
1985	1823.1
1989	2857.4 ↓4

However, it took only nine years (between 1980 and 1989) for the public

debt to triple again—from $908 billion to more than $2.8 trillion. In

**Open Table With Number, Title, Subtitle,
Column Heads, and Notes**

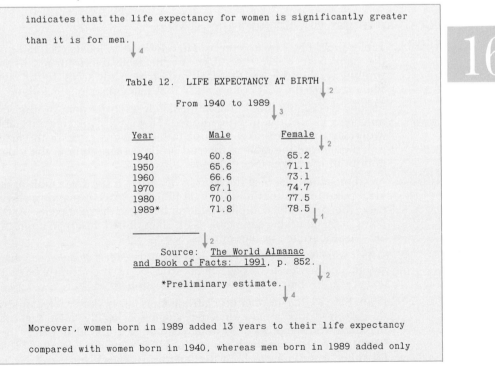

indicates that the life expectancy for women is significantly greater

than it is for men. ↓4

Table 12. LIFE EXPECTANCY AT BIRTH ↓2

From 1940 to 1989 ↓3

Year	Male	Female ↓2
1940	60.8	65.2
1950	65.6	71.1
1960	66.6	73.1
1970	67.1	74.7
1980	70.0	77.5
1989*	71.8	78.5 ↓1

↓2

Source: The World Almanac
and Book of Facts: 1991, p. 852. ↓2

*Preliminary estimate. ↓4

Moreover, women born in 1989 added 13 years to their life expectancy

compared with women born in 1940, whereas men born in 1989 added only

(Continued on page 408.)

**Ruled Table With Number, Title, Subtitle,
Column Heads, and Note**

```
                              ↓ 4
                          Table A-15 ↓
                                     2
                      LIFE INSURANCE IN FORCE
                                          ↓ 2
                         ($000,000 Omitted)
                                          ↓ 1
         _____     ↓ 2

         Year        Ordinary           Group
                                                 ↓ 1

         1910         11,783            . . .     ↓ 2
         1940         79,346          14,938
         1950        149,116          47,793
         1960        341,881         175,903
         1970        734,730         551,357
         1975      1,083,421         904,695
         1980      1,760,474       1,579,355
         1985      3,247,289       2,561,595
         1989      4,939,964       3,469,498  ↓
                                              1

                                              ↓ 2
              Source:  The World Almanac
           and Book of Facts:  1991, p. 837. ↓
                                              4
```

Locating Tables Within Running Text

16

1602 a. Tables should be easy to refer to. Therefore, try to locate each table on the same page where the subject of the table is introduced in the running text. In this way the reader will have ready access to the table while reading the text commentary that may precede and follow.

b. Ideally, every table should fall immediately after the point in the running text where it is first mentioned. However, if placing the table within a paragraph is likely to disrupt the reader's grasp of the material, then locate the table at the end of the paragraph or at the top or bottom of the page. (See ¶1604d.)

1603 a. Avoid breaking a table at the bottom of a page. If starting a table at the ideal point means that it will not all fit in the space remaining on the page, then place the complete table at the top of the next page. (At the point in the text where the table is first mentioned, insert an appropriate cross-reference in parentheses. See ¶1608.)

NOTE: Some software programs have a feature called *block protect*, which automatically prevents a page break from occurring within a block of text. (See the entry on *block protect* in Section 20.)

b. If you have to fit a number of relatively short tables (half a page or less) in a given report, memo, or letter, single-spacing the table text may maximize your chances of locating each table in the ideal place. (See ¶1624 on the issue of single versus double spacing of tables. See ¶1637 for other techniques to limit the length of tables.)

1604 If a table is to appear on a page that also carries running text:

a. It should be centered horizontally within the established margins. (See ¶1609 for guidance on centering a table within these margins.)

b. Try to indent the table at least 5 spaces from each side margin. In any case, the width of the table should not exceed the width of the running text. (See ¶¶1640–1643 for ways to deal with an extrawide table.)

c. The table should be set off by 1 to 3 blank lines from the running text above and below, as follows:

Kind of Table	Spacing in Table Text	Blank Lines Above and Below Table	Illustration
Without column heads or table title	Single	1	¶1601a
Without column heads or table title	Double or 1½-line	2	
With column heads (but no table title)	Single, double, or 1½-line	2	¶1601b, c, d
With table title	Single, double, or 1½-line	3	¶1601e

NOTE: In some software programs, switching from double spacing to triple spacing (in order to leave 2 blank lines) is either difficult or awkward. Therefore, when you are typing a table without a title, leave only 1 blank line above and below the title (instead of the 2 blank lines normally used).

d. Placing a table in the middle of a page (with running text above and below) requires you to leave up to 3 blank lines both above and below the table. If space is tight, place the table at the top or bottom of the page. In that way you can eliminate one set of blank lines and improve your chances of fitting the table on the desired page.

e. Before typing the table, count the number of lines it will require. Be sure to include in your count the blank lines within the table as well as above and below. (See the illustrations in ¶1601 for a quick guide to the allowance for blank lines.) On the basis of this count and an evaluation of the adjacent text material and the space available, you can decide on the best location for the table.

f. Be sure you can fit at least two full lines of running text above or below the table. If the results look unattractive, devote the full page to the table (see ¶¶1605–1608) and resume the text on the following page.

NOTE: If you are using a computer, you do not need to count the number of lines before you start to type. Simply input the table copy at the desired location in the running text. When you are printing out the complete document, if you discover the table will not all fit on the same page, you can move the table as a whole to the top or bottom of the page (as noted in *d* above), make other adjustments (as noted in ¶¶1637–1639), or print the table out on a page by itself (see ¶¶1605–1608). If the software program you are using has a feature called *block protect* and you make use of that feature, then the table as a whole will automatically be moved to the top of the next page.

¶1605

Locating Tables on Separate Pages

1605 When a table occupies more than two-thirds of a page, it can often be difficult to fit on the same page with running text. In such cases type the table on a separate page and place it immediately after the text page on which the table is first referred to.

1606 If a given document contains a number of tables, most of which will each require a separate page, then all the tables (short as well as long) may be executed as an appendix at the back of a report or as an attachment to a memo or letter. This arrangement—which permits the reader to keep the full set of tables alongside the running text (except in the case of bound reports)—can be very convenient, especially if some of the tables are repeatedly cited throughout the running text. (This arrangement also eliminates the problem of trying to fit long tables within the text.)

1607 When a table is to appear on a page by itself, it should be centered horizontally and vertically within the established margins of the page. (See ¶¶1609–1611 for guidelines on centering horizontally and vertically.)

NOTE: If no margins have been established, leave a minimum margin of 1 inch on all four sides of the table.

1608 When a table is not located on the same page on which it is referred to, provide a cross-reference in parentheses to the appropriate page.

(See Table 4 on page 18.)   **OR**   (See Table 2-2 on page 31.)

NOTE: These parenthetical cross-references may be treated as a separate sentence (as shown above) or as part of another sentence (see ¶220).

For the advisability of numbering tables to simplify the matter of cross-references, see ¶1613.

Centering Tables Horizontally

1609 The following procedure (*a–g*) describes how to center a table horizontally in typewritten material and determine the starting point for each column within the table. If you are using electronic equipment, you can in most cases automatically center the table as a whole after it has been input. However, since you may have to plan the tab stops for each column beyond the first, you will need to know how to establish a guide line.

a. Establish a *guide line* as follows:

(1) Select the longest item in each column, whether it occurs in the column head or the column text.

(2) Determine the number of spaces to be left between columns. Normally, you would leave 6 spaces. (See, for example, the illustration on page 404 and the one at the top of page 405, where there are 6 spaces between the two columns.) However, you may use any number of spaces that produces an attractive and readable table. (In the first table illustrated on page 407, there are 12 spaces between columns; in the table at the bottom of page 407, there are 9 spaces between columns.) In any case, do not leave less than 2 spaces.

NOTE: In financial statements 2 blank spaces are customarily used between adjacent columns listing amounts of money.

(3) The combination of the longest item from each column plus an allowance for the space between each pair of columns makes up the guide line. Here, for example, is the guide line used to plan Table 14-4 on page 417:

Year   Personal   Personal   Disposable   Personal
     123456   123456   123456   123456

b. Determine the centering point for the table. If the left and right margins have been established in advance, the centering point will fall halfway between these margins. If the left and right margins have not been established and are to be equal, use the exact center of the page as the centering point.

c. Clear all tab stops.

d. From the centering point, backspace once for each pair of strokes in the key line. If you have an odd stroke left over at the end, do not backspace for it.

e. At the point at which you stop backspacing, set the first tab stop. This tab stop will represent the left margin of the table and of the first column.

NOTE: If the process of backspacing carries you beyond the left margin of the running text, you will know that the table is too wide as it currently stands. (If a left margin has not been established and you backspace to a point that leaves a left margin of less than 1 inch, you will also know that the table is too wide.) As a first step, try reducing the space between columns to as little as 2 spaces; repeat steps *d* and *e* to see if this approach produces an acceptable left margin. (If the table is still too wide, see ¶¶1640–1643 for other solutions.)

f. From the left margin of the table, space forward once for each keystroke in the longest item in the first column. Then space forward again for each blank space to be left between the first and second columns. At the point where you stop, set a tab stop. This will represent the start of the second column.

g. Repeat step *f* until you have set tab stops for each of the remaining columns.

Centering Tables Vertically

1610 To center a table vertically on a full 8½- by 11-inch sheet:

a. Count the number of lines in the table (including the blank lines).

NOTE: There is a total of 66 lines on a standard sheet of paper. In order to maintain a minimum margin of 1 inch (6 lines) at the top and bottom of the page, your count for the table should not exceed 54 lines. Moreover, if you are doing a report and must allow for a page number at the top or bottom of the page, your count for the table should not exceed 51 lines. If it appears that the table is running beyond these limits, consider the various alternatives for reducing the length of the table (see ¶1637). If none of these solve the problem, you will have to continue the table on a second page. (See ¶1638 for guidelines on how to execute a table on two or more pages.)

(Continued on page 412.)

b. Find the difference between the total number of lines in the table (including blank lines) and 66, the total number of lines available on the page. (If a table will occupy a total of 39 lines, then the difference between 39 and 66 is 27.)

c. Divide the difference by 2 to find the line number on which to start the table. (Dividing 27 by 2 yields an answer of 13½.) If your answer has a fraction, ignore it. (In this case, then, you would start typing on line 13.)

1611 If you are using electronic equipment with centering capability, simply input the copy and the table will be printed out centered vertically as well as horizontally.

Table Identification

1612 Tables should be identified by *title* unless they are not very numerous and the significance of the tabular material is clear without some descriptive label.

1613 Tables should also be identified by *number* unless they are quite short, not very numerous, and typically referred to only on the page on which they fall. The use of table numbers simplifies the matter of cross-references, an important consideration if you expect that a number of tables will not fit on the page where they are first mentioned or if you know that certain tables will be referred to repeatedly throughout the running text.

NOTE: Tables may be numbered consecutively throughout a given document or consecutively within each chapter and each appendix (if the document is broken down in this way). With the latter technique, the chapter number (or the appendix number or letter) is used as a prefix in the numbering scheme. For example, Table 3-2 would be the second table in Chapter 3, and Table A-5 would be the fifth table in Appendix A.

1614 The table title may be followed by a *subtitle,* which provides additional information about the significance of the table, the period of time it covers, or the manner in which the information is organized or presented. Since a subtitle should be held to one line if possible (two at the most), a lengthy comment on any of these points should be handled as a note to the table rather than as a subtitle (see ¶¶1634–1636).

1615 Type the elements of table identification as follows:

a. **Table Title.** Type the table title in all-capital letters and center. (See ¶1615d.)

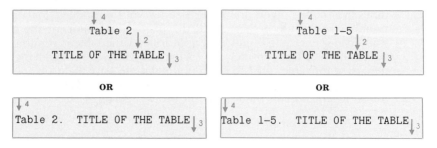

b. **Table Number.** Type the word *Table* in capital and small letters, followed by the appropriate number. To give the table number special emphasis, center it on the second line above the table title. To hold down the length of the table, type the table number on the same line with the table title; in this case insert a period after the table number and leave 2 spaces before typing the table title. (See the illustrations below and at the bottom of page 412.)

NOTE: Within a given document treat all table numbers the same way.

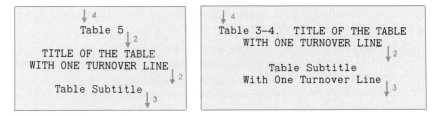

c. **Table Subtitle.** Type in capital and small letters, centered on the second line below the title. The subtitle is usually enclosed in parentheses when it simply comments on the listing of data in some special order (for example, *In Descending Order by Sales Revenue*) or on the omission of zeros from figures given in the table (for example, *In Millions* or *000 Omitted*).

For examples of subtitles enclosed in parentheses, see the tables illustrated on pages 407, 408, 417, 420, and 427.

NOTE: If either the title or the subtitle requires more than one line, break it into sensible phrases and single-space any turnover lines. If possible, try to hold the title or the subtitle to two lines each.

d. To center each line in the table identification, first determine the centering point for the table (see ¶1609b). Then from the centering point, backspace once for each pair of keystrokes in the line. (Do not backspace for an odd keystroke left over at the end.) The point at which you stop backspacing is the point at which to begin typing the line in order to center it.

NOTE: If you are using electronic equipment with centering capability, you will not need to backspace to center each line in the table identification.

e. When a table falls on a page with running text above it, leave 3 blank lines above the first line of table identification. Leave 2 blank lines below the last line of table identification, whether the following copy consists of column heads or the table text.

f. Put all the elements of table identification (the table number, the title, and the subtitle) in boldface if you have that option.

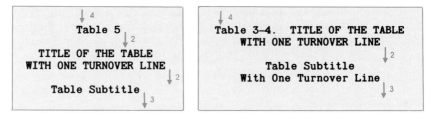

¶1616

Column Heads

1616 a. Unless a table is very simple and the significance of the material is clear without heads, provide a heading for each column. (A heading may be omitted over the first column, also known as the *stub*. See, for example, Table 3 on page 427.)

b. Whenever possible, use singular forms in the column heads. Thus, for example, over a column listing a number of cities, use the heading *City* (rather than *Cities*).

c. In order to hold down the length of column heads, use abbreviations and symbols as necessary. For example:

Acct. No.	Account number
% of Total	Percent of total
FY1993 OR FY93	Fiscal year 1993 (also used to indicate that a company's *fiscal* year does not coincide with the *calendar* year)
1Q/1994 OR IQ/94	First quarter of 1994 (used with 2Q, 3Q, and 4Q to signify the other three quarters of the year)
1993A	Actual results in 1993
1994B	Budgeted results in 1994
1994E	Estimated results in 1994
1995F	Forecast of results in 1995
Sales ($)	Sales results expressed as a dollar amount (in other words, sales revenues)
Sales (U)	Sales results expressed in terms of the number of units sold
Sales YTD ($)	Cumulative sales revenues so far this year (that is, year to date)
% O/(U) Last Year	Percentage by which this year's results are over (or under) last year's results

NOTE: If your reader may not understand some of the abbreviations and symbols you use, explain the unfamiliar ones in a footnote to the table.

    Note: A = actual; E = estimated; F = forecast.

See ¶¶1634–1636 and the illustrations in ¶1623.

d. Column heads should be single-spaced and may be broken into as many as five lines. Column heads are normally centered on the column width (see ¶¶1617–1618), but under certain circumstances the lines that make up the column head may all be blocked left on the column width, that is, start at the left margin of the column (see ¶1619).

NOTE: If you are using electronic equipment with centering capability, each line in a column head can be easily centered. However, in some software programs (especially financial applications), the heads over columns of text often appear blocked *left* on the column width, whereas the heads over columns of figures appear blocked *right* on the column width.

e. In extreme situations, where the column heads are unusually long, it is permissible to type them vertically (reading up). However, because of the awkwardness for the reader and the complications for the typist, consider any alternative that will help you avoid this situation. (See ¶¶1640–1643.)

NOTE: If you are using electronic equipment with the capability of printing smaller type, you may find it possible to get long column heads to fit on a number of horizontal lines.

f. Capitalize the first word of each letter in a column head except articles (*a, an, the*), conjunctions under four letters (such as *and* and *or*), and prepositions under four letters (such as *of* and *in*). See ¶¶360–361, 363 for detailed guidance on capitalizing words in column headings.

For illustrations of different types of column heads, see ¶¶1620–1623.

1617 When a column head is *narrower* than the column text, center the column head over the text as follows:

a. Identify the longest line in the column head and the column text; for example:

COLUMN HEAD: `In-Service`
`12345678901234567`

COLUMN TEXT: `Computer Literacy`

b. Find the difference in the number of keystrokes between the longest line in the column head and the longest line in the column text. (In the example above, the difference is 7.)

c. Divide the difference by 2 (and ignore any fraction in the answer) to find how many spaces to indent the longest line in the column head. (Dividing 7 by 2 yields an answer of 3½, so the longest line in the column head should be indented 3 spaces.)

`###In-Service####`
`Computer Literacy`

NOTE: When this method of centering is used, if a short line cannot be perfectly centered over the long line, the extra space always falls at the right.

d. To center the other lines in the column head in relation to the longest line, follow the same procedure described in *c* above. For example, if the longest line in the column head *(In-Service)* is 10 and another line *(Program)* is 7, divide the difference (3) and discard any fraction in the answer (1½). The resulting figure (1) indicates that the line in question should be indented 1 space.

`In-Service`
`#Training#`
`#Program##`

NOTE: The following examples provide a simple visual check on the correct alignment of lines in a column head.

123456 #	#12345 #	#1234 ##	##123 ##	##12 ###
1234567	1234567	1234567	1234567	1234567

16

1618 When a column head is *wider* than any item in the column text, center the column text under the column head as follows:

a. Type the longest line in the column head, starting at the left margin of the column. (In this case it is the longest line in the column head that will determine the total width of the column.) For example:

```
123456789
Household
```

b. Center any other lines in the column head in relation to the longest line. (See the examples in ¶1617d, note, as a visual check on your results.)

```
123456789
#Median##
#Income##
###per###
Household
```

c. Find the difference in the number of keystrokes between the longest line in the column head and the longest line in the column text. In this example, the longest line in the column head is 9, the longest line in the column text *($19,074)* is 7, and the difference is 2.

d. Divide the difference by 2 (and discard any fraction) to find the number of spaces to indent the longest line in the column text. In this case dividing 2 by 2 gives an answer of 1, so indent the longest text line 1 space.

```
#Median##
#Income##
###per###
Household

#$19,074#
```

e. Once the wide column head has been typed, you can reset the tab stop for this column to establish the starting point for most lines in the column text. In this example the column text will consist almost entirely of five-digit numbers; the dollar sign will appear only in the first entry and in the total line at the bottom of the column. Therefore, it makes sense to set the tab stop at the point at which the five-digit numbers will begin. (You will have to remember to space forward or back for any line that is shorter or longer.)

```
                    ┌─ Tab stop for
                    │  column text
                    │
                    ↓
          $19,074
           17,341
           15,640
           13,242
            9,903
```

NOTE: If you are using electronic equipment, you can easily align the figures in a column by using the decimal or right tab function.

For guidelines on how to align items in column text, see ¶¶1625–1629. The alignment will depend on whether the items are all words, all figures (with or without decimal points), or some combination of words and figures.

16

1619 In drafts and in informal reports, memos, and letters—where the occasion does not justify the time and effort that goes into centering column heads over column text—every line in the column head may start at the left margin of the column. For example:

In–Service Training Program	Average Annual Expenditures	Cumulative Compound Growth	1st–Year Sales Estimates

1620 Open (Unruled) Column Heads

a. Type column heads in capital and small letters, underscored and centered on the column width. (See ¶¶1617–1619).

b. If the column heads in a table do not all take the same number of lines, align the column heads at the bottom.

```
                              ↓4
                        Table 14-4
                                  ↓2
      DISTRIBUTION OF TOTAL PERSONAL INCOME:  1960 TO 1989

              (In Billions of Dollars)
                                        ↓3
                                 Disposable
             Personal    Personal  #Personal#   Personal
    Year     #Income#    #Taxes##  ##Income##   Savings#
                                                        ↓2
    1960      402.3       50.4       352.0        19.7
    1970      811.1      115.8       695.3        55.8
    1980     2165.3      336.5      1828.9       110.2
    1989     4384.3      658.8      3725.5       171.8
                                                       ↓4
```

GUIDE LINE:

```
    Year      Personal     Personal    Disposable    Personal
     123456     123456       123456       123456
```

c. Leave 2 blank lines between the final line of the title or subtitle (whichever comes last) and the first line of the tallest column head.

d. Leave 1 blank line between the column heads and the table text.

1621 Ruled Column Heads

a. When column heads are preceded and followed by horizontal rules running the full width of the table, they are called *ruled* column heads. (If vertical rules are also used between each pair of columns, the heads are referred to as *boxed* column heads.)

b. Insert the first horizontal rule on the line directly below the final line of the title or subtitle (whichever comes last). Extend the underscore the full width of the table, but do not let it overhang the table text on either side.

(Continued on page 418.)

c. On the second line below the underscore, start the column head with the most lines. All the column heads should align at the bottom.

d. Type the column heads in capital and small letters, single-spaced and centered. (For guidance on centering, see ¶¶1617–1619.) Do not underscore the column heads when they are ruled or boxed.

e. On the line directly below the last line of the column heads, insert another horizontal rule the full width of the table. (When both horizontal rules are inserted, the column heads should appear to be centered between them, with 1 blank line above and below the column heads.)

f. On the second line below the second rule, start typing the table text.

<table>
<tr><td colspan="7">↓ 4</td></tr>
<tr><td colspan="7">Table A–14 ↓ 2</td></tr>
<tr><td colspan="7">U.S. FIRE LOSSES FROM 1981 TO 1988 ↓ 1</td></tr>
<tr><td>Year</td><td>Total (000,000 Omitted)</td><td>Per Capita</td><td>Year</td><td>Total (000,000 Omitted)</td><td>Per Capita</td><td></td></tr>
<tr><td>1981</td><td>$5625</td><td>$24.50</td><td>1985</td><td>$7753</td><td>$32.47</td><td></td></tr>
<tr><td>1982</td><td>5894</td><td>25.41</td><td>1986</td><td>8488</td><td>35.21</td><td></td></tr>
<tr><td>1983</td><td>6320</td><td>26.98</td><td>1987</td><td>8634</td><td>35.44</td><td></td></tr>
<tr><td>1984</td><td>7602</td><td>32.15</td><td>1988</td><td>9626</td><td>39.12</td><td></td></tr>
</table>

NOTE: The illustration above of a table with ruled column heads also shows how to treat a table that would be long and narrow if held to its original three columns. A single vertical rule is used to separate the two halves of the table, each with the same set of column heads. If single vertical rules are used between the columns on each side, use a double vertical rule to separate the two halves of the table.

g. If you are using electronic equipment with the capability of executing horizontal lines, space down only once after each horizontal rule in order to achieve the same spacing shown in the illustration above. (See ¶1633d for an explanation.)

1622 Braced Column Heads

a. Some complex tables contain *braced* column heads, that is, heads that "embrace" two or more columns. (They are also called *straddle* heads because they straddle two or more columns.)

b. Type braced column heads in capital and small letters. Single-space any turnover lines, and align braced heads of varying length at the bottom.

c. Center a braced heading over the columns to which it pertains. To do so, follow this procedure:

(1) First plan the arrangement of the column heads and type the ones that are to go below the braced head, centering each over its own column text. Leave room, however, for the braced head.

(2) Count the keystrokes in the longest items in the columns to be braced, and add in the number of blank spaces between the braced columns. (See the illustration in the note below Table 12.)

(3) Count the keystrokes in the longest line in the braced column head, and subtract that number from the figure calculated in step 2 above.

(4) Divide your answer by 2 (and ignore any fraction) to find how many spaces to indent the longest line in the braced head.

(5) Center any other lines in the braced head in relation to the placement of the longest line.

↓4

Table 12.   CABLE DIVISION SALES AND NET OPERATING INCOME
From 1992 to 1996 ↓1   ↓2

Year	Sales		Net Operating Income	
	Thousands of Dollars	Percent of Increase	Thousands of Dollars	Percent of Increase
1992A	1429	-----	252	-----
1993E	1580	10.6	296	17.5
1994F	1500	(5.1)	238	(19.6)
1995F	1300	(13.3)	216	(9.2)
1996F	3000	130.8	480	122.2

Note: A = actual; E = estimated; F = forecast.

↓4

NOTE: In the illustration above a total of 26 keystrokes has to be braced in each case:

```
of Dollars     Percent of      of Dollars     Percent of
12345678901234567890123456     12345678901234567890123456
Sales                          Net Operating Income
```

To center the first braced head, subtract the keystrokes in *Sales* (5) from 26. Dividing the difference (21) by 2 yields an answer of 10½. Ignore the fraction, and indent *Sales* 10 spaces from the start of the first column to be braced. The second braced head, *Net Operating Income*, has 20 keystrokes. Subtracting 20 from 26 yields a difference of 6. Dividing 6 by 2 indicates that the braced head should be indented 3 spaces.

16

1623 Crossheads

a. Crossheads are used to separate the data in the body of a table into different categories. (See the illustration below.)

b. The first crosshead falls immediately below the column heads across the top of the table; the other crossheads occur within the body of the table at appropriate intervals.

c. Type each crosshead in capital and small letters, centered on the full width of the table. Backspace from the centering point to determine where to begin typing each crosshead.

d. Each crosshead should be preceded and followed by a horizontal rule running the full width of the table. (For proper spacing above and below each crosshead, see the illustration below.)

e. If there are vertical rules in a table (as in the illustration below), they should not intrude into the space set aside for the crossheads.

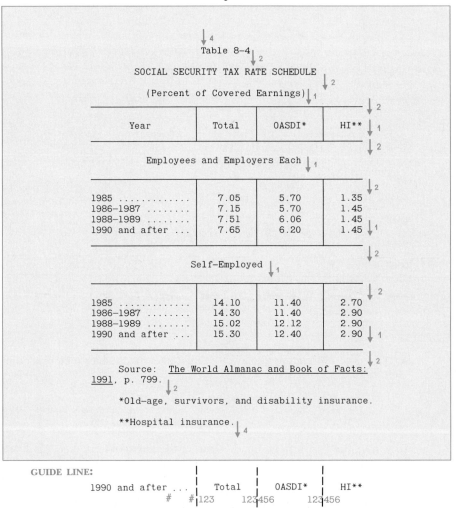

Table 8–4

SOCIAL SECURITY TAX RATE SCHEDULE

(Percent of Covered Earnings)

Year	Total	OASDI*	HI**
Employees and Employers Each			
1985	7.05	5.70	1.35
1986–1987	7.15	5.70	1.45
1988–1989	7.51	6.06	1.45
1990 and after ...	7.65	6.20	1.45
Self–Employed			
1985	14.10	11.40	2.70
1986–1987	14.30	11.40	2.90
1988–1989	15.02	12.12	2.90
1990 and after ...	15.30	12.40	2.90

Source: The World Almanac and Book of Facts: 1991, p. 799.

*Old–age, survivors, and disability insurance.

**Hospital insurance.

GUIDE LINE:

```
1990 and after ... |  Total  |  OASDI*  |  HI**
      #    #|123       123456       123456
```

NOTE: When an asterisk or similar symbol accompanies the longest item in a column, include it in the guide line.

Table Text

1624 Spacing

a. The table text may be typed with single, double, or 1½-line spacing. However, within the same document try to treat all tables alike.

b. Double-space tables for better readability. However, if overall length must be held down and you wish to maximize your chances of locating each table on the page where it is first mentioned, use single spacing. (See also ¶1603.)

NOTE: If a single-spaced table runs quite long, you can break up the solid mass of table text by inserting a blank line or a horizontal rule at regular intervals or at points that serve to group the rows in a meaningful way.

c. If you would like to enhance readability *and* control overall length *and* fit each table in the ideal location, 1½-line spacing may be a good compromise.

d. As a rule, the table text should be typed with the same spacing (or less) used for the running text. Thus when the running text is *single-spaced,* then all the tables are also single-spaced. When the running text is typed in *1½-line spacing,* all the tables may be typed with either 1½-line or single spacing. When the running text is *double-spaced,* then all the tables may be typed with double, single, or 1½-line spacing.

e. The following guide indicates where to begin typing the table text.

If the Table Text Is Preceded by:	Start Typing the Table Text on:
Running text with single spacing	Second line below
Running text with double or 1½-line spacing	Third line below
Column heads—open	Second line below
Column heads—ruled or boxed	Second line below underscore
Table title	Third line below
Table subtitle	Third line below

NOTE: In some software programs, switching from double spacing to triple spacing is either difficult or awkward. In cases where 2 blank lines are called for, use only 1 blank line instead.

For examples of proper spacing, see the illustrations in ¶1601.

1625 Items Consisting of Words

If the table text consists of items expressed entirely in words:

a. Capitalize only the first word of each item in the table text plus any proper nouns and proper adjectives.

NOTE: In special cases, where it may be important to show whether terms are capitalized or written with small letters, the first word in each item need not be consistently capitalized. (See, for example, the second and third columns of the table in ¶1601c.)

b. Use abbreviations and symbols as necessary to hold down the length of individual items. (See ¶1616c for examples.)

(Continued on page 422.)

c. Align each item at the left margin of the column. If any item requires more than one line, indent the turnover line 2 spaces. However, if a column contains both main entries and subentries, begin the main entry at the left margin of the column text, indent the first line of subentries 2 spaces, and indent all turnover lines 4 spaces.

```
Photographs, prints,        Total weekly
   and illustrations ...       broadcast
Scientific or tech-            hours ......
   nical drawings ......    General
Commercial prints .....        programs ...
Reproductions of            Instructional
   works of art .......        programs ...
```

For guidelines on the use of leaders (rows of periods), see ¶1631.

d. If an item in the first column requires more than one line and all the other items in the same row require only one line, align all the items in that row on the bottom.

```
Chemicals and allied products .... 151     201
Petroleum refining and related
   products .................... 69      73  ←  Aligned at
Paper and allied products ........ 391    364     the bottom
```

e. If two or more items in a row each require more than one line, align all entries in that row at the top.

```
Employee benefits report    Prepared       Data based on      ←  Aligned at
                            quarterly       administra-            the top
                                            tive records
```

f. Do not use a period as terminal punctuation at the end of any item except in a column where all entries are in sentence form.

1626 Items Consisting of Figures

a. If a column of table text consists of items expressed entirely in figures:

(1) Align columns of whole numbers at the right.

(2) Align columns of decimal amounts on the decimal point.

(3) In a column that contains both whole numbers and decimals, add a decimal point and zeros to the whole numbers to maintain a consistent appearance.

(4) Omit commas in four-digit whole numbers unless they appear in the same column with larger numbers containing commas. Never insert commas in the decimal part of a number.

```
    325        465.2137
      1       1250.0004
152,657          1.0000
  1,489         37.9898
```

NOTE: Some writers prefer to retain the comma in four-digit numbers under all circumstances.

422   PART 2 □ TECHNIQUES AND FORMATS

(5) If you are using electronic equipment, you can easily align the figures in a column by using the decimal tab or right tab function.

For the way to handle a total line in a column of figures, see ¶1628c.

b. If a column of table text consists entirely of "clock" times (as in a program or schedule):

(1) Align the figures in "on the hour" expressions at the right.

```
11 a.m.
12 noon
 1 p.m.
 8 p.m.
12 midnight
```

(2) Align the figures in "hour and minute" expressions on the colon. (Add two zeros to exact times to maintain a uniform appearance.)

```
 8:15 a.m.
10:30 a.m.
12:00 noon
 1:45 p.m.
12:00 midnight
```

(3) Align expressions of clock time at the left when each item (or some of the items) in the column consists of a starting and ending time. (For another illustration, see page 440.)

```
8:30-9:30
10:30-11:30
12:30-1:30
2:30-3:30
4:45-6:00
```

NOTE: In the "24-hour" system of expressing clock time (in which midnight is 0000 and 11:59 p.m. is 2359), the alignment of clock times poses no problem since all times are expressed in four digits (with no colons and no need for reference to *a.m.* or *p.m.*).

```
0830-0930
1030-1130
1230-1330
1430-1530
```

1627 Items Consisting of Figures and Words

If a column consists of both figures and words (as in the second column below), align the items at the left. Note, however, that a column consisting of words aligns at the left (as in the first column below) and a column consisting only of whole numbers aligns at the right (as in the third column below).

Type of Food	Average Serving	Calorie Count
Bacon	2 strips	97
Beef, roast	4 oz	300
Broccoli	1 cup	44
Tomato, raw	Medium size	30

1628 Amounts of Money

a. In a column containing dollar amounts, insert a dollar sign only before the first amount at the head of the column and before the total amount. The dollar signs should align in the first space to the left of the longest amount in the column.

$ 45.50	$ 165	$ 423.75
2406.05	3,450	584.45
783.25	98,932	1228.00
$3234.80	$102,547	$2236.20

b. Do not insert commas to set off thousands in four-digit numbers unless they appear in the same column with larger numbers. (See the examples above and in ¶1626a.) Moreover, if all the amounts in a column are whole dollar amounts, omit the decimal and zeros (as in the second example above). However, if any amount in a column includes cents, use a decimal and zeros with any whole dollar amount in the same column (as in the third example above).

c. If the table text ends with a *total* line:

(1) In an *open* table (one with no rules between columns of figures), simply type a row of underscores directly under the last amount. Make the underscore as wide as the longest entry in the column. In a single-spaced table, type the total amount on the line directly below the underscore (as in the first example below). To give the total amount greater emphasis, type it on the second line below the underscore (as in the second example below). In a double-spaced table, the amount must be typed on the second line below the underscore (as in the third example below).

$1115.59 ↓1	$ 529,310 ↓1	$21,348.75 ↓2
803.61	1,114,310	
1027.64	1,227,620	2,294.35
528.66		
$3475.50 ↓1	$2,871,240 ↓2	688.50
		$24,331.60 ↓2

1995 SALES REVENUES ↓1

Region	1995B	1995A	Percent of Difference ↓1
Eastern	$ 300,000	$ 345,108	15.0
Midwestern	450,000	467,380	3.9
Southern	260,000	291,849	12.2
Western	240,000	241,005	0.4 ↓1
Total	$1,250,000	$1,345,342	7.6 ↓1

(2) In a *ruled* table (one with horizontal rules only), either treat the underscore as shown in ¶1628c(1) or type a continuous underscore the full width of the table (as shown in the table at the bottom of page 424) or extend it only across the full width of all the figure columns.

(3) In a *boxed* table (one with horizontal and vertical rules), either type a continuous underscore the full width of the table (as shown in the table at the bottom of page 424) or type the underscore the full distance between verticals in any column that contains a total.

d. When a *total* line is being typed, the word *Total* in the first column may be typed with an initial cap only or (for emphasis) in all-capital letters. Start the word at the left margin of the column or (again, for emphasis) indent it 5 spaces—so long as the word does not intrude into the area established for the second column.

1629 Percentages

a. If all the figures in a column represent percentages, type a percent sign (%) directly after each figure unless the column heading clearly indicates that these are percentages.

b. Percentages involving decimals should align on the decimal point. If necessary, add zeros after the decimal part of the number so that each figure will align at the right. If any percentage is less than 1 percent, add one zero to the left of the decimal point.

Increase	Percent of Increase	Increase (%)
55.48%	11.63	24
0.80%	4.00	37
2.09%	25.60	120
13.00%	0.40	8

1630 Special Treatment of Figures in Tables

a. Columns of long figures can be reduced in width by omitting the digits representing thousands, millions, or billions and indicating this fact in parentheses. For example:

(000 Omitted)	OR	(In Thousands)
(000,000 Omitted)		(In Millions)
(000,000,000 Omitted)		(In Billions)

NOTE: The word forms on the right are easier to grasp and are usually shorter than the forms on the left.

b. If the parenthetical comment applies to all columns of figures in the table, it can be given as a subtitle to the table. However, if the comment applies only to one column of figures, insert the parenthetical comment in the column head.

NOTE: Sometimes because of space limitations a comment such as *(000 Omitted)* is reduced to *(000)*. The latter form is permissible if you are sure your reader will understand it.

c. If the parenthetical comment applies to columns of dollar amounts, this fact can also be noted within parentheses and the dollar sign can then be omitted from the column text.

($000 Omitted)   OR   (In Thousands of Dollars)   OR   ($000)

(Continued on page 426.)

16

d. When omitting thousands, millions, or billions from a wide column of figures, you may use rounding or a shortened decimal (or both) to reflect the portion of the number that is being omitted.

Complete Version	Shortened Versions		
Sales Revenues	Sales Revenues ($000 Omitted)	Sales Revenues (In Millions)	Sales Revenues ($000,000)
$ 5,878,044	5,878	$ 5.9	6
29,023,994	29,024	29.0	29
14,229,683	14,230	14.2	14
$49,131,721	49,132	$49.1	49

e. A negative figure in a column may be designated by enclosing the figure in parentheses or by inserting a minus sign (represented by a hyphen) positioned directly to the left of the negative figure.

$1642.38	28.2%	Sales in 1995 ...	$264,238
−82.41	−14.5%	Sales in 1996 ...	262,305
$1559.97	6.1%	Gain/(loss)	$ (1,933)

1631 Leaders

a. If the items in the first column vary greatly in length, use leaders (rows of periods) to lead the eye across to the adjacent item in the next column. The shortest line of leaders should have at least three periods.

b. Solid leaders (....) are preferred to open leaders (. . . .) because they are faster and simpler to type. Open leaders must be aligned vertically.

c. Leave 1 blank space before the start of a row of leaders and before the start of the second column.

d. In a table without vertical rules, you can easily determine in advance where the leaders should end. Simply backspace twice from the start of the second column, and at that point type a period to mark where the leaders are to stop.

NOTE: If you are planning to leave 6 spaces between columns, then between the longest item in the first column and the start of the adjacent item in the second column there should be 1 space followed by four periods and then another space. See, for example, the table at the bottom of page 405. The guide line for this table would appear thus:

```
Amount of substance .... kilogram     Symbol
           123456           123456
```

However, in a table with only two columns, the space between columns (and thus the number of periods) can be adjusted to create the table width you want. In the table at the bottom of page 406, the minimum number of periods (three) has been used. Therefore, the key line for this table would read:

```
Managerial and professional specialty ... 12,588,000
                                       12345
```

e. If you are planning to use leaders in the first column of a boxed table (one with vertical as well as horizontal rules), proceed as follows:

(1) Determine the space to be left between columns. (Assume the standard 6 spaces. Since the vertical rules will be centered between columns, allow 3 blank spaces on either side of each vertical rule.)

NOTE: If you are using electronic equipment to execute the vertical rules, you will have to increase the space between columns from 6 to 7, since the vertical rule requires its own space. See ¶1633d for a fuller explanation.

(2) In planning a key line, take the longest line in the first column and to it add a space, three periods, plus another space. **REASON:** The shortest row of leaders must have three periods (see ¶1631a), and there must be 1 blank space before and after (see ¶1631c). In short, add five keystrokes to the longest line in the first column to arrive at the first vertical rule.

(3) Then add three keystrokes to allow space between the first vertical rule and the start of the second column. (These three keystrokes will balance the 3 spaces that occur between the end of the second column and the next vertical rule; see the illustration below.)

Table 3. NATIONAL INCOME BY SELECTED INDUSTRIES

(In Billions of Dollars)

	1970	1980	1989
Agriculture, forestry, and fisheries	25.9	61.4	101.0
Construction	47.4	126.6	225.1
Finance, insurance, and real estate	96.4	279.5	613.8
Government enterprises ...	132.4	321.8	606.9
Manufacturing	215.6	532.1	803.8
Services	109.8	341.0	883.0

GUIDE LINE:

```
                          |        |        |
                          |  132.4 |  321.8 |   606.9
Government enterprises#...#123   123#456   123#456
```

f. Some software programs have a leader-tab feature that, when engaged, automatically types rows of periods, stopping at the correct point.

1632 Accounting for Omitted Items

When there is no entry to be typed in a given row, it is permissible simply to leave a blank at that point. However, if doing so may raise a question in the mind of your reader, consider these alternatives:

a. Type the abbreviation *NA* (meaning "not available" or "not applicable") centered on the column width.

b. Type a row of periods or hyphens. Use as few as three (centered on the column width), or type the row to the full width of the column.

23,804	23,804	23,804
16,345	16,345	16,345
......	----	NA
38,442	38,442	38,442

See ¶1622 for another illustration.

¶1633

Table Rules

1633 If a table requires rules, use one of the following methods to insert them:

a. Insert all rules on the typewriter, using the underscore. Place a horizontal rule above and below the column heads and at the bottom of the table; do not underscore the column heads. These rules should extend to the full width of the table. As shown in the illustrations in ¶¶1621–1623, type each rule on the line immediately following the preceding copy. This creates the appearance of a blank line above the underscore. Leave 1 blank line between an internal rule and any table copy that follows; leave 2 or 3 blank lines (see ¶1604c) between the bottom rule and any running text that follows. If vertical rules are to be used to separate the columns, insert the page sideways after you have finished typing the table text and type the vertical rules, using the underscore. Do not type rules at the left and right sides of the table; the sides should remain open.

b. Insert all rules with a ballpoint pen and a ruler after the typing has been completed. Be sure to leave space for these rules when typing the table.

c. Insert all horizontal rules on the typewriter, as described in *a* above. Insert all vertical rules with a ballpoint pen.

NOTE: In a table that is to contain vertical rules, leave a minimum of 2 spaces between columns.

d. If you are using electronic equipment with the capacity to execute horizontal and vertical rules, take advantage of this feature. Keep in mind, however, that on a computer each horizontal rule represents a line of space. Therefore, to achieve the effect of 1 blank line between a horizontal rule and a line of text below, space down only once. (On a typewriter you would have to space down twice to create the same effect.)

On a Computer	On a Typewriter
Self-Employed ↓₁	Self-Employed ↓₁
───────── ↓₁	───────── ↓₂
14.10	14.10

By the same token, when you want to execute a vertical rule on electronic equipment, remember that the vertical rule itself represents one space. Therefore, if you want to achieve the effect of 3 blank spaces on either side of a vertical rule between columns (as in the illustration on page 427), you must leave 7 spaces between columns (instead of the customary 6): 3 on either side of the rule plus 1 space for the rule itself.

On a Computer	On a Typewriter
123┊4567	123┊456

Table Notes

1634 a. If a table requires any explanatory notes or an identification of the source from which the table text was derived, place such material at the foot of the table. (Do not treat it as part of a sequence of notes to the running text.)

b. Separate the table text from the table notes by a row of underscores. In a ruled or boxed table, the full row of underscores at the bottom of the table text will provide the necessary separation. In a table without full-width horizontal rules, provide the separation by typing a 1-inch row of underscores (10 keystrokes in 10-pitch or pica type, 12 keystrokes in 12-pitch or elite type) on the line directly below the last line of table text.

c. Begin the first table note on the second line below the row of underscores.

d. If all the notes occupy no more than one full line each, begin each note at the left margin of the table text (for the sake of appearance) and type the notes single-spaced. (For an example, see the illustration in ¶1635b.) However, if any of the notes turn over onto a second line, indent the first line of each note 5 spaces, type all turnover lines starting at the left margin of the table text, and leave 1 blank line between each pair of notes. (For illustrations of indented table notes, see the tables on pages 407, 408, and 420.)

NOTE: To avoid a bad line ending, you can go 1 or 2 spaces beyond the right edge of the table. (See, for example, the illustrations in ¶¶1623 and 1635b.)

1635 If the material in the table has been derived from another source, indicate this fact as follows:

a. Type the word *Source* with an initial cap or in all capital letters, followed by a colon, 2 spaces, and the identifying data. (See ¶¶1508–1522 for models to follow in presenting this bibliographic data.)

b. A source note should precede any other table note.

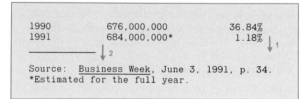

```
1990          676,000,000          36.84%
1991          684,000,000*          1.18% ↓₁
_____ ↓₂
Source:  Business Week, June 3, 1991, p. 34.
*Estimated for the full year.
```

1636 a. If you use abbreviations or symbols that the reader may not understand, explain them at the bottom of the table. This explanation should follow the source note (if any) and precede any other table note. If more than one abbreviation or symbol needs decoding, the explanation can be handled as a series of separate notes (each preceded by a raised symbol or letter), or it may be done all in one note. For examples of both styles, see the illustrations in ¶¶1622–1623.

b. Except for source notes (like the one illustrated above) and a single note explaining symbols and abbreviations (like the one on page 419), every table note should begin with a raised symbol or letter that keys the note to the appropriate word or figure in the table text (or title or subtitle) above. The corresponding symbol or letter should be typed immediately after the appropriate word or figure above, without any intervening space. (See ¶1636d, note.)

c. Use the following sequence of symbols: *, **, *** OR *, †, ‡, §, ¶. The latter set may have to be inserted by hand. (See also ¶1502f.)

(Continued on page 430.)

    d. Use raised lowercase letters ([a], [b], [c], etc.) in place of symbols when there are more than five footnotes for a given table.

       NOTE: Avoid the use of raised *figures* to identify table notes. They could be confusing if used in conjunction with figures in the table text. Moreover, if raised figures are already used for notes pertaining to the main text, it is wise to use letters or symbols so as to distinguish notes that pertain to a specific table.

    e. In assigning symbols or letters in sequence, go in order by row (horizontally), not by column (vertically).

Dealing With Long Tables

1637 To keep a table from extending beyond the page on which it starts, consider these techniques:

    a. Put the table number (if any) on the same line as the table title rather than on the second line above. (See also ¶1615b.)

    b. Use single spacing for the table text. (See also ¶1624.)

    c. Shorten the wording of the table title, subtitle, column heads, and items in the table text to reduce turnover lines. Use abbreviations and symbols toward this end. (See also ¶1616c.) If necessary, provide a brief explanation in the table notes of any abbreviations and symbols that your reader may not immediately understand. (See also ¶1636.)

    d. When the table text entails a long item that is out of proportion to all the other items (or is to be entered in several places in the table text), try to convert the item into a table note, keyed by a symbol or letter appropriately placed in the table above.

    e. If a table is both narrow and long, you can save space by repeating the same sequence of column heads on both the left and right sides of the table. The first half of the table text appears on the left side of the table, and the remaining table text appears on the right. (See the illustration and note in ¶1621.)

       NOTE: In order to achieve consistent treatment of tables throughout a given document, decide on the spacing, the placement of the table number, and the use of abbreviations and symbols before you start typing or printing out the document.

1638 If a table requires more than one page, follow this procedure:

    a. At the bottom of the page where the table breaks, type a continuation line—for example, *Table continued on page 14*—unless it is quite obvious that the table continues on the next page. Type the continuation line in parentheses or brackets, positioned so as to end at the right margin on the line directly below the point at which the table breaks.

       NOTE: If you are breaking a table with ruled or boxed column heads, do not type a full-width underscore at the bottom of the page where the table text breaks off. This underscore should appear only at the very end of the table text.

    b. At the top of the page on which the table continues, repeat the table number (if any) and the table title, followed by the word *Continued* or *Cont.* in parentheses. Also repeat the column heads before resuming the table text.

c. Ordinarily, all table notes should appear only on the page on which the table ends. However, to avoid inconveniencing a reader, place the appropriate notes at the bottom of each page, even if this means that some notes will have to be repeated on two or more pages. Insert a 1-inch row of underscores before such notes (as described in ¶1634).

1639 Do not start a table at the bottom of one page and continue it on the top of the next page if the entire table will fit on one page (either by itself or with running text). In such a case start the table at the top of the next page and insert a cross-reference in the text. (See ¶1608.)

Dealing With Wide Tables

1640 To keep a wide table from extending beyond the margins established for the page, first consider these techniques:

a. Reduce the space between columns to as little as 2 spaces. (To preserve the clarity of the table, you can insert vertical rules.)

b. Use abbreviations and symbols to hold down the length of lines in the column heads and the column text. (In extreme cases the column heads can be typed vertically.)

c. If only a few entries are disproportionately wide or are repeated in the table and make it difficult to fit the table in the space available, consider the possibility of converting these items to table footnotes. (See also ¶1637d.)

1641 Making a Reduced Copy

a. If the suggestions in ¶1640 do not resolve the problem, consider this approach:

(1) If you have access to a photocopier with the capability of producing copies in reduced size, type the extrawide table across the 11-inch dimension of a separate sheet. Reduce the space between columns to as little as 2 spaces in order to limit the overall width of the table.

(2) Then make a reduced photocopy of the table that brings the table width down to the desired size. (You can reduce the table as much as 50 percent and still have readable copy. Naturally, the less you reduce the copy, the better.)

(3) Mount the reduced version of the table horizontally in the desired location, either on a page with running text or on a separate page.

(4) Then make a fresh copy of the pasted-up page so that you wind up with a sheet with all the material on the same surface.

NOTE: In some situations the inclusion of a photocopied page along with typed originals may not be acceptable, and you will have to consider still other alternatives (see ¶¶1642–1643). However, if the use of a reduced photocopy will permit you to insert an extrawide table horizontally at the desired point of reference, the overall convenience to your reader should more than compensate for any sacrifice in appearance.

b. If you are using electronic equipment with the capability of printing smaller type, take advantage of this feature in order to make the table fit within the space available.

1642 Turning the Table

a. Whenever possible, a table should read horizontally, just like the running text. However, when other alternatives do not work or cannot be used, you may turn the table so that it runs vertically on a page by itself. In such a case the left margin of the table will fall toward the bottom of the page and the right margin toward the top.

b. In planning the layout of a turned table, be sure that the overall dimensions of the table will fit within the established margins for the normal pages in the given document. If no margins have been established, leave a minimum margin of 1 inch on all sides of the turned table.

NOTE: Leave a minimum left margin of 1½ inches if the page with the turned table is to be part of a *bound* report. (See also ¶1404b.)

1643 Spreading the Table Over Two Pages

An extrawide table may be spread horizontally over two pages. Each page is typed separately, and then the two pages are taped together to look like one continuous piece of work.

Left-Hand Page   **Right-Hand Page**

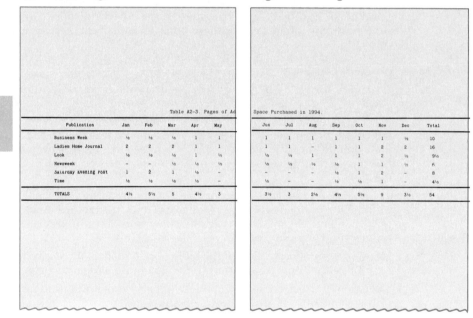

Publication	Jan	Feb	Mar	Apr	May	Jun	Jul	Aug	Sep	Oct	Nov	Dec	Total
Business Week	½	½	½	1	1	1	1	1	1	1	1	½	10
Ladies Home Journal	2	2	2	1	1	1	1	–	1	1	2	2	16
Look	½	½	½	1	½	½	½	1	1	1	2	½	9½
Newsweek	–	–	½	½	½	½	½	½	½	1	1	½	6
Saturday Evening Post	1	2	1	½	–	–	–	–	½	1	2	–	8
Time	½	½	½	½	–	½	–	–	½	½	1	–	4½
TOTALS	4½	5½	5	4½	3	3½	3	2½	4½	5½	9	3½	54

Table A2-3. Pages of Ad Space Purchased in 1994.

a. Select the best place to split the table between columns. Try to break as close to the middle of the table as possible.

b. Also find a good break between words in the title and the subtitle (if any) so that in the finished product these elements will appear to run without any noticeable interruption across the two pages.

c. If the table also carries a number (for example, *Table 8*), place it on the same line with the table title rather than on a line by itself. In that way you can avoid having to position the phrase off center (with *Table* on the left page and *8* on the right).

d. Establish a guide line for each half of the table, and determine on which line the typing should begin.

e. To execute the left half of the table:

(1) Backspace the left half of the title, starting from the right edge of the paper. At the point at which you stop backspacing, begin typing the first half of the title. Repeat this process for the first half of the subtitle (if any).

(2) Next backspace the guide line for the left half of the table, starting from the right edge of the paper, and set the left margin stop and the tab stops.

(3) Then type the column heads and the table text.

(4) If the table involves any horizontal rules, type them to the very edge of the right side of the page.

f. To execute the right half of the table:

(1) Take a fresh sheet of paper and continue typing the title, starting from the left edge of the paper. Make sure that the continuation of the title (and the subtitle, if any) are perfectly aligned with the corresponding copy on the first page. When the two pages are taped together, the title and subtitle should appear to flow without a break. Also be sure that at the point at which the title and subtitle break, there will appear to be only 1 blank space between words when the two pages are taped together.

(2) Use the guide line for the right half of the table to establish appropriate tab stops and a right margin.

(3) If the table involves horizontal rules, make sure that they begin at the very edge of the left side of the paper. When the two pages are taped together, the rules should appear to flow continuously across the entire table.

NOTE: On many computers you can establish a format for the left side of the table and use it for the right side, revising it as necessary.

g. Tape the two pages together, applying the tape on the underside of the sheets. Then fold vertically along the common edge so that the double page can be inserted in sequence with the other pages of the document. The taped fold should appear *at the right* so that the reader may unfold the table to the right.

If the sheet could become caught in any binding or stapling along the left edge, fold the top sheet halfway back toward the right. This should keep the top page from getting snagged.

SECTION

17

Other Business Documents

Section 17 provides models for a number of common business documents. The models reflect formats widely used, but they are not to be regarded as rigid patterns that must be followed without deviation. Feel free to modify these formats to fit the needs of the situation at hand. As always, good sense and good taste (rather than an artificial notion of "absolute correctness") should prevail.

General Format Considerations

Paragraphs 1701–1703 deal with the issues of establishing margins, the treatment of headings, and the choice of alternative type styles if you are using electronic equipment. These format considerations apply to all the specific types of documents discussed in the following paragraphs—executive documents such as agendas and minutes (¶¶1704–1707), financial documents such as balance sheets and income statements (¶¶1708–1711), and various types of résumés (¶¶1712–1713).

Margins

1701 a. **Top Margin.** If you are using plain standard (8½″ × 11″) stationery for the first page of a business document, use a customary margin of 2 inches but reduce it to 1 inch in order to fit more copy on the page and avoid the need for a second page. If you are using letterhead or a printed memo form for the first page, begin typing on the third line below the letterhead or the printed memo heading. If the document requires more than one page, use plain paper for the continuation pages and leave a top margin of 1 inch.

b. **Side Margins.** If you are using standard stationery, leave 1-inch side margins. This provides a 6½-inch line for the text of the document. Use a shorter line for the text if (1) you are using a smaller size of stationery, (2) you want to bring columns of text closer together for easier reading, or (3) you want to achieve a more open look or a more balanced arrangement on the page. (See, for example, the illustration on page 439.) In any case, consult the table on page 301 for the appropriate margin settings.

c. **Bottom Margin.** Leave a bottom margin of at least 1 inch (6 lines).

Headings

1702 a. **Main Heading.** The title of the document or the name of the organization ordinarily appears on the first line, centered in all-capital letters. Additional details (such as a date or a location) appear in capital and small letters on separate lines, with 1 blank line between them. Leave 2 blank lines after the last line of the main heading before starting the body of the document. (For examples, see pages 438–443, 446–448, and 450–451.)

b. **Continuation Heading.** If a document requires more than one page, insert a continuation heading like the one used on the second page of a letter. (See ¶1384 for further details.)

NOTE: The second page of a résumé typically uses a slightly different continuation heading. (See pages 455, 457, and 459 for examples.)

Type Styles

1703 The models shown here in Section 17 have all been done in ordinary 12-pitch (elite) typewriter type. If you are using electronic equipment with the appropriate software, you can use boldface and italic type (as well as different sizes of type) to give special emphasis and distinction to head-ings and other display elements. For example, compare the illustration below with the illustration on page 454.

ALISON L. BUMBRY
Apartment 145
395 West Center College Street
Yellow Springs, Ohio 45387

Home:
513-555-7944
Office:
513-555-0162

OBJECTIVE:

A marketing management position in which marketing and administrative experience plus strong writing and com-puter skills can be used to maximize sales and profit-ability of one or more product lines.

EXPERIENCE:

July 1990–
Present

ADMINISTRATIVE COORDINATOR FOR DIRECTOR OF MARKETING
Zimmer & Boyle Inc., Dayton, Ohio

☐ Created and managed a database to control budgeted expenses for advertising and promotion.
☐ Participated in designing and implementing market re-search studies to determine potential size of market for new product lines.
☐ Coordinated focus group sessions to determine custo-mer attitudes toward our product lines and those of competitors.
☐ Initiated desktop publishing program to create space ads, catalogs, and mailing pieces. Saved the company over $50,000 in the first year of operation.

Executive Documents

The following paragraphs (¶¶1704–1706) present commonly used formats for agendas, minutes, and itineraries. Also provided is a suggested format for a fax cover sheet (¶1707).

17

Agendas

1704 An *agenda* is a list of items to be considered or acted upon. The format of an agenda varies with the circumstances. The agenda for an informal staff meeting may be done as a simple numbered list of topics in a memo addressed to the attendees. (See the illustration on page 438.) The agenda for a formal meeting (for example, of a corporate board of direc-tors) will typically call for a more structured list of topics. (See the illustra-tion on page 439.) The agenda for a formal program (for example, for a conference or a seminar) will be structured around a timetable, with specific time slots allotted to formal presentations by speakers and topical discussions in small groups. (See the illustration on page 440.)

There is no single "correct" way to set up an agenda. The illustrations that follow are intended only to suggest various ways in which an agenda can be formatted. The format you decide to use should be tailored to fit the needs of the meeting or program being planned.

Minutes

1705 *Minutes* provide a record of what was discussed and decided upon at a meeting. The minutes of small committee meetings within an organization are usually done in an informal style, in much the same way that the agendas for such meetings are also prepared. (Compare the informal agenda on page 438 with the informal minutes on page 441.) When the participants at a meeting come from a number of different organizations (as they would, for example, at meetings of professional associations and societies), the minutes tend to be somewhat more formal. And when the minutes may have to serve some legal use, they are typically done in a highly formal style. According to the American Society of Corporate Secretaries, increasing government regulation and stockholder lawsuits make it critically important that the minutes of a meeting of a corporation's board of directors be complete and accurate, since they may have to serve as legal evidence of what the corporation's directors did or intended to do. The *short form* of corporate minutes (illustrated on page 442) simply describes the decisions that were made, along with some brief indication of the key facts on which those decisions were made. By contrast, the *long form* describes in some detail the arguments for and against the decisions finally arrived at. For an analysis of the advantages and disadvantages of the two forms of corporate minutes and for detailed guidelines on the preparation of corporate minutes, write or call the American Society of Corporate Secretaries, Inc., 1270 Avenue of the Americas, New York, New York 10020, 212-765-2620.

Itineraries

1706 An itinerary should clearly set forth the travel arrangements and the appointment schedule of the person making the trip. If the itinerary is intended only for the use of the person traveling, it should be possible to eliminate certain items and abbreviate details that the person is quite familiar with. However, if the itinerary will be distributed to others (who may need to contact the person who is traveling), present the information as fully and as clearly as possible. (For an example, see the illustration on page 443.)

Fax Cover Sheets

1707 As fax (facsimile) equipment shows up in an ever-increasing number of business offices and home offices, it has created the need for a fax cover sheet that in one way or another will indicate (1) the name and fax number of the person receiving the fax, (2) the name and fax number of the person sending the fax, (3) the number of pages being sent, and (4) the name and the telephone number of the person to be called in case the transmission is not satisfactorily completed.

The ready availability of small stick-on labels that accommodate all the essential information in a compact form is appealing to many people, who are pleased to save time and money as a result of not having to create or transmit a separate cover sheet. Therefore, do not feel compelled to create and use a fax cover sheet like the one illustrated on page 444 if commercially prepared stick-on labels will serve your purpose.

(Continued on page 445.)

MEMO TO: Marketing Managers Committee

FROM: Dorothy Innie

DATE: July 10, 19—

SUBJECT: Agenda for July 20 Meeting

Our July 20 meeting will begin at 9:30 a.m. in the small conference room on the second floor. (The large conference room, where we normally meet, has been reserved by Mrs. Harper for an all-day meeting.)

Please come prepared to discuss the following topics:

1. Sales through June for each product line.

2. Year-end sales forecast vs. budget for each product line.

3. Recommendations for changes in this year's marketing plans and requests for supplemental funding.

4. Proposed changes in next year's marketing strategies.

5. Preliminary marketing budgets for next year. (Please put these in writing for me so that I can share them with Bill Carr, our friendly bean counter in the Finance Department.)

DI

ma

Distribution:
G. Albers
R. Fagan
K. Garcia-Lorca
S. Koechlin
F. Li
C. Mandel
T. Pavlick
P. Washington

Memo Format: For the format of a memo done on plain paper (as shown here) or on letterhead stationery, see ¶1393. For the format of a memo done on a printed memo form, see ¶1392.

Numbered List: Note the use of hanging indention for turnovers in the numbered list of items. Leave 1 blank line between items (even if all the items require only 1 line each) so as to make the list easier to read. For further details on the format of a numbered list, see ¶1424e.

End Punctuation: Ordinarily, the items in an agenda require no end punctuation. However, if any item involves the use of a complete sentence (as in item 5 in this illustration), place a period at the end of every item. For details on the use or omission of periods with items in a list, see ¶107.

Agenda—Formal Style

Margins: Note the use of wide (1¾″) side margins and a 5-inch line for the text. This agenda has a number of very short items. If it were done on a standard (6½″) line, it would have an unbalanced look, with a relatively small left margin and a very large right margin.

Numbered List: When a numbered list contains 10 or more items, note that the single- and double-digit figures are aligned at the right. The double-digit figures begin at the left margin.

End Punctuation: Note that no periods are needed at the end of the items in this illustration. (See also ¶107.)

Formal Items: In a formal agenda it is customary to include such items as *Call to order*, *Approval of minutes*, *New business*, and *Adjournment* (or similar types of expressions).

```
                    UNDERLOCK AND KEYE INC. ↓2

                         Agenda ↓2

                 Regular Meeting of Directors ↓2

            Wednesday, September 22, 1993—10 a.m. ↓2

                    Boardroom, Fifth Floor ↓3


 1.  Call to order ↓2

 2.  Approval of minutes

 3.  Report on August operations—G. A. Horn

 4.  Report on corporate financial matters—A. J. McGill

 5.  Report on corporate development matters—L. Soaries

 6.  Review of international operations—W. Burgos

 7.  Discussion of the Real Estate Committee report

 8.  Overview of the performance of major competitors—T. Foy

 9.  New business

10.  Adjournment
```

Agenda—Program for a Conference or Seminar

```
                SOFTWARE APPLICATIONS SEMINAR →2
                     Saddle Brook Marriott →2
                       July 13-14, 19— →3

Wednesday, July 13 →2

8:00-9:00      Registration and Continental Breakfast →2    Lobby

9:00-9:40      Software Applications:  A State-of-the-       Salons A and B
                 Art Overview
                 Speaker: Joyce Stocker-Olsen

9:50-10:30     Word Processing and Communications           Salons A and B
                 Applications
                 Speakers: Louis Serrano and Roy Pfaltz

10:30-10:50    Coffee Break                                 Lobby

10:50-11:30    Desktop Publishing and Graphics Appli-       Salons A and B
                 cations
                 Speakers: Sandra Scroggins and Ed Fcx

11:40-12:20    Spreadsheet and Database Management          Salons A and B
                 Applications
                 Speaker: Esther W. Benoit

12:30-1:45     Lunch                                        Ballroom

1:45-3:15      Concurrent Sessions

               Session 1:  Advanced WordPerfect 5.1         Red Oak Suite
                 Speaker:  Irwin Manoogian

               Session 3:  Harvard Graphics 2.3             Salon D
                 Speaker:  Gary A. Grimes

3:15-3:30      Coffee Break                                 Lobby

3:30-5:00      Concurrent Sessions

               Session 4:  Microsoft Windows 3.0            Red Oak Suite
                 Speaker:  Leola N. Holbrook
```

Headings: (a) The location and date(s) of the conference or seminar should be included in the main heading unless the program is part of a larger document that features this information prominently in some other way. (b) If the program is scheduled to last more than one day, insert an appropriate side heading above each day's listing of events.

Columnar Format: (a) Ordinarily, leave 6 spaces between columns. However, if you plan to use leaders (a row of periods) to visually connect each item in the second column with its counterpart in the third column, you can leave only 1 space between the final period in the second column and the start of the third column. (See ¶1631 for further details.) (b) Align the text in each column at the left, but indent any turnover lines 2 spaces. If you are using electronic equipment that can automatically justify the right margin, the text in the last column (showing room location) may be blocked at the right. (c) For the alignment of "clock" times in a column, see ¶1626b.

Speaker Identification: The speakers listed on the program may be further identified by title, organization, and/or place of residence. These elements of identification should be separated by commas and may, if desired, be enclosed in parentheses. For example:

Gary A. Grimes, software consultant, Newton, Massachusetts

OR: Leola N. Holbrook (vice president, Programmatic Associates, Los Altos, California)

Minutes—Informal (Memo) Style

```
MEMO TO:    Marketing Managers Committee ↓2

FROM:       Paula Washington ↓2

DATE:       July 21, 19-- ↓2

SUBJECT:    Minutes of the Marketing Managers
            Committee Meeting of July 20, 19-- ↓3

Present:    Dorothy Innie (presiding), Georgia Albers, Ruth Fagan,
            Katherine Garcia-Lorca, Sid Koechlin, Charles Mandel,
            Tim Pavlick ↓2

Absent:     Fay Li ↓2

Guest:      Bill Carr ↓3

1.  Sales through June for each product line.  Each product line is behind
    budget for the first six months of the year.  Bill Carr of the Finance
    Department reported that the company as a whole is running 11.2 percent
    behind budget and 6.3 percent behind last year's sales for the first six
    months.

2.  Year-end sales forecast vs. budget for each product line.  Ruth Fagan and
    Sid Koechlin each reported that on the basis of recent reports from the

    sales will be only 5 percent higher than this year's year-end estimate.
    Reworked budgets are due to Dorothy Innie no later than July 28.

The next meeting of the Marketing Managers Committee will be held on August 24
in the large conference room (as usual). ↓2

                              Paula Washington ↓2

nb ↓3

Distribution: ↓2

D. Innie
G. Albers
R. Fagan
```

Memo Format: For the format of a memo done on plain paper (as shown here) or on letterhead stationery, see ¶1393. For the format of a memo done on a printed memo form, see ¶1392.

Subject Line: For better appearance, the entry following *Subject:* has been broken into two lines of roughly equal length.

Attendance Data: This block of copy, which starts on the third line below the typed or printed memo heading, indicates (a) who was present at the meeting (the person who presided is listed first), (b) who was absent, and (c) who attended as a guest.

Content Considerations: (a) List each topic in the order in which it was discussed at the meeting. (Compare these minutes with the agenda illustrated on page 438.) (b) Underscore each topic and end it with a period if the comments are to continue on the same line (as shown here). Omit the period if the comments are to appear below the underscored topic; in that case leave 1 blank line before starting the comments and block each line of the comments on the first word of the topic above (not on the number at the left margin). (c) Give the date and location of the next meeting in a concluding paragraph, starting at the left margin.

Minutes—Formal Style

Heading: (a) Use all-capital letters for the name of the company in the first line. Use capital and small letters for the other lines. (b) For the date line, use the date on which the meeting was held (not the date on which the minutes were prepared).

Format Considerations: (a) Type the text on a 6½-inch line. (b) Indent the first line of each paragraph 5 spaces. (c) Treat resolutions as extracts, indented as a block 5 spaces from each side margin. (d) Type *RESOLVED* in all-capital letters, followed by a comma and *that* (as illustrated). As an alternative, type *RESOLVED* followed by a colon and *That.*

Content Considerations: (a) Use the opening paragraph to indicate the name of the company; the time and the place where the meeting was "called to order" (the first item on the agenda shown on page 439); and whether it was a regular or special meeting. (b) Use the next paragraphs to indicate which directors were present (all were in this illustration); which were absent; which company officers and invited guests were present; who presided; and who recorded the proceedings and prepared the minutes. (c) The body of the minutes should note in each paragraph what business was transacted and what actions were taken. (d) Use the next-to-last paragraph to indicate the date and time of the next meeting. (e) Use the final paragraph to indicate the time of adjournment.

Capitalization Style: Minutes done in a formal style use a formal style of capitalization. Note that short forms such as *Corporation* and *Board* are capitalized. Also note that in formal minutes such titles as *Chairman, Assistant Secretary,* and *Executive Vice President of Operations* are capitalized when used after a person's name. (See ¶313d.)

UNDERLOCK AND KEYE INC.

Minutes

Regular Meeting of Directors

September 22, 19—

A regular meeting of the Board of Directors of Underlock and Keye Inc. was called to order at 4 Riverfront Plaza, Louisville, Kentucky, at 10 a.m. pursuant to the notice sent to all directors in accordance with the bylaws.

The following directors were present, constituting all the directors: Jared G. Allison II, Kenneth L. Calderone, Deborah Dean Daniels, Gary Guyot,

Also present by invitation were William Burgos, Thomas Foy, Gregory A. Horn, Angela J. McGill, George Palmieri, and Lester Soaries.

Jared G. Allison II, Chairman, presided and David F. Rust, Assistant Secretary, recorded the proceedings of the meeting.

The minutes of the last meeting were approved.

Mr. Allison introduced Gregory A. Horn, Executive Vice President of Operations, who reported on August operations. Although sales were still

Henry Koyama reviewed the recommendations of the Real Estate Committee on the matter of building a new facility or renovating the existing facility to accommodate the Corporation's information processing needs over the next ten years.

After further discussion, upon motion duly made and seconded, the following resolutions were unanimously adopted:

RESOLVED, that the Corporation is hereby authorized to undertake construction and rehabilitation activities with respect to renovating the Underlock and Keye building at 321 West Chestnut Street.

The next meeting of the Board will be held on November 24 at 10 a.m.

There being no further business before the meeting, it was, on motion duly made and seconded, adjourned at 1:05 p.m.

Assistant Secretary

442

Headings: If the itinerary is to cover more than one day, insert an appropriate side heading above each day's scheduled list of activities.

Columnar Format: Leave 6 spaces between columns. For the alignment of "clock" times in a column, see ¶1626b.

Spacing: Leave 1 blank line between entries. Single-space any turnover lines, and indent them 2 spaces from the left margin of the column.

Content Considerations: (a) Provide the names of airports only when there is more than one airport serving the city (in this case, Washington, D.C.). (b) Try to provide the first names (rather than simply titles or initials) for all the individuals whom the traveler is scheduled to meet. (c) Try to provide phone numbers for all transportation services, hotels, and restaurants in case plans have to be rescheduled or canceled.

```
                          ITINERARY
                   For Wallace F. Galloway
                      April 12-14, 19—

Tuesday, April 12

6:00 a.m.            Limo to airport: Town Taxi (454-1040)

7:00 a.m.            Depart Rochester, Mohawk Flight 401

8:15 a.m.            Arrive Westchester

                     Limo to meeting:  Arthur's Limo (203-348-5347)
                     Driver will meet you at baggage carousel.

                     Destination:  Burnham & Frye Inc.
                                   West Building
                                   225 High Ridge Road
                                   Stamford, CT
                                   203-555-1216

9:00 a.m.-2:30 p.m.  Meet with Ed Burnham and Norbert Pell. They will
                     make lunch arrangements.

2:30 p.m.            Limo to NYC:  Call Arthur's Limo (203-348-5347) if
                     2:30 pickup time has to be changed.

                     Hotel:  Marriott Marquis
                             1535 Broadway
                             212-398-1900
                             Conf. No. 8941HWXQ; late arrival guaranteed

6:30 p.m.            Dinner with Doris and Jack Cuneen: meet at restau-
                     rant (Palio, 151 West 51 Street, 212-245-4850).

Wednesday, April 13

9:00 a.m.-4:00 p.m.  Board meeting in headquarters building, 49th floor
                     Sam Hurley will drive you to the airport.

5:25 p.m.            Depart Newark, Northwest 1809

6:40 p.m.            Arrive Washington, National Airport
```

Fax Cover Sheet

FAX COVER SHEET →3

DATE: _____ →3

TO: _____ →2

_____

FAX NUMBER: _____ →3

FROM: _____ →2

FAX NUMBER: _____ →2

NUMBER OF PAGES
(INCLUDING THIS
COVER SHEET): _____ →3

MESSAGE: _____

_____

_____

_____

If any part of this fax transmission
is missing or not clearly received,
please call: →2

NAME: _____

PHONE NUMBER: _____

Stationery: A fax cover sheet is usually done on letterhead stationery. If you are using blank paper (as in this illustration) and the material you typically fax does not give your full address and company affiliation, you may want to add blank fill-in lines in the *FROM* section of the form to accommodate this information.

Fill-In Lines: Design the fill-in lines so that all entries can start at a common point and no adjustments in vertical space are required. (See ¶1707a–d.)

Confidentiality Statement: If you are faxing something that is confidential (and this may sometimes not be a wise thing to do), you may want to add an appropriate message to the cover sheet. For example:

CONFIDENTIAL

The contents of this fax transmission
are confidential. If this transmission
has been directed to the wrong office,
please destroy the contents of this fax
immediately and notify [name   ]
at [phone number].

To further ensure the confidentiality of the transmission, call the appropriate person in the receiving office and (a) confirm the fax number to be used and (b) confirm that the person will be standing right by the receiving equipment while the fax is being transmitted.

444

NOTE: Even if you decide not to use a fax cover sheet, the model on page 444 serves to illustrate some useful features you ought to consider whenever you design a form on your own:

a. Lay out the fill-in lines so that as many entries as possible can start at the same point. (In the illustration on page 444, all the entries can begin at a common point of alignment.)

b. Make the fill-in lines long enough to accommodate handwritten as well as typed entries.

Financial Documents

Despite the existence of such professional standard-setting bodies as the Financial Accounting Standards Board (FASB) and the American Institute of Certified Public Accountants (AICPA), no fixed formats have been established for financial documents. The models shown in the following paragraphs (¶¶1708–1710) reflect commonly used formats for balance sheets, income statements, and statements of cash flows. Also provided (in ¶1711) is a format for an operations analysis report that relates certain types of financial results to a current budget, an estimate of year-end results, or last year's actual performance.

Balance Sheets

1708 A *balance sheet* indicates, as of a certain date, what an organization owns (its *assets*), what it owes (its *liabilities*), and how much capital the owner has invested in the organization (referred to as *owner's equity* in the case of a single owner or, in the case of multiple owners, *owners' equity, partners' equity,* or *stockholders' equity*). There are two common formats for a balance sheet. In the *report format* (illustrated on page 446), the section dealing with liabilities and owner's equity comes directly under the section dealing with assets. In the *account format,* the section dealing with assets is positioned on the left and the section dealing with liabilities and owner's equity is positioned alongside on the right. In order to implement the account format on standard (8½″ × 11″) stationery, you will need to turn the paper sideways.

Income Statements

1709 An income statement indicates how much money an organization has taken in (its *revenues*), how much money it has spent (its *expenses*), and how much money it has gained or lost as a result (referred to as a *net gain* or a *net loss*). An ordinary income statement (see the top illustration on page 448) shows these results for a certain accounting period (for example, a full year). A comparative income statement (the bottom illustration on page 448) shows these results for two comparable periods. Both illustrations represent fairly basic versions of an income statement. Many types of businesses require income statements with many additional entries and a more complex sequence of parts. However, the format shown here will accommodate any additional elements.

(Continued on page 449.)

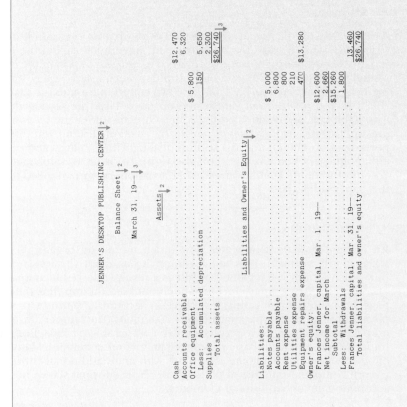

JENNER'S DESKTOP PUBLISHING CENTER |→2

Balance Sheet |→2
March 31, 19— |→3

<u>Assets</u> |→2

Cash		$12,470
Accounts receivable		6,320
Office equipment	$ 5,800	
Less: Accumulated depreciation	150	5,650
Supplies		2,300
Total assets		$26,740 |→3

<u>Liabilities and Owner's Equity</u> |→2

Liabilities:		
Notes payable	$ 5,000	
Accounts payable	6,800	
Rent expense	800	
Utilities expense	210	
Equipment repairs expense	470	$13,280
Owner's equity:		
Frances Jenner, capital, Mar. 1, 19—	$12,600	
Net income for March	2,660	
Subtotal	$15,260	
Less: Withdrawals	1,800	
Frances Jenner, capital, Mar. 31, 19—		13,460
Total liabilities and owner's equity		$26,740

These style notes apply not only to balance sheets but also to the financial documents on pages 448 and 450.

Headings: (a) The main heading—in this case, the name of the organization—is typed in all-capital letters; the title of the document—*Balance Sheet*—and the date are typed in capital and small letters. (b) If the amounts in this document are extremely large, a fourth line may be inserted in the main heading—for example, (*000 Omitted*) or (*In Thousands*)—to indicate that the figures below have been shortened accordingly. (See ¶1630 for further details.) (c) The centered headings over each section of the balance sheet (for example, *Assets*) are commonly typed in capital and small letters and are underscored; they may also be typed in all-capital letters without underscoring.

Capitalization: In this illustration only the first letter of the first word in each text entry (and the first letter of the first word following *Less:*) has been capitalized. An alternative style capitalizes the first letter of all words except for articles, short conjunctions, and short prepositions (see ¶¶360–361). Select one style and apply it consistently in all financial documents you prepare.

Leaders: Use a row of leaders (with 1 blank space before and after) to link each text entry on the left with the figure on the right. The shortest row of leaders should have a minimum of three periods. (See ¶1631 for further details.)

Spacing Between Columns: Leave 1 space between the text column (which ends in leaders) and first column of figures. Leave 2 spaces between the two columns of figures.

Rules in Figure Columns: (a) Type a single underscore rule beneath a sequence of figures that must be added or subtracted. (b) Type a double rule beneath the final figure that represents the total for that section of the column. (Use the platen release lever to turn up the paper slightly before typing the second rule.) (c) Type each rule to the full width of the figures in the column (including the dollar sign), even when the figure directly above the rule is not the widest figure in the column.

Dollar Signs: (a) Insert a dollar sign alongside the first figure in a column. (b) When a sequence of figures appears *below* an underscore rule in the same column, insert a dollar sign alongside the first figure in the new sequence. (c) Insert a dollar sign alongside any figures that represent a total or subtotal.

NOTE: All the dollar signs in a column should be vertically aligned one space to the left of the widest figure in the column.

Income Statements

```
                    BANNISTER AND NEWEL INC. |²
                         Income Statement |²
                   Year Ended December 31, 1995 |³

Revenues:
  Sales ...................................  $1,217,100
  Other operating revenues ................       6,770
    Total revenues ........................              $1,223,870 |²
Expenses:
  Cost of goods sold ......................  $ 536,530
  Research and development expense ........     32,050
  Salaries expense ........................    301,230
  Other operating expenses ................    129,710
    Total expenses ........................                 999,520 |²

Net income before income taxes ...........              $  224,350 |²
```

```
                    BANNISTER AND NEWEL INC. |²
                   Comparative Income Statement |²
               Years Ended December 31, 1995 and 1994 |³

                                                           Increase (Decrease) |²
                                    1995          1994      Amount    Percent |²

Revenues:
  Sales ...............    $1,217,100    $1,034,350    $ 82,750     17.7
  Other operating revenues ..   6,770        15,260      (8,490)    (55.6)
    Total revenues .......    $1,223,870    $1,049,610    $174,260     16.6 |²
Expenses:
  Cost of goods sold ....    $ 536,530    $ 492,420    $ 44,110      9.0
  Research and development
  expense ...............       32,050       104,640    (72,590)    (69.4)
    Total expenses ......      999,520     1,002,400      (2,880)     (0.3) |²

Net income before income taxes ...  $ 224,350    $  47,210    $177,140    375.2
```

Date Line: (a) The date line in these illustrations has been expressed as *Year Ended . . .* (or *Years Ended . . .* in the comparative version). It can also be expressed as *For the Year Ended . . .* or *For Years Ended . . .*, and the word *Ending* can be used in place of *Ended.* The important thing is to select one pattern for the date line and use it consistently in these financial documents. (b) When the date line covers more than one year (for example, *Years Ended December 31, 1995 and 1994),* a comma should precede but not follow the first year cited. It is customary to cite the more recent year first (*1995* before *1994*).

Indentions: Note that main entries start at the left margin and subentries are indented 2 spaces from the left margin. Turnover lines are indented 2 spaces from the start of the entry or subentry directly above. *Total* lines are indented 5 spaces from the left margin.

Negative Figures: (a) Figures that indicate negative amounts or losses are enclosed in parentheses. Take these parentheses into account when calculating column width for centering and spacing purposes, since one or both parentheses could extend one space beyond the positive figures in the column. (b) All negative figures align on the comma signifying *thousands* in the positive figures in the column. (c) A dollar sign that accompanies a negative figure falls outside the opening parenthesis and is aligned vertically with any other dollar signs in the column.

NOTE: The style notes for a balance sheet (on pages 446–447) also apply to the income statements illustrated here.

Statements of Cash Flows

1710 The statement of cash flows is a fairly new document that all business organizations now prepare. It shows the flow of cash into and out of a business as a result of three types of activities: operations, investing, and finance. It also provides a schedule of noncash investing and financing activities. The example on page 450 has fewer entries than would normally appear on this statement, but it serves to illustrate the format for every type of entry that the document is likely to call for.

Operational Analyses

1711 An operational analysis serves to (1) report current financial results in many areas (for example, sales revenues, operating expenses, and net operating income) and (2) relate them to other financial benchmarks (for example, last year's results, this year's budget goals, and next year's forecasts).

The illustration on page 451 shows how the basic format of an operational analysis can be used to analyze promotion expenses for the first nine months of 1994 (referred to in the title as a third-quarter YTD [year-to-date] analysis). For each type of promotion activity listed at the left, the document shows the *actual* promotion expenses for all of 1993 (*1993A*), the *budget* for all of 1994 (*1994B*), and the amount actually spent during the first three quarters of 1994 (*3Q/94 YTD Total*). The analysis then provides an *estimate* of how much will have been spent by the end of 1994 (*1994E*), and it calculates the amount by which the full-year estimate for 1994 will be *over* or *under*—*O/(U)*—the full-year budget for 1994. Finally, the document projects a *budget* for 1995 (*1995B*), and it calculates (as a percentage) the extent to which the budgeted amount for 1995 will be over or under the full-year estimate for 1994.

It is not essential that an operational analysis contain all these elements. Consider the illustration on page 451 simply as a model that can and should be adapted to fit a variety of situations.

(Continued on page 452.)

17

Statement of Cash Flows

The style for balance sheets and income statements (see pages 446–448) applies to statements of cash flows with one exception:

Indentions: A statement of cash flows has several levels of entries. In the fifth block of copy, the main entry (*Reconciliation of net income . . .*) starts at the left margin, the first subentry is indented 2 spaces, and each subsequent level of subentry is indented another 2 spaces. If an entry at any level requires a turnover line, align that turnover line with the first line of the entry (instead of indenting the turnover the customary 2 spaces). In that way you can avoid the confusion that would result from having a turnover line in a given entry start at the same point as a subentry that immediately follows. Compare the following examples:

USE:

```
Reconciliation of net income to
operating activities:
  Net income
  Adjustments to reconcile net
  provided by operating activit
    Depreciation and amortizati
    Changes in assets and liabi
    from purchase of Redd Inc:
      Increase in accounts rece
      Decrease in inventory
    Increase in interest and in
Net cash provided by operating
```

AVOID:

```
Reconciliation of net income to
operating activities:
  Net income
  Adjustments to reconcile net
    provided by operating activ
  Depreciation and amortizati
  Changes in assets and liabi
    from purchase of Redd Inc
      Increase in accounts rece
      Decrease in inventory
      Increase in interest and in
Net cash provided by operating
```

```
BACON AND HAGUE INC.
Statement of Cash Flows
Year Ended December 31, 19—
(000 Omitted)

Cash flows from operating activities:
  Cash received from customers ...............   $12,850
  Cash paid to suppliers and employees .......   (11,000)
  Interest paid (net of amount capitalized)...      (250)
  Income taxes paid ..........................      (310)
    Net cash provided by operating activities ...            $ 1,290

Cash flows from investing activities:
  Proceeds from sale of facility .............   $   880
  Payment for purchase of Redd Inc. net of cash
  acquired ...................................    (1,940)
    Net cash used in investing activities ....             (1,060)

Cash flows from financing activities:
  Proceeds from issuance of common stock .....   $   550
  Dividends paid .............................      (100)
    Net cash provided by financing activities ...             450

Net increase in cash and cash equivalents ...   $   680
Cash and cash equivalents at beginning of year ...  565
Cash and cash equivalents at end of year .....              $ 1,245

Reconciliation of net income to net cash provided by
operating activities:
  Net income .................................              $   625
  Adjustments to reconcile net income to net cash
  provided by operating activities:
    Depreciation and amortization ...........   $   405
    Changes in assets and liabilities net of effects
    from purchase of Redd Inc.:
      Increase in accounts receivable ........      (195)
      Decrease in inventory ..................       180
      Increase in interest and income taxes payable    50     440
    Net cash provided by operating activities ...          $ 1,065

Supplemental schedule of noncash investing and financing
activities:
  Additional common stock was issued upon the conver-
  sion of $550 of long-term debt.

Disclosure of accounting policy:
  For purposes of the statement of cash flows, the
  Company considers all highly liquid debt instruments
  purchased with a maturity of three months or less to
  be cash equivalents.
```

Turned Page: When a financial document is too wide to fit in the 8½-inch width of a standard sheet of stationery, turn the paper sideways and center the document on what is now the 11-inch width. Maintain a minimum margin of 1 inch on all four sides.

Columnar Format: (a) Note the standard use of 2 blank spaces between columns. However, only 1 blank space is used between the second and third columns because the second column ends with leaders. (b) The notation (*$000 Omitted*) in the heading makes it possible to eliminate all dollars signs from the table text and to shorten the figures in each column.

Abbreviations in Column Heads: For a partial list of abbreviations that can be used in column heads, see ¶1616. Because abbreviations like these make it possible to fit wide tables more easily on a page, use them freely whenever you are sure the intended readers will readily understand them. If you are in doubt, either provide an explanation as a note to the table (as is done in the illustration on page 419) or spell the terms out.

Rules in Figure Columns: Make the underscore rules in each column as wide as the widest figure in that column (including any parentheses or a percent sign or a dollar sign that may be adjacent to the figure). Do not extend the rules to the full width of the column when the column head is wider than the figures beneath.

NOTE: The style notes for other financial documents (on pages 446–448 and page 450) also apply to the document illustrated here.

THIRD-QUARTER 1994 YTD ANALYSIS OF PROMOTION EXPENSES →2

($000 Omitted) |3

Account No.	Account Name	1993A	1994B	3Q/94 YTD Total	1994E	1994E O/(U) 1994B	1995B	1995B % O/(U) 1994E
6091440	Fees to consultants	239.9	210.5	172.0	211.0	0.5	159.0	-24.6
6091445	Workshops	0.0	65.0	150.0	310.0	245.0	390.0	25.8
6092003	Brochures	370.5	310.1	240.2	262.0	(48.1)	323.0	23.3
6092008	Catalogs	259.6	355.0	328.0	356.0	1.0	333.0	-6.5
6092012	Newsletters	22.9	27.0	15.3	22.0	(5.0)	12.0	-45.5
6092013	Posters	2.2	46.0	21.0	21.0	(25.0)	15.0	-28.6
6092014	Special promotions	146.1	127.9	125.5	1150.0	1022.1	660.0	-42.6
6092015	Displays	17.8	25.0	18.0	30.0	5.0	48.0	60.0
6093010	Outside advertising	187.7	265.0	181.0	260.0	(5.0)	307.4	18.2
6093150	Conventions	83.9	99.5	91.0	109.0	9.5	148.0	35.8
6093470	Samples	355.1	294.0	387.0	496.0	202.0	601.0	21.2
6097300	Supplies	10.1	0.0	6.0	9.0	9.0	9.0	0.0
6097550	Miscellaneous	9.2	8.0	42.0	46.0	38.0	125.0	171.7
6111445	Sales associates	0.0	180.0	124.0	160.0	(20.0)	200.0	25.0
	Total	1705.0	2013.0	1901.0	3442.0	1429.0	3330.4	-3.2

¶1712

Résumés

Preparing a Résumé

1712 When you prepare a résumé, keep the following things in mind:

a. The purpose of a résumé is not to get you a job but to get you an *interview* for a job.

b. The purpose of a résumé is not to tell a prospective employer about *your* long-term goals and aspirations but to indicate *what you can do for the employer* with the experience you have acquired and the skills you have developed.

c. Do not describe your past jobs in terms of duties and responsibilities. Emphasize things that you have achieved, capabilities that you have acquired, decision-making skills you have put to good use, activities you have initiated, sales and profits that have increased (and expenses that have decreased) because of your efforts and contributions.

d. Describe your achievements and skills in a way that indicates they are readily applicable to other types of jobs and other fields.

e. Do not overstate your achievements by claiming to have done certain things single-handedly when it will be clear to the prospective employer that your "achievement" had to be part of a team effort. In the attempt to come across as a self-starter, don't jeopardize your reputation for honesty.

f. While you want your résumé to stand out from all the others that are submitted at the same time, think of how an employer will view your résumé. If you're applying for a job in advertising, design, or some other creative field, an original format or even an off-the-wall approach may get you the positive attention you crave. But if you're after a job in management, finance, or marketing—where an image of maturity and dependability is important—you'll gain more ground by emphasizing how you can help the employer rather than by taking a far-out approach.

g. Weigh the advantages of preparing a custom-tailored résumé for each situation (in which you organize and focus your strengths in light of a specific employer's needs) over the saving in time and money that comes from preparing an all-purpose résumé designed to fit a variety of job opportunities and a range of employers' needs. If you are using electronic equipment, the prospect of preparing custom-tailored résumés is not as overwhelming as it might be if you are preparing the document on a typewriter.

h. Keep the résumé as short as possible (no more than two pages), and choose a format that yields a clean, uncluttered look. (See the models on pages 454–459.)

i. Do not mention how much you earned in previous jobs or how much you expect to earn in the future.

j. Do not refer to your age, your marital status, your height and weight, your hobbies, or other personal details unless they clearly enhance your suitability for the job in question.

17

k. Do not supply reasons for having left previous jobs or for gaps in your employment history. However, do prepare yourself for dealing with these issues if they come up in the interview.

l. Do not give references on the résumé. It is not even necessary to state that references are available upon request. Be prepared, however, to supply names, addresses, and phone numbers at the interview.

m. Use good-quality paper (of at least 20-pound weight and preferably 24), and consider having your résumé executed and reproduced professionally if you cannot create a crisp-looking document with the equipment you have at your disposal.

Choosing a Format

1713 There is a wide range of formats you can choose from. Indeed, in a number of books dealing exclusively with the topic of résumés, you will find as many as a hundred models showing all kinds of variations in layout and approach. The illustrations on pages 454–459 show three different ways to format a résumé for Alison L. Bumbry, who majored in marketing at college, has had a number of secretarial and administrative positions in the marketing field, and is now attempting to move up to a managerial job in the same field.

The first two models illustrate the *chronological* approach, in which a person's employment history is sequenced by date, starting with the most current job and working backward. This is the approach most widely used and the one many employers feel most comfortable with.

In the first model (on pages 454–455) note that the dates for each job are highlighted in the left column; the corresponding job title, the name and location of the employer, and comments about the job are grouped together at the right. Also note that all the information about job *experience* typically comes before the information about *education*. If you are just out of school and have little job experience to cite, put the educational information first.

The second model (on pages 456–457) also lists the jobs in reverse chronological order, but it highlights the job titles (rather than the dates) in the left column. This approach is especially effective when your employment history shows steady upward progress in a chosen field and you are applying for the next logical position in your career path.

The third model (on pages 458–459) illustrates the *functional* approach, which groups a person's achievements and skills in functional areas such as management, administration, marketing, and writing. The functional approach is harder to implement, but it does have the advantage of grouping your key strengths in meaningful categories (rather than leaving it to the employer to ferret out these patterns of strength from your chronological job descriptions). This approach is especially helpful (a) when you are trying to change from one field to another (since it emphasizes generic types of abilities that can be applied in various settings) and (b) when you are trying to play down gaps or frequent job changes in your employment history.

Résumé—Chronological Style (Emphasizing Dates)

```
ALISON L. BUMBRY                                          Home:
Apartment 145                                                  513-555-7944
395 West Center College Street                            Office:
Yellow Springs, Ohio 45387                                     513-555-0162

OBJECTIVE:        A marketing management position in which marketing and
                  administrative experience plus strong writing and com-
                  puter skills can be used to maximize sales and profit-
                  ability of one or more product lines.

EXPERIENCE:

July 1990—        ADMINISTRATIVE COORDINATOR FOR DIRECTOR OF MARKETING
Present           Zimmer & Boyle Inc., Dayton, Ohio

                  o Created and managed a database to control budgeted
                    expenses for advertising and promotion.
                  o Participated in designing and implementing market re-
                    search studies to determine potential size of market
                    for new product lines.
                  o Coordinated focus group sessions to determine custo-
                    mer attitudes toward our product lines and those of
                    competitors.
                  o Initiated desktop publishing program to create space
                    ads, catalogs, and mailing pieces. Saved the company
                    over $50,000 in the first year of operation.

February 1988—    ADMINISTRATIVE ASSISTANT TO SALES MANAGER
June 1990         Zimmer & Boyle Inc., Dayton, Ohio

                  o Analyzed field sales reports and wrote summaries high-
                    lighting problems requiring immediate action and those
                    suggesting need for changes in product design, order
                    fulfillment procedures, or customer service.
                  o Resolved customer complaints by taking direct action
                    whenever possible or by routing complaint to the ap-
                    propriate person. Followed up to ensure complaint
                    was properly handled.
                  o Supervised a secretary who handled all correspondence
                    and clerical tasks.
```

Heading: The heading should give all the key data an employer needs to get in touch with you. In this arrangement, the data is presented in two blocks: one aligned at the left margin, the other at the right.

Objective: Use your "objective" statement to indicate (a) the type of job you're looking for, (b) the strengths you can bring to the job, and (c) what you think you can accomplish for the employer's benefit.

Experience: (a) In this format the dates for each job are featured in the left column. At the right, each job history begins with the job title (in all-capital letters), followed by the employer's name and location (in capital and small letters) on the following line. (b) The specific achievements in each job history are presented in a series of bulleted entries. The bullets can be created by means of the small letter *o* or a vertically centered period. (c) Note that many entries begin with vigorous verbs (such as *created, initiated, resolved,* and *supervised*) to create the image of a dynamic, take-charge kind of person. Note also that to maintain credibility, the writer uses such terms as *participated in* and *created (with two partners)* to acknowledge the contribution of others whenever appropriate.

Education: Provide information on college and any postgraduate degrees in that order. Provide information about your high school education only if that is the highest level so far attained. If you are currently enrolled in a degree program, note this fact along with an estimated date of completion. For example:

> Pursuing a two-year program in business administration at Glendale Community College; will receive an A.A. degree in June 1995.

Continuing Education: Note any job-related courses you have taken. If you are changing careers or fields, note any other continuing education activity that shows you are a person committed to learning new things.

Special Skills: Note any special skills that could be job-related; for example, mastery of software programs, experience with certain equipment or machinery, speeds achieved in various office skills, mastery of spoken or written foreign languages.

Community Service: Note any activity that is job-related or that shows you to be concerned about the needs of others.

Optional Sections: Also provide job-related information under such labels as these: *Professional Affiliations* (memberships), *Professional Activities* (speeches and published articles and books), *Military Service,* and *Special Interests.*

ALISON L. BUMBRY   Page 2

May 1986–
January 1988
SECRETARY TO MARKETING MANAGER
Crouch and Cowar Incorporated, Toledo, Ohio

o Developed detailed marketing plans, working from rough outlines provided by marketing manager.
o Created and managed a segmented database of names of customers and qualified prospects for direct marketing campaigns.
o Wrote copy for mail campaigns and catalogs.
o Established media contacts to obtain free publicity for new products and special offers.

September 1984–
April 1986
ASSISTANT TO DIRECTOR OF PUBLIC RELATIONS
The Toledo Museum of Art, Toledo, Ohio

o Wrote news releases for new exhibits and special events.
o Wrote, designed, and laid out fund-raising brochures.
o Established and maintained effective media contacts with regional newspapers and TV and radio stations.

EDUCATION:
B.S. in marketing, 1984; minor in English
Arizona State University, Tempe, Arizona

o Wrote feature articles for The Arizona Sundial during sophomore and junior years.
o Created (with two partners) an on-campus birthday celebration service. Managed the service during junior and senior years. Tested various direct marketing techniques to solicit orders from parents of students.

CONTINUING EDUCATION:
Courses in copywriting, telemarketing techniques, niche marketing, and computer graphics. Wright State University, Dayton, Ohio, 1992–1994.

COMPUTER SKILLS:
Advanced WordPerfect 5.1, Microsoft Windows 3.0, PageMaker 4.0, Harvard Graphics 2.3, Lotus 1-2-3 (Version 2.3), dBase IV (Version 1.1).

COMMUNITY SERVICE:
Wrote, designed, and laid out annual fund-raising brochures (since 1992) for the Dayton Homeless Shelter Coalition, using desktop publishing and computer graphics software.

Résumé—Chronological Style (Emphasizing Job Titles)

Heading: In this arrangement all the necessary information is given in a series of centered, single-spaced lines.

Experience: (a) In this format the job titles (rather than the dates) are featured in the left column. At the right the name and location of the organization plus the employment dates are given on one or two lines. (b) Arranging the specific achievements for each job in one paragraph is a common format, but it is not as readable as the "bulleted" format used in the résumés on pages 454–455 and pages 458–459.

```
                    ALISON L. BUMBRY
                     Apartment 145
             395 West Center College Street
                 Yellow Springs, Ohio 45387
                  Home:   513-555-7944
                  Office:  513-555-0162


OBJECTIVE:       A marketing management position in which marketing and
                 administrative experience plus strong writing and com-
                 puter skills can be used to maximize sales and profit-
                 ability of one or more product lines.

EXPERIENCE:

Administrative   ZIMMER & BOYLE INC., Dayton, Ohio, July 1990-Present
Coordinator for
Director of         Created and managed a database to control budgeted
Marketing           expenses for advertising and promotion. Participated
                    in designing and implementing market research studies
                    to determine potential size of market for new product
                    lines. Coordinated focus group sessions to determine
                    customer attitudes toward our product lines and those
                    of competitors. Initiated desktop publishing program
                    to create space ads, catalogs, and mailing pieces;
                    saved the company over $50,000 in the first year of
                    operation.


Administrative   ZIMMER & BOYLE INC., Dayton, Ohio, February 1988-
Assistant to     June 1990
Sales Manager
                    Analyzed field sales reports and wrote summaries high-
                    lighting problems requiring immediate action and those
                    suggesting need for changes in product design, order
                    fulfillment procedures, or customer service. Resolved
                    customer complaints by taking direct action whenever
                    possible or by routing complaint to the appropriate
                    person; followed up to ensure complaint was properly
                    handled. Supervised a secretary who handled all cor-
                    respondence and clerical tasks.
```

Secretary to   CROUCH AND COWAR INCORPORATED, Toledo, Ohio, May 1986–
Marketing   January 1988
Manager
                    Developed detailed marketing plans, working from rough
                    outlines provided by marketing manager. Created and
                    managed a segmented database of names of customers and
                    qualified prospects for direct marketing campaigns.
                    Wrote copy for mail campaigns and catalogs. Established
                    media contacts to obtain free publicity for new products
                    and special offers.

Assistant to   THE TOLEDO MUSEUM OF ART, Toledo, Ohio, September 1984–
Director of   April 1986
Public Relations
                    Wrote news releases for new exhibts and special events.
                    Wrote, designed, and laid out fund-raising brochures.
                    Established and maintained effective media contacts with
                    regional newspapers and TV and radio stations.

EDUCATION: B.S. in marketing, 1984; minor in English
                    Arizona State University, Tempe, Arizona

                    Wrote feature articles for The Arizona Sundial during
                    sophomore and junior years. Created (with two partners)
                    an on-campus birthday celebration service; managed the
                    service during junior and senior years; tested various
                    direct marketing techniques to solicit orders from par-
                    ents of students.

CONTINUING   Courses in copywriting, telemarketing techniques, niche
EDUCATION: marketing, and computer graphics. Wright State Univer-
                    sity, Dayton, Ohio, 1992–1994.

COMPUTER   Advanced WordPerfect 5.1, Microsoft Windows 3.0,
SKILLS: PageMaker 4.0, Harvard Graphics 2.3, Lotus 1-2-3
                    (Version 2.3), dBase IV (Version 1.1).

COMMUNITY   Wrote, designed, and laid out annual fund-raising brochures
SERVICE: (since 1992) for the Dayton Homeless Shelter Coalition,
                    using desktop publishing and computer graphics software.

457

Résumé—Functional Style

Heading: In this arrangement each line is blocked at the left and starts at the same point as the copy in the second column below.

Sideheads: (a) In this illustration the customary sidehead *EXPERIENCE* in the left column has been replaced by *ACHIEVEMENTS* because the term *experience* has been used in two of the four sideheads in the right column. (b) Note how the wording of the "objective" statement (*in which marketing and administrative experience plus strong writing and computer skills*) provides the springboard for the functional sideheads in the right column (*MARKETING EXPERIENCE, ADMINISTRATIVE EXPERIENCE, WRITING SKILLS,* and *COMPUTER SKILLS*). (c) Note how the entries under these sideheads in the right column have been reordered (and in some cases reworded) so as to emphasize the applicant's strengths in each functional area, independent of the job setting in which these strengths were developed.

ALISON L. BUMBRY
Apartment 145
395 West Center College Street
Yellow Springs, Ohio 45387
Home: 513-555-7944
Office: 513-555-0162

OBJECTIVE: A marketing management position in which marketing and
                  administrative experience plus strong writing and com-
                  puter skills can be used to maximize sales and profit-
                  ability of one or more product lines.

ACHIEVEMENTS: MARKETING EXPERIENCE

                  o Participated in designing and implementing market re-
                    search studies to determine potential size of market
                    for new product lines.
                  o Coordinated focus group sessions to determine custo-
                    mer attitudes toward our product lines and those of
                    competitors.
                  o Analyzed field sales reports and wrote summaries high-
                    lighting problems requiring immediate action and those
                    suggesting need for changes in product design, order
                    fulfillment procedures, or customer service.
                  o Developed detailed marketing plans working from rough
                    outlines provided by marketing manager.

                  ADMINISTRATIVE EXPERIENCE

                  o Controlled budgeted expenses for advertising and pro-
                    motion.
                  o Resolved customer complaints by taking direct action
                    whenever possible or by routing complaint to the ap-
                    propriate person. Followed up to ensure complaint
                    was properly handled.
                  o Established and maintained effective media contacts
                    with regional newspapers and TV and radio stations
                    to obtain free publicity for new products and special
                    offers.
                  o Supervised a secretary who handled all correspondence
                    and clerical tasks.

Employment History: Although this section would not appear in a purely "functional" résumé, an employment history provides prospective employers with a brief chronological listing of previous job titles, the name and location of previous employers, and employment dates. Including this section in a functional résumé often serves to mollify employers who are more comfortable with résumés done completely in the chronological style.

ALISON L. BUMBRY   Page 2

WRITING SKILLS

o Wrote copy for mail campaigns, catalogs, and news releases.
o Wrote summaries of field sales reports to underscore need for immediate action.
o Wrote copy for fund-raising brochures for art museum.

COMPUTER SKILLS

o Initiated an in-house desktop publishing program. Saved the company over $50,000 in the first year of operation.
o Designed and laid out space ads, catalogs, mailing pieces, and fund-raising brochures.
o Created and managed a database to control budgeted expenses for advertising and promotion.
o Created and managed a segmented database of names of customers and qualified prospects for direct marketing campaigns.
o Mastered word processing software—Advanced Word-Perfect 5.1 and Microsoft Windows 3.0; desktop publishing and graphics software—PageMaker 4.0 and Harvard Graphics 2.3; and database software—Lotus

EMPLOYMENT HISTORY:
o Administrative coordinator for director of marketing. Zimmer & Boyle Inc., Dayton, Ohio. July 1990-present.
o Administrative assistant to sales manager. Zimmer & Boyle Inc., Dayton, Ohio. February 1988-June 1990.
o Secretary to marketing manager, Crouch and Cowar In-

EDUCATION:
B.S. in marketing, 1984; minor in English Arizona State University, Tempe, Arizona
o Wrote feature articles for The Arizona Sundial during sophomore and junior years.
o Created (with two partners) an on-campus birthday celebration service. Managed the service during

CONTINUING EDUCATION:
Courses in copywriting, telemarketing techniques, niche marketing, and computer graphics. Wright State University, Dayton, Ohio. 1992-1994.

COMMUNITY SERVICE:
Wrote, designed, and laid out annual fund-raising brochures (since 1992) for the Dayton Homeless Shelter Coalition, using desktop publishing and computer graphics software.

PART

3

References

Government Officials (¶1806)
  President of the United States (¶1806a)
  Former President of the United States (¶1806b)
  Vice President of the United States (¶1806c)
  Cabinet Member (¶1806d)
  United States Senator (¶1806e)
  United States Representative (¶1806f)
  Chief Justice of the U.S. Supreme Court (¶1806g)
  Associate Justice of the U.S. Supreme Court (¶1806h)
  Judge of Federal, State, or Local Court (¶1806i)
  Governor (¶1806j)
  State Senator (¶1806k)
  State Representative or Assembly Member (¶1806l)
  Mayor (¶1806m)

Diplomats (¶1807)
  Secretary General of the United Nations (¶1807a)
  Ambassador to the United States (¶1807b)
  Minister to the United States (¶1807c)
  American Ambassador (¶1807d)

Members of the Armed Services (¶1808)
  Army, Air Force, and Marine Corps Officers (¶1808a)
  Navy and Coast Guard Officers (¶1808b)
  Enlisted Personnel (¶1808c)

Roman Catholic Dignitaries (¶1809)
  Pope (¶1809a)
  Cardinal (¶1809b)
  Archbishop and Bishop (¶1809c)
  Monsignor (¶1809d)
  Priest (¶1809e)
  Mother Superior (¶1809f)
  Sister (¶1809g)
  Brother (¶1809h)

Protestant Dignitaries (¶1810)
  Protestant Episcopal Bishop (¶1810a)
  Protestant Episcopal Dean (¶1810b)
  Methodist Bishop (¶1810c)
  Minister With Doctor's Degree (¶1810d)
  Minister Without Doctor's Degree (¶1810e)

Jewish Dignitaries (¶1811)
  Rabbi With Doctor's Degree (¶1811a)
  Rabbi Without Doctor's Degree (¶1811b)

The following forms are correct for addressing letters to individuals, couples, organizations, professional people, education officials, government officials, diplomats, military personnel, and religious dignitaries.

IMPORTANT NOTE: In the salutations that follow the forms of address, the most formal one is listed first. Unless otherwise indicated, the ellipsis marks in the salutation stand for the surname alone.

Because of space limitations, only the masculine forms of address have been given in some illustrations. When an office or a position is held by a woman, make the following substitutions:

For *Sir,* use *Madam.*

For *Mr.* followed by a name (for example, *Mr. Wyatt*), use *Miss, Mrs.,* or *Ms.,* whichever is appropriate.

For *His,* use *Her.*

For *Mr.* followed by a title (for example, *Mr. President, Mr. Secretary, Mr. Mayor*), use *Madam.*

For a detailed discussion of how to construct inside addresses, see ¶¶1317–1343; for further information on salutations, see ¶¶1346–1351; for details on how to handle addresses on envelopes, see ¶¶1389–1390.

1801 Individuals

a. Man With Courtesy Title

Mr. . . . *(full name)*
Address

Dear Mr. . . .:

b. Woman With Courtesy Title

Ms. (**OR** Miss **OR** Mrs.) . . . *(full name)*
Address

Dear Ms. (**OR** Miss **OR** Mrs.) . . .:

NOTE: If a woman prefers one of these titles, respect her preference.

c. Woman—Courtesy Title Preference Unknown

Ms. . . . *(full name)*
Address

Dear Ms. . . .:

OR:

. . . *(full name with no title)*
Address

Dear . . . *(first name and surname):*

d. Individual—Name Known, Gender Unknown

. . . *(full name with no title)*
Address

Dear . . . *(first name or initials plus surname):*

e. Individual—Name Unknown, Gender Known

. . . *(title of individual)*
. . . *(name of organization)*
Address

Madam:
Dear Madam:

OR:

Sir:
Dear Sir:

f. Individual—Name and Gender Unknown

. . . *(title of individual)*
. . . *(name of organization)*
Address

Sir or Madam:
Dear Sir or Madam:

OR:

Madam or Sir:
Dear Madam or Sir:

g. Two Men

Mr. . . . *(full name)*
Mr. . . . *(full name)*
Address

Gentlemen:
Dear Messrs. . . . and . . .:
Dear Mr. . . . and Mr. . . .:

(Continued on page 464.)

h. Two Women

Ms. . . . *(full name)*
Ms. . . . *(full name)*
Address

Dear Mses. (OR Mss.) . . . and . . .:
Dear Ms. . . . and Ms. . . .:

OR:

Mrs. . . . *(full name)*
Mrs. . . . *(full name)*
Address

Dear Mesdames . . . and . . .:
Dear Mrs. . . . and Mrs. . . .:

OR:

Miss . . . *(full name)*
Miss . . . *(full name)*
Address

Dear Misses . . . and . . .:
Dear Miss . . . and Miss . . .:

OR:

Ms. . . . *(full name)*
Mrs. . . . *(full name)*
Address

Dear Ms. . . . and Mrs. . . .:

OR:

Miss . . . *(full name)*
Ms. . . . *(full name)*
Address

Dear Miss . . . and Ms. . . .:

OR:

Mrs. . . . *(full name)*
Miss . . . *(full name)*
Address

Dear Mrs. . . . and Miss . . .:

i. Woman and Man—No Personal Relationship

Ms. (OR Mrs. OR Miss) . . . *(full name)*
Mr. . . . *(full name)*
Address

Dear Ms. (OR Mrs. OR Miss) . . .
and Mr. . . .:

OR:

Mr. . . . *(full name)*
Ms. (OR Mrs. OR Miss) . . . *(full name)*
Address

Dear Mr. . . . and Ms. (OR Mrs.
OR Miss) . . .:

1802 Couples

a. Married Couple—No Special Titles

Mr. and Mrs. . . . *(husband's full name)*
Address

Dear Mr. and Mrs. . . . *(husband's surname):*

b. Married Couple—Husband Has Special Title

Dr. and Mrs. . . . *(husband's full name)*
Address

Dear Dr. and Mrs. . . . *(husband's surname):*

c. Married Couple—Wife Has Special Title

Senator . . . *(wife's full name)*
Mr. . . . *(husband's full name)*
Address

Dear Senator and Mr. . . . *(husband's surname):*

d. Married Couple—Both Have Special Titles

Dr. . . . *(wife's full name)*
Dr. . . . *(husband's full name)*
Address

Dear Drs. . . . *(husband's surname):*

Captain . . . *(husband's full name)*
Professor . . . *(wife's full name)*
Address

Dear Captain and Professor . . . *(husband's surname):*

e. Married Couple—Wife Retains Maiden Name

Ms. (OR Miss) . . . *(wife's full name)*
Mr. . . . *(husband's full name)*
Address

Dear Ms. (OR Miss) . . . *(wife's maiden name* and Mr. . . . *(husband's surname):*

OR:

Mr. . . . *(husband's full name)*
Ms. (OR Miss) . . . *(wife's full name)*
Address

Dear Mr. . . . *(husband's surname)* and Ms. (OR Miss) . . . *(wife's maiden name):*

For forms of address for teenagers and younger children, see ¶¶1322d–e.

f. Married Couple With Hyphenated Name

Mr. and Mrs. . . . *(husband's first name and middle initial, plus wife's maiden name followed by hyphen and husband's surname)*
Address

Dear Mr. and Mrs. . . . *(wife's maiden name followed by hyphen and husband's surname):*

g. Unmarried Couple Living Together

Ms. (OR Miss) . . . *(full name)*
Mr. . . . *(full name)*
Address

Dear Ms. (OR Miss) . . . and Mr. . . .:
OR:
Mr. . . . *(full name)*
Ms. (OR Miss) . . . *(full name)*
Address

Dear Mr. . . . and Ms. (OR Miss) . . .:

1803 Organizations

a. Organization of Women and Men

. . . *(name of organization)*
Address

Ladies and Gentlemen:
Gentlemen and Ladies:
Gentlemen: (see ¶1350)
Dear . . . *(name of organization):*
    (see ¶1350c)
OR:
Mr. . . . *(name of organization head)*
President *(or other appropriate title)*
. . . *(name of organization)*
Address

Dear Mr. . . .:
OR:
Chief Executive Officer *(or other appropriate title)*
. . . *(name of organization)*
Address

Sir or Madam:
Madam or Sir:
Dear Sir or Madam:
Dear Madam or Sir:

b. Organization of Women

. . . *(name of organization)*
Address

Mesdames:
Ladies:

c. Organization of Men

. . . *(name of organization)*
Address

Gentlemen:

1804 Professionals

a. Lawyers

Mr. . . . *(full name)* *
Attorney-at-Law
Address
OR:
. . . *(full name),* Esq.†
Address

Dear Mr. . . .:*

b. Physicians and Others With Doctoral Degrees

Dr. . . . *(full name)*
Address
OR:
. . . *(full name),* M.D.†
Address

Dear Dr. . . .:

1805 Education Officials

a. President of College or University

. . . *(full name, followed by comma and highest degree)*
President, . . . *(name of college)*
Address
OR:
Dr. . . . *(full name)*
President, . . . *(name of college)*
Address

Dear President . . .:
Dear Dr. . . .:

(Continued on page 466.)

18

---

*See the note at the top of page 463.

†When an abbreviation such as *Esq., M.D.,* or *Ph.D.* follows a name, do not use a courtesy title such as *Mr.* or *Dr.* before it. (See also ¶¶518c, 519c.)

OR:

President . . . *(full name)*
. . . *(name of college)*
Address

Dear President . . .:
Dear Dr. . . .:

b. Dean of College or University

. . . *(full name, followed by comma and highest degree)*
Dean, . . . *(name of school or division)*
. . . *(name of college)*
Address

OR:

Dr. . . . *(full name)*
Dean, . . . *(name of school or division)*
. . . *(name of college)*
Address

OR:

Dean . . . *(full name)*
. . . *(name of school or division)*
. . . *(name of college)*
Address

Dear Dean . . .:
Dear Dr. . . .:

c. Professor

Professor . . . *(full name)*
Department of . . . *(subject)*
. . . *(name of college)*
Address

OR:

. . . *(full name, followed by comma and highest degree)*
Department of (OR Professor of) . . . *(subject)*
. . . *(name of college)*
Address

OR:

Dr. . . . *(full name)*
Department of (OR Professor of) . . . *(subject)*
. . . *(name of college)*
Address

Dear Professor (OR Dr.) . . .:
Dear Mr. . . .:*

d. Superintendent of Schools

Mr. (OR Dr.) . . . *(full name)*
Superintendent of . . . Schools
Address

Dear Mr. (OR Dr.) . . .:*

---

*See the note at the top of page 463.

e. Member of Board of Education

Mr. . . . *(full name)**
Member, . . . *(name of city)* Board of Education
Address

Dear Mr. . . .:*

f. Principal

Mr. . . . *(full name)**
Dr. . . . *(full name)**
Principal, . . . *(name of school)*
Address

Dear Mr. . . .:*
Dear Dr. . . .:*

g. Teacher

Mr. . . . *(full name)**
Dr. . . . *(full name)**
. . . *(name of school)*
Address

Dear Mr. . . .:*
Dear Dr. . . .:*

1806 Government Officials

a. President of the United States

The President
The White House
Washington, DC 20500

Mr. President:*
Dear Mr. President:

b. Former President of the United States

The Honorable . . . *(full name)*
Local address

Dear Mr. . . .:

c. Vice President of the United States

The Vice President
United States Senate
Washington, DC 20510

OR:

The Honorable . . . *(full name)*
Vice President of the United States
Washington, DC 20510

Sir:*
Dear Mr. Vice President:*

d. Cabinet Member

The Honorable . . . *(full name)*
Secretary of . . . *(department)*
Washington, DC   ZIP Code

Sir:*
Dear Mr. Secretary:*

e. United States Senator

The Honorable . . . *(full name)*
United States Senate
Washington, DC 20510
OR:
The Honorable . . . *(full name)*
United States Senator
Local address

Sir:*
Dear Senator . . .:

f. United States Representative

The Honorable . . . *(full name)*
House of Representatives
Washington, DC 20515
OR:
The Honorable . . . *(full name)*
Representative in Congress
Local address

Sir:*
Dear Representative . . .:
Dear Mr. . . .:*

**g. Chief Justice of the
U.S. Supreme Court**

The Chief Justice of the
   United States
Washington, DC 20543
OR:
The Chief Justice
The Supreme Court
Washington, DC 20543

Sir:*
Dear Mr. Chief Justice:*

**h. Associate Justice of the
U.S. Supreme Court**

Mr. Justice . . . *(last name only)*
The Supreme Court
Washington, DC 20543

Sir:*
Dear Mr. Justice:*

---

*See the note at the top of page 463.

**i. Judge of Federal, State, or
Local Court**

The Honorable . . . *(full name)*
Judge of the . . . *(name of court)*
Address

Dear Judge . . .:

j. Governor

The Honorable . . . *(full name)*
Governor of . . . *(state)*
State Capital, State   ZIP Code

Sir:*
Dear Governor . . .:

k. State Senator

The Honorable . . . *(full name)*
The State Senate
State Capital, State   ZIP Code

Sir:*
Dear Senator . . .:

**l. State Representative or
Assembly Member**

The Honorable . . . *(full name)*
House of Representatives
   (**OR** The State Assembly)
State Capital, State   ZIP Code

Sir:*
Dear Mr. . . .:*

m. Mayor

The Honorable . . . *(full name)*
Mayor of . . . *(city)*
City, State   ZIP Code
OR:
The Mayor of the City of . . .
City, State   ZIP Code

Sir:*
Dear Mr. Mayor:*
Dear Mayor . . .:

1807 Diplomats

**a. Secretary General of the
United Nations**

His Excellency . . . *(full name)**
Secretary General of the United Nations
United Nations Plaza
New York, NY 10017

Excellency:
Dear Mr. Secretary General:*
Dear Mr. . . .:*

(Continued on page 468.)

b. Ambassador to the United States

His Excellency . . . (*full name*)*
Ambassador of . . . (*country*)
Address

Excellency:
Dear Mr. Ambassador:*

c. Minister to the United States

The Honorable . . . (*full name*)
Minister of . . . (*department*)
Address

Sir:*
Dear Mr. Minister:*

d. American Ambassador

The Honorable . . . (*full name*)
American Ambassador
(OR The Ambassador of the United
States of America)
Foreign address of U.S. embassy

Sir:*
Dear Mr. Ambassador:*

1808 Members of the Armed Services

The addresses of both officers and enlisted personnel in the armed services should include title or rank and full name followed by a comma and the initials USA, USN, USAF, USMC, or USCG. Below and in the next column are some specific examples with appropriate salutations.

a. Army, Air Force, and Marine Corps Officers

Lieutenant General . . . (*full name*),
USA (OR USAF OR USMC)
Address

Sir:*
Dear General . . .:†
(NOT: Dear Lieutenant General . . .:)

b. Navy and Coast Guard Officers

Rear Admiral . . . (*full name*), USN
(OR USCG)
Address

Sir:*
Dear Admiral . . .:†

For officers below the rank of commander, use:

Dear Mr. . . .:*

c. Enlisted Personnel

Sergeant . . . (*full name*), USA
Address

Seaman . . . (*full name*), USN
Address

Dear Sergeant (OR Seaman) . . .:

1809 Roman Catholic Dignitaries

a. Pope

His Holiness the Pope
OR:
His Holiness Pope . . . (*given name*)
Vatican City
00187 Rome
ITALY

Your Holiness:
Most Holy Father:

b. Cardinal

His Eminence . . . (*given name*)
   Cardinal . . . (*surname*)
Archbishop of . . . (*place*)
Address

Your Eminence:
Dear Cardinal . . .:

c. Archbishop and Bishop

The Most Reverend . . . (*full name*)
Archbishop (OR Bishop) of . . . (*place*)
Address

Your Excellency:
Dear Archbishop (OR Bishop) . . .:

---

*See the note at the top of page 463.

†Use the salutation *Dear General* . . . whether the officer is a full general or only a lieutenant general, a major general, or a brigadier general. Similarly, use *Dear Colonel* . . . for either a full colonel or a lieutenant colonel and *Dear Lieutenant* . . . for either a first or a second lieutenant. Also use *Dear Admiral* . . . for a full admiral, a vice admiral, or a rear admiral.

d. Monsignor

The Reverend Monsignor . . . *(full name)*
Address

Reverend Monsignor:
Dear Monsignor . . .:

e. Priest

The Reverend . . . *(full name, followed by comma and initials of order)*
Address

Reverend Father:
Dear Father . . .:
Dear Father:

f. Mother Superior

The Reverend Mother Superior
Address

OR:

Reverend Mother . . . *(name, followed by comma and initials of order)*
Address

Reverend Mother:
Dear Reverend Mother:
Dear Mother . . .:

g. Sister

Sister . . . *(name, followed by comma and initials of order)*
Address

Dear Sister . . .:
Dear Sister:

h. Brother

Brother . . . *(name, followed by comma and initials of order)*
Address

Dear Brother . . .:
Dear Brother:

1810 Protestant Dignitaries

a. Protestant Episcopal Bishop

The Right Reverend . . . *(full name)*
Bishop of . . . *(place)*
Address

Right Reverend Sir:
Dear Bishop . . .:

b. Protestant Episcopal Dean

The Very Reverend . . . *(full name)*
Dean of . . . *(place)*
Address

Very Reverend Sir:
Dear Dean . . .:

c. Methodist Bishop

The Reverend . . . *(full name)*
Bishop of . . . *(place)*
Address

OR:

Bishop . . . *(full name)*
Address

Reverend Sir:
Dear Bishop . . .:

d. Minister With Doctor's Degree

The Reverend Dr. . . . *(full name)*
Address

OR:

The Reverend . . . *(full name)*, D.D.
Address

Reverend Sir:*
Dear Dr. . . .:

e. Minister Without Doctor's Degree

The Reverend . . . *(full name)*
Address

Reverend Sir:*
Dear Mr. . . .:*

1811 Jewish Dignitaries

a. Rabbi With Doctor's Degree

Rabbi . . . *(full name)*, D.D.
Address

OR:

Dr. . . . *(full name)*
Address

Dear Rabbi (OR Dr.) . . .:

b. Rabbi Without Doctor's Degree

Rabbi . . . *(full name)*
Address

Dear Rabbi . . .:

---

*See the note at the top of page 463.

Glossary of Grammatical Terms

This glossary provides brief definitions of common grammatical terms.

Adjective. A word that answers the question *what kind* (*excellent* results), *how many* (*four* laptops), or *which one* (the *latest* data). An adjective may be a single word (a *wealthy* man), a phrase (a man *of great wealth*), or a clause (a man *who possesses great wealth*). An adjective modifies the meaning of a noun (*loose* cannon) or a pronoun (*unlucky* me, I was *wrong*).

Adjective, predicate. See *Complement.*

Adverb. A word that answers the question *when, where, why, in what manner,* or *to what extent.* An adverb may be a single word (speak *clearly*), a phrase (speak *in a clear voice*), or a clause (speak *as clearly as you can*). An adverb modifies the meaning of a verb, an adjective, or another adverb.

> We closed the deal *quickly.* (Modifies the verb *closed.*)
>
> Caroline seemed *genuinely* pleased. (Modifies the adjective *pleased.*)
>
> My presentation went *surprisingly* well. (Modifies the adverb *well.*)

Adverbial conjunctive (or **connective**). An adverb that connects the main clauses of a compound sentence; for example, *however, therefore, nevertheless, hence, moreover, otherwise, consequently.* (See also ¶178.)

Antecedent. A noun or a noun phrase to which a pronoun refers.

> She is the *person who* wrote the letter. (*Person* is the antecedent of *who.*)
>
> *Owning a home* has *its* advantages. (*Owning a home* is the antecedent of *its.*)

Appositive. A noun or a noun phrase that identifies another noun or pronoun that immediately precedes it. (See ¶¶148–150.)

> Mr. Mancuso, *our chief financial officer,* would like to meet you.

Article. Considered an adjective. The *definite* article is *the;* the *indefinite, a* or *an.* (See *a–an* on page 252.)

Case. The form of a noun or of a pronoun that indicates its relation to other words in the sentence. There are three cases: nominative, objective, and possessive. *Nouns* have the same form in the nominative and objective cases but a special ending for the possessive. The forms for *pronouns* are:

Nominative	Objective	Possessive
I	me	my, mine
you	you	your, yours
he, she, it	him, her, it	his, hers, its
we	us	our, ours
they	them	their, theirs
who	whom	whose

Nominative case. Used for the subject or the complement of a verb.

She publishes a newsletter. (Subject.)

The person who called you was *I*. (Complement.)

Objective case. Used for (1) the object of a verb, (2) the object of a preposition, (3) the subject of an infinitive, (4) the object of an infinitive, or (5) the complement of the infinitive *to be*.

Can you help *us* this weekend? (Object of the verb *help*.)

Brenda has not written to *me*. (Object of the preposition *to*.)

I encouraged *her* to enter the biathlon. (Subject of the infinitive *to enter*.)

They believed me to be *her*. (Complement of the infinitive *to be*.)

Possessive case. Used to show ownership. (See ¶¶627–651.)

Clause. A group of related words containing a subject and a predicate. An *independent* clause (also known as a *main clause* or *principal clause*) expresses a complete thought and can stand alone as a sentence. A *dependent* clause (also known as a *subordinate clause*) does not express a complete thought and cannot stand alone as a sentence.

I will go (independent clause) if I am invited (dependent clause).

Adjective clause. A dependent clause that modifies a noun or a pronoun in the main clause. Adjective clauses are joined to the main clause by relative pronouns *(which, that, who, whose, whom)*.

Their bill, *which includes servicing,* seems reasonable. (Modifies *bill.*)

Adverbial clause. A dependent clause that functions as an adverb in its relation to the main clause. Adverbial clauses indicate time, place, manner, cause, purpose, condition, result, reason, or contrast.

These orders can be filled *as soon as stock is received.* (Time.)

I was advised to live *where the climate is dry.* (Place.)

She worked *as though her life depended on it.* (Manner.)

Please write me at once *if you have any suggestions.* (Condition.)

Because our plant is closed in August, we cannot fill your order now. (Reason.)

Coordinate clauses. Clauses of the same rank. They may be independent or dependent clauses.

Carl will oversee the day-to-day operations, and *Sheila will be responsible for the finances.* (Coordinate independent clauses.)

When you have read the user's manual and *you have mastered all the basic operations,* try to deal with these special applications. (Coordinate dependent clauses.)

Elliptical clause. A clause from which key words have been omitted. (See ¶¶102, 111, 119, 130b, 1082d.)

Now, for the next topic.   Really?   If possible, arrive at one.

(Continued on page 472.)

19

Essential (or restrictive) clause. A dependent clause that cannot be omitted without changing the meaning of the main clause. Essential clauses are *not* set off by commas.

The magazine *that came yesterday* contains an evaluation of new software.

Nonessential (or nonrestrictive) clause. A dependent clause that adds descriptive information but could be omitted without changing the meaning of the main clause. Such clauses are separated or set off from the main clause by commas.

Her latest book, *which deals with corporate financial analysis,* has sold quite well.

She has had a lot of success with her latest book, *which deals with corporate financial analysis.*

Noun clause. A dependent clause that functions as a noun in the main clause.

Whether the proposal will be accepted remains to be seen. (Noun clause as subject.)

They thought *that the plan was a failure.* (Noun clause as object.)

Then he said, *"Who gave you that information?"* (Noun clause as object.)

Comparison. The forms of an adjective or adverb that indicate degrees in quality, quantity, or manner. There are three degrees: positive, comparative, and superlative. (See ¶1071.)

Positive. The simple form; for example, *new, efficient* (adjectives); *soon, quietly* (adverbs).

Comparative. Indicates a higher or lower degree of quality or manner than is expressed by the positive degree. It is used when two things are compared. It is regularly formed by adding *er* to the positive degree *(newer, sooner).* In longer words it is formed by adding *more* or *less* to the positive *(more efficient, less efficient; more quietly, less quietly).*

Superlative. Denotes the highest or lowest degree of quality or manner and is used when more than two things are compared. It is regularly formed by adding *est* to the positive degree *(newest, soonest).* In longer words it is formed by adding *most* or *least (most efficient, least efficient; most quietly, least quietly).*

Complement. A word or phrase that completes the sense of the verb. It may be an object, a predicate noun, a predicate pronoun, or a predicate adjective.

Object. Follows a transitive verb. (See *Verb.*)

I have already drafted the *contract.*

Predicate noun or pronoun. Follows a linking verb. It explains the subject and is identical with it. (Also called a *predicate complement, subject complement,* and *predicate nominative.*)

Miss Kwong is our new *accountant.* (*Accountant* refers to *Miss Kwong.*)

The person responsible for the divestiture decision was *I.* (The pronoun *I* refers to *person.*)

Predicate adjective. Completes the sense of a linking verb. (Also called a *predicate complement.*)

These charges are *excessive.* (The adjective *excessive* refers to *charges.*)

NOTE: In this manual, the term *complement* is used to refer only to a predicate noun, pronoun, or adjective following a linking verb. The term *object* is used to denote the complement of a transitive verb.

Conjunction. A word or phrase that connects words, phrases, or clauses.

Coordinating conjunction. Connects words, phrases, or clauses of equal rank. The coordinating conjunctions are *and, but, or,* and *nor.*

Correlative conjunctions. Conjunctions consisting of two elements used in pairs; for example, *both . . . and, not only . . . but (also), either . . . or, neither . . . nor.*

Subordinating conjunction. Used to join subordinate clauses to main clauses. A few common subordinating conjunctions are *when, where, after, before, if.* (See ¶132.)

Connective. A word that joins words, phrases, or clauses. The chief types of connectives are conjunctions, adverbial conjunctives, prepositions, and relative pronouns.

Consonants. The letters *b, c, d, f, g, h, j, k, l, m, n, p, q, r, s, t, v, w, x, y, z.* The letters *w* and *y* sometimes serve as vowels (as in *saw* and *rhyme*).

Contraction. A shortened form of a word or phrase in which an apostrophe indicates the omitted letters or words; for example, *don't* for *do not.* (See ¶505b–e.)

Dangling modifier. A modifier that is attached either to no word in a sentence or to the wrong word. (See ¶1082–1086.)

Direct address. A construction in which a speaker or a writer addresses another person directly; for example, ''What do you think, Sylvia?''

Elliptical expressions. Condensed expressions from which key words have been omitted; for example, *if necessary* (for *if it is necessary*). (See also *Clause; Sentence.*)

Essential elements. Words, phrases, or clauses needed to complete the structure or meaning of a sentence. (See also *Clause; Phrase.*)

Gender. The characteristic of nouns and pronouns that indicates whether the thing named is *masculine (man, boy, stallion, he), feminine (woman, girl, mare, she),* or *neuter (book, concept, it).* Nouns that refer to either males or females have *common* gender *(person, child, horse).*

Gerund. A verb form ending in *ing* and used as a *noun.*

> *Selling* requires special skills. (Subject.)
>
> I enjoy *selling.* (Direct object of *enjoy.*)
>
> She is experienced in *selling.* (Object of preposition *in.*)

> **Dangling gerund.** A prepositional-gerund phrase that is attached either to no word in a sentence or to the wrong word. (See ¶1082c.)

Imperative. See *Mood.*

Indicative. See *Mood.*

Infinitive. The form of the verb usually introduced by *to* (see ¶¶1044–1046). An infinitive may be used as a noun, an adjective, or an adverb. (See *Phrase, infinitive.*)

NOUN: *To find affordable housing* these days is not easy. (Subject.)
          She is trying *to do a hatchet job on my proposal.* (Object.)

ADJECTIVE: I still have two more contracts *to draft.* (Modifies *contracts.*)

ADVERB: He resigned *to take another position.* (Modifies *resigned.*)

Interjection. A word that shows emotion; usually without grammatical connection to other parts of a sentence.

> *Oh,* so that's what he meant.   *Wow!* What a weekend!

Modifier. A word, phrase, or clause that qualifies, limits, or restricts the meaning of a word. (See *Adjective; Adverb; Dangling modifier.*)

Mood (mode). The form of the verb that shows the manner of the action. There are three moods: indicative, imperative, and subjunctive.

> **Indicative.** States a fact or asks a question.

> Our lease has expired.   When does our lease expire?

(Continued on page 474.)

19

Imperative. Expresses a command or makes a request.

> Call me next week.   Please send me your latest catalog.

Subjunctive. Used following clauses of necessity, demand, or wishing (see ¶¶1038–1039); also used in *if, as if,* and *as though* clauses that state conditions which are improbable, doubtful, or contrary to fact (see ¶¶1040–1043).

> I demand that we *be* heard.   It is imperative that he *be* notified.
> We urge that she *be* elected.   If he *were* appointed, I would quit.
> I wish I *were* going.   If she *had* known, she would have come.

Nonessential elements. Words, phrases, or clauses that are not needed to complete the structure or meaning of a sentence. (See also *Clause; Phrase.*)

Noun. The name of a person, place, object, idea, quality, or activity.

Abstract noun. The name of a quality or a general idea; for example, *courage, freedom.*

Collective noun. A noun that represents a group of persons, animals, or things; for example, *audience, company, flock.* (See ¶1019.)

Common noun. The name of a class of persons, places, or things; for example, *child, house.* (See ¶¶307–310.)

Predicate noun. See *Complement.*

Proper noun. The official name of a particular person, place, or thing; for example, *Ellen, San Diego, Wednesday.* Proper nouns are capitalized. (See ¶¶303–306.)

Number. The characteristic of a noun, pronoun, or verb that indicates whether one person or thing (singular) or more than one (plural) is meant.

> NOUN: beeper, beepers   PRONOUN: she, they   VERB: she *works,* they *work*

Object. The person or thing that receives the action of the verb. An object may be a word, a phrase, or a clause.

> I need a new desktop *computer.* (Word.)
>
> She prefers *to work with hard copy.* (Infinitive phrase.)
>
> We did not realize *that your deadline was so tight.* (Clause.)

Direct object. The person or thing that is directly affected by the action of the verb. (The object in each of the three sentences above is a *direct* object.)

Indirect object. The person or thing indirectly affected by the action of the verb. The indirect object can be made the object of the preposition *to* or *for.*

> Molly gave (to) *me* a hard time about my sales performance this quarter.

Ordinal number. The form of a number that indicates order or succession; for example, *first, second, twelfth.* (See ¶¶424–426.)

Parenthetical elements. Words, phrases, or clauses that are not necessary to the completeness of the structure or the meaning of a sentence.

Participle. A word that may stand alone as an adjective or may be combined with helping verbs to form different tenses (see ¶¶1033–1034). There are three forms: present, past, and perfect.

Present participle. Ends in *ing;* for example, *making, advertising.*

Past participle. Regularly ends in *ed* (as in *asked* or *filed*) but may be irregularly formed (as in *lost, seen,* and *written*). (See ¶1030a–b.)

Perfect participle. Consists of *having* plus the past participle; for example, *having asked, having lost.*

19

When a participle functions as an *adjective*, it modifies a noun or a pronoun.

The *coming* year poses some new challenges. (Modifies *year*.)

Having retired last year, I now do volunteer work. (Modifies *I*.)

Because a participle has many of the characteristics of a verb, it may take an object and be modified by an adverb. The participle and its object and modifiers make up a *participial phrase*.

Seizing the opportunity, Orzo offered to buy the business. (Object is *opportunity*.)

Moving aggressively, we can soon control 40 percent of the market. (*Aggressively* modifies *moving*.)

Dangling participle. A participial phrase attached either to no word in a sentence or to the wrong word. (See ¶1082a.)

Parts of speech. The eight classes into which words are grouped according to their uses in a sentence: verb, noun, pronoun, adjective, adverb, conjunction, preposition, and interjection.

Person. The characteristic of a word that indicates whether a person is speaking *(first person)*, is spoken to *(second person)*, or is spoken about *(third person)*. Only personal pronouns and verbs change their forms to show person. All nouns are considered third person.

	Singular	Plural
FIRST PERSON:	*I* liked this book.	*We* liked this book.
SECOND PERSON:	*You* liked this book.	*You* liked this book.
THIRD PERSON:	*She* liked this book.	*They* liked this book.

Phrase. A group of two or more words that lack a subject and a predicate; used as a noun, an adjective, or an adverb.

Noun phrase. A phrase that functions as a noun (such as a gerund phrase, an infinitive phrase, or a prepositional phrase).

I like *running my own business*. (Gerund phrase as object.)

To provide the best possible service is our goal. (Infinitive phrase as subject.)

Before 9 a.m. is the best time to call me. (Prepositional phrase as subject.)

Adjective phrase. A phrase that functions as an adjective (such as an infinitive phrase, a participial phrase, or a prepositional phrase).

Adverbial phrase. A phrase that functions as an adverb (such as an infinitive phrase or a prepositional phrase).

Gerund phrase. A gerund plus its object and modifiers; used as a noun.

Delaying payments to your suppliers will prove quite costly in the long run.

Infinitive phrase. An infinitive plus its object and modifiers; may be used as a noun, an adjective, or an adverb. An infinitive phrase that is attached to either no word in a sentence or to the wrong word is called a *dangling* infinitive (see ¶1082b).

To get TF's okay on this purchase order took some doing. (As a noun; serves as subject of the verb *took*.)

The decision *to close the Morrisville plant* was not made easily. (As an adjective; tells what kind of decision.)

Janice resigned *to open her own business*. (As an adverb; tells why Janice resigned.)

NOTE: An infinitive phrase, unlike other phrases, may sometimes have a subject. This subject precedes the infinitive and is in the objective case.

I have asked *her to review this draft for accuracy*. (*Her* is the subject of *to review*.)

(Continued on page 476.)

19

Participial phrase. A participle and its object and modifiers; used as an adjective.

The committee *considering your proposal* should come to a decision this week.

I prefer the cover sample *printed in blue and yellow.*

Prepositional phrase. A preposition and its object and modifiers; may be used as a noun, an adjective, or an adverb.

From Boston to Tulsa is about 1550 miles. (As a noun; serves as subject of *is.*)

Profits *in the automobile industry* are up sharply this quarter. (As an adjective; indicates which type of profits.)

You handled Dr. Waterman's objections *with great skill.* (As an adverb; indicates the manner in which the objections were handled.)

Prepositional-gerund phrase. A phrase that begins with a preposition and has a gerund as the object. (See ¶1082c.)

By rechecking the material before it is set in type, you avoid expensive corrections later on. (*By* is the preposition; *rechecking,* a gerund, is the object of *by.*)

Essential (or **restrictive**) **phrase.** A phrase that limits, defines, or identifies; cannot be omitted without changing the meaning of the main clause.

The study *analyzing our competitors' promotion activities* will be finished next week.

Nonessential (or **nonrestrictive**) **phrase.** A phrase that can be omitted without changing the meaning of the sentence.

The Stanforth-Palmer Company, *one of the country's largest financial services organizations,* is expanding into satellite communications.

NOTE: The term *verb phrase* is often used to indicate the individual words that make up the verb in a sentence. Sometimes the verb phrase includes an adverb. A verb phrase can function only as a verb.

You *should work together* with Nora on the report. (The verb phrase consists of the verb form *should work* plus the adverb *together.*)

Positive degree. See *Comparison.*

Predicate. That part of a sentence which tells what the subject does or what is done to the subject or what state of being the subject is in.

Complete predicate. The complete predicate consists of a verb and its complement along with any modifiers.

Barbara *has handled the job well.*

Simple predicate. The simple predicate is the verb alone, without regard for any complement or modifiers that may accompany it.

Barbara *has handled* the job well.

Compound predicate. A predicate consisting of two or more predicates joined by conjunctions.

Barbara *has handled the job well* and *deserves a good deal of praise.*

Prefix. A letter, syllable, or word added to the beginning of a word to change its meaning; for example, *a*float, *re*upholster, *under*nourished.

Preposition. A connective that shows the relation of a noun or pronoun to some other word in the sentence. The noun or pronoun following a preposition is in the objective case. (See ¶¶1077–1080.)

Martin's work was reviewed *by Hedley and me.*

Principal parts. The forms of a verb from which all other forms are derived: the *present,* the *past,* the *past participle,* and the *present participle.* (See ¶¶1030–1035.)

Pronoun. A word used in place of a noun. (See ¶¶1049–1064.)

    DEMONSTRATIVE: *this, that, these, those*

    INDEFINITE: *each, either, any, anyone, someone, everyone, few, all,* etc.

    INTENSIVE: *myself, yourself,* etc.

    INTERROGATIVE: *who, which, what,* etc.

    PERSONAL: *I, you, he, she, it, we, they*

    RELATIVE: *who, whose, whom, which, that,* and compounds such as *whoever*

Punctuation. Marks used to indicate relationships between words, phrases, and clauses.

    Terminal (or **end**) **punctuation.** The period, the question mark, and the exclamation point—the three marks that may indicate the end of a sentence.

    NOTE: When a sentence breaks off abruptly, a dash may be used to mark the end of the sentence (see ¶207). When a sentence trails off without really ending, ellipsis marks (three periods) are used to mark the end of the sentence (see ¶291b).

    Internal punctuation. The comma, the semicolon, the colon, the dash, parentheses, quotation marks, the underscore, the apostrophe, ellipsis marks, the asterisk, the diagonal, and brackets.

Question.

    Direct question. A question in its original form, as spoken or written.

    He then asked me, "What is your opinion?"

    Indirect question. A statement of the substance of a question without the use of the exact words of the speaker.

    He then asked me what my opinion was.

    Independent question. A question that represents a complete sentence but is incorporated in a larger sentence.

    The main question is, Who will translate this idea into a clear plan of action?

Quotation.

    Direct quotation. A quotation of words exactly as spoken or written.

    I myself heard Ed say, "I will arrive in Santa Fe on Tuesday."

    Indirect quotation. A statement of the substance of a quotation without the use of the exact words.

    I myself heard Ed say that he would arrive in Santa Fe on Tuesday.

Sentence. A group of words representing a complete thought and containing a subject and a verb (predicate) along with any complements and modifiers.

    Simple sentence. A sentence consisting of one independent clause.

    I have no recollection of the meeting.

    Compound sentence. A sentence consisting of two or more independent clauses.

    Our Boston office will be closed, and our Dallas office will be relocated.

    Complex sentence. A sentence consisting of one independent clause and one or more dependent clauses.

    We will make an exception to the policy if circumstances warrant.

    Compound-complex sentence. A sentence consisting of two independent clauses and one or more dependent clauses.

    I tried to handle the monthly report alone, but when I began to analyze the data, I realized that I needed your help.

(Continued on page 478.)

Elliptical sentence. A word or phrase treated as a complete sentence, even though the subject and verb are understood but not expressed.

Enough on that subject.   Why not?

Declarative sentence. A sentence that makes a statement.

Our company is continually testing cutting-edge technologies.

Interrogative sentence. A sentence that asks a question.

When will the conference begin?

Exclamatory sentence. A sentence that expresses strong feeling.

Don't even think of smoking here!

Imperative sentence. A sentence that expresses a command or a request. (The subject *you* is understood if it is not expressed.)

Send a check at once.   Please let us hear from you.

Sentence fragment. A phrase or clause that is incorrectly treated as a sentence. (See ¶102, note.)

Statement. A sentence that asserts a fact. (See also *Sentence, declarative.*)

Subject. A word, phrase, or clause that names the person, place, or thing about which something is said.

The law firm with the best reputation in town is Barringer and Doyle.

Whoever applies for the job from within the department will get special consideration.

Compound subject. Two or more subjects joined by a conjunction.

My wife and my three sons are off on a white-water rafting trip.

Subjunctive. See *Mood.*

Suffix. A letter, syllable, or word added to the end of a word to modify its meaning; for example, trend*y*, friend*ly*, count*less*, receiver*ship*, lone*some*.

Superlative degree. See *Comparison.*

Syllable. One or more letters that represent one sound.

Tense. The property of a verb that expresses *time.* (See ¶¶1031–1035.) The three *primary* tenses correspond to the three time divisions:

PRESENT: they think

PAST: they thought

FUTURE: they will think

There are three *perfect* tenses, corresponding to the primary tenses:

PRESENT PERFECT: they have thought

PAST PERFECT: they had thought

FUTURE PERFECT: they will have thought

There are six *progressive* tenses, corresponding to each of the primary and perfect tenses:

PRESENT PROGRESSIVE: they are thinking

PAST PROGRESSIVE: they were thinking

FUTURE PROGRESSIVE: they will be thinking

PRESENT PERFECT PROGRESSIVE: they have been thinking

PAST PERFECT PROGRESSIVE: they had been thinking

FUTURE PERFECT PROGRESSIVE: they will have been thinking

There are two *emphatic* tenses:

PRESENT EMPHATIC: they do think

PAST EMPHATIC: they did think

Transitional expressions. Expressions that link independent clauses or sentences; for example, *as a result, therefore, on the other hand, nevertheless.* (See also ¶138a.)

Verb. A word or phrase used to express action or state of being. (See also *Mood.*)

Enniston *has boosted* its sales goals for the year. (Action.)

My son-in-law *was* originally a lawyer, but he *has* now *become* a computer-game designer. (State of being.)

Auxiliary (helping) verb. A verb that helps in the formation of another verb. The chief auxiliaries are *be, can, could, do, have, may, might, must, ought, shall, should, will, would.*

Transitive verb. A verb that requires an object to complete its meaning. (See also *Object.*)

Fusilli *has rejected* all offers to purchase his business.

Intransitive verb. A verb that does not require an object to complete its meaning.

As market growth *occurs* and customer interest *builds,* our sales expectations *are rising* and top management's excitement *has increased.*

Linking verb. A verb that connects a subject with a predicate adjective, noun, or pronoun. The various forms of *to be* are the most commonly used linking verbs. *Become, look, seem, appear,* and *grow* are often used as linking verbs. (See ¶1067.)

Laura *seemed* willing to compromise, but Frank *became* obstinate in his demands. Was he afraid that any concession might make him *appear* a fool?

Principal parts of verbs. See *Principal parts.*

Verbal. A word that partakes of the nature of a verb but functions in some other way. (See *Gerund; Infinitive; Participle.*)

Voice. The property of a verb that indicates whether the subject acts or is acted upon.

Active voice. A verb is in the active voice when its subject is the doer of the act.

About a dozen people *reviewed* the report in draft form.

Passive voice. A verb is in the passive voice when its subject is acted upon.

The report *was reviewed* in draft form by about a dozen people.

Vowels. The letters *a, e, i, o,* and *u.* The letters *w* and *y* sometimes act like vowels (as in *awl* or in *cry*). (See also *Consonants.*)

Glossary of Computer Terms

As the world of the office continues to undergo a series of rapid technological changes, a whole new vocabulary continues to evolve—a vocabulary that often seems more dazzling or bewildering than the actual changes themselves. The following glossary provides brief and simple definitions of the key terms and concepts that are part of this new vocabulary.

NOTE: When boldface type is used to highlight a word or phrase within a definition, it signifies that the highlighted word or phrase is defined elsewhere in this glossary.

Access. To call up information out of **storage;** also, to transfer newly **keyboarded** information into storage.

> **Random access.** A technique that permits stored **text** to be directly retrieved, regardless of its location on the **storage medium.**

> **Serial access.** A technique for retrieving stored information that requires a sequential search through one item after another on the **storage medium.** (Serial access is needed, for example, to locate information stored on **magnetic tape.**)

Access time. The amount of time it takes a **computer** to locate previously stored information; also, the time needed to transfer newly **keyboarded** information into **storage.**

ADP. Automatic **data processing.**

Alphanumeric. Consisting of letters and numbers.

Applications software. Computer **programs** designed to perform **information processing** tasks for a specific type of business or activity (for example, **spreadsheets, desktop publishing, database management**).

Archive. Storage of duplicate **text** on **disks** or **diskettes.** Usually refers to data that is infrequently used or stored as **backup** material.

Artificial intelligence. Computer systems that attempt to imitate human processes for analyzing and solving problems.

ASCII (American Standard Code for Information Interchange). A standard eight-**bit** code that permits the computer equipment of different manufacturers to exchange **alphanumeric** data with one another. The acronym ASCII is pronounced *as-kee*. (See also *Compatibility*.)

Author. The creator of a **document** that passes through an **information processing system;** also called *principal* or *originator*.

Automatic carrier return. The ability of a **computer** to advance automatically to the beginning of the next line during **keyboarding** without requiring the operator to touch the Return key. (See also *Wraparound.*)

Automatic centering. The ability of a **computer** to center **text** between margins, tab settings, or other designated points.

Automatic decimal tab. The ability of a **computer** to automatically align columns of figures on the decimal point as they are **keyboarded.** Columns of whole numbers are automatically aligned on the last digit.

Automatic file select. The ability of a **computer** to pick out certain items from a collection of information on the basis of the **characters** that appear in certain positions. (For example, the computer can examine a list of subscribers and choose only those whose subscriptions expire in a certain month.)

Automatic file sort. The ability of a **computer** to rearrange a collection of information into alphabetic or numeric order on the basis of the **characters** that appear in certain positions. (For example, the computer can arrange a randomly typed list of names and addresses into numeric order by ZIP Code and then alphabetically by name within each ZIP Code.)

Automatic footnote tie-in. The ability of a **computer** to automatically position footnotes on the same page as the **text** they refer to. If the text is moved to another page, any related footnotes will also be transferred to that page. Also known as *footnote drag.*

Automatic hyphenation. The ability of a **computer** to automatically hyphenate and divide words that do not fit at the end of a line. If the **text** is later revised so that the divided word no longer begins at the right margin, the hyphen is automatically removed and the word prints solid. (See also *Hyphen drop.*)

Automatic line or paragraph numbering. The ability of a **computer** to automatically number each line or paragraph sequentially in the rough-draft copy of a **document.** The line or paragraph numbers are automatically deleted during final **printout.**

Automatic line spacing. The ability of a **computer** to automatically change vertical line spacing during **printout** (for example, from double to single to double again) on the basis of **commands** given at the time of **text entry.**

Automatic page numbering. The ability of a **computer** to automatically print sequential page numbers on the pages that make up an entire **document.** If the document is revised, with a gain or loss in the total number of pages, the page numbering is automatically adjusted in the next **printout.**

Automatic pagination. The ability of a **computer** to take a continuous piece of **text** and automatically divide it into pages with a specified number of lines per page. If the text is changed because of the addition, deletion, or rearrangement of copy, the computer will automatically repage the material to maintain the proper page length.

Automatic printer control. The ability of a computer to make automatic adjustments for line spacing, underlining, **boldface printing,** type size, and so on. (See also *Automatic line spacing.*)

Automatic record selection. See *Automatic file select.*

Automatic underlining. The ability of a **computer** to automatically underscore **text** without requiring the operator to touch the underscore key once for each underlined **character.** The underscoring is done on the basis of a **command** (at the time of **text entry**) that indicates how much text to underline.

Background printing. The ability of a **computer** to print a **document** while other work is being done on the **keyboard** and the **display screen** at the same time.

Backup. Storage of duplicate text on **disks** or **diskettes** as a safety measure in the event the original medium is damaged or lost.

Batch processing. Performing a single operation on a group of items at the same time rather than processing each item completely as it comes up.

Baud. See *Bits per second (bps).*

20

Binary numbering system. A numbering system in which all numbers are represented by various combinations of the digits 0 and 1.

Bit. Binary digit. The smallest unit of information that can be recognized by a **computer.** Bits are combined to represent **characters.** (See also *Byte.*)

Bits per second (bps). A measurement that describes the speed of data transmission between two pieces of equipment. Also known as *baud.*

Block delete. A **command** to **delete** (or erase) a segment of **text.**

Block move. A **command** to reproduce a segment of **text** in another place and at the same time erase it from its original position.

Block protect. The ability of a **computer** to automatically prevent a page break from occurring within a block of text (for example, a table).

Boilerplate. Standard wording (for example, sentences or paragraphs in form letters or clauses in legal documents) that is held in **storage.** When needed, it can be used as is, with minor modification, or in combination with new material to produce tailor-made **documents.** Also known as *repetitive text.*

Boldface printing. A method of printing in which certain **characters** appear darker than the surrounding **text.** (See also *Shadow printing.*)

Boot. (Short for *bootstrap.*) A **program** that instructs a **computer** to store its operating system and prepare to **execute** an applications program. (See also *Applications software.*)

Buffer memory. See *Memory, random-access.*

Bug. A defect in a **program** that causes the **computer** to malfunction or cease to operate. (See also *Debug.*)

Byte. The sequence of **bits** that represents a **character.** Each byte has eight bits.

Card. See *Circuit board.*

Cassette. A cartridge holding **magnetic tape.** (See also *Magnetic medium.*)

Cathode-ray tube (CRT). See *Display screen.*

Central processing unit (CPU). The brains of an **information processing system;** controls the interpretation and execution of instructions.

Character. A single letter, figure, or symbol produced by a **keystroke** on a **computer.**

Character set. The complete set of **characters** displayable on a **computer.** These characters can be alphabetic (in capital or small letters), numeric, or symbolic.

Character string. A specified sequence of typed **characters,** usually representing a word or phrase. A character string is often used to locate a particular word or phrase wherever it appears in a **document** so that it can be automatically replaced with another word or phrase. Thus if a person's name has been consistently misspelled or a date has been given incorrectly in several places, the error can be easily corrected. (See also *Search and replace.*)

Characters per second (cps). The number of **characters** printed in one second; a measurement frequently used to describe the speed of a **printer.**

Chip. An **integrated circuit** used in **computers.**

Circuit board. A board or card that carries the necessary electronics for a particular computer function (for example, **memory**). The circuit boards that come with the original equipment perform the standard functions identified with that type of equipment. Additional circuit boards can be fitted into the computer to expand the kinds of functions that the equipment can perform.

Clear. A **command** to erase material from **storage.**

Code. The language used to translate **bytes** into recognizable **characters.** Also, the pattern or system of signals recorded on media that stand for alphabetic or numeric characters or machine functions.

Code key. A special key on the **keyboard** used to **command** a **computer** to perform a function. (See also *Function keys; Mnemonics.*)

Column move or delete. A **command** that permits a **computer** to move or **delete** vertical blocks of **characters** with a minimum number of steps. In unsophisticated systems, where columns must be moved or deleted one line at a time, the operator must go through a time-consuming process.

Columns. The horizontal spaces across the screen of a **computer.** An 80-column screen holds 80 characters on each line.

Command. An instruction, given through a special **keystroke** or series of keystrokes, that causes a **computer** to perform a function.

Compatibility. The ability of one type of **computer** to share **storage media** or to communicate with another. (See also *ASCII.*)

Computer. An electronic device that is capable of (1) accepting, storing, and logically manipulating data or **text** that is **input** and (2) processing and producing **output** (results or decisions) on the basis of stored **programs** of instructions. Some computers are also capable of processing graphics, images, and voice input. The term **computer** is now used generically to refer to all types of electronic equipment, such as **word processors** and **electronic typewriters,** which have more limited capabilities.

Configuration. The components that make up a **computer;** also referred to as **hardware.** Most computers include a **keyboard** for **text entry,** a **central processing unit,** one or more **disk drives,** and a **printer.** Most systems also have a **display screen.**

Control character. A special **character** that is never printed but causes a visible result during printing. For example, spacing, tabulation, and carrier return are all achieved by means of control characters.

Control code display. The ability of a **computer** to display instructions, **commands,** or **control characters** on the **display screen** or a **printout.**

cps. See *Characters per second.*

CPU. See *Central processing unit.*

Crash. A malfunction in a computer's **hardware** or **software** that prevents the computer from functioning.

Crossfooting. The ability of a **computer** to total numeric amounts arranged in rows and columns. The answers are then placed at the end of each row or at the bottom of each column.

CRT. Cathode-ray tube. (See *Display screen.*)

Cursor. A special **character** (usually a blinking underscore, dot, arrow, or box) that indicates where the next typed character will appear on the **display screen.**

Cursor positioning. The movement of the **cursor** on the **display screen.** Most **computers** have four keys to signify *up, down, left,* and *right* movement. Some require the use of a **code key** plus another key to move the cursor.

Daisy wheel. A printing element made of plastic or metal and used on certain impact **printers.** Each **character** is engraved at the end of a spoke, so that the entire element resembles a daisy. Daisy wheels come in many type styles.

Data processing. The mathematical or other logical manipulation of numbers or symbols, based on a stored **program** of instructions. Also known as *electronic data processing (EDP).* (See also *Information processing.*)

Database. A stored collection of information.

Database management system. The **hardware** and **software** needed to establish and maintain a **database** and manage the information held in **storage.**

Debugging. The procedure for locating and eliminating defects in a **program.** (See also *Bug.*)

Default format statement. An instruction on **format,** built into a **software** program or the computer's **memory,** that will be followed unless the operator provides a different instruction. (A 6½-inch line, with 1-inch side margins, is a common default format and will be used unless the operator specifically establishes other margin settings.)

Delete. A **command** to erase something held in **storage**—from as little as a single **character** to as much as a page or more of **text.**

Desktop computer. A **microcomputer.**

Desktop publishing. A system that processes text and **graphics** and, by means of page layout **software** and a laser **printer,** produces high-quality pages suitable for printing or in-house reproduction.

Dictionary. A **program** used to check the spelling of each word entered in the **computer.** If the **keyboarded** word does not agree with the corresponding item in the dictionary or does not appear in the dictionary, it is highlighted on the **display screen** as a possible misspelling. The operator must then either make the necessary correction or confirm that the word is correct as keyboarded.

Directory. A list of the **files** stored on a **disk.**

Disk. A random-**access,** magnetically coated storage medium, shaped like a phonograph record, with high storage capacity (500-plus pages). May be hard or flexible. (See also *Diskette.*)

Disk drive. The component of a **computer** into which a **disk** is inserted so that it can be read or written on.

Diskette. A small, nonrigid **disk** with limited storage capacity (normally 30 to 200 pages). Also known as a *floppy disk.*

Disk operating system. See *DOS.*

Display screen. A device similar to a television screen and used on a **computer** to display **text** and **graphics.** Also called a *cathode-ray tube (CRT),* a *video display terminal (VDT),* or a *monitor.*

Distributed logic system. A system in which several **computers** share **storage** and an internal processor, but each individual computer retains some internal processing capability. (See also *Shared logic system.*)

Document. Any printed business communication—for example, a letter, memo, report, statistical table, or form.

Document assembly. The creation of a new **document** by combining pieces of previously stored **text** and sometimes newly typed material. (See also *Boilerplate; Merge.*)

DOS (Disk Operating System). A **program** that allows the **computer** to manage the storage of information on **disks** and to make use of compatible **software.**

Dot matrix. The use of closely spaced dots to form **characters** on some **display screens** and **printers.** (See also *Printers, dot matrix.*)

Downtime. The period when equipment is unusable because of a malfunction.

Dual display. The capability of a **computer** to show two or more video images simultaneously on the same display screen. See also *Split screen.*

Dual-sheet feeder. A device that can automatically insert two different types of paper (for example, letterhead and plain paper) into a **printer.**

Duplexing. A procedure that permits two **computers** to transmit data to each other simultaneously.

Editing. The process of changing **text** by inserting, deleting, replacing, rearranging, and reformatting.

EDP. Electronic **data processing.**

Electronic mail (E-mail). The transfer of **documents** through **telecommunication channels** without the physical movement of paper.

Electronic typewriter. A **word processor** with limited functions.

Elite type. Any typeface that allows the printing of 12 characters to the inch. Also known as *12-pitch type.* (See also *Pica type.*)

Encryption. Coding confidential data so that only **computers** equipped with an appropriate decoding device can receive such transmissions and convert them into an intelligible form.

Enter. To **keyboard** data into **memory.**

Ergonomics. The science of adapting working conditions and equipment to meet the physical needs of workers.

Escape key. A **function key** that permits the operator to leave one segment of a **program** and move to another.

Execute. To perform an action specified by the operator or the **program.**

Expert system. See *Artificial intelligence.*

Fax (n.). A shortened form of the word *facsimile.* A copy of a **document** transmitted electronically from one machine to another.

Fax (v.). To transmit a copy of a **document** electronically.

Field. A group of related **characters** treated as a unit (such as a name); also the location in a record or **database** where this group of characters is entered.

File. A stored **document;** a group of related documents or data stored under a common file name.

Floppy disk. See *Diskette.*

Font. An assortment or set of type of one size or style. Includes all letters of the alphabet, arabic numerals, and punctuation marks. (See also *Character set.*)

Footer. Repetitive information that appears at the bottom (the foot) of every page of a **document.** A page number is a common footer. (See also *Header.*)

Footnote drag. See *Automatic footnote tie-in.*

Format. The physical specifications that affect the appearance and arrangement of a **document**—for example, margins, spacing, **pitch.**

Forms mode. The ability of a **computer** to store the **format** of a blank **document** or form so that it can later be displayed on the screen and completed by the operator. Once a fill-in has been entered, the **cursor** automatically advances to the beginning of the next area to be filled in. (See also *Mask.*)

Function keys. Keys on a computer **keyboard** that give special **commands** to the computer—for example, to set margins or tabs. (See also *Code key; Control character.*)

Global. Describing any function that can be performed on an entire **document** without requiring individual **commands** for each use. For example, a global search-and-replace **command** will instruct the **computer** to locate a particular word and replace it with a different word wherever the original form occurs in the text.

Graphics. Pictures displayed or printed by means of horizontal, vertical, diagonal, and curved lines.

Hard copy. **Text** printed on paper; also called a **printout.** (See also *Soft copy.*)

Hard disk. A rigid **magnetic** storage **medium** that can store large amounts of **text.**

Hardware. The physical components of a **computer:** the **central processing unit,** the **display screen,** the **keyboard,** the **disk drive,** and the **printer.** (See also *Software.*)

Hardwired. Describing a **computer** that has its **programs** built into the circuitry of the machine. These programs cannot be changed.

Header. Repetitive information that appears at the top (the head) of every page of a **document.** A page number is a common header. (See also *Footer.*)

Home. The upper left corner of the **display screen;** the starting position of a page or **document.**

Hot zone. The area before the right margin, usually seven to ten characters wide. Words in this area may have to be divided or moved to the next line.

Hyphen drop. The ability of a **computer** to automatically delete a hyphen previously inserted to divide a word at the end of a line if the **text** is later revised and the word reappears elsewhere in a line.

Icon. A picture or symbol that represents a particular function or **command;** for example, a picture of a trash can means "destroy."

20

Indexing. The ability of a **computer** to accumulate a list of words or phrases that appear in a **document** (along with their corresponding page numbers) and to print out or display the list in alphabetic order.

Information processing. The coordination of people, equipment, and procedures to handle information, including the **storage, retrieval,** distribution, and communication of information. Because the term **word processing** no longer refers solely to the processing of **text** and the term **data processing** no longer refers solely to the processing of numerical information, the term **information processing** is increasingly used generically to embrace the entire field of processing words, figures, graphics, images, and voice input by electronic means.

Input. Information entered into the system for processing. *Inputting* information means **entering** it on the keyboard.

Insert. To add **text** to a **document.**

Integrated circuit. A tiny complex of electronic components produced as a solid unit. May be used as circuitry for logic or as storage modules.

Integrated software. Software that combines in one **program** functions normally performed by separate programs.

Interface. The electrical connection that links two pieces of equipment together so that they can communicate with each other.

I/O. Input/output. (See also *Simultaneous input/output.*)

Justification. A method of printing in which additional space is inserted between words or **characters** to force each line to the same length.

K. The abbreviation for *kilo,* meaning "1000." In **information processing,** K stands for *kilobyte* (1024 **bytes**). K is often used to describe a **computer's** storage capacity. Thus, for example, 256K means 256 kilobytes of storage.

Keyboard. The device for entering **input** into a **computer.**

Keyboarding. Entering **characters** into the **memory** of a **computer.**

Keystroke. The depression of one key on a **keyboard.**

Kilobyte. See *K.*

Language. The **characters** and procedures used to write **programs** that a **computer** is designed to understand.

Laptop computer. A portable **microcomputer,** normally battery-powered.

Load. To feed data or **programs** into a **computer.**

Local area network (LAN). A system that uses cable or other means to permit high-speed communication between various kinds of electronic equipment within a small area.

Mag. Short for *magnetic;* used in expressions like *mag card* and *mag tape.*

Magnetic card. A card coated with magnetic material that can store one or two pages of information. Also called a *mag card.*

Magnetic medium. Any device coated with a magnetic material that can be used to store information entered in a **computer**—for example, **magnetic cards, magnetic tapes, disks,** and **diskettes.**

Magnetic tape. Tape coated with a magnetic material that can store information.

Mainframe. The **central processing unit** of a large **computer** system.

Mask. A **document** or form stored in a **computer** and displayed on the **display screen** with blank areas that must be filled in. A form letter on which an operator enters a name, an address, and a salutation is an example of a mask. (See also *Forms mode.*)

Memory. The part of a **computer** that stores information. (See also *Storage.*)

> **Random-access memory (RAM).** The temporary memory that allows information to be stored randomly and accessed quickly and directly (without the need to go through intervening data). Also known as the *buffer memory.*

20

Read-only memory (ROM). The permanent memory of a **computer;** a set of instructions that has been built into the computer by the manufacturer and cannot be **accessed** or changed by the operator.

Menu. A list of choices or questions programmed into a **computer** to guide the operator through a function. For example, a "printing" menu would ask about the desired paper size, the **pitch** to be used, and so on.

Merge. A **command** to create one **document** by combining **text** that is stored in two different locations. For example, a **computer** can merge the standard text of a form letter with a mailing list to produce a batch of letters with a different name, address, and salutation on each letter. (See also *Document assembly.*)

Microcomputer. A small and relatively inexpensive computer system commonly consisting of a **display screen,** a **keyboard,** a **central processing unit,** one or more **disk drives,** and a **printer,** with limited **storage** based upon a **microprocessor.** Also referred to as a *desktop computer* or a *laptop computer.*

Microprocessor. The electronic component of a **microcomputer** consisting of **integrated circuits** contained on a silicon **chip.**

Mnemonics. A **computer's** system of **commands,** structured to assist the operator's memory. Often, the commands are abbreviations of the functions they perform (for example, *C* for *center, U* for *underline).*

Modem. Abbreviation for "*mo*dulator/*demo*dulator." A device that converts electrical signals into tones for transmission over telephone lines or converts the tones back into electrical signals at the receiving end.

Monitor. The **display screen** of a **computer.**

Mouse. A hand-operated electronic device used to move the **cursor** around on the **display screen.** Mostly used with **microcomputers.**

Off-line. Refers to an operation performed by electronic equipment not tied into a centralized **information processing system.**

On-line. Refers to an operation performed by electronic equipment controlled by a remote **central processing unit.**

Optical character reader (OCR). A device that can read **text** and enter it automatically into a **computer** for **storage** or **editing.** Also called an *optical scanner.*

Originator. See *Author.*

Orphan adjust. The ability of a **computer** to prevent the first line of a paragraph from being printed as the last line on a page. When the first line of a paragraph does appear as the last line on a page, it is referred to as an *orphan.* (See also *Widow adjust.*)

Outlining. The ability of a **computer** to automatically number and letter items typed with an indented format. If **text** is added or deleted, the numbering sequence may be automatically corrected. Also known as *paragraph numbering.*

Output. The results of a **computer** operation.

Overwriting. Recording and storing information in a specific location to destroy whatever had been stored there previously.

Page break. A **command** that tells the **printer** where to end one page and begin the next.

Paragraph numbering. See *Outlining.*

Password. An identification code required to **access** stored material. A device intended to prevent **documents** from being viewed, **edited,** or printed by unauthorized persons.

Peripheral. Any device that extends the capabilities of a **computer** but is not necessary for its operation (for example, an **optical character reader**).

Permanent memory. See *Memory, read-only.*

Personal computer (PC). A **microcomputer** for personal and office use.

Pica type. Any typeface that allows the printing of 10 characters to the inch. Also known as *10-pitch type.* (See also *Elite type.*)

20

Pitch. Measurement indicating the number of characters in a horizontal inch. For example, *12-pitch type* yields 12 characters in 1 inch; *10-pitch type* yields 10 characters in 1 inch.

Playback. The process of displaying or printing **text** after it has been entered.

Principal. See *Author.*

Printers. Devices of various types that produce copy on paper.

> **Impact printers.** Devices that produce **characters** on paper by striking a printing element against a ribbon.
>
> **Nonimpact printers.** Devices that produce characters on paper without striking a ribbon or the paper. *Ink-jet printers* form characters by spraying tiny, electrically charged ink droplets on paper. *Laser printers* use a narrow beam of pure red light to burn characters onto light-sensitive paper.
>
> **Character printers.** These print one character at a time.
>
> **Line printers.** These print an entire line at a time and thus produce work more quickly than character printers.
>
> **Letter-quality printers.** These printers produce high-quality work that looks as if it had been done on a carbon-ribbon typewriter.
>
> **Dot matrix printers.** Substantially cheaper than letter-quality printers, these use needles or bristles to produce characters made up of small dots. The work they produce, while legible, is usually considered acceptable only for personal or in-house use; for documents being sent outside or even to top-level management, letter-quality printing is normally required.
>
> **Twin-track printers.** Devices capable of producing two different type styles within the same **document** without requiring the operator to change the printing element. Also known as *dual-head printers.*
>
> **Bidirectional printers.** Devices that can print from left to right and from right to left. Because they eliminate unnecessary carriage returns, they speed up printing.

Printout. The paper copy of a **document** produced on a **computer;** also, the process of printing the copy.

Printout queuing. A procedure that allows the **printer** to line up a number of **documents** for printing. Having given the **command** to print, the operator is free to go on to other jobs while all the documents are being printed.

Printwheel. See *Daisy wheel.*

Program. An established sequence of instructions that tells a **computer** what to do.

Prompt. A message given on the **display screen** to (1) indicate the status of a function (for example, "Command Incomplete"), (2) help the operator complete a function, or (3) indicate that an attempted function cannot be performed.

Protocol. A formal set of rules that governs the transmission of information from one piece of equipment to another.

RAM. See *Memory, random-access.*

Read. To transfer information from an external storage medium into internal storage. (See also *Storage, external* and *internal.*)

Read in. To store data in a specific location.

Read out. To copy information held in internal storage and transfer it to some form of external storage. (See also *Storage, external* and *internal.*)

Reconstruction. The ability of a **computer** to salvage information stored on a damaged **disk** or **diskette** and transfer it to an undamaged one.

Record (n.). All the information pertaining to a particular subject. Records are often typed in a list format so that the information can be easily manipulated and combined with other **text** to create new **documents.** (See also *Document assembly.*)

Record (v.). To store the **keystrokes** entered into a **computer** or the sounds spoken into a dictation device.

20

Response time. The time a **computer** takes to execute a **command.**

Retrieve. To transfer a **document** from **storage** to **memory.**

ROM. See *Memory, read-only.*

Save. To store a **program** or data on a storage device such as a **disk.**

Scanning. Examining **text** on the **display screen** for **editing** purposes.

Scroll. The capability to display a large body of **text** by rolling it past the **display screen** either horizontally or vertically. As text disappears off one edge of the screen, new text appears at the opposite edge of the screen.

Search and replace. A **command** that directs the **computer** to locate a **character string** wherever it occurs in a **document** and replace it with a different character string.

Shadow printing. A method of printing darker **characters.** The **printer** strikes each character twice; because the second image is not exactly on top of the first character, it creates a shadow and makes the character appear darker than the surrounding characters. (See also *Boldface printing.*)

Shared logic system. A system in which a number of **computers** share the processing and **storage** capabilities of one **central processing unit.** If the central processor malfunctions, each computer is affected.

Shared resource system. A clustered system in which **workstations** have their own internal processors but share resources, such as **printers** and central **storage.** Each **computer** can function independently.

Sheet feeder. A device that inserts sheets of paper into a **printer.**

Simultaneous input/output (I/O). The ability of a **computer** to allow the **text** of one **document** to be entered or edited while a different document is being printed. (See also *Background printing.*)

Soft copy. Text displayed on the **display screen.** (See also *Hard copy.*)

Software. The operating instructions or programming of a **computer.** (See also *Hardware.*)

Sort. To arrange **fields,** records, or **files** in a predetermined sequence.

Split screen. The ability of some **computers** to display two or more different video images on the screen at the same time. A type of **dual display.** (See also *Windowing.*)

Spreadsheet. A program that provides a worksheet with rows and columns to be used for calculations and the preparations of reports.

Stand-alone unit. A self-contained **computer** that functions independently, without the aid of other equipment.

Status line. A line of information on the **display screen** that indicates the position of the **cursor.**

Stop code. A **command** that causes the **printer** to halt during printing; used to allow the operator to change the **font** or paper on the printer.

Storage. The **memory** of a **computer.**

> **External storage. Magnetic cards, magnetic tapes, disks,** and **diskettes** used to store information; can be removed from the computer.
>
> **Internal storage.** An integral component of a computer, used to store information.

Storage medium. See *Magnetic medium.*

Store. To place information in **memory** for later use.

Subscript. A **command,** given at the time of **text entry,** that instructs the **printer** to print one or more **characters** slightly below the regular line of type, usually by a half or quarter of a line (for example, H_2CO_3). (See also *Superscript.*)

Superscript. A **command,** given at the time of **text entry,** that instructs the **printer** to print one or more **characters** slightly above the regular line of type, usually by a half or quarter of a line. (See also *Subscript.*)

Switch code. A **command,** given at the time of **text entry,** that tells the **computer** to go from one storage station to another to find text for the **document** being prepared.

Tab grid. A series of indentions (usually 5 spaces apart) that are preset in a **computer.**

Telecommunication channels. Telephone and other communication channels used to transmit information from one location to another.

Temporary memory. See *Memory, random-access.*

Terminal. Any device that can transmit or receive electronic information.

Text. The written material to be displayed on a screen or printed on paper.

Text entry. The initial act of **keystroking** that places **text** in **storage.**

Turnaround time. The time it takes for a **document** to be entered, **edited,** proofread, corrected, printed, and returned to the person who created it.

Typeover. See *Overwriting.*

User-friendly. Describes equipment and **applications software** that are easy to master.

Variable. Information in a standard **document** that changes each time the document is produced (for example, the name and address in a form letter).

Video display terminal (VDT). See *Display screen.*

Widow adjust. The ability of a **computer** to avoid printing the last line of a paragraph as the first line on a page. When the last line of a paragraph does appear as the first line on a page, it is referred to as a *widow.* (See also *Orphan adjust.*)

Windowing. The ability of a **computer** to split its **display screen** into two or more segments so that the operator can view several different **documents** or perform several different functions simultaneously. (See also *Split screen.*)

Word processing. A system of personnel, procedures, and automated equipment designed to handle communications efficiently and economically. *Word processing* also refers to the electronic manipulation of alphabetic and numeric characters to serve various communication purposes. (See also *Information processing.*)

> **Centralized word processing.** A system that locates all word processing activities within a single area in an organization.

> **Decentralized word processing.** A system that locates separate word processing facilities in different departments of an organization. The separate facilities are often called *satellite word processing centers.*

Word processing system. A specific combination of personnel, procedures, and automated equipment designed to handle the production of communications.

Word processor. The components that make up an **information processing** system. Most systems include a **central processing unit**, a **keyboard,** a **display screen,** a form of magnetic **storage,** and a **printer.**

> **Blind word processor.** A **word processor** without a **display screen.**

> **Communicating word processor.** A **word processor** that can transmit **text** and **graphics** to and receive them from a computer or another word processor via telephone lines or other electronic transmission links.

> **Dedicated word processor.** Electronic equipment designed specifically to perform text **editing** functions.

Workstation. The basic components of a **word processor** (**keyboard, display screen,** and **printer**). *Workstation* also refers to a work area for an individual worker.

> **Dumb workstation.** A word processor in a **shared logic system,** which is entirely dependent on a remote **central processing unit** for operating instructions and **storage.** (Often called a *dumb terminal.*)

> **Intelligent workstation.** A word processor equipped with its own **central processing unit** and **storage.**

Wraparound. The ability of a **computer** to automatically move words from one line to the next (*word wraparound*) or from one page to the next (*page wraparound*) as a result of insertions, deletions, or margin adjustments.

Index

This index contains many entries for individual words. If you are looking for a specific word that is not listed, refer to ¶719, which contains a 12-page guide to words that are frequently confused because they sound alike or look alike (for example, *capital—capitol—Capitol* or *stationary—stationery*).

NOTE: The **boldface** numbers in this index refer to paragraph numbers; the lightface numbers refer to page numbers.

Boldface numbers refer to paragraphs; lightface numbers refer to pages.

Boldface numbers refer to paragraphs; lightface numbers refer to pages.

INDEX   **493**

Boldface numbers refer to paragraphs; lightface numbers refer to pages.

INDEX   495

Boldface numbers refer to paragraphs; lightface numbers refer to pages.

Boldface numbers refer to paragraphs; lightface numbers refer to pages.

INDEX   497

Boldface numbers refer to paragraphs; lightface numbers refer to pages.

Boldface numbers refer to paragraphs; lightface numbers refer to pages.

INDEX   499

Boldface numbers refer to paragraphs; lightface numbers refer to pages.

INDEX   501

Titles, personal *(cont.)*
  government officials, **310, 312–
    314, 317, 1806–1807**
  hyphenation, **612, 808**
  in letters, **1322–1325, 1348,
    1349, 1364–1368**
  military (*see* Military titles)
  Miss, Mr., Mrs., Ms., etc., **517,
    1322–1324, 1347, 1349,
    1366**
  occupational designations vs.,
    312c
  plurals, **618–619**
to, verbs with (*see* Infinitives)
To whom it may concern, **1349c**
together, 257
together with, **146, 1007**
too, **143**
toward–towards, 271
Transitional expressions, 479
  at beginning of clause, **142,
    178–181**
  at beginning of sentence, 139
  colon with, **181–182**
  comma with, **122c, 138–143,
    178–183**
  dash with, **183, 204**
  at end of sentence, **140, 182**
  lists of, **138a, 178**
  parentheses with, **183**
  semicolon with, **178–182**
  within sentence, **141, 183**
Triple spacing, alternatives to,
  1385a, 1406, 1425g, 1604c
try and, 271
type (see *kind,* 263)
Typewriting (*see* Business
  documents; Letters,
  correspondence;
  Manuscripts; Memos;
  Postcards; Reports;
  Spacing; Tables)

Underscore, **285–290**
  for definition of word, **240, 286**
  for foreign expressions, **241,
    287**
  inserting, **290**
  italics and, **289,** 73
  for letters referred to as letters,
    285
  for titles of artistic and literary
    works, **289**
  for words referred to as words,
    285
Unfinished sentences,
  punctuation of, **208, 275,
    291f**
unique, 271
United States, **525, 1021**
up, 271
upon–up on, 266
Usage, 251–272
used to, 271

Verb phrases, 476
  compound nouns and, **802**
Verbal, 479
Verbs, **1030–1048,** 479
  adjectives and adverbs
    following, **1066–1067**
  agreement with subjects, **1001–
    1029** (*see also* Subjects)
  auxiliary, **1030c, 1032–1034,**
    479
  in clauses
    with *as if* or *as though,* **1042–
      1043**
    with *if,* **1040–1041**
    of necessity, demand, etc.,
      1038
    with *that,* **1047**
    with *wish,* **1039**
  compound, **811–812, 1048**
  in compound nouns, **612a, 802**
  gerunds (*see* Gerunds)
  helping, **1030c, 1032–1034,** 479
  infinitives (*see* Infinitives)
  intransitive, 479
  linking, **1066–1067,** 479
  participles (*see* Participles)
  passive forms, **1036–1037**
  principal parts and tenses of,
    1030–1035, 476, 478–479
    future (see *shall–will,* 268–
      269)
    future perfect, **1033c**
    future perfect pro-
      gressive, **1034d**
    future progressive, **1034c**
    omitting parts, **1048**
    past, **1030, 1032, 1039–1043**
    past participle, **1030, 1033,
      1036**
    past perfect, **1033b, 1039b,
      1040**
    past perfect progressive,
      1034d
    past progressive, **1034b**
    present, **1030, 1031, 1035,
      1038b, 1041, 1043**
    present participle, **1030, 1034**
    present perfect, **1033a**
    present perfect pro-
      gressive, **1034d**
    present progressive, **1034a**
    sequence of tenses, **1047**
  of the senses, **1067**
  transitive, 479
  troublesome, 228
very, 271–272
vice, hyphenation with, **808b**
Voice, 479
Voting results, **451**
Vowels, 479

ways, 272
we for *I,* **1059**
Weights, **429–430, 535–538, 621**

well–good, 261
were, subjunctive, **1039a, 1040,
  1042**
west (*see* Compass points)
what, sing. or pl., **1026**
where–that, 272
whether–if, 261
which–that, **132, 1062**
who–which–that, **1062**
who–whom, **132, 1061**
whoever–who ever, 272
whoever–whomever, **1061**
whose and *who's,* **1063**
wide (as a suffix), **820b**
Widows, prevention of, **1356,
  1407, 1408e,** 490
will–shall, 268–269
wise, 272
wish clauses, **1039**
Women (*see also* Sexism in
  language)
  forms of address, **1321b, 1322,
    1801**
  salutations for, **1347–1350**
  signatures of, **1366**
  titles of, **517, 1322–1323**
Word division, **901–922**
  basic rules, **901–906**
  compound words, **907–908**
  in paragraphs, **916–918**
  preferred practices in, **907–918**
  prefixes, **909, 911–912**
  suffixes, **910–912, 922a–b**
  syllabication, **901–904, 921–922**
  within word groups, **919–920**
Word processing terms, **365, 544,**
  480–490
Words used as words
  plurals, **626**
  quoted, **239**
  underscored or italicized, **285,
    290c**
would have, 272
would–should, 269

Years
  abbreviated, **412, 460**
  in sequence or range, **458–460**
yes
  capitalization, **233, 273d**
  comma following, **138b, 139–
    142, 227, 233, 256a**
  exclamation point following,
    119–120
  period following, **102, 120**
  in quotation marks, **233**
your–you're, **1056e**

ZIP Code, **161, 1311–1313, 1318,
  1331, 1339, 1341**
  space before, **1389d, 1390a,
    1390d**

Boldface numbers refer to paragraphs; lightface numbers refer to pages.